SCIENTISTS
AND JOURNALISTS
Reporting Science as News

SCIENTISTS AND JOURNALISTS

Reporting Science as News

Edited by

Sharon M. Friedman, Sharon Dunwoody, and Carol L. Rogers

American Association for the Advancement of Science

Originally published for AAAS
by The Free Press, A Division of Macmillan, Inc.

Printed in the United States of America

printing number

1 2 3 4 5 6 7 8 9 10

Library of Congress Cataloging in Publication Data

Scientists and journalists.

　Originally published: New York: Free Press, c1986.
　　1. Journalism, Scientific.　2. Science news.　I. Friedman, Sharon M.
II. Dunwoody, Sharon.　　III. Rogers, Carol L.
PN4784.T3S34　1988　　　　　　　　　　070.4′495　88-7874
ISBN 0-87168-340-7

Contents

Acknowledgments

The editors would like to thank the authors of the chapters in this book who contributed their time and energy to this endeavor. We are also grateful to the Scientists' Institute for Public Information and to the editors of *Science, Technology & Human Values* for giving us permission to reprint information contained in their publications. Finally, our thanks go to those friends, colleagues, and family members who encouraged us to produce this book.

Introduction

The woman sitting next to me on the bus was trying to be subtle. But she was obviously interested in an article I was reading about the use of an injection as an alternative to surgery for some patients with severe back problems. Finally, she asked to see the piece, confessing that her father had just recently undergone the injection procedure, and she had been casting about for some understandable account of it.

For me, this brief encounter on the bus was not at all unusual. I ride the bus to and from my university job each workday partly to save gasoline but mainly to give myself time to pore over the growing pile of popular science magazines to which I subscribe. And hardly a week goes by that doesn't find me passing a magazine to a fellow rider who has spied something of interest. One week it may be a story about ceramics, another week a story about the late anthropologist Margaret Mead. Recently a woman who turned out to be a graphic artist waxed enthusiastic over some drawings accompanying a story about attempts to regulate scientific exchanges between the United States and other countries.

—Sharon Dunwoody

T HIS ANECDOTE DEMONSTRATES two important points. The first is that many people with little formal training in science have a compelling interest in all kinds of science. The second is that when nonscientists are looking for scientific information, they turn to the mass media.

These are not novel discoveries, for both the interest of nonscientists in science and their dependence on the mass media as major sources of scientific information have been well documented in the research literature. Many studies show that following the end of formal schooling, most people utilize the mass media as their primary "teachers" about science. Thus the mass media are important keys to the public understanding of science, for it is primarily through the media that scientists can get functional information into the public domain. And it is the *human* aspect of this link between science and the mass media that this book examines.

It is important to distinguish the argument that science and the mass media *ought* to work together for the betterment of the human race from the argument that—like it or not—science and the mass media *are intrinsic* to the process by which nonscientists come to understand (or misunderstand) science. While some authors in this book take the first position, the editors hew most vigorously to the second. This volume was not designed to *prescribe*, but rather, to *describe*, the relationship between science and the mass media by looking at interactions between scientists and journalists through the eyes of both.

The plethora of science offerings in the mass media suggests that scientists and journalists are in frequent contact. Since the late 1970s there has been an explosion in science coverage—most notably in magazines—with editors and reporters eager to capitalize on what appears to be a substantial audience for science information of all kinds.

Yet it is difficult to characterize the interactions between scientists and journalists. When members of the two groups interact across professional boundaries, what are their respective motivations and assumptions? Who controls the situation and with what results? How does the quality of the resulting information vary with the rules of the "game" and the expertise and motives of the players?

No single term aptly describes the interactions. The word "partnership" implies something far too consensual; most journalists and scientists do not engage in a long-term pursuit of common goals. The word "coalition" is somewhat more satisfactory because it conveys a sense of transience. Diverse groups of people often form coalitions to pursue *common* goals, and journalists and scientists do constitute two diverse groups. However, they may have very *different* goals that lead them to participate in the science communication process. Scientists, for example, often feel that media coverage of science should educate nonscientists about the field. Science journalists, on the other hand, see their job not as pedagogical, but simply informational. Journalists say they emphasize what's new or problematic about science in their reports because there is neither time nor space for basic science instruction. Perhaps the most accurate term for scientist–journalist interactions is "symbiosis," that condition in which diverse entities coexist for mutual benefit. But important elements of the interaction between journalists and scientists remain a mystery, a "black box" from which emanates scientific information packaged for public consumption. This book ventures into that "black box" in all its complexity through the personal experiences of some of its authors and the research of others.

A Bit of History

One thing about scientist–journalist interactions is certain: *regular* contact between these two occupational groups is of relatively recent vintage.

This is not to say that the mass media have ignored science in the past or that scientists have ignored the media. Not totally. But prior to the world wars, science was not part of a newspaper's steady diet of news. Scientists rarely served as sources. They were summoned only to comment on crises of major proportions, such as the San Francisco earthquake.

However, the world wars were catalysts for greater mass media coverage of science. The large-scale human devastation of World War I had obvious scientific antecedents. Tear gas, TNT, and the staggering health problems of the wounded and disfigured all promoted a vigorous dialogue about the public's need to know more about science. The American Chemical Society responded in 1919, a year after the Armistice, by setting up a news service. It was the first of its kind to be established by a scientific society in this country. In addition, a newspaperman, E. W. Scripps, in collaboration with University of California biologist W. E. Ritter, set up his own science news service in 1921. Called "Science Service," the Scripps operation attempted to sell science news to newspapers throughout the country. At its height, the service was sending daily packets of science news to some two hundred newspapers and other periodicals. Today Science Service continues to publish *Science News,* a weekly newsmagazine of science.

The 1930s found a handful of journalists working as science writers. But it was only a handful. When science journalists banded together in 1934 to form their own professional organization, the National Association of Science Writers, their numbers totaled only a dozen. And when Science Service did a head count in 1939 of "science writers and editors of newspapers, syndicates, and magazines," it came up with sixty.

Then came World War II. Again the weapons of war focused attention on science. This time those weapons were even more frightening, especially the atomic bomb. The federal government invested much money in weapons research and other scientific efforts supporting war-time activities. And mass media researchers found themselves with grant money if they could direct their work toward investigations of the ability of media to "persuade" soldiers to fight or the enemy to surrender.

Following the war, other events prompted mass media attention to science. In 1957 the Soviets launched *Sputnik*. Both science and journalism in the United States scrambled to catch up. Before the war, of the sixty science writers Science Service had identified in various media, thirty-four covered science for newspapers. When the service did another head count in 1960, it found that about 25 percent of the 1500 daily and Sunday newspapers reported employing a full- or part-time reporter who gave special attention to science, medicine, and technology. That is about a tenfold increase in twenty years. Attempts to place men on the moon in the 1960s and 1970s spawned the generation of science writers who today work for many of the major media in this country. The environmental movement of the early 1970s focused journalists' attention on science's social, economic, and political contexts.

Counts of mass media science reporters today are difficult to come by. No comprehensive list exists, although the 1984 membership list of the National Association of Science Writers—still the dominant professional organization for media science journalists—lists about 575 individuals who cover science for newspapers, magazines, radio, or television, or who work as freelance writers.

The pervasiveness of media science coverage is obvious. As the interest of the media in science has blossomed, scientists have been drawn into the science communication process. Some have resisted strongly, but others have welcomed the chance to share their information with people outside the scientific community.

In fact, some scientists have been engaged in communicating science information to the public for centuries. In the nineteenth century, for example, British field naturalist Frank Buckland devoted much of his time to writing about science for popular periodicals. Other scientists of that time staged public lectures on a wide variety of topics. But as nineteenth-century science evolved from a hobby for the rich to its twentieth-century status as a profession, most scientists retreated from public communication activities. Today, while public understanding of science is high on the agenda of many scientific societies, it is still relatively low on the personal agendas of many scientists. This seems to be changing, but more from media prodding than from any change in science as a culture.

The Goals of This Book

This book describes the connections between scientists and journalists that characterize the science communication process today. Three things about these connections should be noted:

• First, when describing interactions, it is important to get beyond the "public faces" or masks that participants may wear while pursuing their activities. Within the scientific and journalistic cultures, these masks become almost stereotypical. Surveys show that scientists generally disparage journalists and their work, while the traditional view of journalist–source relationships as adversarial mandates that reporters treat scientists not as allies, but as potential foes. In each case, however, the masks seem to clash with individuals' specific experiences; both scientists and reporters often have positive experiences with each other. The contributors to this book—most of them either scientists or journalists—work to shed these masks and explore relationships realistically.

• Second, understanding interactions between groups requires getting beyond anecdotes. Anecdotal experience can be colorful, but it sometimes is a poor predictor of the way things *generally* are. This anthology combines anecdotal experience with empirical evidence. While some of the contributors speak from the heart, others speak from their data.

• Third, relationships are seldom simple. One goal of this book is to show that connections between scientists and journalists are complex. Each person in the process is embedded in a social milieu that affects his or her reactions to others. Each person brings very different individual experiences to such encounters. While some patterns of interaction may become evident as one reads through the book, illustrating the rich complexity of interactions that make the patterns hard to discern is this book's main goal.

Some Important Definitions

The terms "science" and "mass media" are used in this book in their widest sense. Thus, "science" comprises not only the biological, life, and physical sciences but also the social and behavioral sciences and such applied fields as medicine, environmental sciences, technology, and engineering. "Science writing" includes coverage of these fields as well as the political, economic, and social aspects of science.

"Mass media" refers to any medium of communication that reaches large numbers of people. Under that umbrella are newspapers, radio, television, and magazines. One also could include books, newsletters, and cable TV programs; however, only the major mass media forms are discussed here.

One other semantic note is in order: there are a variety of strategies for coping with gender references in the various chapters. Some authors have elected to use "he or she"; others switch from "she" to "he" as anecdotes change; and others stick with the traditional "he" pronoun as a generic reference. As no standard for style yet exists, the editors have decided to allow this variety to remain.

How This Book Came About

The genesis of this book was a set of formal sessions at the 1982 annual meeting of the American Association for the Advancement of Science (AAAS). The three editors organized both a workshop and a symposium on the public communication of science, and the response to both was so great that a distillation of the oral material into a book seemed in order. The book is organized around updated and expanded material from the speakers from the symposia and the workshop. A few individuals who presented relevant material at other AAAS meetings also have been included.

Whom Is This Book For?

Just as "science" and "media" are defined very broadly, so is this book's audience. Scientists, journalists, and students can benefit from these readings. Ultimately, what all readers will have in common is an intrinsic interest in the public communication of science.

Providing a book for such a broad spectrum of readers requires careful writing strategies. The contributors were urged to adopt an informal, easy-to-read style that makes points without a lot of qualifying verbiage and academic language. Those who wish to read further about specific topics can turn to the copious notes that accompany some of the chapters and to the bibliographies in the appendixes.

This book is a "reader," a volume that can be both substantive and entertaining. However, there are a number of things the book is not:

• This is *not* a how-to book. It provides only limited strategies for dealing with the media, specifically in Appendix A.

• This is *not* an exhaustive compendium of available science communication materials. Although the contributors address many science communication issues here, they by no means examine them all. Nor is each issue treated comprehensively. However, the notes and the annotated bibliographies in Appendixes E and F provide further information.

• This is *not* an unbiased text. It is important to remember that the editors and all the contributors think that it is crucial for scientists and journalists to interact, that scientific information belongs in the public domain, and that scientists must be a major and active part of the process. Obviously, there are individuals who would disagree. They do not appear in this volume.

A Brief Outline

Part I: This section examines the actors in the science communication process: scientists, journalists, public information persons, and different segments of the audience for scientific information. These chapters cite current science communication research.

Part II: The views of scientists and science journalists dominate the second part of the book. The relationships between the two are emphasized, and chapter authors freely discuss their perceptions of what makes scientist–journalist connections so rocky at times and so smooth at others. The AAAS workshop included a panel of journalists and scientists who spoke frankly about their perceptions of media coverage of science; an expanded version of that discussion is included.

Part III: Although media coverage of science is more sophisticated today than it has ever been, in this section both media practitioners and researchers explore what they feel are shortcomings in recent media offerings. Some of the criticisms are based on case studies of specific events such as the accident at Three Mile Island in 1979.

Part IV: A hardy and slowly growing band of scientists have chosen to bypass journalists as intermediaries and take their information directly to the people. These scientists have, in effect, become journalists, and in this final section of the book three of them discuss their reasons for doing so and some of the strategies they use.

Finally, the appendixes include a basic guide for scientists on interacting with journalists, examples of science writing, and annotated bibliographies of science communication research and of popular media science offerings.

As noted earlier, the mass media play a crucial role in the public knowledge of science. Whether intentionally or not, scientists and journalists are caught in a web of relationships that greatly affect both the quantity and the quality of the scientific information that the public consumes. This book attempts to convey not only the complexity of these connections but also their richness and their value.

S. D.
S. M. F.
C. L. R.

PART I

Understanding
the Actors

Certain types of individuals appear time and time again in the science communication process. While they may not be the only actors, they play key roles in bringing scientific information into public view. These individuals are the scientist, the journalist, the public information person, and the interested member of the public who ultimately consumes the information. In Part I, we examine each of these actors in turn.

CHAPTER 1

The Scientist as Source

Sharon Dunwoody

The principal role of the scientist in the public communication of science is as a source of scientific and technical information for both journalists and the public. Because they carry out the actual experimentation, scientists have the most direct knowledge of research. But they face many problems in communicating this knowledge to the public because they are subject to a host of constraints and pressures from their own professional world. Social science researchers have looked at some of these constraints, and Sharon Dunwoody discusses what they have found in this chapter.

Sharon Dunwoody is a former newspaper science writer who went on to earn her Ph.D. in mass communications. She now teaches science writing at the University of Wisconsin (Madison), in the School of Journalism and Mass Communication, and conducts research in various aspects of science communication. One of her studies concerns the work characteristics of science journalists during scientific meetings; see Chapter 12 for a discussion of that research.

I<small>N THE EARLIER DAYS</small> of this century, a scientist rarely encountered a journalist. Newspaper reporters found much of what scientists did to be complicated and of limited interest to their readers. Scientists considered reporters to be—quite simply—irrelevant. The mass media played no role within their professional culture, so scientists had no need to accommodate the journalistic enterprise.

Things have changed a bit since then, however. Many reporters still think what scientists do is hard to understand, and most scientists still don't give much thought to journalism. But the level of interaction between the two groups has increased dramatically. Science is now an established "beat" for media organizations. The popular science magazines that emerged in the late 1970s and 1980s graphically illustrate the discovery by American mass media of the public's interest in science. As a result, the scientist is becoming an institutionalized source of information. She is no longer contacted only when the media encounter an unusual story; rather, she is part of the legitimate arsenal of sources for reporters.

Who is this scientist-source? We have known for some time that some scientists receive more media attention than others, but only in the last few years have researchers attempted to sketch a portrait of the typical scientist-source. This chapter examines that sketch as drawn from a number of studies of both scientists and journalists. In addition, we explore the attitudes of scientists who communicate with the public through journalists and some of the costs and benefits to scientists who assume such a public role.

Sketching the Portrait

It's a rare scientist who calls a journalist and volunteers a story. Instead, the journalist typically initiates the contact. But that process is inconsistent; some scientists are besieged by journalists while others are never contacted. Why the difference? No doubt there are dozens of factors, but researchers have isolated a handful that bear examining.

Type of Employer

Unlike the owner of the little mom-and-pop grocery store on the corner, scientists are rarely self-employed. Instead, they work within organizations: universities, government laboratories, private companies. Scientists working for private industry seem to encounter journalists much less often than do scientists working in government or in public institutions such as universities (Table 1–1). The difference may be attributable in part to industry priorities, but news selection patterns of journalists seem to play a role as well.

Private companies are often more interested in protecting informa-

Table 1-1. Amount of Journalistic Contact of Scientists, by Employer*

Amount of Contact by Journalists in 12-Month Period (1980–1981)	Type of Employer		
	University n = 182	Government n = 31	Industry n = 50
0 contacts	31.9%	29.0%	58.0%
1–2 contacts	28.0	25.8	20.0
3 + contacts	40.1	45.2	22.0
	(100.0)	(100.0)	(100.0)

*These data are based on a survey of scientists from both the physical/biological and the social/behavioral sciences. The national survey was conducted in 1981 and was based on a systematic random sample of scientists included in the reference work *American Men and Women of Science*. For further methodological details, please see Sharon Dunwoody and Michael Ryan, "Scientific Barriers to the Popularization of Science in the Mass Media," *Journal of Communication*, 35 (Winter 1985): 26–42, or Sharon Dunwoody and Michael Ryan, "Public Information Persons as Mediators Between Scientists and Journalists," *Journalism Quarterly* 60:4 (Winter 1983), 647–656.

tion than disseminating it. As a result, industry-employed scientists often feel that their employers restrict both their freedom to communicate with other scientists outside their companies[1] and their freedom to convey information to the public.[2]

Even when information from industrial scientists does get to the media, journalists may ignore it. A group of British researchers compared the information flowing across the desks of science journalists to what actually became news. They found that while the bulk of the information came from industry, industrial sources accounted for only 6 percent of the material ultimately printed or aired by the journalists.[3] The researchers concluded that journalists are wary of industrial information and that they view company-issued press releases as promotion, not information. To avoid these perceived public relations attempts, the journalists seek information from sources such as scientific journals which they believe contain information reflecting science as it is being practiced.

Type of Scientist

The most popular scientific source for the media is the social scientist. A recent survey found that while nearly 50 percent of the physical and biological scientists interviewed had encountered no journalists within the year, the same percentage of social scientists had talked with at least three journalists during the period (Table 1–2).

This finding is surprising because science reporters seem to have little regard for the social sciences and rank them quite low on their list of

Table 1-2.   Amount of Journalistic Contact, by Type of Scientist*

Amount of Contact by Journalists during a 12-month period (1980–1981)	Type of Scientist	
	Social/Behavioral n = 127	Physical/Biological n = 144
0 contacts	23.6%	48.6%
1–2 contacts	26.8	25.0
3+ contacts	49.6	26.4
	(100.0)	(100.0)

*See note, Table 1-1.

personal interests.[4] Reporters also readily admit that they are not very well equipped to evaluate social science research.

What, then, makes social scientists so popular in the media? It appears that while science journalists view social science topics with disdain, their editors have quite a different reaction: they welcome them. To illustrate, let's look at media coverage of a major scientific event, the annual meeting of the American Association for the Advancement of Science (AAAS). The AAAS meeting offers information about all areas of science, and it is treated as a major news event each year by the media. At one particular meeting, reporters for the two major U.S. wire services, Associated Press (AP) and United Press International (UPI), filed stories on fifteen topics. Of those fifteen, only four dealt with social science.[5] Yet three of those four topics were picked up by more daily newspapers throughout the United States than were any other stories from the meeting. Clearly, editors found the social science topics to be more "newsworthy" than other science stories from the meeting.[6]

Editors like social science stories because they think readers will like them, and they are probably right. Much social science research seems directly relevant to our own lives. A story about television viewing and violent behavior in children appears more applicable to everybody's daily concerns than does a story about a fraudulent scientific experiment. Also, even when talking "science-ese," social scientists can sound like they are talking plain English. Thus editors may feel that the social sciences are easier to understand than are other areas of science such as physics or zoology. Some scholars caution that such an assumption is misleading,[7] but it may be the reason why so many general reporters are assigned to cover social science stories.

Source Credibility

Journalists pick sources their readers will believe are credible. But deciding what makes a source credible can be tough. When a reporter needs information from a scientist about a controversial pesticide, for example, whom does he choose and why? Recent research points to three credibility factors: (1) mainstream status, (2) administrative credentials, and (3) previous contact with the media.

At least two studies have found that journalists are more likely to tap mainstream scientists than dissident scientists for information.[8] Establishment scientists get better press, these researchers argue, because journalists are very dependent on their scientific sources and don't want to alienate them by going to dissident scientists. Also, after covering science for long periods of time, many science journalists may come to think like their mainstream sources and may themselves regard fringe scientists as aberrant and not worthy of media attention. Finally, one sociologist has found that media organizations deploy their reporters to "legitimated institutions," where reporters will be more apt to run into mainstream scientists than fringe scientists.[9]

Administrative credentials may seem like an odd criterion for scientific credibility. After all, scientists are supposed to do research, and the more research done, the more credible one ought to be. However, at least one study indicates that active researchers were not used as the primary sources for the stories about their research fields. Instead, journalists turned to scientific administrators. In this study, a social scientist examined 275 newspaper and magazine stories dealing with the health effects of smoking marijuana and found that the majority of sources the mass media deemed credible had done no marijuana research at all. Instead, 70 percent of the sources were administrative officials from such agencies as the National Institute of Mental Health and the Food and Drug Administration.[10]

Prior media visibility also seems to be a good source-credibility factor. In the 1960s, some Norwegian researchers suggested that one strong determinant of what is news today is what has been news in the past.[11] A scientist may be deemed a newsworthy, credible source of information simply because he has been a source in the past. The social scientist who examined the marijuana stories found evidence of this. Some of the sources selected by the media, he noted, were "highly prominent scientists in fields tangentially related to marijuana research" who had become media celebrities in their own right.[12] Rae Goodell, associate professor of science writing at MIT, also documents the media popularity of some scientist-sources in her book *The Visible Scientists*,[13] but emphasizes that these scientists have usually established their reputations in their own professional areas before venturing into the public domain. However, she found that while they were highly regarded in their own areas, these scientists rarely discussed those areas with the media; rather, they usually were asked about topics tangential to their scientific expertise.

In summary, the composite scientist-as-mass-media-source is likely to be a social scientist employed by either a governmental agency or a university. He—and it is indeed most likely to be a "he"—is probably an established scientist, and it is somewhat likely that he has been interviewed by reporters in the past. Finally, chances are good that he is being asked by journalists to comment on topics other than his own research.

It is important to remember, however, that this portrait of the scientist-as-source is only a composite sketch of an individual who may be evolving even as he is being described.

The Risks and Benefits of Serving as a Source

Certain people in our society might be characterized as media "hounds." Politicians, for example, actively cultivate journalists because media visibility is vital to their survival. But scientists generally do not. Every science reporter has a closet full of stories about the scientist who hangs up the phone rather than talk to her, or about the physician who won't talk to a journalist unless the journalist signs the equivalent of a legal contract specifying what is and is not legitimate behavior during an interview.

Some researchers trying to understand scientists' touch-me-not attitude approach the problem in terms of risks and benefits. What are the risks for scientists of dealing with the mass media? What are the benefits? If the potential risks outweigh the possible benefits, we might then have a clue to scientists' recalcitrance.

Risks

For *any* source, working with journalists is risky. A source can only hope that her information will pass relatively unchanged through the journalistic production process and into the public domain. But does being a scientist make the risks of dealing with journalists different, or more severe?

The answer seems to be yes. Scientists are part of a culture that still remains relatively indifferent to the public understanding of its work. The scientific community does not reward its members for informing the public, and in some instances it may punish them for doing so. Consider these hypothetical examples:

• A medical researcher agrees to talk to a local newspaper reporter about his work, and the reporter writes an accurate story. However, when the researcher applies for membership in a prestigious society related to his field, he is rejected. Society members tell him they object to the use of his name in the newspaper story, a practice that the society considers tantamount to "unethical advertising."

• A university chemistry professor obtains a grant to produce a series of television programs on the relationship of chemistry to today's society. The television series is a big hit, but the professor's colleagues around the country criticize him for "wasting" time that could better be devoted to research. They imply that if he were a "good" scientist—that is, a productive researcher—he wouldn't have to "go public" for gratification.

In neither case would the scientist have been fired, demoted, or otherwise abandoned by his colleagues. Nonetheless, the cost of public communication would be high in both cases. In a self-governing culture such as science, it is important to conform to the rules.

The most important of these rules is that to be a "good" scientist is to be actively engaged in research that fellow scientists consider to be of high quality. The more such research is done, the greater the rewards within the system. But this premium on research activity means that a scientist isn't recognized for doing other things. Charismatic teachers don't win Nobel Prizes.

Among activities that rank low on the reward scale is communicating with the public. Scientists are well aware of this. Surveys indicate that scientists realize that public understanding of science efforts don't play a defined role within the scientific community,[14] and that they feel that engaging in public communication is more likely to hurt than help them professionally.[15] Interestingly, one study found that social scientists were somewhat more likely than others to see potential scientific rewards in public communication.[16]

Ultimately, the research shows that—unlike other kinds of journalistic sources—scientists don't *need* the media to advance in their fields. On the contrary, they probably are better off avoiding the media until they've "made it" within science. Once they are established, however, they can talk to the media without fear of reprisals from their peers. So it is reasonable that researchers have found younger scientists more likely to avoid contact with journalists than older scientists.[17] And, not surprisingly, Rae Goodell's "visible scientists" all had "made it" in science before stepping into the public arena.[18]

Benefits

If scientists were punished every time they talked to reporters, there would be no scientist–journalist interactions to write about. Some scientists obviously get rewards from public communication activities. Among likely rewards are the following:

Personal Satisfaction. Some scientists are genuinely concerned about increasing the public's understanding of science and are willing to devote a share of their time to it despite occasional pressure from colleagues.

Public Recognition. The mass media are pervasive. They are the only avenues open to the scientist who—for one reason or another—wants her name to become a household word.

Employer Recognition. The scientific culture may not encourage scientists to deal with journalists, but employers often do. Scientific societies and a variety of industries now recruit scientists from within their ranks to act as media spokespersons. Universities often consider public information activities to be a form of community service for which a scientist may reap psychological or financial rewards.

Political Recognition. Scientists spend lots of time soliciting grant money. For the most part, money comes from governments, foundations, or private industry. Scientists must convince those who control the purse strings that their research is of value, and they have begun to realize that media visibility can help them make that argument. One recent survey found scientists quick to acknowledge a potential link between getting their names in the newspapers and obtaining research funds.[19] A national science writer has noted that when scientists call her with story ideas she now routinely asks if their grants are up for renewal.[20]

Peer Recognition. As disparaging as scientists can be about the mass media coverage of their disciplines, it appears that like the lay public, they use the media to monitor what is going on in science, including developments in their own fields. In one study 60 percent of a medical school faculty reported that they sometimes learned of new medical developments through the mass media.[21] And the experience of one sociologist may be quite telling. A story about a small research project she had conducted was published in *The New York Times* and subsequently was spread, via the *Times's* wire service, throughout the country. She reported that by far the largest category of mail she received came from other sociologists who had seen or heard a media story and wanted a copy of her research report.[22] In addition, this small research project was included in a number of sociological anthologies. The project's originator argues that the piece's eventual success in the field had less to do with its value as seminal research than with its having become widely known among sociologists via the media.[23]

Thus scientists may be rewarded for cooperating in the public understanding of science effort. But most rewards will be *outside* of science, and even today they may come at the expense of rewards within the system.

Knowledge: Another Critical Variable

Many scientists don't know much about either journalism or reporters. Scientists-in-training rarely take courses in journalism or have formal training in dealing with the mass media. Respondents in one recent survey of scientists heartily agreed with the statement that "most scientific training does not adequately teach those who go through it to communicate with media representatives."[24] Perhaps more importantly, however, scientists may know little about journalists because they have no incentive to learn. For most of us, for example, there's no reason to learn much about plumbers. We encounter them so intermittently that it doesn't make sense to invest a lot of our time in studying their levels of education or their occupational norms. Scientists can make the same argument about journalists. Since most scientists see journalists only occasionally, they have no reason to invest time in understanding what makes a journalist tick.[25]

But that ignorance can complicate relationships between scientists and journalists if—in the absence of information—scientists make inaccurate assumptions about the way journalism works. For example, a scientist may harbor a stereotypical image of a reporter as someone not interested in facts but only in "sensational" information; that image may not even be based on personal experience, but may derive from the comments of colleagues who have been "burned" by journalists in the past. Like any stereotype, it may accurately depict a few individuals but offer only a distorted view of most.[26]

Another way of dealing with strangers is to make assumptions about their behaviors based on your own, a strategy that scientists may employ in trying to predict journalistic behavior. For example, scientists are actively engaged in publishing, and so are journalists. In fact, the lives of both are governed by the quality and quantity of their published work. So, reasons the scientist, I can safely assume that the rules governing my publishing experience will generalize to the mass media experience. Not surprisingly, scientists who make such assumptions are in for a shock.

The publication of a research journal article and the publication of a media story are two very different processes. Most scientists acknowledge that differences exist. But those scientists who don't know much about the mass media seem to *behave* as if the two enterprises were governed by the same rules. For example:

• The scientist herself is the author of a journal article, and as author she maintains a great deal of control over her manuscript throughout the publishing process. She can negotiate changes suggested by editors or reviewers, and she sees the manuscript at a variety of points in the process; this gives her the chance to make changes even after the manuscript has been set in type. However, if she expects the same kind of control over a news story, she is in for a surprise. For one thing, the scientist is not the author; the journalist is. For another, even the journalist doesn't have much control over the publication process. In the mass media, production is highly decentralized, making it difficult for one person to shepherd a story from interview to print. Editors step in at various stages to take over, and for many reporters control of the story ends as soon as it is handed over to an editor.

• An issue of a journal may take months to get published. Scientist-authors have plenty of time to check their manuscripts at various stages of production and can even solicit the opinions of others as they go. Media stories, on the other hand, often go from raw manuscript to finished product in a matter of hours, and the production process is inflexible. Consequently, reporters sometimes don't have the luxury of checking facts or of rewriting. Of course, numerous media have less-than-daily production schedules: monthly magazines, weekly newspapers, or television programs. But even for these media, production schedules are defined in terms of days, not weeks or months. Inevitably, most mass media production schedules seem to run, not walk. And the scientist who assumes there will be plenty of time to rework material is almost always wrong.

• Finally, there are big differences between the content of a scientific research article and that of a media science story. Media stories are shorter than their journal counterparts and contain less information. Information is organized differently. While journal articles proceed from rationale to methods to findings, media stories operate in reverse order. Moreover, research articles and their media counterparts are written in two different languages. The former is in the scientific language appropriate to the topic, while the latter attempts a nontechnical translation of the work.

These differences exist primarily because the products serve two very different audiences. While journal articles are "must" reading for scientists in the field, the mass media audience must be lured into the story. Newspaper readers, for example, don't have to read anything if they don't want to, so one major task of the journalist is to bring readers up short as they skim their newspapers, literally grabbing their attention so they will pause long enough to ingest information. To keep them interested, the media use simple versions of words and concepts and eschew detail. This last point is important. While readers of a journal article will pore over the most minute methodological and philosophical points of their colleagues' research, readers of a newspaper science story will read for only a few main points. To burrow into methodological or theoretical detail is to lose them, for most of these readers will be interested primarily in what the researchers found and why it is important to their daily lives.

Given this last strategy, it is interesting to note that scientists' *primary* criticism of the content of media science stories is that details are omitted.[27] This may indicate that scientists are using the same criteria to judge media stories and refereed journal articles. Not surprisingly, this generalization from their own publishing experience finds the media account running a poor second to the journal article.[28]

A Shared Culture

Sociologists Jay Blumler and Michael Gurevitch suggest that journalists and their sources participate in a "shared culture" in which rules guiding their interactions are established and followed. The rules are not explicit, of course, and individual participants may not embrace them with equal fervor. But members of the culture all know what the ground rules are, and they abide by them.[29]

For example, sources and reporters may all share similar definitions of what is news. They may all implicitly agree on what constitutes "balance" in a news story: the ground rules may call for journalists to obtain responses from certain individuals or agencies, for instance, to balance comments from other kinds of persons or agencies. If someone violates the rules, both reporters and sources may retaliate. A reporter who repeatedly ignores sources' requests to publish information only after a certain date, for example, may be ostracized not only by her sources but also by fellow reporters.

A shared culture emphasizes cooperation rather than conflict. As such, it seems to be the antithesis of the traditional perception of journalist–source interactions as adversarial, dominated by distrust and wariness. But a shared culture offers advantages to all concerned; for example, it allows sources and reporters to exchange information efficiently, and its emphasis on cooperation allows a level of trust necessary to maintaining long-term relationships, something that reporters often need.

Shared cultures are shaped in settings where sources need journalists as much as journalists need sources. Thus to characterize the culture shared by particular sets of sources and journalists is to describe the degree of one group's dependence on the other.

The symbiotic relationship between journalists and such sources as police and politicians, for example, is almost palpable. But it is hard to find evidence of a shared culture of scientists and reporters. As noted above, the two know little about each other, and they certainly have evolved few joints rules governing their behaviors. One need only listen to the arguments surrounding the question of a scientist's "right" to review a journalist's story to realize this latter point.

The crux of the problem seems to be that while journalists need information from scientists, scientists rarely need what journalists have to offer. Traditionally, public visibility has brought with it no cachet for scientists.

The picture is changing, however. In almost every scientific organization journalists can now find a few scientists who are genuinely willing to serve as sources. For these scientists, talking to a journalist is not a form of punishment; rather, they claim to enjoy the experience. And the more frequently they work with journalists, the more favorably they view media coverage of science.[30]

Interestingly, increasing numbers of scientists are bypassing journalists altogether and are communicating directly with the public through books, popular magazine articles, newspaper columns, and television shows. (In Part IV of this volume, three scientists describe their rationales for such activities.) And now even scientists-in-training are becoming sensitive to the mass media; such institutions as the Massachusetts Institute of Technology, Lehigh University, and The Johns Hopkins University are among those offering science communication training to science and engineering students. Teachers of science communication in more traditional journalism settings also have noticed a steady increase in the number of science students enrolling in their courses.

In many ways, the interactions of scientists and journalists offer us a chance to watch the evolution of a "shared culture." Already that culture has progressed from being nonexistent to a kind of fragile, neophyte state. Those who are committed to the public understanding of science expect it to develop eventually into a full-blown relationship, for, despite all their problems with one another, scientists and journalists are at last beginning to realize that they need each other to accomplish their respective goals.

Notes

1. William Kornhauser, *Scientists in Industry* (Berkeley: University of California Press, 1963); Stephen Cotgrave and Steven Box, *Science, Industry, and Society* (London: George Allen & Unwin, 1970).

2. Sharon Dunwoody and Michael Ryan, "Scientific Barriers to the Popularization of Science in the Mass Media," *Journal of Communication*, 35 (Winter 1985): 26–42.

3. Greta Jones, Ian Connell, and Jack Meadows, "The Presentation of Science by the Media" (Mimeo., Primary Communications Research Centre, Leicester, Great Britain, 1978).

4. Sharon Dunwoody, "The Science Writing Inner Club: A Communication Link Between Science and the Lay Public," *Science, Technology, & Human Values* 5(1980): 14–22 (reprinted as Chapter 12 in this volume).

5. The four topics were levels and types of violence found in the home, the long-term benefits of early intervention programs such as Head Start, a change in U.S. migration patterns from migrating to urban areas to migrating away from cities, and the election of controversial scientist Arthur Jensen to an honorary position at AAAS (Jensen's research on the relationship between race and IQ would be considered social science). The other eleven topics were sunspots and their effects on weather, the *Viking* mission to Mars, federal regulation of research, weather modification, recombinant DNA techniques, wind energy, coping with large-scale environmental problems, the physics of karate, drought in the West, development of nuclear weapons, and earthquake forecasting.

6. Sharon Dunwoody, "Tracking Newspaper Science Stories from Source to Publication: A Case-Study Examination of the Popularization Process" (Paper presented to the meeting of the Society for the Social Studies of Science, Toronto, 1980).

7. Robert B. McCall and S. Holly Stocking, "Between Scientists and Public: Communicating Psychological Research Through the Mass Media," *American Psychologist* 37 (September 1982): 985–995.

8. Nancy Pfund and Laura Hofstadter, "Biomedical Innovation and the Press," *Journal of Communication* 31 (Spring 1981): 138–154; Rae Goodell, Chapter 13, this volume.

9. Gaye Tuchman, *Making News: A Study in the Construction of Reality* (New York: The Free Press, 1978).

10. R. Gordon Shepherd, "Selectivity of Sources: Reporting the Marijuana Controversy," *Journal of Communication* 31 (Spring 1981): 129–137.

11. Johan Galtung and Mari Holmboe Ruge, "The Structure of Foreign News," *Journal of International Peace Research* 1 (1965): 64–90.

12. Shepherd, "Selectivity of Sources," 135.

13. Rae Goodell, *The Visible Scientists* (Boston: Little, Brown & Co., 1977).

14. Luc Boltanski and Pascale Maldidier, "Carrière Scientifique, Moral Scientifique et Vulgarisation," *Social Science Information* 9 (1970): 99–118.

15. Roy E. Carter, "Newspaper 'Gatekeepers' and the Sources of News," *Public Opinion Quarterly* 22 (1958): 133–144; Dunwoody and Ryan, "Scientific Barriers to the Popularization of Science."

16. Dunwoody and Ryan, "Scientific Barriers to the Popularization of Science."

17. Boltanski and Maldidier, "Carrière Scientifique"; Sharon Dunwoody and Byron Scott, "Scientists as Mass Media Sources," *Journalism Quarterly* 59 (Spring 1982): 52–59.

18. Goodell, *Visible Scientists*.

19. Dunwoody and Ryan, "Scientific Barriers to the Popularization of Science."

20. Cristine Russell, "How Does the Science News Network Operate?" (Paper presented at a conference, "Communicating University Research: The Next Step," sponsored by the Council for the Advancement and Support of Education, Alexandria, Va., 1982).

21. Donald L. Shaw and Paul Van Nevel, "The Information Value of Medical Science News," *Journalism Quarterly* 44 (1967): 548.

22. Laurel Richardson Walum, "Sociology and the Mass Media: Some Major Problems and Modest Proposals," *The American Sociologist* 10 (1975): 28–32.

23. Personal interview by the author with Laurel Richardson Walum, Columbus, Ohio, 1978.

24. Dunwoody and Ryan, "Scientific Barriers to the Popularization of Science."

25. Carter develops this particular point with respect to physicians in "Newspaper 'Gatekeepers' and the Sources of News."

26. For more details about the problems of stereotypical responses to journalists by scientists, see Sharon Dunwoody and S. Holly Stocking, "Social Scientists and Journalists: Confronting the Stereotypes," in Eli Rubinstein and Jane D. Brown, eds., *The Media, Social Science, and Social Policy for Children: Different Paths to a Common Goal* (Norwood, N.J.: Ablex Publishing Corp., in press).

27. See, for example, Phillip J. Tichenor, Clarice N. Olien, Annette Harrison, and George A. Donohue, "Mass Communication Systems and Communication Accuracy in Science News Reporting." *Journalism Quarterly* 47 (1970): 673–683; James Tankard and Michael Ryan, "News Source Perceptions of Accuracy of Science Coverage," *Journalism Quarterly* 51 (1974): 219–225; and S. C. Borman, "Communication Accuracy in Magazine Science Reporting," *Journalism Quarterly* 55 (1978): 345–356.

28. For an expansion of this point, see Sharon Dunwoody, "A Question of Accuracy," *IEEE Transactions on Professional Communication*, PC–25 (December 1982): 196–199.

29. Jay G. Blumler and Michael Gurevitch, "Politicians and the Press: An Essay on Role Relationships," in Dan D. Nimmo and Keith R. Sanders, eds., *Handbook of Political Communication* (Beverly Hills: Sage Publications, 1981), 467–493.

30. Dunwoody and Scott, "Scientists as Mass Media Sources."

CHAPTER 2

The Journalist's World

Sharon M. Friedman

The scientific world is not the only one to place constraints on the science communication process. The world of journalism also applies many pressures. An understanding of science communication requires knowledge about how the mass media operate. This chapter reviews the literature to present a primer on science communication and the mass media.

Sharon M. Friedman is an associate professor of journalism and director of Lehigh University's Science and Environmental Writing Program. Before joining the Lehigh faculty in 1974, she was the associate information officer at the National Academy of Sciences and information officer for the International Biological Program. Friedman, who has degrees in both biology and journalism, has written more than twenty articles on science and technical communication and has edited five volumes of conference proceedings and two books. Her research concentrates on how well small and medium-sized newspapers cover science and technology issues, and her study of how local newspapers covered the Three Mile Island nuclear plant before the accident is presented in Chapter 14.

SINCE THE EARLIEST DAYS of science writing, the profession has been beholden to the two worlds of science and journalism, functioning under the rules and constraints of both. But the influence of these two worlds has not been equal, for, above all else, science writing is a creature of the mass media, and the journalistic world has shaped science writing to its own needs.

The influence of journalistic style and training has added good and bad aspects to the profession, some of which are not well understood by scientists or laypersons. Journalistic needs also have bent science writing goals, and in some instances, made them harder to attain. Such constraints have often inhibited what scientists and some science writers would like to see in science articles, such as more explanation, more in-depth coverage, more attention to details. These goals, however, do not always mesh with the needs of the mass media.

Just what are these needs and how is their influence felt? One of the first places to start in such an examintion is to look at the variety of organizations encompassed within the term "mass media." Another is to examine the constraints imposed on science writing by the structure and operation of the media, including such factors as the size of various organizations, lack of space or air time, "hard news" requirements, deadlines, source use, editorial pressures, and reporter and editor education. Last, the broadcast media have special problems that impose additional constraints on science coverage. Examining these also will help clarify the influence of the mass media on science communication.

What Are the Mass Media?

When many people think of the "mass media," they envision a monolith of organization and purpose. Yet the media are made up of numerous organizations separated into distinct groups by their operations and needs, and beyond that into individual publications and broadcast stations. While they do have at least one unity of purpose—that of providing information to people—the differences among them are important, particularly in understanding the behavior of the organizations and the news professionals operating within them.[1]

First, there is the obvious division between the print and electronic media. In the print area, there are newspapers, magazines, wire services, and newspaper syndicates. In broadcast, there are radio and television. However, these divisions are not really sufficient. There are differences in size, structure, and autonomy to be considered. Differentiations also can be made by frequency of publication, depth and breadth of coverage, locality, and credibility.[2]

Even in as specialized an area as science coverage, there are several levels of differentiation. For example, among the print media are those for the general public such as daily or weekly newspapers or general magazines like *Time* or *Newsweek* that cover science as well as other subjects. Then there are science magazines, including *Science 85, Discover,* and *Science Digest,* that cover only science but also are for the lay reader.

Publications for scientists also break down into several areas. There are the more general types such as *Chemical and Engineering News,* and then there are journals which are technical and only for specialists in a particular field.

Among newspapers, there are national ones such as *The New York Times,* the *Washington Post,* and the *Los Angeles Times.* Then there are large city and smaller regional and local newspapers, each with its own aims and needs. However, the influence of the national publications is greatly felt at the local level. Reports in *The New York Times* on national and international news appear in newspapers all across the nation because of syndication. Similarly, other stories that appear in numerous cities and towns originate on the wire services. The national influence also is present in television, and it helps create a "common world view" for viewers and readers on many issues.[3]

Yet, along with this common view, there is another one that is very specific for each publication, broadcast station, and medium. This view relates to each organization's own audience of readers or viewers. Whatever a news outlet produces needs to be keyed to the interests of its particular audience. Knowing about and writing for a particular audience is a prime journalistic rule, and it is something that must be considered as very important when trying to understand how the media operate.

Another point concerning audience to keep in mind for science writing is that audience size decreases as technical level increases. In other words, the more people a publication or broadcast station wants to reach, the more understandable it has to be. To reach the greatest number of newspaper readers or television viewers, science news must be simplified and translated into lay terms. Sometimes this can be done easily, but it also can lead to problems of oversimplification and even distortion, particularly if there are no specialists or science writers working for the organization.

Size of the Organization

The size of a news organization has resounding effects on how that organization operates. Size, for example, plays a large role in determining whether there are specialty or "beat" reporters working for an organization. Sociologist John Johnstone found that within smaller organizations there is less specialization, and that as news organizations get larger, journalists' duties become more specialized, including assignment to full-time news beats. In his 1971 study, in organizations with fewer than 25 editorial employees, 33 percent of the reporters said they covered just one type of news, while in organizations with 25 to 100 employees, 52 percent of the reporters covered a beat, as did 57 percent in organizations with more than 100 employees. Control of editorial operations also becomes more centralized in larger organizations and fewer people share in key editorial decisions, according to Johnstone.[4] This has important effects on what stories get published and the manner in which they appear, as shall be seen later.

Science writing is considered a specialty beat, and it is usually found at newspapers or broadcast stations with large staffs. According to most science writers, there are no more than 100 full-time science reporters working for newspapers or wire services in the United States. Far fewer work for broadcast stations. Science is covered on smaller publications or stations by general assignment reporters or by articles picked up from the wire services or news syndicates. Besides the science writer, other specialists writing about scientific topics would include medical, energy, health, and environmental writers; probably more than half of these reporters would be included in the above estimate of numbers working for newspapers and wire services, since titles and scope of beat vary throughout the country.

The size of a news organization also affects the type of reporting done. The news organizations most likely to engage in in-depth reporting are the newsmagazines, followed by the large national newspapers. The wire services, small daily newspapers, and broadcast stations are least likely to have the time or money for this type of activity, and they follow the standard "hard news" format to be discussed below.[5]

The number of sources used for articles also is affected by size. Having multiple information sources should be the goal of media outlets. As with in-depth reporting, multiple source use appears to increase as the size of the organization increases, with newsmagazines and large daily newspapers the most likely to require multiple sources.[6]

Closely interrelated with size is the economic condition of a news organization. Smaller organizations cannot afford to allow their reporters to spend a great deal of time on one subject because there are many subjects to cover and a limited number of reporters to handle them. Also, a smaller economic base means a smaller publication or station with less space or air time for science articles and fewer resources to use to get news and develop features. In addition, it could mean a more locally oriented audience, demanding, for example, more county government, school, sports, or cultural news within this smaller publication or on the local television or radio newscast. Frequently, such concerns edge science news out of the newspaper or broadcast.

Space and Air Time

There is not a great deal of space for news in a daily newspaper. On a heavy advertising day, for example, the "news hole," as it is called, may constitute only 30 percent of the newspaper, with advertisements taking up the rest of the space. Out of this 30 percent comes room for columns, comics, editorials, and regular features. This leaves about 5 percent or less for the news of the day—national, international, local—plus other features. So the length of an article is important, and brief is better. Time allotments for television and radio are even tighter; generally there is only time to read a headline and maybe a few short paragraphs on the air.

The amount of space or air time given to cover a science story is a crucial factor. This is because complex subjects need much explanation. Patrick Young, a science writer for the Newhouse News Service, says that his biggest problem is trying to explain adequately, accurately, and interestingly a complex technical subject in 900, 1000, or 1200 words.

> It's a very difficult thing to do. If we're trying to explain, for example, the various research techniques used in high-energy physics, we really can get bogged down. So, frankly, I tend to limit the number of stories involving a great deal of complexity. I prefer to talk about what's been found and explain the significance of it because that's what I can do best in 800 or 1200 words. And if it's the type of story in which I have to explain the technique itself, the chances are good that it won't be written for Newhouse. It's not a situation I'm particularly happy with, but I think I do a better service to readers if they can walk away from a story understanding it rather than being confused. The other problem is that if the editors get confused by a story, they're not going to run the piece.[7]

Warren Leary, science writer for the Associated Press (AP) wire service, notes that at AP "we have to look at our audience, our time constraints, and our space restraints. I don't frequently have 900 or 1200 words to explain something in a story. I might have 400 or 500 words." Leary's readership is a general audience, served by 1300 newspapers and 3500 radio and television stations. Anything he writes has to be condensed for broadcast, too. "If I can't cover a subject in 500 words for a newspaper, I certainly can't condense it to 100 words for a broadcast story," he points out.[8]

Understanding why such space limitations exist is important. David Perlman, science editor for the *San Francisco Chronicle,* worked a stint as the newspaper's city editor. In this role, he had to weigh the "latest news from the plasmid front against the latest news on Proposition 13." He knew that space for plasmids had to go when property tax cuts demanded more lineage.[9]

But not all science writers are unhappy with their space limitations.

In a national study of science writers I did in 1973, 56 percent of those responding said they were satisfied with the amount of space they received in their publications.[10] However, my 1979 study of general assignment reporters from smaller eastern Pennsylvania newspapers found major complaints about the amount of space given articles, even when they were not on a scientific topic.[11] This disparity appears to be related to the size of the publication involved and the priorities given to science news coverage. Smaller publications, more often than not, squeeze in science articles when and where they can, but only if these are judged to be of specific interest to the publication's readers.

Broadcast constraints are even more demanding concerning air time. According to broadcasting researcher F. Leslie Smith, "The script of an evening thirty-minute network newscast, if set into type, would not even fill the front page of *The New York Times*. Thus television news editors must be extremely selective in choosing items for the newscast, and the writer must be extremely selective in the amount of detail to include in each story."[12]

Roger Field, health and science editor for WBBM–TV in Chicago, calls the time crunch a major problem. He may have to shoot a story in an hour or two; scripts may be written in fifteen minutes. Research time for reporters is practically zero, with only the chance to get one or two calls out to sources. Field explains that if a story breaks at 11:15 a.m., he has to do an interview at 12:15 p.m. By 2:15 he and his crew return from shooting and he writes a script. Besides working with these excruciating deadlines, he notes, he and others reporting science news on television have to "beg and scrape" for two minutes of air time, including the introduction and closing, on a typical day. Editors "have fits" if he asks for more than three minutes, because deducting commercials, sports, and weather may leave only six to eight minutes for news of the world.[13]

Robert Bazell, science reporter for NBC News, reported at an American Association for the Advancement of Science (AAAS) symposium on science and the media in 1978 that he usually gets no more than ninety seconds for a story. He jokingly said that if the Ten Commandments were to be delivered in the contemporary world, network news would report, "The Lord issued ten commandments today. The three most important were. . . ." Bazell did note, however, that there is a trend to longer feature stories on network news of four to six minutes.

The Hard News Aspect

Hard news, sometimes called spot news, is what generally occupies the first three to five pages of a newspaper and most of a television or radio newscast. Because this type of article is written according to a rigid formula with strict requirements, it causes many problems for scientists, who don't find it contains enough information or detail. One prime requirement for hard news is currentness, or a news peg, something that makes the story immediate, or, in journalistic terms, makes it news.

The hard news story is written in an inverted pyramid style, with the conclusions placed first in the story. Ninety percent of all news stories are written in this format, which depends heavily on the opening or lead sentence. Reporters are told by editors to make the lead sentence a "grabber," something to draw the audience into the story. Yet the first sentence also must be simple and not too long. Trying to do all of this with a science topic is often difficult and contributes to charges by scientists of oversimplification and distortion. The lead sentence is followed by items written in descending order of importance. Very detailed material is at the bottom of the story or is not included at all.

Another prime requirement for a hard news article is what journalists call the "5Ws and H." The initials stand for *who, what, where, when, why,* and *how,* and these elements are supposed to be present in all news stories within the first few paragraphs. When several of these are found in the lead sentence, it is called a summary lead. The rest of the article is written in short paragraphs, using easy-to-understand language in short sentences.

This rigid formula is highly successful in getting information across to readers, particularly those who are reading quickly. Skimmers get the message even if they read only the first paragraph. The formula also makes for short articles easy to edit. With the most important information at the top, an editor can delete the bottom to shorten the article and still keep the theme of the story intact. In addition, the formula requires less writing time, which is important for reporters faced with short deadlines.

Besides the hard news approach, there are other ways to write articles, including feature, interpretive, and investigative modes. Feature articles are generally longer and are not constrained by a hard news peg, although they still need some element of timeliness. They vary in length from stories that are one paragraph to those that are several pages or minutes long. No standard formula is used here and the conclusions do not have to come first. Also there is no cutting from the bottom by an editor.

While hard news attempts to tell what is happening, features have more room to develop why and how and provide more perspective. There are a number of different types of features, but the one most often used in science writing is the explanatory feature, which does exactly what it says: it explains something that is already in the news or some particular topic of interest, such as the controversy over radical versus simple mastectomies.

Interpretive reporting overlaps with feature article writing. Interpretive articles provide the reader with the meaning or significance of a development. They frequently deal with controversial subjects, but sometimes even they cannot tell the whole story in one article because of space or time limitations, so often they evolve into series of articles. These articles try to relate various viewpoints, including the costs and the benefits of particular actions.

Investigative reporting involves looking below the surface of a story and digging into aspects that normally are not covered. This type of reporting takes much longer than hard news or feature reporting and frequently involves extended document searches and numerous interviews with sources. It often is invoked for studying aspects of highly controversial subjects, such as nuclear power safety, and is most frequently done by larger news organizations.

Most science writers prefer to write explanatory features and interpretive or investigative articles, because they feel these stories get more science across to their readers and have more influence on readers' attitudes. Writers participating in the 1973 national study said that they felt hard news stories were misleading and a disservice to readers, and that trying to fit a science story into a hard news mode was like trying to put a size nine foot into a size five shoe.[14]

This study also showed that these journalists had been moderately successful in overcoming the news media's tendency toward the hard news approach. Fifty-one percent of 144 science writers said the greatest number of stories they wrote were interpretive rather than straight news.[15] A later national study of science writers in 1978 indicated that 37.5 percent said they wrote features, 32.4 percent produced spot or breaking news, 16.8 percent wrote background pieces, 9.8 percent did investigative reporting, and 3.5 percent wrote other types of pieces, including columns. Everette Dennis and James McCartney, the authors of this study, concluded that most science journalists worked in traditional breaking news and feature modes with some attention to analytical work in background reports. Few did investigative reporting. The authors pointed out that feature and background work accounted for 54 percent of the science journalism output on metropolitan dailies, a strong emphasis indicating more attention to interpretation and process-oriented stories.[16]

Both the 1973 and 1978 national studies found a greater tendency for stories to be more consumer-oriented and relevant to readers. They also found that when investigative reporting was done, the writers who engaged in it were more likely to see themselves in an adversarial relationship to sources than reporters doing feature or background pieces. The 1973 study found that reporters then under the age of thirty did more investigative reporting than their older peers.

Despite these trends, hard news is still the most prevalent format in journalism, and its practice has some detrimental effects on science communication. For example, its emphasis on currentness creates problems for science writers because scientific discoveries do not happen overnight and so do not have a natural news peg. This leads those seeking media coverage to use various devices to provide a news peg, such as holding press conferences, putting out press releases, or giving speeches. In that way, the discovery takes on the timeliness of the event taking place. Since these activities are not real but contrived news events, reporters call them "pseudo-events."

In environmental reporting, the need for a news peg creates an emphasis on covering fast-breaking disasters like oil spills, or staged events like protest marches, or announcements by "newsworthy" people like politicians and actors, according to David Sleeper, formerly of the Conservation Foundation and now an editor of *Blair & Ketchums' Country Journal*. The net result, he says, is reporting that is "woefully out of context, what William James called 'criticism of the moment at the moment.' "[17]

Sleeper notes that a Connecticut environmental writer has charged that most newspaper coverage of land-use issues in his home state provides "stories that mean little to most readers and give no sense of their communities' growth." Reporters focus solely on what happens at zoning hearings and may overlook vital issues, according to the writer. A wire service energy reporter quoted by Sleeper relates that few journalists are willing to take a long view. "All of us seem to cover the energy story on a blow-by-blow basis—fights in Congress, between Congress and the White House, and occasionally some of the agency disputes. It's blow-by-blow, rather than the long view. But it's easier to be sure that you're presenting accurate information."[18]

One reason for this short-term approach, according to John Mansfield, former executive producer of "Nova," a science television show on the Public Broadcasting System (PBS), is that credit goes to the person who breaks a story, not to the one who does the more responsible, in-depth followup of the story. He explains that in all media the emphasis is not on depth but on a new angle, citing as an example his desire to do an update of a "Nova" show on hazardous wastes called "Plague on Our Children." Despite the fact that this show had won numerous prizes, his producers told him that there was nothing really new about the subject and that they had already "done it." Mansfield maintains that they had only scratched the surface in the first show, but that the need to feature new subjects, rather than follow up on old ones, is very strong, particularly in television, because of the cost and time commitment required for new shows.[19]

Another problem created by the hard news approach is the influence it has on deciding what constitutes a good story in the eyes of editors and reporters. According to most news personnel, the best stories are those that have drama and human interest, although the 1973 national study of science writers indicated that their primary criterion for a good science story was relevance to or application for the reader.[20] Many reporters find that writing about applied aspects of science such as medical or environmental issues is easier than writing about basic science, and such stories constitute better reading for their audiences. Leary of AP says that stories on basic research are hard to get across to readers. There is no active aversion to writing about basic research, but it is just difficult to do within the constraints of the work, he explains.[21]

Among other problems the hard news approach brings to science writing is the unrealistic picture it often paints of the scientific enterprise. Science is portrayed as something made up of "breakthroughs" every other day, rather than a long, laborious process. Scientific advances appear to be the products of individual researchers rather than of teams of scientists building on each other's work.

The need for drama and simplification frequently leads to charges of sensationalism from scientists and other media critics. Sleeper complains that at the beginning of the environmental movement, events were dramatized by environmentalists and heavily covered by the mass media. Now, he explains, with major environmental legislation in place, environmentalists have shifted from drama to implementation, but the media have not. They still prefer controversy, heroes, and villains, the continuing big story, according to Sleeper. He feels that environmental coverage in the news media is too conflict-oriented, that too much emphasis is given to "hot" news, and that journalists often are uncritical of claims by special interest groups.[22]

Deadlines

Most hard news articles are written under tough deadlines of hours and not days. A reporter may be assigned to cover a city council meeting at 8:00 p.m. that breaks up at 10:30, and she has an hour to prepare a story for the next morning's edition.

With most science articles, unless they are about events that have just occurred, deadlines are not quite that tight. But many reporters covering a scientific meeting such as that of the American Association for the Advancement of Science have to file one or two stories a day. That is why they will base most of their articles on the five or six press conferences that occur each day, rather than sit through long symposium sessions.

Feature deadlines are somewhat longer—two to three days, sometimes even two or three weeks, depending on the subject, the newspaper or broadcast station, and the size of the news organization's staff. Generally, the larger the organization and its staff, the more time reporters can take to develop feature articles.

Cristine Russell, science/medical writer for the *Washington Post*, describes deadline pressures:

> So often we are faced with a very short deadline. For example, we hear someone at a congressional hearing say ten minutes worth of something and we have to create a story out of that—so that's what we cover at one end of the spectrum. Fortunately, in the science area, we have more luxury than many of our journalism colleagues in that we can spend an incredible amount of time on one subject. For one series I wrote recently on modern maternity, I spent more than two years researching the subject.[23]

Working for a wire service, Leary has much shorter deadlines. He says that sometimes he does not "even have the luxury of ten minutes to get a story out. We are more or less composing and thinking about a story as we are dictating it over a telephone."[24]

The speed of the wire services is legendary, and it can be of great benefit in bringing people the news quickly. But it also can lead to mistakes, such as the one in 1981 following the attempt to assassinate President Ronald Reagan, when AP and at least one of the three television networks declared presidential press secretary James Brady dead without positive confirmation. Too much speed also can lead to superficial coverage and lack of interpretive or investigative reporting.

In a study of the behavior of science writers during the 1977 AAAS meeting, Sharon Dunwoody found that reporters operating under a greater number of newsroom constraints—principally deadlines—were more dependent on press conferences, and, therefore, on the sponsoring organization that set up the press conferences, than were reporters with few constraints. The more stories a reporter was expected to write, the more likely he was to rely on the press conferences as an efficient means of gathering information. She also found that more than 50 percent of the stories produced by reporters with daily deadlines were single-source stories, while the majority of stories written by reporters with fewer constraints used two or more sources.[25] (Other findings of this study are discussed in Chapter 12.)

Source Use

Using a number of sources of information, including books, periodicals, and people, is important for good science reporting. Often, however, reporters, particularly general assignment reporters, use only one or two sources when writing about scientific or science-related topics. General assignment reporters attending a science writing workshop in Pennsylvania in 1979 listed their lack of knowledge about where to go for information about science-related issues as one of their prime problems.[26] Limited source use also was a problem with coverage of the Three Mile Island (TMI) nuclear plant before the accident. Only one out of thirty-six reporters, news directors, and editors interviewed in the Harrisburg region said he had used an outside source to help him understand nuclear information from TMI, and that source was the Nuclear Regulatory Commission (see Chapter 14).

In a study of the media coverage of the swine flu issue, communications researchers David Rubin and Val Hendy noted that a "reporter, particularly when under deadline pressure and dealing with a complex story, is a captive of his or her sources." They found a strong relationship between the quality of coverage in a news medium and the number of sources consulted during the week for information on the inoculation program. "*The New York Times* named twenty-two different sources in its articles, the *Washington Post* seventeen, and the *Miami Herald* twelve. On the other end of the scale, the *Denver Post* named two, the *St. Louis Post-Dispatch* five, and the *Casper Star-Tribune* one."[27]

Even if reporters do know where to find sources—as most experienced science writers do—there is a problem with getting too close and being manipulated by them. Perlman of the *San Francisco Chronicle* feels that too many long-term science writers have become "inside dopesters." He notes, "So many scientists are personal friends; so many others have shared their feelings so intimately; so many have been so candid about grantsmanship and research dead-ends and the problems of publish-or-perish, that one often becomes over-protective—like police reporters when the cops misbehave."[28]

There is also the tendency to be in awe of scientific sources. Joel Shurkin, a former science writer for the *Philadelphia Inquirer,* is quoted as saying, "There's a tendency on our part to believe anyone who has a Ph.D. or M.D. after his name. We automatically assume he knows what he's talking about, and we rarely think he's either wrong or self-serving."[29]

Because of this belief, science writers and other reporters can be misled. One reason for this is differences in educational background that sometimes keep reporters from asking skeptical yet informed questions. Another relates to their susceptibility to public relations efforts. Environmentalists charge, for example, that the media—especially local media in industry-dominated towns—rarely question industry-generated information regarding occupational health hazards, such as asbestos or cotton dust, or large development projects.[30] Industry similarly claims that reporters use environmentalists' "hyped" information to get headlines, even if the information is not very sound or scientifically proven.

Jim Sibbison, a press officer for fifteen years with the U.S. Public Health Service and the Environmental Protection Agency, charges that health agencies under the Reagan administration have been manipulating reporters by suppressing most of the information about cancer-causing chemicals. According to Sibbison, the Carter administration used to provide information about cancer-causing compounds to reporters, but the Reagan personnel have shut off the cancer news spigot. This clamping down is possible, he says, because reporters are not actively trying to ferret out reports or documents to the contrary. He blames the nature of the news-gathering process, explaining that many Washington-based environmental reporters do not conduct interviews, consult documents, and then sit down and write their stories. Rather, they have one source of news—government handouts in the form of press releases, official speeches, or staged news conferences. He accuses these reporters of failing to cultivate independent sources within the health agencies and environmental organizations—sources who could tell them, for example, that the government hasn't been doing much about cleaning up the chemicals.[31]

Sociologist R. Gordon Shepherd, in a study of coverage of the marijuana issue, found that the "press appears to rely primarily on a few 'science celebrities,' rather than specialists conducting relevant research, for their scientific information."[32] Rae Goodell of MIT discovered that certain scientists are better at communicating with the public and reporters, and they become "visible" and are frequently quoted, even in areas beyond their scientific expertise.[33]

Media doses of newsworthy people—stories based on *who* said something at the expense of *what* someone said—are frequent in environmental reporting, according to Sleeper. He cites the example of President Carter's Sun Day pledge of $100 million for solar energy as an excellent example of this, noting that because the television networks and wire services were on deadline, they had to report the president's pledge almost verbatim. As a result, they did not have time to find out and report that the $100 million represented transferred, not additional, funds, and that it was substantially less money than considered necessary by the Department of Energy and several congressional committees.[34]

However, some science writers complain that they receive too much information from sources, particularly public relations sources. Russell of the *Washington Post* told university science information officers in 1980 that "we're being haunted a lot with press releases and nonstories . . . if we got fewer releases on more important topics, we would all be happier. It's frustrating spending a lot of time just getting through the mail and discovering that half of this box that has been piling up for the last week contains announcements of people getting new titles."[35]

Editorial Pressures

Editors play a vital role in getting information into the media, from assigning reporters to cover stories to clarifying format and copy to writing headlines. Managing editors frequently decide on the priorities given to various types of news, including science news. City editors make many of the day-to-day or weekly decisions about reporter assignments. In a 1973–1974 Canadian study of science writing in the media, Orest Dubas and Lisa Martel, of the Ministry of State for Science and Technology, found that thirty of the forty-eight managing editors they queried said that the city editor was the decision maker for assigning science news. Another eight managing editors said the news editor was the person in charge of science assignments.[36]

In their role of assigning stories, or, as the case for the wire service editor, selecting the stories that come over the wire to place in a newspaper or read on the air, editors as a rule do not appear very discriminating when it comes to science topics. Alton Blakeslee, retired science editor for the Associated Press, related that he could get a story on the front page of every newspaper subscribing to AP by mentioning in his lead paragraph something about the treatment of piles, ulcers, or sexual impotence. This was because every wire service editor either had these three conditions or worried about them, Blakeslee explained.[37]

Since the early 1960s, public opinion studies have shown an interest on the part of readers in getting more science articles, yet editors did little to fill the demand until the late 1970s. Susan West, a staff writer for *Science 85*, explains that editors don't believe people are interested in science stories. "When I was working on a newspaper," she says, "the editors would cut any science story down to 500 words. They didn't believe there was anything important enough in science that couldn't be said in 500 words. And they didn't want a story to explain how scientists work, how they carry out the process of science."[38]

Perlman of the *San Francisco Chronicle* tells of a city editor's request for him to do an article about an English faith healer who was visiting San Francisco by coming up "with a new wrinkle, such as having a doctor or two confront him [the faith healer] or getting someone he can heal." Although Perlman did not do the article, he says this is the idea many city editors have of what constitutes a good science story.[39]

Both the 1973 and 1978 national surveys of science writers found discontent among reporters with their editors. Many respondents mentioned the need to make editors more aware of the nuances of science news. One wrote for the 1978 study, "Educate editors. They are irresponsible and derelict in their duty to the American people. They like to scare the public with half-fact and wrong information to attract readership. They neglect to present the steady continuing story of say, aviation, which is important to everyone. They waste news space on junk. They waste TV air time on junk."[40]

The Canadian study found that editors gave business and financial topics highest priority in terms of specific coverage and reporter assignments, but that this contrasted sharply with public preferences, which gave highest priority to local news, followed by education, medicine and health, pollution, ecology or the environment, and social science issues. It is no wonder that 43 percent of the lay respondents to this study felt the media were not providing enough science coverage.

Despite this, managing editors from many large-circulation Canadian dailies felt that having a reporter specializing in science was either too costly or unnecessary, or both. As a result, they relied on the wire services for the bulk of their science news.[41]

Headlines written by editors are a major concern for science writers because so many of the headlines are misleading or sensational, and angry scientists blame the writers for them. On daily newspapers, a number of people can write headlines for science stories. The Canadian study found that the news editor and the news desk staff wrote them in nearly half the cases, while one-third said headlines were done by the city editor and his or her staff. Sixteen of the dailies surveyed said that wire editors decided what headlines should be used for stories from the wire services. Copy editors were involved in the process on nine papers. Only four papers, all with large circulations, had assigned a specific desk person to handle science news, and, for two of these, the arrangement was informal and irregular.[42]

Besides assigning reporters to cover stories and determining headlines, editors also decide whether an article is written in an acceptable manner or needs revision. Because of this crucial role, they exert a major influence on how reporters write stories. Sometimes reporters choose to write in a way that ensures easy acceptance and few changes. For example, several general assignment reporters covering science-related topics said they downplayed important research results and played up more general information because they knew their editors and readers would more readily accept this approach.[43]

Journalism professor Mark Popovich, in reviewing research of editorial influence on reporters' writing, notes that several studies have found that reporters were not working for their audiences but instead were trying to survive and succeed in the newsroom. One study of 120 newspersons in the northeastern United States, according to Popovich, showed that "the reporter's source of reward was located among his peers in the newsroom." Another study found that reporters frequently relied on the city editor's perception of audience needs and demands.[44]

Phillip Tichenor, Clarice Olien, Annette Harrison, and George Donohue of the University of Minnesota found in their study of the interactions among reporters, editors, and scientists that "specific editor interest was a crucial factor in reporter performance, and . . . editors present both an energic [motivating] and control factor" in the newsroom.[45]

Popovich explains that according to his review of the research it appears that

> when it comes to selecting the news, reporters have their own ideas of what constitutes news, but they also have some inkling of what constitutes news for their editors. Research studies have implied that reporters are faced with a personal conflict because of those two sets of cognitions. On the one hand, they know what they like in the way of news; but on the other hand, since they think they know what the editor wants, they try to give it to him. Frankly, the reporter, if he wishes to continue in employment, carries out the wishes of his superiors.[46]

Education of Editors and Reporters

One of the reasons that editors seem to have so much trouble with science news is their lack of scientific background. The Canadian study found that of the forty-nine editors responding to the survey, fewer than one in three had had any science courses in college. Only fifteen had taken courses in political science; eleven had enrolled in sociology, psychology, or business/economics courses. Fewer than one in ten had taken courses in biology, mathematics, chemistry, physics, agricultural sciences, or engineering.[47]

This lack of scientific background also is often characteristic of general assignment reporters who cover science-related subjects. At the 1979 Pennsylvania science writing workshop, general assignment reporters said their chief problem was lack of background or scientific training. Of fifteen reporters providing background data, two had bachelor's degrees in biology and one in the social sciences. Four had degrees in English and eight had degrees in journalism (two of these had journalism double majors, one with government and the other with psychology).[48]

A 1975 study of seventy-three newspaper and twenty television reporters in the Twin Cities area of Minnesota by Arnold Ismach and Everette Dennis found that 62 percent had majored in journalism, 35 percent in the humanities, 21 percent in the social sciences, and 3 percent in science or engineering. (Some people had double majors or different majors in graduate or undergraduate school, accounting for the 121 percent.)[49]

In studies of coverage of the TMI accident and the swine flu debacle, reporters' backgrounds proved to be a vital issue. Particularly during the TMI accident, reporters lacking scientific backgrounds had a difficult time with the terminology and concepts of nuclear reactors (see Chapters 14 and 15).

Science writers usually have more science background than general assignment reporters and consequently have an easier time dealing with complex scientific subjects. In fact, a number of science writers feel that much of the blame heaped on their shoulders by scientists for sensational, inaccurate, or distorted stories rightly belongs to general assignment reporters. "They don't have enough background to ask intelligent questions or write intelligent stories," according to Ron Kotulak, science writer for the *Chicago Tribune*. He notes, "They take the easy way out; they go for the jugular."[50] Field of WBBM–TV in Chicago points out that no broadcast executive would expect a general assignment reporter to do "play by play" coverage of major sports events, yet any reporter that's available gets sent to cover a science story.[51]

Because general assignment reporters frequently cover important local science-related topics such as pollution, sewage treatment problems, dam sitings, farming problems, and hazardous waste sites, their lack of scientific background is a serious concern. These reporters often do not know where to go for information, they have a hard time with technical jargon, they have difficulty in deciding what information is important, and they have a problem getting scientists to talk to them.[52]

And while the specialized science writer isn't faced with all of these problems, even she can't know everything about all scientific topics. A medical reporter can have a hard time writing about neutron stars, and what does an energy reporter know about monoclonal antibodies?

The education of science writers has been moving toward more undergraduate and graduate training in science over the years. The first group of science writers, recruited in the late 1950s and early 1960s, had little science training and were predominantly general reporters assigned to cover science. A number of them went back to graduate school to pick up some training in either science writing or science later in their careers. In the early 1970s, more science-trained people got jobs as science writers, bringing a far better background and a more skeptical eye about science to the profession.[53] Recently, with the advent of a number of science-writing programs in universities, future science writers are being trained in both science and science-writing subjects.

Yet, despite this increased science training, science writers still have some status problems with both scientists and their journalistic peers.

Victor Weisskopf, Institute Professor Emeritus at Massachusetts Institute of Technology, notes:

> Science writers, with some impressive exceptions, are not well enough informed. This, I think, is also due to their lack of status among their colleagues in print or broadcast journalism and, perhaps more important, among those in the scientific community. That has to be changed. Science writers and TV people should be invited to conferences, not only as observers, but as members of the scientific community. There is nothing more important than status. More than money, status makes people work and take things seriously.[54]

Even among their colleagues, science writers have to fight for status and respect. According to Perlman of the *San Francisco Chronicle*, specialists such as science writers are not considered team players.

> They demand expensive reference books and shelf room for journals. They disappear on out-of-town trips to meetings, rocket-launchings, and laboratories. They insist that their stories cannot be written in less than two columns. They balk at explaining what a proton or a molecule is every time they use such words. They argue—all too often in vain—with the copy editors who incorrigibly top their carefully qualified stories with headlines heralding "cure" and "breakthrough."[55]

During the TMI accident, many newspapers sent political or general reporters to the scene and kept their science writers back in the office. While some science writers felt this was the best approach, others were quite unhappy. Edward Edelson, science editor of the *New York Daily News* and then president of the National Association of Science Writers, proposed in its newsletter in 1979 that "science writing is a ghetto of journalism." He got the idea, he said, by looking at the coverage of TMI and of the plan to publish material on the hydrogen bomb in *The Progressive* magazine. "Both were stories in which science and technology intruded into politics and everyday life. In both cases, most of the coverage was done by people other than science writers," Edelson said. He continued:

> . . . I have the feeling that science writers generally are treated like plumbers. . . . A plumber is someone you call in when you need technical information. You pay well for the information, but you have no particular respect for the plumber as anything but a fixer of plumbing. In the same way, a science writer is paid well for writing about genes or whatever technical, and is sent to the back row when affairs of real importance arise.[56]

Special Problems of Radio

Some of the problems in dealing with science for the broadcast media arise from the fact that radio stories have to be written to be heard and not seen. Science news must be brief, straightforward, and easy to understand. Most radio stations only broadcast five minutes of news every hour. These few minutes of news generally come from wire service copy, which is read on the air. This practice is so prevalent that it has its own name: "rip 'n' read." For the most part, major news items are repeated on each newscast with few changes, and, as a result, these broadcasts amount to a "headline service."[57]

All-news radio stations broadcast continuous news interspersed with features and commercials, with the news usually repeated in twenty-minute cycles. Several radio networks provide a news service, while some even feed features, commentary, and sports.[58] Under these conditions, there is little place for science on radio newscasts except in very boiled down, simplified presentations.

One of the places that listeners can find radio science reported is on National Public Radio. Ira Flatow, a science reporter for NPR, feels that doing science on radio is tougher than writing it for the print media for two reasons. The first involves the limited amount of detail a reporter can put in a radio story. "You can't fill it up with numbers and facts and details that you can put in print. In radio, once it's gone, it's gone, not like in print where you say, 'Oh, what was the number again?' and you can go back and look," says Flatow.

The other reason is that radio reporters must tape all their material. Flatow has to tape a whole story off the phone or go and tape in person, and this is time-consuming and sometimes difficult.[59]

Interviewing someone for radio is not easy, either. Because most news reports fed to commercial networks and local radio stations must be no longer than thirty to fifty seconds, interviewees must speak in clean, ten- to twenty-second "bites." Interviewers also must have "strong stomachs" in order to ask simple questions they often feel are embarrassing but required by the time constraint, according to Flatow. He recalls one colleague asking Nobel Prize winner David Baltimore to explain in twenty seconds or less how recombinant DNA worked.

He points out that because radio reporters need good taped spots, they are easy prey for special interest groups, some scientists, and lobbyists. These people know that the radio medium is "an animal with an insatiable appetite for news spots."

However, Flatow notes that radio has a potential for excellent science coverage, particularly in documentaries, and that it has one overriding advantage over any of the other media—its immediacy. "If you want to know about it first, listen to the radio," he declares.[60]

Special Problems of Television

The television medium is perhaps the hardest of all for science communication because it has many of the constraints of print and radio, plus some of its own, including special production criteria and the need for good visuals and large audience appeal.

While restricted air time for science news is a severe limiting factor, as already discussed, so is the manner in which television news stories are produced. Describing how a press conference is covered, Frank Field, longtime television health and science editor, explains:

> The television science reporter walks in with a team of specialists— cameramen, light man, and sound man. While that very costly technical crew sets up the lights, readies the camera, and checks out the sound, the reporter talks with his subject and gets the story in the subject's own words. All the while, the reporter is thinking about what the camera and microphone see and hear and will bring to the audience in the two to five minutes (three minutes on the average) he will have on the air that night.

The reporter tells the sound man to pick up the sounds he wants and the cameraman what to shoot. According to Field, it is impossible for a television crew to cover a science press conference the way a print reporter does. Time is too precious, videotape and film too expensive, and the general question-and-answer patterns are too complex to use on television. In all, between 400 and 1200 feet of videotape or film might be shot at the scene. Then this has to be edited and the science reporter needs to point out what is significant, what needs to be shown, Field says. Film from libraries might be added, as might a special diagram. Interest and pacing have to be created by intercutting from the scientist to the reporter to other visuals and then back again. Then this product is screened, and it may be reedited, and perhaps even bumped by a fast-breaking story. Field says, "There are no guarantees; the limited air time and the tremendous daily news activity make competition quite keen."[61]

The visual needs of television news require covering events that are predictable, where camera crews can be assigned easily. Sometimes this results in trivial events getting more coverage than important ones because they supply more than "talking heads." This also allows television news to be manipulated by demonstrators and others who can play up the drama of their particular concern visually. Drama is a prime concern—television is an entertainment medium, even in its news segments—and action, blood and chaos are good visual elements to have.[62] Only stories of enormous significance are aired whether or not they lend themselves to visualization, according to Field.[63]

While hour-long science documentaries do not suffer from the time constraints of regular newscasts, they do have many other limiting factors. One of the most important is funding for the project; another is getting air time. Television subjects must appeal to a wide share of the audience. Several science shows such as "Walter Cronkite's Universe" and "Discover, the World of Science" tried to appeal to large numbers by taking the "wonders of science" approach. Others, including PBS's "Nova," combine wonders with intelligent presentations of science policy issues. Neither approach has led to sustained, regular programming on the national commercial networks. Ratings for "Universe" varied from a 17 to 24 percent share, averaging around 21. Although the ratings were respectable, the show was canceled in the fall of 1982.[64]

Leon Jaroff, former managing editor of Discover magazine, explains that he felt two problems undid "Universe." First, it was not promoted well; and second, its half-hour length required too much squeezing of material. He says that the hour length of the "Discover" television show allows it to go into more depth. The "Discover" programs have been presented periodically and at first were syndicated. In 1985 they moved to PBS. Jaroff points out, however, that the big problem with television shows is the cost. "Discover" costs $1 million a program, including production and promotion costs, he relates.[65]

"Nova" has been on the air since 1973. Yet despite its longevity, it is highly unlikely "Nova" would have survived on a commercial network. During its long stint, it has been supported by government grants as well as corporate underwriting.

The entertainment factor—focusing on the human drama of a scientific endeavor—is high in documentaries. According to John Angier, former executive producer of "Nova" and now a principal of Chedd-Angier Productions, "We like to entertain first, and then the information and public understanding can come along later."[66] Mansfield, another former executive producer of "Nova," says that the show very consciously intersperses the occasionally "cuddly, furry wildlife show"—an almost guaranteed audience winner—with programs about quarks or particle physics. This is essential, he explains, when one is attempting to entertain as well as educate.[67]

Understanding Media Constraints

It is clear that journalists for both the print and electronic media work under a rigid set of rules and a deadly set of pressures. A reporter has many decisions to make about a science story—what aspect to emphasize; what material needs explanation; how much research detail to present; how to translate the scientific jargon for the audience in question; how much background information to include; and, if the subject is controversial, how to achieve a balanced piece. Influencing these decisions are deadline and editorial pressures, the need for visuals, the problem of getting complex material across to a lay audience in a short article or even shorter television or radio presentation, and, perhaps, hostility or lack of cooperation from scientists.

It is important for scientists and others who interact with the mass media to understand these constraints, these rules, and these pressures, so that they can work with reporters rather than against them. The saying "Nothing is so dead as yesterday's news" may not be much solace to a scientist or other source who has been misquoted or feels misrepresented by the media, but it is a fact. It is important to remember the true role of the mass media.

According to Howard Simons, former managing editor of the *Washington Post* and science writer, the job of the media "is to catch history on the run and that's all it is. I don't think we ought to do it differently. When we see a story with a science component, such as TMI or the energy crisis, we have to run to get it. We have a crisis mentality and a crisis response. I see nothing wrong with that as long as you have good people and good standards. . . . More often than not, we do a better job than we're given credit for."[68]

Notes

1. Lee B. Becker, "Organizational Variables and the Study of Newsroom Behavior: A Review and Discussion of U.S. Research" (Paper presented at the Eleventh Conference of the International Association for Mass Communications Research, Warsaw, Poland, September 1978), 1.
2. Peter M. Sandman, David M. Rubin, and David B. Sachsman, *Media: An Introductory Analysis of American Mass Communications,* 3rd ed. (Englewood Cliffs, N.J.: Prentice-Hall, 1982), 245.
3. Michael Novak, "Journalism, the Academy and the New Class," in P. L. Alberger and V. L. Carter, eds., *Communicating University Research* (Washington, D.C.: Council for the Advancement and Support of Education, 1981), 79.
4. John W. C. Johnstone, "Organizational Constraints on Newswork," *Journalism Quarterly* 53 (Spring 1976): 7.
5. Becker, "Newsroom Behavior," 8.
6. Ibid.
7. Warren Leary, Susan West, and Patrick Young, "The Genuine Article: Reporting Real Research," in Alberger and Carter, eds., *Communicating University Research,* 171.
8. Ibid., 172.
9. David Perlman, "Science News as Viewed by the City Desk," *Newsletter of the National Association of Science Writers* 26 (December 1978): 17.
10. Sharon M. Friedman, "Changes in Science Writing Since 1965 and Their Relation to Shifting Public Attitudes Toward Science" (Unpublished master's thesis, Pennsylvania State University, 1974), 50–53. Also in "Science Writers and Public Attitudes Toward Science," *Newsletter on Science, Technology, & Human Values,* June 1976, 6–8; and "Changes in Science Writing," *Decline*

in the Global Village, James E. Grunig, ed. (New York: General Hall, 1976), 263–268. Page numbers in this text refer to the unpublished thesis.

11. Sharon M. Friedman, unpublished data from surveys of general assignment reporters and editors attending a science writing workshop at Lehigh University, 1979–1980.

12. F. Leslie Smith, *Perspectives on Radio and Television* (New York: Harper & Row, 1979), 141.

13. Roger Field, "What's Wrong with TV Science Reporting?" (Paper presented at the Symposium on Science and the Mass Media, Loyola University, Chicago, April 14, 1981).

14. Friedman, "Changes in Science Writing Since 1965," 37–50.

15. Ibid., 39.

16. Everette E. Dennis and James McCartney, "Science Journalists on Metropolitan Dailies," *Journal of Environmental Education* 10 (Spring 1979): 10–11.

17. David Sleeper, "Do the Media Too Often Miss the Message?" *Conservation Foundation Newsletter*, January 1979, 4.

18. Ibid.

19. "Science in the Media," *SIPIscope* 10 (Winter 1982/1983): 6.

20. Friedman, "Changes in Science Writing Since 1965," 57.

21. Leary, West, and Young, "The Genuine Article," 173.

22. Sleeper, "Media Miss the Message?", 2.

23. Cristine Russell, Warren Leary, Patrick Young, and David Perlman, "How I Cover Science: Newspapers," in Alberger and Carter, eds., *Communicating University Research*, 117.

24. Ibid., 118.

25. Sharon Dunwoody, "The Science Writing Inner Club: A Communication Link Between Science and the Lay Public," *Science, Technology, & Human Values* 5 (1980): 14–22 (reprinted as Chapter 12, this volume).

26. Sharon M. Friedman and Walter Trimble, *Science Writing Workshop* (Bethlehem, Pa.: Lehigh University, 1981).

27. David M. Rubin and Val Hendy, "Swine Influenza and the News Media," *Annals of Internal Medicine* 87 (December 1977): 772–773.

28. Perlman, "Science News as Viewed by the City Desk," 17.

29. David Shaw, "Science News: Experts See Distortions," *Los Angeles Times*, January 13, 1977, 3 in reprint.

30. Sleeper, "Media Miss the Message?", 5.

31. Jim Sibbison, "Whitewashing Cancer at EPA," *Environmental Action*, December 1982/January 1983, 25–26.

32. R. Gordon Shepherd, "Selectivity of Sources: Reporting the Marijuana Controversy," *Journal of Communication* 31 (Spring 1981): 129.

33. Rae Goodell, *The Visible Scientists* (Boston: Little, Brown & Co., 1977).

34. Sleeper, "Media Miss the Message?", 5.

35. Russell et al., "How I Cover Science," 117.

36. Orest Dubas and Lisa Martel, *Media Impact: A Research Study on Science Communication* (Ottawa: Ministry of State, 1975), 105.

37. Goodell, *Visible Scientists*, 134.

38. Leary, West, and Young, "The Genuine Article," 174.

39. Russell et al., "How I Cover Science," 121.

40. Dennis and McCartney, "Science Journalists on Metropolitan Dailies," 14.

41. Dubas and Martel, *Media Impact*, vi–vii.

42. Ibid., 105–106.

43. Friedman and Trimble, *Science Writing Workshop*.

44. Mark Popovich, "Coorientation in the Newsroom: An Analysis of the News Preferences of Reporters, Editors, and Publishers" (Paper presented at a meeting of the Association for Education in Journalism, Seattle, Washington, August 1978), 2–5.

45. Ibid., 5.

46. Ibid., 12.

47. Dubas and Martel, *Media Impact*, 111.

48. Friedman and Trimble, *Science Writing Workshop*; and Friedman, unpublished data.

49. Arnold H. Ismach and Everette E. Dennis, "A Profile of Newspaper and Television Reporters in a Metropolitan Setting," *Journalism Quarterly* 55 (Winter 1978): 741.

50. Shaw, "Science News," 2 in reprint.

51. Field, "What's Wrong with TV Science Reporting?"

52. Friedman and Trimble, *Science Writing Workshop*.

53. Friedman, "Changes in Science Writing Since 1965," 72–82.

54. Victor E. Weisskopf, "The Problem of Informing the Public About Basic Research," in Alberger and Carter, eds., *Communicating University Research*, 56.

55. David Perlman, "Science and the Mass Media," *Daedalus*, Summer 1974, 212.

56. Edward Edelson, "The President's Letter," *Newsletter of the National Association of Science Writers* 28 (November 1979): 13.

57. Smith, *Perspectives on Radio and Television*.

58. Ibid., 140.

59. Rex Buchanan, "Science on the Radio," *SCIPHERS* 3 (Spring 1982): 3.

60. Ira Flatow, "Radio Science Reporting Is an Honorable Estate," *Newsletter of the National Association of Science Writers* 27 (April 1979): 10–11.

61. *Science on Television* (Washington, D.C.: American Association for the Advancement of Science, 1975), 13–14.

62. Smith, *Perspectives on Radio and Television*, 141.

63. *Science on Television*, 13–14.

64. Rex Buchanan, "Run Over by the Fonze," *SCIPHERS* 3 (Fall 1982): 7.

65. "Science in the Media," *SIPIscope,* 11.

66. Judy Klein, "The Medium Gets a Message," *Science News,* June 2, 1979, 365.

67. "Science in the Media," *SIPIscope,* 7–8.

68. Friedman and Trimble, *Science Writing Workshop,* 67.

CHAPTER 3

The Practitioner in the Middle

Carol L. Rogers

The role of the science information person has been almost totally unexplored, and consequently is not well understood by scientists or journalists. Yet this practitioner may be more integral in the science communication area than in other fields of inquiry. This is because most scientists work for institutions, such as universities, government agencies, and hospitals, that employ public information personnel, and journalists often contact scientists through these individuals. Carol Rogers examines the vital link they provide in the scientist–journalist connection.

Carol L. Rogers has spent more than fifteen years developing and implementing public understanding of science and science communication activities. As head of communications and membership for the American Association for the Advancement of Science, she directs the operation of its large and busy annual meeting newsroom, coordinates publicity efforts for its magazines, supervises media relations and membership development activities, and oversees production of two radio programs. She has taught a short course on science and the media for teachers and university research faculty and frequently lectures on public understanding of science issues.

• *It was late afternoon when we heard the rumor that the president of the United States had eliminated all funding for science education from the National Science Foundation's budget for the next fiscal year. We checked it out, found it to be true, then called a couple of key science writers to tell them about it. We gave them more background details as well as the names of persons who could confirm the story's validity. The administration had not yet made the proposed cuts public, so the journalists had been unaware of them. The story made the front page in a major national newspaper.*

• *The debate about scientific freedom and national security was heating up, so we called the producer of a nationally syndicated television show and suggested a program on that topic. We then assisted her in developing the program, outlining some of the key issues and recommending articulate spokespeople who could present different points of view. The program aired shortly thereafter.*

• *The Nobel Prize in physics was announced. A science writer called us and several other public information officers at universities and scientific organizations to get the names of physicists who could explain the work that led to the award and comment on its significance.*

T HESE EVENTS HAPPENED. The "we" and "us" are the American Association for the Advancement of Science (AAAS) Office of Communications staff, but they could have been any of dozens of science information people around the country. These events are specific, but they are also typical of scenes repeated daily in universities, industries, scientific organizations, and government agencies.

These examples reflect only part of the job of the practitioner in the middle—the science information person. But they demonstrate the key role this person plays in the science communication process. That role is often overlooked, and of all the actors—the scientist, the journalist, the public, and the science information person—the last has been the least studied.

In this chapter we take a closer look at science information (SI) professionals, those often invisible links between scientists and journalists, and, more broadly, between scientists and the public. We see who they are, how their roles evolved, what they do, and some of the problems they encounter. We show that any understanding of the science communication process, and any attempts to work within it and improve it, must consider this practitioner in the middle.

Who They Are

Who are these SI people, and what are their backgrounds and skills? Where are they, and how did they get there? We have more questions than answers, for little hard data exist, and much of what we know is anecdotal. But we can begin to sketch a picture of them.

First, their titles and responsibilities are as varied as the organizations in which they work. They are usually in offices called public information, public relations, communications, public affairs, news service, or media relations. These different names may actually differentiate types of activities, but more often they simply signify the style or preference of the organization.

Regardless of title, SI people are now working in most large scientific societies, universities, major research laboratories, and industrial organizations. Many science-based institutions have large staffs who devote all their time to providing information to the media and the public about the institution's work and about scientific and technical developments generally.

Little is known about the backgrounds of SI people, or their education and training as a group. Many that I know personally began as reporters and moved into science information work later. They often have little or no formal training in science and are similar in that way to their science journalism colleagues in the mass media. Others do have science backgrounds, and chose communication as a profession rather than research or teaching.

Still others are journalism graduates who specialized in science communication. In fact—if anecdotal evidence can be trusted—most of the young persons trained in science journalism are going into public information work rather than mass media journalism. This probably has as much to do with the job opportunities in science information (especially in high-technology industries) and concurrent lack of immediate opportunities in the mass media as it does with initial job preferences.

Successful science information people possess good communication skills, both oral and written. They also must have organizational and administrative talents—more so than their mass media colleagues. Flexibility and adaptability plus coolness under pressure are decidedly important attributes. Successful SI practitioners have either brought these skills to the job or have acquired them early in the game.

How Their Roles Evolved

Science information operations developed like those of most other professions—as a response to a perceived need. In this case, the primary need was to provide the public with information—to anticipate and answer its questions about science. In addition, some organizations wanted to generate public support for their activities, while still others had a negative public image they wanted to counter.

As science expanded rapidly in this century, many of its new developments had a profound impact on the public. As we have seen (Chapter 2), few reporters were equipped to deal with a multitude of different scientific topics. Even now, when the number of writers skilled in covering science has grown tremendously, the volume and complexity of the information with which they have to deal has outpaced them. And of course, many reporters covering science today still have no formal science background.

Early on, scientific societies tried to help. The American Chemical Society (ACS) set up a news service in 1919. Today that news service continues to issue news releases, runs pressrooms at meetings, produces radio programs, and disseminates in other ways a great deal of information about chemistry and chemists to the media and the public. The ACS news service is now part of a much larger public relations operation that also includes television activities and planetarium shows.

The American Institute of Physics (AIP) created a public relations department in 1956 and began running a pressroom at the American Physical Society meeting. The following year, the Soviet Union launched *Sputnik* and physics was "in." Reporters needed help with such concepts as parity, transistors, and plasma physics, so AIP began holding a series of one-day seminars for science writers. Over the next ten years, AIP seminars dealt with most fields of physics. From those early beginnings evolved a diverse and wide-ranging public information effort which today encompasses print, television, and radio.[1]

The current communications activities of the American Association for the Advancement of Science can be traced only to the mid-1970s, although the organization had been engaging in public information activities to some extent virtually since its inception in 1848. Most of the media-related work over the years centered on a newsroom at the large AAAS annual meetings. Now this activity is supplemented by radio programs, seminars, reporters' guides, and much more.

The growth of science information efforts in universities, government agencies, and industries has paralleled the growth of scientific research and development itself. In many instances, an organization which might have had no one designated to handle scientific information twenty years ago may currently have several people with responsibilities as varied as television production and speech writing.

What They Do

Science information people fill many roles within their institutions. Sometimes they serve as spokespeople for their organizations, appearing before community groups and the media. They often set up and run speakers' bureaus and coordinate special events such as open houses, lecture series, and seminars. They may also produce brochures, booklets, special reports, and other printed materials.

Of all their diverse roles, the three that have the most impact on that sometimes fragile connection between scientists and journalists are those of adviser, communicator, and media facilitator (mediator). Making distinctions among these roles is difficult because they are so interrelated, but we will try to do so as we look closely at each.

Adviser

Most SI professionals spend quite a bit of time in an advisory role. Sometimes they might be advising, in the traditional sense, top officials within their own organizations. At other times they will be helping scientists to work better with the media. Success as an adviser often is determined quite directly by the amount of credibility a science information person has within his or her institution. However, the backgrounds and perspectives of the persons being advised, the time available, the institutions' policies, and the sensitivity of various issues all can affect the outcome of the activity.

To be effective advisers, science information persons must know their institutions, the media, the sciences, the public, and the world at large. They must keep up with scientific research, issues in science policy and higher education, and key industrial science concerns. Only then will they know what issues are especially important for their institution and which of its activities are especially important to the public.

To know an institution is to know its goals, strengths, weaknesses, history, primary interests now and in the past, and its people, including administrators, researchers, and other key personnel. To work effectively, the SI person must know the best institutional spokespersons on particular topics and be able to get through to them on a moment's notice.

And, of course, SI people must understand the media, know what their needs are, how they operate, who the science journalists are, and who among general assignment reporters, producers, editors, and a host of other media people may also be interested in science information.

Some SI professionals have an important role in advising the top administrative officer of their institutions, and for this they must have ready and easy access to that person, as well as a good working relationship with him or her. At times this can mean being the bearer of bad news: for example, that a certain proposed policy can reflect unfavorably on the institution, or that information *should* be provided to the media even though it could put the institution in an unfavorable light. Such situations are never easy, but their outcome can be a test of the effectiveness of the science information person and of the credibility of the institution.

Fortunately, in most cases the advisory role is not fraught with quite such tension. More typically, the advice concerns how scientists can work effectively with the media. Usually the SI person gives this type of advice on a one-to-one basis, focusing on the technical aspects and likely public impacts of a particular new scientific development or science policy issue.

To reinforce such advice, some SI offices have developed booklets on how to work with the media. One, "The Scientist's Responsibility for Public Information," was the outcome of a discussion between scientists and science writers arranged by the Society for Neuroscience. (It provides practical information useful to scientists in any discipline and is reprinted in Appendix A.) Both the American Physical Society and the American Chemical Society have developed similar manuals for their members.[2] These formal "how-to" booklets are tangible evidence of one part of the science information advisory role. And as more and more scientists become involved with the media, and as more and more science enters the public domain, it is likely that the advisory role of the science information person will become even more pronounced.

Communicator

Many SI people are, in effect, science journalists within their own organizations. The newspaper columns, magazines, and radio and television programs they produce are often indistinguishable from those produced by the commercial media. Unfortunately, we have no definitive data on the extent and scope of these communication activities, but we do know of numerous examples.

There are literally scores of university magazines, newspapers, and booklets that deal with research and are produced by science information people. Some cover a single topic in depth; others follow the traditional commercial magazine format and cover a variety of topics. Some of the best deal with research topics in a broad context, including information about work being done in both home institutions and elsewhere.[3]

Scientific societies also produce booklets and other types of publications about research developments in their disciplines. Government agencies publish extensive materials about scientific research, including magazines and newsletters. Industrial organizations also disseminate many types of printed materials. Produced for a variety of audiences, most of these publications also serve as sources of information for the mass media. They not only alert reporters to research being done but also provide extensive background on particular topics.

Some science information staffs also write for newspapers. One research news editor at a major public university, for example, writes a regular science column for the local newspaper. Another university's science information person is, in effect, the science reporter for the local newspaper, which does not have a science specialist on staff.

A number of scientific organizations and universities provide regular short science news feature items to small newspapers and other media around the country. These may be reprinted exactly as written by the SI person and under his or her byline. In many cases these features provide the only science news a small weekly newspaper publishes.

SI people also actively use the broadcast media. In fact, several of the nationally syndicated radio science programs on the air today were begun by public information staffs at science organizations and universities and are still produced by them as a public service. University information people often provide science clips for local television news programs. At least one scientific society is producing its own television news segments.[4]

Institutional SI people are involved in communicating science information directly to the public for a variety of reasons. Some view themselves primarily as journalists; others want to help satisfy the desire of the public for more science information; still others choose to take their message directly to the public rather than have it translated and modified by the mass media.

This communicator role poses particular challenges for science information professionals. When their primary audience is the general public, they are not the "practitioner in the middle," but are actually journalists. Their duties are the same and require the same standards of journalistic excellence as those of their mass media colleagues. They cannot afford to go to the public as advocates for their organizations, yet they have a relationship to those organizations that is impossible to ignore.

Facilitator and Mediator

Probably the most familiar role of the science information person is as facilitator—mediator or liaison—between scientists and the media. He or she typically maintains media contacts, prepares and distributes news releases, arranges news conferences, and undertakes other activities that facilitate the flow of information between science and the public via the media. Sometimes, however, these duties also include restricting access to the scientists by the media, either because the scientists do not want to talk with reporters or because the institution has policies that limit such interaction.

To some extent, SI people guide the media to the scientific research that is going on—where it is, who's doing it, why and how it's important. Central to that role is making information easily accessible to the people who need it. SI people may serve as alerting mechanisms, as one of the examples at the beginning of this chapter points out. They may also provide extra sets of arms and legs, tracking down people and background information; checking facts; and providing highlight summaries, tip sheets, and news releases.

All parts of the facilitator role come into play in the busy newsroom of a scientific meeting. The activities of the AAAS newsroom are typical.

The five-day AAAS annual meeting is the largest general scientific meeting in the country and is a major source of news about science. Hundreds of reporters attend each year, representing national and local newspapers, radio stations, television programs, general interest magazines, science publications, and every other conceivable media organization. Some are experienced science writers. Others are general assignment reporters covering scientific news for the first time. The AAAS communications staff assists reporters in their almost overwhelming task of getting a handle on the meeting so that the information the public gets is current, interesting, and important.

To do this, we operate a large newsroom with facilities for writing and filing stories. We provide news releases and copies of speakers' papers, and we arrange news conferences on topics we consider especially newsworthy. Some of the more experienced science writers and those operating under fewer organizational constraints take the time to seek out their own story ideas, but most reporters covering the meeting rely primarily on our press conferences.[5] Checks of print and other media have shown these to be the major sources of information disseminated from the meeting.

We also initiate and arrange many radio, television, and print interviews, suggesting guests and topics and assisting media representatives in lining them up.

The AAAS annual meeting newsroom activities differ only in scale from those of many other organizations. Reporters count on the organizations' public information people to set up interesting and relevant news conferences; to know what about the meeting is new, different, or important; to arrange interviews with speakers who are articulate (especially important for radio or television); to supply copies of the presentations; to provide adequate on-site work space and a means of transmitting stories to their papers or magazines (telephone, telecopier, telex);

and, in the case of television interviews, to help line up visuals (film footage, slides, scale models, and so on).

How do science information people view their facilitator role? One good description comes from the person who ran the public relations operation for the American Heart Association for ten years: "I saw my job as a surrogate reporter. I didn't have an ax to grind. I saw myself as being a friend to the science reporters, as someone to help them find a story, not because I had something to convey or to push; that wasn't my job, and I don't think it's any of our jobs. I think our interest is to get information out."[6]

A busy newsroom like that at the AAAS meeting is a microcosm of the interactions among scientists, journalists, and science information persons throughout the year. During our meeting, we try to persuade reluctant scientists to participate in news conferences or interviews; we attempt to dissuade other scientists from holding press briefings on topics we know do not warrant it and will get little media attention; and we provide scientists with tips on meeting with reporters during news conferences or interviews and encourage them to make copies of their papers available. Concurrently, we will be providing reporters with additional background information about a scientist or meeting topic, and setting up a last-minute interview to meet a producer's deadline. And at the same time, we might be working with the AAAS Board of Directors to issue a last-minute policy resolution it has just approved on a controversial issue. In some cases, we ourselves will be writing a news item about the meeting for some internal or external publication.

Mass communication researchers have called this "mediator" role one of the most difficult of all tasks performed by public information persons in science research organizations, primarily because of the different goals and concerns scientists and journalists have and the different languages they use.[7]

Is the public information officer an effective mediator between scientists and the media? One study found that scientists perceived that the public information office played almost no role in their interactions with the media. They believed that journalists initiated most of the contacts.[8] Another study, of medical school information activities, concluded that public information offices have little influence in bringing scientists' research to the attention of the mass media.[9]

On the other hand, the science editor of the *San Francisco Chronicle* told a group of university information officers, "No matter how many reporters tell you that they never listen to a university 'flack' or that they don't care about news releases, it isn't true. You are the people we depend on probably more than any other source." He noted that public information persons can steer reporters to the right person on a campus and can pave the way to scientists who don't know the reporter.[10]

At the same meeting, another national science writer said, "It's helpful sometimes to have an information officer who will open the door for you if you know a scientist is going to be difficult." And he singled out one institution that gets a lot of media attention, which he attributed not only to its being a fine research institution but also to its having public information people who are "very aggressive, knowledgeable, and helpful."[11]

Also at the same meeting, the person who arranges an annual briefing for science writers identified public information persons as the ones who can tell him who their most articulate scientists are and which ones are exciting and doing the most interesting work.[12]

In an extensive study of how science reporters cover the AAAS annual meeting, Sharon Dunwoody found that AAAS could essentially decide what was news about its own meeting by making available certain papers and by setting up press conferences (see Chapter 12). In another example, the public information staff of Battelle Memorial Institute, a large science research institution in Columbus, Ohio, generates nearly 100 percent of what becomes news about Battelle by phoning journalists or city desks, or taking calls from journalists who ask to speak with experts on various topics.[13] And more than half of the scientists in one study reported that some mediation has taken place in their interaction with reporters and that it has resulted in more accurate stories.[14]

These seemingly conflicting data are not surprising. First, most SI persons view their roles as background ones. They often are relatively invisible in the science communication process and probably need to be to do their jobs effectively.

As for journalists, they can easily overlook the assistance provided by science information people and are often unaware of the extent of the interaction between the SI person and the scientist, even when that interaction might have been the key to their being able to get the story. In other cases, some journalists may feel that their sense of independence is compromised if they admit to getting story ideas from a science information person rather than originating the ideas themselves.

Finally, scientists typically do not know how science information gets communicated and have no idea what the science information person in their organization does. And when a reporter calls them, they seldom think that the impetus might have come from the science information officer.

The Problems SI Officers Encounter

Some science information people work in institutions which accord them the respect and resources they need to do their jobs effectively.

Others, unfortunately, do not. And most SI people find that within the journalistic community, there is often a less-than-positive attitude about their work.

Within their own institutions, SI people may find themselves low in the hierarchy and with too many competing responsibilities. They may be expected to attract national media attention to their institutions and keep themselves up-to-date in science and technology, yet their budgets may be so small that doing these things well is not possible. There may not be any encouragement to upgrade their professional skills, and within their institutions their positions may be classified in such a way that they become low-paying, dead-end jobs.

Within the journalistic community, SI people may find themselves disparagingly referred to as public relations "flacks," while their work is accepted by the media entirely without acknowledgment. The National Association of Science Writers, the main organization for professional science journalists, does accept SI people as associate members, but does not permit them to vote or hold office.[15] This occurs in spite of many similarities in backgrounds, training, activities, and outlooks of the two professions.

The job of supplying science information can be personally frustrating because public recognition is hard to come by. An SI person's news release or article may be printed verbatim in a newspaper or magazine, yet carry the byline of a reporter. Similarly, the SI person's role in setting up radio and television programs may often be ignored, as may efforts in working with scientists to help them prepare for media-related activities.

Understanding the Process

These problems aside, what is it like to be the practitioner in the middle?

First, it is hardly ever dull—especially on Friday afternoons at 5:00 P.M., when a call comes from a journalist who needs information right away to meet a deadline and everyone else seems to have left for an early weekend. We have to be very creative in tracking down people who have the information we need.

Then, too, it is seldom simple, for we must serve many different and often conflicting constituencies. Scientists with whom we work see us as representatives of the media; reporters with whom we work see us as representatives of the scientists. And both scientists and reporters may see us as representatives of our institution and its administration. We are indeed in the middle.

On the most basic level, we must carry out the goals and aims of our institution while working with the scientists within that institution, who are very independent beings. While they may have allegiance to the institution, they often have a stronger allegiance to their work and their discipline.

We must have a good relationship with the media, for reporters are one of our prime constituencies. And while we keep the needs and interests of the media in mind, we must never forget that our ultimate responsibility is to the public, to provide them with interesting, reliable information about science and technology.

What happens when the needs and demands of these different constituencies are in conflict? How does one respond when a scientist wants to announce research results but the institution does not, or when a reporter wants information that will cause particular embarrassment to the institution or individual scientist? And what about the public's right and need to know? Should the public have to wait weeks or months until research is actually published in a major scientific publication before hearing about important new scientific developments?

There are no easy answers to these questions, nor is there any single answer that will hold true in all situations. How well science information people do their jobs has a lot to do with how well they are able to satisfy the needs of their often-conflicting constituencies. Their credibility with all of them is the key to their success.

Notes

1. Audrey Likely, "Talking Science to the Public," a talk presented as part of a panel discussion, "Communicating Science to the Public," at the annual meeting of the American Association for the Advancement of Science, Washington, D.C., January 3, 1982.

2. "The Scientist's Responsibility for Public Information," produced by the Society for Neuroscience, is reprinted as Appendix A, this volume. It is also available from the Scientists' Institute for Public Information (355 Lexington Avenue, 16th floor, New York, N.Y. 10017). The other two "how-to" booklets are "Physics Goes Public," produced by the American Physical Society (335 East 45th Street, New York, N.Y. 10017), and "The Chemists and the Media," published by the American Chemical Society (1155 16th Street, NW, Washington, D.C. 20036).

3. Among the really good university publications are *OSU Quest*, a newspaper published by Ohio State University; *UCSF Magazine*, published by the University of California, San Francisco; *Bostonian Magazine*, published by Boston University; *The Research News*, published by the University of Michigan; and *RE:SEARCH*, published by Northeastern University.

4. These radio programs include "Dimensions in Science" (formerly called "Man and Molecules"), which the American Chemical Society public relations office has been producing for more than twenty years; "Science

54 UNDERSTANDING THE ACTORS

Editor," produced by the University of California; "Science Report," produced by the American Institute of Physics; and "Report on Science" and "Focus," both produced by the AAAS communications staff. The television initiatives include "Science TV Report," produced by the American Institute of Physics public information division.

5. Sharon Friedman provides an explanation of how the media operate, including the constraints under which they work, in Chapter 2.

6. Sharon Dunwoody, Ben Patrusky, and Carol Rogers, "The Gatekeepers: The Inner Circle in Science Writing," in P. L. Alberger and V. L. Carter, eds., *Communicating University Research* (Washington, D. C.: Council for the Advancement and Support of Education, 1981), 152–161.

7. Sharon Dunwoody and Michael Ryan, "Public Information Persons as Mediators Between Scientists and Journalists," *Journalism Quarterly*, 60 (Winter 1983): 647–656.

8. Ibid., 652.

9. Susan Holly Stocking, "Mass Media Visibility of Medical School Research: The Role of Public Information Initiatives, Scientists' Publishing Acitivity, and Institutional Prestige" (Ph.D. dissertation, Indiana University, 1983).

10. David Perlman, "Informing the Public About Research: The Media," in Alberger and Carter, eds., *Communicating University Research*, 109–115.

11. Cristine Russell, Warren Leary, Patrick Young, and David Perlman, "How I Cover Science: Newspapers," in Alberger and Carter, eds., *Communicating University Research*, 116–127.

12. Dunwoody, Patrusky, and Rogers, "The Gatekeepers."

13. Ibid., 157.

14. Dunwoody and Ryan, "Public Information Persons as Mediators."

15. The National Association of Science Writers is the professional organization for science writers and science information persons. The membership classifications include an active category for those who write primarily for the mass media (including freelance writers) and an associate category for science-writing educators and for those who are primarily engaged in public information activities for institutions. Although the membership is about evenly divided between these two categories, only the active members can vote and hold office.

CHAPTER 4

Reaching the Attentive and Interested Publics for Science

Jon D. Miller

Not everyone pays attention to scientific information in the mass media. But the question of who seeks out such information has long gone unanswered. Journalists particularly, with their emphasis on satisfying audience wants and needs, must know how to separate the publics for scientific information from the rest. Knowing one's audience permits a reporter to tailor the message, and a scientifically attentive or interested audience may need a very different kind of message than would a disinterested group. Jon Miller has conducted some of the most influential recent research on the attentive and interested publics for science. In this chapter he outlines some of his findings and then offers his views of what these findings mean for the mass media and science journalists.

Jon D. Miller is the director of the Public Opinion Laboratory and associate professor of political science at Northern Illinois University. He received his doctorate in political science from Northwestern University in 1970 and has devoted most of the last decade to studying public attitudes toward science and technology. He is the author of *Citizenship in an Age of Science, The American People and Science Policy* and many articles and book chapters on the subject. Miller is a member of the AAAS Committee on the Public Understanding of Science.

COMMUNICATING SCIENTIFIC INFORMATION[1] to the public successfully requires the recognition that "the public" is not a single homogeneous entity but rather a complex structure of segments defined mainly by interests, knowledge, and broader life goals. Marketing analysts have used the concept of population segments for decades, but communicators have been slower to adopt this approach. The major television networks, for example, still make prime-time programming decisions on the basis of viewership data that amount to undifferentiated counts of the number of sets tuned to a given channel. Newspapers still base advertising rates on simple circulation counts. Only magazines have made extensive use of specialized population segments in their editorial, circulation, and advertising sales strategies.

In this chapter I would like to introduce the concept of an attentive public, one segment of the public that may be important to those who communicate scientific information. The presentation of this basic concept will lead to a discussion of the objectives of communicating scientific information. And the final section will examine the media consumption patterns of selected segments of the public and will suggest some strategies for the communication of scientific information.

Making Choices

The single most important factor affecting someone's receptivity to scientific information appears to be interest. Unlike our frontier ancestors, who suffered from boredom and isolation, we are faced with an extraordinary range of activities, each competing for the finite number of hours in our day. On a typical day in most urban areas, an individual can choose among numerous motion pictures, several plays or musical performances, amateur and professional athletic contests, informal or formal courses on a wide array of topics, recreational sports, topical discussion groups, political meetings, and a rapidly increasing number of television and cable offerings.

The competition for our time is intense, reflecting the richness and diversity of our industrialized society. Some persons will be interested in science and technology; others will not. Some will be interested in foreign affairs; others will not. Some people will follow professional baseball avidly; others will not. The important point is that no individual can follow every interest or issue. We all make choices—consciously or unconsciously.

This process of interest specialization is important for two reasons. First, it suggests a similar specialization in participation by citizens in the formulation of science policy. Second, it implies differences in people's receptivity to scientific information. It is important to explore each of these implications in greater detail.

Different Levels of Participation in Science Policy

Participation in the formulation of public policy in any area requires time and other resources that are limited. Writing or calling a legislator, attending a meeting, or persuading others on any issue all make demands on our time. Almost half of American adults report that they do not follow any public policy area closely.[2] Among those citizens who follow one or more issues, relatively few say they are able to follow more than three issues.

This issue specialization process was described first by Gabriel Almond, who was concerned about the small number of Americans who appeared to follow foreign policy matters.[3] Almond suggested that those citizens who demonstrated (1) a high level of interest in an issue area, (2) a functional level of knowledge about that area, and (3) a pattern of relevant information gathering could be labeled *attentive* to that issue. Collectively, these individuals constitute the *attentive public* for any given issue.

National survey data indicate that 20 percent of American adults are attentive to science policy.[4] In contrast to other segments of the population, the attentive public for science policy is younger, predominantly male, better educated, and more likely to have taken a college-level science course (Table 4–1).

A second important segment of the public is comprised of persons who have a relatively high level of interest in science and technology but lack a functional understanding of the process or the terminology of science. Referred to as the *interested public* for science policy, this group includes about 20 percent of American adults. In contrast to the attentive public, the interested public is slightly older and somewhat less well educated, and they are less likely to have taken a college-level science course. The interested public represents the pool from which additional attentives might emerge should conditions stimulate wider public concern about science policy issues.

Public involvement in the formation of public policy can be viewed as pyramidal in form (see p. 59). For specialized and technical areas such as science, public policy is made by a small number of decision makers who have the power to make binding decisions. The decision makers for science policy would include the president, relevant executive officers, congressional leaders, and relevant committee and subcommittee chairs and members. Judges may occasionally become science policy decision makers.

Table 4-1. Comparative Demographics of Attentive Public for 1979 and 1981*

	Attentive Public		Interested Public		Nonattentive Public	
	1979	1981	1979	1981	1979	1981
Age						
17–24	24%	18%	17%	19%	18%	18%
25–34	32	33	21	18	19	22
35–44	12	16	15	15	17	17
45–54	12	15	17	17	14	16
55–64	13	10	14	15	14	10
65 and over	7	8	17	16	17	18
	(100)	(100)	(101)	(100)	(99)	(101)
Gender						
Female	35	40	55	54	58	57
Male	65	60	45	46	42	43
	(100)	(100)	(100)	(100)	(100)	(100)
Education						
Less than high school	7	8	26	19	36	24
High school	59	48	63	69	55	61
Baccalaureate	19	32	8	9	6	10
Graduate degree	16	12	4	3	3	5
	(101)	(100)	(101)	(100)	(100)	(100)
College science courses						
None	46	NA	79	NA	82	NA
Some	54	NA	21	NA	18	NA
	(100)		(100)		(100)	
N =	319	637	328	617	988	1940

*Due to rounding, percentages do not all total to 100.

The primary representatives of science reside at the second level of the pyramid. This group consists of persons from universities, corporations, independent research centers, and the media. These policy leaders normally define the science policy agenda, present policy requests to decision makers, and negotiate to resolve policy differences among themselves and with decision makers. When there is a high degree of agreement between the decision makers and the science policy leaders on any given matter, policy decisions are made and there is no wider public participation in the process. In the United States, most science policy matters are resolved in this way, without broader public involvement.

There are, however, at least three circumstances in which a broader segment of the public participates in making science policy. First, when

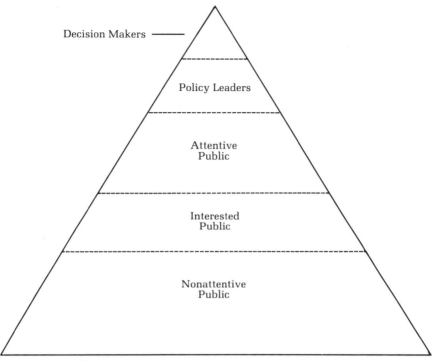

Decision Makers ———

Policy Leaders

Attentive
Public

Interested
Public

Nonattentive
Public

A Stratified Model of Participants in Science Policy Formulation

there are serious differences among science policy leaders over a specific issue, both sides tend to appeal to interested and informed citizens—the attentive public—to contact decision makers and to make their views known. The current controversy over the safety and desirability of nuclear power plants illustrates this type of public involvement.

Second, even when there is agreement among science policy leaders, some decision makers may reject specific policy demands. In this case, science policy leaders often try to mobilize the support of the attentive public, asking them to contact the appropriate decision makers to argue for a specific policy. Arguments in the early 1980s over federal funding for scientific research and for science education illustrate this type of public involvement. Faced with substantial reductions in federal spending, the leadership of science policy attempted to generate political pressure from those attentive to science policy. Most of the appeals for public involvement were channeled through disciplinary societies, educational associations, and professional groups.

Finally, a few issues have become electoral issues, primarily through the direct referendum mechanism. The fluoridation referenda of the 1950s and 1960s were the first major examples of placing essentially scientific judgments on an electoral ballot. More recent referenda have focused on nuclear power and laetrile. Issues such as fluoridation and laetrile have reached the ballot when individuals and groups who were not a part of the mainstream science policy leadership group found the traditional executive and legislative channels closed but sensed that there was popular support for their cause. The genesis of the nuclear power referenda is more complex, since a segment of the traditional science policy leadership group has been active in the anti–nuclear power movement. When issues reach a formal referendum, the interested and nonattentive publics become involved in the formulation of science policy. While the number of science-related referenda has been relatively small, this avenue of public participation remains available, especially at the state level.

Different Information Needs

Given the different levels of citizen involvement in the formulation of science policy, we expect individuals to have different science information needs.

At the top of the policy pyramid, decision makers have specialized science information needs. As the range and frequency of science policy matters on the national political agenda have grown in recent years, decision makers have increasingly had to make comparative judgments concerning science and technology matters and have sought empirical measures of scientific activity and output. Efforts to measure the state of science by the National Science Foundation in recent years illustrate this type of information.[5]

Decision makers also need information about major science policy problems and alternatives. To a large extent, this information comes from policy leaders who are seeking to implement a given policy or arguing for one policy solution over another. While I don't devote any space here to the information needs of decision makers, it is important to understand these needs, since many of the science information needs of other groups in the system reflect and respond in part to these needs.[6]

The science information needs of science policy leaders are similar in nature to those of the decision makers, but they are broader since it is also important for science policy leaders to understand the substance of much of the scientific work for which they seek support and to be sensitive to the relative needs of various areas of scientific work. To a large extent, these matters are discussed and resolved within the structure of disciplinary societies and interdisciplinary organizations within the scientific community. The policy committees of groups such as the

American Chemical Society, the Industrial Research Institute, or the American Association for the Advancement of Science have traditionally provided a forum for the exchange of information and the resolution of policy differences. As the size of the scientific community increased in the postwar years, the need for more formal information exchange increased and a number of specialized scientific journals emerged. The more traditional journals such as *Science* and *Nature* have continued to provide an important forum for science policy leaders.

The attentive public for science policy also has important science information needs. In line with its role in the policy formulation process, the attentive public needs to be informed about specific controversies for which its involvement is sought. If science policy leaders wish to generate broader public response on issues such as scientific research funding or nuclear power, it is imperative that the attentive public be informed of the nature of the problem, that it learn about alternative solutions to the problem, and that it become sensitive to the longer-term implications of various solutions. The very process of seeking to mobilize the support of the attentive public does convey some of this information. It also is important for the attentive public to have a general understanding of the process of scientific study and some functional understanding of the major constructs used in scientific discourse (for example, molecule, gene, cell). This background knowledge of science might be characterized as basic scientific literacy.

To a large extent, the information needs of the attentive public have been neglected until very recently. Science reporting in mass-circulation magazines and newspapers has been too general to provide the level of information needed for basic scientific literacy, while magazines such as *Scientific American* have become too technical for most of the attentive public. The emergence of a new generation of science magazines such as *Science 85, Discover,* and *Omni* and the inclusion of more sophisticated science information in older magazines such as the *National Geographic* have begun to address the information needs of the attentive public for science policy. Similarly, science television programming such as "Nova" and "The Ascent of Man" have contributed to the information needs of this group.

The information needs of the interested public are a somewhat more difficult market to address. This segment of the public has a high level of interest in scientific matters but lacks both a basic understanding of scientific concepts and the confidence to tackle communications that appear to be "scientific." They are unlikely to try to read a magazine such as *Scientific American* but may be more receptive to less sophisticated magazines such as *National Geographic.* To communicate scientific information to this segment of the public, the approach must be nontechnical, and the format should be simple and pictorial when possible.

Little agreement exists about the information needs of the non-attentive public at the bottom of the policy pyramid. The traditional view of science educators has been that all citizens ought to be scientifically literate in order to participate in the democratic processes that lead to science policy. This view is still widely held within the scientific community. More recently, some observers—including myself—have advanced the proposition that universal scientific literacy is not feasible, that a significant portion of the population is not attracted to science and technology.[7] If this is the case, then their scientific information needs may be characterized as consumer-oriented or practical in nature.

Different Patterns of Information Gathering

Are persons who are attentive to science matters more likely to read scientific material than others? Do they use the same sources as others? If there are differences in information consumption patterns, it may be possible to develop specific strategies for satisfying the information needs of the various segments of society. Since the attentive public is more active than either the interested public or the nonattentive public in the formulation of science policy, it will be useful to look at how this group—as well as the interested public—uses each of the major media sources.

Looking first at television viewing, data from a 1981 national survey indicated that 59 percent of the attentive public were regular viewers of a science television show (Table 4–2).[8] "National Geographic Specials" were the science programs most frequently viewed by both the attentive and interested publics, with 45 percent of the attentive public reporting

Table 4-2.   Patterns of Television Viewing: 1981

Watched Each Show "most of the time"	Attentive Public	Interested Public
National Geographic Specials	45%	29%
Walter Cronkite's Universe	24	22
Nova	22	6
At least one of above	59	40
Evening news	72	75
Morning news	24	31
ABC's Nightline	22	31
At least one of above	78	81
60 Minutes	61	59
N =	637	614

that they watched the show most of the time. Only 24 percent of the attentive public reported regular viewing of "Walter Cronkite's Universe," and 22 percent were regular viewers of "Nova." The interested public for science policy was significantly less likely than the attentive public to be regular viewers of these television science shows.

Almost 80 percent of the attentive public reported that they watched a television news show regularly, with the greatest number viewing the evening television news. The interested public was just as likely to view these general news shows regularly as was the attentive public.

Looking at newspaper readership, the data from the 1981 survey indicated that almost three-quarters of the attentive public for science policy were regular newspaper readers but that only 9 percent of the attentive public rated the newspaper to be a very good source of science news (Table 4-3). The interested public for science policy was slightly less likely to read a newspaper regularly, but somewhat more likely to view the paper as a good source of science news.

Half of the attentive public reported that they were regular readers of one or more science magazines (Table 4-4). Approximately a third of the attentive public reported that they read the *National Geographic* most of the time. Ten percent reported that they read *Psychology Today* regularly, while fewer than 10 percent were regular readers of *Science, Omni, Discover, Scientific American, Science Digest,* and *Science 81.* The interested public reported a similar—but significantly lower—pattern of science magazine readership.

Just over half of the attentive public reported reading a general news magazine most of the time (Table 4-4). *Time* was the most frequently read general news magazine among attentives, with *Newsweek* close behind.

Table 4-3. Patterns of Newspaper Readership: 1981

	Attentive Public	*Interested Public*
Frequency of reading		
Most of the time	72%	64%
Occasionally	21	24
Not at all	7	12
Evaluation of newspaper as source of science news		
Very good source	9	14
Moderately good source	45	52
Not a good source	46	34
N =	637	614

Table 4-4. Patterns of Magazine Readership: 1981

Read "most of the time"	Attentive Public	Interested Public
National Geographic	31%	17%
Psychology Today	10	5
Science	8	6
Omni	8	3
Discover	6	3
Scientific American	6	2
Science Digest	4	3
Science 81	3	2
At least one science magazine	50	27
Time	32	21
Newsweek	28	14
U.S. News & World Report	22	11
At least one newsmagazine	53	30
N =	637	614

Beyond the formal communications channels, the attentive public uses a variety of informal information and learning resources including zoos, aquaria, botanical gardens, and museums. Data from the 1981 survey indicated that 82 percent of the attentive public for science policy utilized one or more informal learning resources during the year prior to the interview (Table 4–5). Approximately 60 percent of the attentive public reported visiting a zoo at least once in the preceding twelve months, half reported visiting a botanical garden or arboretum, and the same proportion said they had visited a science and technology museum at least once during the last year. The interested public reported slightly lower utilization rates.

Table 4-5. Patterns of Informal Learning: 1981

Visited at Least Once in Last Year	Attentive Public	Interested Public
Zoo	61%	54%
Botanical garden or arboretum	51	37
Science or technology museum	52	28
Natural history museum	43	33
Aquarium	37	37
At least one of the above	82	71
N =	637	614

The Purposes of Scientific Communication

In general social terms, two purposes for scientific communication to the public are (1) the creation or enhancement of scientific literacy, and (2) the dissemination of information relevant to the formulation of science policy. A substantial portion of mass media science writing has as one of its goals increasing the scientific literacy of the reader. *Scientific American* articles on particle physics, plate tectonics, or recombinant DNA illustrate this type of communication. Similarly, pictorial essays in *National Geographic* on crystal structures or microscopic organisms are directed toward increasing the scientific literacy of the reader. Much of the material in the newer science magazines such as *Science 85*, *Discover*, and *Omni* may be motivated by a similar objective.

In contrast, articles on the safety or risks of nuclear power plants, the problems of nuclear waste disposal, the long-term effects of PCBs, or acid rain illustrate communications designed to inform the reader about actual or potential science policy issues. The major characteristic of this type of communication is that it relates directly to a current or emergent science policy issue.

It is important to understand the difference between these two purposes for communicating scientific information to the public and to realize the implications of that difference for effective communication. At the most basic level, the improvement of scientific literacy is a complex, long-term task. It is not an impossible task, but it most certainly is not a short-term project. A 1979 national survey indicated that only 7 percent of American adults met a minimal test of scientific literacy.[9] Adults who did not acquire some degree of scientific literacy during formal schooling tend to lack both the interest and vocabulary to understand communications intended to improve such literacy.

While there is some evidence that scientifically literate persons tend to feel more positive about organized science than nonattentives, the linkage is not perfect, and this is a long route toward policy support. For adults, communications designed to influence policy views should focus on the policy issue and provide an intelligent discussion of the policy alternatives. Given the relative sophistication of the attentive public for science policy, one-sided exhortations are unlikely to be effective in mobilizing support.

Some Strategies for Communicating Science to the Public

As stated above, the task of increasing scientific literacy among adults is complex and long-term. The need is great in all strata of the public, but it is especially critical among the members of the attentive public. Miller has reported that two-thirds of those persons who are attentive to science policy cannot pass a relatively minimal test of scientific literacy.[10] These individuals have sufficient policy-relevant information to be able to discuss specific policy issues, but when probed on the meaning of scientific study and on specific scientific constructs such as radiation or DNA, they cannot demonstrate a minimal level of understanding. Since these persons sometimes participate in the formulation of science policy, it is important that their level of scientific literacy be increased as much and as early as possible.

Fortunately, this is the most interested and receptive segment of the public and the easiest with which to communicate. It would appear that this group can be reached through focused television science programming such as "National Geographic Specials" or "Nova," through specialized magazines such as the National Geographic, Discover, or Science 85, and through informal learning resources such as zoos and museums. Since this segment of the population is interested in scientific and technological matters, communications can begin with some presumption of interest and can focus on scientific substance. The general approach and level of sophistication of a "Nova" show illustrates the most effective level of communication for increasing the scientific literacy of the attentive public for science policy.

While I believe that the improvement of the scientific literacy of the attentive public is the highest priority for scientific communication, the improvement of scientific literacy among the interested and nonattentive publics is also desirable. The interested public expresses a high level of interest in scientific and technological matters but knows even less about science than does the nonliterate portion of the attentive public for science policy. The interested public is more likely to use broadcast media than print media and is more likely to watch a commercial television channel than public television. Network shows such as "Walter Cronkite's Universe" would appear to be the most effective approach to this group. As with the attentive public, a moderately high level of interest can be assumed, but the level of scientific vocabulary will be very low and the level of understanding of the process of scientific investigation even lower. Pictorial essays such as those in National Geographic may also be effective in reaching the interested public.

Efforts to increase the scientific literacy of the nonattentive public face formidable barriers, because the nonattentive public is not interested in scientific and technological matters. If a magazine article or a television show deals with science or technology, the nonattentive public may not even read or view it. So a major communication task in regard to this segment of the population is to persuade them that it is important to be scientifically literate. An increase in the volume of science programming or articles will have little effect on the nonattentive citizen until he or she first develops an interest in the subject area.

When it comes to information about science policy, the most receptive segment of the population will be the attentive public. This segment of the public is already very interested in the issue area and at least moderately knowledgeable about science policy issues. In the transmission of policy-relevant information to the attentive public, general news media—television newscasts, newspapers, and weekly newsmagazines—can effectively alert this group to an issue in the public arena or to its movement toward a critical decision point. It appears that the attentive public does not view newspapers as a very good source of science news; thus, these more general media may serve either as early warning systems or as news bulletins. For the communication of more sophisticated and detailed background information, specialized science magazines and selected television science programming seem to be the best approaches. A recent "Nova" program on the condition of science education and the demise of federal support for science education illustrates an effective background, policy-relevant communication. Articles in *Discover, Science 85,* or other science magazines would serve a similar function.

While a growing number of media have communicated science to the attentive public in recent years, national survey results suggest that the attentive public is still seeking more sophisticated presentations of current science policy matters. This group will be relatively unreceptive to one-sided exhortations on policy issues. On the other hand, given some of their difficulties with basic scientific constructs, they are unlikely to be responsive to excessively technical presentations.

The interested public plays only a marginal role in policy formulation, and previous studies have found that this group is relatively unlikely to participate in the formulation of science policy even when the opportunity is available. I don't think it would be wise to make a major investment to convey policy-relevant information to this group, but some of the communications targeted for the attentive public will inevitably reach the interested public. Some persons in this segment who are particularly interested in a given policy matter may use attentive-directed communications to become informed and to participate in the policy process. But the proportion of the interested public that actually participates in the policy process will be relatively small.

Although I don't think any useful purpose would be served by directing policy-relevant information to the nonattentive segment of the public under normal circumstances, when a science policy issue reaches an electoral referendum, the nonattentive public may become an important part of the process. Studies of public involvement in nuclear power referenda have indicated that the nonattentive public tends to look to opinion leaders for guidance when confronted with a technical issue such as nuclear power.

The best long-term solution to both increasing scientific literacy and increasing the size of the attentive public for science policy is the improvement of science education in the pre-college and college years. If an interest in science can be stimulated early in life and an understanding of the basic processes of scientific study conveyed, there will be a higher level of receptivity to scientific communication. Once these formative years have passed and no interest in science, or a fear or dislike of it, has been created, the effectiveness of later communication efforts will be very low.

Notes

1. The term "scientific information" is meant to include a wide array of information concerning basic science theories, applied scientific problems and impacts, and technical and consumer information. The scope of substantive content would include the physical and biological sciences, the social sciences, medicine, engineering, and related applied fields.

2. J. D. Miller, K. Prewitt, and R. Pearson, *The Attitudes of the U.S. Public Toward Science and Technology,* final report to the National Science Foundation under contract SRS78–16839 (Chicago: National Opinion Research Center, 1980); J. D. Miller, *A National Survey of Public Attitudes Toward Science and Technology,* report to the National Science Foundation under grant 8105662 (DeKalb, Ill.: Public Opinion Laboratory, 1982); and J. D. Miller, *The American People and Science Policy* (New York: Pergamon, 1983).

3. G. A. Almond, *The American People and Foreign Policy* (New York: Harcourt, Brace, & Co., 1950).

4. Science policy refers to governmental decisions concerning basic science, applied science, and technology; see Miller, *American People and Science Policy.*

5. National Science Board, *Science Indicators—1976, 1980,* and *1982* (Washington, D.C.: U.S. Government Printing Office, 1977, 1981, and 1983, respectively).

6. D. K. Price, *The Scientific Estate* (Cambridge, Mass.: Belknap Press, 1965); J. D. Miller and K. Prewitt, *A National Survey of the Nongovernmental Leadership of American Science and Technology,* a final report to the National Science Foundation under NSF grant 8105662 (DeKalb, Ill.: Public Opinion Laboratory, 1982).

7. J. D. Miller, "The Scientific Literacy of the American People: A Reinterpretation," in *AAPT Pathways: Proceedings of the Fiftieth Anniversary Symposium of the AAPT,* ed. M. Philips (Stony Brook, N. Y.: AAPT, 1981); and J. D. Miller, "Scientific Literacy: A Conceptual and Empirical Review," *Daedalus,* 112 (Spring 1983): 29–48.

8. The survey was sponsored by the National Science Foundation and conducted by the Public Opinion Laboratory at Northern Illinois University. Approximately 3200 individuals were interviewed and 637 were identified as attentive to science policy. A complete description of the survey design, sample plan, response rates, and interview schedule is provided in Miller, *A National Survey of Public Attitudes Toward Science and Technology.*

9. Miller, "Scientific Literacy: A Conceptual and Empirical Review."

10. Ibid., 45–46.

PART II

Analyzing
the Interactions

T HE WORKING RELATIONSHIP between scientists and journalists is not always a smooth one. How these two sets of individuals interact with one another is the subject of Part II. Authors in this section examine these interactions at both the local and national level, and scientists and journalists comment on each other's participation in the science communication process.

CHAPTER 5

Scientists and the Local Press

David W. Crisp

The majority of people in the United States read local, small-town newspapers rather than large national papers. Most of these smaller newspapers do not employ full-time specialty reporters. Yet science-related problems such as toxic wastes, air pollution, and groundwater contamination all hit home in small communities, where they must be covered by general assignment reporters who have little training in or understanding of science. These reporters face many problems, including not knowing where to go to get information, or, if they have found it, not knowing how to interpret it or translate it into lay terms for their readers. David Crisp found himself in just such a situation in Palestine, Texas, a town of about 15,000 people in the eastern part of the state, when that region was being considered as a potential storage site for nuclear wastes. This is his account of the problems he faced. His prizewinning series of articles about the Palestine nuclear waste storage issue can be found in Appendix B.

David Crisp worked as a general assignment reporter for the *Palestine Herald–Press* from 1979 to 1981, following a year's stint at the State Legislative Reference Library in Austin and graduation from Stephen F. Austin State University. In 1980 he won the AAAS–Westinghouse Science Journalism Award for science writing in newspapers with less than 100,000 circulation. From 1981 to 1982 he was the city hall reporter for the *Bryan–College Station Eagle*. He received his master's degree in English from Texas A&M University in August 1983, after which he rejoined the *Eagle* as a sports reporter.

O<small>NE OF THE DIFFICULTIES</small> of reporting science news at the local level is the absence of a larger perspective. It is a bit like trying to make a sketch of Mount Rushmore while standing on George Washington's nose. I am neither a scientist nor a science writer but I was a general assignment reporter who covered science news when it came up, when I had time for it, and when a siren did not call me away to a car wreck or a fire.

I came to the attention of the American Association for the Advancement of Science (AAAS) and vice versa because of a series of articles I wrote in 1980 when the federal government was considering three salt domes near Palestine, Texas, as possible sites for the nation's first high-level nuclear waste repository. Much of what I know about scientists and science writing comes from the two years I spent sorting out confusing claims about the safety of nuclear waste disposal, looking at questions such as what could be done about nuclear wastes, who was doing something, and—of paramount importance to my readers—where nuclear wastes would go.

Nuclear waste disposal is an endless—and endlessly fascinating—problem, bringing together as it does elements of the international debate over nuclear proliferation, the energy crisis, states' rights, the environmental movement, acts of Congress, the nuclear power controversy, and that wonderful, emotionally charged, almost magical word, *radiation*, with all its connotations of nuclear holocaust, science fiction mutants, cancer, and a whole catalog of damages to unborn generations.

I thought then, and I believe now, that small communities that fall by geographical accident into the forefront of the nation's search for the solutions to its most haunting problems should be first in line to get the most complete and accurate information possible. Otherwise, those people can't be blamed for taking the familiar point of view that "I know it has to go somewhere, but I don't want it in my backyard."

That is a morally bankrupt position. It is well that in places like Palestine—which are left out of the debate on most national problems—people should have to openly confront the real issue: nuclear wastes do have to go somewhere, and they do have to go into somebody's backyard.

It is one thing for federal bureaucrats and scientists to figure up worst-case scenarios, risk-benefit analyses, threshold levels, and definitions of reasonable certainty. It is quite another matter when one can, as I could, thumb through a thick government document and find a little red circle on a map that shows where the nuclear garbage is going to go, and inside that circle is a dot that shows where your house is.

I believe it is critical that the people who live inside that red circle know what's going on, but I sense a reluctance on the part of some scientists to talk with those people who need help the most. This reluctance is understandable. It takes personal courage bordering on the heroic to return all the calls, to answer the naive questions, to go to the public meetings, to weather the irrational and emotional attacks, to take the risk of having one's name linked in print to a misquotation or a misinterpretation of fact.

I think scientists also sometimes feel that there is no use talking to local people, because they don't understand the subject and they aren't going to change their minds anyhow. This feeling also is understandable. An East Texas state representative, who has since mercifully been defeated, summed up the feelings of a lot of Palestine people about nuclear wastes when he said, "I don't believe anyone can prove beyond a shadow of a doubt that it won't hurt anything. To me, that's all we need to know." He was quite right, of course. Science can prove very little beyond a shadow of a doubt. His statement captured the mood of his constituents.

But the effort to inform should not be abandoned just because no one is going to be convinced. People don't need to be told what to think, but they do need some facts to think about. I began the study of nuclear wastes with the goal of finding some firm, final answers. To my surprise, I found instead that as my knowledge increased, so did my objectivity and tolerance. This phenomenon, I believe, is a natural consequence of the search for knowledge. It is easy and entertaining to ridicule people who react irrationally to things they don't understand, but those people aren't stupid; they just don't have good information and they don't know where to get it.

An East Texas county judge, appearing at a public hearing in Dallas on what was obscurely called a "generic environmental impact statement," complained eloquently that he couldn't get a copy of the 1400-page document until a few days before the hearing, which was far too late to even read it, much less comment on its highly technical contents. He asked for more information, and he asked that it not be worded "in scientific or bureaucratic mumbo-jumbo our rural counties may not understand." The judge's situation improved after that, or at least changed. The last time I talked to him, he was getting plenty of documents—so many, in fact, that he didn't know where to put them all. He said he didn't know how he would ever find time to read them.

The judge's dilemma touches on many of the problems that small-town newspaper reporters face in getting information on complicated issues. There are the problems of getting information in time, of getting the information one needs, and of getting information one can understand. The difficulties can be enormous. Small towns have small libraries with very few, often very old books. Bookstores carry a few antitechnology volumes, which for some reasom seem to move off the shelves better than more serious stuff. Newspaper office reference materials typically consist of an unabridged dictionary, a 1974 *World Almanac*, a thirty-five-year-old set of *World Book* encyclopedias, and a framed copy of the paper that came out the day Japan attacked Pearl Harbor. Even major newspapers and magazines can be hard to find. The reporter feels abandoned somewhere in the eighteenth century, waiting anxiously for the next carriage to arrive with the latest news long after it has happened and long after he has botched his story.

The information that is available often is full of sentences like this: "The purpose is to evaluate the extent to which data and information requirements for high-level waste program implementation can provide the basis for strong involvement by state and local levels of government." This is not a particularly bad example. I am pretty sure it means something and I think I know what it is. But I doubt that there are many people who can read a sentence like this without having to think at least twice about how requirements for implementation can provide a basis for involvement. It is language without communication, words fired off like blank cartridges into the air. The danger for the reporter is that the better one gets at reading this stuff, the harder it is not to write that way.

Because it is so hard to get good information, reporters on small papers find themselves turning to scientists as primary sources rather than going to them armed with facts and finely honed questions. This approach strains the patience of the scientist and the credibility of the reporter.

Scientists and small-town reporters aren't used to working with each other, and their relationship can be tenuous at best. The scientist who deals with the national media has an idea of what he is dealing with, and what the risks and benefits are. He can choose to talk to or avoid the national press on the basis of selfless motives—the desire to improve society through understanding—or for more practical reasons: the desire for fame, to grind an ax, or to drum up research funding. On the small paper, most of the practical reasons don't apply. Nobody ever became famous by talking to the *Palestine Herald-Press*. The scientist knows that whatever he says will be read intently by a small number of people, then will disappear overnight into garbage cans and bird cages. No guest appearances or book offers will follow. He also knows that the message will be transmitted, perhaps transmogrified, to that small public by a reporter who probably lacks the time, the skill, and the experience to do the job right. Small newspapers are staffed by young reporters on their way up and by old reporters who can barely get up. It's the reporter's job to ask dumb questions, but it is disconcerting for the scientist when all the reporter understands are dumb answers.

For the reporter, talking to a scientist can be intimidating and a little overwhelming. It's hard to admit that you not only failed to catch the subtle implications of his laboriously constructed explanation, but that you didn't even understand the words. And it's embarrassing to have to call back, minutes before deadline, to ask if that was four rems or four millirems he was talking about, and what's the difference?

But dealing with scientists can often be a pleasure, for they tend to be intelligent, articulate, and dedicated to their work. They also can be the only way for the desperate reporter, working on deadline and a limited budget, to overcome the frustrating obstacle of not knowing where to turn for information.

Government spokesmen can play a reporter like the scales on a piano, shuffling him up and down the keyboard of bureaucracy but never teaching him the tune. They can't understand that what is just one of dozens of pinpoints on a map to them is a matter of front-page concern to the people who live under those pins.

Industry is no better as a credible source because it is widely perceived, rightly or wrongly, as being willing to say anything to make a buck. Because scientists depend on government funding, they, too, often are seen as having a vested interest in the work they do.

Many people in places like Palestine see scientists in the same light as Ogden Nash's Professor Twist, the conscientious scientist who, as you may recall, "Camped on a tropic riverside,/One day he missed his loving bride./She had, the guide informed him later,/Been eaten by an alligator./Professor Twist could not but smile./'You mean,' he said, 'a crocodile.' " A lot of people see scientists that way: as amoral observers who stand on a platform of neutrality while fueling the fires of a society exploding with change. People see their children being devoured while scientists are busy putting names on crocodiles.

So the reporter who finds a selfless scientist who is willing to talk, who will return his phone calls and explain it all one more time, has found a treasure beyond price. Those of us who have found scientists like that are grateful, and we show our gratitude by calling them again and again. But experts usually aren't indigenous to the community, so they are hard to find and it takes a lot of long-distance phone calls to talk to them. And because they aren't local people, science news outside of controversy often just isn't covered in local papers, which live and breathe for the local angle, for that is the only thing they do that no bigger paper can do better.

Such coverage as there is in small papers often just boils down to gauging the emotional reactions of people to things they are scared of but don't know much about. In Palestine, we could have interviewed

14,000 people who adamantly opposed a nuclear waste site. Or we could have interviewed the one person in town who was all for it—but everybody already knew who he was. Those kinds of stories have their place, but they only reinforce the one thing people already know: they are scared.

Newspapers try to print something for everybody, a little unlike television, which seems to aim everything at everybody. At the local level, small papers try to do a little of everything with very little more than nothing. While serving as unofficial chief science writer for the *Herald-Press*, I also covered at one time or another—and occasionally all at the same time—the county, the courthouse, the police, business, the schools, city hall, property tax reform, and state politics. That does not include occasional but insistent demands to write a feature, a review, a travel piece, an obituary, or a high school football story. That kind of diversity at a small paper is not at all unusual, and it is not hard to imagine that science stories, which often lack a timely news peg and take a long time to write, usually get set aside in the stack of "things to do tomorrow." In the newspaper business, tomorrow never comes. The deadline is always today.

The time it takes to research and edit a good science story, or even a mediocre one, often has to come out of a reporter's own spare time, such as that is. A few obscure paragraphs about "data requirements" and "program implementation" can ruin a whole weekend. It's also hard to check out sources, to find out who is a good scientist and who isn't. A newspaper may occasionally catch a politician with his hand in the till, but it does not have the resources to catch a scientist who juggles his test tubes to improve his results.

Because they are so pressed for time and money, local reporters also have few chances to get out of the community and acquire outside training. In two years in East Texas, I attended one event that might loosely be considered a scientific training exercise. It was an industry-sponsored tour of a nuclear power plant, accompanied by lectures on the wonders and safety of nuclear power, and by generous servings of Johnny Walker Black. We didn't learn a lot of science, but I did pick up a few pointers about Scotch.

Opportunities to come to a meeting like that of AAAS are a rare blessing because of the chance to find out what's going on, to feel a part of an international community of people interested in science. These meetings are good places to see some of the fundamental differences between the scientific method and journalistic method. Reporters are always looking for answers; scientists try to find more elegant questions. Scientists want to get it right; reporters want to get it today. Scientists define their terms with precision and sprinkle their statements with qualifiers and exceptions that sound wishy-washy to a reporter, who must paint in broad strokes for a broad audience.

But good scientists and good journalists also have a great deal in common: an ingrained skepticism toward established dogma, conventional wisdom, and the tyranny of common sense; an eye for accuracy and detail; the ability to deal impartially with facts that don't fit the theory; and contempt for the pernicious notion that all passionately held ideas are of equal value.

Unlike many subjects reporters cover, science writing actually comes easy once the basic principles are grasped and the vocabulary is mastered, because science is comparatively logical, orderly, and precise. The study of long-term radiation effects hold no terror for someone who has tackled the Texas Property Tax Code, and I would rather debate relativity with Einstein himself than to try to explain Texas politics.

Reporters and scientists also can be of use to each other, even at the local level. When I covered the National Scientific Balloon Facility, which is an East Texas site for launching balloon experiments, I consistently heard scientists say that the best coverage they ever got in the local paper was by a paper-thin old reporter known as Bones Jones. That surprised me at first. Bones, in his twice-weekly column, "Rattling around with Bones Jones," has retained at the age of eighty a lively curiosity and a sharp mind, but he also has reached the age where he can afford to indulge himself in opinions that might get a younger man shot. His solution to the nuclear waste problem was to pile all the wastes up on the ground and let them burn their way through the center of the earth, so the Chinese would have to worry about them.

But the scientists at the balloon base liked Bones because he would come out with a camera and a notepad every time a new team was ready to launch a balloon and take a picture to run in the paper showing who they were and what they were trying to do. After that, when the scientists went into town with their strange clothes, their beards, and their foreign languages, people knew who they were. They became, during their brief stay, a part of the community. No metropolitan daily could have duplicated that service.

That is a small thing, but the relationship between scientists and reporters also can be of immense value when a national issue hits a small town. The effort to understand the nuclear waste problem in Palestine eventually became almost a community project: people formed citizens' groups and brought in scientists, politicians, and university professors for public meetings; high school students organized debates, conducted surveys, and invited speakers to their classes.

In the absence of experts, even this reporter found himself in the uncomfortable position of making talks and trying to answer dozens of questions over the phone, things like "Won't it hit the groundwater?" and "Should I buy land on a salt dome?" One fellow even told me he had laminated the articles I wrote, which I figure must be about as close to immortality as a newspaperman ever gets. But the role that I and others tried to fill belonged to a scientist.

Besides the big issues, there are dozens of opportunities for science stories in even the smallest towns, if scientists are available to help. You can't write a good story about the city sewers without knowing something about gravity flow and bacteria. You can't evaluate a standardized test or a poll without knowing something about probability theory and sampling error. You can't write a good story about the price of gasoline without knowing where the oil is and what it takes to get it out.

Local papers always will be more interested in local politics than in science, and that is proper. Newspapers are the errand boys of democracy. But local science reporting, which has so much room for improvement, can blossom if scientists and journalists can work together against the natural obstacles that keep them apart.

CHAPTER 6

The View from the National Beat

Cristine Russell

Reporters who work for large mass media outlets can influence a very large number of readers through articles in their own newspapers plus syndication in other publications throughout the country. Cristine Russell examines the roles that science journalists play at this level and explores some of the conflicts that arise between these journalists and their sources.

Cristine Russell is a national science and medical reporter for the *Washington Post*. She also appears regularly on public television's "Washington Week in Review." Russell reported on science for the now-defunct *Washington Star* from 1975 to 1981 and earlier worked for several science-oriented magazines. She was a 1971 Phi Beta Kappa graduate in biology from Mills College. Her numerous science writing awards include the National Association of Science Writers' Science-in-Society Award, the National Society for Medical Research's Claude Bernard Award, and the American Chemical Society's James T. Grady Award.

- *University of Utah doctors implant the world's first permanent artificial heart in a dying dentist. Two years later doctors at Loma Linda University transplant a baboon heart into a two-week-old infant.*

- *Researchers track the mysterious cause of AIDS, a new immune-system disease that may be the most deadly affliction of modern times.*
- *A popular headache remedy, Tylenol, falls prey to an unknown terrorist's tampering.*
- *NASA launches a new-generation flying machine, the space shuttle.*
- *Revelations of fraud in science threaten the traditionally sacred tenet of integrity in research.*
- *Scientists invade the mysteries of the human brain, unraveling its complex chemical pathways, visualizing its workings for the first time.*
- *A decade-long war on cancer fails to provide across-the-board cures but shows successes in treating a variety of tumors. At the same time, studies identify commonly used chemicals, from pesticides to food additives, that may cause human cancer.*
- *An assassin's bullet threatens the life of President Reagan.*
- *Genetic engineering moves out of the laboratory and into practical studies of new products of benefit to medicine and agriculture, but critics raise questions about the possible environmental impact of the release of genetically engineered organisms.*
- *A malfunction at Pennsylvania's Three Mile Island nuclear plant undermines the national future of this form of power.*

THIS IS A SAMPLING of significant scientific and medical stories that attracted national and international attention over the past decade. Many of them exploded on the front pages of newspapers or captured the lead spot on television and radio news. Others evolved more slowly, an accumulation of advances that added up to a major research trend. Some provided major new hope to the public; others frightened an already nervous lay audience, bringing added uncertainty about their own health.

The communication of each involved a far-from-perfect exchange between members of the news media and a variety of scientific "experts." The sources of information included doctors, basic researchers, and technicians, who were, in turn, often shielded from direct contact with the press by official spokespersons and public relations specialists. The pursuers of information ranged from general assignment reporters covering science on a one-shot basis to experienced science reporters devoting their full-time efforts to this area.

And the settings varied, from standing-room-only press conferences to exclusive one-on-one interviews. The outcome often was determined by time, the news commodity generally in shortest supply. The emergency at Three Mile Island meant a barrage of often-conflicting information at hurried press conferences and on-site encounters. Surgery to implant an artificial heart started with an around-the-clock vigil in a crowded cafeteria pressroom and tapered down to terse medical announcements before the patient's death; no reporter had an opportunity to interview artificial heart recipient Barney Clark before his death.

Unraveling the intricacies of gene-splicing of neurotransmitters in the brain, however, largely stayed in the domain of science writers with the inclination to spend hours with scientists willing to explain how a piece of DNA can be manipulated or how the complex pathway of a brain chemical can be traced. At other times, the journalistic pursuit required tracking down data that had not reached the public domain or jumping in the middle of a controversial debate that experts had not resolved—for example, the cancer-causing potential of a chemical of public concern.

How well the connection between the press and the scientists works depends on the individual participants in both groups. The range of scientists and their attitudes toward cooperating with the press—from willingness to extreme reluctance—is as varied as the experience of the journalists who indulge in science writing. The skills of the players on both sides, from their grasp of substantive knowledge to their ability to translate the difficult languages of science, are just as divergent. Generally speaking, scientists are becoming more sophisticated in dealing with the press, and science journalists are sharpening their skills in writing difficult stories that express the complexities, and often uncertainties, of scientific studies. But each group approaches the public communication task from a different perspective. To discuss these perspectives, let's start with the scientists.

The Reluctant Scientists

First of all, the obvious should be stated. For scientists, science communication with a lay audience is almost always a secondary issue. Of first importance, from a professional standpoint, is the business of science itself, whether experimental research or clinical testing in any given line of scientific endeavor.

Whether communication of that work to the public is considered of major importance by the scientist—for altruistic or selfish reasons or both—partially depends on his or her view of the media. While it's a bit simplistic, scientists can be put into two basic categories, those who are willing to cooperate with journalists and those who can think of nothing worse.

In the reluctant group are those who truly hate the press, who cite worst-case examples of how their own work or that of others has been mistakenly reported to the public and how those reports have damaged their reputations. These scientists appear to assume that every reporter is a sensational tabloid–type writer who will hype research to sell papers.

Others in the reluctant group just don't place any personal importance on dealing with members of the media. They are too busy to bother with reporters, they say; instead, they place their priorities on communicating with fellow scientists. One senses an elitism in their tendency to keep to themselves and snobbishly reject those colleagues who "stray too far" in parading their work before the public.

Whatever their reasons, these reluctant scientists are difficult to track down. If they return telephone calls, it's often days later, long after the deadline has passed. If you do get them on the phone, you've got to talk fast to convince them, first, of your journalistic credentials and, second, that their work deserves public attention. Even then, they still talk in the most technical language possible and are fearful of being misquoted. When you ask them to predict the practical implications of their work, there is a sigh and a lecture about how there is no way to know and anyway that's not why they are doing the work in the first place—they are pursuing basic scientific truths. When the interview is completed, they insist on reviewing your story before it's printed and are angry when you tell them that this is not possible.

Consider this example. In 1980, while covering national science and medicine for the now-defunct *Washington Star,* I became interested in doing a series on the use of artificial intelligence in medicine. I learned that Stanford University played a big role in this area and phoned a scientist there to get more information. When I offered to fly out and interview those involved, I was met with considerable hesitancy and told it would be better if I attended an upcoming conference being organized for practicing physicians.

I agreed, but when I got to the conference I encountered a group of scientists who, almost to a person, were extremely reluctant to speak to a member of the press. Apparently, most of them felt their field had been "burned" in earlier years by press predictions about how fast artificial intelligence research was proceeding. They seemed to have made an informal pact among themselves not to speak to reporters at all.

Despite the fact that the conference was open to reporters, no attempts were made to provide information to the press, even though this is usually done at such meetings. And university public information officers who tried to be helpful were just as frustrated in their attempts to get leaders of the conference to talk about their work. (One scientist, despite calls ahead of time, absolutely refused, but finally gave in only after being pursued in person.)

I persevered at the conference, finally completing a two-part series that, as far as I know, was perfectly acceptable to those who had initially been so uncooperative in getting it done.

I don't think journalists should hold to the self-centered assumption that everyone has to talk to us. If scientists are conducting privately funded research, they certainly have a right to refuse. But I do feel scientists have an obligation to provide information if their work is being publicly funded. In this case, many of the researchers were getting large sums of money from the federal National Institutes of Health.

The Overly Cooperative Scientists

Fortunately, the above example illustrates an extreme subgroup of scientists. But they are not the only "extremists." At the other end of the continuum are those who might be considered a bit too helpful in their efforts to utilize the press.

Some researchers are interested in popularizing not only science, but also their own reputations. They even seek writers out with the help of their own public relations agents. While the practice of hiring public relations assistance started with scientists who had written books, it seems to be spreading. At a recent scientific convention, one scientist had advance texts of his speech prepared and distributed by a commercial public relations agency. Such salesmanship can be a problem if it overpromotes a particular presentation and draws a busy science writer's attention away from other potentially valuable pieces of research.

It's not only concern for personal reputations that sends scientists seeking reporters. Financial considerations also come into play. With belt-tightening by federal funding agencies, there is an incentive for some scientists to get attention in Washington via the media if their grant is up for review. Others, particularly those involved in genetic engineering work that is going commercial, also have a monetary concern that can be greatly aided by publicity.

The overly cooperative category also includes scientists with a cause to push or a political point of view to promote. They sign highly publicized petitions, come to Washington to appear before Congress, or take their cause to science journals or newspaper editorial pages. Sometimes their causes are generally supported by the scientific community —for example, concern about the plight of fellow scientists in repressive countries such as the Soviet Union, or the need for more research funds from the federal government. Science reporters in the nation's capital frequently receive calls from scientific groups that bring Nobel Prize–

winning scientists to Washington to argue before major congressional committees reviewing science budgets.

Other causes are a matter of debate within the scientific community and often create confusion for the public when argued on the pages of the nation's newspapers. One example of this is the late 1970s debate over whether the artificial sweetener saccharin caused cancer. It began with a precipitous 1977 announcement by the federal Food and Drug Administration (FDA) that an animal study had shown saccharin to be carcinogenic and therefore federal law required that it be banned from the marketplace. Saccharin, of course, was a big business item, a major ingredient in diet soft drinks and foods. At the time, there were no other artificial, noncaloric sweeteners on the market. So not only industry but also the diet-conscious public were reluctant to give up this popular weight-controlling substance.

Congress came under strong pressure to intervene, and scientists were used by all sides to argue their positions. The industry-backed Calorie Control Council lined up prominent scientists to dismiss the saccharin–cancer connection and make fun of the animal research, suggesting people had to drink 800 bottles of soda a day in order to get cancer. Consumer groups sought scientific experts who strongly pushed the other point of view, saying that a substance shown to cause cancer in animals should be presumed to pose danger to humans unless proven otherwise.

Because cancer can take more than a decade to develop after exposure and because it is difficult to conduct human studies to prove a substance actually causes the disease, such a debate inevitably comes down to a philosophical choice about the degree of risk that is acceptable. In this case, the prevailing pressures led Congress to set aside the FDA's ban, and, in a frequently used postponing tactic, ask for more studies. A later review by the National Academy of Sciences concluded that saccharin is a weak cancer-causing agent that may also promote cancer-causing effects of other chemicals. Needless to say, all contenders in this issue sought as much media coverage as possible to get their views out to the public.

Another, more recent case in which scientists have conducted a public tug-of-war in the mass media concerns the purported link between a commonly used medication, aspirin, and a rare, life-threatening disease in children called Reye's Syndrome.

Initially, the federal Centers for Disease Control supported several studies showing a link between aspirin and this frightening childhood illness, and consumer groups took the FDA to court for failing to act. In June 1982 the Department of Health and Human Services announced it would put a warning label on aspirin, cautioning against its use in youngsters with flu or chicken pox. The aspirin industry was outraged and brought together scientific experts to criticize the studies. Many of them appeared before a sympathetic congressional committee and received extensive media attention.

The American Academy of Pediatrics, which represents doctors who care for children, initially supported the aspirin restrictions but later backed off and communicated its reservations to the Reagan administration. In late 1982 the FDA compromised, announcing it would conduct a public information campaign but would postpone the labeling proposal until more research had been done.

Again, consumer, parent, medical, and industry groups solicited a wide range of often-differing scientific viewpoints and used the mass media to put government agencies and Congress under conflicting outside pressures.

I don't think scientists have to be or even should be neutral, particularly as science enters into more public policy issues. But it is clear that when they use the media to get their points across, they are not acting just as neutral, objective researchers. As journalists we have an obligation to point out when someone is acting as both a scientist and an activist for some cause, or when there might be a financial consideration involved, and let our readers judge the relevance of these nonscientific connections.

The Valuable Sources

Fortunately, many scientists today are neither reluctant nor overly cooperative. These vital information sources don't have an ax to grind, aren't out to oversell their own work, and genuinely wish to be helpful in the preparation of science stories for the public. Such professionals are crucial to science writers. We come to depend upon them to give us guidance when we are writing about new and difficult topics or complicated societal problems. They also are the people we rely upon when disasters occur and deadline pressures are greatest. Increasing dissemination of science in the lay press and scientists' recognition that the public is not only interested but also paying for much of their research has helped create a new generation of researchers who are more responsive than ever before.

Among those helping to popularize science are the "visible" scientists. They are usually well-known researchers who are quite willing to talk to the press, and they are frequently sought out by journalists for quotes on numerous subjects. However, a danger exists both for these "big name" researchers and for the journalists who quote them when the scientists begin to stray from commenting on their fields of expertise and become "instant" experts on almost any scientific subject under the sun.

Other scientists hold more loyalty to selected reporters. These sources may spring from a single story or stories well done. A writer who reports accurately and fairly on a given scientist's work or a difficult and complicated issue probably will find that expert happy to take a call when another story comes along. And on many occasions, these scientists volunteer information, contacting a reporter on their own initiative with a good lead for a possible story. For example, an expert on medical ethics I contacted for a story on the artificial heart called me months later with a terrific national story with dramatic ethical implications about a leukemia patient seeking a bone marrow transplant.

Increasing opportunities for scientists to meet and work with journalists occur at large gatherings such as the annual meeting of the American Association for the Advancement of Science (AAAS). Regular press conferences create an excellent opportunity for easy contact, while symposium sessions provide common ground for discussions between scientists and media people about various kinds of research.

Although their motives may vary, most national medical and scientific organizations also offer a variety of opportunities for bringing scientists and journalists together. For more than twenty-five years, the American Cancer Society has held an annual science writers seminar (it usually takes place in a warm spot such as Florida or California, where the casual atmosphere is most conducive to new friendships between the two camps). The American Heart Association has a similar gathering, and federal research institutes have frequent background seminars for reporters.

The Journalists

Journalists, like scientists, come in many shapes and colors. Relations between the two groups often are determined by how well scientists understand these differences. Perhaps the greatest difference exists between general assignment reporters, who are confronted with scientific issues on a sporadic basis, and those who report on science all of the time. There also are differences between journalists who report for different types of media—newspapers, magazines, television, and radio— all of which have audiences with varying degrees of sophistication and deadlines that place constraints on the gathering of news.

Any organization with a big story has faced head-on the problems posed by the variety of appetites of the journalistic animals they are trying to tame. A classic example of the zoo-like atmosphere created under such circumstances resulted from the University of Utah's announcement that a permanent artificial heart would be implanted in a human subject for the first time.

The news came across the wires on the evening of Tuesday, November 30, 1982, that the feat would be attempted in an operation Thursday morning. Contacted by my editor, I quickly flew to Salt Lake City—just in time. Because of the patient's worsening condition, an emergency operation had to be performed on Wednesday evening. By the next day, the literally massed media numbered well over 100, with the handful of full-time medical reporters overwhelmed by their general assignment and electronic colleagues.

All of us had differing needs. While we all shared a common interest in getting the basic details of the surgery and the doctors' thoughts about the future, out-of-town reporters needed more information on various aspects than hometown reporters who had been covering the story for months. Some of us desperately needed lengthy details on the medical aspects, while for many reporters this was a human interest story, pure and simple. A dying patient had been saved, at least temporarily. Medical writers from the print media needed information on the technical issues of blood pressure, just what drugs the patient was receiving, the fine points of what risks he faced in the days ahead. These issues were not of great concern to reporters from the electronic media, who only had seconds or minutes of on-air time to tell the story.

Everyone made the best of a difficult situation, and as the days wore on, the numbers of reporters dwindled. Eventually the story became a daily update for the wire services and local reporters, with few big press conferences until the death of the patient after more than three and a half months on the artificial heart. By then the whole world knew of Barney Clark and his ordeal. But the coverage of larger issues, such as the long-term prospects and the ethical and economic implications of artificial heart research, tended to be done in greater depth by science rather than general assignment reporters.

Even in more routine daily reporting, differences in degrees of sophistication between general assignment and science reporters are evident. Problems in science coverage often arise when inexperienced general reporters get a "scoop" on a local science or medical story that they perceive to be of major significance. Because of their lack of background, general assignment reporters are more likely to portray a story as "newer" or "bigger" than it actually is. Science writers for the major wire services related that they often put out brushfires started by local reporters who get involved in scientific and medical stories—from unorthodox cancer cures such as laetrile to the latest diets—that may be oversold.

Nevertheless, many good general assignment reporters are able to tackle tough subjects of any kind and often outdo specialty reporters by asking basic questions that readers want answered. I don't envy the reporter covering everything from local politics to the chief of police who suddenly must write a very technical story. In such cases, experts need to talk in the simplest terms and help put the research or problem in context; unfortunately, they often don't, and the resulting story may contain inaccuracies and misunderstood points, which they blame fully on the reporter. Had they taken the time to become familiar with the reporter's background and not assumed a great deal of scientific knowledge, the story might have turned out far better for all concerned.

The Science Writers

Full-time science writers generally have good scientific backgrounds, acquired either through taking science courses in college or graduate school or through learning on the job by talking with scientists and reading numerous scientific journals and magazines. Among younger science journalists, the trend is to have training in both some field of science and science journalism.

There are far fewer full-time science writers than general assignment reporters. The National Association of Science Writers, the profession's major organization, includes about 500 active members who write about science directly for the public. Many cover science and medicine across the board; others concentrate in one area such as medicine. Still others specialize even further, covering only physics, energy, environment, space, biomedicine, or the social sciences.

The largest group is composed of freelance writers who sell their work to outlets such as magazines or who concentrate on books. Science writers employed by media organizations are far fewer in number; probably no more than 100 full-time science reporters work on U.S. newspapers, for example. At the *Washington Post,* we now have three full-time national science and medical reporters, and a separate weekly health feature section. *The New York Times,* which carries a weekly supplement called "Science Times," has a large crew of more than ten specialists. But generally newspapers that have science writers—the large metropolitan dailies primarily—only have one or two. Most smaller newspapers have no science reporter at all.

Other science writers work for science magazines specially designed for the public, a field that has undergone a renaissance since the late 1970s and early 1980s. Several science magazines were started, such as *Discover* (published by Time Inc.), *Science 85* (published by AAAS), and the science fiction–science hybrid *Omni,* as well as a consumer health magazine, *American Health.*

Some science and medical journals, such as *Science* (published by AAAS) or the *Journal of the American Medical Association,* also carry special news sections written by science writers. Many science journalists also work for an endless stream of newsletters and special science publications.

The smallest subgroup of science writers resides in the electronic media. The major networks traditionally have one science or medical correspondent. These journalists appear to have limited exposure, however, on evening news shows. Local stations generally don't assign a reporter to science, although a local science reporter for Washington's CBS affiliate, WDVM, has been a model example of how well this can work in both medical and science coverage. Radio science specialists, with the exception of several excellent National Public Radio science correspondents, are an even rarer breed.

Years of experience and daily reading of mounds of mail and journals have provided science journalists with a skeptical eye when sorting through the myriad stories that come our way. While we are peppered with a few somewhat sensationalist souls, we are, for the most part, a rather cautious lot. At a recent AAAS annual meeting, for example, science writers attending a press conference on crime were surprised by the outspoken comments of one scientist on the contribution of heredity to criminal behavior. We were all taken aback. This issue had come up many times before and is fraught with touchy social and political ramifications. The researcher presented sketchy details about research he had done in Denmark that, if true, were sensational. It would have been easy to take what he said and run back to our editors with a front-page story about the criminal gene. We didn't. Several reporters spent much of the day trying to get more information about the scientist and his work, talking to his colleagues and federal officials who funded his study. It turned out to be a legitimate story, but our skepticism prevented it from being blown out of proportion.

A Legitimate Tension

When working on stories, most science writers seek to get beyond the press conference, the press release, or the journal article, and talk, whenever possible, to the scientists involved and to those who are familiar with the scientists' work. Underlying these interactions is an essential tension between scientists and journalists that can sometimes get in the way of an honest attempt by both parties to present science to the public. In part, the tension is a natural one because both sides have different purposes. The scientist may wish to tell his or her story in all its complexity, while the journalist must necessarily reduce it to a manageable and more simplistic form for his or her audience. But the tension can be exacerbated when there is a lack of awareness of the journalistic process by scientists involved, a confusion of roles, or a struggle for the control of information.

A crucial constraint—and one often not well understood by experts we contact—is the time allowed to write a given story. Obviously, a breaking story written on deadline in a matter of minutes or hours will be less comprehensive than a well-researched feature piece or series.

We also face problems when there is a confusion over the roles played by the scientist and the writer, particularly concerning the issue of independence. While the role of scientists is to conduct their research and present it in their own light, our role as journalists is not to accept it simply at face value. In addition to translating it for the reader, without all the technical jargon, we must point out if it is controversial or well re-garded in the field. We have all heard from scientists who were hurt that we didn't use precisely their language in the story or that we included some criticism of their work, however justified. We need to make it clear that most science journalists are not agents or advocates for a given cause, but simply are trying to present a balanced story.

I might add that the investigative journalism bug that bit many re-porters in the wake of the Watergate scandal of the early 1970s and the resignation of then-president Richard Nixon has generally been less evi-dent in science reporting. In fact, some critics feel that science journal-ists have been too complacent, too fact-oriented, and sometimes too sym-pathetic to science itself.

Increasingly, there also is a struggle between journalists and the sci-entific establishment for control of information. At a personal level, many scientists insist, at least at first, on the option of reading a story before it appears in print. On a practical level, at least for a daily news-paper reporter, this is impossible. But even if all the time in the world were available, I don't think such checking would be advisable. Most reporters are willing to check specific facts or quotes, if there is any problem. But few of us feel that it is appropriate to subject our work to the approval of a given institution or scientist. While scientists would be offended if we suggested that reporters help them design their experi-ments or write them up for publication in a prestigious journal, they don't seem to think the reverse is a problem for us. We need to convince them that we, too, are professionals doing our jobs as best we can.

At an institutional level, there is the problem of conference organi-zers or journals seeking to restrict access to information. Reporters, for example, almost were excluded from the historic beginning of the debate over the risks of genetic engineering research. The 1975 Asilomar Con-ference (named for the beautiful coastal site in California where the meeting took place) brought together, by invitation only, an interna-tional group of biomedical researchers concerned about a revolutionary new gene-splicing technique. While the procedure offered future benefits to humanity, some prominent scientists believed that the work should proceed cautiously because of the unknown potential for creating novel, dangerous organisms. The specter of a bug that could carry a cancer gene was raised.

Because of the sensitivity of the issue, some organizers of the conference initially sought to keep the press out. Only after protests from science writers and the intercession of the National Academy of Sciences' public information chief, Howard Lewis, were a dozen or so reporters allowed to attend. The ground rules were strict and unusual: reporters who attended had to agree not to write about the week-long conference until it had ended, but the meeting itself was open completely to their scrutiny.

This compromise worked well. The informal exchanges during the conference as well as the formal proceedings helped break down barriers between the scientists and the journalists involved. Each side understood the other better, and the stories that resulted were far superior to those that would have been written by reporters hearing about conference results after the fact, had they been barred from attending. The proceedings also paved the way for more in-depth coverage of the important issue of genetic engineering in the years to come. In this instance, not restricting access to information allowed scientists and journalists to work together and helped each group reach particular goals.

An ongoing debate continues, however, on another troublesome restriction—the attempt to keep scientists from talking to the press before their work is published in a scientific journal. This is carried to an extreme by the prestigious *New England Journal of Medicine (NEJM)*, which over the years has won a reputation among researchers and journalists as the premier place for publication of new medical studies. This journal has a controversial, inflexible rule—dubbed the "Ingelfinger Rule" after its late editor, Franz Ingelfinger—that it will reject any manuscript that has appeared in other journals or has been detailed in the lay press. The rule is intended to prevent premature publicity and also helps promote the journal's exclusive image.

While there are advantages for journalists in writing about research that has undergone scientific review, waiting for peer review and publication in order to cover a story can sometimes become a practical disservice, particularly if there is a public health problem involved. Scientists often are torn between wanting to be helpful in the preparation of an accurate press account and fearful that the result will be banishment from the pages of *NEJM*. Some are even afraid to talk to reporters after presenting their work at a scientific meeting that is open to the press.

In one instance, government officials initially tried to restrict press access to the findings of a National Institutes of Health conference because they were seeking *NEJM* publication. They backed off after reporters complained.

When the AIDS (Acquired Immune Deficiency Syndrome) epidemic began, some doctors were hesitant to talk to public health officials from the federal Centers for Disease Control about their research on this disease, even though these officials represented the lead government agency investigating the problem. The doctors were concerned that reports of their cases in government publications would interfere with their chances for later journal publication. The problem also appeared at a National Institutes of Health symposium on the cause of AIDS in the spring of 1983 when a government cancer researcher declined to present his research to his colleagues because it was not yet published and reporters were attending the meeting.

The debate about these and other restrictions imposed on science writers continues. But I would argue that *NEJM*'s inflexible rule should be modified. Using unreviewed research puts more responsibility on science writers and the researchers who talk to them, but this has been done in the past successfully. Those reporters who choose to write about unpublished work have an added obligation to seek comments from other scientists in the field and to point out the preliminary nature of the studies.

Despite these problems, the climate for science writing is improving and opportunities are expanding. In fact, the difficulties we encounter in covering science at the national level are outnumbered by the problems we have in choosing from the many good stories out there to write about.

The stories themselves and the way they are covered have changed dramatically over the last decade. Enthusiastic "gee whiz" reporting of the wonders of scientific discovery has expanded to encompass the public implications of science and technology. Coverage of societal impact —ethical, environmental, and economic—often is as important today as accurate reporting of the scientific research itself. For example, what impact will the expense of the artificial heart have on medical costs and who should receive it? Will the first genetically engineered bacterium to be tested for agricultural applications also pose an environmental hazard? How have nuclear plants changed since the Three Mile Island accident?

Answering these questions is a challenge science writers face in addition to keeping up with the explosion of scientific information itself. Fortunately there also is, at least for the time being, an explosion in the number of new magazines, and the media that present science to the public.

More importantly, public interest in the subject has never been stronger.

CHAPTER 7

Physicians and Reporters: Conflicts, Commonalities, and Collaboration

Dennis S. O'Leary, M.D.

While reporters and physicians obviously perform very different tasks, Dennis O'Leary argues that the two have many professional aspects in common. He also explores factors that create tensions between the two, particularly when a prominent public official is being treated for a serious illness or injury in a hospital. O'Leary approaches his task from a unique perspective, having served as hospital spokesman for The George Washington University Medical Center during the treatment of President Ronald Reagan and Press Secretary James Brady after an assassination attempt in 1981.

Dr. Dennis S. O'Leary has been a member of the faculty and administrative staff of The George Washington University Medical Center for the past decade. He is currently dean for clinical affairs and acting medical director of The George Washington University Hospital and holds the academic appointment of professor of medicine. A native of Kansas City, he received his undergraduate degree from Harvard College and his M.D. from Cornell University. Active in a variety of professional activities, he has served as president of the District of Columbia Medical Society.

MEDICINE AND THE MASS MEDIA are both rather unusual segments of our society. They may represent the last bastions of rugged individualists in the world. Oftentimes we refer to them collectively as "medicine" or "the media," but they are collectives only in the broadest sense. Even their respective professional associations are built upon the cornerstone that the individual must be permitted to do his job his own way so long as he stays within certain broad ethical boundaries. And these ethical boundaries can change from time to time.

An important characteristic of rugged individualists is that they seek to control their work environments. Acknowledging certain practical constraints and the moderate duress of peer pressure and competition, they determine what they will do, when they will do it, and with whom, if anyone, they will collaborate. Journalists and physicians expect to, and do, control their worlds with reasonable effectiveness. Control is not used in a negative sense; rather, it is a commentary on the independent nature of the individuals who choose to enter these professions.

There are, of course, practical constraints. Physicians do have to keep appointments with patients; journalists do have to meet deadlines. But both seem to have an inherent reluctance to collaborate or to develop interdependent relationships with colleagues. Some physicians go to great effort to avoid calling in a consultant. Consultation somehow seems to cast a pall upon the physician's ability to manage his own patient. One encounters much the same attitude among journalists.

The issue at hand, however, is not collaboration within medicine or within the media, but rather the broader matter of collaboration and cooperation between the two professions. This is a difficult marriage, but one that must take place. There is a substantial public investment in medicine: large amounts of federal funds are invested in research, and there is a major commitment of public money to patient care and medical education. The acceptance of such funds implies accountability to the public. Meeting that responsibility requires transmission of information to the public. And the media—print and electronic—are the principal vehicles for that transmission. There are many good examples of how well this has worked in certain instances, but there remain some real separations between the two professional worlds of journalism and medicine.

Both worlds are, in fact, at significant risk in this collaboration— medicine for being misunderstood and the media for misunderstanding. Each views the other as powerful, sometimes arrogant, and therefore dangerous, even in an at-arms-length relationship. Each regards the other suspiciously, because rugged individualists are like that, and also because past misadventures have laid a valid foundation for suspicion. However, successful collaborations have been achieved, attesting to the professionalism of the individuals involved.

Professionalism is the critical issue. Professionals serve someone else—an individual, a group of people, a society. Medicine has traditionally viewed itself as a profession, and the vast majority of physicians are professionals in the service sense. Where *self*-serving motives become preeminent, whether financial or otherwise, the physician becomes a tradesman. As in medicine, there are journalists who devote themselves to the public through providing objective and understandable information, but the journalistic profession has its tradesmen as well.

The distinction between profession and trade is important, for a third party—the public—is also involved. The public benefits if both groups fulfill their obligations in this joint venture; it is at risk if either the media or medicine fails to communicate effectively.

Whether medicine and the media are both truly professions is less important than the perceptions individual physicians and journalists have of each other, for an individual's perception is his truth. I believe the average physician is just as likely to view journalists as professionals as he is to view them as tradespeople. That perception has significant bearing upon the physician's behavior: whether he will cooperate with journalists, and how he will communicate with them.

For the science writer, understanding the medical profession, its ethos and problems, is helpful. Medicine, tradition-bound, zealously protects the privacy of the doctor–patient relationship and extends that privacy to its whole domain. Medicine is also hard-nosed about its science—perhaps because so much of medicine is an inexact science—and has traditionally accepted as valid observations only those published in refereed journals.

But medicine's world is changing. There are increasing intrusions into the doctor–patient relationship by third-party insurers, legislators, lawyers, economists, regulators, and others; health care costs have escalated; the investment of public and private funds in research and medical education is large. Privacy for medicine, if not gone, is at least severely eroded. Without passing judgment on this change as either good or bad, medicine accepts the need for better and broader communication with the public it serves.

Still, relatively few physicians feel comfortable communicating with the media and the public. Physicians learn skills for communicating with people, but these people are usually patients. Even so, any doctor who can interact effectively with a patient ought to be able to interact effectively with a journalist.

The basic principles of effective communication are simple and obvious. First, it is absolutely critical that information be transmitted at the other person's level of understanding. If it is not, the communicator wastes his own and his listener's time. Since each profession and trade has its own jargon, it is easy to obfuscate, even without intent, and therein lies a major risk of being misunderstood. Indeed, it is not unusual to find medical school professors, quite comfortable in communicating with senior trainees, who must struggle to adjust to the level of understanding of junior medical students. Successful teachers, however, understand the importance of this transition and can easily make the adjustment.

Second, one must never sell other people short. Simply put, people are not stupid. Not only do they have the ability to comprehend, but also they can accept cautions, caveats, and bad news. In fact, people cope much more effectively with concrete bad news than with an information void that creates anxiety, fear, and speculation.

Third, one should periodically place oneself in the position of listener. The listener's concerns, needs, and responsibilities differ from those of the speaker. Empathy and understanding help create a clearer message. If the message is not received, or is received with skepticism, the source of the problem is not necessarily the other person. It may be the communicator's problem. A second effort never hurts.

Those physicians and journalists who have not had positive experiences with each other should try again. Physicians must understand that just as members of their own profession vary in quality and commitment, so, too, do journalists. If a physician has a story to communicate to the public, he should select a journalist the same way he would select a physician—very carefully. And a good journalist is someone who sees his responsibility as extending beyond presenting the facts and who knows there is no such thing as an unbiased presentation. The bias is inherent, beginning with the headline. The determinant of a successful story is whether the public correctly interprets the story, be it negative, positive, or neutral. Therefore, the essential ingredients, above and beyond the facts, are the balance and tone conveyed by the story. Balanced, accurate stories will foster increased physician cooperation with the media; the converse also is true.

The medical profession generally views its colleagues who communicate with the public through the media with some favor, even admiration. A well-done professional representation in the media is generally respected, notwithstanding irreducible but rather inconsequential professional jealousies. Such activities are not tied into the traditional reward system in medicine, but if the system typically does not reward such performances, neither does it punish them. There is, however, little tolerance for self-aggrandizing media reports or promotion of medicine that does not have an established scientific basis. Publication of information in a refereed scientific journal and its simultaneous release to the media generally are not mutually exclusive, either ethically or otherwise. Only a few scientific journals have politics that are an exception to the rule.

Even so, many physicians are reluctant to work with the media. The world of the physician differs from that of the journalist. The physician is, in a sense, insulated from the rest of the world, with his own time schedules to meet, conferences to give, rounds to conduct, patients to see, and a reward system that derives from these activities. The physician may be involved in important work of interest to the public, but he may not understand this, and he may have little if any understanding of the media systems that could inform the public.

Indeed, the naiveté of physicians cannot be underestimated. Many do not know that their institutions have public relations offices. The few who do know are not sure what these offices do, and they probably wonder if the money might not be better spent on more important matters. Their appreciation of the outside world is largely passive. While most read newspapers and magazines, listen to radio, and watch television, they have essentially no grasp of the major differences in the mechanisms through which information is disseminated by these various communication modes.

Similarly, many physicians think that if they have talked with one reporter, that's all that's necessary. They simply assume that one reporter will pass the information along; there is no sense of the independence or variety of media or of wire services or of how stories are picked up and spread across the country.

Even if a physician thinks he has a story, he isn't sure how to enter the media system. Many public relations offices have endless problems in ferreting out stories. At a still more practical level, the physician may not understand that when a reporter calls him, a timely return call is mandatory. Commonly, the physician feels a little busy and thinks it will be quite satisfactory to call back the next day. Of course, the story is long since finished by then.

One of the most difficult interactions between physicians and journalists, and also one of the most important, occurs when a person of public prominence, such as a high government official, is badly injured or falls seriously ill and enters a hospital. The central news element is the implication of this person's injury or illness for the public. When will the individual be able to function again in his job? How long will he be impaired and to what degree? Here, the public's right and need to know must be delicately balanced against the patient's right to privacy.

Some information about a serious injury or illness of a prominent person almost invariably reaches the public before the patient arrives at the hospital. The public is concerned for the patient as a person and for the void that now exists in this person's public office or role. Until some definitive details are known and made public, an information vacuum exists. In this situation, the media must rely on secondhand accounts and speculation by outside experts and others. These news accounts clearly aggravate the public's anxiety and are emotionally taxing to all. Thus, release of specific and detailed clinical information related to the individual's public role may be appropriate. This approach serves the public interest as well as the interest of the patient.

Of course, even in this situation, the nature and amount of information released should be governed by what has happened since the patient was hospitalized and by the extent of the clinical information available for predicting his progress and outcome. When definitive surgical or medical treatment has been undertaken and the outlook appears good, a hospital spokesman not only can provide details about the treatment but also can give some reasonable, if cautious, reassurance to the public about the patient. However, if the prospects for recovery or even survival are uncertain, the public's ability to deal with negative information and an uncertain outcome must be weighed against media and public anxiety created by sparse information, external rumors, and speculation.

Whether the news is good or bad, the manner in which it is provided is important. Information should be presented in a matter-of-fact manner and in unembellished and understandable lay terms. This type of presentation will help limit the tendency of some media organizations to sensationalize the situation.

The extent to which reassurances can or should be offered is a judgmental issue. Without question, no hospital spokesman should distort the clinical accuracy of available information. But a hospital spokesman who is a physician has the capacity to interpret this information and discuss possible outcomes. Generally, various pressures as well as the unpredictability of human biology lead physicians to offer conservative projections. But in the circumstance of a prominent patient, this approach may not give due weight to the public interest. At the other extreme, overly rosy optimism creates obvious hazards for everyone and certainly is not in the public interest.

The ability of a physician to provide balanced interpretations can make him the most appropriate choice to serve as hospital spokesman in tense and delicate situations. However, in choosing the best spokesman, the hospital must consult with all the parties involved. These include the patient, his family, his physician, and the organization or agency with which the patient is associated. The hospital must not overlook the fact that some prominent individuals have personal press officers or are associated with organizations that have highly structured and sophisticated press offices.

Once the spokesman has been selected, in order to provide consistency and clarity this person should be the *only* information source. If two or more official information sources exist, the risk of misinterpretation increases greatly. Even if these sources have the same information, they may use different terminology, potentially providing varying meanings to the media and the public.

Assuming that a physician has been selected as spokesman, he must assume this role with care and sensitivity, for media and public expectations of him are greater because of his stature and knowledge. He is expected to have considerable clinical information about the patient, to know its significance, and to be able to provide a professional judgment about the likely progress of and outcome for the patient. Terse or bland statements, which may be intended to protect the patient, may instead convey the impression that important information is being concealed and may increase the public's anxiety. This approach hurts the physician's credibility with reporters, and, in the long run, may be detrimental to the patient, the hospital, and the public.

Timing the release of information is a prime concern. When a patient first arrives, a physician's general instinct is to wait until more about the patient is known. At the same time, reporters are under pressure to get information at once, and the physician must consider the external information vacuum and its rumor-spawning capability. Some compromise must accommodate the reality of patient care and the legitimate demand for public information.

The primary source of information about any patient is his physician, whether he himself is spokesman or he briefs another to serve in that capacity. But the first obligation of the physician is to the patient, and only later can he be expected to communicate his findings, actions, and opinions to reporters and others, no matter how great the demand. In reality, a reasonable opportunity to summarize the treatment should occur within a few hours of hospitalization.

The frequency of press releases and public statements will be governed by the specific situation, but rarely are they needed more often than twice a day. To the extent that flexibility exists, timing should be sensitive to print and electronic media deadlines and needs. The result will be a better working relationship with the media.

The physician spokesman also must be aware of the types of reporters and media with whom he is dealing. When an acute injury or illness befalls a public official, this is "spot" news, and the initial media coverage will usually involve general news reporters whose level of medical sophistication tends to be quite basic. Special care should be taken at this time to communicate with them in understandable terms. Within twenty-four to forty-eight hours after the initial event, news coverage will progressively involve science or medical reporters whose level of medical sophistication is considerably greater. This may ease certain communications problems for the spokesman, but he will find himself dealing with more searching and complex questions. He should assist these specialized reporters not only in translating medical facts but also in providing balance in emphasis among these facts. Given a good reporter, the eventual story will reflect the spokesman's degree of success in conveying accurate and balanced information.

In dealing with reporters of any type, however, the physician spokesman must remember that there are certain elements of the patient's care that are no one else's business. The public may have the right to know about certain aspects of the health status of public officials as related to their ability to carry out their public duties, but the obligation to inform the public lies with the public official, not with the hospital or its spokesman. And if a patient does not want certain information released to the media, then the hospital should not release it, no matter how much reporters and the public want it. Further, the spokesman must respect a patient's privacy concerning health-related information prior to and after his hospitalization. No matter how interested reporters and readers are, the physician spokesman should discuss only the patient's current hospitalization.

Obviously, when public individuals require hospitalization, the tenets of the two professions of medicine and journalism come closely into play, and sometimes they appear to work at cross purposes. However, these tenets, like the physicians and reporters who live by them, are similar in that they are both concerned with "rights." The question of which "right"—a person's right to privacy or the public's right to know—is more important is steeped in constitutional interpretation and is not confined just to encounters between medicine and the media. Both physicians and reporters should deal with each other fully informed about each profession's needs and limitations. In this way, the public interest can best be served, as can the goals of the two professions.

The barriers between medicine and the media are beginning to come down, as indeed they should. There are risks involved for both, but there are benefits as well. Most importantly, there is a public need for the barriers to fall. Major health issues face this society today, and only an informed public can participate knowledgeably in addressing these issues. Increased cooperation between reporters and physicians is essential in providing this knowledge.

CHAPTER 8

What Makes
a Good Science Story?

*Panel Discussion with Ira Flatow,
Dennis S. O'Leary, Joann E. Rodgers,
Stephen H. Schneider, and Robert J. Trotter*

The "perfect" science story is an elusive entity. In this discussion—an updated and expanded version of a panel discussion that took place during the 1982 Annual Meeting of the American Association for the Advancement of Science—a group of scientists and science reporters explore some serious questions for the field of science communication.

Ira Flatow has worked as a science reporter for National Public Radio since the early 1970s. His broadcasts are heard frequently on the morning news and on NPR's celebrated "All Things Considered." In addition, he is the writer/host for the PBS science show "Newton's Apple." In 1981 he received the Science and Society Award of the National Association of Science Writers for his coverage of the creationism–evolution controversy. He was a co-winner of the 1983 AAAS–Westinghouse Science Journalism Award in both the radio and television categories.

Dennis S. O'Leary became something of a household word in 1981 when he assumed the role of spokesman for The George Washington University Medical Center in Washington, D.C., during the tense days following the attempt to assassinate President Ronald Reagan. His comments on "Physicians and Reporters: Conflicts, Commonalities, and Collaboration" appear in Chapter 7.

Joann E. Rodgers, currently deputy director and director of media at the Johns Hopkins Medical Institution's Office of Public Affairs, was a science writer for the Hearst Newspapers for eighteen years, serving as both a columnist and a national science correspondent between 1973 and 1984. Additionally, she was a contributing editor to *Science 81, 82, and 83* and is a frequent contributor to *Science Digest.* She has received awards for her writing from the Lasker Foundation, the American Heart Association, the American Cancer Society, the National Council for Medical Research, and the Cystic Fibrosis Foundation. She is immediate past president of the National Association of Science Writers and a director of the Council for the Advancement of Science Writing.

Stephen H. Schneider is the deputy director of the Advanced Study Program at the National Center for Atmospheric Research in Boulder, Colorado. He is nationally known for his writings on climatology, and his comments on "Both Sides of the Fence: The Scientist as Source and Author" appear in Chapter 16.

Robert J. Trotter worked for *Science News* from 1969 to 1981, spending his last four years as editor of the magazine. During much of his tenure there, Trotter specialized in covering the social sciences, and in 1980 he won a special media award from the American Psychological Association for "making a sustained contribution in communicating psychology to the general public." Since leaving *Science News,* he has worked as a freelance science writer in Washington, D.C., and he is currently a senior editor at *Psychology Today.*

T HE MODERATORS, Sharon Dunwoody and Sharon Friedman, posed the questions for this panel discussion.

QUESTION: One major area of disagreement between scientists and journalists is over something called "accuracy." Do scientists and journalists disagree over what makes a statement inaccurate? And why is this such a sensitive and continuing issue for both groups?

TROTTER: Accuracy should be one of the most important concerns of any reporter, but it is especially important in science stories. Not only do inaccuracies infuriate scientists and prejudice them against journalists, but inaccuracies also can have dangerous and far-reaching effects.

Science stories deal with hard facts. And because many readers tend to take the word of scientists as gospel, any inaccuracy can lead to serious misunderstandings. A misleading story about a "cancer cure," for instance, could give false hopes to victims or send hundreds of people to a possibly dangerous laetrile clinic in Mexico. Inaccuracies could eventually prejudice readers against both scientists and journalists and make it harder for all concerned to do their jobs.

There should be no disagreement between scientists and science writers about the importance of accuracy, but there may be some disagreement about what constitutes accuracy. In many cases, scientists want to see a full, dispassionate discussion of their work—including all pertinent details and background information. But reporters, who have to deal with deadlines, space problems, and editors, may have to sacrifice some of the more technical details and emphasize some of the more striking aspects of a story. In doing so, they may be less accurate or less complete than the scientists would like. But if science writers care about what they are doing, they can learn to be both accurate and readable.

Good science writers are the ones who can satisfy both editors and readers and present an accurate science story. Good scientists in this context are the ones who understand the problems reporters face and try to work with them in order to end up with a story that is both accurate and printable. The solution to the "accuracy problem," I think, is mutual, professional respect between scientist and journalist. Accurate stories can help journalists earn this respect.

SCHNEIDER: Scientists often are offended when they say "3.65" and it comes out in an article as "about 4." This doesn't bother me, but it is often deemed inaccurate and irresponsible by many of my colleagues. More serious, perhaps, is the "paraphrase problem." I refer to the reporting of a scientist's opinion on a sensitive issue, when the journalist simplifies through paraphrasing a point of contention and that paraphrasing subsequently gets the scientist in trouble with colleagues—at least in his or her perception—because the scientist's own statements to the journalist were more precise and careful than the printed version. What the scientist does not realize is that his or her own words were probably not easily quotable (or even comprehensible) in their often involuted, Germanic form.

Finally, it is not infrequent, especially for general assignment journalists, to completely mix up basic points and quantitative statements in a story in which the technical component is complex or subtle. I think both scientists and journalists could agree that this is simply bad work and should be dealt with by stricter forms of internal controls within journalism that would warn, punish, and ultimately fire people who repeatedly put in such inaccurate performances, regardless of how beautifully they may write, how glamorous they may look, or how popular they may be with certain segments of the public. This is especially a problem for television journalists.

O'LEARY: The problem of accuracy lies in the fact that people live in their own worlds and thus see the world from their own perspectives. The journalist probably has a better sense of what will sell newspapers or catch the interest of the public. But in acting on this knowledge, the average journalist may not pay attention to enough of the details from the scientist's perspective. As far as the scientist is concerned, accuracy is lost in the translation.

The scientist who reads a newspaper story about himself or his work is reading it as a scientist and is probably concerned that his colleagues are reading the story as well. He is wondering how those colleagues may react to that story, because they do not read it in the same way as does the public. It might be a terrific story from the standpoint of the lay public, but the scientist will be wondering, "Will I be reviled by my colleagues?"

Often, the scientist has provided the facts, but the story just does not come out in a way that makes sense to him as a scientist. This gets into issues of balance and tone. An example is when a scientist feels that some fact has received undue attention in an article, or when another fact that he felt was very important has not received sufficient attention. Or an article may convey too great a degree of promise or hope. For instance, let's say that a scientist has made a discovery that would make it possible to produce an important new vaccine. The reality, though, from a production standpoint, is that a new product will not be on the market for three to ten years. If this is not conveyed in the story, then public demand for the vaccine may be immediate.

An important caveat is that when the scientist is dealing with science writers rather than general reporters not experienced in covering science, the sophistication of the reporting is quite different. Relatively few scientists or physicians understand the difference between a science writer and a general reporter; they do not appreciate the level of sophistication of a lot of the science writers.

FLATOW: Scientists usually refer to "accuracy" when they are critical of the way journalists convey the importance or meaning of their work. A scientist may feel that his work is meaningful because it is leading in such-and-such a direction. However, a reporter may disagree not with the content of the research itself but with the scientist's feeling about where his work is leading. The two may disagree over its ramifications, in other words. Sometimes, when a scientist does not fully understand or agree with the reporter's point of view about such implications, he or she may call a story "inaccurate."

This is a continuing issue between reporters and scientists, because the accuracy or integrity—a better word—of the research project is not being questioned. Rather, it is the implications that are at issue. Scientists do not like to think about those implications. They like to think they are doing pure science while others—technologists—are taking their work and applying it.

That's what made the debate over recombinant DNA research so unusual. Scientists in this rare case stopped their work to consider the ramifications of the genetic engineering research they were doing. Yet even here a typical conversation between a scientist and a reporter might have resulted in clear agreement over how the DNA research was accomplished but in disagreement (and, consequently, "inaccurate" reporting) over where the research might lead (for example, "monsters" escaping from the lab).

QUESTION: What some of you seem to be saying is that judgments about accuracy may in fact be value-laden, with scientists and journalists essentially disagreeing over what information belongs in a story and how that information should be played. Is that correct? Could you give us some examples?

SCHNEIDER: Often scientists who have made discoveries greatly valued by their peers are disappointed when they find that journalists have primarily repeated what is already well known to the scientific community and at most have made only peripheral mention of the new discovery in the article. These scientists fear that they may appear to their colleagues as unoriginal, self-appointed spokespersons for the field rather than "sticking" to their areas of acknowledged expertise. However, they are more upset because the journalists do not recognize them for the importance of their discovery—their little detail, in which a total of twelve people may have an intense interest but about which the rest of us could hardly care.

In addition, journalists often tend to stress issues of obvious significance to people now, sometimes missing the more subtle or long-range aspects of new work that have less "immediate" value.

Finally, there is the whole journalistic style of putting unqualified, headline-like statements in the first paragraph, with increasing details and qualifiers banished to the following paragraphs, and with—especially in the view of scientists—*necessary* caveats appearing last. I have on more than one occasion known editors to chop off the bottom few paragraphs that responsible journalists had loaded with appropriate caveats. I still remember a story in my local newspaper quoting me. The headline, "Scientist Predicts Ice Age," was followed by a total of two paragraphs that attempted to tell readers all about what the ice age would do to the economy, population, and other things of social interest, all described in the most dramatic terms. The editor—who in my opinion was completely irresponsible and should have been disciplined—had chopped out the bottom paragraph, in which I was properly quoted as saying, "but we have 10,000 to 20,000 years before it happens!"

Science journalists, in particular, are going to have to be very tough with their editors, some to the point of threatening to resign, in order to minimize this problem. The journalists could point out that they will lose their best sources of information if people who are not involved with the story make arbitrary editing decisions after a writer has spent a great deal of time assembling a balanced presentation. Perhaps the best journalists already know how to write a scissors-proof piece by including the right degree of caveats along with each paragraph. If so, then the problem is one of merely spreading this art more widely among the general practitioners.

QUESTION: Several people have suggested that scientists and journalists sometimes disagree on what constitutes a valid scientific source. For example, some scientists argue that journalists often give too much space to "extremists" in the interest of balancing their stories. How do you feel about this issue?

RODGERS: American journalistic tradition seeks "truth" with what someone has called a two-handed approach. That is, reporters attempt to balance information "on the one hand" with information "on the other hand." For the novice science writer, especially, there is security and comfort in this formula. It provides at least a patina of "fairness," and if enough "hands" are investigated, visible evidence of a lot of work.

The charge that journalists often give too much space to "extremists" may arise from scientists who misunderstand or ignore this traditional approach to reporting. It is as deeply entrenched among journalists as is the scientist's commitment to scientific method. In our efforts to get all sides of a story, presenting fringe positions is inevitable.

However, I agree with some of the scientist-critics of this tradition, because the practice may do little more than provide cover for a science journalist's unwillingness to make a judgment. The journalist is more than a stenographer; he or she is also a gatekeeper. At some point a position must be taken. There is not always an "other hand."

On the other hand (sorry!), scientists often take the position that "accuracy" requires an unwillingness to take a position. Or they may practice their own form of timid investigation and operate from the philosophical base that there is no "truth." Existentially, I may agree. But followed to its logical conclusion, this stance denies a social conscience to some of the best educated and most thoughtful human beings on this planet. Real people who must make real decisions on the basis of always imperfect information must come away from a science story with at least some basis for getting off the dime.

In sum, what I'm saying is that the processes of both science and science writing take some guts and some willingness to commit to a point of view or a conclusion, on paper or on the airwaves. Good science journalism can be objective, but the finished product can never be neutral.

FLATOW: Moderation is not what makes "news." Rightly or wrongly, newspaper journalists and broadcasters do not make a living reporting that "nothing is wrong."

However, I think that many times extremists are given too much space in stories because "balance" is missing. Sometimes this balance can only be supplied by reporters knowledgeable enough to know where to look for the other side of the story. Remember, too, that extremists can turn out to be right!

SCHNEIDER: This issue of balance can take several forms. For example, many scientists are nettled when a journalist feels his or her responsibility for fairness has been discharged simply by quoting one lunatic fringe against another. It is imperative both for the credibility of the scientific community and the education of the public that reporters have a reasonable sense of what the spectrum of prevailing scientific opinion is on some complex subject so that they can choose where the middle is and avoid being caught in a fruitless debate between jargon-wielding, often special-interest extremes. Sometimes this is difficult to do because it means getting involved enough in the subject to find out where the middle is, but frankly, people unwilling to do so should turn in their press cards.

Another form of balance often nettles some scientists, including myself. I have often been "used" by journalists who have quoted me accurately on a particular topic and then used that quote to balance a story. So if the story was balanced, why do I complain? Primarily because the quote dealt with something only peripheral to my interest and, in fact, could well have been outside my principal field and outside the principal thrust of the interview. Thus, when colleagues see me in print talking about, say, nuclear power, even though I only used it briefly as an analogy to carbon dioxide's effect on the climate, they begin to wonder why I've become an instant expert in all subjects and why I don't spend the bulk of my time talking about my field. Many scientists feel they have been abused when their principal points are ignored and only peripheral comments—usually dramatic or quotable ones—are taken out of the context of the overall presentation. Consequently, this practice bothers scientists even when the quotes are fair representations of the limited context in which they were made.

TROTTER: Scientists may complain that journalists give too much space to extremists. But if properly done, this can be a useful ploy. In some cases, it is possible to give the extremists enough rope to hang themselves. In other cases, it is possible to set up the extremist position and then knock it down with a more rational view. Either way, the story should leave the reader with a balanced or accurate view—and the journalist still has the extremist viewpoint to use for a "grabber" lead. The question of extremists is related to the question of accuracy. Extremists often are used because they make good copy, but they should be used only if the end result is an accurate and balanced story.

QUESTION: A perennial point of confrontation between scientists and journalists is "fact checking." Scientists often want to examine a journalist's story before publication to check for inaccuracies. Journalists, on the other hand, are loath to turn their manuscripts over to any source at any point. What are your experiences with this dilemma (if, in fact, you consider it a dilemma) and how do you personally react to it?

SCHNEIDER: If there is one thing I can't stand, it's the flimsy excuse that phoning back a source to check the facts—or even the whole story—is somehow compromising "journalistic independence." There is no way a source can hold the pen in his or her hand that could change any word the journalist wishes to write. On the other hand, the source can make it very uncomfortable, ethically or otherwise, for a journalist who doesn't wish to change something that is incorrect or exploitative of the source.

I can't for the life of me understand how independence is compromised when a journalist checks back with a scientist on complex and often politically sensitive issues to be sure that—*in the opinion of the scientist*—the story is accurate and balanced. If the journalist simply believes that the scientist is trying to "cover his tail," then he or she should by all means avoid making the changes the scientist has requested. But that journalist also must be prepared to defend him- or herself later on.

On the other hand, scientists tend to be about as dense as lead in understanding the problems that science journalists face in dealing with their editors and with the public. So I don't see scientist–journalist problems as a one-way street. But if journalists checked back more and were perceived as more responsible, I'm sure that scientists would be more willing to talk to them. Right now, when somebody mentions to scientific colleagues that he or she has just gotten off the phone with "that newspaper reporter," a frequent response is snickers.

RODGERS: "Fact checking" is at best a euphemism and at worst a con. The issue in the flap over fact-checking privileges, for both scientists and journalists, is mutual trust and respect or the lack thereof.

It is certainly a worthwhile goal to enhance mutual trust and respect between the scientific and journalistic communities. I personally believe it is. But the primary goal of journalists is to get information out as accurately and quickly as possible. Furthermore, there is a certain "adversariness," to coin a word, built into the pursuit of this goal that has stood the test of time as a means to serve the public interest.

The process is imperfect. Inaccuracies get into print. Some journalists fail to uphold high standards. But before we apply corrective measures, let's make certain they do not rely solely on simplistic "fact-checking" formulas. Otherwise, the cure may be worse than the disease.

I have worked with many of these formulas. All have benefits; all have risks. Broadly speaking, the benefits include some peace of mind on the part of the scientific source and an expert hedge against inaccuracy for the journalist. The potential risks are, however, important concerns, because implicit in any—repeat, any—system of "checking back" are promises of power and penalty.

The journalist knows that when she goes back to a source to read her story, she is offering that source some say over more than the facts. It is both a professional and human quality to exercise that say, particularly, as Schneider notes, when the issues are complex, politically sensitive, or linked to social policy.

The scientist who offers to cooperate with a journalist only if he is allowed to "fact check" knows this very well. For again, implicit in the system is the promise of penalty if the journalist refuses. Perhaps the source will not cooperate, or he may complain to the journalist's editor or publisher. Aggravating the situation are deadlines and the inevitable misunderstanding on the part of scientific sources about the role of science journalism. Science reports in newspapers, magazines, and on the air are at best tentative. They are not meant as stenographic reports, final words, or monuments.

Let's suppose, however, that the journalist agrees to check back. While theoretically, or in the best of all possible worlds, it is true that the source cannot force the journalist to change what he or she has written, the reality is often in my experience, otherwise. Women's and other mass circulation magazines are a case in point. They have some of the most ferocious fact-checking systems in use anywhere in the free world. They send full manuscripts not only to particular sources but often to consultants who sit on their boards. The upshot has been galloping timidity in scientific and medical copy. When a journalist knows that sources are given unlimited access to copy, after a while he begins to avoid making certain inquiries or reporting certain information. This self-censorship is born of the journalist's long experience with frustration in trying to defend material that a source questions.

In the hands of sensitive, knowledgeable, and professional editors, these abuses of the fact-checking system are minimal. I know because I have worked with such editors. They do exist. Unfortunately, they are not in the majority. Even on science magazines, there are some editors who, as a matter of policy, opt to placate a vocally unhappy source at the expense of a science journalist's report. Recently, an editor whom I respect elected to remove an entire reference to a piece of *published* research because the scientist who wrote it refused to confirm the current validity of the work unless he got to make major additions to the manuscript.

So where does that leave us? To my way of thinking, we're left with an imperfect but nevertheless workable process of challenge, compromise, and standard-setting. It's a feel-your-way system all up and down the science journalism front lines; it's a system to muddle through. My guidelines are as follows:

1. During the interview process, or certainly before leaving the source, science journalists should periodically and carefully go back over technical, complicated, or sensitive ground. I say things such as, "Let me make sure I have my facts straight," and "If I interpret your conclusions thus and such, would you agree?" This approach serves two purposes: one, to check on accuracy, and two, to reassure the scientific source that I am determined to be accurate and that I will take care not to misinterpret what he says or does.

2. I ask my sources to tell me who in their field would agree and disagree with them and who else in their field they think I should speak with. Again, this approach serves two purposes: to let the source know that I intend to check out what she says very carefully and to reassure her that I want to give her view a fair treatment.

3. I say nothing to a source at the beginning of the interview about going off the record or fact checking unless the source asks. If he brings the subject up, I ask that the source be as specific as possible about what is to be on or off the record. This gives me a sense of what the source is anxious about and a clue to how I can reassure him.

4. If the source insists on seeing the manuscript or on having me read back material, I may offer to read back direct quotes and specific technical matter. I also try to tell the source in what context *generally* I plan to place her material.

5. If a source wants to know why I am reluctant to send the manuscript to him or read it to him, and if I have time, I briefly summarize what I've written above. I don't, by the way, plead my case on the basis of "compromised independence."

6. When a source complains about an inaccuracy, I check it out fast and respond personally.

I think Steve Schneider hits an interesting note in his statement that "if journalists . . . were *perceived* as more responsible . . . scientists would be more willing to talk to them." In order for mutual trust and respect to enhance accurate science reporting, *both* journalists and scientists must perceive those traits to be in place.

QUESTION: In journalism there appear to be no explicit ground rules governing the *kinds* of information that belong in a science news story. When writing about research, for example, how much and what kind of details belongs in a journalistic account? How does a journalist know when to stop?

FLATOW: The detail, of course, depends upon the audience. A more technical readership needs and deserves more detail, but they may rightfully expect to find it in a technical journal rather than in the mass media.

Unfortunately, the question of detail becomes more and more important as our technical society gets more and more complex. In a society that depends upon high technology, decision makers and the public must continually juggle their need to know with their ability to understand.

In daily news broadcasting, detail is usually kept to a minimum. Broadcasters realize that they cannot and should not attempt to take the place of the written word by providing detail. Usually, once a broadcast story goes by, it is lost. There is no way to go back and "hear" a sentence again as one might reread it in a newspaper or magazine. That's why broadcast writing is as simple as possible. However, there are times that cry out for details, such as life-and-death situations, and these details must be repeated as often as necessary to make the point.

O'LEARY: A good science writer puts a certain amount of background research into a story in order to help readers understand the broader context within which the story falls. For example, while serving as a spokesman for the medical center during the Reagan assassination attempt, I spent a tremendous amount of time with reporters on background, on broad context. I was concerned about translating medical facts for a lay public, but much more important to me were balance and tone. Reporters had to understand what a fact meant, how important it was, and that it should be presented as neither more or less important than it was.

If reporters have done their homework, then they understand the context within which facts lie, and they are going to produce a better story regardless of the circumstances.

TROTTER: Journalists writing about research should include enough detail to explain how important conclusions were reached. The amount of detail provided, however, will differ depending on the audience. Readers with a technical or scientific background may feel cheated if they do not get enough information. Less sophisticated readers may not be able to follow anything more complex than the basic steps of a research project.

Communication is the goal, and the wants, needs, and abilities of the audience must be considered if the communication is to be effective.

SCHNEIDER: I generally tend to side with the journalists in the sense that their stories are primarily intended for the public and thus should contain a reasonable background summary of the issues, regardless of whether such a summary is "original" from the scientist's point of view. I also think that emphases on policy or other "vague" issues of public interest constitute perfectly legitimate foci for stories.

On the other hand (there is always an "other hand"), a few strokes for the fragile egos of specialized scientists whose chief rewards come through recognition of their major achievements (even if those achievements are really minor in the general scheme of things) is more than a nice gesture. It may even add information of interest to some readers. At the least it will gain for the journalist a friend who could act as a reliable evaluator of the accuracy of future stories that deal with the same subject.

RODGERS: The amount of detail in a journalistic account and the extent to which the science journalist sticks to the scientific account are determined largely by the peculiarities of the topic, the medium, and the contingencies of preparation time and space allotment.

If I am writing about prostaglandin synthesis for the *Ladies' Home Journal*, I will not describe the biochemical pathways of the pituitary in detail. I will describe what the research is likely to mean to women with fertility or menstrual problems. If I am writing the same place for *Science 85*, I might focus on benchmarks in the history of prostaglandin research and on the people who carried the research along. And if I am writing it for *Scientific American* or a high-technology publication, I would want to provide great detail on lab methodology. If I am writing on the subject for a daily tabloid, the story would probably be a newsy account of a published paper or meeting report.

QUESTION: How should journalists deal with the need for immediate information during a crisis that has scientific or technological aspects—crises such as the accident at Three Mile Island or the Reagan assassination attempt—when only incomplete information is available and when sources need time to put such information together? In other words, how does the public's right—and need—to know get balanced with the potential for delivering erroneous information?

FLATOW: This is one of the most difficult decisions facing science journalists: how much incomplete information can still be labeled "responsible journalism"? Should a reporter tell "all" that he or she knows, realizing that this may entail communicating information that could be inaccurate, misleading, or potentially dangerous?

In the case of Three Mile Island, the public's right to know was overriding because a disaster might have occurred. Word of a crisis might have helped people make decisions about whether their lives were in danger. In this case, though, it turned out that no one knew at the time how dangerous the situation really was; they didn't know how much damage had been done to the core. Conflicting information from company officials and federal investigators only served to make the picture even fuzzier.

The Reagan shooting resulted in a different kind of panic. No lives were in danger on a mass scale. But the sheer scope of the situation—the shooting of the president—made it an event of the utmost public attention.

Having experienced the TMI confusion firsthand, I decided during the Reagan crisis that the best way to deal with the overload of incomplete information was to simply tell my listeners that "we don't really know what the truth is. Here is the best we can do. You'll have to live with the 'facts' as we know them at this moment." Thank goodness we did not air an obituary for presidential press secretary James Brady, as did other media. Those premature announcements of Brady's death were undoubtedly caused by the pressure to be "first" with the news, but in this case the journalists who were "first" were also wrong.

SCHNEIDER: It seems to me that there is a simple operating rule: don't offer as truth what you know to be rumor, speculation, or soon-to-be-revised statements. By all means report what is known or said, but give people a sense of what it is worth! Use plausible alternative scenarios, if you can get some, and try to explain the ramifications of "what happens if." At least this will enable readers or viewers to anticipate the options and to deal with the truth when it ultimately comes out. While headline writers will never do such things as scenario analysis, good journalists need not always be reduced to the lowest common denominator in their writings.

TROTTER: The public has a right to get accurate, not erroneous, information. In times of crisis, such as Three Mile Island, a good journalist will have or find sources who can discuss the situation and evaluate it based on the information available. But the resulting story should always indicate that it is based on incomplete information. Even an incomplete story can be good if the reporter explains why it is incomplete. Again, the emphasis should be on accuracy.

O'LEARY: First of all, there's no such thing as a well-organized disaster. The more complex the disaster situation, the more unlikely it is that leadership will emerge quickly, not only to take charge of the situation but also to provide understandable information to the public.

The situation I dealt with (the Reagan assassination attempt) was in a sense much easier to handle than something like Three Mile Island, where there was the potential for multiple injuries. If one is going to be the spokesperson pulling together information, there has to be some way to gather that information and to make some sort of coherent presentation to the public. The public is probably not well served by fragmentary, piecemeal information. Since gathering information takes a finite period of time, there is going to be a delay in relaying that information to the public.

The next question is how much of a delay is reasonable. At The George Washington University Medical Center we delayed in producing information at first because our patient was in surgery. The people with the information were the doctors who were taking care of him. Their first responsibility was to care for the patient, and then, secondarily, they were responsible for relating information about him. Once surgery was completed, we were able to move forward in preparing a response for the public.

Through the early days of that period we were producing press releases and meeting with the media twice a day. But when it was time for, say, the afternoon press briefing and something was going on, we would delay the briefing as long as we could in order to provide as much information as possible. For example, on the fifth day of his hospitalization, President Reagan underwent a bronchoscopy to remove some secretions from his chest. We held up the afternoon briefing long enough to know the results of the bronchoscopy procedure.

We must be sensitive to the needs of the media, but meeting these needs may be a juggling act. You cannot serve only your own needs and you cannot serve only the media's needs. Invariably there are going to be some compromises and you do the best you can.

RODGERS: For good or ill, the public demands immediate gratification of its news hunger. It's a fact that must be dealt with, not an issue to be debated or something to be blamed on someone. If that fact is the starting point, then the goal of science communication must be to keep channels open. That requires coordination of effort on both sides: those with the information and those who transmit it to the public.

Those with the information and expertise can perform best when they equip spokespersons with frequent updates on information, when they give them free rein to respond to press inquiries, and when they provide sufficient round-the-clock access for the press. Otherwise, they inevitably create communications bottlenecks that frustrate reporters to the degree that some journalists will go with rumors, guesses, or other questionable information.

My approach to crisis science journalism, in general, is to maintain a home base through which information can be filtered and checked. That base gives the journalistic specialist better access to his or her expert sources, files, libraries, and other media, including wires, television, and competing newspapers. During a crisis the science journalist functions best, in my opinion, as a resource and gatekeeper rather than as a street reporter. During Three Mile Island, for example, I believe I did a better job sitting in my newsroom, talking to health physicists and nuclear engineers to supplement and explain the information coming out of the chaos at the Pennsylvania press site. During the Reagan assassination attempt, the need was similar.

Finally, I have a bias about science communications that may be as unpopular with science reporters as with scientists. It is this: if the choice is between getting some information out—even though it has a high risk of carrying some inaccurate or misleading material to the public—and getting no information out, I choose the former.

In my experience, attempts to guarantee 100 percent accuracy by withholding information are a poor trade-off. And they almost never work. The good science journalist will *always* strive to be 100 percent accurate and will never fail to report her reservations about the veracity of information along with that information. But there comes a point when the science journalist must "go with what she's got," even if in her heart of hearts she suspects it won't stand the test of time. Good communications is a process; it has to start somewhere. Unless initial information gets out, that process will be short-circuited and stunted, possibly with worse consequences than would result from a piece of inaccurate or incomplete information. Without the first report, there is no opportunity to rebut, discuss, challenge, explain, or educate.

PART III

Critiquing the State of the Art

T HE FIELD OF SCIENCE COMMUNICATION has grown and evolved since its origin in the 1930s. During this time, it has gone through at least two general stages: an early one that concentrated on writing about the excitement and wonders of science, and a more recent stage of looking at science's policy aspects as well as its wonders.

Part III examines the current state of the science communication field from the view of content, style, and media and news source behavior. It looks at the impact of the explosion of interest and activity in science communication in the late 1970s, and it also presents classic case studies of media coverage of an annual meeting of the American Association for the Advancement of Science, the recombinant DNA issue, and the accident at the Three Mile Island nuclear plant. These important retrospective studies provide a historical perspective on the field from which to assess its effectiveness and question who actually sets the agenda for science communication. Since Chapters 12 through 15 are historical in approach, all titles and affiliations in them are those current at the time of the case study.

CHAPTER 9

The Medium Is Large, but How Good Is the Message?

William Bennett

Between 1978 and 1980, several new science magazines came into being, while others enlarged or otherwise changed their formats, bringing the public a greater variety of scientific coverage than ever before. That journalists rather than scientists became the prime writers for these magazines provided some advantages for readers, but it also brought about some problems of style and content that William Bennett believes can have serious consequences.

William Bennett graduated from Harvard Medical School and then spent several years in research before becoming the science and medicine editor at Harvard University Press. Since 1977 he has worked as a freelance science writer, except for a one-year stint as director of the Writing Program at Massachusetts Institute of Technology. He is now editor of *The Harvard Medical School Health Letter*. With Joel Gurin, he is coauthor of *The Dieter's Dilemma: Eating Less and Weighing More*.

T HE TITLE CHOSEN FOR A BOOK lives after it; the text is often interred with its author. The late C. P. Snow and Marshall McLuhan both wrote slim volumes of cultural criticism and prophecy that a few decades later, can only be called minor—if not merely wrong.[1] But their titles have gone on to an independent life. The notion of "two cultures," one scientific, the other literary, has a kind of workaday plausibility to those of us who struggle to make science accessible to the public. In reality, however, our readers probably know even less of history or literature than they do of science. Whatever we popularizers are doing, we are not bridging Lord Snow's chasm. And although we often speak of the "media" as our medium, we are actually doing our work in print and according to traditional formulas. Television and other electronic novelties have done little to convey an understanding of science to the viewing public. They may, indeed, prove incapable of doing so.

Instead of trying to write about the "message" of science as "communicated" through the "media," I want to look at popular science *writing*, mainly as it appears in current magazines. In asking how "good" it is, I will be more concerned with such traditional concepts as style and substance, as opposed to "messages" or market penetration.

Despite some setbacks in readership and income figures, most of the new science publications are meeting the survival test of quality quite handily, and on that ground alone one could argue that there is little to criticize. Yet it has become second nature for science journalists to worry about the state of their craft. There is a collective sense in the science press that what it does, although noble in purpose, is somehow problematic, even suspect. The science story is seen as debasing the pure gold of real science into the dross of popularization—by a kind of reverse alchemy. Committed, as all of us are, to the belief that science is something true and good and beautiful, we carry around a slight chronic sense of guilt that we are misrepresenting the real McCoy in order to make it comprehensible, palatable, marketable to those with even less grasp of the subject than we have.

This discomfort is too often abetted by the scientists we write about. Many of them persist in disparaging science journalism as a failed attempt to transmit the pure light of research results to the public's blind eyes. The science writer, in this caricature, is fated to be, at best, a diligent polisher of dark glass. Such extreme pessimism, which is really just cheap elitism, can be dismissed out of hand.

But given an agreement that science ought to be popularized, I think it is harder to deal with the question of *who* should be doing this work. The new science magazines have answered in a remarkably uniform way. Their editors have turned to professional writers, not scientists, for their copy. Most of them depend on freelancers (although *Discover* is written mainly by its staff), but they all have made the basic decision not to rely on stories written by scientists. This was a thoroughly conscious choice and was justified at the time by the assertion that *Scientific American's* formula was no longer working very well, at least for a large number of potential readers. The reluctance to use practicing scientists as authors was reinforced by the failure of *Human Nature,* an ill-fated harbinger of the new flock of popular science magazines. Devoted primarily to behavioral science, *Human Nature* was often criticized for failing to find its level during the fifteen months of its life, from late 1977 to 1979. The magazine's editorial problems were attributed in part to the fact that it chose a course of respectability at the price of readability by seeking scientists as its principal contributors.

In choosing the other course—to rely on professional writers, most of whom have little or no experience as practicing scientists—I think the new magazines' editors were responding to a much broader problem than the fact that scientists often write muddy sentences or load their prose with jargon. The differences in the way scientists and writers use language go deeper than that and have to do with their respective places in the social system of science.

To be sure, scientists often do not write nicely polished sentences, and that might be reason enough to go elsewhere. But I don't think that's really the issue; sentences can be cleaned up by an editor if the text is fundamentally open to its intended audience. The underlying problem is that scientists have professional goals and rules that keep them from *wanting* to make their work truly accessible to a popular audience—and disable them from doing so when they try. Virtually all professions display a tendency to isolate themselves intellectually; it is a way of reinforcing their identity and status within society at large. This is as true of law, architecture, and literary criticism as it is of science. Professional jargon, to take just one obvious example, helps to serve this purpose— just as the argot of criminals or the slang of teenagers serves to reinforce social boundaries or to protect members of the in-group from infiltration by outsiders.

Not only do members of a profession, often quite unconsciously, use their prose to exclude the "unqualified," they also employ it to manage their relations and status within the field. Thus, even the scientist who is addressing a popular audience is likely to have more on his agenda than straightforward exposition. He may well take the occasion of a popular article to acknowledge or assert priority of discovery, to recite a scientific genealogy, or otherwise to delineate social relations with colleagues in his field.

These traits are conspicuous in many articles written for *Scientific American.* Appearing in the pages of that magazine has become one of the earmarks of status for American scientists. Indeed, the editors appear to have self-consciously taken on that function, to have integrated their publication into the reward system of science. Thus, the reader, at least *this* reader, becomes terribly conscious that the author of an article is writing in part about the fact that he has been selected to write the article—an honor to be acknowledged and justified without slighting the contributions of his colleagues. The main text of the article, about a scientific subject, is closely interwoven with a subtext that attends to professional courtesy. In trying to follow the thread of discourse, the reader is subject to the mental equivalent of eyestrain.

A related but somewhat distinct reason that most scientists are not successful popularizers is that they have been trained to write for a controlled—really a censored—press, the refereed journals. Censorship has a vital, constructive role to play in the social system that Spencer Klaw, editor of the *Columbia Journalism Review*, has termed the "scientific estate." But the journalistic fourth estate operates according to a set of values that does not cheerfully tolerate this form of news "management." Accustomed to reading and writing in one mode, scientists often find it difficult to adjust to the seeming unruliness of popular journalism.

By weeding out substandard contributions, the refereed science press serves to maintain the credibility of the research establishment as a whole. It also provides a way to draw the boundaries of membership and status within the scientific elite, and it serves as a kind of registry in which the ownership of intellectual property can be recorded. The intellectual property of scientists is their principal asset, and it has real value; it is convertible to money and power. Because scientists are, with increasingly rare exceptions, public employees, the rate of conversion is determined by the commitment of the public and their political representatives to continued government funding of research.

In the simplest terms, then, the role of censorship in the scientific press is to see that science as a collective endeavor maintains the brightest possible image, puts its best foot forward. That's a sensible, even laudable, aim, but it brings the scientist, committed to "managing the news," into potentially sharp conflict with journalists, who are, or should be, acting as representatives of the reading public, not of the scientific establishment. Even though scientists and journalists ostensibly share a commitment to telling the truth, they have a fundamentally different professional interest in what is selected for the telling, and in how it is told. However discreetly, the scientist is likely to use publication to blow his own horn, or that of his field—and properly so. A journalist's job, on the other hand, is to evaluate the pitch.

In summary, I am somewhat skeptical of the notion that scientists are, as a rule, motivated to foster public understanding of their work. I think there are many reasons, mostly not consciously appreciated, for scientists to prefer a polished public image to genuine public understanding of their work. The science magazine editors' decision not to employ scientists to do their own popularizing was, therefore, consistent with a journalistic tradition that, at its best, maintains a potentially adversarial relationship between the writer and his subject. Generals are not hired to report on their wars.

There was bound to be a trade-off, however, as a consequence of the turn to professional writers, and I think it might have been natural to assume that the loss would be in scientific accuracy, not literary quality. Journalists might be expected to garble scientific facts, blow up a tentative finding, make unwarranted extrapolations from the data—all the historical sins of sensationalist science reporting. Yet that is precisely what has *not* happened in any significant degree, as far as I can tell. Of course, I can't be dead certain that every detail I read, even in an article on a familiar subject, is correct. But in the areas I know something about, the facts seem to be accurate; research findings seem to be judiciously cited; caveats are appropriately inserted. Naturally, there are errors, but on the balance the level of accuracy seems pretty high. Likewise, the choice of subjects and the balance with which they are presented seems to me reasonable from the point of view I would expect a scientist to take. The findings that are highlighted, the lines of research that are chronicled—these seem to correspond pretty well with what scientists themselves are choosing to emphasize in their journals and reward with their prizes. Although a couple of the magazines sport lurid cover graphics and make comic attempts at raciness in their headlines, across the board, I would say, the editors are policing their content pretty respectably.

What I would not have predicted is what has happened. The prose in the new science press, with rare exceptions, proves to be somewhat dull and predictable, despite clear efforts to dress it up with bright phrases, narrative interludes, and well-chosen similes—not to mention aggressive graphics that sometimes altogether overwhelm the text. I have been surprised that this is my reaction to the new magazines. But it occurs repeatedly and appears to be shared by at least some of the people I talk with, so I am tempted to think that it points to something real.

If the stuff isn't interesting, why is it selling? My answer has to be that I think there is a large and avid audience for science stories. The new magazines would have had to make a determined effort in order to fail abjectly, right off the bat. Even *Scientific American,* which few people argue is a scintillating read, has maintained its circulation of some 700,000 for many years now. Moreover, the writing in the new magazines is far from *bad,* but it lacks an intensity, a sparkle, a sense of mission, all of which I would have expected given both the intrinsic brilliance of the scientific work there is to write about and the human implications, exhilarating or painful, that it portends. So I am not proclaiming science journalism a disaster area—far from it. But I do think there has been a shortfall, a subtle but nonetheless real failure to take the writing beyond the upper reaches of the ordinary, and inasmuch as we might have anticipated brilliance during this period of expanded opportunity, I think it's worth looking for some of the reasons that we are not seeing much better writing.

Now I grant that the prose in the new magazines is competent—to a remarkably uniform degree. The stories are smoothly, professionally written and are well edited. But although there are few clinkers, the gems are fewer still. Rarely do I suck in my breath and say, "Wow, what a sentence," or "That idea was elegantly developed." Even less often do I laugh or snicker or feel a surge of rising gorge. There is a stylistic monotony, a shallowness in the reporting, a lack of texture and allusion. And the very blandness of science writing becomes a flaw in the journalism because it is misleading. Science is not bland; it is not a well-oiled mechanism; it is not necessarily going about its business in a way that calls only for periodic progress reports. Somehow the blandness about which I am complaining fosters the impression that personal eccentricity, politics, or ideology are to be treated as material for anecdotes and not as fundamental influences on the practice of research.

I'm disinclined to think that this state of affairs reflects incompetence or a deficiency of writing talent, or that it's anyone's fault. I think the causes are systematic and that we are all more or less captives of the same situation.

For starters, our prose suffers because we still haven't been able to determine who our real audience is. When we write, we do not have a happy, internalized sense of the person who will read our words. The most obvious sign of this basic uncertainty is that stories about relatively sophisticated scientific developments still include elementary definitions of such terms as DNA, electron, and nucleus. It becomes a kind of water torture to pick up a popular article on some aspect of molecular biology, for example: you *know* that sooner or later you must read yet one more definition of DNA, with a description of the fundamentals of inheritance. Do we really need to go on defining DNA? Isn't it a little as though political writers found it necessary to define "prime minister," or military writers to explain what a bomb does?

I recently read the manuscript of a popular essay on modern genetics. It was written by a professional science writer who used the quaint term "blood heat" for the temperature 37°C and "caustic soda" instead of sodium hydroxide. In selecting these words, the author seemed to imagine that he was writing for an audience of nineteenth-century classicists. But he introduced "hydrogen bonding" without flinching and "amber mutants" with barely a nod of explanation. Although egregious, I think this example of oscillation between labored definition of familiar terms and casual introduction of obscure ones is far from isolated, and it is an important symptom. It reflects real uncertainty as to who our audience may be, and this doubt has serious consequences for a writer. At the least it has a chilling effect: you cannot write at blood heat if you are perennially in doubt about your readers' fundamental vocabulary.

Granted, this uncertainty about what readers can be trusted to know is a problem in other areas as well as science writing. As the total body of human knowledge has grown, the core of information that any "educated" reader can be expected to command has diminished, not necessarily because people are less well educated but because education leads them in disparate directions at a relatively early age. The first essayist, a Frenchman writing in the sixteenth century, could and did assume a fluent knowledge of classical authors; nowadays, we cannot assume that our readers know who Montaigne was, let along that they might recognize a quotation from his essays. This is a much more fundamental problem than the divergence of two cultures. It reflects the fragmentation of a single culture that has grown too large to be shared by its members. There is, in other words, no such thing as a "general" reader once you leave a rather basic level of reporting. Yet many editors persist in asking their writers to address prose to an imaginary reader who was educated two generations ago, hasn't read anything of science since, and on a sudden whim has picked up one of their magazines. I would like to remind them that Lewis Thomas' essays in *The Lives of a Cell,* his best work, were first published in the *New England Journal of Medicine* and were written for an audience that he assumed would have basic scientific literacy. The essays were reprinted without change in the book, which became a best-seller despite—or perhaps on account of—any textual difficulties they present to the common reader.

A related observation: I think many science writers or their editors don't really trust their material. They don't expect readers to find it entertaining. To compensate, they resort to a kind of stock theatricality in their prose. For example, in one issue of *Science 83* (by far the best written of the popular science magazines), four of the seven features began with narrative leads—all in the present tense:

- "Jim Curran is making one last phone call. His voice cracks. . . ."
- "Hans Goedicke is angry at George Michanowsky, but in a bemused way."
- "In the early afternoon on January 11, 1982, four Hopi Indian men walk into the Smithsonian's Museum of Natural History, a golden-domed science building. . . ."
- "Jim Anderson stands at the edge of a graveled hilltop with his eyes lifted and the fingers of one hand resting against his lower lip. . . ."

There is, perhaps, a hint of false advertising in these leads; what follows is not to be a sustained narrative. Rather, the little story gets the reader into the tent; thereafter the exposition begins. Leads such as these—in such profusion—betray a fear that the audience does not care to read about ideas. This audience could not be trusted, perhaps, to read beyond any of the following sentences:

- "It is a truth universally acknowledged, that a single man in possession of a good fortune must be in want of a wife."
- "Happy families all resemble one another; every unhappy family is unhappy in its own way."
- "Under certain circumstances there are few hours in life more agreeable than the hour dedicated to the ceremony known as afternoon tea."

Yet these sociological generalizations begin three of the finest real narratives in literature.[2]

Not only is the science writer likely to be hampered by uncertainty about what his audience knows and by mistrust of its tastes, but as a journalist he is in a peculiarly ambiguous relationship to the material about which he writes. The real reporters of science are not the journalists who write for the public but the scientists themselves; the researchers are really the only ones in a position to write eyewitness accounts. It may be one of our cultural tragedies that scientists are so pressured to squeeze the eyewitness excitement out of their writing. Meanwhile, however, science journalists become, in their way, incumbents of the rewrite desk—at least in their posture as interpreters of scientific knowledge to the lay public.

This relationship of journalist to scientist—or rewrite man to front-line reporter, puts the writer at an important psychological disadvantage. It leads to an inhibited style. The journalist, not feeling entitled to his own point of view, succumbs to an excess of caution.

There are several conceivable ways out of this bind, some more effective, no doubt, than others. One commonly chosen approach is to disguise a science piece as a story about a scientist. This device tends to fall flat, though, especially when the story-about-a-scientist boils down to an elaboration of the sentence "Researcher makes discovery," which really amounts to reporting "Dog bites man." We have come to *expect* that researchers will make discoveries, especially beneficial ones. It is normal behavior for them, so trying to punch up the interest of a science story by writing about the process of discovery runs the paradoxical risk of seeming banal.

On the other hand, writing about scientists in unexpected ways presents hazards of another sort. It is not all that easy to act on *Washington Post* medical writer Victor Cohn's wonderful dictum, "Scientists are to journalists what rats are to scientists," for scientists are also to science writers what "sources" are to journalists in other fields. When journalists write critically about scientists as entrepreneurs, for example, or when they question the conduct of science or the social value of a research effort, they put their scientists on the defensive. And a defensive scientist is also authoritative, articulate, disdainful, and not above pulling rank. It's not an easy reaction to handle. And yet, if science writing is to fulfill its potential, I think it has to venture some independent criticism and to brook the response. The new magazines and their writers have seemed to me relatively unwilling to do this—to take hard inquisitive looks at science as a *human* institution, at the politics, economics, sociology, and psychology of research and researchers.

Now obviously, journalists shouldn't be irresponsible when they seek to criticize science or scientists. Mothers shouldn't be irresponsible either, but that doesn't mean they should stop mothering. It is not irresponsible to risk making mistakes. There are bound to be excesses in any free press and even serious errors of commission. But I don't believe that it is preferable to make the error of omission that seems, at present, to predominate.

I think that this error is, in essence, to treat science unscientifically. As June Goodfield writes in her book *Reflections on Science and the Media:*

> The public needs to know about the actual nature of the scientific process, for this, as much as the content of science, should be comprehended. . . . the methodology of science and the spirit of science should also be conveyed. . . . (this) task practically no one has done at all, for journalists generally don't know how to, and scientists either have not bothered or, in some cases, have not wanted to be observed that closely.[3]

What really matters about science is the method, not the facts. Facts, in themselves, have exceedingly limited power, as the nineteenth-century English writer Thomas De Quincy points out: "What do you learn from a cookery-book? Something new, something that you did not know before, in every paragraph." Yet such a book is "wretched" and "provisional," to be discarded when new facts supersede the old.

It is the power of science that it transcends wrong results, that good research can yield an erroneous or incomplete picture of the world—but in a way that moves the discussion along. Yet most science writing focuses on the putative "facts" of science and scants the process. The result is a disturbing overemphasis on the authority of science as a source of truth, rather than on its revolutionary potential as a way of thinking. The scientist comes off as an authority, and the validity of his work is justified by his standing, not the other way around.

There is a great hazard here—even to scientists—which is that they come to be perceived as one of a competing array of equally plausible authorities. The reader who is not already a convert, who has not fully bought into the scientific world view (presumably the intended audience of the magazines), can easily react by dismissing the scientist-authority as a bully and instead opting for an alternative, underdog "expert" who presents himself or herself as knowing about UFOs, vitamins, or extra-sensory perception. Now "scientists" may or may not be right about any of these subjects. UFOs could exist. That doesn't matter. What matters is the nature of the evidence that is sought and proffered by any of the parties to the discussion.

In sum, I think that the new science magazines are running the risk of fostering a seriously unscientific, or even antiscientific, frame of mind in their own readers. And these readers may even be people who are moderately well informed about the body of information that we call scientific and who identify their own interests with those of science. Reorienting the tenor of science writing—while keeping it salable—can hardly be an easy thing to accomplish. But if we don't try, I'm not sure science writing is worth doing at all.

Notes

1. C. P. Snow, *The Two Cultures and a Second Look* (Cambridge: Cambridge University Press, 1964); Marshall McLuhan and Quentin Fiore, *The Medium Is the Message* (New York: Random House, 1967).
2. The three books are, respectively, Jane Austen's *Pride and Prejudice*, Leo Tolstoy's *Anna Karenina*, and Henry James' *The Portrait of a Lady*.
3. June Goodfield, *Reflections on Science and the Media* (Washington, D.C.: American Association for the Advancement of Science, 1981), 88.

CHAPTER 10

Humanizing Science Through Literary Writing

Jon Franklin

Science coverage typically reports new developments, but Jon
Franklin believes this is an inadequate way of defining science for the
public and that it contributes to the gap between science and the
public. He suggests expanding the subjects covered by science writers
as well as changing the usual writing style. The style he proposes is
exemplified by this chapter and his 1979 Pulitzer Prize–winning
article, "Mrs. Kelly's Monster," reprinted in Appendix C.

Jon Franklin, science writer for the *Baltimore Evening Sun*, is the
author of several books, including *Shocktrauma, Not Quite a Miracle*,
and *The Guinea Pig Doctors*. He describes his genre as "literary
journalism," arguing that modern literature must by necessity deal
more and more with the human aspects of scientific progress. His
work has won him a variety of prizes, including the American
Chemical Society's Grady Medal in 1975 and, in 1979, a Pulitzer Prize
for feature writing. In 1984 he received the Helen Carringer Journalism
Award from the National Association of Mental Health for a series of
articles on molecular psychology. He won the 1984 Pulitzer Prize for
explanatory writing for a series called "The Mind Fixers."

F OR A SCIENCE WRITER, covering a meeting of the American Association
for the Advancement of Science is a lot like one of those five-day vaca-
tions in which you visit nine countries.

Maybe on the first morning you do a story about warm-blooded dinosaurs, followed that afternoon by a take-out on neutrinos. That night your editor calls in a lather because the husband of somebody who just got kidnapped is a janitor in your hotel, and you should get hopping.

The next day you're tired, and you want something sweet and easy.

That was my situation in Denver a few years ago when two public relations guys from Rocky Flats showed up at the AAAS pressroom. They were pushing a story about a new electricity-generating windmill that was being tested at nearby Rocky Flats.

Rocky Flats, of course, was the place where hydrogen warheads were manufactured, and at the time it had a little PR problem. Something about spilled plutonium.

And these guys desperately wanted to see stories about their windmill testing program and about what a wonderful environmental boon it was.

If I did a story, they promised, they could get me a quickie glimpse of Rocky Flats, up close. I couldn't resist. Besides, what the hell, I'm an Okie. I like windmills. So I did the story.

And that night there was a wind. Not a roof-snatcher, but a little more of a blow than normal. And guess what blew over? You got it. The windmill.

So I had to do a follow-up, on deadline. I called Rocky Flats and was informed that suddenly everybody was out of the office and would return the call, someday. Or would I like to call back next month, perhaps?

And then, while you're trying to write a second-edition lead on Rocky Flats forgetting how to speaka da English, you miss a story on a new virus and another one on the social habits of South American farm workers. That afternoon, naturally, paleoastronomy and abused children are both scheduled for two o'clock.

It's a strange existence, chasing the news in science.

Ours is a borderline world, part science, part art, part smoke, part mirrors. As an art form—and I'm going to argue that it's just that—science writing is a new, mysterious force in the world.

Until World War II, science was a private and privileged business. Sometimes it was an arm of commerce. Other times it was secret and had to do with gizmos for steering torpedos.

When writers of that day wrote about science, they usually focused on the weird. The Wizard of Menlo Park,[1] the newspapers announced, had performed another act of magic. Or an inventor had devised a machine for sending messages through thin air.

Somewhere, the novelist wrote, in a decaying castle in Denmark or Transylvania, a biologist worked patiently on corpses, intent on creating life.

It was all the same to the citizen, whose daily existence on the farm was not much affected either way. And their separate status didn't hurt the scientists at all.

And then there was a war. The world was forever changed.

The people weren't farmers anymore. Suddenly science was everywhere, everybody's business . . . political business.

Overnight the scientist graduated from shaman to high priest. The image makes you wince, but how else was the public to visualize this mysterious, sinister figure in a white smock?

The scientist put up with it because, like a priest, he needed, you know, support. Funding. Tax money. Call it anything but tithes.

The change from private to public science had enormous consequences, and one of those was the birth of science writing. Scientists who needed support started buttonholing reporters.

The reporters immediately made two fundamental discoveries.

One, the stuff was fascinating to research and an incredible challenge to write.

Two, unless it had to do with flying saucers, the Loch Ness monster, or the use of hypnotism to solve capital crimes . . . almost nobody wanted to buy it.

The scientist made a discovery, too. He found that when he clipped a *New York Times* story about his work and attached it to his grant request, then, somehow, some way, fate smiled benevolently on him.

If all else was equal, the wisdom was, a newspaper clipping could save the day.

Beneath the wisdom there was a dirty rumor that it made a big difference even when all else was nowhere near equal.

There was ambivalence on both sides, but writer and scientist both persevered. For one thing, both tended to be idealistic, and there was a matter of public duty.

While the world hung under the shadow of the bomb, doctors cured polio. Computers kept our bank accounts straight and were soon put to work compiling dossiers on pinko peace creeps. Before, politicians had called the shots. Now scientists acted, and politicians reacted.

There was definitely a need for, as the scientists put it, "communication with the public."

It was an admirable ideal, but it talked a whole lot easier than it lived.

There were some real disasters.

My favorite occurred in the late 1960s, when the first pulsar was discovered. I will repeat the story, more or less as it was told to me, by one of the scientists who was there.

The tale begins down at Arecibo, in the Caribbean, where the United States had built the world's largest radio telescope. The radar dish was nestled in a natural crater in the Puerto Rican hills. It was too big to aim, so it pointed straight up. Each day, as the earth turned, it swept across the heavens.

One of the first discoveries that the astronomers made was that each time the dish swept across one specific section of sky, it picked up a series of sharp, short bursts of radio energy.

In effect there was something up there beeping at them, very fast, beep-beep-beep-beep-beep, like that.

We know now that it was a pulsar, the cinder of an exploded star. It was spinning incredibly fast and giving off a radio beacon. With each revolution there was a beep.

But all the Arecibo scientists knew was that there was something up there beeping at them. And, since they had never run across anything like that before, it *had* to be important.

Being responsible citizens as well as good scientists, they had a sit-down meeting. They knew they were obligated to announce their discovery to the world, but they weren't too sure how to go about it.

Eventually they decided to look up the largest newspaper in the United States and call an editor there. That ought to take care of it.

Well, the best-read newspaper in the United States turned out to be a publication printed in, of all places, Lantana, Florida, just a few hours' flight to the north.

A while later, in Lantana, an editor picked up a telephone.

Yes, he was interested.

Man, oh man, was he interested. One of his best reporters was on the next plane south.

The astronomers sat the fellow down and explained that something was up there beeping at them . . . beep-beep-beep . . . like that. They let him listen to the tape-recorded beeps, and they gave him a lesson in radio astronomy.

Finally, he asked, thoughtfully, "So you don't really know for sure what's doing the beeping?"

No, of course not. All they really knew was the beeping.

Well, then, it could be anything, right? It could even be intelligent life trying to start a conversation?

The astronomers laughed, sort of pleased that the fellow was beginning to grasp the basic vagueness of science. Sure, I suppose, sure. It could be anything.

They started talking about the wonders of radioastronomy again, but the reporter was suddenly in a hurry. They drove him to the airport, saw him off, and went back to their work.

And so it was that the most important astronomical discovery of the decade was announced on the front page of *The National Enquirer*. The banner headline, in 72-point type, said something like: ALIENS CON-

TACT EARTH. The story, if I remember correctly, ran near a piece about an arthritis cure and one on Elvis' sex life.

In any revolution, you've gotta expect a little bloodshed.

This didn't happen very many times before scientific institutions started opening public relations offices and science writers were hired. The institutions got good people, despite low pay and poor working conditions, because it was one of the few ways that a science writer could support a family.

And each year, there were a few more artists in science.

Scientists didn't think of it that way, of course. They didn't think about art at all, just that money was tight, and it wouldn't hurt to have a few clips to attach to the ole grant request.

Periodically, they sent their PR people down to scrounge up some ink at the local newspaper.

Down in the city room, the fellow who covered science knew as soon as he saw the PR person that the story was a plant. If it was any good, she wouldn't have come to the local paper; she'd have called *The New York Times.*

Sometimes, a deal was struck. The reporter would write the story and the PR person would owe him a favor. The next time, before she called *The New York Times,* the local reporter would get an off-the-record call first.

For years, local science writers eked out an existence based on a multiplicity of such under-the-table deals between newspapers and PR people.

It was a complicated game, made more so by the lack of enthusiasm on the part of our creditors. A lot of us were right at the poverty level and operated as little more than mouthpieces for the scientists we interviewed.

And the stories read like a cross between a bureaucratic announcement and a scientific paper.

The science writer, not quite understanding the material, did the best he could and handed a story in. The editor understood it even less, but, having no time to pursue a boring matter further, lopped off the last four inches and scheduled it around a tire ad on page F–17.

The scientist read the story when it was printed, and dictated a letter praising the reporter for his accuracy.

The story had two other readers. One was a disgustingly intelligent seventh-grader who wanted to impress her science teacher. The other was an elderly man who mistakenly thought it had something to do with his rare but miserable bone condition.

Even so, the system limped along, getting better, as we love to say, all the time. Sure, there were growing pains, but things quit falling apart so often, and *The New York Times* usually got its stuff right, and no one announced anything really big any more in *The National Enquirer.*

Things were okay.

That is . . . unless you wanted to count laetrile and vitamin E.

Unless you wanted to count environmental panic, and Agent Orange, and the unseen radiation that was going to kill you if you didn't give money to the right research program.

If you discounted falling research budgets, and sporadic book-burnings, and a renewed attack on Charles Darwin, and a few other scattered whitecaps out there on the sea of ignorance.

But those things aside, the system limped along and seemed to improve steadily.

It's a real system, today. Manipulation is still a part of the game, but outright lying has been banned by both sides. The scientists pass their data to us. We print it. We pass questions back. We're gentlemen about it now.

But science is still an island of rationality in a sea of ignorance, and we can't afford to forget about that sea. We don't dare forget that its storms are sometimes fierce.

And things are getting better, okay, but . . . somehow . . . it doesn't . . . quite . . . work.

You've just got to count the environmental panic.

You've got to count the terror of Three Mile Island. Put it in any category you want, but you've got to count it.

You've got to count Shockley.[2]

And the antivivisectionists.

And the creationists.

When you live on an island, you always have to count the gathering clouds and rising waves.

In a crisis we all revert to type, and science writers were writers before they were scientists. Newton was a very fine fellow, but our basic allegiance is to the muse.

And on a black day, as you try to piece together a story about why the military wants to launch shuttle missions into polar orbit, the muse appears.

What's a nice young artist like yourself doing in a mess like this?

And you sort of have to answer the muse. You have to say something like "Well, you see, I been workin' hard, crankin' data through my typewriter, Ma'am."

And the muse looks at you real funny.

"*What?* You've been putting *what* in your typewriter, boy?"

Data?

So you get real sheepish and try to explain to the muse about C. P. Snow and his two societies.[3] You know. Scientists on one side and everybody else on the other.

And you try to tell her about how you enlisted in science writing to communicate across the chasm between the two.

But she doesn't listen.

"Data?" she asks, shrilly.

Information?

Communication?

Then the muse stares at you and says, "You been brainwashed." And then she disappears, and you go back to trying to explain the military advantages of polar orbits.

After a few conversations in the woodshed with the muse, her argument gets through.

Science is a dramatic process powered by the toil and dreams of human beings. It is beating back the darkness. It is a great chess game with God.

But none of your stories are remotely human. They are never about people, only about things.

And you call yourself a writer!

An artist who gets himself in that kind of a pickle has to rethink his entire life. Since we writers are big on staring at our navels in the first place, the rethinking takes us all the way down to first principles and Old Truths.

Like for instance, consider the notion that scientists want to communicate with the public. We assume this, because, well . . . mostly because they say so.

Of course, they *do* send their PR people around, and they grant you interviews, usually.

And on the appointed day you show up in the scientist's office, where he and the PR person are waiting. The scientist sends his secretary after coffee.

While you wait, the scientist mentions that the PR person assured him that you will read him a copy of the final story before it goes to press.

The PR person is overcome by a spasm of coughing, which you interpret to be a vigorous denial.

The scientist is offended when you say no.

Why not? After all, he says, people review his copy!

That's true, of course, but he doesn't have to write a scientific paper, turn it in, and rush off to a legislative hearing on CAT scanners, either. Neither does he have to deal with the world of editors and readers.

You try to explain and he doesn't understand, but neither does he kick you out of his office.

His story lies in the fact that of sixteen cohorts of mice, 17.3 percent of them had the expressed genetic defect, while 23 percent of them had the biochemical marker. Anything beyond that is conjecture.

And if you're going to print this, be sure you include the names of the three biologists in New York and the seven statisticians in Texas who contributed. And please credit our granting agency, without which none of these data would have been forthcoming.

As he talks, he never forgets for a moment that you're not going to show him your story. He pauses between sentences, thinking ahead, choosing his words carefully.

When he's defensive, he prefers what he considers very precise language. Precise, concise, and very obscure, with many syllables.

Now, I guess it's the nature of science to specialize, to focus down on specific questions . . . and it's the nature of specific questions to spawn long, Greek-like words to describe obscure (but important) relationships.

Some of this is unavoidable. There is simply no word for *quark* but *quark*.

I have no quarrel with the necessary invention of language. Nothing can be done about it except to try to fight the tide and to translate the more fundamental discoveries into words and metaphors we can all understand.

Nevertheless, science-ese is the single most obvious barrier between scientists and everybody else. And scientists, perhaps without thinking about it, are continually adding unnecessarily to the problem.

Consider, as exhibits, all those scientific words that have found their way into the common tongue . . . only to be quickly altered by the scientific community, which apparently feels compelled to speak differently than the rest of us.

The word *data*, with a long *a*, is one of my favorite examples. *Data* was originally introduced into the American language as a group noun, like *society*. That made it singular. You'd say the data *was* primitive, the same way you'd say a society *was* primitive.

But as soon as the word drifted down to the high school level and truck drivers started using it, scientists softened the *a* and started saying *daaata*, and started making it plural. Suddenly it was necessary to say, "The *daaata* were primitive."

Likewise, as soon as the folks at home started saying *coronary* instead of *heart attack*, the cardiologists switched to *infarct*.

And so it was that *kilometer* became *kil-o-meter* and *centimeter* became *sonometer*, and there is a movement among gynecologists to change the name of their profession to . . . and I hope I have this right . . . *genecologist*.

I can understand the instinct to hide behind language, and to use words that will guarantee the ignorance of the lay public—words designed to obfuscate, to intimidate, and to confuse pesky reporters like me.

I can also understand why kids speak pig latin. It shields them from outsiders, and it makes them special.

But it also makes them . . . *different.*

That's something people notice.

Scientists talk different from us.

Alien. That's another word for people who talk different. Alien. Cold.

They clone things.

They experiment on people.

They build bombs that kill human beings while leaving buildings intact.

They've banished God from school. They worship Darwin, and they're making our children do it, too. Instead of Jesus, our children have birth control pills.

Didn't you hear about that scientist in Silver Spring?[4] Dreadful story, dreadful. The poor monkeys!

And the scientists . . . they knew it was wrong. You didn't notice them standing up and defending that fellow, did you?

They know what they're doing. Mark my words, they know.

There is an old building in downtown Baltimore, and I go by it a lot. It makes me think.

It's a stately, rectangular brick building, two stories tall and with a huge columned porch across the entire front. It sits on the corner of Greene and Lombard, and it's the oldest building on the University of Maryland campus.

Inside, there is a great hall, shaped like an octagon, for lecturing, and . . . .

And why put an *octagonal* hall in a *rectangular* building? Why waste all that space?

Clever of you to ask!

The space wasn't really wasted. The angles of the hall concealed a series of secret autopsy rooms.

Just a short time ago, as cultural evolution is measured, a lynch mob cornered some grave-robbing medical perverts in there. The mob swung a length of rope over an oak tree.

Focus your mind, if you will, on those two young pathologists inside.

Imagine their terror as the flickering light of the torches danced on the ceiling, as they searched frantically for the trap door, found it, slipped through, and ran . . . .

And ran, and ran, and ran.
The storms can be fierce, on the sea of ignorance.

So who is the mob, anyway?
Who is the public?
Who are those people on the other side of the great chasm that C. P. Snow described?

The first thing we see is that the situation, as usual, isn't quite that simple. Society isn't cleft by one deep chasm but is more . . . well . . . shattered. The public, the mob, includes some unlikely folks.

Physicists, for instance, are rarely comfortable with the science of psychology and are often skeptical of its premises. Biologists can't as a rule follow much physics, chemists have their own special view of biology, there are lots of sociologists who believe in astrology, and I've met astronomers who think blacks are genetically inferior to whites.

At the root of those misunderstandings is science's intrinsic complexity. If you're going to play the great research game, you've got to focus your attention, and therefore your life, on the ways of science and scientists.

Graduate assistants would be, in any other religion, called novices. They spend years as apprentices, and by the time they become, say, biochemists, they are biochemists mind and soul.

We can't fault them for this. It has been necessary.

But consider for a moment the fellow who doesn't have a scientific bent, a guy who, say, majored in journalism or business.

His college required him to take one course in chemistry, and he put it off as long as he could. Finally he gritted his teeth, took a deep breath, and signed up.

Somehow, thank God, thanks to staying up all night, thanks to black coffee and pep pills, he remembered enough on the final to pull a low C. He took it, gladly, and fled the science department.

For the rest of his life, every time he thinks of chemistry, he feels stupid. He copes by not *thinking* very much about chemistry.

Now he takes vitamin C because Linus Pauling won a Nobel Prize.[5] He watches the situation at Loch Ness with interest. His fear of cancer-causing chemicals borders on paranoia.

He's not stupid, though, or lazy, and he advanced in the newspaper business. Now he's a senior editor.

Or maybe he's not an editor.

Maybe he sells cars, or builds houses, or runs for Congress and gets—God help us—elected.

He hears about a book, Lewis Thomas' *Lives of a Cell.* He hears about it, but he doesn't read it. The whole subject makes him think of recombinant DNA.

Half the time that scares him witless, and the other half it makes him wish he'd bought Genentech.[6]

He wonders, sometimes, about the world that's forever closed off to him. Not wonders, really, because to him there's no wonder in it. "Worries" is a better word.

What are they doing, anyway? he asks himself.

Would they tell me?

Would I understand it if they did?

No. And they know it.

He doesn't go to church regularly, although recently, with times so tough, he's been going more often. His Christian faith is a rock in a very stormy sea of . . . he doesn't see it as a sea of ignorance. To him, the rising winds are those of change.

And this business of abortion . . . .

Who are scientists, to say when life begins?

Who are they, to say what it is?

They talk funny, you know.

Not like you and me. Big words. Scary words. Words that make you feel stupid.

And sometimes, a mob forms, and gasoline is poured over a pile of books.

A science writer learns to appreciate the suddenness with which a wave can rise and break.

Sometimes, when my cynicism gets really bad, I'll buy a copy of one of those supermarket rags, those journals that chronicle the life of the Widow Onassis. I'll hide it inside a *Wall Street Journal,* take it to my bedroom, lock the door . . . and let myself be wonderfully, deliciously horrified.

I'm especially fascinated by all the quack remedies you can get through the mail for $12.98 plus handling plus shipping plus batteries.

You know, pyramids that will keep your teeth free from cavities, and the secret formula salve that will give you a bustline like Dolly Parton.

So the time came, a half-dozen years ago, when I had been doing a lot of heavy stuff and wanted to give my readers a break. Some comic relief. I planted my tongue firmly in my cheek and began writing.

Hey, folks.

Hey, look at all the stuff the docs have been holding out on you. The AMA would go broke if you knew you could prevent cancer for the price of a magnetic coil and a vial of vitamins. That sort of thing. I thought it was pretty cute.

The day the column ran I was sitting at my desk when my managing editor walked by.

He went about ten steps farther, stopped, seemed to consider something for a minute, and backed up. He stared at me.

Franklin, he said, finally . . .

Franklin, *you're going to regret that.*

I got my first call about an hour later.

And I got calls, and I got letters, more than ever before in my entire career.

And these folks were hoppin' mad. Here I was, went and whetted their interest, and then didn't even have the common decency to tell them where they could get all this wonderful stuff!

The best way to handle a journalistic pratfall is to make a joke of it, so I tacked a couple of the letters up on the bulletin board.

Then, on about the third day, I picked up the telephone and found myself talking to a woman whose son had brain cancer.

I had to tell her that I was sorry, but there wasn't any cancer cure. No, ma'am. The story was a joke.

Funny, see. Ha, ha.

Funny.

Only it wasn't at all.

She didn't hang up on me, and I stammered an awkward apology. She listened, and I guess she accepted the apology because we talked for a while.

I was surprised to find that she was a rather intelligent lady. She had a college education, occupied a responsible position in a shipping office, and was fluent in French.

But, in the words of Will Rogers, each of us is a fool in his own way.

Her son had a brain tumor, and there her intelligence stopped. The doctors said they could do nothing, so she had moved on to something else. Her son was on laetrile.

She was, in that way, a fool. But who was I to fault her? What would I have done, had it been one of my daughters?

After I hung up the telephone I spent several weeks refusing to think about it, but it wouldn't be ignored. Finally I went back, found the letters other people had sent me about that column, and started making telephone calls.

With very few exceptions, the people I contacted were intelligent. They led productive lives, raised children, endured divorces, saved money for retirement, and honored their mothers and fathers.

The only thing they had in common was that they were all sick or had someone close who was. One woman's husband had died of cancer the day before I called.

They were intelligent except for one area in which they were threatened—in this case, the area of medicine. On that subject they were completely irrational. They were, in Will Rogers' words, all fools when it came to health care.

In each instance, the blind spot occurred in a location where the psyche had been disturbed by an emotional upheaval.

In having these blind spots, my readers were really no different from the rest of us.

How many scientists have misjudged the results of an experiment because of what they *wanted* to see, or *needed* to see?

How many reporters have biased a story, unconsciously, to conform to their own strongly held theory about what society is and how it works?

Of course, neither scientist nor writer can afford to do that often.

The biologist can't afford to be blind in the area of biology, but he *can* safely indulge himself in a few cornball prejudices about physics. Physicists do not have to accept evolution in order to succeed, which is probably why several physicists have rallied to the creationist cause.

A hurricane, an artist might say, a hurricane of ignorance.

A circular wind of fright and distrust, fueled by large words and the distant vision of the scientist. The scientist does not smile, in this vision. He is stony-faced and uses big words.

He makes announcements that make sense for a moment and filter through the mind and are gone, leaving no trace.

In the background there is machinery . . . and a blue spark jumps across a Van de Graff generator . . . and the smell of ozone . . . .

And economic clouds close in, and jobs are threatened, and the world turns turbulent, and fear grows.

The blind spots search restlessly for a simple answer, any port in a storm, and soon the blind spots find one another and align, and there forms a brotherhood of fools.

Did you read, they ask each other, about that scientist in Silver Spring? The one with the poor, helpless monkeys? Did you hear what he did to them?

Where did thalidomide come from?

Where did the babies with no arms and legs come from, tell me that?

Who invented the Pill? A scientist!

And Agent Orange?

And I remember those hidden autopsy rooms, and the crowd with the torches, and the rope. I think about those two young pathologists, running, running, running through the Baltimore night.

And the artist in me knows exactly what's wrong.

For openers there's the *daaata* we've been running through our typewriters. We did it that way because *daaata* was what the scientists wanted to, as they put it, communicate about.

But the result has been a disaster.

We have given the public the picture of the scientist as the scientist wants to be viewed by himself, as a man of fact, cold fact, four cohorts of dead white rats measured against the regeneration rates of salamander tails.

Put that way, it sounds very much like witchcraft.

These are perceptions that rise from deep within us, from the psychological forces that equate "alien" with "evil." And those are forces, I must point out, that have always been considered fair game for artists. Literature has a claim on that turf, along with psychology.

So, for that matter, does the exploding new science of neurobiology. Scientists are actually beginning to see the physical structure for our behavior.

From an artist's viewpoint, the clues they provide have a direct bearing on the human condition.

Consider, for instance, the artistic implications of Dr. Paul Maclean's work, and his sobering theory of the triune brain.

One day several years ago I spent several hours with Dr. Maclean.

He got out his brain slides to demonstrate to me that both human and animal brains were divided into three distinct subbrains. I was immediately struck by the haunting similarity, here, to Freud and his ideas about a three-part psyche.

The most primitive brain sits at the very base of the cranium, where the spinal cord comes up.

Dr. Maclean calls it the lizard brain, because that's pretty much what it looks like. Its shape and organization were ancient even in the day of the dinosaur.

Nature never throws anything away if she can avoid it, so the next subbrain developed on top of the lizard brain, covering and dwarfing it. The second brain characterizes the mammal.

Finally, in a sudden spurt of growth almost yesterday, the wondrous cerebral cortex appeared as a separate growth of cells atop the mammalian brain.

Each of the three brains is organized differently and has its own function.

What can the lizard brain do?

Study a lizard. It can think territoriality, for one thing. It can do things by rote. A male lizard can chase female lizards.

When there are no females to chase, or territory to defend, a lizard sits for hours, bobbing its head, bobbing, bobbing, keeping a perfect rhythm. Rhythm is characteristic of the lizard.

The poet speaks to the lizard brain, speaks of the rhythmic pounding of the ancient sea. The lizard responds to iambic pentameter and to the light, dancing melody of Lewis Thomas.

The mammalian brain speaks a much different and richer language. It converses with itself in love and hate, in fear and joy, in the emotion that clothes the reptilian act of sex.

Literature speaks directly to the mammalian brain in story and plot and a fabric of human action. The second brain is emotion, and it makes life worth living.

But it is also the beast that drives the hurricane and blinds us all, each in our own way, and makes us fools.

And then the cortex . . . the fabulous cortex. It speaks data, precise English, mathematics, truth. Cold, cruel, metallic truth.

Truth, the mammalian brain says, is nice. It can be handy, at times. But if overused, it tends to interfere with the more serious affairs of the mammal and the lizard. The cortex needs, as the euphemism goes, to be "supervised."

The cortex, Dr. Maclean told me, seems by the circuitry to be under the direct control of the lower brains.

All messages between mathematics and biology must go through the lower two brains.

There, of course, they are censored.

And blind spots develop.

If your son has a brain tumor, and the doctors say he must die, well . . . well, courage is all, Jesus loves me, doctors are crooks and fools, and the peddlers of laetrile are wealthy.

So that, from the neurobiological point of view, was what a blind spot was!

It was dark and snowing when I left Dr. Maclean's office, and I never will forget the drive home, muse sitting on my shoulder, refusing to use a seat belt as usual. Both of us were ecstatic.

The blind spots were emotional, and emotions responded to stories.

Not data, as the muse was petty enough to point out. Stories.

Writers weren't supposed to be "communicating," whatever that was. They were supposed to be telling stories.

In the year and a half following my interview with Dr. Maclean, I kept his articles in a stack under my favorite chair, to peruse at every opportunity.

I talked to several other science writers, most notably Don Drake of Philadelphia, and found that they had reached many of the same conclusions.

Because we were awed by scientists we had painted them as they had wanted their peers to see them, down at the dearly beloved granting agency.

We had done quite well at it, and the public saw them exactly as we portrayed them. The public had diagnosed them as cold and analytical and didn't trust them an inch.

I mean, what would *you* think if you read in a newspaper that some guy had collected three tons of cow pancreases. Sure, he made some endocrine breakthroughs, but that's not the question. You need more than the science.

You need to know what kind of guy collects three tons of cow pancreases. If you don't know, you get perhaps a little suspicious of him.

Science writers are remembering, now, why we got involved in this mess in the first place. And it wasn't *daaata*. It was dreams and adventure and tales of human struggle.

One last revolution now comes into play, and that is the revolution in literature generally attributed to Truman Capote. He gave us the ability to write dramatic nonfiction, true-life dramas, and in so doing to use the techniques of literature.

Those techniques are as abstract as anything a theoretical mathematician tangles with, so I'll spare you what, to me, are the consuming details.

But you need to know they are the techniques that put the *feeling* into good books.

They are what drives the reader to read on and on, until it's long after bedtime.

The new literary technology allows us not only to educate the reader but also to touch him and, yes, even to *change* him.

The scientists wants us to ignore the drama that proceeds in his laboratory, and, more important, in his mind.

He denies that he has feelings about salamander tails and that he hopes for things and dreams of things, odd things such as, maybe, a clear solution suddenly turning blue, and a discovery.

He is deeply ashamed that in his most secret thoughts, he yearns to be chosen to go to Stockholm.[7]

And yet these characteristics make him human, make him real. They make his efforts, his frustrations, and his mistakes interesting and understandable. And *dramatic*.

Drama.

A novelist, if she has the fire in her guts, can write a thing like *Uncle Tom's Cabin* and throw her gentle reader into the filthy bonds of slavery and help start a civil war.

Or if he has the consummate skill of a John Steinbeck, he can take you, in *The Grapes of Wrath,* to the dust bowl in depression Oklahoma. John Steinbeck can make you understand what it feels like to have hungry children and to drive off across the desert in a rickety Ford, westward to California with a crazy hope and, in the back of a pickup, a dying mother.

A novelist can . . .

. . . look. Where did *you* learn to love science?

From a textbook?

Or from Arthur Clarke?

Or Asimov's robots?

Or the poet, Bradbury?

Those writers used the drama in their stories as a carrier wave for their ideas and for scientific fact and theory.

We have to take readers into science the way John Steinbeck took them into Oklahoma.

Only by using emotion, and literary structure, can we send our truths in through the blind eye of the hurricane and calm it.

Science writers are moving in that direction, now, through dramatic nonfiction.

Suddenly, we have a whole new world of stories to choose from . . . stories of discovery, of dashed hopes, of geniuses and fools. Stories that are never dull, and that never get printed around tire ads.

We have stories about dreamers, perhaps, who look at stars and find something up there, beeping at them, and they don't know what it is, but they know it's the most important sound that they ever heard in their lives.

We have tales about physicists and about how they play dice—or is it poker?—with God and about how they sometimes are deeply religious and about why it is reasonable that that is so.

We have stories about psychologists who look for madness, and, having looked, find it all around them.

What kind of a man tortures animals?

It's time to tell the whole story, all of it, at the same time, about the people who suffer from the diseases these men and women are trying to understand, using monkeys. Let's tell the story of the people whose lives are destroyed, who die in agony from such diseases.

Let's take the reader into the hospitals, if we have to, and let them hear the screams.

Science is a collection of people with oddities and problems, and husbands and wives and children, and phobias about crowds in the night and ropes.

It also happens to include many of our finest minds, today. Each is locked, for its own reason, in desperate and dramatic battle with forces unknown.

Right now those people offer the greatest hope and the only viable dream that we have.

That, I submit, is modern literature's most important theme.

Notes

1. Thomas Edison was often referred to as the Wizard of Menlo Park.

2. William Shockley shared the Nobel Prize in physics in 1956 for development of the transistor. During the 1970s, he came into prominence for his controversial views on intelligence and race, particularly for his belief in the inferior intelligence of the black race. Many people do not consider his expertise in applied physics sufficient grounds to seriously support his theories on genetics.

3. C. P. Snow, *The Two Cultures and a Second Look* (London: Cambridge University Press, 1964).

4. In 1981, police in Silver Spring, Maryland, raided the Institute for Behavioral Research, an animal research laboratory that had been funded by the National Institutes of Health for eleven years. They took away seventeen allegedly abused monkeys, claiming that the monkeys were untended and in poor condition.

5. Linus Pauling is a chemist who won the Nobel Prize for chemistry in 1954 and the Nobel Peace Prize in 1963. Recently he has urged people to take megadoses of vitamin C to help mediate effects of the common cold and cancer.

6. Genentech is a California company using recombinant DNA technology to manufacture such biological products as human growth hormone. When its stock was first placed on the open market, its price skyrocketed, only to drop a short time later.

7. Nobel Prizes are awarded in Stockholm.

CHAPTER 11

Gee Whiz!
Is That All There Is?

Fred Jerome

In the early days of science writing, articles were written to excite the reader with new events and discoveries. This technique became so prevalent that it earned the name of "gee-whiz" science journalism. In more recent times, science writers have become more analytical and policy-oriented. Now, however, Fred Jerome wonders if the advent of a number of new science magazines in the 1970s and 1980s has not led to a wholesale return to the "gee-whiz" school of science writing.

Fred Jerome is director of the Media Resource Service, a program of the Scientists' Institute for Public Information. The service maintains a computerized file or more than 18,000 scientists around the country who have agreed to answer questions from journalists. He also serves as adjunct professor of journalism at New York University and the School of Visual Arts and has published numerous articles on science and the media.

WHEN THE ELI LILLY COMPANY ANNOUNCED, in the summer of 1982, that its new drug Oraflex would be available, one television newscaster—quoting the company's press release—called the drug a "real break-through." One can imagine William Safire, in his witty, weekly *New York Times Magazine* column, "On Language," scowling at the redundant use of the word "real." A breakthrough is a breakthrough, after all, and needs no underscoring.

The Oraflex announcement was just one more sign of how prevalent "gee-whiz journalism"—the headline and magazine-cover overselling of "sensational" new technological inventions, laboratory discoveries, and archeological finds—has become in mass media coverage of science and technology. A typical case in point was the March 1983 issue of *Health* magazine, the "Fourth Annual All-Breakthroughs Issue," whose cover headlines heralded the arrival of "E.T. Drugs," "Micro Miracles: Surgery Under Glass," and "New Ways to Lengthen Lives." No wonder the PR people at Lilly felt the need to distinguish Oraflex from the run-of-the-mill breakthroughs (many of them not real) that bombard the mass media audience every day. Indeed, in view of the subsequent revelations about the health hazards of Oraflex and the drug's recall from the market, we can probably expect future headlines announcing a "*really* real breakthrough."

Back in 1981, I criticized the popular science media, and especially the three then-new mass audience science magazines—*Discover, Science 80,* and *Science Digest*—for their heavy emphasis on "gee whiz"; on discoveries, breakthroughs, and inventions; and for their avoidance of science policy issues. This criticism was not intended to deny the need for coverage of scientific successes, but rather it served as a plea for balance, an argument that the public needs, *and* is interested in, more than simple phenomenology.

It was my contention then that most of the major debates in science and technology policy—such as nuclear and toxic waste disposal, military technology, the crisis in science education—were generally ignored by the popular science magazines and science television programs. At a time of widespread public cynicism and disenchantment with society, I argued that the surging public interest in science presented an opportunity to reach a mass audience with discussions of critical issues facing our country and that the opportunity was being missed.

Finally, I asserted that "gee-whiz journalism" also neglected another crucial aspect of science: the mystery, the things scientists don't yet know; indeed, the careful, repetitious, often tedious scientific *process* that underlies the breakthroughs—the real breakthroughs—that do occur.

The presentation brought numerous favorable responses from scientists and journalists alike and was quoted, broadcast, excerpted, and, in a revised version, published in *Technology Review*,[1] one of the few science magazines that does focus on policy. Heartening response. But has anything changed since then? The answer is yes—but not enough. For the most part, science in the mass media has remained a sales contest in which headline makers, cover illustrators, and TV admen scramble to come up with the newest new-ness, and major policy issues continue to be downplayed or ignored.

Mixed Signals

Important changes *have* occurred in the three popular science magazines that were the new kids on the block in 1981, but the signals are still mixed. Despite a number of welcome improvements, discussed below, major gaps remain in their coverage of science and technology issues, gaps that are hard to explain unless they reflect a continuing second-class status for policy questions.

In identifying the most important science policy issues, leaders of the U.S. science and technology communities almost unanimously include the crisis in science and engineering education, international technological competition, funding for basic research, the debate over missiles and other nuclear weapons, and environmental health hazards and the government's response to them. Yet most of these have been neglected or avoided by the three science magazines.

But it is not the job of the popular science magazines to present what the scientific establishment thinks should be presented, argues Allen Hammond, editor of *Science 85,* who notes, "Our first responsibility is to our readers." In other words, the readers want medical breakthroughs and space shots and animals, not science policy.

Perhaps. But there is at least some evidence that readers *are* interested in, if not eager for, more stories on science policy controversies. Regular coverage of policy in the "Science Times" section of *The New York Times* has not affected readership. Indeed, a 1981 *Times* market survey reported the science section was second only to the front page in reader popularity.

Another barometer of which aspects of science draw public interest is the Media Resource Service sponsored by the Scientists' Institute for Public Information, which receives nearly 2500 calls a year from journalists around the country who are writing about science and technology and need sources. Since most of the callers work for mass media outlets, electronic as well as print, the topics they call about are a fair reflection of what their editors and executive producers believe will "sell"—in other words, a reflection of the public's interest.

The calls cover just about every conceivable aspect of science and technology, and, to be sure, many deal with medical breakthroughs, new technology, astronomy, and space. But from January 1982 through March 1983, the most popular subject was hazardous wastes—including dumps, disposal, incineration, recycling, transport, and, specifically, PCBs, PBBs, and dioxin. Another frequent topic was acid rain. Yet not a single feature article on either toxic wastes or acid rain appeared from January 1981 through March 1983 in any of the three science magazines mentioned above.

In that same period, *Discover* ran 46 feature stories on medical developments and biomedical research, 23 on space or astronomy, and 23 or more on the latest technological achievements; *Science 81, 82,* and *83* featured 26, 14, and 13 articles on those three areas; and the figures for *Science Digest* are similar.

All too often, the "Eureka!" approach to reporting science prevails. A review of cover headlines in *Discover, Science 82,* and *Science Digest* for the first half of 1982 shows that "New!" was still the headline-writers' favorite word: "New Science and Fireworks," "New Facts Stun Paleontologists," "New Physiology," "A New Science That Can Predict Winners and Losers at Sex," "A New Geometry of Nature," "New Windows on the Body." And in the same spirit of salesmanship, "Engineers Unveil Their Plans . . . ," "Secrets of the Curve Ball," "Celebrating Innovation," and on and on.

Changes

But things are changing. At least in the print media, considerably more attention is being devoted to science and technology policy today than three years ago. All three of the magazines discussed above are now running more public policy–related articles. *Science 85* editor Hammond says he deliberately avoided controversy during the magazine's first year to allow the publication to become established, but he has since been devoting increasing space to policy questions. In a conversation in 1983, Scott DeGarmo, then editor of *Science Digest,* insisted that his magazine had always been concerned with societal issues, "particularly the role of individual entrepreneurship in our society," but acknowledged that in the past year "our commitment to public policy has become more explicit. Our staff needed to mature, both as individuals and as a team, before taking on some of those challenges." And Leon Jaroff, then managing editor of *Discover,* said his writers "increasingly cover the science and technology components of the major issues of the day because we've found people are thinking about those issues and have been stimulated to want to read more."

Since 1981 all three magazines have printed major articles on such issues as evolution versus creationism, the use of animals in laboratory research, fraud in science, the nature–nurture controversy, and the debate over new military technology. In addition:

- *Discover* now provides monthly coverage of the ongoing military technology discussion, and the June 1983 issue featured an in-depth critique of the new antimissile super-weaponry advocated by President Reagan. Other recent *Discover* features have dealt with the crisis in nuclear energy, Soviet chemical warfare, and whether boxing should be outlawed. In addition, former managing editor Jaroff's regular column, "The Skeptical Eye," has offered insightful and often iconoclastic policy analysis.

- *Science 82* (which went on to become *Science 83,* etc.) acknowledged the need for more policy coverage by initiating, in March 1982, a regular column called "Advice and Dissent" in which guest commentators discuss current controversies. (The first column, by Clifford Grobstein, was titled "When Does Human Life Begin?") More recently the magazine has carried thoughtful articles on, among other issues, genetic screening of employees, the lie detector as a reliable (or unreliable) criminal-justice tool, and orphan drugs.
- For its part, *Science Digest* is the only one of the three to have provided feature coverage of the international technology race between the United States and Japan, as well as of the potential role of high technology in reviving the U.S. economy.[2] Moreover, the Hearst-published magazine boldly took on the Chevron Chemical Company in a detailed investigative article titled "Paraquat Coverup" in its June 1983 issue.

But perhaps the most significant change that has occurred has not been in magazines but in the growing number of newspaper science sections. When the "Science Times" section of *The New York Times* first appeared several years ago, its editors eschewed news-related articles. ("That's for the front section.") Presumably after much internal evaluation, the section now features at least one article a week on such current-event topics as missile technology, science education, nuclear proliferation, and the technology of verification of test-ban treaties. A number of leading Knight-Ridder newspapers have followed suit in their weekly science sections, and it is reasonable to expect other newspapers to follow the *Times'* successful example.

Quite possibly, the success of the "Science Times" in policy-related coverage by such leading science journalists as Philip Boffey, William Broad, Bryce Nelson, and Bayard Webster has had an effect on the content of the monthly science magazines. In any case, there appears to be a growing awareness among editors and publishers that the public *is* interested in and *will* buy science policy discussions, at least as part of the weekly or monthly science package. In fact, R. Timothy Leedy, former advertising sales director for *Discover,* credits the publication's growth specifically to its rejection of science salesmanship. An article in the December 1982 issue of *The New York Times* describing *Discover* as

"America's largest science magazine with a circulation of 850,000" reported that Leedy attributes that first-place status to the magazine's "non–gee-whiz" approach.

Assuming this trend continues, and all indications are that it will, the public—at least the science-section and science-magazine readers—will become more familiar with the critical issues in science and technology policy, better informed, and better able to participate in the decision-making process. That's not a panacea for all our political problems, of course, but it's a lot better than cynicism.

Vacuum Tube

There is still a long way to go, however. Commercial television, the only truly *mass* medium in this country, continues to be a vacuum tube when it comes to science policy issues. The few network science "specials" continue to focus on the wonders of nature and the miracles of modern technology. Certainly those are valid and valuable areas to cover, and they lend themselves beautifully to the graphics needed by television; but gee whiz, is that all there is?

Even the Public Broadcasting System, which seems, by default, to have cornered the television science market, appears to be infatuated with "wow" programming: colorful, magnificently filmed productions by such groups as the National Geographic Society and the Smithsonian Institution.

In recent years, we have seen the rise and fall of the two attempts by the major networks to provide regular prime-time science programming: "Walter Cronkite's Universe" on CBS and "Omni: The New Frontier" on ABC. Neither of these dealt to any meaningful extent with policy questions. In fact, "Omni" was the quintessence of "gee-whiz journalism." Both these efforts failed because of low audience ratings. Is it possible that their failure was related to their "gee-whiz" approach? Is it possible that wonderment alone will not work week in and week out, that all this amazement becomes boring? If so, perhaps the cancellation of those two programs will encourage network decision makers to add a little meat to their future science program menus.

Of course, there are other possible explanations for the failure of those programs. Insiders at CBS point out, with some bitterness, that the network never promoted "Universe" the way it promotes most sitcoms, and it relegated the program to summer weekday evenings, sandwiched between reruns, thereby almost certainly sealing its fate. Some observers argue that the mass (network) television audience simply isn't interested in science. Others, such as Barbara Culliton, news editor of *Science* magazine, disagree. According to Culliton, "People want more interesting, but not necessarily less, science on television . . . . "Universe" had many attributes, one of them being Cronkite. But "Universe" . . . was boring."[3]

One can't help but wonder whether another approach, one with more emphasis on the critical science policy issues our country faces, might not have worked better. It should be made quite clear that the argument for more coverage of science policy debates is *not* based on the promise of advertising sales or commercial success. It is based on our society's need for an informed public. Even if it's boring (and it definitely doesn't need to be), as *New Yorker* columnist Michael Arlen has written, "It wouldn't kill us to know a little bit more about the so-called boring stuff, and it might in fact kill us *not* to know about it."

In a similar vein, journal editor Marcel La Follette wrote:

> Concentrating only on the entertainment aspect of popular science communication will do little to improve scientific literacy. All too often this "gee-whiz" science serves merely the same soothing function as soap operas, baseball games, and "I Love Lucy" re-runs, but for a different audience.[4]

How ironic it is that at a time of growing national alarm about scientific illiteracy among the American public and growing national determination to intensify science and engineering education in the classroom, no major effort is being made to provide serious science programming for the vast majority of scientifically illiterate Americans who depend on the television networks for most of their information.

For some, it is comfortable to rationalize that there is simply no mass audience for science policy, that the tens of millions of television viewers are "inattentive" to science—"tube-boobs" desiring nothing more after a hard day's work than to settle into the oblivion of a can of beer and "Dallas." Despite the ominous consequences of a public that is uninformed about public policy—for example, cynicism and susceptibility to demagogues—it is argued that "if they don't know anything about public policy, that's a shame, but it's their own fault and nothing can be done about it."

Serious Science During Prime Time?

Before embracing such an elitist view, however, consider the continuing and growing popularity of "Nova," the exceptional PBS series that covers both "gee-whiz" science and science policy. Former producer John Mansfield reported that the 1982–1983 "Nova" series had been more popular than ever: "Even competing with the World Series, our ratings have doubled compared with fall '81." "Nova" consciously intersperses what Mansfield calls the "cuddly, furry, wildlife show" with issue-oriented programs such as:

- "Adventures of Teenage Scientists," which pays tribute to Westinghouse Award winners but also focuses on the deteriorating state of science education.
- "Cobalt Blues," an investigation into America's strategic mineral resources and the political and economic controversy surrounding current international metal strategy.
- "Asbestos: A Lethal Legacy," on the consequences of asbestos exposure and the controversy over social and legal responsibility.
- "The Dawn with No Tomorrow," a look at the latest generation of nuclear weapons and the views from Moscow and Washington.

But, some would argue, "Nova" is not really a valid test of audience interest, since PBS is "educational television"; when it comes to the major networks, the bottom line is big bucks.

Mansfield insists that the mass audience for science programs such as "Nova" is definitely out there, citing a weekly half-hour science "magazine" television series in his native Great Britain that, after nearly twenty years on the air, now commands between 11 million and 13 million viewers, one-sixth of the total population of the British Isles. "Science is now recognized as the vital stuff of everyday life," he argues convincingly, "and it's merely a production and promotion problem to bring the viewers to it."

It is interesting to speculate on just how popular science policy issues might turn out to be—in spite of their social value—given half a chance on commercial television. Surely, the creative genius of American communication could find a way to capture the public's enthusiasm by presenting the excitement, the challenge, and the risk–benefit choices involved in virtually all current science policy debates as regular, prime-time fare.

Unfortunately, most network executives appear firmly convinced that serious treatment of science policy simply won't sell shaving cream. And so millions of Americans will probably continue to view science as little more than breakthroughs. And *real* breakthroughs. And *really* real breakthroughs. And . . . .

Notes

1. Fred Jerome, "The Great Science and Technology Bazaar," *Technology Review* 83 (May/June 1981):16–18.
2. See Robert Jastrow, "Science and the American Dream," *Science Digest* 91 (March 1983):46–48.
3. Comments from "A Symposium: Science in the Media," *SIPIscope* (special issue) 10 (Winter 1982):4–5.
4. Marcel La Follette, "Editorial," *Science, Technology, & Human Values* 7 (Spring 1982):3.

CHAPTER 12

The Science Writing Inner Club: A Communication Link Between Science and the Lay Public

Sharon Dunwoody

Journalists ultimately decide what information becomes news or is ignored. Although most newswriting textbooks offer criteria for selecting news, the process by which information actually is chosen is poorly understood. This chapter reprints an article about how science writers select news at a major scientific meeting. Although a number of the journalists mentioned in this piece have gone on to other jobs, the article remains something of a classic because it provides an important inside view of a group of influential science reporters at work, and delineates the pressures, problems, and influences that affect them as they cover a major scientific meeting.

Sharon Dunwoody is an associate professor at the School of Journalism and Mass Communication at the University of Wisconsin (Madison). She has conducted research on science journalists as news *makers* and on scientists as news *sources* (Chapter 1).

SINCE THE MID-1960s, a relatively small group of specialty reporters has played a large part in determining what the U.S. public has learned

This article was originally published in *Science, Technology & Human Values* 5 (winter 1980): 14–22. Copyright 1980 by the Massachusetts Institute of Technology and the President and Fellows of Harvard College. Reprinted by permission of John Wiley & Sons, Inc.

about significant scientific happenings. Nonscientists depend primarily on print media for news about science;[1] therefore, science writers employed by major newspapers and wire services have played crucial roles within the last fifteen years as translators of scientific information for a wide range of publics. However, although the names of these journalists may be familiar to many of us, we know very little about how they do their jobs.

In an effort to find out, I studied the news-gathering behaviors of a sample of the top U.S. mass media science writers at the annual meeting of the American Association for the Advancement of Science.[2] The study, conducted during 1976–1978, consisted of three parts: (1) face-to-face interviews with the journalists, with questions primarily directed to reporters' perceptions of how they select news and gather information; (2) observation of the journalists as they covered the AAAS annual meeting; and (3) content analysis of the nearly 800 stories about the meeting that were published in U.S. daily newspapers.[3]

The study found that the U.S. mass media science writing community is dominated by a relatively small group of newspaper, magazine, and wire service reporters who, since the mid-1960s, have largely determined what the public has read about significant scientific events. These individuals, who at any one time total no more than twenty-five or thirty journalists, form a closely knit, informal social network that I call an "inner club."[4] Many of its members have been a part of this club for more than ten years; in fact, its stability over time may be unique among informal networks. And the club is worth studying precisely because it affects the news-selection and news-gathering behaviors of its members.

It does so mainly by emphasizing *cooperative* behaviors among reporters in situations that should be highly *competitive*. Cooperation provides a number of benefits for members, but it also exacts certain costs when the larger notion of "responsible science coverage" is taken into account. For example, inner club membership enhances story accuracy by making a wider pool of resources available to a journalist. But cooperative story selection also has the negative effect of reducing variety in science news coverage by fostering a homogeneous notion of "what's news" at a given event.

The Genesis of the Inner Club

Members of this informal science-writing network readily acknowledge the bond that exists among them. Said one, for example:

> There is a group of very experienced science writers in this country, and we do form—gee, I hate to use the term—something of a clique. We keep each

other apprised of what's going on . . . . A bond of trust has grown up between us.

Another similarly viewed the relationships among his colleagues as something akin to a "fraternity," characterizing the club as "kind of an in-group . . . we're all friends. We've worked together for a long time and, obviously, . . . it evolves over time."

Most of the members agree that the group coalesced in the 1960s when some of them were suddenly dubbed science writers and sent by their newspapers or wire services to cover the great science story of the decade: the manned landings on the moon. Many of the journalists who journeyed to Cape Canaveral or to Houston possessed little scientific expertise. They had been pulled from general reporting backgrounds and their educations had been primarily journalistic. Their editors knew even less about science, however; so, despite their lack of experience, these new science journalists were expected to know what they were doing. This meant they were responsible for front-page stories that were both substantive and accurate, yet they could not expect much help from home.

Consequently, they turned to one another. Away from their city rooms for weeks, they became socialized to *each other* rather than to their peers in the home newsroom.[5] As one science writer noted:

> At the height of it (the space program), they were making a major launch every three months, and you would be down there at the Cape for two-and-a-half weeks at a time. The result was that it (the group of science writers) became your family. There were love affairs, there were hates and fights . . . . It became a traveling road show with the same people showing up time and time again, going to the same places and doing the same things. There was great cohesiveness.

Another agreed that covering events away from the city room played a large part in the evolution of the group:

> We see more of each other because of going to these meetings, covering these stories. You're with each other for several days at a time, most of the day and most of the evening; you tend to go out and eat dinner together. So you get to be very good friends. You've got a common interest, like I have more in common with science writers from other papers than I do with reporters here on the_____, because we're covering the same stories, we interview the same people, and we see each other not just casually. So we all get to be pretty good friends.

The major emphasis of the club as it evolved was on cooperation. Cooperation seemed a good strategy because by sharing expertise, the group could evaluate scientific information better than could an individual with limited knowledge. Also, when the normal reporter–source

problems arose, the journalists could close ranks and collectively negotiate a solution, a procedure that promised more success than did individual efforts. The science writers had also become close friends, so
cooperative behavior seemed a better strategy for preserving those relationships than did competitive behavior. Finally, the quality of a
reporter's work was judged by his editor in relation to what the other
reporters were producing. The reporter, therefore, could satisfy his
editor not by "scooping" his fellow science writers but by producing the
same story each day. Cooperative behavior helped to ensure that.

The Inner Club Today

Inner club members (Table 12–1) share several characteristics. They
generally are affiliated with the prestige print media, media that can afford to make science a national or even international beat. Unlike most
reporters, they travel regularly, spending days at a time away from the
city room. They see each other regularly at large scientific meetings, at
events such as the 1976 Viking landings on Mars (covered at the Jet Pro-
pulsion Center in California), or the Legionnaire's disease crisis in Pennsylvania. They have been working as science writers for a number of
years, long enough for close personal relationships to develop. And they
share an intense concern for professional aspects of science writing, for
the quality and accuracy of what they do.

The majority of inner club members in this study are male; most
hold bachelor's degrees in journalism or some other nonscience field,
but have taken graduate courses in science or science writing. As students, they had no interest in becoming science writers, and most
worked as general reporters for some years before concentrating on science reporting.

As of 1979, the average inner club member in this study had been a
full-time science writer for fifteen years. They are most likely to work for
a morning metropolitan newspaper with a circulation of 300,000 or
more. The majority prefer space, astronomy, and the hard sciences to
other areas of science and perceive themselves to be very autonomous of
the newsroom, with the option of selecting their own story topics at least
80 percent of the time.[6] In fact, they are likely to act as science editors on
their newspapers whether they actually have the title or not. Editors may
defer to their judgment when evaluating the quality of science stories
written by others. The majority of respondents in this study travel at
least five times a year, usually to scientific meetings. And the news
criteria they perceive themselves to be using are quite similar to those
utilized by other journalists in other coverage areas: reader interest, potential significance of information to reader, newness of information, in-

Table 12-1. Names of Science Journalists Suggested by Colleagues for Inner Club Status, with Titles and Media Affiliations at Time of Study

*George Alexander	Science writer	*Los Angeles Times*
Stuart Auerbach	Medical/Science writer	*The Washington Post*
*Jerry Bishop	Staff reporter	*The Wall Street Journal*
Al Blakeslee	Science writer	Associated Press (retired)
Jane Brody	Medical writer	*The New York Times*
Victor Cohn	Science writer	*The Washington Post*
*Bob Cooke	Science editor	*Boston Globe*
Lewis Cope	Science writer	*The Minneapolis Tribune*
Donald Drake	Science/Medicine writer	*Philadelphia Inquirer*
*Ed Edelson	Science editor	*The New York News*
*Peter Gwynne	General editor	*Newsweek*
Bill Hines	Science writer	*Chicago Sun-Times*
*Don Kirkman	Science writer	Scripps-Howard Newspapers
*Ron Kotulak	Science editor	*Chicago Tribune*
*John Langone	Medical/Science editor	*Boston Herald-American*
Harry Nelson	Medical writer	*Los Angeles Times*
*Tom O'Toole	Science editor	*The Washington Post*
*David Perlman	Science editor	*San Francisco Chronicle*
David Prowitt	Science correspondent	Public Broadcasting System
*Judy Randal	Science correspondent	*The New York News*
*Joann Rodgers	Medical writer	*Baltimore News-American*
*Al Rossiter	Science editor	United Press International
*Joel Shurkin	Science writer	*Philadelphia Inquirer*
Art Snider	Science editor	*Chicago Sun-Times*
*Brian Sullivan	Science writer	Associated Press
*Walter Sullivan	Science editor	*The New York Times*
John Noble Wilford	Science writer	*The New York Times*
*Patrick Young	Science writer	*The National Observer*

n = 28
*Participants in study (n = 17)

formation that interests either the journalist or his editor, prominence of source, uniqueness of information, proximity, and the intrinsic importance of the information to science.

The Inner Club's Effects on News Gathering

The inner club network has an effect on news making primarily when science journalists converge on one event or meeting. Although this is not a daily (or even weekly) occurrence, it does increase the likelihood that coverage of any scientific event significant enough to attract groups of journalists will be affected by the network. Understanding the workings of the inner club may not help us to interpret the how's and why's of daily newspaper science coverage; but when a major scientific "happening" takes place, knowledge of inner club effects can provide some insight to mass media coverage of that event.

The effects are substantial. Inner club journalists may constitute only a small proportion of science writers who converge on any scientific event, but they significantly affect news coverage primarily because they work for either the major wire services (Associated Press and United Press International) or the elite print media, who also participate in wire service operations (such as *The New York Times* wire service, Scripps-Howard, Knight-Ridder, and the *Los Angeles Times/Washington Post* service). Wire copy accounts for a substantial portion of the editorial diet of most newspapers in this country. Thus, although only a few science journalists belong to the inner club, they can greatly influence what the public eventually will read about an event.[7]

To study the inner club in action, I chose as a "laboratory" the annual meeting of the American Association for the Advancement of Science. The meeting is one of the largest scientific gatherings in the country and annually draws more journalists than almost any other scientific occurrence; average newsroom attendance ranges from 300 to 600. The event is so popular among science writers, in fact, that the National Association of Science Writers, Inc., conducts its business meeting each year at AAAS.[8] Since most inner club reporters consider it a "required" annual trip, the meeting provided an ideal setting for observation of inner club interactions.[9]

Various cooperative behaviors among inner club members affected two points in the newsmaking process at the meeting: topic selection and information gathering.

Topic selection. The most frequently mentioned type of cooperation was helping one another select stories. At a meeting like that of AAAS, much of the practice seems to be a matter of discussing story possibilities informally and listening to colleagues weigh the potential of particular press conferences or evaluate the "quotability" of particular scientists. The result is a consensus among club members about what or who is news at a given moment. Such a consensus seems to provide three major benefits for participants:

1. It allows them to "neutralize" the competitive aspects of the coverage situation. Journalism is traditionally a competitive business, with one newspaper pitted against another, one journalist trying to scoop his or her colleagues. But at events such as the AAAS meeting, the inner club member is faced with a paradox. Since the club is made up of journalists from the prestige media, members are not only close friends but also each other's main competition. The inner club member handles this contradiction by nullifying the competitive aspects. Each journalist knows that his editor is watching the competing newspapers and wire services and is evaluating what he produces *in relation to* what the competition

publishes. If he produces something different, he may be in trouble; at the very least he will have to defend his choice. But if all competitors produce the same story for the day, then each editor assumes his reporter has done a good job. As one inner club member noted:

> A science writer will come back and say "Hey, I've found a good one," and ears will prick up. I'll sometimes do the same. You share with friends and they share with their friends and it gets around. Everybody's in the same boat, trying to please editors and get a good story done.

2. Collective story selection provides each reporter with the personal reassurance that he has found a "newsworthy" story. Just as editors gauge the quality of their reporters' story selections against the competition, the reporters come to depend on each other to validate what is news on a given day. It is difficult to select one story and then watch one's colleagues choose another. One journalist who is not an inner club member remarked that "everybody tends to agree on what is the important story" at a meeting and she finds that "a little bit unsettling. When you go to those meetings . . . there's a little bit more of that pack mentality in terms of everybody pressuring everybody else" to agree jointly on a major story for the day.

3. Selecting stories collectively allows the inner club also to pool its expertise. One reporter may be able to warn another away from a risky story; a third writer may be able to suggest a different story possibility altogether. As one inner club member noted, "I'm likely to change my mind (about a story topic) if it's an area that I don't know much about and if I know some other reporter knows a lot about it."

One example from the 1978 AAAS meeting sheds some light on this process. A number of inner club members attended a press conference at which a scientist presented findings of a study of Seventh Day Adventists that indicated consumption of red meat is linked to increased rates of heart attacks, increased cancer rates, and decreased life expectancy. After the press conference, one inner club member warned her colleagues to obtain a copy of the research findings before writing anything; she felt the study may not have controlled for other confounding factors in the respondents' lifestyles and suggested the journalists make sure the study was a valid one before going ahead with a story. Several club members took her advice.

Information gathering. Although science writers are not eager to talk about cooperative information-gathering behaviors, I observed at least four types of information sharing during the 1977 AAAS meeting.

1. Providing scientific information. Perhaps most common among information-gathering behaviors was the tendency of the inner club to act as a pool of resources for its members. Journalists with science questions would corral one another, searching for definitions, clarifications,

examples, and analogs. At times, the rooms where reporters typed their stories would be alive with questions and answers, as one reporter depended on another's expertise. Information was always freely given.

2. Sharing notes and interviews. Inner club members respect one another's journalistic abilities, and cooperative information gathering would sometimes extend to the actual sharing of interview notes or of the interview sessions themselves. In one instance, the science writer for a large eastern newspaper set up an interview with an astronomer and then invited a colleague—who happened to work for a competing eastern newspaper—to sit in with him. Another journalist recounted an instance, at an earlier AAAS meeting, when he and a fellow science writer wanted to attend four different symposia at the same time and managed to do so by each attending one and leaving tape recorders at the other two. "We wound up—the two of us—covering four separate meetings simultaneously," he said. "And we swapped notes . . . covered ourselves that way."

3. Supportive questioning at press conferences. Journalists generally find press conferences frustrating because they have so little control over the "event"; reporters rarely work together, so questions are disparate with little or no followup. This is not the case among the inner club. The cooperative nature of the group encourages reporters to take their leads from each other, to ask follow-up questions, to work together. By doing so, reporters can gain some control over the interview situation and can focus lines of questioning as necessary. At the 1977 AAAS meeting, for example, three inner club members attended a press conference at which a scientist discussed his attempts to identify infant behaviors that might be useful predictors of Sudden Infant Death Syndrome (SIDS). The three inner club members had written frequently about SIDS in other contexts, and when one began questioning the scientist closely about the predictive nature of his work, the other two joined what became a rather heated exchange. The journalists argued that they did not want to write stories that might provide false hope to readers, and the scientist in turn argued that he could not generalize any further from his data than he had already done. In the end, none of the three journalists wrote stories about the SIDS research. Both scientist and journalists were angry, but one science writer on the sideline felt that such intense, cooperative questioning was justified in cases such as this. He explained that a number of writers have been "burned" by scientists claiming to have found the explanation for SIDS. He felt that when a journalist is writing a SIDS story, he is justified in pushing the scientist to the limit, and the technique of following up on one another's questions at a press conference is a good way of doing that.

4. Acting as warning systems for one another. Just as inner club members warn each other away from potentially risky topics or scien-

tists, so do they also flag information that must be interpreted cautiously. And if they feel a colleague is "going beyond the data" in drawing conclusions, they will take the time to warn him or her about it. An incident that took place at the 1977 AAAS meeting illustrates this point. One of the most popular press conferences at that meeting was on new Viking data about Mars and its moon, Phobos. During the press conference, astronomer Carl Sagan noted that new measurements of Phobos indicated it was made up to some extent of carbonaceous chondrites and constituted "a big lump of organic matter orbiting Mars." The main point of the discussion was that the data lent credence to the hypothesis that Phobos may be a captured asteroid. But one science writer came away from the press conference with the news that "there's oil on Phobos. Phobos is a little Saudi Arabia!" He apparently had made the conceptual leap from long-chain hydrocarbons to oil. Several inner club members were visibly disturbed by the oil comment and talked further with Sagan. One reporter then corralled the colleague who had come up with the Saudi Arabia statement and warned him, "Sagan just called (another reporter) down on that (mentioning oil). You can have long-chain hydrocarbons without it being anything like oil." Ultimately, the idea of oil on Phobos was either played down in or even eliminated from inner club stories.

Advantages and Disadvantages of Inner Club Membership

The main function of the inner club, then, seems to be to turn what should be a highly competitive media situation into a cooperative one for its members.[10] Resulting cooperative strategies seem to help inner club members to produce news more efficiently and more accurately.

Most inner club members come to science meetings saddled with deadline demands. They do not have the luxury of taking two or three days to gather information for a story; in many cases they may be expected to produce two stories a day, and time is of the essence. Sharing information is one way to cut down on the gathering time. Being able to look at a colleague's interview notes means you do not need to interview the scientist yourself. Collaborative questioning in a press conference may provide sufficient information to eliminate the need for further discussion with the scientists after the conference. Sharing information is, thus, an efficient strategy for news production.

Sharing also may increase accuracy. Because the information they cover is so technical, science writers worry about the accuracy of their products. Accuracy is enhanced when a journalist avails him- or herself of a pool of resources—such as the inner club. A number of science writers have accumulated expertise in specific areas of science and are able to provide detailed information to their colleagues. By emphasizing sharing, the club encourages interaction and the type of behavior monitoring illustrated by the Phobos incident.

However, while these behaviors probably increase the accuracy of the scientific information presented to the public, I think they also have had two negative effects on inner club coverage of science. One is standardization in story selection, and the other is the emphasis on some areas of science to the neglect of others. When the inner club attends a meeting such as that of AAAS, most factors encourage a homogeneous output. Cooperative newsgathering favors duplication; a large number of talented writers concentrate on a relatively small number of topics. The concentration of time and effort is not intrinsically bad—any one reporter could not possibly produce stories about more than a miniscule part of the meeting. However, if reporters ignore topics at a science meeting, they should do so according to some relevant criteria. What readers see or read about the event should in some way be more important, more relevant to them perhaps, than what they don't.

It is not clear that cooperative story selections by the inner club are based on such criteria. Members may define news less by judgments of the intrinsic importance of information than by the notion that if others have done this story, then it must in fact be important. In other words, duplication may be a strategy for satisfying *internal* (organizational) pressures but may have little meaning outside the reporting selection process. Inner club standardization of story choices at a scientific event thus means that lay readers will be exposed to only a small portion of the event itself and, in addition, will be given no help in understanding the criteria used to select that small pool of stories.

My data indicate that these journalists also tend to cover areas of science with which they are familiar. Such a situation is not a problem if backgrounds are diverse, but homogeneous science interests among reporters lay the groundwork for neglect of certain areas of science by the club's majority. As Table 12–2 attests, there is a certain amount of homogeneity in reporter interests within the club. Since many members spent most of their early science-writing years with the space program, the physical sciences and astronomy rank high. Others have developed interests in specific fields such as climatology or geology,[11] but areas of little interest to most club members are likely to be neglected. And the fields generating the *least* amount of interest among these respondents are the social sciences.

Science writers—of all journalists—should be equipped to report on the social sciences; in fact, they are not. Few feel they know enough about social science research techniques to evaluate studies and make news decisions. The typical response is to avoid social science or at least to view lack of evaluative skills as no great barrier to writing. "I'm not

Table 12-2. Scientific Interests of the Inner Club Ranked by Frequency of Mention

Topic	Number of mentions
Space	14
Astronomy	13
Other physical sciences, particularly geology	12
Medicine/biology	10
Environment/energy	9
Anthropology/archeology	8
Technology	7
Political/social aspects of science	6
Social science/behavior	4

Total number of respondents in study: 17

very well equipped to evaluate sociology," said one inner club member, "but it can't hurt anybody so I figure it's not going to do too much damage if I get it a little screwed up." So what's news to the inner club is *not* likely to be social science. And even when a social science story is picked up, inner club membership may not be of much help in ensuring accuracy. None of the inner club members studied in this project professed to have any social science expertise. A social sciences "pool of resources" simply may not exist among these elite science writers.

The Future of the Inner Club

The inner club will continue to influence science news coverage in the United States for some time; members are relatively young and show no intention of stepping aside. Nevertheless, I believe that the club's influence *is* likely to diminish over time.

Science writers appear to be shifting emphasis and resources away from coverage of discrete *events* to coverage of complex *issues,* such as the nationwide use of solar technologies or the industrial potential of recombinant DNA techniques. This shift may be partly adaptive; few scientific events today can rival the manned space shots for excitement and front-page potential. The shift also may signal a recognition that science's important effects on society do not lend themselves to an event orientation in news stories. Such a switch from event to nonevent coverage of science does, however, reduce the frequency with which the inner club is coming together. An informal network that depends on personal interactions will be likely to suffer.

A second major reason for the club's diminishing influence is that a number of "new" journalists moving up in the mass media ranks have not become socialized to the inner club.[12] Most simply have not been around long enough—less than ten years in most cases—but they also bring very different backgrounds to the profession.

Many of them majored in science in college, knew as students that they wanted to become science reporters, and began their mass media careers not as general reporters but as science writers. Few of them were around when the manned space program was in full swing, and they seem to be very interested in covering political, economic, sociological, and technological aspects of science. Although inner club members do not avoid such areas, the younger journalists seem to place higher priority on the integration of "pure"science with its social ramifications.

The inner club will, of course, not disappear. However, as young science journalists are hired and opportunities to become socialized to one another at scientific events decline, the incidence of intense cooperation among journalists that so characterizes the inner club today should decrease. Such an evolution may give individual science writers sufficient independence to allow development of personal news-making strategies while at the same time enabling the science writing *community* to retain enough cooperative behaviors to give members access to some of the distinct advantages of peer monitoring and assistance.

A Brief Postscript . . . from the Perspective of 1985

When this study was published five years ago, I predicted the gradual demise of the inner club, and, consequently, of its impact on national media coverage of science. Although five years may not be enough time for significant change to occur, my own observations during the period have altered my prediction somewhat. My current educated guess is that the inner club itself may prove to be quite resilient but that its ability to affect media coverage of science on a national scale may decrease nonetheless.

It was my contention in 1980 that the combination of more independent, young science writers emerging on the scene and the availability of fewer events at which journalists could coalesce would bring about the gradual demise of the inner club. That prediction hasn't held up so far. For one thing, the number of events at which science reporters can gather has, if anything, increased with the launching of the space shuttle on a regular basis. And for another, a number of young science writers who in the late 1970s were not members of the inner club now seem securely entrenched in the ranks. So, at present, the group seems as vigorous as ever.

But I think the club's impact on media science coverage has diminished and may continue to do so. Since the late 1970s, science has become a major interest of a growing array of mass media. New magazines, a bevy of science and health newsletters, and increased science offerings in newspapers and by broadcast outlets have resulted in a larger, more heterogeneous pool of science reporters. The impact of the inner club is felt when that small group can literally account for the bulk of stories produced. In the current setting, that ability to dominate seems to be decreasing.

Notes

1. See, for example, Hillier Krieghbaum, *Science, the News, and the Public* (New York: New York University Press, 1958), pp. 12–16; James W. Swinehart and Jack M. McLeod, "News About Science: Channels, Audiences and Effects," *Public Opinion Quarterly* 24 (Winter 1960): 583–589; and Orest Dubas and Lisa Martel, *Science, Mass Media and the Public,* vol. 2 of *Media Impact* (Ottawa: Information Canada, 1975), pp. 34–36.

2. Study findings discussed in this article constitute a part of the author's doctoral dissertation, "Science Journalists: A Study of Factors Affecting the Selection of News at a Scientific Meeting," Indiana University, 1978. Data were collected with the aid of a grant from the Gannett Newspaper Foundation via the Indiana University Center for New Communications. Other components of the larger study *not* discussed here include comparisons of the news selection patterns of the top mass media science writers with those of journalists with much less expertise in science. Also included in the dissertation are analyses of the stories produced about the meeting, including comparisons between newspaper and broadcast coverage, between local (Denver) and nonlocal coverage, between media that sent reporters to the meeting and media that did not, and between wire service organizations and newspapers.

3. Details of the study methodology are available from the author. I suspected that I would find a small but cohesive network of experienced science writers in the United States, so I set out to construct a sample of those very individuals through a self-selection method. Three prominent science writers and four public information persons who work for national scientific institutions were asked to provide names of journalists whom they *regularly* encounter in major science news situations. Those providing names were David Perlman, then science editor of the *San Francisco Chronicle*; Ron Kotulak, science editor for the *Chicago Tribune*; Ed Edelson, science editor for *The New York News*; Don Phillips, senior project specialist for the American Hospital Association; Audrey Likely, director of public relations for the American Institute of Physics; Dorothy P. Smith, manager of the news service for the American Chemical Society; and Carol Rogers, public information officer for the American Association for the Advancement of Science. The resulting lists were then merged and the names ranked according to the

number of mentions they received. Those science journalists named by three or more of the seven persons were considered likely candidates for this experienced "inner circle" of science writers that I wished to study. (Table 12–1 provides names of all persons on that final list.) I then included in the sample *all* persons on the list who indicated they intended to cover the 1977 AAAS annual meeting, the event around which the study was designed. Of the twenty-eight names on the list, seventeen ultimately were included in the study.

4. This term originally was used by Timothy Crouse to describe the social network established among national political reporters who were covering presidential candidates during the 1972 U.S. election. His book, *The Boys on the Bus* (New York: Ballantine Books, 1973), provides a number of accounts of behaviors that closely parallel what I observed among the science writing inner club.

5. Socialization across media organizations, the situation described here, is not common in journalism. Studies such as the classical one by Warren Breed ("Social Control in the Newsroom," *Social Forces* 33 (May 1955): 326–335) have consistently found that journalists become socialized to peers *within* their own newsrooms. The exceptions to the rule seem to be specialty reporters, who establish relationships with similar reporters from other news organizations. Descriptions of this specialist phenomenon are provided by Jeremy Tunstall, *Journalists at Work* (London: Constable, 1971) and by Steve Chibnall, *Law-and-Order News* (London: Tavistock Publications Limited, 1977).

6. This percentage represents a high level of autonomy when compared to editorial personnel in general. A national study of American journalists by Johnstone, Slawski, and Bowman titled *The News People* (Urbana: University of Illinois Press, 1976) found that only 46.2 percent of the respondents were able to make any of their own story assignments independently of their editors. In large media organizations with more than 100 editorial employees, where science writers are likely to be employed, the percentage drops to 36.2.

7. Additional data gathered for this study corroborate this argument. A total of eighty-eight mass media print journalists covered the 1977 AAAS meeting. Of that group, fourteen were inner club members. Although the inner club constituted only 16 percent of all reporters, the group accounted for 56 percent of the 772 newspaper and news magazine stories published throughout the country in ensuing weeks. When coverage by the two local (Denver) newspapers was eliminated from the analysis, the percentage of stories attributable to inner club members increased to 64 percent (n = 583).

8. It should be emphasized that the AAAS meeting was selected primarily because it is a setting that *predictably* attracts the inner club each year. The meeting is sufficiently different from other scientific meetings to make one cautious about generalizing the study results to them, but the number of science stories generated by the AAAS meeting alone is sufficient to warrant examination of the event. And subsequent discussions of the study findings with science writers involved in this research have elicited numerous

acknowledgments that behaviors observed at the AAAS meeting parallel those that take place when the inner club gathers to cover other events as well. I would like to thank AAAS and particularly Arthur Herschman, head of the meetings and publications division, and Carol Rogers, public information officer, for their cooperation with the study.

9. Data were gathered at the 1977 AAAS meeting in Denver through the use of four trained observers who were stationed at points throughout the press area of the meeting. Additionally, I subsequently gathered further observational data at both the 1978 Washington and 1979 Houston meetings.

10. Observation of the inner club at several AAAS meetings indicates that the kinds of information sharing discussed here take place primarily among members. The informal network is based on close personal ties that have developed over time and, like anyone, an inner club member will interact most with his or her friends. Members will certainly provide information to nonmembers when asked, but they will rarely initiate communication with journalists outside the network. This means that reporters who are new to science writing, who perhaps need more help with information than anyone, are often the most isolated at these meetings.

11. Don Kirkman of Scripps-Howard, for example, developed an interest in weather from several years as a weather observer for both the U.S. Navy and the U.S. Weather Bureau. Al Rossiter of UPI majored in geology as an undergraduate and even spent a year in graduate school taking geology courses before turning to journalism.

12. Among these journalists are Ira Flatow, science reporter for National Public Radio in Washington, D.C.; Cristine Russell, science-medicine reporter for the (now-defunct) *Washington Star;* Jon Franklin, science writer for the *Baltimore Evening Sun;* Bob Gillette, science writer for the *Los Angeles Times;* and David Salisbury, science writer for the *Christian Science Monitor.*

CHAPTER 13

How to Kill a Controversy: The Case of Recombinant DNA

Rae Goodell

Journalists often feel they are the ones who decide what becomes news, but some communications researchers suggest instead that *sources* significantly influence what gets covered and how it gets covered. In this case study, Rae Goodell provides an in-depth look at the agenda-setting function of the scientific sources involved in the recombinant DNA issue.

Rae Goodell is an associate professor of science writing at the Massachusetts Institute of Technology. She is the author of *The Visible Scientists* and a number of articles analyzing the relationship between the scientific community and the mass media. She serves on the board of directors of the Council for the Advancement of Science Writing and on the AAAS Committee on Public Understanding of Science.

IN 1979, WHEN THE GENETIC ENGINEERING FIRM Biogen first proposed establishing its U.S. headquarters in Cambridge, Massachusetts, Mayor Alfred Vellucci tried to stimulate press and public interest in possible health hazards associated with recombinant DNA technology. But, whereas in 1976 Vellucci's efforts to ban all recombinant DNA experiments in the city of Cambridge had helped precipitate a major national controversy, this time press and public were unimpressed. Biohazards were perceived to be a dead issue, and the isolated efforts of a few local politicians could not resurrect it. Similarly, recent efforts to regulate recombinant DNA research in other communities, and major changes in federal guidelines, have generated fleeting attention at best.[1]

Most scientists hardly mourned the demise of the recombinant DNA safety controversy, but the circumstances surrounding its passing are nonetheless disturbing. Particularly troubling is the extent to which the scientific community has shaped press coverage and hence public perceptions of the issue, sometimes inadvertently, sometimes intentionally. A gradual increase in the influence of the scientific community on press coverage of recombinant DNA can be observed by following developments in the scientific community and in the press through three major phases: first, the development of the recombinant DNA safety controversy from about 1974 to 1977; second, the curtailment of the controversy, from about 1977 to 1979; and third, the shift of attention to the genetic engineering industry, from about 1979 to the present.

The Development of the Safety Controversy

In the first—experimental—period, 1974–1977, a group of scientists, many of them politically inexperienced, tried a number of different approaches to press and public involvement as they deliberated on the risks and regulation of recombinant DNA research. In some ways these years were tumultuous ones: widely divergent viewpoints were exposed in the press and generated controversy far beyond the scientific community's control. Even in this period, however, some scientists had significant effects on the press.

It was, for example, largely at the initiative of leading DNA researchers that the recombinant DNA safety issue originally came to the attention of press and public. These scientists were not deliberately seeking publicity—far from it—but they recognized that their efforts to reach their colleagues for an internal discussion of the issues, particularly with letters in *Science* and *Nature*, would probably also bring the subject to the attention of reporters. In fact, early in 1974 Victor McElheny, then a reporter for *The New York Times*, had already stumbled upon the story but had agreed not to print it until the scientists were ready.

That time came at a press conference on July 18, 1974, called to explain that a National Academy of Sciences (NAS) committee was publishing a letter in scientific journals asking for a postponement of certain types of recombinant DNA experiments until the following February, when an international scientific meeting could be held to assess risks and devise guidelines. Only then did major press reports appear, although aspects of the story had been around since the summer of 1971, when early gene-splicing experiments provoked debate among participants at a Cold Spring Harbor workshop, and particularly since the fall of 1973, when a letter calling for assessment of risks had been published in *Science* and explained in an article in *New Scientist,* both of which are commonly read by science reporters.[2]

For a number of reasons, most notably the organizers' own inexperience, many of the stories emerging from that July 1974 press conference were everything the scientists might have feared, emphasizing as they did the vivid potential risks of the research and the unusual interim moratorium or "ban" on experiments. Some of the headlines read, for example, "Scientists Fear Release of Bacteria" (*Los Angeles Times*), "Genetic Scientists Seek Ban—World Health Peril Feared" (*Philadelphia Bulletin*), "A New Fear: Building Vicious Germs" (*Washington Star-News*).[3]

Dismayed, some of the leaders of the DNA safety discussion sought to exert more control over press coverage of their future deliberations. They succeeded. Laying plans for the upcoming safety conference at Asilomar in California, the principal organizers at first sought to exclude the press entirely. When it became clear that such a move would be politically untenable (Stuart Auerbach of the *Washington Post* threatened to invoke the Freedom of Information Act, for example), the organizers agreed to a small contingent of reporters, ultimately sixteen, arguing that a larger number would create a media circus. The reporters were also required to agree to an embargo on stories until the end of the three-and-a-half-day meeting. Although the meeting was supported by public funds, in general the few reporters who were turned down accepted their fate, including a correspondent for Canadian Broadcasting Corporation and freelance writers for *New Times* and *Harpers.*[4]

Indirectly, the embargo influenced much more than the number and timing of stories. For one thing, it allowed the reporters, often hassled by the demands of daily journalism, to produce some excellent, widely praised reporting. But the embargo also encouraged the reporters to focus on the point of view of the scientists who were present, rather than checking with experts who had not been included. Thus, much of the press largely accepted the scientists' definition of the problem—a narrow question of health risk—and the scientists' approach to a solution: self-regulation by the researchers. Both organizers and press failed to anticipate later criticisms about the technical importance of including experts from other fields, such as epidemiologists and occupational health specialists, and the political importance of opening the meeting to more lay participants. Ironically, although many of the Asilomar organizers were reluctant to admit the press, they later would point to the reporters' presence as evidence that the meeting had had "public participation."[5]

In the months and years that followed, the nature of DNA press coverage continued to depend on the nature of the information that the scientific community made available. The summer after Asilomar, a few scientists began to criticize publicly the guidelines being prepared by a National Institutes of Health (NIH) committee on the basis of the Asilomar recommendations. These critics were duly quoted, and their views juxtaposed with those of the DNA researchers—"opponents" versus "proponents," risks versus benefits. When Senator Edward M. Kennedy called hearings, emphasizing the need for public input, his views, together with the scientists' responses, led to another juxtaposition: "public involvement" versus "freedom of scientific inquiry."[6]

As the controversy spread around the country, generating federal, state, and local efforts to regulate the research, events seemed increasingly beyond the scientists' control. But again, the influence of the scientific community was substantial. Although scientists did not determine the settings, frequency, and circumstances for debate, they continued to guide its content. Scientific spokesmen, called upon to give testimony, continued to define the issue primarily as a question of immediate health risk, separate from ethical and social implications. Press and public took little initiative to broaden the discussion, except when stimulated briefly by events such as scholarly conferences on ethical issues.[7] Also, scientists holding views between the polar positions had less incentive to speak out, and the press and public largely did not seek them out.

Curtailment of the Safety Controversy

In 1977, a dramatic change occurred in the way the DNA issue was being handled by the scientific community, and consequently by the press, drastically curtailing the safety controversy. At the beginning of the year, the academic research community seemed reconciled to the notion that federal regulation was inevitable, given public sentiment, and perhaps necessary, given difficulties in enforcing the existing NIH guidelines, particularly in the burgeoning genetics industry. Also, some recombinant DNA proponents favored uniform, preemptive federal legislation to counteract the threat of a patchwork of local initiatives that would put some universities at a competitive disadvantage.[8]

Although legislation sounded logical in theory, the actual introduction of bills in the Senate and House had a chilling effect. Some called for national commissions staffed predominantly by nonscientists, heavy fines for offenders, and the right of local communities to institute regulations more stringent than the federal ones. Scientific leaders perceived the measures as a dangerous precedent in regulating basic research. Also, among DNA researchers, momentum was building to get on with the research: laboratories that had been under construction were ready to go, ideas were ripe, European competitors were forging ahead.

To counteract the legislative drive, political leaders of the scientific community joined with DNA researchers to lobby against the bills. Strategies began to emerge at a research meeting in Miami in January 1977, at a conference of academic leaders at NIH in February, and at a National Academy of Sciences forum in March. In April the NAS sent a resolution to Congress, and in June and July participants at Gordon Research Conferences in New Hampshire sent letters to Congress. Harlyn O. Halvorson, at the time president of the American Society for Microbiology, organized a coalition of scientific societies and leaders, sending delegations and letters to key legislators during the summer. By September, Senator Kennedy had withdrawn support for his bill and the other legislators were backing proposals for minimal measures. Nothing reached the Senate floor by the end of 1977, and in 1978 the same process was repeated on a smaller scale with weaker bills. By October 1978 it was clear that barring a major accident involving recombinant DNA technology, there would probably be no legislation at all.

The lobbyists' remarkable success came largely from two particularly persuasive lines of argument. The first contended that significant new data showed the risks of recombinant DNA techniques to be much less serious than originally feared. According to a report by Barbara Culliton in *Science,* this "new data" argument was stressed at least partly because Halvorson had been advised by seasoned lobbyists to offer members of Congress an "escape clause," an explanation for changing their minds on the issue.[9] Among the documents quickly disseminated to Congress and the press was the official summary of a June 1977 conference at Falmouth, Massachusetts, reporting that the consensus of the experts present had been that the risks from the strains of *E. coli* bacteria ordinarily used in recombinant DNA research were very small. Also circulated that summer was the as-yet-unpublished report of a research project headed by Stanley Cohen of Stanford University School of Medicine, which was interpreted by the lobbyists as demonstrating the activities such as those proposed or done by gene splicers also commonly occurred in nature.

The lobbyists' second major argument was that the vast majority of scientists, including some of the biologists who had originally urged caution, now believed recombinant DNA research to be safe. The remaining critics, it was argued, were a small minority, a fringe group, who, like the public, did not have the expertise to judge the merits of the DNA issue. This argument represented a culmination of pressure against the critics that had been building for some time. As a recent congressional report states:

> Scientists were happy to debate the possible hazards of gene splicing among themselves until 1975 or so, but from the moment that the subject became a matter of public interest, the atmosphere of debate changed sharply. There was a closing of the ranks, and the emergence of a deep hostility toward the scientific critics of the NIH guidelines, which differed sharply from the academic welcome traditionally accorded dissenting views.[10]

As the lobby intensified, suggestions were made, even in print, that opponents of DNA research were mystics, hysterics, political opportunists, incompetents.[11] If such public epithets were not sufficient deterrent to speaking out, critics were also approached privately, with hints that their research grants, jobs, promotions were in jeopardy.[12] Also, leaders in the recombinant DNA field began refusing to grant interviews to reporters who also planned to talk with opponents.[13] And so, the number of DNA critics indeed decreased, in some cases because they revised their estimates of the safety of the research, but in other cases because they revised their estimates of the safety of speaking out against the research.

Also important to the lobby's success was the acceptance of its position by the press, creating a very different climate of opinion from that of 1974 to 1976. The increase in availability of DNA proponents and decrease in availability of opponents coincided with a similar shift in their representation in press coverage. Studies show that beginning in 1977, coverage of the views of critics dropped sharply, and the lobbyists' claims for the new data were reported largely without reservation.[14] Allegations that opposition was being suppressed were not checked out, despite opportunities to do so—at meetings of the NIH Recombinant DNA Advisory Committee, for example. As legislation and lobbying activity faded, press coverage faded with it, until the safety aspects of the issue were considered history.

The Shift in Attention to Biotechnological Industry

The lull in press coverage was short-lived, however, because a new story quickly emerged to fill the vacuum: the blossoming of the genetic engineering industry. While Congress was actively considering legislation, industry downplayed its involvement in recombinant DNA technology. For example, when the brain hormone somatostatin was first synthesized, the announcement was made at Senate hearings in November 1977 by Philip Handler, then president of the NAS, and Paul Berg, a senior researcher from Stanford University. There was initially no mention of the company—Genentech—for whom the work had been done.[15]

As the threat of regulation faded, however, industry began an impressive public relations campaign. Press conferences were timed to capitalize on each new development, and interviews with company spokesmen were arranged to highlight the technology's potential. Having left industry alone earlier, much of the press responded to the public relations campaign with frequent newspaper coverage of breakthroughs and magazine features on benefits, rarely balanced by the reservations of financial analysts, occupational health experts, labor, or scientific observers.[16] *Newsweek*, for example, called the phenomenon "The Miracle of Spliced Genes"; *Life*, the "Miraculous Prospects of Gene Splicing"; *The New York Times*, the "Industry of Life."[17]

Ironically, while simultaneously covering such issues as Three Mile Island and Love Canal, the press generally treated the genetics industry as if it could be expected to be free of unwanted side effects. More recent coverage has mentioned the tensions created by the close relationship between companies and universities in the development of the technology. But, again, these issues were first raised primarily by scientists rather than by reporters.

The Future

The pattern throughout the history of the recombinant DNA issue has been one in which the scientists willing to speak out—whether they were the Asilomar conference organizers, the established scientist-critics, the congressional lobbyists, or the industrial leaders—have largely determined the timing, extent, and direction of press coverage. The scientists, rather than the journalists, have in effect set the press' agenda and made the news decisions.

Judging from other case studies of coverage of scientific controversy, the pattern is a common one. Expressed in different forms, one of the most frequent criticisms of press coverage of controversial issues involving science and technology has been its passivity, its lack of initiative, its tendency to use what is readily available from established scientific leaders without further investigation.[18] A study of coverage of the risks of marijuana, for example, found that the most frequently cited sources for news stories were administrators in government and private agencies and Nobel Prize–winners and other celebrities not in the marijuana research field.[19] According to another case study, the California press missed the existence of a serious asbestos occupational health problem within the state because reporters were checking only with governmental sources, not labor leaders and others.[20] And again, as described by June Goodfield's *Reflections on Science and the Media*, most of the press also missed the facts behind the exposé of William Summerlin's fabrication of data on transplants of mice's coats at Sloan-Kettering Cancer Center because reporters talked only to Sloan-Kettering leadership, and not, for example, to Summerlin's colleagues.[21] A study of press coverage of the Apollo space program blamed the press for accepting a "myth of invincibility" about NASA experts and not following up strong clues that there were flaws in the program; if these flaws had been exposed, the author argues, corrections might have been made that would have prevented the fire in January 1967 that killed three astronauts.[22]

Other studies suggest that many writers and scientists accept this close interdependence between an inner group of scientists and press as a matter of course. Recent critiques of Three Mile Island and swine flu coverage, for example, contend that reporters were indignant when designated experts could not give them a consistent explanation and missed the fact that the experts' very confusion was an important part of the story.[23] And other studies have found that scientific leaders, in turn, sometimes become indignant when the press does not cover exclusively their points of view.[24]

This kind of symbiotic relationship between sources and reporters is to some degree common to all kinds of journalism, but there are a number of reasons why it may be particularly strong—and unhealthy— in science journalism. To begin with, the press, like the public, generally finds science somewhat intimidating, so editors are likely to insist that sources have obvious credentials and well-established credibility. In moderation, such a policy is appropriately cautious; carried too far, it is unnecessarily confining. Moreover, inexperienced writers and editors are unlikely to have the confidence in their own judgment necessary to do investigative stories, to search out and evaluate information that the scientific community is unaware of or does not volunteer. Experienced writers and editors, however, are aware of the scientific community's sensitivity to criticism, and are likely to fear that investigative stories will jeopardize the trusting relationship that they have worked hard to build with scientist sources. Veteran writers also tend to share scientists' enthusiasm for the process, values, and discoveries of science and to be less interested in conveying political aspects of science. They are concerned, too, as are scientists, that political stories may tarnish the image of science and increase public hostility toward it. Finally, editors, especially at daily newspapers, sometimes misunderstand the nature of science and deny their reporters the time and flexibility to do in-depth reporting. With a peculiar kind of chauvinism, scientists and science reporters have frequently assumed that the views of scientists on scientific issues are definitive, the product of expertise and collective wisdom, and that the views of lay participants, such as environmentalists, labor leaders, or religious leaders, are somehow inferior or extraneous.

On political issues, however, the scientific community necessarily functions as an interest group—or as a number of them. As John Ziman put it:

> It is the wisdom of the pluralistic society to doubt the competence of any authority to choose wisely on behalf of every citizen. It is not so much that they cannot be trusted not to feather their own nests; it is simply that the questions debated within such organizations are seldom correctly posed. They refer far too much to what is technically possible or technically optimal, rather than what is socially desirable. [25]

Such an observation is hardly new, but, as the recombinant DNA safety issue exemplifies, it has yet to have a major impact on the conduct of science journalism. When science becomes part of the political process, science writing should become part of political reporting and be judged accordingly. [26] In the long run, the result will be more solid public confidence in science—based on realistic assessments, not public relations; on information, not image.

Notes

1. Information on the history of the recombinant DNA issue is based, except as indicated, on documents and transcripts of interviews deposited in the Recombinant DNA Controversy Oral History Collection (MC100), Institute Archives and Special Collections, MIT Libraries, Cambridge, Massachusetts. Information on press coverage is based on analysis of the press clipping files in the same collection. For a brief published history of the recombinant DNA safety controversy, see S. Krimsky, *Genetic Alchemy: The Social History of the Recombinant DNA Controversy* (Cambridge: MIT Press, 1982). On patterns in press coverage of the recombinant DNA debate, see R. Goodell, "The Gene Craze," *Columbia Journalism Review* 4 (November/December 1980): 41–45; and M. Altimore, "The Social Construction of Scientific Controversy, "*Science, Technology, & Human Values* 7 (Fall 1982): 24–31.

2. An exception to the lack of coverage of the potential risks of recombinant DNA prior to July 1974 was an article by R. Cooke, "Scientists Worry That New Lab Organisms Could Escape, Do Harm," *The Boston Globe*, November 11, 1973, 66.

3. For additional comments on the July 1974 press conference and resulting coverage, see R. Hutton, *Bio-Revolution: DNA and the Ethics of Man-Made Life* (New York: New American Library, 1978).

4. A few reporters appeared at the meeting uninvited, one of whom broke the embargo, but the invited press abided by their earlier agreement nonetheless.

5. Stuart Auerbach, then science writer for the *Washington Post*, objected to the labeling of press attendance as "public participation" in a letter to the

editor, "Writers at Asilomar," *Hastings Center Report* 5, no. 4 (August 1975): 4.

6. A tendency for science news to present two opposing viewpoints, rather than a number of differing views, also is indicated in B. J. Cole, "Science Conflict: A Content Analysis of Four Major Metropolitan Newspapers, 1951, 1961, 1971," master's thesis, School of Journalism and Mass Communications, University of Minnesota, Minneapolis, 1974. The study also found an increase in the amount of conflict in science news between 1951 and 1971, from 17.6 percent to 28.3 percent of sampled stories.

7. A number of scholarly conferences in 1975 on ethical implications of gene engineering helped to stimulate articles: for example, by Albert Rosenfeld in *Saturday Review*, July 26, 1975, and by Victor McElheny in *The New York Times*, December 15, 1975. For further discussion of the lack of coverage of social and ethical aspects of recombinant DNA technology, see N. Pfund and L. Hofstadter, "Biomedical Innovation and the Press," *Journal of Communication* 31, no. 2 (Spring 1981): 138–154. A similar lack of coverage of ethical concerns is observed in early heart transplant coverage in W. R. Oates, "Social and Ethical Content in Science Coverage by Newsmagazines," *Journalism Quarterly* 50, no. 4 (Winter 1973): 680–684.

8. By the end of 1978, regulatory action had at least been considered in Cambridge, Massachusetts, which passed an ordinance, after widely publicized deliberations, in January 1977; Bloomington, Indiana; San Diego; New Haven; Amherst; Princeton; Berkeley; Madison, Wisconsin; Oakland (where the company Cetus is located); Nutley, N.J. (where Hoffman–La Roche is located); Shrewsbury, Massachusetts (where Worcester Foundation for Experimental Biology is located); Worcester, Massachusetts (where the University of Massachusetts Medical School is located); and at the state level in California, New York, Maryland, New Jersey, Massachusetts, and Illinois. For a summary of regulatory efforts as of 1982, see S. Krimsky, A. Baech, and J. Bolduc, *Municipal and State Recombinant DNA Laws: History and Assessment* (Medford, Massachusetts: Department of Urban and Environmental Policy, Tufts University, June 1982).

9. B. Culliton, "Recombinant DNA Bills Derailed: Congress Still Trying to Pass a Law," *Science* 199 (January 20, 1978): 276.

10. "Genetic Engineering, Human Genetics, and Cell Biology: Evolution of Technological Issues, Biotechnology (Supplemental Report III)." Report prepared for the Subcommittee on Science, Research, and Technology of the Committee on Science and Technology, U.S. House of Representatives, 96th Congress, Second Session, August 1980, p. 48. See also N. Wade, "Gene-Splicing: Critics of Research Get More Brickbats Than Bouquets," *Science* 195 (February 4, 1977): 466–467.

11. See, for example, J. D. Watson, quoted as accusing several DNA opponents of incompetence, in A. Lubow, "Playing God with DNA," *New Times* 8 (January 7, 1977): 58. DNA opponents are charged with "uninformed fear, mysticism, and political opportunism" in M. F. Singer, "The Recombinant DNA Debate," editorial, *Science* 196 (April 8, 1977): 127. The hazards of recombinant DNA research "exist largely in the imaginations of a very small

group of scientists," according to an excerpt from the annual report of the National Academy of Sciences, "Philip Handler on Recombinant DNA Research," *Chemical and Engineering News* 55 (May 9, 1977): 3. In a speech to the 1978 American Association for the Advancement of Science annual meeting, Representative Richard L. Ottinger deplored the "vilification" of critics, which he likened to the early years of the nuclear debate; see "DNA: Scientists' Social Responsibility," *Congressional Record* 124, no. 17 (February 14, 1978).

12. Based on interviews conducted by the author with recombinant DNA critics. Permission to cite by name has not been granted.

13. Based on interviews conducted by the author with science writers. Permission to cite by name has not been granted.

14. A decline in representation of critics in DNA coverage is described in Goodell, "The Gene Craze," and Pfund and Hofstadter, "Biomedical Innovation."

15. Genentech's involvement was mentioned by witnesses later in the hearings and at a press conference on the somatostatin work the following month. The hearings were "Regulation of Recombinant DNA Research," Hearings before the Subcommittee on Science, Technology, and Space of the Committee on Commerce, Science, and Transportation, U.S. Senate, 95th Congress, First Session, November 2, 8, 10, 1977.

16. Pfund and Hofstadter, "Biomedical Innovation."

17. M. Clark, "The Miracles of Spliced Genes," *Newsweek*, March 17, 1980, 62–64; "Weaving New Life in the Lab: The Miraculous Prospects of Gene Splicing," *Life*, May 1980, 48–55; and A. J. Parisi, "Industry of Life: The Birth of the Gene Machine," *The New York Times*, June 29, 1980, F1.

18. Similar observations are made in other reviews of criticism of science news. See Pfund and Hofstadter, "Biomedical Innovation"; and E. Lambeth and R. Ferguson, "The *Columbia Journalism Review* and Scientific Controversy: An Overview and Commentary" (Paper presented at "When Experts Differ: The Role of the Mass Media in Scientific and Technological Controversy," Association for Education in Journalism annual meeting, Boston, August 10, 1980).

19. R. G. Shepherd, "Science News of Controversy: The Case of Marijuana," *Journalism Monographs*, no. 62 (August 1979).

20. B. Medsger, "Asbestos: The California Story," *Columbia Journalism Review* 16, no. 3 (September/October 1977): 41–50.

21. J. Goodfield, *Reflections on Science and the Media* (Washington, D.C.: American Association for the Advancement of Science, 1981).

22. J. A. Skardon, "The Apollo Story: What the Watchdogs Missed," *Columbia Journalism Review* 6, no. 3 (Fall 1967): 11–15; and "The Apollo Story (Second Part)," Ibid., no. 4 (Winter 1967/1968): 34–39.

23. P. M. Sandman and M. Paden, "At Three Mile Island," *Columbia Journalism Review* 18, no. 2 (July/August 1979): 43–58; D. M. Rubin and V. Hendy, "Swine Influenza and the News Media," *Annals of Internal Medicine* 87, no. 6 (December 1977): 769–774.

24. B. J. Culliton, "Science, Society, and the Press," *New England Journal of Medicine* 296 (June 23, 1977): 1450–1453; D. S. Greenberg, "Let's Hear It for Science," *Columbia Journalism Review* 13, no. 2 (July/August 1974): 16–22.

25. Quoted from a 1974 radio broadcast in Goodfield, *Science and the Media,* 14.

26. Some leading science writers have discussed the need for more investigative reporting of science. See, for example, "Science, Technology, and the Press: Must the 'Age of Innocence' End?" *Technology Review* 82, no. 5 (March/April 1980): 46–56.

CHAPTER 14

A Case of Benign Neglect: Coverage of Three Mile Island Before the Accident

Sharon M. Friedman

Probably the most analyzed scientific event in recent times was the March 1979 accident at the Three Mile Island nuclear plant located some ten miles south of Harrisburg, Pennsylvania. One segment of this analysis examined media coverage of the accident, and, in an unusual step for studies of this kind, two researchers gathered data about what information the utility and the local media had provided to area residents *before* the accident. Sharon Friedman describes communication flow patterns that prepared no one for an accident and contributed to the communications chaos that occurred during the accident itself. This case study, too, asks who sets the media agenda, this time at the local level.

Sharon M. Friedman served as a consultant to the Public's Right to Information Task Force of the President's Commission on the Accident at Three Mile Island. She conducted this research with Nancy C. Joyce, another task force staff member. In total, fourteen staff members and consultants constituted the task force that evaluated the mass media coverage of the TMI accident.

DURING AN EMERGENCY, correct and complete information can save lives, but during the accident at the Three Mile Island (TMI) nuclear plant at Middletown, Pennsylvania, in March 1979, correct and complete information was a rare commodity. Although no lives were lost, the communications breakdown that occurred during the accident affected thousands of area residents and others who wanted to know what was happening and the degree of danger involved.

Key aspects of the communications breakdown were lack of planning, primarily because no one acknowledged the possibility that an accident such as this could occur, and lack of a common understanding and a common language, primarily because the mix of engineers and the media was something akin to the mix of oil and water.

Elements of this breakdown appeared very early in the history of TMI. The public information programs and policies that were developed from 1965 on by Metropolitan Edison (Met Ed), the utility that operated TMI, set the stage for how the utility would handle information about TMI during the accident. Coverage by local media before the accident helped determine what local residents knew about TMI and the safety of nuclear plants in general and colored their later response to the emergency. This chapter reconstructs the history of Met Ed–TMI–media interactions.[1] From it emerges a blueprint for the communications crisis that was to come.[2]

Public Information Activities at Med Ed

The public information programs at Met Ed were the prime sources of information about TMI before the accident, both for the media and the public. The programs fell into three major categories: those dealing with Met Ed and TMI in general, those dealing specifically with TMI, and those dealing directly with area residents (community relations program).[3]

General Public Information Efforts

A four-person professional staff at Met Ed's Office of Communications Services in Reading, Pennsylvania, handled a multitude of general public information tasks for the utility, including press releases, media relations, advertising, employee relations, radio spots, and bill inserts for the entire Med Ed system, not just TMI. This was an unusually small staff for all these functions, but upper-level management saw the operation as "cost-effective" and refused to hire additional personnel.[4]

The four staff members were not well prepared to handle nuclear public information. None had scientific training, and three had spent little time on the job—an average of about seven months at the time of the accident. The staff dealt only with the local media; all national contacts were handled by the communications office at General Public Utilities (GPU), a holding company in New Jersey which is Met Ed's parent corporation. Policy input from Met Ed's Communications Services Office had always been minimal, even on public relations issues. According to the manager of this office, Blaine Fabian, "The public relations function . . . was not the overpowering operation in the company." He noted, "Quite frankly, our executives are not accustomed to having . . . PR advice, or accepting it."[5]

This tradition of ignoring public relations advice proved important during the accident, as Met Ed's top-level engineers and executives made information blunders that led to media and public distrust. Met Ed's public information staff also lost its credibility quickly because there was no way it could respond to the deluge of calls for information and to the demands of reporters at the scene. Small staff size, lack of understanding of nuclear technology, and inexperience, particularly in dealing with the national media, made the utility's public information specialists ineffectual during the accident.

TMI Information Efforts

The TMI information program was quite different from the general public relations program, primarily because it had been started and was run by engineers in the utility's generation department. Met Ed's public information specialists were only minimally involved. The vice president for generation determined what information could be made available about TMI–1 and TMI–2, the two reactors at the facility, and who was to clear that information before its release to the media.[6] Although the vice president for generation at the time of the accident was aware of and interested in the need for public relations, it was not one of his main concerns. Nor was it anyone else's.

As a result, a striking omission occurred in the plant's emergency plans: only one sentence in the main body of the plan and two paragraphs in the annex dealt with public information needs. The reference in the body of the plan said that Met Ed headquarters in Reading, Pennsylvania, would provide technical support in a number of areas, one of which was public relations.[7] No person was charged with this operation, no specifics were detailed, no plans were made. The reference in the plan's annex noted that during a general emergency, the most serious of all such events, "it may be deemed necessary to notify the general public that an abnormal operation condition exists at the Three Mile Island Nuclear Station."[8]

None of the thirteen persons interviewed at Met Ed or GPU after the accident could identify any plan that delineated what specific information tasks were to be done by utility information specialists and others during an emergency. One major result of this lack of preparation was that chaos reigned at Met Ed during the first few days of the accident (see Chapter 15).

Lack of an emergency information plan, however, did not imply any lack of public information about TMI. In fact, Met Ed had provided, through weekly press releases, a great deal of information about the status of TMI to the local media before the accident. These weekly releases, written to a rigid format, briefly described the operating status of the two reactors and listed all "events" Met Ed had reported to the Nuclear Regulatory Commission (NRC) that week. These events, or problems, ranged from minor fuse blowouts to major equipment breakdowns and reactor shutdowns. Met Ed began to issue these releases in 1974, and utility officials were quite proud of them, pointing out that most other utilities did not do this as a practice. They said they issued the releases because they wanted to keep the public informed and to show they had nothing to hide.

Unfortunately, however, the weekly releases were written by engineers who did not know what the public could understand or what the media could use. They used technical jargon throughout the releases, including such terms as "deenergized power distribution buses," "automatic actuation," and "redundant valves." Most science writers, let alone general assignment reporters, would have trouble with such terminology.

The releases also failed to describe what events reported to the NRC meant for the plant or area residents, and, in some instances, appeared to purposely avoid this. For example, a major plant shutdown occurred at TMI–2 on April 23, 1978, because of problems with the main steam release valves. These valves are not on the nuclear side of the plant and were not involved in the accident. They are important, however, for energy generation. Med Ed called the problem with the valves minor at the time and predicted TMI–2 would be in operation shortly.[9] Its next major statement on the valves was on May 26, a month later. A press release explained that the plant was undergoing extensive testing of these valves and that this problem would be resolved in the next few weeks.[10]

The problem was that the valves would not shut properly, according to a May 8 Licensee Event Report filed by the utility with the NRC. Eventually twenty new valves had to be installed, resulting in a twenty-week plant shutdown. At the time of the May 26 press release, information about the projected long delay had already been sent to the NRC, but Met Ed did not tell reporters until June 23 that it would take until September to replace the valves.[11]

Journalists who received these weekly releases also were misled about when events had occurred. These events were "reported to the NRC this week," the releases said. Reporters naturally assumed they had occurred during the past week because news depends on timeliness. Such was not the case, however. The NRC required many reports: some immediate, some weekly, some monthly. Met Ed lumped information from all these reports into its releases, so that an event that had happened on March 29, for example, was reported in a release on May 5.[12]

These delays had important consequences. When reporters occasionally queried the utility about an event, they were assured it had already been easily corrected and there was no danger. They accepted these statements at face value and assumed Met Ed had everything under control.

The weekly Met Ed press releases were positive and upbeat, emphasizing startups, not shutdowns. While they did list problems at the plant, they described them as minor and part of the effort to get commercial operation under way. Almost every release described such events as not affecting "the health and safety of the public."

Cumulatively, however, the releases revealed a serious pattern of sloppy operational discipline and consistent equipment problems. The plant was not operating during about 70 percent of its "startup," or testing period, from March through December 1978. The industry average for plants being nonoperational during this period is 40 percent.[13] There had been at least eleven reactor shutdowns and numerous stops and starts of the plant's turbine.[14]

But these harbingers were largely ignored by local reporters, who frequently discarded the weekly releases or condensed them for filler stories or occasionally printed them verbatim. Perhaps the releases could have alerted the media and the public to problems at TMI if they had been better written and more understandable. Unfortunately, what they did instead was lull people into a complacent state about the safety of the nuclear plant, a state that was shattered when the accident occurred.

Community Relations

The third major segment of Met Ed's information program, directed at local residents, was designed to convince citizens that TMI was a good and desirable neighbor. It was aimed at utility customers, government officials, business and community leaders, and students and teachers.

One of the keystones of this wide-ranging program was the TMI observation center, located near the plant. The center was opened in March 1970 so that people from the area could "watch the plant grow from the ground floor up," according to William Gross, Met Ed's supervisor of information, who was charged with running the center.[15]

Before the accident, an average of 15,000 visitors per year came to view displays on energy sources, the atom, fuel assemblies, uranium (called a "Gift of Mother Nature"), and the economic benefits of nuclear power. They also saw slide shows and took home booklets about the plant and nuclear power. When visitors could not travel to the center, it came to them in the form of slide presentations by Gross. From September 1978 to March 1979, he spoke to more than 3000 school children.[16]

The message Gross and the center emphasized was that nuclear plants were exceptionally safe. "The nuclear industry has logged millions of hours of operation, and it is consistently listed as one of the safest industries by the National Safety Council," declared one slide show script.[17] During these shows, Gross pointed out that all nuclear plants released minute quantities of radioactive materials, but that regulations were so strict that any radioactive water released had to meet government standards for drinking water.

In addition to Gross's visits, Met Ed also sponsored numerous events designed to persuade youngsters to support nuclear power, including school programs presented by the utility and Pennsylvania State University's Department of Nuclear Engineering. Max Frye, a mathematics teacher in York, Pennsylvania, about fifteen miles from TMI, remembered that the basic theme of one of these programs was "to assure us that radiation was perfectly safe." In one part of the program, a student volunteer was given a can of soda to drink and then a Geiger counter was held to the student's stomach. It clicked loudly, giving the appearance that the student had drunk radioactive material without apparent ill effects, he recalled. When Frye charged that it was illegal to administer radioactive material without a license, the demonstrator replied that he had simply held a small amount of radioactive material in his hand near the student, making the soda appear radioactive. He said he usually explained this hoax to his audience, but in this instance there had not been enough time.[18]

The utility also paid teachers to attend nuclear conferences, encouraged them to set up nuclear science courses, and gave them numerous pamphlets, bibliographies, and audiovisual aids. From 1970 to 1973, it held a series of nuclear science conferences for students.

Met Ed sent nuclear safety messages to adults in newspaper and radio advertisements, pamphlets, handouts, and even customer bill inserts. They, too, emphasized the positive—the nonpolluting nature of nuclear power and the safety record of the industry. Negative aspects, such as low-level radiation and radioactive waste disposal, were not discussed.

One pamphlet, "Your Personal Radiation Inventory," assured readers about the safety of TMI:

> It is obvious that Three Mile Island's contribution to the background radiation will be quite insignificant. In fact, if the worst conceivable accident were to occur at Three Mile Island Nuclear Station, because of safeguards, a man could remain at a spot less than a half mile from the reactor for 24 hours a day for an entire year and be exposed to only 2 mrem (millirems) of radiation.[19]

Met Ed's intensive efforts to assure its customers and neighbors of the safety and nonpolluting nature of TMI were accepted with few questions. There was little support for the meager and scattered antinuclear groups in the vicinity, despite long licensing hearings on the plant in both Harrisburg and Washington, D.C. Very little questioning on health hazards occurred.[20] "Everything we read and heard (about the plant) was good," said a member of Middletown's League of Women Voters.[21] Because the 1979 accident so shook residents' faith in Met Ed as an accurate information source, the communications breakdown during and after the accident became even more severe.

Mass Media Coverage of TMI Before the Accident

Newspapers

Six daily newspapers serve the region surrounding TMI: the *Harrisburg Patriot* and the *Harrisburg Evening News,* which are jointly owned and part of the Newhouse chain; the *Lancaster Intelligencer-Journal* and the *Lancaster New Era,* also jointly owned; the *York Daily Record;* and the *York Dispatch.* Middletown, the home of TMI, is also served by the weekly *Press and Journal.* Local media performance was assessed by interviewing staffs and examining TMI clippings from the papers.[22]

Editorial policies for all of these newspapers except the *Lancaster Intelligencer-Journal* were mildly in favor of nuclear power before the accident. A view expressed by the city editor of the *Harrisburg Patriot* was typical: "Nuclear power is good, but it would be nice if it were a little safer."[23] The *Intelligencer-Journal* had earned a mild antinuclear reputation. Its editor said: "We didn't condemn nuclear power per se; we were concerned about the way it was run. We raised the questions on whether plants were being run properly. No plant is better than the person at the button."[24] However, most of the newspaper's questions dealt with the Peach Bottom nuclear facility south of Lancaster and not TMI.

Each newspaper was able to identify one person who had written about Met Ed and TMI for a period of time before the accident. TMI, per se, was not a "beat" for the newspapers; it and Met Ed were generally covered as part of the utility, energy, or business beat. Reporters who wrote about Met Ed had no scientific or technical backgrounds, nor did the editors who handled their articles. All appeared to be better versed in financial than science writing.

Most of the reporting was superficial in nature, straight "hard news" on what had happened. There was very little in-depth reporting, such as investigative articles, series, or interpretive or background pieces. One major exception was a series done by the *York Daily Record* on TMI, which will be discussed below. Editors said this lack of in-depth coverage was largely because of small staffs or the absence of anyone with enough technical expertise to pursue and investigate stories about the plant and its machinery. No one felt able to question Met Ed's explanations that it was always testing one thing or another, explained the city editor of the *Harrisburg Evening News*.[25]

Reporters found Met Ed's weekly releases on the status of TMI hard to understand and expressed frustration with them. Many said they had a difficult time judging when something was newsworthy in the releases and what the significance of an event was for the plant and the community.

Those who called Met Ed to find out about an event usually received a standard assurance that there was no threat to public health or safety and that the problem was being or had been handled successfully. A reporter from the *York Daily Record* said that when safety questions were asked, Met Ed information staff members tended to smooth things over.[26] Others agreed that the utility played down safety questions and that its staff was not very cooperative about answering them. Given the technical jargon and pat assurances, few reporters bothered to call Met Ed to ask for explanations of terms or make inquiries about the significance of various events. Only one reporter said he went to outside sources for assistance in understanding the releases or happenings at TMI.

Very few of the newspapers kept the weekly TMI releases on file for more than a week or two (although several reporters said they kept their own files), so that it was difficult for them to see any cumulative effect of reported problems. During the accident, the *Harrisburg Patriot* and the *Lancaster New Era* had to send people to Met Ed's Reading headquarters to get duplicates of the releases so they could use them for references and backtracking.

In retrospect, the majority of reporters and editors did not feel they had done a good job in covering TMI and providing information to the public. They should have paid more attention to details, they agreed. Saul Kohler, executive editor of both Harrisburg newspapers, declared they should have been aware of every shutdown, every misstep, every bending of the rules that Met Ed made. But he added that this was an ideal, not an achievable reality.[27]

A number of newspeople placed much of the blame for the poor local coverage on Met Ed. Most felt that while Met Ed did inform the media of TMI events, it did so in a way that was not useful. The city editor at the *Harrisburg Evening News* accused Met Ed of hiding the seriousness of the problems encountered and propagandizing when it could.[28] With few exceptions, the reporters and editors agreed that Met Ed had misled them about the severity of events.

However, a reporter for the *Lancaster Intelligencer-Journal* said that if the utility misled him he was willing to be misled, and thus it was partly his own fault. "If you don't ask the right questions, you don't get the right answer. Or if you don't know what questions to ask. You have to really understand what people are saying—you must really *know* it. Otherwise you get half-truths all the time and you miss the guts of the issue."[29]

Staff members on both Lancaster newspapers also took the NRC to task, saying it was the commission's responsibility to tell the media what the problems were. "The NRC was lax. We were counting on them and they failed."[30]

By four months after the accident, several of the newspapers had made changes so they could cover nuclear power and TMI more thoroughly. Some had assigned a full-time reporter to cover TMI specifically or energy issues in general. Most reporters said they had become much more skeptical of what Met Ed and the NRC had to say.

Newspaper Content

The two Harrisburg newspapers provided the TMI coverage for most readers in the region, and this coverage was analyzed in detail using the library file of the newspapers. Together, they published sixty articles on TMI from 1977 through March 1979, showing a generally good level of coverage of major TMI issues but little coverage of events reported in the weekly press releases. When information from the weekly TMI releases was used, it was rewritten with some indication that a Harrisburg reporter had called Met Ed for more information. Licensing hearings for TMI–2 held in both Harrisburg and Washington received heavy coverage, with the views of antinuclear groups well represented.

The *Patriot* and *Evening News* ran nineteen TMI articles during 1977 on a variety of issues including antinuclear protests, plant evaluations, licensing hearings, safety and plant events, and security problems (Table 14–1). Subjects ranged from a barrel's radiation leak to beefing up plant security to favorable evaluation of the plant. Coverage in-

Table 14-1.   Combined Number of Staff Articles on Three Mile Island in the *Harrisburg Patriot* and the *Harrisburg Evening News*, by Subject, from 1977 to March 1979

Subject	1977		1978		Jan.–Mar. 1979		Total	
	N	%	N	%	N	%	N	%
Antinuclear protests	1	(5.3)	—		—		1	(1.7)
Plant evaluations	4	(21.1)	—		—		4	(6.7)
Licensing hearings	3	(15.8)	15	(48.4)	4	(40)	22	(36.7)
Safety and plant events	7	(36.8)	6	(19.4)	—		13	(21.7)
Security problems	—		4	(12.9)	—		4	(6.7)
Miscellaneous	4	(21.1)	6	(19.4)	6	(60)	16	(26.7)
Totals	19	(100.1)	31	(100.1)	10	(100)	60	(100.2)

creased in 1978, with thirty-one articles primarily concerning licensing hearings. These long articles explored many issues, including complaints against the plant, its closeness to the Harrisburg airport, and the danger of planes crashing into the cooling towers or the reactor, and its relation to radon tailings and radiation exposure. A number of articles also related "good news" about TMI, including the dedication of TMI–2, a good rating for TMI–1 from the NRC, and the beginning of commercial operation of TMI–2. During the first three months of 1979, ten articles on TMI were published in the Harrisburg newspapers, including a history of the licensing hearings and a report on a press tour of TMI facilities. In addition to these locally based articles, both the *Evening News* and the *Patriot* ran several hundred articles during this time on nuclear power, problems related to it, and antinuclear protests. These articles were generated by the wire services, syndicates, and the Newhouse chain. [31]

While the Harrisburg newspapers did not pay much attention to plant operations or the weekly releases, they did provide more than adequate coverage in their sixty articles of major issues and events including security problems at TMI, the licensing hearings, and efforts by antinuclear groups to halt TMI–2. However, they did not seek the added depth needed to cover the whole picture. Their coverage was event-oriented and did not serve an alerting function. Readers of their coverage might have known the plant was having a few problems, but the newspapers emphasized the legal situation more than any other aspect of the plant startup.

To evaluate TMI coverage for four of the other newspapers in the region, clippings from Met Ed files were used. (The extremely tight deadline for completion of this study precluded reviewing each newspaper's library files as was done for the Harrisburg newspapers.) Met Ed's files might have been incomplete, reflecting a lower number of articles than actually appeared, but they did provide a general idea of the coverage by these four newspapers between 1976 and 1978. (Clippings for the *Lancaster New Era* were not available, and all clippings for 1979 were disregarded as being incomplete.)

These four newspapers published between twenty-seven and seventy-one articles on TMI between 1976 and 1978 (Table 14–2). This coverage was devoted mostly to the major news stories covered by and already described for the Harrisburg newspapers, but, with one exception, was considerably more sparse. Included were most of the "good news" stories, occasional accounts of major plant problems, and rare stories on protests by antinuclear groups. The exception was the weekly *Middletown Press and Journal,* which ran a total of seventy-one articles (twenty-two in 1976; eight in 1977; and forty-one in 1978), the most published on TMI between 1976 and 1978 by any newspaper in the area. However, this coverage consisted almost entirely of printing the weekly press releases, often verbatim, and rarely included any of the major news events in detail or the activities of antinuclear groups. Few readers could understand what the articles said. So despite the fact that this newspaper printed the greatest number of articles on TMI, because its coverage parroted the technical jargon used in the weekly releases, its readers were not well informed.

The *Lancaster Intelligencer-Journal* ran nineteen TMI articles in 1976, including a number of the weekly releases in condensed, rewritten form. Its TMI coverage dropped off to only nine articles each in 1977 and 1978, with few weekly releases used. It printed about half of the major news stories on TMI and had very little coverage of the licensing hearings in Harrisburg or Washington. As noted earlier, this newspaper appeared more concerned about the Peach Bottom nuclear plant than about TMI. Even so—assuming the Met Ed clippings were complete—printing just nine articles per year about the plant during 1977 and 1978 is not a very good record.

Before April 1978, when the *York Daily Record* changed hands, the newspaper had been considered a conservative, pro-business publication, with a "hands off" policy toward Met Ed. During 1976 and 1977,

Table 14–2. Number of Three Mile Island Articles by Other Area Newspapers Found in Metropolitan Edison Files, 1976–1978

Newspapers	1976		1977		1978		Total	
	N	%	N	%	N	%	N	%
Middletown Press and Journal	22	(34.4)	8	(21.6)	41	(60.3)	71	(42)
Lancaster Intelligencer-Journal	19	(29.7)	9	(24.3)	9	(13.2)	37	(21.9)
York Daily Record	11	(17.1)	13	(35.1)	10	(14.7)	34	(20.1)
York Dispatch	12	(18.8)	7	(18.9)	8	(11.8)	27	(16)
Totals	64	(100.0)	37	(99.9)	68	(100.0)	169	(100.0)

there were eleven and thirteen articles published about TMI, most nearly verbatim versions of the weekly press releases. During 1978, under its new ownership, the newspaper published ten articles, bringing its total for the three-year period to thirty-four. It also adopted a more liberal policy and viewpoint, and its new executive editor was more in favor of investigation. This and several other factors resulted in a four-part series on problems at TMI, published two weeks before the accident.

The series was inspired by a statement from the Union of Concerned Scientists that a fire, such as the one that had occurred in Alabama at the Browns Ferry nuclear plant, could happen at TMI. The series also discussed radioactive waste, evacuation plans, economics, and health effects. However, the series never discussed the events reported in the weekly releases. The reporter who wrote the series said he had not known about them at the time.[32] Arguments of many of the antinuclear groups were presented, but they were balanced by extensive quotes from Met Ed officials. Even so, Met Ed was quite upset with the series, and eventually Walter Creitz, Met Ed president, wrote an op-ed piece (at the invitation of the paper's publisher) about TMI that assured everyone of the plant's safety. It appeared two days before the accident.

The *York Dispatch*, a much more conservative newspaper than the *Daily Record*, published twenty-seven TMI stories between 1976 and 1978, covering about half the major newsworthy events. Most of its articles were short and provided little information. However, when considering the relatively few TMI articles printed by the *York Daily Record* and the *York Dispatch*, thirty-four and twenty-seven, respectively, over a three-year period, one must take into account that York's electricity comes from Met Ed, while Harrisburg and Lancaster are served by another utility. Therefore, some TMI coverage may have been sacrificed in the York newspapers in order to cover non-nuclear Met Ed issues. According to reporters, people in York were more concerned about higher electricity costs and retroactive rate increases than safety issues at TMI.

Radio and Television Coverage

Small staffs, perceived public disinterest in nuclear power plants, and disinterest on the part of Met Ed in broadcast coverage resulted in minimal broadcast attention to TMI before the accident. News reports by radio and television stations focused on significant events in the pre-operational stages such as starting the nuclear reaction and placing the plant "online." Once TMI–2 was operating, little attention was given to safety matters, with the exception of the security violations that plagued TMI between 1974 and 1978. Rate matters, including petitions for increases, were considered by the broadcast media to be more news-worthy.

Broadcast reporters also complained about the Met Ed weekly press releases, saying they provided skeletal information and were repetitive and not timely. "They didn't make enough effort to explain the nature of problems. . . . Even if the problems were minor, there was no explanation of why they were minor, or what exactly was the nature of any given problem," said the news director of WNOW Radio in York.[33] As a result, broadcasters tended to discount the significance of the events in the releases. Most had the impression from the weekly releases that things were going exactly as expected and any problems were insignificant.

Broadcasters inquiring about plant problems received the same pat assurances as did press personnel. Hal German, former anchorman at WHP–TV in Harrisburg, explained that Met Ed answered questions in such a way that unless reporters knew what they were talking about, they could not follow them up. "Our questioning had to be right on the money. Nothing was volunteered."[34]

The number of weekly releases used by area broadcast stations ranged from one or two a year to many. Some stations appeared to make an effort to cover the antinuclear point of view by interviewing members of these groups and by covering issues involved in the licensing hearings. However, like the area newspaper reporters and editors, the broadcasters conceded they could have done a better job covering TMI.

Why Did Things Go Wrong?

Metropolitan Edison and the local media were both to blame for not keeping local residents properly informed about TMI before the accident. However, the practices they followed were not that different from those used elsewhere in the nation. Very few utilities in 1979 had emergency information plans and still fewer provided weekly press releases on the status of their reactors. Area newspapers and broadcast stations acted like others of similar size, faced with similar economic constraints and limited resources. This case study is representative of how science and other technical subjects get covered by small media outlets across the country. Of the numerous factors that affected the TMI situation, three are of overriding importance: complacency, size, and the lack of mutual understanding by engineers and reporters.

Complacency was prevalent in the citizens of the area, the utility, and the media. Citizens living nearby had been told that nuclear plants were safe, clean, efficient operations and an economic boon. The TMI facility had, in fact, helped bring some jobs to the area when a nearby air-force base had closed, and it had replaced a heavily polluting, coal-burning generating plant owned by Met Ed nearby. Also, nuclear power was not new to this region, since other nuclear plants were already operating downstream on the Susquehanna River at the Peach Bottom nuclear facility in York County. According to public opinion surveys done for the utility, only a few people objected to TMI or to nuclear plants in general.

The utility's complacency related primarily to operational matters and exemplified the feeling throughout the nuclear industry that nuclear power was very safe and that planning for evacuation and public information in case of a major accident was not needed. Most industry and government attention was focused not on a slowly building, long-term accident such as actually happened at TMI, but on a quick "loss of coolant accident." With the latter, the need to inform the public would have been after, nor during, the incident—as it had been with previous events such as the fire at Browns Ferry. Consequently, no one worried about developing a public information plan for use during an emergency.

The media's complacency related to their superficial reporting of TMI events described in the weekly press releases and to their use of very few, if any, outside information sources. It is hard to severely fault the region's media for not paying attention to the weekly releases; they believed the public was not interested in TMI, and the releases came in week after week noting something else wrong at the plant but assuring that the problems were not dangerous to the residents near the plant. Given the deadly sameness of the releases and the technical jargon, one could see how reporters and editors would not pay much attention to them.

What is less acceptable, however, was the news personnel's lack of any enterprise in seeking out information sources other than Met Ed to help them understand the jargon or the technicalities. Even though these reporters were not technology specialists, many of them had reported consistently about TMI, and they should have tried to develop sources who were impartial and willing to help them understand Met Ed information. Additionally, in much of their coverage the media followed Met Ed's lead on what should be reported about the plant, particularly in the "good news" articles. For a large portion of the time between 1976 and 1979, Met Ed helped set the media agenda for TMI coverage in the region.

Size, both of the utility and of the media outlets, was a second major factor in their failure to keep citizens aware of TMI events. In 1979 Met Ed was one of the smaller utilities in the nation, employing a much smaller work force than most. Its public relations staff of four writing professionals was nowhere near that of its neighboring utility, Pennsylvania Power & Light Company, which employed some fifteen professional writers. Perhaps also because of its size but probably due to other factors as well, Met Ed's executives had a very old-fashioned view of corporate public relations. They believed their information personnel should only write press releases and put out employee newsletters—that is, perform a publicity function. They appeared to be unaware of the high-level advisory role played by many public relations individuals regarding corporate policies. As a consequence, during the accident Met Ed officials had their public relations chief setting up plans for site facilities rather than providing the advice they desperately needed in order to deal with the mass media.

At the area's media outlets, both print and electronic, staffs were small, and none had the personnel, time, or financial resources to pursue topics for weeks or even days on end. They could not afford to have reporters poring over each week's list of reported events or nosing around in government document rooms to see what Met Ed had told the NRC. When the weekly releases came in, according to one editor, they were put on a stack that was about ten inches high every day. There was no time in a busy city room to ponder significance, he added.

These smaller media discouraged in-depth reporting, catering to a "hard news" format that presented the who, what, when, and where without much emphasis on the why and how. The need for a news peg or currency and short deadlines also dictated what was printed or broadcast. Interpretive and investigative reports, which require time to do and more than usual newspaper space or air time to present, were the exception rather than the rule. Had they been done more frequently, they would have helped clarify events and nuclear issues for both reporters and readers.

In addition, these small organizations did not have many specialty reporters, including science writers. Most of their work was done by general assignment reporters, jacks-of-all-topics. While a few newspapers and broadcast stations did have one person looking at Met Ed information, others assigned it to whoever was available at the time, thereby losing any chance for continuity of coverage.

Lack of mutual understanding between Met Ed engineers and reporters was the third important factor. The reporters, untrained in any field of science or technology, did not understand the engineer's language, nor did they pay much attention to scientific detail. In addition, their lack of specialized training probably held them back from developing scientific contacts at a state or national level to help them interpret technical information. This is a particularly serious concern even today in issues such as nuclear power, where each side has its "experts." Without some scientific background or assistance, it is very difficult for reporters to understand the technical issues relevant to thorough comprehension of a problem. Consequently, they have a tendency to play up political and legal issues, which are easier than technical ones to understand and relate to readers. This tendency certainly was evident in TMI coverage before the accident.

Met Ed made little effort to overcome the reporters' lack of technical knowledge by making its releases more understandable. In fact, the engineers who wrote the weekly releases did not even know there *was* a problem. One senior-level engineer was astounded when told that reporters did not understand the releases. He said there had never been any complaints about them and that the language was simple. (The Met Ed public information staff did know the releases were not being used, but they did not provide this feedback to the engineers.) By not bothering to find out what reporters could use and comprehend, the engineers contributed to the lack of understanding and undercut their own efforts to keep citizens informed about TMI.

In retrospect, neither Met Ed nor the media worked as hard as they should have on providing TMI information to the public. However, Met Ed is more at fault. Its public relations programs about TMI were misleading to both the media and the public, and its planning for emergency information needs was nonexistent.

Media representatives said they did not pay enough attention to detail, and they were right. Generally, they performed to a reasonable degree, but their reporting of TMI was uninspired and flaccid. With the exception of the *York Daily Record,* no newspaper or broadcast station went beyond adequate reporting to do what was required for excellent or even very good reporting. They did not make that extra effort that sets apart a truly good media organization from an average one—at least not on the coverage of TMI. That this situation is not uncommon at smaller media outlets throughout the country does not bode well for coverage of nuclear power or any other scientific or technical subject.

All these factors helped set the stage at TMI for a communications breakdown during a serious accident. And when that accident occurred, no one was prepared—not Met Ed, not the media, and certainly not the residents of the region.

An Update

The accident at Three Mile Island did not end when the TMI–2 reactor was shut down in 1979. Even today, so many issues still remain that many people consider the accident an ongoing event. In the years following the accident, questions over cleanup procedures for TMI–2, numerous hearings on restarting the undamaged TMI–1 reactor, various plans to finance the cleanup, lawsuits, operator cheating scandals, decisions by the Nuclear Regulatory Commission, antinuclear demonstrations, and congressional hearings all were of concern to area residents.

Had the local media learned any lessons from the accident and the media criticism that followed? Were they providing better coverage of TMI issues for area residents than they had before the accident?

A study of newspaper coverage of TMI during 1981 and 1982 in Harrisburg, Lancaster, and York found a major improvement in the quantity of articles being produced for citizens.[35] In all six newspapers studied, the number of articles had increased tenfold over that done before the accident. The total number of articles for the six newspapers was 1897 in 1981 and 1982, compared to 155 before the accident.

However, most of these articles still were straight news stories about events at TMI or reports or announcements by the utility, the Nuclear Regulatory Commission, antinuclear groups, and others involved in TMI activities. Few contained in-depth explanations or put events or issues into perspective for readers. There was very little investigation and the newspapers were still event-oriented, rarely following up stories.

General assignment or business reporters at four of the six newspapers had part-time TMI beats, spending more time on its coverage than they had before the accident. Only one reporter had any technical background, while one had taken a course in nuclear power operations when assigned to the beat. All the others had no scientific or technical background, and although there had been opportunities at five of the six newspapers to hire science writers to cover TMI, no editor had chosen to do so.

Use of news sources had improved considerably, but due more to the increased number of parties now involved in TMI issues and events than to newspaper enterprise. Still missing from the ranks of news sources were objective scientists and others not involved in the TMI controversy.

The utility operating TMI, now called GPU Nuclear, had improved its public information operation considerably. It had moved its offices onto the TMI site and increased the number of its professional employees, hiring experienced newspaper or television reporters. A public information emergency plan had been devised and was practiced during various drills by the utility. The TMI weekly releases that had been written by engineers were replaced with press releases prepared by professional writers when required by events. Most local reporters and editors now gave information staff members good grades, saying they were well versed in the issues, helpful, and very accessible. The reporters felt TMI press releases were accurate, understandable, and mostly free of technical jargon.

Considering all these factors, were complacency, size, and problems in understanding technical information still affecting coverage of TMI in

1981 and 1982? For the most part, the answer is yes, although to a lesser extent than before the accident. While the quantity of information had increased, providing area residents with considerably more coverage about TMI than before the accident, quality had not improved considerably. Because of the media's complacency, citizens were not getting enough in-depth information to help them understand the complex issues surrounding TMI. Size was still preventing the newspapers from devoting time or people to provide perspective for readers. And while understanding of nuclear terminology had improved to some extent, the reporters' lack of technical or scientific backgrounds was still hindering their performance and making them dependent on sources for technical explanations.

These six newspapers did learn to pay attention to nuclear plant problems and report about them in detail, and compared to other newspapers of their size, they are doing a better job in covering TMI and nuclear power issues in general. But they still fall down on the job in going beyond hard news reporting. As was said of their coverage before the accident, they still are not making that "extra effort that sets apart a truly good media organization from an average one."

Notes

1. An earlier version of this chapter appeared as "Blueprint for Breakdown: Three Mile Island and the Media Before the Accident," in *Journal of Communication* 31, no. 2 (Spring 1981): 116–128. Both versions are based on "Met Ed Public Relations: What the Public Knew About TMI Before the Accident," *Report of the Public's Right to Information Task Force, Staff Report to the President's Commission on the Accident at Three Mile Island* (Washington, D.C.: Government Printing Office, 1979), 29–46; and a 150-page unpublished report of the same title, filed in the U.S. National Archives.

2. Nancy C. Joyce, an information specialist with the President's Commission on the Accident at TMI, served as a research associate for this study, interviewing broadcast personnel and citizens in the TMI area. She also reviewed many subpoenaed documents, surveyed TMI coverage by the Harrisburg newspapers, and helped analyze Metropolitan Edison's community relations program.

3. Information on Metropolitan Edison's public information programs was gathered from subpoenaed utility documents. Thirteen employees of Metropolitan Edison and its parent corporation, General Public Utilities, were interviewed, including all professional members of the public relations staffs and key engineers involved in TMI information policies and programs. Thirteen members of antinuclear groups and area citizens provided additional information, as did industrial trade groups and other utilities.

4. Ernest Schleicher, Metropolitan Edison vice president for consumer affairs. Personal interview, July 26, 1979.

5. President's Commission on the Accident at Three Mile Island. Transcript of the Public's Right to Information Task Force interview with Blaine Fabian, manager of communications services, Metropolitan Edison, Summer 1979, pp. 58, 109.

6. Metropolitan Edison. "Preparation, Approval, and Release of Public Announcements Concerning Generation Stations." GP0021, Revision 2, 1978, p. 3.

7. Metropolitan Edison. "Three Mile Island Site Emergency Plan 1004." Section 2, Revision 2, February 15, 1978, p. 13.1.

8. Metropolitan Edison. "Station Health Physics Procedure 1670.13, vol. 1, Emergency Plans and Procedures, Release of Information to the Public." Three Mile Island Nuclear Station, Revision 1, June 23, 1977, p. 1.

9. Metropolitan Edison. Press Release no. 61–78c, April 28, 1978; Press Release no. 70–78c, May 12, 1978.

10. Metropolitan Edison. Press Release no. 81–78c, May 26, 1978.

11. Metropolitan Edison. Press Release no. 92–78c, June 23, 1978. Licensee Event Report (LER) Output on Events at Three Mile Island 1 and 2 from 1969 to Present, Nuclear Regulatory Commission. Docket no. 05000320, LER no. 78–033/01T–0, Event Date, 4/23/78, Report Date, 5/8/78, p. 72.

12. Metropolitan Edison. Press Release no. 66–78c, May 5, 1978. LER Output on Events at Three Mile Island 1 and 2 from 1969 to the Present, Nuclear Regulatory Commission. Docket no. 05000320, LER no. 78–021/03L–0, Event Date, 3/29/78, Report Date, 5/1/78, p. 70.

13. Robert Arnold, Metropolitan Edison senior vice president. Personal telephone interview, August 1, 1979.

14. Michael L. Bancroft, Robert B. Stulberg, and Robert McIntyre, "Death and Taxes: An Investigation of the Initial Operation of Three Mile Island No. 2," Public Citizen, Washington, D.C., April 5, 1979, p. 1. Ernest Schreiber and David Osterhout, "3-Mile Plant Had 36 Problems in 6-Month Period Before Accident," Lancaster New Era, April 7, 1979, pp. 1–2. Rod Nordlund, "Workers Talk of 'Rush Job' in 3 Mile Island Preparation," Philadelphia Inquirer, April 16, 1979, pp. 1 and 6.

15. William Gross, supervisor of information, Metropolitan Edison. Personal interview, July 18, 1979.

16. Ibid.

17. Metropolitan Edison. "Nuclear Power—Building a Better Tomorrow." Speech–slide show, 1972.

18. Max Frye, York citizen. Telephone interview with Nancy Joyce, July 1979. Personal telephone interview, April 1980.

19. Metropolitan Edison. "Your Personal Radiation Inventory," Flier, no date.

20. Christopher Sayer, Lee Musselman, and Kay Pickering, members, Three Mile Island Alert. Personal interview, July 17, 1979.

21. Middletown League of Women Voters. Interview of six members with Nancy Joyce, July 20, 1979.

22. Twenty-three newspaper reporters and editors and thirteen radio and television reporters and news directors were interviewed individually or occasionally in groups. Articles on TMI from the *Harrisburg Patriot* and *Evening News* from 1977 to 1979 were reviewed using clipping files from the newspapers' library, as were clippings of nuclear power stories not related to TMI from wire services and syndicates. TMI articles from four other area newspapers were evaluated using clipping files subpoenaed from Metropolitan Edison. While these files may have been incomplete, time constraints on the study prevented any further review.

23. Patrick Carroll, city editor, *Harrisburg Patriot*. Personal interview, July 19, 1979.

24. William Schultz, editor, and Charles Shaw, reporter, *Lancaster Intelligencer-Journal*. Personal interview, July 20, 1979.

25. Dale Davenport, city editor, *Harrisburg Evening News*. Personal interview, July 17, 1979.

26. Wiley Brooks, executive editor, Kathryn Duncan, city editor, and James Hill, reporter, *York Daily Record*. Personal interview, July 19, 1979.

27. Saul Kohler, executive editor, *Harrisburg Patriot-News*. Personal interview, July 19, 1979.

28. Dale Davenport, op. cit.

29. William Schultz and Charles Shaw, op. cit.

30. Ibid. Also Daniel Cherry, editor, Robert Kozak, news editor, and Charles Kessler, Ernest Schreiber, and Timothy McKeel, reporters, *Lancaster New Era*. Personal interview, July 20, 1979.

31. Because of problems encountered in viewing wire service and syndicated articles on nuclear power in the library of the Harrisburg newspapers, the number of articles reviewed is only approximate.

32. Wiley Brooks, Kathryn Duncan, and James Hill, op. cit.

33. Jerry Edling, news director, WNOW Radio, York. Interview with Nancy Joyce, July 19, 1979.

34. Hal German, producer/anchor, WHP–TV, Harrisburg. Interview with Nancy Joyce, July 20, 1979.

35. Sharon M. Friedman, "Environmental Reporting: Before and After TMI," *Environment* 26, no. 10 (December 1984): 4–5, 34.

CHAPTER 15

Not Just Another Day in the Newsroom: The Accident at TMI

Ann Marie Cunningham

In a companion piece to the preceding chapter, Ann Marie
Cunningham describes the confusion that characterized reporters'
attempts to get information and sources' attempts to provide it during
the accident at Three Mile Island. She examines why the information
process broke down.

Ann Marie Cunningham was on the staff of the Task Force on the
Public's Right to Information of the President's Commission on the
Accident at Three Mile Island. She interviewed foreign and American
journalists who covered the accident and public information officers
who worked with them. Currently a freelance investigative reporter
who frequently writes about nuclear issues, she is the coauthor of two
books about new technology, *The Technopeasant Survival Manual*
and *Future Fire: Weapons for the Apocalypse.* Her articles have
appeared in many publications, and she is a contributing editor of
Nuclear Times magazine. She also is coeditor of a collection of essays
on how the press covers nuclear weapons and arms talks.

Even BEFORE THE 1979 ACCIDENT at the Three Mile Island nuclear power
plant operated by Metropolitan Edison (Met Ed) near Harrisburg, Pennsylvania, many journalists were familiar with the history and issues of

the debate over nuclear power. One study by the Battelle Human Affairs Research Center, for example, estimates that there was a 400 percent increase in print media coverage of nuclear power issues between 1972 and 1976. But covering Three Mile Island posed new and different problems.[1]

For the first time, reporters had to cover a potentially serious nuclear plant accident as it was happening. Past accidents—none as serious as TMI—had ended before the media were fully aware of the problem. Coverage of accidents such as the 1975 fire at the Browns Ferry plant in Alabama was largely retrospective, lacking the drama and urgency of breaking news. In contrast, news from Three Mile Island broke on the front page over several days; the unfolding situation at the plant actually appeared more serious on the fourth day of the accident than it had on the first.

A Brief Chronology

The accident began in the early hours of Wednesday morning, March 28, 1979, but local residents did not learn about it until 8:25 a.m., when a local radio station broadcast that a general emergency had been declared at the plant. Met Ed's declaration of a general emergency set the tone for public information dissemination that characterized the accident: neither it nor any other of the groups involved, such as the Nuclear Regulatory Commission (NRC) or Pennsylvania state officials, explained clearly what a general emergency meant—that radiation had been released beyond the boundaries of the plant site and represented a risk to public health. Much of the news on the first day of the accident consisted of contradictory statements from various individuals within the utility and the NRC, state officials, and scientists over how much radiation had been measured off-site, how much damage the reactor core had sustained, and what had caused the accident.

On Wednesday evening, Met Ed announced that it had succeeded in starting a reactor coolant pump and that the plant was under control. Thursday, things indeed did appear under control on the surface. However, Met Ed and the NRC were embroiled behind the scenes in a conflict over dumping approximately 400,000 gallons of industrial waste water, slightly contaminated with radioactivity, into the Susquehanna River. Confusion and misinformation about the dumping (the utility did not inform the media about it until ten hours later) badly damaged the utility's already weakened credibility with reporters and contributed to their impression that the accident was more dangerous to the public than Met Ed maintained.

On Friday, two new developments seemed to indicate that the accident was far from under control. In the early morning, Met Ed released a 1200-millirem burst of radioactivity into the atmosphere. Confusion at the NRC about the nature of the release and the amount of radioactivity led Pennsylvania's governor to order a precautionary evacuation of pregnant women and very young children within a 5-mile radius of the plant. Later on Friday, the NRC announced that there was a large bubble of hydrogen gas in the top of the reactor vessel. NRC and Met Ed officials at the TMI site disagreed with officials at the NRC headquarters in Bethesda, Maryland, over the bubble's potential dangerousness—specifically, whether it might contribute to a meltdown. By Saturday evening, officials at Bethesda were saying the bubble might explode, but the on-site utility and NRC representatives seriously disagreed: they saw no immediate danger.

On Sunday, in an effort to calm the public, President Jimmy Carter visited the plant. On Monday, the NRC confirmed the utility's report that the bubble had shrunk, and finally, on Tuesday, April 3, the NRC announced that the risk of the bubble's exploding no longer existed. [2]

Public Information Officials: Confused Sources

Instead of remaining a regional story, TMI almost immediately became a national and international drama that attracted a worldwide press corps numbering at any time from 300 to 500 journalists. NRC and Met Ed officials were besieged with inquiries almost as soon as the news media learned that a general emergency had been declared at the plant site. Reporters arrived in three waves. The first on the scene, on Wednesday, March 28, were not regulars on science and technology beats but either general assignment reporters who happened to be available or "firemen," reporters with reputations for covering breaking stories efficiently. By the second day of the accident, editors realized the magnitude and complexity of the story and began to dispatch their science and technology specialists. By the third and fourth days, reporters had begun to arrive from abroad, many from countries with heavy investments in nuclear power. They included press from Spain, Great Britain, Japan, France, West Germany, Sweden, and Italy.

Once at the TMI site, both reporters and public information officers had to operate under conditions that made it almost impossible for adequate news reports to reach the public. The public information problems of Met Ed and the NRC were rooted in lack of planning. Neither expected that an accident of this magnitude—one that went on for days, requiring evacuation planning—would ever happen. In a sense they were victims of their own reassurances about the safety of nuclear power. As a result, neither had an emergency public information plan. Neither had personnel trained in disaster public relations. Coordination between the utility and the NRC was so weak that neither knew who was responsible for informing the public in the first crucial hours of the accident. For example, the NRC did not know whether to send its own public information people to the site or when or where to set up an NRC press center.

Met Ed's public information department had occupied a low rung within the corporation and had had no voice in policy before the accident. It had never dealt with a national press corps and was inexperienced at fielding specific questions about nuclear power from critics or probing journalists. The utility also lacked an appropriate spokesperson during the accident.

Perhaps the most serious failure in planning was that neither the utility nor the NRC made any provision for transmitting information from those who had it—in the control room or elsewhere on site—to those who needed it to manage the accident or to make decisions about the evacuation. Those who needed this vital information included other utility executives, the governor of Pennsylvania, the NRC's Incident Response Center in Bethesda, public information officials, journalists, and the public.

Met Ed officials at company headquarters in Reading, Pennsylvania, or officials at the parent company, General Public Utilities (GPU) in New Jersey, often did not know what employees at the crippled plant knew. NRC officials and engineers at the Bethesda center, which dealt with nuclear "events" throughout the country, did not know what their colleagues in the Region One office in King of Prussia, Pennsylvania, knew. (TMI is in Region One's territory, and Met Ed personnel generally reported to NRC officials there.) Neither of the NRC offices knew what Met Ed was planning. These fundamental communication problems proved particularly damaging to Met Ed because the inadequate flow of information was often mistaken by journalists for intentional coverup. On Wednesday morning, for example, while Met Ed president Walter Creitz was telling some reporters that there had been small off-site radiation releases, Met Ed public information officials in the same building, who did not know what Creitz knew, were telling reporters there had been none. This negligence in passing information along to staff dealing with the press was one reason why the utility lost credibility early in the accident. In addition, the NRC made little effort until the sixth day of the accident to supply the media with technical briefers who could answer complex questions. Both the NRC and the utility left reporters pretty much to their own devices.

The Working Press on the Scene

Given this confusion among sources and given that reporters were almost entirely dependent on such sources for their information, it is not surprising that media coverage of the accident in the first few days also was confused. A reporter with no particular nuclear expertise who arrived at TMI on the afternoon of the first day of the accident, Wednesday, March 28, found no central Met Ed information facility. No one was distributing schematics of the plant or answering basic technical questions about the reactor. No one was describing what a general emergency was or why it was important. There was no central or good source of up-to-date information about radiation—not on Wednesday and not on any day during the first week, when this was, arguably, the most crucial information the public required. There were no telephones for reporters.

The utility was answering phone queries from its Reading headquarters, nearly sixty miles from the site, but the information being dispensed was late, and, as things turned out, much too optimistic about conditions inside the plant. There was no official spokesman for Met Ed until John Herbein, vice president for generation, took on the role at an impromptu press conference early Wednesday afternoon. Herbein made no effort to translate his engineering expertise and jargon for reporters, and no transcript was made of his remarks to aid reporters or Met Ed public information staff who missed the press conference.

The situation was no better for those reporters who tried to reach the NRC's Region One Office in King of Prussia, or the agency's Incident Response Center in Bethesda, or the NRC's chief public information officer in downtown Washington, D.C. These people had almost as much difficulty obtaining up-to-date information from the site as did Met Ed's public information staff, and no effort was made to coordinate information among NRC staff who were dispensing it to reporters. Complicating matters further, some members of Congress were receiving different, often more speculative and pessimistic reports from the NRC on such subjects as damage to the nuclear core and errors made by the operators of the nuclear plant. Reporters who had not received this information heard it secondhand from congressional sources. One result was that reporters became suspicious of information they got from Met Ed and from NRC officials on-site. The NRC made no effort to coordinate information going to Congress with that going to the news media.

What, then, was a journalist during the first two days of the accident collecting? Generally, all that was available were fragmentary and often contradictory bits of information from a variety of uncoordinated sources. Often reporters fed the fragments they got from one source to other sources ignorant of the information, so that reporters were, in a sense, briefing information officers with what they heard elsewhere. For example, the utility's chief public information officer learned from a reporter that a general emergency had been declared at the plant site on Wednesday morning. He should have been given this information immediately by the plant operators for dissemination to the press.

In the information vacuum created by primary sources at TMI, many journalists responded with initiative. Peter Stoler of *Time*, for example, suspecting that the utility was having bigger problems than it was admitting, went to a library in nearby Harrisburg to check a metallurgy text for the temperature at which zirconium cladding on nuclear fuel rods melts. Ben Livingood of the *Allentown Morning Call* teamed up with another *Call* reporter, Gary Sanborn, who had been a reactor operator in the Navy aboard the U.S.S. *Enterprise*. Sanborn could interpret the technical language used by Herbein, and he prompted Livingood to ask the right questions.

However, for a number of issues during the accident—such as the danger posed by the hydrogen bubble or the size of the radiation release that prompted the partial evacuation of nearby communities on Friday—the only type of accurate reporting possible under the circumstances was to present the contradictory statements of a variety of officials.

The news media, like their sources, also were unprepared. Few—though by no means all—who covered TMI had more than a rudimentary knowledge of nuclear power. Some, by their own admission, did not know how a pressurized light water nuclear reactor worked or what a meltdown was. Few knew what questions to ask about radiation releases so that their reports could help the public evaluate health risks.

But some reporters with regular science or energy beats were assigned to the story, such as John Fialka of the *Washington Star*, Richard Lyons of *The New York Times*, and Paul Hayes of the *Milwaukee Journal*. The *Chicago Tribune* sent Casey Bukro, who had written on environmental issues since 1967 and had visited all seven of the nuclear plants operating in Illinois. Stuart Diamond of *Newsday* had made nuclear power one of his specialties and had produced, by his own estimate, perhaps a thousand stories on nuclear power for the newspaper. *Time*'s Stoler had spent nine years specializing in science, the environment, and medicine; in 1978, he had traveled to the Soviet Union on a tour sponsored by the Atomic Industrial Forum to study nuclear energy in that country. Jonathan Ward, the CBS producer in charge of the network's coverage at the site, and CBS reporter Robert Schakne had been working for a year to compile a dossier on every operating nuclear power plant in the country. (Unfortunately, they had not yet investigated TMI.) Ward also had produced stories on decontamination and radioactive waste disposal.

But even for journalists familiar with nuclear power, the effort required to make sense of the story was enormous. It was not like covering a political campaign or an airplane hijacking, when at least the vocabulary of the sources and the vocabulary of the reporters are the same.

The nuclear industry had developed its own language, and this was a handicap for the many journalists who did not speak it. A seemingly simple question from reporters about whether the core of the reactor had been uncovered and damaged elicited responses couched in terms of "ruptured fuel pins," "pinholes in the cladding," "melted cladding," "cladding oxidation," "failed fuel," "fuel damage," "fuel oxidation," "structural fuel damage," or "core melt." The technical distinctions between these terms are real, but for reporters who did not speak the language, covering TMI was like suffering from color blindness at a watercolor exhibition.

William Dornsife, a nuclear engineer with the Pennsylvania Bureau of Radiation Protection, described the language barrier from his side: "It's difficult for an engineer to respond to a technical question with anything but a technical answer. And I knew by the questions I was getting back that the press people just didn't understand what was going on." Robert Bernero, the NRC's assistant director for material safety standards, functioned as a technical briefer for the NRC at its press center in Middletown beginning on the sixth day of the accident and was one of the few technicians at the agency who could communicate with the press and the public. He said the root of the problem was that "many technical people don't like public affairs. And they can be less than constructive because they frequently become apprehensive about what they are saying and retreat to the shelter of technical language. And then they can say (if misquoted), 'I said exactly what I would say in writing a technical report.' "

Neither the NRC nor Met Ed provided enough technical briefers in the first five days of the accident to help journalists interpret what they were being told. When Bernero arrived on the sixth day of the accident, he was surprised by the number of reporters who still needed his basic briefing on how the reactor worked. Reporters also found Harold Denton, the NRC's director of nuclear reactor regulation, less than satisfactory. Denton went to the site on Friday, the third day, to help manage the recovery operation and became the agency's chief spokesman. According to Bukro of the Chicago Tribune, "Denton was the hero of Harrisburg because he was the only one talking. But he should learn to talk English like the rest of us."

Reporters also arrived at TMI with different objectives. Some were science writers with an interest in the reactor itself. Some were medical writers with an interest in public health and safety. Others were sent to write "color" stories and focus on reactions of citizens and evacuees.

And some reporters had been awaiting this type of accident because of the way the nuclear industry had aggressively sold its safety record. "For twenty years," said Stuart Diamond of *Newsday,* "the nuclear industry has pointed to its chin and said, 'Hit me right here, brother.' I think they set themselves up for a fail." National Public Radio's science reporter Ira Flatow echoed Diamond's sentiments: "We knew nuclear power was on trial at Three Mile Island, and we knew it was losing."

Why the Public's Right to Know Was Not Served

A number of factors contributed to the communications chaos during the TMI accident. Beyond those already discussed, one that must be considered is the different goals of the reporters and the engineers. The journalists had a blunt and uncompromising view of what the public has a right to know during an accident—everything, as soon as it is available. But the engineers' priorities centered on getting the reactor under control first and communicating their actions later. Some engineers also were concerned with protecting their colleagues, their utility, and the nuclear industry. As a result, certain kinds of information were slow to reach the news media and the public. A close examination of utility and NRC press releases and public statements during the first few days showed their reluctance to discuss operator error as a cause of the accident, blaming it instead on equipment malfunction. Utility officials minimized the extent of damage to the reactor core, and they were not forthcoming about the present (and the likelihood of future) radiation releases beyond the plant's boundaries. In light of what was known at the time, their early statements to the media on radiation releases and core damage were sketchy and misleading.

The NRC's behavior is more difficult to characterize. Along with antinuclear groups, some NRC officials provided the news media with some of the most frightening information during the accident. On the other hand, the commissioners who led the NRC were frequently less candid than their own staff. While there is no unambiguous evidence of coverup, some NRC officials, like those from Met Ed, showed a marked capacity for self-deception, while others hid behind technical jargon to obscure answers to troublesome questions.

The complexity of the accident and the many needs of the reporters covering it would have made it difficult for even an ideal public information program to function properly. Given the information program in place when reporters arrived, it proved an impossibility.

While the media can be criticized for missing some stories and failing to provide context for others, they were generally not guilty of the most common criticism leveled at them: that they presented an overwhelmingly alarming view of the accident. Headlines throughout the first week of the accident were actually more sober than the confusion at the site and within the NRC warranted.

During the accident, neither Met Ed or NRC public information officials nor journalists got word of events to the public in an effective or prompt manner—something that must be achieved in the event of future accidents. Each side failed for different reasons, and to a different degree. The most common explanations—that the utility lied, that the NRC covered up to protect the nuclear industry, or that the media engaged in an orgy of sensationalism—do not hit the mark. Indeed, reporters often showed great skill in piecing together the story, and some NRC officials disclosed information that was truly alarming and damaging to the industry's image because they thought the public had a right to know about it. Even the utility's shortcomings in the public information area—and they were many—are attributable to self-deception as well as a lack of candor. Given the enormous investment at stake for Met Ed, the company's unwillingness to recognize the severity of damage to the reactor is not surprising.

One positive result of the TMI experience is that reporters and nuclear engineers were introduced to each other's problems, needs, and peculiarities. Nuclear experts should now realize that technical language, which to them offers precision and economy of expression, can be maddeningly opaque when aimed at reporters under deadline pressure. Instead of leading to more accurate stories, technical language can produce ambiguity, confusion, and frustration.

To the extent that journalists learn about nuclear technology and develop a standard of comparison for future accidents, they can help reduce the confusion that surrounds such accidents. But a major and initial burden in the area of public information falls on those who operate and regulate the nuclear plants.

Many lessons can be learned from the accident at TMI, but one of the most important is that all parties need to know more about each other's needs and goals in order to serve the public's right to know in the future.

Notes

1.   This chapter is based on the *Report of the Public's Right to Information Task Force, Staff Report to the President's Commission on the Accident at Three Mile Island* (Washington, D.C.: Government Printing Office, 1979). I thank my thirteen fellow task force members, who helped interview reporters and public information officers who were on the scene during and immediately after the accident.

2. For a more complete chronology of the accident and the events that followed, see *Report of the President's Commission on the Accident at Three Mile Island, The Need for Change: The Legacy of TMI* (Washington, D.C.: Government Printing Office, 1979); Daniel F. Ford, *TMI: Thirty Minutes to Meltdown* (New York: Penguin, 1982); Mike Gray and Ira Rose, *The Warning: Accident at TMI* (New York: W. W. Norton, 1982); and Mark Stephens, *Three Mile Island* (New York: Random House, 1980).

PART IV

Talking to the Public: Scientists in the Media

MORE OFTEN THAN EVER BEFORE, scientists are actively communicating directly with the public. In Part IV, three scientists who have taken on this role in three very different ways share their experiences. And immediately afterward, in Appendix A, we reprint a guide for other scientists who might be interested in either working more effectively with the media or communicating directly with the public.

CHAPTER 16

Both Sides of the Fence: The Scientist as Source and Author

Stephen H. Schneider

Although the most frequent role for a scientist in the science communication process is that of an information source for journalists, a growing number of scientists are becoming public communicators themselves. Stephen Schneider fills both roles, as source and communicator, and in this chapter he suggests strategies for surviving and thriving in this dual capacity.

Stephen Schneider is head of the Visitors Program and deputy director of the Advanced Study Program at the National Center for Atmospheric Research in Boulder, Colorado. He has written three popular science books, coedited several others, and appeared on numerous television shows. Additionally, he has written some 100 scientific papers, proceedings, legislative testimonies, and book chapters. The editor of *Climatic Change,* he is a member of numerous national and international committees on climate, food, water, energy, and environmental and societal issues. Most recently he has been involved in research on the problem of "nuclear winter."

How—AND WHY—DOES A SCIENTIST one day find himself or herself both a source and author of science information for the public? There are, no doubt, many different answers. I'll offer mine from the perspective of personal experience. My initial moment as a source occurred early in my first postdoctoral year, when a Radio Sweden reporter found me at an international meeting, backed me against a locked door, stuck a microphone in my face, and asked, "Dr. Schneider, you have said in a recent paper that human pollution will [actually, I had said "could"] bring on the next ice age. So when will it begin?" I no longer recall how I answered that question, but I vividly remember my feelings: fright, exhilaration, and a (somewhat overblown) sense of self-importance. I also learned from this first loss of scientific innocence that being interviewed poses a substantial element of hide-and-seek between a reporter looking for juicy quotes and a scientist trying to minimize damage to his reputation from oversimple public pronouncements or outright media distortion. The game viewed from my side is simple enough, although the solution is difficult: try to say something with sufficient impact to keep me in the story which at the same time will keep me in my job. Steering a safe course between scientific respectability and good copy isn't easy, particularly for a young scientist. It's even tougher when the pen—or editing pencil—is not in your own hand.

It was, ironically, several additional encounters as a source that ultimately led me to become an author. At the center where I work we have a public information office that has a clipping service. Every time my institution's name appears in one of several hundred newspapers or journals, we receive a clipping. In addition, every six to eight weeks the public information office compiles all these clippings and mails them out to a rather sizable fraction of the atmospheric science research community. About ten years ago I got an eye-opening lesson in the perils of being a young—that is, pre-tenure—source of public science. At an AAAS conference I delivered a paper on some possible inadvertent effects of human pollution on climate. Unknown to me, the distinguished silver-haired gentleman sitting near the front taking careful notes was Walter Sullivan of *The New York Times*. Although the story that later appeared was both responsible and a great delight to my New York City relatives, its trail across the country left me truly shocked. At first things went fine. In addition to the *Times'* use of the article, several other newspapers picked up the story within a few days of its initial publication. These not only acknowledged the source, but they also included Sullivan's byline. Perhaps a dozen other publications condensed or paraphrased the story, attributing much of it to Sullivan and the *Times*.

Then, things began to change as clippings of variously edited versions of Sullivan's story came out of the hinterlands. By the time some newspapers were finished, bylines of local reporters had appeared and Sullivan's role had vanished. One newspaper, in a drought-prone area of the Great Plains, had even changed Sullivan's emphasis on weather modification to a distorted story on water modification. Ultimately, I learned that even good stories pose risks after one of my colleagues posted this last, distorted clipping on the door of the weather map room where nearly everyone could see it.

Paraphrases of the source by the reporter—or by another newspaper—are often believed by the scientist's colleagues to be accurate reflections of his statements; implications and conclusions of the story are, likewise, usually assumed to be coincident with the source's views. Thus, only a few bad stories can cause a lot of damage to a source. Because of this bad early experience and several similar ones over the next half-dozen years, I eventually concluded that there were only two ways I could ever expect my colleagues to get a fully balanced account of the totality and tone of my public statements: (1) send them all the diverse and sometimes contradictory clippings put together, since, *taken together,* the ensemble of stories coming in from our clipping service almost always yielded something close to what I had said; or (2) do my own writing and be responsible for it. Since the former was difficult to achieve, I chose to do my own books.

From Source to Author, and Back Again

I discovered two things in the wake of writing and promoting my first book. First, those who don't like the idea of popularizing by scientists will take any opportunity to discredit the popularizer. Second, the message of most scientists who do their own writing is really not carried to the general public by his or her own words (with the rare exception of a Carl Sagan or a Margaret Mead); rather, its transmission still is dependent on science journalists. In this case, the reporters write stories based on the scientist's writings rather than taking the usual route of a personal interview.

There are probably two generalizations I can make from my experiences in dealing with journalists. First, science journalists almost always do a better job of "getting the story straight" than general assignment reporters sent out into what many perceive as the intimidating—or dull—science beat. Second, in my field at least, the quality of science writing from the hard core of full-time science writers who regularly attend the annual meeting of the AAAS has improved immensely since the early 1970s. Indeed, some reporters have become so sharp in climatology that they can even quote back to me previous years' statements which were slightly different from this year's, wanting to know why things have changed. Reporters with such a steep learning curve tend to be those who call up to check back with me to be sure that the facts of their story accurately reflect my views. Over time I've learned whom I can trust. These reporters get juicier quotes simply because they can be relied on to put such statements in a context that doesn't do violence to the balance of my own views. Ironically, as mentioned earlier, I've found that my popular writings have primarily helped to inform this group of reporters and thus have helped improve the general quality of stories on weather and climate they write. These journalists, more than I, have communicated my written ideas to lay audiences. My attempt to break into the scientist-as-author category has merely reinforced my initial role as a source.

Controlling the Interview: Finding the Compromise

While most scientists' roles as popular authors cannot really be separated from their roles as scientific sources because their books have their primary impact on the public through the science press rather than directly, some practical distinctions can be made between the role of scientist as source and scientist as author. Let's discuss the source role first.

As a source, I have come to realize that a journalist who interviews a scientist often is stuck between an editor demanding a jazzy news peg or a dramatic storyline and a source hoping to put his best scientific face forward, with "best" defined within the value system of the scientist's colleagues. Often, what impresses these colleagues is of little interest (or use) to lay persons grappling with their own scientific illiteracy.

After a decade of experience, I have developed several strategies as a source. First, I try to anticipate what I believe the public wants—and needs—to know about atmospheric science problems. Rather than stress my own work in interviews, I generally try to present a broad overview of the entire field with very little specialized detail; then, later on, I hone in on the particular specifics to which my own research contributions may be relevant. At first this was resented by many of my colleagues as taking credit for other scientists' work, but by now most of my peers have become used to me as a self-ordained "mouthpiece" for the field, and thus they expect me to describe more than my own work in interviews, and they even encourage me—as long as the product isn't too wild.

Second, I try to get a reporter to include in a story some notion of the longer-term, global-scale, policy implications of scientific research, and the recognition that public decisions to deal with these issues are *value judgments* for which scientific expertise is only an input, not a special license to choose for society how to act. I admit that I often bring these policy issues in, even though I may not be asked about them in an interview. However, I feel that being a source is a two-way street: the reporter is getting information that can help lead to a credible story, and I am getting public exposure for ideas that I think are important and for which the media are my best routes to the public. While I never expect a writer to hammer out a story that reflects all—or even most—of what I want said, I do expect that at least some of the material I want aired will appear. Very often, and particularly with veteran science reporters who understand the interplay involved, we both seem pleased with a compromise outcome.

Third, I use analogies and metaphors that are common to the experience of most readers but don't do violence to the scientific content that the metaphor is to illustrate. Economic analogies—in particular, personal budgets—are very useful in my field of climatology.

Some Tough Standards for the Scientist-as-Author

Except when I am writing very narrowly about those subjects in which I have research experience, I, too, am a science journalist in my popular writings. Yet there is a difference, for I believe that the scientist-author has special standards to maintain. For example, my book-writing technique usually involves at least four drafts. The first one or two are negotiated between myself and a coauthor, typically a science writer. Third drafts follow after consideration of comments from sharp, close friends—typically my graduate students and postdoctoral fellows. Then the third-draft chapters go out to perhaps a dozen outside scientists who are experts in the diverse fields from whose work I have drawn. I ask them to be tolerant of the popular purpose of the book but to be brutal in order to keep me honest in their respective disciplines.

The other side of this coin is that my nonclimatologist manuscript critics can send me their writings containing climatic components, and I do for them what they've done for me. Over the years I have built up a network of such contacts in a variety of fields, and I feel that these critics of my journalistic activities distinguish science writing by a scientist from science writing by most nonexperts.

There are other distinctions as well. For instance, I firmly believe that it is not sufficient to simply put down a quote or two from scientist A and an opposite set of views from scientist B, judging that my obligation for fairness to the reader is met. I feel that the public expects me as a scientist to do more than quote fairly the differing views of other scientists; I also should provide an assessment of the worth of these views. *If I repeat in print someone else's opinion without criticism or comment, then it has implicitly become my opinion.* After all, am I not supposed to be in a better position to judge the validity of other scientists' opinions than the lay reader? That may not always be true, but I believe it to be a widespread perception of lay readers of books by scientists.

In contrast, most science journalists present opinions of various scientists fairly, often juxtaposing one extreme view against another. Occasionally, a journalistic author takes sides, but this is not enough. The public needs to know not only which extreme expert is at the throat of which counterpart but also something about the *spectrum of scientific opinion* on the subject, with some indication of where extremes fit on that spectrum. People need a sense of the *likelihood* that any scientific opinion might be correct, and they should be told of the possibility that we can't tell yet who is correct or if indeed any of the present theories might ever prove right. There are exceptions, of course, but most popular scientific writings by journalists don't go far enough to give a true sense of the spectrum of scientific opinions on an issue, nor do they offer probabilities as to who might be right or even discuss what it will take to resolve the uncertainties.

On the other side, many scientist-popularizers are not very interesting storytellers or are not very good writers. Even if they correctly describe the spectrum of opinion in their field, they may be doing it to an audience of a few hundred specialized or professionally interested readers. Of course, there are a few notable exceptions, such as those scientist-authors who tend to get on the best-seller list and command large public followings.

Trial by Television

Finally, let me come to a point where "scientist as author" merges with "scientist as source": television and radio appearances. Whether pushed into the electronic media by one's publisher or invited by the networks, scientists who write popular books often have a surprisingly easy time getting such media appearances. For me, few things are more frustrating than having to condense 500 meaty pages into 500 words that must include two good jokes and one dramatic conclusion. However, such talk-show appearances have at least one distinct plus: you live by your wits and what is said is not paraphrased, misquoted, distorted, or interpreted, for what you say is what the viewer gets. If things go wrong, it is probably your fault.

One also may be involved in serious interviews on film or tape by serious evening news reporters or feature media journalists. These may be less frustrating encounters than entertainment shows but present the same risks for a scientist as do interviews with the print media: journalists can paraphrase and select quotes.

Like print interviews, those on television require simple statements of complex materials and are helped by everyday metaphors. To communicate successfully one learns to fashion carefully worded—yet suffi-ciently dramatic—quotable quotes. The primary difference between the studio and the notepad interview is the pressure: the camera catches your eyes, your twitches, your crumpled suit, your uncertainty, and your five o'clock shadow. Perhaps these added stresses help to explain why only a relatively small number of scientists are interviewed and reinter-viewed on a variety of scientific subjects on television. Print journalists, on the other hand, can draw from a much wider pool of scientific tal-ent for their sources, since a scientist's nervous demeanor or other appearance-related aspects do not matter. The scientist can be laun-dered by the pen of the writer.

Scientists and Journalists: Partners in Communication

In summary, then, my views from both sides of the fence are surprisingly similar: the scientist-as-source and scientist-as-author are usually not very independent roles. The public learns about most of a scientist's popular writings through journalists who report on them rather than through firsthand reading of the scientist's own words—with a few spec-tacular, best-selling exceptions.

However, there are differences between these roles, too, since I believe the scientist-as-writer has the obligation to provide readers with critical evaluation of the spectrum of scientific views in his or her field—and the likelihood of their validity. The scientist-as-source is less obliged to fashion such broad perspectives and more constrained by the narrower subjects imposed by the interviewer. However, I believe that the source should still go beyond the narrow technical questions and of-fer some overview and implications of his or her work—assuming, of course, that the source has thought seriously and read widely about such implications and isn't merely talking off the top of his or her head!

Scientists-as-writers emphasize those points they believe the public should know, whereas scientists-as-sources have to work hard to con-vince journalists to write about what they think the story should contain. Some compromise between interviewer and interviewee probably leads to the best story, for few scientists or journalists could, by themselves, capture the essence of what's important in a complicated field and com-municate it in an interesting way to the public.

Therefore, I don't see the science journalist, scientist-as-journalist, or scientist-as-source in their conventional roles as independent or adversarial entities. The public needs information from all of these in-carnations to get a readable and honest impression of what is going on in science and what it means for them. Reducing tensions among these groups, primarily through better appreciation of each other's interdependent roles, is a major priority for our respective professions. Given the increasing importance to a democracy of a scientifically literate public, this priority for better communication among the communicators is also part of our obligation to society.

CHAPTER 17

Newspaper Columns for Fun and Profit

William Doemel

The efforts of scientists to become active communicators range from large national ones such as Carl Sagan's "Cosmos" television series to small-scale local activities. One example of the latter is "Science Notebook," a newspaper column that was written for thirteen years by members of the biology department at Wabash College in Indiana. Faculty member William Doemel describes the evolution of the column and discusses why his department considered it to be a relevant activity for scientists. Four sample columns appear in Appendix D.

Chairman of the biology department at Wabash College, William Doemel is interested in interactions between science and its several publics. A microbiologist with degrees from Heidelberg College and Indiana University, he has published research papers on the biology of organisms in extreme environments and on responses of photo-synthetic organisms to phosphates and optical brighteners, both components of synthetic detergents. Under a fellowship from Lilly Endowment, he co-organized a workshop for college teachers on science, technology, and public policy.

FOR THIRTEEN YEARS I AND MY COLLEAGUES at Wabash College wrote a regular column about biology and science. We called the column

"Science Notebook," and it appeared biweekly in two Indiana newspapers, the *South Bend Tribune* and the *Indianapolis News,* until late 1983. Nine authors—all scientists who teach and conduct research in biology at Wabash, an undergraduate liberal arts college located in Crawfordsville, Indiana—wrote more than 300 one-thousand-word columns. Each of us contributed three to six columns yearly. Believing that other biologists and scientists in other fields ought to be talking to the public, I agreed to share our experiences here, and to describe some of the problems we encountered.

We began writing our column for two reasons. First, we believed that the public wanted to understand the facts, processes, and structure of science; and second, we believed that newspaper editors, recognizing the interest of their readers, would pay for columns. We wanted to further the public understanding of science, and we needed the money to pay undergraduate biology majors for summer research projects. Fortunately, we were supported in our journalistic effort by a strong academic environment and a departmental heritage that encouraged all of us to participate in the project.

I was a first-year faculty member when the biology department faculty began to consider writing the column. I had chosen to teach at Wabash College because of its strong credentials as an undergraduate liberal arts college. When I arrived, three members of the department were in the final stages of writing an introductory college textbook. The authors believed that every liberally educated student ought to have an understanding of biology. I soon discovered that all the members of the department shared this belief and that the most important course of the biology curriculum was the introductory course. All of us participated in teaching that course and contributed to its design. Since at that time biology was a required course, the students included those majoring in the humanities and social sciences as well as in the sciences. During each lecture period, the entire biology faculty would gather with the students to learn from a colleague about a particular aspect of biology. Through this experience, all the faculty came to share common values and beliefs about education and about the importance of understanding biology.

When the American Association for the Advancement of Science and other scientific organizations began to encourage scientists to communicate their knowledge more effectively to the general public, Thomas Cole, then chairman of the department, urged the department to broaden its definition of education to include the general public. Significantly, everyone agreed. Although all of us knew that we would receive little recognition for our efforts from colleagues outside the institution, we were in an environment that encouraged the liberal education of the public. All administrators of the college, from the president to the chairperson of the department, supported our individual efforts. As an untenured member of the staff, I would not have become involved with an undertaking so seemingly alien to the development of my scientific career were it not for the unqualified support of the administration. With that support, everyone agreed to participate in the writing of the column, and everyone placed a high priority on its development.

Even though research funds were plentiful during the early 1970s, grants to support undergraduate research were limited. Believing that research is an essential part of being a biologist and that undergraduate students ought to have an opportunity to do research, we all agreed to donate our earnings from the column to an endowed fund for undergraduate research. I can't recall our discussions during those early meetings, but I do remember that we expected to earn a reasonable sum for each article. We also believed that we could write a newspaper column that would interest and inform the average reader.

On October 6, 1971, the first column, "Fall Coloration" by Austin Brooks, appeared in the *Indianapolis News*. The editor agreed to pay $20 for each column, and we agreed to provide a column each week. Fifty-two columns were written and published during the first year. Nine faculty members had contributed from one to thirteen articles each. We soon discovered that writing comprehensible articles about topics ranging from interferon to Mendelian genetics to continental drift is extremely time-consuming and intellectually draining. Some of us found the writing to be easier than did others, but after the first year we all recognized that we could not continue to write a weekly column. Fortunately, the editors agreed to accept the column on a biweekly basis, so during the second year we had to write only twenty-six columns,

By September 1978, we had written 207 columns for the newspaper. The editors of the newspaper demonstrated their support by increasing the payment to $30 per column. Although there were not many direct comments from readers, we had received many indirect comments and compliments. Now confident in our ability to write articles, we began to explore the possibility of syndication. We prepared a portfolio of our published columns and sent them to several national syndicates for comment. We heard nothing. The director of publications for the college suggested that we establish our own syndicate and agreed to help. We visited editors of several newspapers, and two editors agreed to publish revised columns on a weekly basis, paying a reduced rate of $15 to $20 per column.

Beginning in the fall of 1978, the *Columbus* (Ohio) *Dispatch* and the *South Bend Tribune* published "Science Notebook," increasing our distribution to close to a million readers. The *Columbus Dispatch* featured the column each Sunday on its op-ed page. Also, the *Dispatch* distributed the Sunday newspaper to local schools, and the column became a part of high school education in the Columbus area. Our articles were now illustrated with photographs or artwork prepared by Wabash students or faculty members, an addition that clearly enhanced reader interest. Although our column in the *Indianapolis News* still was appearing only on a biweekly basis, the addition of the two newspapers and our decision to provide artwork significantly increased the burden on all of us. When the student artists graduated, we stopped providing the artwork. Even so, the newspapers continued to publish the column, supplying their own pen-and-ink drawings. By 1980, we had used all of our previously published articles and could not continue to supply a weekly column to the *Dispatch* and the *Tribune* unless we wrote more columns. The editor of the *South Bend Tribune* agreed to continue on a biweekly basis and sent a complimentary letter to us about the column, but the editor of the *Columbus Dispatch* chose to discontinue the column. As of October 1983, we had written and published 318 original articles and 141 rewritten articles. For these articles, we received more than $11,000, an amount that earned sufficient money for us to employ one student during the summer.

In January 1983, the *Indianapolis News* discontinued the column for space and financial reasons. In September 1983, we chose to stop writing the column for the *South Bend Tribune* because the amount of time required to produce it was too much for the financial return we would receive from only one newspaper.

How Did We Write "Science Notebook"?

When I write an article for a science journal, I assume that the reader has some knowledge about the subject and is motivated to read the article. When I wrote for "Science Notebook," neither assumption was valid. Not only did I have to entice the reader to continue reading, but I also had to provide, within the 1000 words of the column, a clear understanding of the topic. All of us found this to be a significant challenge, particularly when we were writing about abstract concepts such as DNA, genes, enzymes, and even microorganisms.

Also, we were not fully prepared to relinquish control of the final content of the published column. As scientists, we had always had some control. Journal editors suggested changes, but they didn't change meaning and content of articles without consulting us. Journal editors even gave us the opportunity to review the galley proofs. However, with the newspaper column, once the articles left the college we had no control. We were dependent upon the judgment of the newspaper copy editor. When the title was misstated or the arguments were garbled, our colleagues assumed that we were responsible. Although our column was a feature rather than a news column, often, because of space limitations, an editor would delete its last paragraph. Since we were inexperienced newspaper writers, that last paragraph often contained the essence of the article. Even when we mastered the art of writing news columns, the copy editor would delete paragraphs or segments from within the column, seemingly at random, creating havoc with the published article.

We also looked forward each week to reading the editor's headlines for the column. Limitations of space, time, and understanding often caused interesting twists in that short summary that introduced the column to the reader. "Pop Goes the Popcorn," "Don't Pooh-Pooh Pawpaw, It's the Poor Man's Banana," and "Sugar-Binding Lectins Not Always a Sweet Tale" were creations of the imaginative mind of a copy editor who had to fit a title to the available space and to the content of the article. Sometimes the headline had little relationship to the article. Gradually, both we and the copy editors learned about science news columns, and we encountered fewer surprises when we read the published piece.

Of course, sometimes we did garble or misstate the argument. We tried to reduce that possibility through a process of internal review. One faculty member served as the "managing editor" and coordinated the writing and editing assignments. Every article was reviewed by two other faculty members for comprehension level, science errors, grammatical errors, and stylistic problems. Although all of us believed this review was necessary, we also discovered that such a review posed problems for writer and reviewer alike. Often the ego of the writer suffered from the return of a preliminary column that was covered with red ink and perhaps even included a critical comment about its quality. Criticism from close colleagues is much harder to accept than criticism from distant, anonymous reviewers. The faculty reviewer, too, suffered from conflicting demands, for he or she had to assure the quality of the column and still maintain a friendly relationship with the writer. We reduced these potential conflicts by insisting that the writer had the final authority, with the reviewer a friendly critic, not a censor.

Our public was distant, faceless, and, usually, silent. This was new to us. As teachers we lecture to students who respond by facial expressions or with questions. Articles we publish in science journals also initiate direct response. However, our "Science Notebook" readers seldom responded. Compliments or criticisms were rare, and the letters we did receive generally either sought solutions to medical or botanical problems or prayed for our redemption. In the first instance, general articles about human, pet, or plant diseases often elicited letters seeking solutions to very specific problems. When I wrote an article about algae and eutrophication, I received several letters from individuals who wanted to control algal growth in their recreational ponds. When one of our group wrote an article about evolution, he received several "hellfire and brimstone" letters. We hoped to increase reader participation by encouraging letters and asking questions of the readers, but these efforts were not successful.

Why Scientists Should Write About Science

"Science Notebook" is no longer published. When we started the column there were few journalists who were knowledgeable about science, and fewer still who called themselves science writers. Then, there seemed to be opportunities and a real need for scientists to write about their science for the public. Today the public has many sources of news about science. *Science News, Science 85, Discover, Science Digest,* and other popular magazines offer comprehensive, current, and well-illustrated articles. *The New York Times* has a Tuesday section about science that is read throughout the country. Generally, articles appearing in these publications are written by professional journalists, not scientists. While we have returned to our teaching and research, the question remains: Should scientists, just as we, be communicating science to the public? I contend that the scientist provides the reader with a different perspective from that of the science writer, and that this perspective is important.

Having spent almost half my life immersed in science, first as an undergraduate and graduate student, then as a teacher and researcher, I am part of the scientific community. So when I wrote articles for the public, I was writing from *within* that community, constrained but also informed by its traditions and its paradigms. While I lacked the freedom of the external, knowledgeable observer, I had ready access to the history, people, and literature that define the scientific community. In this way, my perspective differed from that of the external observer, however knowledgeable. Both perspectives are different, both are valid, and the public benefits by seeing many different images of science.

"Science Notebook" was not written for the reader of *The New York Times;* it was written for the reader of the small local newspaper. Although many such readers attended college, for most of them a formal education ended with high school. Today, that latter public is still not being well served. Whereas college sophomores readily understand articles published about science in the public science magazines, college freshmen find those same articles challenging.

There still is a need for "Science Notebook." But for such a column to succeed, it must be published weekly and it must be well illustrated. We couldn't meet that schedule, nor could we provide any illustrations. "Science Notebook" withered, but I hope somehow other scientists will seek to share their excitement about science through the news media in a format understandable to the average reader.

CHAPTER 18

A Scientist in TV Land

Gerald F. Wheeler

Television provides one of the best ways of reaching large numbers of people, but it imposes many special constraints. Few scientists have had as many and as varied experiences with the medium as has Gerald F. Wheeler. In this chapter, he traces his involvement with both local and national science television productions.

Gerald Wheeler is both a scientist and a teacher. Trained as a nuclear physicist at the State University of New York at Stony Brook, he has spent most of his energies in the past decade on the issues and problems of getting science to nonscientists. The author of three books, two for elementary school teachers and one college-level physics textbook, Wheeler has been awarded the Lindback Teaching Award for excellence in university teaching and the American Association of Physics Teachers' Millikan Award for creative contributions in physics education. During the past decade, he has been involved in the production of more than 100 television programs dealing with science and technology. He is currently a W. K. Kellogg Fellow, studying telecommunications and their role in education.

W OULD YOU LIKE TO HAVE YOUR OWN TV SHOW?
    I had just finished my first TV appearance—explaining energy concepts on a late-night talk show—when the show's producer asked me

that question. As a traditional nuclear physicist, I normally would have said no immediately; any project this far from research has to be avoided. However, at the time the producer popped the question I was spending more and more time in the classroom and less and less with accelerators. Although I harbored no secret hopes of being "discovered," the possibility of expanding the size of my classes from hundreds to thousands was too good to pass up. Without much thought about whether I was good enough, whether I had time, or whether I could even think of show topics, I said, "Sure."

As the "crank-call" physicist at Temple University, I got all the "unusual" requests. So three weeks earlier, when the local CBS-owned TV station had called looking for a physicist for a talk-show debate on the energy crisis, they got me. They had chosen the teams and needed one more player. I refused, citing my lack of knowledge of the issues. But I couldn't hang up without giving my opinion. "Most TV debates about science-related issues are useless because the viewers don't understand the science behind the issues. The moderator needs an interpreter—a token scientist," I said. The caller from the station graciously listened and essentially replied, "Thanks—don't call us; we'll call you." They did, about an hour later. Apparently the host liked the idea of having someone on his side.

The show went well. Periodically the host would stop the debate and turn to me. "What are they talking about?" I'd give a quick description of the difference between fission and fusion or an explanation of why one should even try to get energy from sun rays. The host would then thank me and return to the debators. The taping ended with the producer asking me, "Would you like to have your own TV show?"

This was the beginning of rich experiences that taught me about television, and, consequently, about the differences between the worlds of television and science. These differences are important to anyone planning to use television to get science to the public.

Science is our collective interpretation of the entire universe. Our descriptions go forward and backward in time and span distances from the subnuclear to uncountable light-years. Getting science on television means presenting an unimaginably large variety of phenomena, many of which are beyond the human experience. Television offers options not found in the classroom. The "magic" of television allows one to walk through 93 million miles of empty space, to travel at relativistic velocities, and to peer into the core of an atom.

This power of television comes with some definite constraints. In the past decade I've been involved in about a dozen science-on-television projects. I want to discuss three projects that, with hindsight, turned out to have common messages for a scientist in TV land.

A Local Commercial Station

My first example is my own Saturday-afternoon science show aimed at a young audience. I called the show "Sidewalk Science" to convey the casual approach I had planned. I had a great deal of freedom with this production, since the station wanted more children's programming and they knew little about science. I could choose my own topics, create my own dialogue, and even design my own set. Anything I suggested was fine, provided it didn't cost any money.

The first thing I learned has followed me through all subsequent productions: what a scientist calls interesting is worlds apart from what the general public calls interesting. At first I refused to consider the possibility that there was a difference. Since I had the TV series, I simply expected to choose my topics and present them. My first show was going to be on forces, a good physicist's topic. I made a list of all the cute demonstrations I could think of; gathered my ropes, springs, bathroom scales, and other paraphernalia; and made a rough draft of the script (actually I copied my Physics 101 lecture notes). I was ready. I arranged a meeting with the producer to put the final touches on the notes before the taping session.

His first question was, "What's your tease?" A tease, I was told, is a short lead-in that entices the viewer to stay tuned for exciting things to come. Somehow that didn't seem very professional to me. After a little thought I announced that I would stand in front of the camera and in a very excited voice say, "Today we are going to experiment with forces!" The producer dismissed my suggestion as boring and detailed his idea, which involved a gorilla playing tug-of-war with me. Subsequently, we had these battles each week. Each week I would tell him about the inherent beauty of physics, and each week he would remind me that there would be no show if we didn't interest the viewers. The tease questions always got resolved. In retrospect, I suppose he won. I relaxed and submitted to ideas that would make any self-respecting physicist cringe at the mere mention of them. We created some good teases, but I did draw the line at gorillas.

My premiere aired on a spring Saturday afternoon. I felt it was the best half-hour presentation on forces that I had ever done. Most of my colleagues conceded that they also liked it. But one frank critic—a nonscientist—said, "You did a good job, your demos were clear, but who cares about forces?" I was flabbergasted. Obviously, I thought, this critic just didn't appreciate the importance of forces in our understanding of nature. With each new show, my critic returned with the same question, "Who cares?"

It took quite a while for me to realize that most people don't care, at least not in the way scientists care about these staples of physics. As scientists we probably get this biased view of the rest of the world from our students. They "care" because the topics will be on an exam in their near future. The person on the street is not being tested. Ask a ten-year-old, "Would you like to talk about forces?" The response will probably be, "No thanks, but may it always be with you."

In addition to misreading the public I also misread the medium of television. Somehow I was trying to use TV to teach the public science, and I was determined to do it my way. I failed. I tried to change television to match science rather than change my style to match television. Television styles conflict with the ways of science. Television moves fast. Success in front of the camera means moving at a high pace. There's nothing like it in science. Scientists are trained to be cautious, not to make quick, glib statements. When we write research articles, for example, we carefully moderate our statements with qualifications. After the newness of seeing myself on television wore off, my finished product each Saturday would usually depress me. "My God, my hand is covering the most crucial part of the demonstration!" I started viewing the show in the studio immediately after taping it, but often that didn't help because there wasn't money to pay for the extra studio time to reshoot it. I also think the producer felt I was being a little picky; it looked fine to him.

My colleagues were even more picky. Those who occasionally saw the show on a Saturday had comments that were quite different from those I heard in the studio. A colleague greeted me at the physics department door early one Monday morning: "Did you know that you implied that hardness varies linearly with melting points?" I replied, "Did I say that?" My professional critic corrected me—I had *implied* it. I now have a graph of hardness versus melting temperatures on my office wall that shows that it is not actually such a bad implication. On that particular Monday morning I just said, "Oh," and sheepishly went on my way. The fast pace is only partly to blame for the "mistakes" my colleagues thought I made. On television, where the audience is the general public, things are said more simply. But whenever we stray from the precise mathematical structure of physics, whenever we attempt to put mathematical ideas in words, we reproduce the phenomena with less fidelity. On television, scientists are translators, and a good translator must know both languages well.

Television's fast-delivery style plus the need to translate science results in a tension between two imperatives. There's a complementarity principle in modern physics that says there are certain pairs of quantities in the universe that seem to be holding an investigator hostage. As he or she attempts to know one of the pair better, the other becomes less and less knowable. There's an analogous "complementary pair" in television called "Accuracy and Clarity." We can make something very clear as long as we don't worry too much about accuracy. On the other hand, if we go for total accuracy, we make it unclear in this medium. It's unclear because television demands minimal explanation. As soon as one tries to get very accurate, clarity slips beyond the viewer's grasp. Television demands fast explanations.

I went into the production of this local science-for-children series believing that the inherent beauty of science was of equal interest to everyone, that since I delivered successful classroom lectures I could "deliver" a television explanation, and that I could communicate scientifically accurate information. Producing "Sidewalk Science" taught me that my classroom and research experiences were a necessary but hardly sufficient background for getting science on television. I had to learn more about what interests the general public; I had to change my presentation; and I had to come to grips with the fact that I couldn't be as accurate as I would have liked.

A National Program

A few years after this first television project I joined Children's Television Workshop in the production of "3-2-1 Contact," a series on science and technology for young viewers. I expected this experience to be different, since I would be "behind the camera" in a consulting and development role. That change turned out to be less important than I had suspected. When I was freed from the pressure of performing, all my scientific modes of operating snapped right back into position. I still had a great deal to learn about science on television.

I was now part of a very large professional team with what seemed like limitless resources. I assumed that my team experiences in nuclear physics would be good training for this new experience. I was wrong, On research teams, arguments are related to the substance of the data, but we are all talking from the same world view. In television we were all talking in different languages. When science and television people get together even their vocabularies are different. My team meetings now were with editors, animators, story researchers, scriptwriters, assistant producers, producers, and an executive producer. We all had different meanings assigned to common words like "good," "bad," "right," and "wrong."

One team decision sent a crew to interview an engineer who used an infrared-TV system to measure heat losses in buildings. The following week, the producer scheduled a viewing of a rough cut (the draft) of the final piece. Everything went fine until the end of the viewing when the interviewer turned to the engineer and said, "So, hot things reflect hot colors and cold things reflect cold colors." The engineer—probably nervous in front of the camera and completely unfamiliar with television's pace—incorrectly said, "Right!" I immediately jumped up shouting, "Wrong!" The producer argued that I was being picky. It couldn't be *that* wrong; it was just right for the piece since it concluded the segment and visually cued the ending. I stayed put: it was *scientifically* wrong.

The producer was missing the point of the argument: in science one word, or one result, can make something totally wrong. This type of falsification, so central to the process of science, is nonexistent in television. But television people demand excellence in a way that's strange to scientists, and I was missing that point in the argument. In deciding what is right or wrong in television, there is more debate, there are more valid opinions, and there is more intuition than is used in science. There are good and bad producers, good and bad editors, and good and bad animators. Some people "have it" and others don't. In television it's the people; in science it's the data. The executive producer understood both languages, and she changed the piece so that an off-camera narrator gave the correct explanation, leaving the visual tone nearly untouched.

Even when team members understand the language differences, the task of blending science and television styles into a final product is difficult. The topics on "3-2-1 Contact" were suggested by the scientists and the dialogue was created by scriptwriters. The writers, while very talented in creating dialogue, had no idea what physical phenomena could be connected in a show to highlight a particular theme. A writer and I had an especially difficult time with a part in a week's theme on an already familiar topic to me, "forces." We had acquired *Skylab* footage for the gravity show. I wanted to stress that while the astronauts were weightless, they were still pulled by gravity. (In fact, as any physical scientist knows, gravity's the key issue here!) The writer's problem was that dialogue must sound natural and my insistence on an accurate scientific explanation made for dull dialogue. There was no debate about the fact that gravity's the key issue, there was a little debate about its importance, and a lot of debate about how to say it naturally. We struggled for two days to merge the right dialogue with the right science.

While my science colleagues didn't quibble with me about the correctness of the science in "3-2-1 Contact," some wondered why we didn't do more. Why, for example, didn't we explicitly talk about Newton's Laws of Motion? We didn't because "3-2-1 Contact" had to capture the attention of youngsters and hold it for the whole show. It was inappropriate to do the same things one would do in a classroom. The shows had to be bright and lively and at the right level; failing at that would mean no viewers.

Being at the right level is as important on television as in the classroom. The rules of science can be set to music in jingles and skits.

I'm sure we could have created situation comedy about action/reaction or centrifugal forces, but we didn't. We didn't because, at this level, children aren't even aware of the idea of forces as they are conceptualized in the physics world view. By looking at the motion of a roller coaster or a Frisbee, by talking about the actions of a football player or a figure skater, "3-2-1 Contact" provided experiences that, while seeming casual, were actually carefully filled with words like "friction," "forces," and "gravity." In short, "3-2-1 Contact" both then and now teaches kids to talk science.

I left that premiere season at Children's Television Workshop with a new sense of the importance of teams, of the value of different kinds of experts, and of the need to get those experts communicating. The scientist has to have a limited veto power on a science show, but he or she should not have the freedom to control the whole production. "3-2-1 Contact" succeeded in creating interesting and scientifically meaningful experiences for its viewers. This happened by carefully defining the boundary conditions of expertise.

A University Production

My last example, a production at a university TV center, grew from a desire to capitalize on the public's general interest in astronomy. I worked with a faculty member from the film and television department to produce twelve short programs, called "Skywatch," that have been inserted into existing regional programs. In much the same way that a weather person announces the upcoming weather, this series had me highlighting the upcoming constellations. Since the constellations are relatively constant, this particular series has the unique feature of having reruns that will remain current years later.

"Skywatch" had some attributes of the first two projects. I was in front of the cameras again, producing a broadcast-quality program for a commercial network on a low budget, and, as in the second example, I was part of a team of people with many different world views.

The first insight I gained from "Skywatch" seems obvious in hindsight: merging science's concepts with television's medium demands the testing of many ideas before the final taping can occur. As I reflect on the past ten years, I realize that this newfound insight has been following me around since the beginning. It surfaced so clearly during the "Skywatch" venture because I *had* the time to experiment with presenting science concepts on television. Some ideas were as simple as showing a laser beam, others involved simulating a black hole. The academic setting gave me more studio time.

The second insight I got from "Skywatch" is related to the role that television can play in raising the scientific literacy of the public. My relationship with television had been rocky. After starting with a false hope of television's power to educate the public, I recoiled to a feeling of powerlessness. I began to believe that commercial television couldn't be much help to science communicators. I lamented that the gap between scientists and the general public was too big for television to span; good television was just inherently too superficial.

The "Skywatch" experience helped me realize that television can be part of a larger conduit for reaching the public. I became convinced that increasing the scientific literacy of my audience is not a continuous process, but, rather, a layered one. Television naturally lends itself as a springboard to other layers, or conduits, which strengthen, deepen, and expand the superficial layer initially presented.

After production of the "Skywatch" programs finished, our project evolved into creating other ways to use the broadcasts to reach the public. Being a smaller, less expensive production and having a smaller audience gave us a chance to try new modes of outreach. We could create different levels, or layers, of literacy. In this layered-literacy approach, the TV programs do what they do best: they "tease" one into an involvement with new ideas. The caveat, however, as I learned in my first experience, is that the tease must be done in the style of television. Our "Skywatch" audience is small enough that we can encourage write-in requests for more information. When that happens, the text literacy layer has been initiated by the viewer. In its first season, "Skywatch" generated a monthly correspondence with 100 interested citizens. They received a one-page flyer that gave diagrams, definitions, and more viewing tasks. Additional literacy layers can be tested. One possibility is forming a skywatchers' network with monthly telephone conference calls. That layer is particularly attractive to a rural area; others might be better for cities.

Some of the developments in telecommunications—videotext, interactive cable television, and low-power broadcasting, to name a few—also hold exciting possibilities for new experiments. The number of "Skywatch" viewers is too small for a national broadcast project, but it is manageable as a university or small community project. Whichever way science-on-television projects evolve, the payoff in just the numbers of viewers is mind-boggling to scientists. "Skywatch" and "Sidewalk Science" had "classes" numbering in the thousands, while millions of children around the world see "3-2-1 Contact." These numbers alone make an investment of time, money, and effort in science on television a wise one.

Appendixes

APPENDIX A

The Scientist's Responsibility for Public Information: A Guide to Effective Communication with the Media

Neal E. Miller

As science and technology become increasingly crucial to this nation's policy decisions, public understanding of these areas becomes increasingly vital. Both good scientists and good journalists share a responsibility to provide clear, accurate, and timely information. But journalism, like laboratory research, has certain rituals that appear mysterious to the uninformed. This article addresses those "never stated practices" in an attempt to remove some of the fears, doubts, pitfalls, and misunderstandings that scientists may have in dealing with the press.

The following comments are a summary prepared by Neal Miller of the discussion between science writers and scientists at a Science Writers' Seminar organized by the Public Information Committee of the Society for Neuroscience at Airlie House, Virginia, May 3–6, 1976. While they are understandably oriented toward the medical sciences, we believe they are generally applicable to problems scientists face in dealing with the media.

Miller and the Society for Neuroscience have been gracious enough to permit the Scientists' Institute for Public Information to republish this article for the benefit of those scientists participating in

SIPI's Media Resource Service as well as any scientist who may have the opportunity to "meet the press."

Significance of Public Information

The growing importance of science in our society and its increasing dependence on the taxpayers' support make it a duty of the scientist to cooperate with the science writer in educating the public. Unless reputable scientists supply accurate information to the popular media, the public is left at the mercy of the charlatans, the sensationmongers, and of exposes by the anti-intellectuals.

Science plays a vital role in our technologically developed society, and it is important for citizens to understand something about it in order to make wise decisions. The public pays for our research; how intelligently they support it depends on how well they are informed. Since the chief source of public education about current research is science writing, we have a vital stake in trying to help with this work.

The purpose of this article, prepared cooperatively by scientists and science writers, is to help you to understand the writer's problems, which are different for the different types of media, and to give you practical hints on how to work with science writers so that accurate information is effectively communicated.

> The more visible you people become, the more that helps us. Your willingness to talk with us, your willingness to just exchange the excitement you have about this research gives us new ideas. You have to be vocal and you have to be visible and you have to be willing to talk about what you're doing.
>
> Ira Flatow
> *Science Editor, National Public Radio*
> *at the 1976 Science Writers' Seminar*
> *hosted by the Society for Neuroscience*

General Points Applicable to Most Media

You Can Control the Interview

Some scientists fail to do their share of informing the public because they are afraid. They should know that by considering in advance what they want to say and what they don't want to say they can control the interview.

As with most things in life, there are some risks. This article is designed to help you to understand and to minimize these risks. On the average, helping to inform the public will yield benefits to science, to your institution, and even to you that far outweigh the risks.

Avoiding Criticism from Colleagues

Investigators being interviewed should consider themselves as providing information to a public that requires it, and thus doing a service for the scientific community as a whole. As more scientists realize how important public information is for the support of science and understand the practical conditions under which the media must operate, the danger of being reproached by one's scientific peers for self-glorification is being rapidly reduced.

By following a few simple rules, you can avoid legitimate criticism. First, the press is not a place for announcing primary data or new findings to the scientific community. Material presented to the press should have appeared or at least been accepted for publication in a scientific journal, been presented at a meeting, and had adequate refereeing or peer criticism. Publication of an article or the presentation of a paper at a meeting is an event that may justify a news story. It also provides the writer with a "hook" on which to hang the story.

Credit to Colleagues

Although the average newspaper article, radio, or television program typically does not have space to give citations or list additional names, you should, when relevant, briefly but pointedly mention one or two key antecedents to your work and the fact that similar work is being done in either several other unnamed laboratories or, if there is only one, a specifically named laboratory. Where such credits are especially important, explain this to the interviewer. You can suggest that other investigators be interviewed, though often it may not be possible for the writer to follow that suggestion.

Feature stories in Sunday supplements, magazines, or special-interest publications can specifically mention more investigators and laboratories. For such stories, be especially careful to give adequate credit, or if there is time, to refer the writer to other investigators.

The experienced interviewer knows that any segment of scientific research fits into a larger picture. He or she may in fact judge your reliability and accuracy by how well you clarify the context in which your work is done. The novice writer may need to be reminded that research is a *process* and that apparent "breakthroughs" are usually no more than advances on a very long continuum and are almost always the result of a great deal of previous research.

Need to Achieve Simple Exposition

The science writer must explain things simply and clearly so that the average layman can understand them. Most science writers have to deal with a wide range of topics, from asteroids to zygotes, and those from local papers may also have to cover crime, sports, and politics. Therefore, it is up to you to explain your work to them simply, clearly, and unambiguously in everyday language. The less translation the interviewer has to do, the less opportunity there is for errors and distortions to intrude.

Never underestimate the intelligence of science writers, but understand how unfamiliar they may initially be with your special topic, its background, methods, and terminology. Ask how much background the writer has in your particular field so that you will know what level is appropriate for your explanation. State your major finding, how it fits into the larger picture, its implications, future needs for research, where it may lead. Do not "talk down" to a writer. If you have to repeat an explanation, it could be that you were not clear enough the first time.

Off-the-Record and Background Information

At your discretion, you are always free to advise the interviewer that your comments should be "off the record" or "for background information only." In most cases, it is a firm rule of journalism that "off-the-record" or "background" comments are never publicly attributed. But you should reconfirm this understanding *before* making off-the-record comments. Naturally, a journalist and readers prefer to know the identity of sources and, whenever possible, this is desirable. But you should know your options.

Preparing a Written Statement

Providing a clear and simple written summary can help the science writer to write an accurate story. Ideally, your statement should be prepared in the newspaper format, with the main idea in the first paragraph and progressive elaboration in subsequent paragraphs. Longer, more thoughtful articles that review the work of several individuals always seem more effective and accurate.

Interest and Implications

Science writers must compete for space or time with other news events and stories. In this competition they must publish or perish. Their stories must interest the audience. Therefore you should point out the meaning and implications of your results, for theory, application, or both. But you must distinguish clearly between a step toward a possible application and the discovery, or even the imminence of one. If the work has clinical implications, avoid raising any false hopes of a quick cure that cannot presently be delivered. Ask writers to exert whatever control they can over the composition of misleading or sensationalized headlines for your story.

Form Letter for Mail Inquiries

Sometimes a report of a discovery with clinical implications will bring in letters from desperate people seeking help. A form letter can be used to correct misunderstandings or to give guidance. To deal with special cases a few sentences can be added to the basic form letters.

Brevity

The competition for space or time is intense, especially in the news media. The length of a newspaper column is 750 words; a 500-word story (a little less than two double-spaced pages of typescript) is typical. A radio story can range from an eight-minute feature segment to a thirty-second news spot. Most TV presentations are short, one to three minutes. In all media, there are occasional longer, in-depth presentations, but these are most likely to appear in specialized or monthly journals, Sunday supplements, documentaries, or special features. All news stories, including scientific ones, must provide information in a hurry and must be made up of factual statements simply presented without technical detail and without ambiguity.

Cuts: Caution About Claims

An editor may have to cut a story severely to fit a column or to make room for urgent last-minute news. Similarly, a tape or film may be cut. Therefore you should avoid making statements that will claim too much if subsequent qualifications are deleted. The possibility of cuts is the reason for the newspaper format suggested above for your written statement.

Racing the Clock

Many writers work against imminent deadlines. They need immediate answers and do not have time for extensive research or any revisions. Those who work for daily news media may have only an hour or two. It seldom helps them to be referred to a book or technical journal in some distant library. Writers working for weekly news media may have more time. Newspaper feature stories, articles in specialty magazines, and television or radio documentaries allow more time. Authors of popular books on scientific topics are relatively well off, but even they must work fast to produce a book in a reasonable time so their earnings can be equivalent to a decent hourly wage.

Some researchers, with the best of intentions, will return a writer's phone call three, four, five or more days later, noting simply that they have been busy. This perhaps is understandable in a world where research results involve weeks, months, and years of work, but often it is totally worthless in the world of the newsroom, which measures life in hours.

The scientist must remember that to the science writer, deadlines may be enemies, but they cannot be ignored. The experienced reporter who telephones a scientist for comment, advice, or information will indicate the subject of the story and when the deadline is. It may be mutually advantageous for the researcher to suggest that the reporter telephone his/her home that night, if the deadline is close. Or they may agree that a collect call by the scientist to the writer's home is better for both their schedules.

Checking What Is Attributed to You

Often writers need to make a direct quote or to specify you as a source; they cannot attribute a statement to "a source close to Mother Nature." Usually, it is possible to get a writer to agree in advance to check the accuracy of direct quotes or statements attributed to you by reading them over the telephone, perhaps with one or two of the preceding and following sentences in order to establish the context. When time allows, writers will often agree to let you see the part of their manuscript that deals with the materials you have supplied, along with the material that establishes the context. Most science writers are highly responsible professionals who are eager to check accuracy whenever possible. But the scientist should confine suggested corrections to definite errors of fact or grossly misleading errors of emphasis.

You must realize that the requirements of popular exposition are quite different from those of an article in a technical journal, that the writer is a professional craftsman who has developed his or her own style, and that condensation and clarification inevitably involve a certain amount of oversimplification and even distortion—but may be much more accurate than what the reader had in his mind before!

Some writers will not check accuracy with you. When the time is too short for such a check, that is the time for you to be most cautious.

Inquiring About Credentials

There are a very few writers or producers who, in asking for an hour or more of your time, may give you the impression that they have been commissioned to do a story or show for a prestigious publication or network, when, in fact, they only hope to sell something there. Diplomatic questioning can determine the exact nature of the publication or station involved and the writer's or producer's relation to it. Most producers or writers are willing to cite or show samples of their previous work. This can help you to decide how much time to invest.

Public Relations Office in Your Institution

Before making any major commitment, check a writer's credentials through the public relations, information, or news office in your institution. Although most science writers are professionals with high standards for improving the public's understanding, there are a few exceptions and a few publications that specialize in sensationalism or headlines with exaggerated claims. Alert public relations professionals can check the credentials of the writer who is contacting you and can find out whether the individual is a member of one of the three professional organizations of science writers (the National Association of Science Writers, the American Medical Writers Association, or the

American Society of Journalists and Authors). Public relations offices can also give the neophyte useful advice and guidance, arrange interviews, prepare press releases, and help with other interactions with the media.

Judging Reliability: A Two-Way Street

The field of science journalism is growing as a specialty, and the number of writers uniquely qualified to bridge the gap between scientists and laymen is increasing. Some have degrees in science or science journalism. Others have, during years of experience with reputable publications, developed a special interest in the biological sciences. Writers of this calibre are perfectly capable of following developments in neuroscience research and choosing the right time to produce a well-researched article on a "hot" topic. You will probably recognize the names or at least the affiliations of such people and should consider yourself fortunate if they seek you out.

However, such highly skilled and specialized writers are still a small part of the spectrum that includes the neophyte from a local daily who may arrive at your laboratory fresh from a flower show. Always take pains to ascertain the level of sophistication you are dealing with and adjust your approach accordingly.

Remember that the best interviewers are anxious to avoid being "burned" by inexact or incomplete information, and may have checked *your* credentials to find out where you have published and who recommended you as a reliable source. A healthy degree of skepticism on both sides should have a favorable end product: science news that is informative and interesting without encouraging credulity or predicting imminent wonders.

A Personal Relationship

By observing the media, you can learn who the reliable science writers are in your area. It usually is easy to establish a good personal relationship with them. There is no substitute for such a relationship.

Supplying Specific Facts or Referrals

Sometimes a science writer may telephone you to secure a simple scientific fact, to check on the definition of a technical term, to learn which authorities to interview on a topic, or to secure an opinion on the reliability of someone else's statement. Answers to such questions can be extremely valuable in helping a conscientious writer prepare an accurate story; your aid can mean the difference between the dissemination of incorrect or correct information. In answering such questions, bear in mind the pressures of time and other practical constraints on the science writer. If in doubt, ask how much time and effort is available; for example, it may be much more useful to refer the writer to an adequate local authority than to a more eminent distant one. It usually is useless to refer the writer of a news story to a "great" review in a journal.

Supplying Frank Criticism

Be candid; while trying to be perfectly fair, do not hesitate to point out that a claim made by a colleague is controversial and to suggest a good representative of the other side of the controversy. Point out, when necessary, that certain claims are greatly exaggerated. If you can't take responsibility for a criticism, as a last resort refer the writer to a criticism that has appeared in print—ideally, finding it promptly and reading it over the phone. As one science writer aptly said: "A major value of disagreement is that it is a demonstration of truth at work."

Special Points Relevant to Television

Television has more impact than any other medium. It has become the focal point of most homes. Many children spend more time with TV than they do attending school. In its brief history, it has changed the lives of its viewers by opening up the world to them in a way no print or other electronic medium could. But its potential for education has only been partially realized.

Because of the power of TV, permitting a television crew and cameras to come into your laboratory can have great value for science. This may disrupt your work for half a day, but those few hours can make a powerful contribution to the public understanding of science.

Good science programs do not just happen; they must be carefully planned. TV's strongest point is the presentation of interesting material, ideally involving movement. Use your imagination in calling to the producer's attention various possibilities in your laboratory for telling the story through dynamic views of research in progress, the blackboard, animation, or diagrams. If you are taking high-quality motion pictures of any of your research for any reason, you should save a print with the idea that excerpts from it may possibly be useful in some television program.

Determine in advance the range of the time likely to be allotted to the final presentation and don't be surprised if this is quite short—30 seconds to 8 minutes—because of the high premium on television time. Be prepared to have many times that amount of film taken. The producer will need adequate materials from which to choose.

Because of the impact of TV, you should be sensitive to any shots that might be disturbing if seen out of context (e.g., an operation without the viewer's being told that the animal is under surgical anesthesia). Most producers will be at least as sensitive to this problem as the scientist. The extremely rare producer who tries to sneak in a few tasteless shots should be shunned. Before agreeing to appear on a live program, you should know something about the general nature of the program, the other participants in it, and, ideally, the producer.

If the TV shots are being recorded, ask about the possibility of repeating a small portion if you believe you could give a much better answer to the same question (or one phrased in a more relevant way) the second time. Do not ask to do this too often!

It is sometimes useful to give a TV producer a relevant reprint, especially if it is not too technical, or a lay-language version of your work—conceivably even to develop a tentative script, which certainly will be altered. Inquire first how much written material would be appreciated.

While a live interview on politics or sports may be best if it is completely spontaneous, this does not necessarily hold true for science unless the interviewer is quite familiar with the material. Thus, it is best to go over the material first with the interviewer and agree on a rough outline. This does not mean a completely stereotyped, memorized sequence, but rather spontaneity within a sequence of ideas that has been generally agreed upon. Ignore the camera, look at the interviewer; let him/her lead you along. Keep your answers short and clear.

Often, a TV producer is willing to give you a copy of the completed film or videotape or your portion of it. Occasionally, producers are even willing to give copies of material not used. Such material can be very useful in teaching, either in its original form or with excerpts joined together by black leaders, so that a fifteen-second bit of illustrative action can be used as an "animated slide." Obviously, you should never release such material to a competitor of your benefactor without the latter's permission.

Special Points Relevant to Radio

Many of the considerations that apply to television apply also to radio. But in radio the medium is exclusively sound. While the sound of the human voice is adequate for communication, it is highly desirable to incorporate background sounds, laboratory sounds, or animal sounds to enliven the dullness of a straight exposition.

Commercial radio coverage of the neurosciences usually is limited to short "filler" notes in the news as brief as thirty seconds or package spots of one to three minutes. In addition, news of prize awards, major findings, or government support announcements is handled much as it is by the print media, but radio is expected to provide an even greater measure of immediacy and entertainment. Full-length feature shows exploring a field or a discovery in some depth are rare in commercial radio.

The National Public Radio System, chartered by Congress, is part of the Corporation for Public Broadcasting, which funds radio and television. Most of the 200 public radio stations are located on college campuses across the country. More science news is likely to be heard on this network than on commercial radio.

The science writers for radio compete with other news for air time. The average story runs between three and six minutes, equivalent to three or four news columns, but there are some twenty-minute in-depth features.

Special Points Relevant to Newsprint

The primary function of newspapers and news magazines is to provide information on "what's new" to a broad readership, but entertainment is also a consideration. The news must be presented simply and must be interesting enough to hold attention. *Science news will be read only if it is presented in a simple, direct, and graphic way, and it will be printed only if the editor believes that it will be read.* While the primary content is the printed word, a good photograph or diagram can occasionally be useful.

It is important to remember that the journalists are first and foremost surrogates for their readers. As such, the journalist's primary obligation is to news as he or she perceives it—not to the sensibilities of the scientist or the scientist's institution. Moreover, controversy and scandal are *every* journalist's meat—and even better if they can be found hidden in some ivory tower. Remember the painted mouse . . . .

There are very different kinds of newspapers and news magazines, each of which takes pride in its individuality and unique qualities. The following is a rough categorization.

Large Dailies

These include "world" newspapers such as *The New York Times, The Times* (of London), the *Washington Post,* and *Christian Science Monitor.*

Since one of their functions is to record ongoing history, they attempt to report news in all subject categories, even the scholarly and technical, if the event has broad significance. But all stories must compete for available space. Thus, depending on the vagaries of politics, military conflict, or earthquakes, a news development involving science may or may not make publication.

Newspapers must have a specific event as the point of departure for most of their stories. Since yesterday's news is stale, the reporter is racing a deadline. Wherever possible, it is merciful to give the writer a news release in advance of a specific event such as a scientific meeting. The story can have a release date that will be honored. It is useful to find out the paper's deadline and to schedule press conferences accordingly or, better yet, to arrange their timing in advance with the reporter.

Feature Stories. The large newspaper will occasionally publish a longer story that may or may not arise from an important new development. This feature story will review the subject area, providing background to recent developments, and attempt to give a broader understanding of the field to the general reader. Such stories are generally preplanned and researched, include information from interviews, and may take days or weeks to prepare instead of the minutes or hours that the news story is allowed. Feature stories are short versions of the more leisurely and literary feature articles that appear in weekly or monthly magazines.

Medium-Size and Small Dailies

These make up the majority of newspapers in the country. Their needs and the coverage they provide differ from those of the large metropolitan paper. Usually they will not have a writer who specializes in science or medical topics; the writer assigned to a science story one day may cover a fire the next. Most of the world or national news coverage in such papers comes from the wire services. Local names and places are important to these papers, and their primary interest may be in clinical developments rather than basic research. A major story from the wire service about a scientific breakthrough in another part of the country may be ignored in favor of a lesser story coming from the local school or hospital and featuring the names of local scientists.

Wire Services

A scientist may think he or she is talking to a small hometown newspaper in Oregon about a small clinical study, and the next thing that happens is that Mother calls from Maine with congratulations about the Nobel-quality work she read about in *her* local paper. This is the work of the wire services, the most powerful—though least understood—organs of American journalism.

Polls show that most Americans get their news from television, but most of the news they hear on television is generated by the wire services—at least anything from out of town. And frequently, these wire services—the Associated Press (AP), United Press International (UPI), and Reuters—get *their* news from local papers.

So if you are talking for any print reporters, no matter how small the newspaper, no matter where you are, always consider that what you say may wind up in newspapers or on TV all over the country, maybe all over the world. The scientist must take time to help the reporter get it right. The reporter may overemphasize clinical implications, trying to make page one with the work of a local scientist, or may misunderstand the implications entirely. Frequently, a wire service will pick this story up, without checking back with the scientist, and it will get national exposure at perhaps four paragraphs' length. This is the perfect length for a newspaper to fill out a column. So be forewarned.

The wire services have their own competent science and medicine correspondents, but they are powerless to keep off the wire these small out-of-perspective stories from local bureaus—often written by young, ambitious reporters looking for the big story to start them up the ladder.

Large-Circulation Weeklies

Examples of this type of publication are *Time, Newsweek, Parade,* and *U.S. News and World Report.* (The *National Enquirer* poses special problems. It is frankly sensational and the distortions generated here can produce real harm in patients looking for "cures." Unfortunately, it has such a large readership that one regrets to see its reporters left exclusively to the less reliable sources they frequently use.) These publications cannot cover fast-breaking news the way the dailies do, but they attempt to provide more in-depth coverage of events and trends in the world. Their reporters have somewhat more time to research their stories than do those for the dailies; sometimes an article can be several days or even several weeks in preparation. Because their resources and circulations are so large, their impact is powerful.

News Periodicals for Physicians

These organs attempt to update professionals on all the new developments in their fields. *Medical World News, Medical Tribune, Hospital*

Practice, and *AMA News* are examples. For the most part, their readers are busy practitioners who can manage to stay current in their own specialties but need to be aware of what is new in all areas of medicine, including basic research. Stories of new developments are brief but provide enough data and names of individuals for the reader to follow up in the literature a story that is close to his/her needs. The occasional feature article gives more perspective. Writers for these publications are necessarily highly skilled professionals with special training in one or more branches of medicine. They attend professional meetings and cull professional journals for leads to news. These writers can take time to prepare excellent articles. They are writing for a sophisticated and influential audience. Nonetheless, their requirements are closer to those of a newspaper than to those of a technical scientific journal.

Magazines and Books

Magazines that are not primarily oriented toward the news (e.g., the *New Yorker, Ladies' Home Journal, Cosmopolitan, Esquire*) will occasionally run a feature story on a scientific topic. The requirements for these stories are similar to those of feature stories in newspapers or Sunday supplements. Sometimes they are written by staff writers who have little background in science; at other times, a science writer may be commissioned to produce a specific story or, as a freelance writer, may sell one to a magazine. There is more time for research, more opportunity to interview a number of different investigators, more chance to check facts and allow the scientist to check what has been written.

A popular science book must have the same level of simple, clear exposition as the other printed media, but because of its greater length, can deal with more complicated subject material in more detail. The writer has more time to research the material, but unless there is some type of grant support, in the long run he or she must average a reasonable number of words per day in order to earn a living.

Explaining the Process, or Beyond the Products of Science

The conditions that confront most of the media, especially the pressure for time, space, and interest, favor stories that emphasize the end-products of science—the practical results, the new techniques, surprising phenomena—rather than the process by which science develops and sometimes, often quite unexpectedly, leads to important practical consequences. Yet, in order to make intelligent decisions concerning science, the public needs to know something about the process by which it advances—the fumbling trial-and-error, the logical way in which a scientist devises tests to choose between alternative hypotheses, the long chain of small advances gradually leading to new understanding, and the unexpected discoveries. Of course, all these points cannot be covered in a single story, but sometimes a story can illustrate one or another part of that process. Realizing the constraints upon the media, the scientist should seize every possible opportunity to illustrate the scientific process as simply and clearly as possible, to make it interesting, and to try to persuade the writer of a feature article or TV show to cover a somewhat narrower range of materials in greater depth. If this can be done via the media (and also in the introductory courses over which we have vastly more control!), it will become more difficult for an otherwise intelligent politician to make a ridiculous statement such as: "We're not paying you people at NIH to satisfy your curiosity about the *causes* of disease, we're paying you to *cure* it!"

APPENDIX B

Nuclear Waste: A Problem That Won't Go Away

David W. Crisp

Winner of the 1980 AAAS–Westinghouse Science Writing Award for newspapers of less than 100,000 circulation. The five-part series was published in the *Palestine Herald–Press*, Palestine, Texas, February 24–28, 1980.

Part I: A Look Back at Our Future

In 1995, high-level waste canisters begin to arrive, most of them by rail . . .

In the summer of 1980, a drilling rig goes up almost overnight in the center of the Keechi salt dome. Law Engineering Testing Co., subcontracted by the Office of Nuclear Waste Isolation to study the Gulf Coast interior, takes a core sample and finds the salt solid and dry.

Water tests on all four sides of the dome show no dissolving of the salt. Engineers discount a 1926 report that water from the Carrizo-Wilcox aquifer occasionally leaches salt from the dome and carries it to the surface.

In 1985, the site is selected as the best in the Gulf Coast interior. After reviewing studies of the Keechi and other sites in Nevada, Washington, and New Mexico, the Department of Energy recommends licensing of the site as a nuclear waste repository.

An environmental impact statement is filed and accepted over strong local opposition. Environmental groups from Austin and Dallas come to Palestine to protest and Keechi becomes as much a code word for nuclear opposition as Three Mile Island.

Some real estate deals fall through. A few industries considering Palestine decide to go elsewhere. Others, anticipating an influx of new workers and an expanded tax base, move in.

In 1990, the government buys land over the Keechi salt dome. The major landowners there—the Links, Lights, and Grumbles—move.

Besides 440 acres for the site itself, another square mile or so around the dome is bought as a buffer zone. Subsurface rights are acquired for a couple more square miles to prevent drilling near the site.

Preliminary construction begins. State Highway 19 is rerouted and railroad spurs are built north of town toward the dome. Growth of Palestine toward the northwest stops.

Workers, about 1500 of them, build two sets of receiving buildings, one for high-level wastes and another for low level. The high-level building is two stories high and made of concrete. They build administration, storage, emergency generation, refrigeration, and ventilation buildings.

They also build locker rooms, showers, a laundry, cafeteria, firehouse, and living quarters. The buildings are surrounded by two fences, one a high isolation fence to discourage saboteurs and terrorists.

Three mining shafts are excavated: one to transport radioactive wastes, one to move men and materials, and one for ventilation.

Two-hundred underground rooms are dug out, occupying more than 87 million square feet—74 million square feet for nuclear waste storage —the rest is occupied by shafts, service areas, and corridors.

As the Department of Energy predicted in 1979, nine workers are killed in construction and mining accidents, none by radiation. When building is complete, all but 300 workers move on to other jobs. The crime rate, buoyed by the twenty-seven major crimes the excess population has contributed every year, begins to taper off.

In 1995, high-level waste canisters ten feet long and a foot in diameter begin to arrive, most of them by rail. They are shipped in heavy, shielded reusable casks. Each cask contains several canisters, each railroad car carries one cask.

The casks have proven themselves in extensive testing as long ago as 1977 at the Sandia Laboratories in New Mexico. They have been dropped onto reinforced concrete from a height of thirty feet; they have endured fire hotter than 1475 degrees; they have been smashed broadside by railroad locomotives traveling eighty miles an hour.

Still, the railroad industry does not accept the test results, claiming scientific criteria were not met. And eleven substances commonly shipped can fuel fires as hot as 4275 degrees.

During shipment, the heat of the wastes raises the surface temperature of the casks to 180 degrees. Palestinians living along the tracks receive minute radiation doses from each passing cask—doses so small that 10,000 casks give off as much radiation as a single X ray.

At the repository, the casks are lifted by crane from the railcars and placed in transfer cells, where the canisters are removed and inspected. All handling of high-level wastes is by remote control.

Damaged canisters are taken to overpack cells and fitted into new containers. Then they are moved to the mine shaft and lowered into the repository.

Meanwhile, low-level wastes, which are far less toxic, arrive by truck in 55-gallon drums. They are unloaded with shielded forklifts, moved to the shaft, and taken underground. Low-level waste drums are stacked two high along the walls of underground rooms. High-level waste canisters are placed ten meters apart in holes or trenches and covered over with salt.

When a room is full, it is sealed off with a steel plug so that the wastes remain retrievable for five to twenty-five years. In case the site fails, the wastes can be removed.

By the year 2015, the repository is full. It contains more than 68,000 canisters. The rooms and shafts are backfilled with salt, though the fill salt is only 80 percent as dense as it was before mining. Total cost to this point: $20 billion.

Most of the workers move on to one of the two or three other repositories that will be in operation. They leave behind nine school teachers and extra doctors and policemen the county has hired because of them. They also leave behind a small security force, in the unlikely event some terrorist group is willing to attempt the immense and dangerous task of unearthing the wastes.

The surface buildings are dismantled and the site is turned into a wildlife refuge. The radioactive heat beneath raises the temperature at ground level about half a degree. It also causes the salt to expand, lifting the surface over the dome five feet over several centuries.

More than 2000 feet below the surface, each canister heats the salt around it to about 85 degrees over a forty-year period. Water, usually found in tiny quantities in salt, migrates toward the heat. Eventually, each canister is surrounded by about six gallons of water.

Radiation emanates from the canisters, creating chemical reaction with the salt and water. Hydrochloric acid forms and corrodes the stainless steel canisters within a few years.

The wastes themselves have been incorporated into a boron silicate glass similar to Pyrex. Some scientists say the glass will hold the wastes in place for centuries. Others say the wastes will leach through in a few weeks.

Either way, the salt itself eventually becomes the waste container. Cesium-137 and barium-137, which make up the bulk of the wastes, give off gamma rays for 1000 years before their radiation is spent. At that point, according to the University of Pittsburgh's Bernie Cohen, a person would have to eat half a pound of the wastes to incur a 50 percent chance of getting cancer.

Without steel canisters, the wastes slowly leach through the salt, reaching the Carrizo-Wilcox Aquifer within 30,000 years of their release. Within another 400 years, they reach the surface and become part of the drinking water.

After 100,000 years they give off less radiation than a granite building. But they remain radioactive for a million years or longer.

That time is as far from 1980 as Neanderthal man. Whether anyone is around to drink enough contaminated water to be harmed by it is a matter of pure speculation.

If men live above the Keechi dome then, the memory of nuclear wastes may be lost to them.

Or the wastes could be a legend, or a nearly forgotten religious taboo, with its own priesthood and holy ground, calling far back to the days when nuclear power was a fact, not some ancient science fiction.

PART II: Salt Dome Storage Idea Came Up in 1957

When humans first began splitting atoms in World War II, storing the wastes that resulted was the last thing on anyone's mind. Winning the war came first.

When civilian nuclear waste began to appear in 1957, it came in quantities so small it was considered negligible. Even today, if all the electricity in the United States was produced by nuclear power (about 14 percent actually is), each person's annual share of nuclear waste would be about the size of an aspirin tablet.

To be sure, it would be a toxic aspirin tablet. And the volume of wastes produced by the military weapons program is vastly larger, making up as much as 99 percent of all radioactive wastes.

Still, military and commercial wastes present comparable problems. Military wastes, which were stored in tanks in liquid form, are being solidified for final storage, as federal policy requires.

And military wastes are proportionately less toxic than commercial wastes, since plutonium is used by the military to make bombs but is part of the waste problem in the civilian program. And, while military wastes accumulate steadily but slowly, commercial wastes are increasing geometrically, as the number of operating plants expands from seventy one now in operation to five hundred plants either planned or under construction world-wide.

In 1957, nuclear power was a small-scale operation, and the National Academy of Sciences suggested the wastes could be safely and inexpensively stored in repositories mined out of salt formations.

In 1980, salt remains a preferred method of storage, for a number of reasons: it is abundant, inexpensive to mine, nearly as strong structurally as concrete, and shifts to "heal" holes and fractures.

And salt formations are as old as 100 million years, which shows they are geologically stable. Salt dissolves rapidly in water, which means its existence is evidence it is not contaminated by groundwater.

But salt also has disadvantages. Southern Methodist University's Dr. George Crawford said neutrons from nuclear waste canisters could penetrate the salt and fracture it, allowing canisters to sink to the groundwater beneath. Studies he conducted on salt from 1955 to 1959 were "very promising," Crawford said, but now he is "totally against it."

While serving as nuclear research officer in the School of Aerospace medicine at Brooks Air Force Base from 1959 to 1963, Crawford said he was a nuclear energy supporter.

But in 1971, as a visiting scientist at the Nuclear Research Laboratory in Switzerland, he said he saw a melt-down of an experimental reactor and changed his position.

"Your only recourse is to protest," Crawford said. "We are not a throw-away society."

The U.S. Geological Survey, in a 1978 report, did not go that far but did call for more study. While scientists can find sites that have been stable in the past, the report concluded, they cannot predict what will happen in the future. The effects of water on salt and possible chemical reactions between salt and the wastes themselves remain uncertain.

Early efforts to find a suitable repository have raised more uncertainties. An Atomic Energy Commission proposal to store wastes near Lyons, Kansas, was withdrawn in 1971 after 175,000 gallons of water pumped into a nearby salt mine disappeared.

And the Waste Isolation Pilot Project near Carlsbad, New Mexico, designed to demonstrate successful storage in salt, has been cancelled for technical and political reasons.

In Germany, low- and intermediate-level wastes already are being stored in 55-gallon drums in an abandoned salt mine near the East German border.

And in the United States, studies of salt continue on the Gulf Coast, in the Permian Basin of west Texas, and in the Salina Basin, which includes parts of Ohio, Michigan, and New York.

Of more than 500 domes on the Gulf Coast (about half of them underwater), all but seven have been eliminated from further study. Three are in Mississippi but are located near or under a wildlife refuge, national forest, or town. Two Louisiana domes have been studied for five years by Louisiana State University, but a 1978 law against nuclear waste storage in Louisiana salt is now hampering further studies, according to engineer Dean Klotz.

In Texas, testing on the Oakwood dome has been delayed, and extensive study of the Keechi dome near Palestine has not begun. The Keechi is in a stable area—the largest earthquake in the entire Gulf Coast was recorded in Rusk in 1891. Some scientists now think that was no earthquake at all but only a severe windstorm.

The Keechi area also contains little oil or gas, which means it is less valuable economically and not as penetrated by drill holes as the Oakwood dome.

However, there is evidence that the Keechi may be too small to meet the government's requirement of 1800 acres underground. And some fractures, possibly major ones, have been found on the dome. The Texas Bureau of Economic Geology's Dr. E. G. Wermund said it will take more study to know for sure.

Meanwhile, the Department of Energy is mulling over other proposals for nuclear waste disposal, none of them as well understood as salt.

President Carter's February 12 message to Congress put methods other than geologic storage on the back burner, but some funds will still be devoted to them as "longer range options."

The wastes could be loaded onto rocketships and fired into the sun, but that could cost $1.4 million per reactor each year, and rockets have been known to fall back to earth.

Wastes could be loaded onto ships, taken to the middle of the ocean, and dropped or lowered deep into sediments that have remained undisturbed for millions of years. The bottom of the ocean is five times more barren than the Sahara Desert, but deepwater flow is not well understood and international political complications could prove insurmountable.

International politics also could block storage in polar ice caps, which are far away, cold, and barren. And heat from radioactive wastes would melt some of the ice, which could affect climate and raise ocean levels.

Wastes could be stored in holes 30,000 feet below the surface of the earth, or they could be bombarded with neutrons until they turn into nondangerous elements. Both ideas present technical problems, and they share a disadvantage: they render the wastes permanently irretrievable.

Current guidelines call for wastes to be stored retrievably for five to twenty-five years. Some scientists say that isn't long enough.

"Current technology sees no use for spent fuel rods," Crawford said. "Future technology will consider them a gold mine."

Calling the wastes "resources of the future," Crawford proposes they be stored on-site by nuclear power plants or at decommissioned plants, which he said will be too radioactive to use for anything else anyway. Stainless steel canisters encasing the wastes could be replaced as they corrode, until uses for the wastes are found.

Wastes are now being stored on-site, though nuclear plants are running out of room in storage pools. Predictions that lack of space would cause some plants to close in the 1970s did not come true, but it could happen in the 1980s.

DOE's Curtis Carlson said expensive sites to store overflow wastes will have to be built in the next few years. A bill authorizing one or more sites is under consideration in Congress.

Meanwhile, radioactivity eats away at the metal that encloses it. At the Hanford Reservation in Washington, where 70 percent of the nation's military wastes are stored, at least eighteen leaks of radioactive materials have occurred, including one that lasted forty-eight days and spilled more than 115,000 gallons.

Radioactivity has been found in streams near a waste site in West Valley, New York, and plutonium was found hundreds of yards away from the Maxey Flats site at Moorhead, Kentucky.

It is a problem that has outstripped attempts to find a solution, and the lack of a solution casts doubt on the government's ability to find one. But the problems are not simply federal, nor are they all technical.

They also are political. And as the federal government pushes toward a solution, state governments are blocking the way.

PART III: Measuring the Danger

Nuclear scientists' opinions mixed
over effects of radiation on humans

The wastes generated each year by a nuclear power plant are small enough to fit under a dining room table. But if all the wastes from all the plants were dumped into rivers, spread on crops, or sprayed into the air, they could cause up to a billion cancers, according to one estimation.

High-level commercial wastes contain more than 100 different isotopes of uranium, some of which give off all their energy and disappear in a few days. The more radioactive something is, the faster it decays.

Atoms in a nuclear reaction can either absorb or be split by neutrons. Atoms that are split by neutrons, called fission products, include strontium-90, cesium-137, barium-137, and iodine-129, which are among the most dangerous waste products.

But all those products have half-lives of thirty years or less. Within thirty years, half of the radioactivity has decayed. Within another thirty years, half of the remainder is gone.

Since it takes ten or twenty half-lives to decay to harmless levels, the fission products are nearly gone after 600 years. At that point, the nuclear wastes as a whole are only about as radioactive as natural uranium ore.

But the atoms in the reactor that were not split by neutrons, but rather absorbed them, will have only begun to decay.

Known as transuranics, they include isotopes of neptunium, americium, curium, and plutonium, all of which are toxic and have long half-lives. Some of them even become more dangerous as time passes.

Americium-243, for example, has a half-life of 7300 years; then it eventually decays to plutonium-239, which is more toxic and has a half-life of 24,000 years.

Because transuranics decay so slowly, they give off only small amounts of radiation. They tend to stay where they are put, and their radiation cannot penetrate very far.

However, scientists admit the effects of small doses of radiation over a long period are not well understood. Cancer can take thirty years to develop, and its causes are difficult to trace.

It is possible that there is a minimum level of radiation that has no effect at all. But it is also possible that some radiation effects are cumulative, building up in the body until dangerous levels are reached.

A 1972 report even indicated that low levels of radiation may be more dangerous than higher ones, because high doses kill cells outright, while lower ones only damage them, making them cancerous.

One way to measure the danger from living near nuclear wastes is to compare their effects with natural background radiation from the sun and rocks and minerals in the earth.

Under normal operation of a waste site, the total radiation dose from wastes to the whole population would be only about 3 percent of the natural dose. A single X ray, by comparison, exposes one to more radiation than an entire year of natural radiation in Texas.

In fact, radiation doses given off during routine operations throughout the nuclear cycle are so low that Bernie Cohen of the University of Pittsburgh has argued that it is safer to mine uranium, burn it, and store it safely deep underground than it is to leave it lying unused and unguarded in the earth.

Predicted doses from accidents are larger, but remain small enough that Dr. Margaret Maxey of the University of Detroit said of the nation's worst nuclear accident that "people who flew in to Washington to protest Three Mile Island got more [radiation] exposure on the flight than they would have standing at the fence at Three Mile Island."

The Department of Energy calculates that a bad accident, such as a 75-foot thick meteorite crashing directly into a nuclear waste storage site, could damage the health of up to 140,000 people if the area was densely populated. But DOE oddsmakers say such an accident would occur only once every 20 trillion years.

On that basis, the risk from the accident is quite small. Automobile accidents will kill that many people in the next three years. But not everyone accepts government estimates.

Dr. George Crawford, chairman of the physics department at Southern Methodist University, said the government "is determined to prove [waste storage] will work. They do set up a few straw men and proceed to knock them down," he said, but warned that government researchers have been "less than completely honest."

A 1969 study by John W. Gofman and Arthur R. Tamplin and a 1977 study by Dr. Thomas Mancuso charged that even at federally allowed dosages levels, low-level radiation can cause cancer. The studies have become so controversial that they serve as a sort of watershed for pro- and antinuclear forces.

But proponents of nuclear energy argue that radiation dangers are comparable to danger from other energy sources, especially coal.

A lignite-burning plant the size of Big Brown, near Fairfield, can send as much as 600 pounds of carbon dioxide into the atmosphere every second. Worldwide use of such low-grade coal could affect the world's climate within 100 years, according to industry sources, perhaps even melting polar ice caps and flooding seacoast cities.

A coal plant puts up to thirty pounds of ash into the air every second, emits benzpyrene (the cancer-causing agent in cigarettes), and puts out as much nitrogen oxide as 200,000 automobiles.

Since lignite ore contains radioactive elements, a coal plant can even burn up to ten tons of uranium each year, releasing the radioactivity into the air.

Expensive scrubbers and tight regulation reduce dangers from coal, but increased burning of low grades partly offsets safety measures.

In any case, some scientists think coal will never be as safe as nuclear power—and waste disposal is considered the safest part of the nuclear cycle.

An operating nuclear reactor, for example, contains as much radioactivity as is given off by the 4 billion tons of uranium dissolved in the world's oceans. The 200,000 kilowatts of heat a reactor generates while running declines to 8500 kilowatts a week after it stops.

But neither coal, solar, nor geothermal energy present alternatives to nuclear waste storage. More than half a million cubic meters of high-level wastes already exist and 10,000 more are being added each year.

Where to put them forever is a problem the federal government is just beginning to seriously address.

"The Greek God of Hell"

Plutonium most controversial new element

The most controversial, useful, and dangerous product of nuclear energy production is an element found nowhere in nature, but which lasts half a million years after man creates it.

It is plutonium—named after the Greek god of hell, as nuclear critics often point out. Some of its properties are hellish indeed.

In amounts as small as 3 millionths of a gram, it has caused cancer in dogs. In amounts as small as ten or twenty pounds, it can make a small nuclear bomb.

A pound of it is, in theory, enough to cause cancer in every living human being, a statistic the University of Detroit's Dr. Margaret Maxey scoffs at.

"That makes as much sense," she said, "as saying that one ejaculation can fertilize every woman in the world—the problem is the delivery system."

(Continued)

Radiation from plutonium is so weak it can penetrate neither a sheet of paper, nor human skin. Even if it's swallowed, the mucus layer protecting the stomach blocks most of the radiation.

It is most dangerous if inhaled, which is what could happen "if some cataclysm catapults it into the upper atmosphere to rain down as global fallout," as a National Academy of Sciences report has pointed out.

The chances of such a cataclysm would increase, nuclear critics argue, if the federal government allows the nuclear industry to recycle plutonium or use it in breeder reactors.

Because plutonium burns in a nuclear reactor like uranium does, the industry has assumed that wastes recovered from spent fuel rods would be processed to remove unburned uranium and plutonium.

The elements could then go back into the reactor, extending uranium supplies by 20 to 40 percent.

However, no commercial reprocessing plants were operating in 1977 when President Carter issued a reprocessing ban.

Three plants had been built before the ban came. The first operated in West Valley, New York, from 1966 to 1972, but failed to recover costs and was approaching contamination limits when it was closed. 600,000 gallons of reprocessed high-level wastes remain stored on the site.

Two other reprocessing plants—in Illinois and South Carolina—never opened because of technical problems and uncertain economics.

Carter's ban was not for economic reasons but to help fight the proliferation of nuclear weapons. Unlike a nuclear power plant or commercial enrichment plant, a reprocessing plant produces weapons-grade materials. And countries receiving nuclear technology from the United States may be as interested in weapons as in electricity.

Besides that, the plants make a tempting target for saboteurs and terrorists. And though the nuclear industry argues that reprocessing is essential, a 1977 Ford Foundation study concluded its economic benefits are "questionable," at least until the price of uranium ore soars because of scarcity.

More expensive and difficult to build, but potentially more energy-efficient, are breeder reactors. Such reactors could end dependence on uranium altogether, since they are theoretically capable of producing forty times more fuel than they consume.

But they also can explode, unlike conventional nuclear plants. Although the expected force of such an accident would be at least

2000 times smaller than the impact of the atomic bomb that fell on Hiroshima, it could be powerful enough to fracture its containment vessel.

The only commercial breeder reactor built in the United States was the Fermi reactor in Detroit. The plant suffered a partial core meltdown during testing in 1969, prompting an engineer's famous remark, "We almost lost Detroit." Construction was halted by economic and licensing problems in 1972.

A second attempt, the Clinch River Breeder Reactor, is scheduled to be completed with government aid in 1983, despite presidential opposition.

Neither reprocessing nor breeder reactors solve the problem of nuclear waste. Waste would still be produced and it would contain small but toxic amounts of plutonium. Concentrations of other heavy elements, such as americium, would be increased. The total volume of waste would be about the same.

Part IV: Materials May Return to Earth

Under present federal plans, unburned radioactive materials will eventually wind up where they came from—deep underground.

How they get out of the ground, how they will be put back in, and what happens in between is a process that costs a lot of money, poses some risks, and produces about 14 percent of the nation's electricity, as well as all of her nuclear weapons.

Uranium, mined in concentrations of ten to twenty pounds per ton of ore, is the source of it all. Most of it comes from the Rocky Mountains, but production in Texas is growing rapidly, increasing from 1.9 million pounds in 1977 to an estimated 6 million pounds this year. It takes about 200 tons of mined uranium per year to power one nuclear plant.

Texas uranium comes from an area south and southeast of San Antonio, and accounts for many of the more than 2000 shipments of radioactive materials daily in Texas. (Oil-well logging, radiography, X rays, and weapons production account for most of the rest.)

Uranium mining releases radon gas and its decay products, including lead. By falling on crops, the products can enter the food chain, a 1976 Nuclear Regulatory Commission found.

Uranium miners inhale radioactive dust, which can get into lungs and cause cancer. A Ford Foundation study found that radiation exposure from mining may cause four delayed cancer deaths a year—about a third as many deaths as are caused by mining accidents.

Mined uranium ore is taken to a mill, usually nearby, where it is crushed, ground, and concentrated into solid yellowcake form. Some unused elements in the ore—called tailings—are radioactive for thousands of years. They were used as landfill and concrete mix in Grand Junction, Colorado, and other western cities in the 1960s, but have since been linked to increased cancer rates and birth defects.

Today tailings remain in shallow trenches at the mill, and the yellowcake uranium goes to a conversion plant. It is made into uranium hexafluoride, which is a gas at temperatures above 135 degrees.

The gas is needed for the next step, which is enrichment. Natural uranium is made up 99.3 percent uranium-238 and 0.7 percent uranium-235, which produces the power.

The enrichment plant raises the percentage of U-235 to about 3 percent in a process that consumes large amounts of electricity—as much per plant as the city of Cleveland, according to one estimate.

Even at 3 percent U-235, nuclear fuel is too weak for a nuclear plant to explode like a bomb. But enrichment plants have the technical capacity to produce weapons grade materials of 90 percent uranium-235 or higher. That is one reason all three enrichment plants now in operation —in Tennessee, Kentucky, and Ohio—are owned by the federal government.

Enriched uranium makes one more stop—at a fuel fabrication plant—before it can be used. There it is converted into solid pellets less than an inch long. Each pellet, according to Homer Schmidt of Texas Utilities, can produce as much energy as a ton of coal.

The pellets are loaded into fourteen-foot-long metal tubes, called fuel rods. From 64 to 256 fuel rods go into one fuel assembly, and a single reactor contains 150 to 700 fuel assemblies. Total initial fuel cost: about $60 million.

Fuel assemblies are placed into a reactor core, the heart of a nuclear power plant. In the core, a chain reaction begins. U-235 atoms spontaneously give off neutrons, which strike other atoms in the core. Some struck atoms absorb the extra neutrons, changing their basic structure and creating new elements, such as plutonium. Other atoms are split, or fissioned, by the neutrons. Split atoms give off energy, and more neutrons, which strike other atoms.

Fission produces energy and a tremendous amount of heat, which boils water in tubes that pass through the reactor core in loops at a rate of 4 million gallons an hour.

Boiling water produces steam, which turns a turbine and generates electricity. A plant the size of Comanche Peak, now being built near Glen Rose, has a capability of more than a million kilowatts in each of its two reactors.

But as the chain reaction consumes U-235, the plant operates less and less efficiently, so about one-third of the fuel rods must be replaced each year.

The replaced rods are so hot the wastes inside self-boil for years after removal. They can give a lethal dose of radiation to a person standing ten yards away for ten minutes. They are placed in pools of water, where the heat and radiation disperse rapidly at first, then more and more slowly as time goes by.

The federal government, fearing plutonium inside could be made into weapons, will not allow them to be cut open so plutonium and uranium left in them can be reused. Federal efforts to find a permanent repository for them remain in the planning stages.

They will continue to give off heat and radiation for thousands of years. They are a problem that will not go away.

PART V: Opposition Developed to Storage

In July 1978, 300 persons gathered in Anderson College Center as a panel discussed testing of three proposed nuclear waste storage sites in Anderson, Freestone, and Leon Counties.

The reception was cool, fearful, and occasionally hostile, just as it has been in three other public meetings since then. Congressmen, scientists, and Department of Energy officials alike have either fueled opposition or failed to dissipate it.

"What is minimal danger?" asked Nancy Wise of Fairfield at one meeting. "One life? Is this theoretically safe or absolutely foolproof safe?"

No one could say for sure.

In the year and a half since the first meeting, with one local site removed from consideration and the other two questionable, opposition to waste storage has grown.

Commissioners' courts in Anderson and Freestone counties have opposed it, and so has the Palestine Chamber of Commerce, after canvassing the results of a survey of its members.

One hundred and six of 108 people polled in Palestine Plaza said they oppose a local storage site, and more than 3000 people have signed petitions against it.

The Action Committee for the Retention of Environmental Safety

(ACRES) purchased newspaper ads and has held three meetings, the last of which drew more than 250 people, including U.S. Representative Charles Wilson and three state legislators.

Wilson said he believes Texas should store the nuclear wastes it generates, but State Representative Fred Head of Athens asked the Texas Energy and Natural Resources Advisory Council on December 7 to ban nuclear waste sites near populated areas, including East Texas.

At that meeting, TENRAC tabled a decision on a nuclear policy for Texas. The proposed policy calls for Texas to "encourage the implementation of one or more demonstration sites" for high-level waste disposal.

The policy recommends locating a low-level waste site in Texas but that Texas "seek the right of concurrence" over any site.

Governor Bill Clements, cochairman of TENRAC, now says he opposes storing radioactive wastes from other states in Texas.

Other states have taken stronger stands. Eleven states, including some under consideration for storage sites, have said they will not accept nuclear wastes.

A 1978 Louisiana law prohibiting storage of nuclear wastes in salt domes has slowed DOE testing. One Louisiana official predicted waste storage there would "probably put an end to dreams of prosperity and expectations for a better life" among residents of affected parishes.

In Michigan, where the Salina basin is under study, 90 percent of those voting in nonbinding referenda said they would not consent to radioactive waste repositories in their counties. In 1977, Michigan's governor formally requested the state be removed from consideration.

Local or state opposition also has halted or delayed studies in New Mexico, Nevada, Ohio, and New York. "Is it true," a Freestone County resident asked DOE's Keith Klein, "that since we're agreeable and you're here, they'll win by default and we'll lose?"

Klein replied that the department "has no authority to allow a state to veto DOE's decisions on nuclear waste repositories."

However, a policy decision last year by former energy secretary James Schlesinger prevents DOE from investigating sites over state objections.

A State Planning Council appointed by President Carter February 12 will instead work on developing a policy of "consultation and concurrence."

Consultation means that government intends to keep states involved in site selections, even to the point of funding state staffs to review federal actions.

But DOE's attempts to inform have been widely criticized. At Dallas hearings on a generic environmental impact statement, speaker after speaker said a highly technical 1400-page statement had been mailed too late for proper study, or that the meeting had not been properly publicized, a complaint also made by Freestone and Anderson County judges Sam Bill Bournias and N.R. Link.

Dr. Howard K. Settlemyre, who owns most of the land over the Oakwood dome, said tests had been under way there for four to six weeks before he learned they were not simple water tests.

At the time of the Fairfield public meeting on October 22, DOE had already decided to defer testing on the Oakwood dome. However, this decision was not announced until November 20.

Joe Grumbles, who owns land over the Keechi dome, has said he believes that field crews, ostensibly from oil companies, have conducted DOE tests on his land.

Some local residents, including Link, argue that the studies themselves have caused undue fears and economic damage locally.

DOE has acknowledged in a recent report that the studies "appear to many citizens to be evidence of a federal commitment to put nuclear wastes at a proposed site."

There is "substantial citizen pressure," the report went on, to delay all federal activities until controversial issues are settled. "Yet answers are not available until the activities are complete," the report pointed out.

But concurrence, the policy of winning state approval for a proposed site, may present the thorniest problems. Though DOE has not yet proceeded where locally blocked, Congress may have the final say.

Should a state legally challenge a selected site, Congress could require "a preponderance" or "clear and convincing" evidence of harm to residents to justify objections.

Or Congress could give states final say by passing states' rights legislation on nuclear waste siting. Bills to that effect have been proposed but not yet passed.

Or Congress could give tax breaks or other political plums to states willing to take on nuclear wastes.

As testing goes beyond early stages and the need for a storage site worsens, pressures on Congress and the states will increase. The United States could eventually need as many as ten repositories, according to some estimates.

If wastes from other countries are accepted to control nuclear proliferation, as has been suggested, the figure could go even higher. The nuclear waste problem in the United States would double if all of the world's commercial nuclear wastes were accepted.

If other states follow Clement's lead and reject out-of-state wastes, the number of repositories could soar as high as fifty, a site in each state, increasing risks and expense.

For now, the DOE is seeking only four, possibly five sites. Plans call for them to be distributed as widely as possible to reduce transportation of wastes, provide a hedge against site shutdown, and distribute the storage burden among the states.

But the very first site, wherever it turns out to be, is likely to be the hardest of all to find.

APPENDIX C

Mrs. Kelly's Monster

Jon Franklin
Winner, 1979 Pulitzer Prize for Feature Writing [1]

In the cold hours of a winter[2] morning Dr. Thomas Barbee Ducker, chief brain surgeon at the University of Maryland Hospital, rises[3,4] before dawn.[5] His wife serves him waffles[6] but no coffee. Coffee makes his hands shake.[7]

---

[1] This story was originally written as a single piece without footnotes. It was then cut in two for publication in *The Evening Sun,* December 1979. I have recombined the two pieces here and added footnotes to explain the various writing techniques I used in its creation.

[2] You must set the mood early in the story. Dr. Ducker also rose to a warm house and a bright future, but those facts are not relevant to the story being told.

[3] It is no accident that the first verb in this story is active.

[4] The use of present tense tends to make the story more immediate, but it increases the pressure on the writer, who must supply an endless stream of detail to make the immediate nature of the story seem real. Because of the increased technical problems with present tense, the technique must never be used lightly. Also, present tense is usually unsuitable for longer pieces.

[5] This provides sense of time. Sense of place is implied, here: It's in Dr. Ducker's house, in Baltimore.

[6] Be specific with symbolism. Also note how the food imagery here dovetails with the food imagery in the ending. Food is a life process. In the morning the food is warm and served lovingly. In the end, the food is dry, cold, and packed in an anonymous paper bag.

[7] Straight news technique requires the writer to sum up the story in the first paragraph. Feature style often requires that it be implied. The implication here is that it is very important that Dr. Ducker's hands *don't* shake.

In downtown Baltimore,[8] on the twelfth[9] floor of University Hospital, Edna Kelly's husband tells her goodbye.[10] For fifty-seven years Mrs. Kelly shared her skull[11] with the monster[12]: No more. Today she is frightened but determined.

It is 6:30 a.m.[13]

"I'm not afraid to die," she said[14] as this day approached.[15] "I've lost part of my eyesight. I've gone through all the hemorrhages. A couple of years ago I lost my sense of smell, my taste. I started having seizures. I smell a strange odor and then I start strangling. It started affecting my legs, and I'm partially paralyzed.

"Three years ago a doctor told me all I had to look forward to was blindness, paralysis, and a remote chance of death. Now I have aneurysms; this monster is causing that. I'm scared[16] to death . . . but there isn't a day that goes by that I'm not in pain, and I'm tired of it. I can't bear the pain. I wouldn't want to live like this much longer."[17]

As Dr. Ducker leaves for work, Mrs. Ducker hands him a paper bag containing a peanut butter sandwich, a banana and two Fig Newtons.[18]

Downtown, in Mrs. Kelly's brain, a sedative takes effect.

Mrs. Kelly was[19] born with a tangled knot of abnormal blood vessels in the back of her brain. The malformation began small, but in time the vessels ballooned inside the confines of the skull, crowding the healthy brain tissue.

---

[8] Place transition.

[9] Be specific . . . but only when it doesn't interfere with the story being told. You need a good *literary* reason for the inclusion of each fact. In this case, it was rhythm.

[10] This implies danger, building on the implications of the "shaking hands" line above.

[11] Note the perception that Mrs. Kelly *is* her brain. Such a unity, once established, must be carried out throughout the piece.

[12] This perception was Mrs. Kelly's, not the author's nor the surgeon's. Your subject will do much of your head work for you, if you'll be observant.

[13] Pacing. Pacing must begin before the need for it becomes apparent. This story picks up a definite beat later. It begins here, with the stipulation of an exact time. To make it an odd number, such as 6:32, would have been enameling the lily, and would have lost the effect when the story shifts to specific time later, as the pace increases.

[14] Flashback to material gleaned in an early interview.

[15] This sentence marks the transition from the opening, or lead, into the complication.

[16] And we're back to present tense.

[17] The reader must clearly understand the motivations of your characters. In this case, Mrs. Kelly has decided to go for broke because the disease had made her life not worth living.

[18] Foreshadowing is the magic of the dramatic feature writer. In this part of the story, the lunch helps get Dr. Ducker out of the house and shifts the reader's attention toward his work. (The information does double duty, another hallmark of good dramatic writing.)

[19] Flashbacks provide supportive, background, and character information.

Finally, in 1942, the malformation announced its presence[20] when one of the abnormal arteries, stretched beyond capacity, burst. Mrs. Kelly grabbed her head and collapsed.[21] After that the agony never stopped.

Mrs. Kelly, at the time of her first intracranial bleed, was carrying her second child. Despite the pain, she raised her children and cared for her husband.[22] The malformation continued to grow.

She began[23] calling it "the monster."

Now, at 7:15[24] a.m. in operating room eleven, a technician checks the brain surgery microscope and the circulating nurse lays out bandages and instruments.[25] Mrs. Kelly lies still on a stainless steel table.

A small sensor has been threaded through her veins and now hangs in the antechamber of her heart. The anesthesiologist connects the sensor to a 7-foot-high bank of electronic instruments. Oscilloscope waveforms begin[26] to build and break. Dials swing. Lights flash. With each heartbeat a loudspeaker produces an audible popping sound. The steady pop, pop, popping[27] isn't loud, but it dominates the operating room.

Dr. Ducker enters the O.R. and pauses before the X-ray films that hang on a lighted panel. He carried those brain images to Europe, Canada and Florida in search of advice, and he knows them by heart.[28] Still, he studies them again, eyes[29] focused on the two fragile aneurysms that swell above the major arteries. Either may burst on contact.

---

[20] This personifies the malformation. Personification of objects is a tricky, tricky business and should be done only with the greatest care—and only with the principal forces in the story. It would not do, for instance, to personify the peanut butter sandwich.

[21] The story does not say how Mrs. Kelly felt. Rather it implies and shows it. Action (grabbing one's head and falling) tells much more than attempts to describe her feelings. The first rule of feature writing is "Show, don't tell."

[22] She is never said, specifically, to be courageous. Rather, by her actions, she is shown to be.

[23] Today I would hesitate to use "began." I would say, instead, "She called it 'the monster.'" Words like "begin," "began," "commenced," and "started" are usually unnecessary and tend to give sentences in which they reside a distant and passive cast.

[24] Fifteen minutes past the hour is more specific than thirty minutes past. A minor point, but the tempo is building.

[25] Always use action. If you want to tell the reader that the operating room is ready, then show the crew getting it ready.

[26] This word is unnecessary.

[27] The value of sound as a pacing and descriptive device is widely overlooked. Clocks tick. Babies cry in the background. Pencils tap restively on tables. Rain clatters on a tin roof. Notice those things, and use them.

[28] This serves to emphasize the danger.

[29] By using the eyes, what's going on in the brain can be illustrated.

The one directly behind Mrs. Kelly's eyes is the most likely to burst, but also the easiest to reach. [30] That's first.

The surgeon-in-training who will assist Dr. Ducker places Mrs. Kelly's head in a clamp and shaves her hair. Dr. Ducker checks to make certain the three steel pins of the vice have pierced the skin and press directly against Mrs. Kelly's skull. "We can't have a millimeter [31] slip," he says.

Mrs. Kelly, except for a six-inch crescent of scalp, is draped [32] with green sheets. A rubber-gloved palm goes out and Doris Schwabland, the scrub nurse, lays a scalpel in it. Hemostats snap over the arteries of the scalp. Blood spatters onto Dr. Ducker's sterile paper booties. [33]

It is 8:25 a.m. The heartbeat goes pop, pop, pop, 70 beats a minute, steady.

Today Dr. Ducker intends to remove the two aneurysms, which comprise the most immediate threat to Mrs. Kelly's life. Later, he will move directly on the monster. [34]

It's a risky operation, designed to take him to the hazardous frontiers of neurosurgery. Several experts told him he shouldn't do it at all, that he should let Mrs. Kelly die. But the consensus was that he had no choice. The choice was Mrs. Kelly's.

"There's one chance out of three that we'll end up with a hell of a mess or a dead patient," Dr. Ducker says. [35] "I reviewed it in my own heart and with other people, and I thought about the patient. You weigh what happens if you do it against what happens if you don't do it. I convinced myself it should be done."

Mrs. Kelly said yes. Now Dr. Ducker pulls back Mrs. Kelly's [36] scalp

---

[30] If you're taking your reader into unfamiliar territory, it's necessary to step back periodically and tell the reader, in brief and nontechnical terms, what's going on. Otherwise, certain readers will become disoriented and quit reading.

[31] The word "millimeter" is rather unfamiliar to the reader. It is necessary to run it through the reader's mind once, in a relatively slow-paced situation, so that it will seem more familiar later when it's used under more dramatic tension. The rule is never to use an unfamiliar word for the first time in a fast-paced part of your story, because it'll slow the narrative down. (It is, incidentally, not relevant here exactly how large a millimeter is. It is sufficient that the reader know it's small.)

[32] Here, you'll note, she's draped. Later, the image is "shrouded."

[33] Gore, like sex, is sometimes more effective when it occurs off camera.

[34] This is another orientation paragraph. Note that it is used also as a pacing device, to keep the action from getting too fast here. We want the action to build.

[35] Says to whom? The reporter, of course. But imagine how awful it'd sound to say, "said to this reporter." Keep yourself out of the copy and let your subject talk directly through you to your reader. Remember, as a feature writer who puts himself into the action, you are a surrogate for your reader, and your existence on the scene is totally unimportant.

[36] Were I to write this today, I'd use "her," instead of "Mrs. Kelly's."

to reveal the dull ivory of living bone. The chatter of the half-inch drill fills the room, drowning the rhythmic pop, pop, pop[37] of the heart monitor. It is 9 o'clock when Dr. Ducker hands the two-by-four-inch triangle of skull to the scrub nurse.

The tough, rubbery covering of the brain is cut free, revealing the soft gray convolutions of the forebrain.

"There it is," says the circulating nurse in a hushed voice. "That's what keeps you working."[38]

It is 9:20.[39]

Eventually Dr. Ducker steps back, holding his gloved hands high to avoid contamination. While others move the microscope into place over the glistening brain the neurosurgeon communes[40] once more with the X-ray films. The heart beats strong, 70 beats a minute, 70 beats a minute.[41] "We're going to have a hard time today," the surgeon says to the X rays.[42]

Dr. Ducker presses his face against the microscope. His hands go out for an electrified, tweezer-like instrument. The assistant moves in close, taking his position above the secondary eyepieces.[43]

Dr. Ducker's view is shared by a video camera. Across the room a color television crackles,[44] displaying a highly magnified landscape[45] of the brain. The polished tips of the tweezers move into view.

[37] Pacing devices must be heavily foreshadowed. The pops are going to be critical later, so they have to be firmly embedded in the front of the story.

[38] Greek choruses are very useful. Watch for the opportunity to use them.

[39] The times are getting more specific.

[40] The difference between the right word and the almost-right word, Mark Twain said, is the difference between lightning and the lightning bug.

[41] Repetition can add dramatic tension and emphasize building tensions in the story. Most professional writers understand that events and ideas must be foreshadowed, but few apply the principle to gimmicks, like repetition, as well.

[42] Actually, of course, he doesn't expect the X rays to hear him. The words are directed to the occupants of the operating room—or to the readers, in the persona of a reporter, who is standing beside him. Here is another example of physical action (his voice is aimed at the X rays) being used to keep the story concrete while implying moods and tensions.

[43] This is the pause before battle. A romantic novel uses the same technique when the writer describes the knights settling into their stirrups just before the heroic charge. Some things never change.

[44] Sounds, like smells, are extremely effective in putting the reader into your story. The senses of hearing and smell are ancient, and are more closely connected to the emotional brain than is the sense of sight. That's a good anatomical fact for a professional writer to know.

[45] This is the hardest-won word in the piece. I wanted something that implied a bigness. The word "landscape" is commonly applied to continents and planets, and so carries an aura of great spaces. Few people realize how big a drop of water becomes under a microscope, and how the viewer can actually get lost and disoriented in it. Getting disoriented and lost is one of the most important dangers of neurosurgery.

It is Dr. Ducker's intent[46] to place tiny, spring-loaded alligator clips across the base of each aneurysm. But first he must navigate[47] a tortured path from his incision, above Mrs. Kelly's right eye, to the deeply buried Circle of Willis.

The journey will be immense. Under magnification, the landscape of the mind[48] expands to the size of a room. Dr. Ducker's tiny, blunt-tipped instrument[49] travels in millimeter leaps.

His strategy is to push between the forebrain, where conscious thought occurs, and the thumb-like projection of the brain, called the temporal lobe, that extends beneath the temples.[50]

Carefully, Dr. Ducker pulls these two structures apart to form a deep channel. The journey begins at the bottom of this crevasse.[51] The time is 9:36 a.m.

The gray convolutions of the brain, wet with secretions, sparkle beneath the powerful operating theater spotlights. The microscopic landscape heaves and subsides in time to the pop, pop, pop of the heart monitor.

Gently, gently, the blunt probe teases apart the minute structures of gray matter, spreading a tiny tunnel, millimeter[52] by gentle millimeter, into the glistening gray.[53]

---

[46] Any time you start talking about something that happens in the subject's head, you almost automatically slow the narrative and move into background discussion. So, when you do that, make sure you're doing it at a place you can afford to slow down. Also, this does double duty as another orientation paragraph.

[47] "Navigate" is something you do over a landscape, or seascape. See the footnote on "landscape," above.

[48] Now, the perception of "landscape" fully established, we can make the story's most important metaphysical leap, from the brain to the mind. When I wrote this piece I was beginning an unusually technical series on the brain, focusing on the brain-mind connection. I decided to do this story as the lead piece because I thought it would embed that point firmly in the reader's brain/mind.

[49] As the instrument and its movement become the focus of the reader's attention, it becomes a surrogate for Dr. Ducker. Thus the instruments get a very specific personification.

[50] More orientation. Note the regularity of orientation paragraphs, and how they fall off as the pace picks up.

[51] This paragraph should have read, ". . . Dr. Ducker pulls these two structures apart to form a deep *crevasse*. The journey begins at the bottom. The time is 9:36 a.m." Some heat-of-the-moment awkwardness is, sigh, unavoidable in the newspaper feature writing business.

[52] Never use an awkward word for the first time in a poetic passage. It takes the reader's brain longer to process it the first time, and that will throw off the rhythm you're trying so hard to establish. Foreshadow!

[53] Count the number of *m* sounds in this paragraph. Then count the number of g sounds. That is a very, very tricky gimmick and can be used only in pacing. Very much of it, and an otherwise elegant piece turns saccharine.

"We're having trouble just getting in," Dr. Ducker tells the operating room team.[54]

As the neurosurgeon works, he refers to Mrs. Kelly's monster as "the AVM," or arteriovenous malformation.[55] Normally, he says,[56] arteries force high-pressure blood into muscle or organ tissue. After the living cells suck out the oxygen and nourishment, the blood drains into low-pressure veins, which carry it back to the heart and lungs.

But in the back of Mrs. Kelly's brain one set of arteries pumps directly into veins, bypassing the tissue. The unnatural junction was not designed for such a rapid flow of blood and in fifty-seven years it slowly swelled to the size of a fist. Periodically it leaked drops of blood and torrents of agony.[57] Now the structures of the brain are welded together by scar tissue, and to make his tunnel, Dr. Ducker must tease them apart again.[58] But the brain is delicate.

The screen of the television monitor fills with red.

Dr. Ducker responds quickly, snatching the broken end of the tiny artery with the tweezers. There is an electrical bzzzzzt[59] as he burns the bleeder closed. Progress stops while the blood is suctioned out.

"It's nothing to worry about," he says. "It's not much, but when you're looking at one square centimeter, two ounces is a damned lake."[60]

Carefully, gently, Dr. Ducker continues to make his way into the brain. Far down the tiny tunnel the white trunk of the optic nerve can be seen. It is 9:54.

Slowly, using the optic nerve as a guidepost, Dr. Ducker probes deeper and deeper into the gray. The heart monitor continues to pop, pop, pop, 70 beats a minute, 70 beats a minute.

The neurosurgeon guides the tweezers directly to the pulsing carotid artery, one of the three main blood channels into the brain. The carotid twists and dances[61] to the electronic pop, pop, popping. Gently, ever

---

[54] Here, action is used to foreshadow.

[55] Shift here to background.

[56] This attribution is unnecessary and slows down the flow.

[57] Parallel construction tugs compellingly at the mind. It makes things seem related that aren't, and makes for slick stream-of-consciousness transitions. The concepts "drops of blood" and "torrents of agony" come from separate universes . . . or do they? That was the question this piece was written to make the reader ask.

[58] This statement brings us back to story action.

[59] A good feature writer learns to observe noises and, when possible, bring them to his reader. Sometimes this can be tricky. I've got an hour invested in "ka-Glup, ka-Glup, ka-Glup," used to describe a heart sounds amplifier in an upcoming book.

[60] Driving home the idea, again, that the microscope magnifies everything, including the problems.

[61] Verbs are everything.

gently, nudging aside the scarred brain tissue, Dr. Ducker moves along the carotid toward the Circle of Willis, near the floor of the skull.

This loop of vessels is the staging area from which blood is distributed throughout the brain. Three major arteries feed it from below, one in the rear and the two carotids in the front.

The first aneurysm lies ahead, still buried in gray matter, where the carotid meets the Circle. The second aneurysm is deeper yet in the brain, where the hindmost artery rises along the spine and joins the Circle.

Eyes pressed against the microscope, Dr. Ducker makes his tedious way along the carotid.

"She's so scarred I can't identify anything," he complains through the mask.

It is 10:01 a.m. The heart monitor pop, pop, pops with reassuring regularity.[62]

The probing tweezers are gentle, firm, deliberate, probing, probing, probing, slower than the hands of the clock. Repeatedly, vessels bleed and Dr. Ducker cauterizes them. The blood loss is mounting, and now the anesthesiologist hangs a transfusion bag above Mrs. Kelly's shrouded[63] form.

Ten minutes pass. Twenty. Blood flows, the tweezers buzz, the suction hose hisses. The tunnel is small, almost filled by the shank of the instrument.

The aneurysm finally appears at the end of the tunnel, throbbing, visibly thin, a lumpy, overstretched bag, the color of rich cream,[64] swelling out from the once-strong arterial wall, a tire about to blow out, a balloon ready to burst, a time-bomb the size of a pea.[65]

The aneurysm isn't the monster itself, only the work of the monster, which, growing malevolently, has disrupted the pressures and weakened arterial walls throughout the brain. But the monster itself, the X rays say, lies far away.[66]

The probe nudges the aneurysm, hesitantly, gently.

"Sometimes you touch one," a nurse says, "and blooey, the wolf's at the door."

[62] This implies that irregularity is not reassuring, and foreshadows trouble ahead. When the heart slows, the reader will know instantly something is wrong. He won't need an explanation, which would slow him down.

[63] Note the switch from "covered" to "shrouded." This kind of foreshadowing operates on the reader's mind at a subconscious level. With such subliminal devices, the reader never knows what hits him. But hit him it does.

[64] When you've taken the reader to an alien and frightening place, it's necessary to use as many familiar images as possible. But they have to be very apt. If it's the almost-right word, you end up looking like an idiot.

[65] Relate sizes to something the reader knows.

[66] This should have been foreshadowed, first, very early in the piece. Another example of deadline-related awkwardness.

Patiently, Dr. Ducker separates the aneurysm from the surrounding brain tissue. The tension is electric.

No surgeon would dare go after the monster itself until this swelling killer is defused.

Now.[67]

A nurse hands Dr. Ducker a long, delicate pair of pliers. A little stainless steel clip, its jaws open wide, is positioned on the pliers' end. Presently the magnified clip moves into the field of view, light glinting from its polished surface.

It is 10:40.

For eleven minutes[68] Dr. Ducker repeatedly attempts to work the clip over the neck of the balloon, but the device is too small. He calls for one with longer jaws. Soon that clip moves into the microscopic tunnel. With infinite slowness, Dr. Ducker maneuvers it over the neck of the aneurysm.

Then, in an instant, the jaws close and the balloon collapses.

"That's clipped," Dr. Ducker calls out. Smile wrinkles appear above his mask.[69] The heart monitor goes pop, pop, pop, steady. It is 10:58.

Dr. Ducker now begins following the Circle of Willis back into the brain, toward the second, and more difficult, aneurysm that swells[70] at the very rear of the Circle, tight against the most sensitive and primitive structure in the head, the brainstem. The brainstem controls vital processes, including breathing and heartbeat.

The going becomes steadily more difficult and bloody. Millimeter, millimeter after treacherous millimeter the tweezers burrow a tunnel through Mrs. Kelly's mind. Blood flows, the tweezers buzz, the suction slurps. Push and probe. Cauterize. Suction. Push and probe. More blood. Then the tweezers lie quiet.

"I don't recognize anything," the surgeon says. He pushes further and quickly finds a landmark.

Then, exhausted, Dr. Ducker[71] disengages himself, backs away, sits down on a stool and stares straight ahead for a long moment. The brainstem is close, close.[72]

---

[67] A paragraph is, most of all, a unit of thought. If the thought is elegant, the paragraph is short.

[68] When you've got rapid action, keep writing down times in your notebook. Later, you can select what you need for pacing.

[69] Action can sometimes be heightened by hinting at it. The alternative would have been, "He smiled behind his mask." That's a more direct statement of fact but has less dramatic impact. Both statements are accurate.

[70] Word choice can be used to bolster imagery. In this case, the word tends to remind the reader of the nature of the aneurysm.

[71] It should have been "he."

[72] Again, repetition emphasizes. If you're interested in rhythmic techniques, by the way, read Edgar Allen Poe's poetry. Bells bells bells bells bells bells. And not one single bell more.

"This is a frightening place to be," whispers[73] the doctor.

In the background the heart monitor goes pop, pop, pop, 70 beats a minute, steady. The smell of ozone and burnt flesh hangs thick in the air.[74] It is 11:05 a.m., the day of the monster.

The operating room door opens and Dr. Michael Salcman,[75] the assistant chief neurosurgeon, enters. He confers with Dr. Ducker, who then returns to the microscope. Dr. Salcman moves to the front of the television monitor.

As he watches Dr. Ducker work, Dr. Salcman compares an aneurysm to a bump on a tire. The weakened wall of the artery balloons outward under the relentless pressure of the heartbeat and, eventually, it bursts. That's death.

So the fragile aneurysms must be removed before Dr. Ducker can tackle the AVM itself. Dr. Salcman crosses his arms and fixes his eyes on the television screen, preparing himself to relieve Dr. Ducker if he tires. One aneurysm down, one to go.

The second, however, is the toughest. It pulses dangerously deep, hard against the bulb of nerves that sits atop the spinal cord.

"Technically, the brainstem," says Dr. Salcman. "I call it the 'pilot light.' That's because if it goes out . . . that's it."

On the television screen the tweezer instrument presses on, following the artery toward the brainstem. Gently, gently, gently, gently it pushes aside the gray coils. For a moment the optic nerve appears in the background, then vanishes.[76]

The going is even slower now. Dr. Ducker is reaching all the way into the center of the brain and his instruments are the length of chopsticks. The danger mounts because, here, many of the vessels feed the pilot light.[77]

---

[73] "Whispers" is a word that amplifies the nature of the frightening place in which Dr. Ducker finds himself. Reserve this category of attribution trick for dramatic passages only. Usually, the word "said" will suffice. Repetition of the word "said" is rarely a serious problem.

[74] Pacing images are used to put the reader into the scene while also serving to slow the story action down. This implies that you've got to have enough action that you can afford some slow passages. If you don't have enough action to withstand the imagery slowdowns, you've probably got a boring story.

[75] Minor characters do not have to be introduced at the top of a story, but, if not, they must be foreshadowed. In this case that was easy, since Dr. Salcman came in and hung around for a while before he started taking important (structural) action.

[76] A glance at something he's met before, in this case the optic nerve, gives the reader the sense that he understands where he is. That is strictly smoke and mirrors, of course, but it puts his mind at rest and he can read on. After all, the reader isn't here to learn brain anatomy. He's here to find out what happens, and how the story comes out. Don't explain any more than the reader needs to understand the story. Explanations beyond that are flab.

[77] In a less rushed world, this would have been better foreshadowed.

The heartbeat goes pop, pop, pop, 70 beats a minute.[78]

The instrument moves across a topography of torture, scars everywhere, remnants of pain past, of agonies Mrs. Kelly would rather die than further endure.[79] Dr. Ducker is lost again.

Dr. Salcman joins him at the microscope, peering through the assistant's eyepieces. They debate the options in low tones and technical terms.[80] A decision is made and again the polished tweezers probe along the vessel.

Back on course, Dr. Ducker works his tunnel ever deeper, gentle, gentle, gentle as the touch of sterile cotton. Finally the gray matter parts.

The neurosurgeon freezes.[81]

Dead ahead[82] the field is crossed by many huge, distended, ropelike veins.

The neurosurgeon stares intently at the veins, surprised, chagrined, betrayed by the X rays.

The monster.

The monster, by microscopic standards, lies far away, above and back, in the rear of the head. Dr. Ducker was to face the monster itself on another day, not now. Not here.

But clearly these tangled veins, absent on the X-ray films but very real in Mrs. Kelly's brain, are tentacles of the monster.

Gingerly, the tweezers attempt to push around them.

Pop, pop, pop . . pop . . . pop . . . . pop . . . . pop.[83]

"It's slowing!" warns the anesthesiologist, alarmed.

The tweezers pull away like fingers touching fire.

. . . . Pop . . . pop . . pop . pop, pop, pop.

"It's coming back," says the anesthesiologist.

The vessels control blood-flow to the brainstem, the pilot light.

Dr. Ducker tries to go around them a different way.

Pop, pop, pop . pop . . pop . . . pop . . . .

And withdraws.

---

[78] And the beat, now in a separate paragraph, begins to take on a life of its own.

[79] And a tip of the hat to Abe Lincoln. Immature poets, some guru said, create. Mature poets steal. When possible, steal from the masters. Steal from romance novels and other trash at your peril.

[80] Going too deeply into the technical would only confuse the reader and is not necessary to the action. Deciding what to leave out is one of the writer's most important functions. The iron rule is that if you don't need it to make the climax work, then you don't need it at all. Some of the best stories are written backwards. This one was, sort of, and at times.

[81] When your action is being carried along by active, fine-scale description, then *action* is defined not as motion, but as change. Thus freezing in the face of danger is, in this story, a very active thing for Dr. Ducker to do.

[82] Symbolism can be layered on top of symbolism. The word "dead" is symbolic in its own right, and the phrase "dead ahead" is a term used for *navigating* across *topography*.

[83] Consider the foreshadowing that led up to this.

Dr. Salcman stands before the television monitor, arms crossed, frowning.

"She can't take much of that," the anesthesiologist says.[84] "The heart will go into arrhythmia and that'll lead to a . . . call it a heart attack."

Dr. Ducker tries a still different route, pulling clear of the area and returning at a new angle. Eventually, at the end of a long, throbbing tunnel of brain tissue, the sought-after aneurysm appears.

Pop, pop, pop . pop . . pop . . . pop . . . .

The instruments retract.

"Damn," says the neurosurgeon. "I can only work here for a few minutes without the bottom falling out."

The clock says 12:29.

Already the gray tissue swells visibly from the repeated attempts to burrow past the tentacles.

Again the tweezers move forward in a different approach and the aneurysm reappears. Dr. Ducker tries to reach it by inserting the aneurysm clip through a long, narrow tunnel. But the pliers that hold the clip obscure the view.

Pop, pop . pop . . pop . . . pop . . . .

The pliers retract.

"We're on it and we know where we are," complains the neurosurgeon, frustration adding a metallic edge to his voice. "But we're going to have an awful time getting a clip in there. We're so close, but . . . ."

A resident who has been assisting Dr. Ducker collapses on a stool. He stares straight ahead, eyes unfocused, glazed.[85]

"Michael, scrub," Dr. Ducker says to Dr. Salcman. "See what you can do. I'm too cramped."

While the circulating nurse massages Dr. Ducker's shoulders, Dr. Salcman attempts to reach the aneurysm with the clip.

Pop, pop, pop . pop . . pop . . . pop . . . .

The clip withdraws.

"That should be the aneurysm right there," says Dr. Ducker, taking his place at the microscope again. "Why the hell can't we get to it? We've tried, ten times."

At 12:53, another approach.

Pop, pop, pop . pop . . pop . . . pop . . . .

Again.

It is 1:06.

And again, and again, and again.

Pop . . .pop . . . pop, pop, pop . . . pop . . . pop-pop-pop . . .

---

[84] Note the absence of the phrase "told this reporter." Unless you're writing about yourself, *stay out of your story.*

[85] This makes Dr. Ducker's fatigue more real.

The anesthesiologist's hands move rapidly across a panel of switches. A nurse catches her breath and holds it.

"Damn, damn, damn."

Dr. Ducker backs away from the microscope, his gloved hands held before him. For a full minute, he's silent.

"There's an old dictum in medicine," he finally says. "If you can't help, don't do any harm. Let nature take its course. We may have already hurt her. We've slowed down her heart. Too many times." The words carry defeat, exhaustion, anger.[86]

Dr. Ducker stands again before the X rays. His eyes focus on the rear aneurysm, the second one, the one that thwarted him. He examines the film for signs, unseen before, of the monster's descending tentacles. He finds no such indications.

Pop, pop, pop, goes the monitor, steady now, 70 beats a minute.

"Mother Nature," a resident growls, "is a mother."

The retreat begins. Under Dr. Salcman's command, the team prepares to wire the chunk of skull back into place and close the incision.

It ends quickly, without ceremony. Dr. Ducker's gloves snap sharply as a nurse pulls them off.[87] It is 1:30.

Dr. Ducker walks, alone, down the hall, brown paper bag in his hand. In the lounge he sits on the edge of a hard orange couch and unwraps the peanut butter sandwich. His eyes focus on the opposite wall.

Back in the operating room the anesthesiologist shines a light into each of Mrs. Kelly's eyes. The right pupil, the one under the incision, is dilated and does not respond to the probing beam. It is a grim omen.

[88] If Mrs. Kelly recovers, says Dr. Ducker, he'll go ahead and try to deal with the monster itself, despite the remaining aneurysm. He'll try to block the arteries to it, maybe even take it out. That would be a tough operation, he says without enthusiasm.

"And it's providing that she's in good shape after this."

If she survives. If. If.

"I'm not afraid to die," Mrs. Kelly had said. "I'm scared to

---

[86] It is better to let action carry emotion, even if the action is no more than inflection on words.

[87] This punctuates the end of the action. It is a specific, active, concrete, sensual (sound is used) symbol.

[88] This paragraph and the two short paragraphs that follow are worse than unnecessary. They bring up images that are irrelevant (Mrs. Kelly is going to die and Dr. Ducker knows it) and distract the reader. Some readers were left uncertain as to whether or not Mrs. Kelly died. These paragraphs are the culprit. Together, they comprise the worst structural failing of the story, and if the rest of it hadn't worked well enough to offset the problem, the piece as a whole would have failed. (After I made the preceding statement at a Council for the Advancement and Support of Education seminar where this treatment was originally presented, a participant approached me afterwards to argue that the vagueness introduced by this section added suspense to the piece. I can't decide whether or not her point, in this instance, is valid.)

death . . . but . . . I can't bear the pain. I wouldn't want to live like this much longer."[89]

Her brain was too scarred. The operation, tolerable in a younger person, was too much. Already, where the monster's tentacles hang before the brainstem, the tissue swells, pinching off the source of oxygen.

Mrs. Kelly is dying.

The clock on the wall, near where Dr. Ducker sits, says 1:40.

"It's hard to tell what to do. We've been thinking about it for six weeks. But, you know, there are certain things . . . that's just as far as you can go. I just don't know. . . ."

He lays the sandwich, the banana and the Fig Newtons on the table before him, neatly, the way the scrub nurse laid out the instruments.[90]

"It was triple jeopardy," he says finally, staring at his peanut butter sandwich the same way he stared at the X rays. "It was triple jeopardy."

It is 1:43, and it's over.

Dr. Ducker bites, grimly, into the sandwich.[91]

The monster won.

[89] Flashbacks late in the story provide dramatic perspective. It is time that the reader remember that Mrs. Kelly went into this with her eyes open. Otherwise, our hero becomes tarnished by failure. One of the points of the piece is that he is *not* tarnished, because he tried.

[90] Foreshadowed, this becomes a very dramatic, human action.

[91] He must go on. Food symbolizes life.

Examples from "Science Notebook"

Thomas Cole, William Doemel,
David Krohne, and Robert Petty

SUGAR-BINDING LECTINS
NOT ALWAYS A SWEET TALE

THOMAS COLE

In 1969, Georgi Markov, a Bulgarian playwright, defected to the West and eventually wound up working for the British Broadcasting Corp. and Radio Free Europe.

Markov's broadcasts included some remarks critical of the Bulgarian government. On September 7, 1978, Markov was waiting for a bus in London when he was stabbed in the thigh with a sharp-tipped umbrella. Markov fell ill with a high fever and died four days later.

Autopsy revealed poison in Markov's blood and a 2mm (about the size of a pinhead) metal capsule in the thigh muscle. By the end of the month, toxicologists associated with the case concluded Markov died from the poison ricin, introduced in the metal capsule. At least one other Bulgarian refugee, who also was critical of the Bulgarian government, was shot with a ricin bullet.

Ricin is a poison derived from the castor bean (*Ricinus communis*) and belongs to a class of compounds now called lectins. The simplest

The four articles in Appendix D are reprinted with permission from "Science Notebook," published by Wabash College, Crawfordville, Indiana; copyright Wabash College.

definition of a lectin is a "sugar-binding protein" and the toxicity of ricin is related to that property.

"Modern" Information

The lectins first were described in 1888 by a worker who studied the ability of toxic extracts from castor beans to agglutinate red blood cells. The majority of information about lectins has been discovered since 1947. Interaction of lectins with sugars is analogous to the binding interaction of antigens and antibodies, the major components of immunology and immunity. The interactions of lectins and sugars is not immunological, but the interactions are quite specific just as are interactions of antigens and antibodies.

Lectins now have been found in many kinds of cells, including those of bacteria, fungi, and animals, but most is known about lectins from plant seeds—peas, beans, and wheat.

The functions of lectins in nature is not known, but despite this lack of information, these sugar-binding proteins are useful in studying a number of problems in biology.

Some of the properties of lectins that result from the sugar-binding capability include agglutination of cells, stimulation of division of white blood cells, inhibition of certain enzymes, and inhibition of fungal growth.

Cell Membrane

These events are related to the nature of the cellular membrane. In the last few years, the fluid-mosaic model for the structure of the cell membrane has received much support.

The fluid-mosaic model proposes that the structure of the cell membrane is a double-layered sheet of fat or lipid with proteins embedded in it. The proteins have the ability to move about in the fatty double-layered sheet and the pattern of various proteins on the surface of the membrane may vary greatly with time. These two properties give rise to the fluid and mosaic concepts of the model.

Many membrane proteins are glycoproteins; that is, these membrane proteins have sugars and chains of sugars attached to them.

A good example of the glycoprotein nature of membrane proteins is seen in human blood typing. Red cells from type A and type B persons have different sugars in their glycoproteins and therefore are distinguishable by anti-A and anti-B blood-typing antibodies. Interestingly enough, some lectins can distinguish between various blood types.

Con A

The first lectin to be purified greatly (crystallized) was concanavalin A from the jack bean *(Canavlia einsformis)*.

In 1936, workers at Cornell University discovered that Con A, as concanavalin A is abbreviated, will combine with starch and the two components precipitate from solution. They also noted that glucose, the simple sugar making up starch, or mannose (a very simple sugar), would prevent the precipitation of starch by Con A. These studies were important in suggesting that the primary event in lectin action is the binding of sugar.

One of the current uses of lectin is distinguishing between normal and malignant or cancerous cells.

For example, normal mouse cells in tissue culture are not agglutinated by Con A. After being transformed to malignancy with a virus, the same mouse cells are agglutinated by Con A.

In general, malignant cells are agglutinated by lectin concentrations which are 1/20th of the strength needed to agglutinate normal cells.

What does this discussion of lectins have to do with the murder of Georgi Markov?

Understanding the lectin action may lead to an understanding of the action of ricin toxin and other toxins such as diphtheria toxin.

Ricin and similar plant toxins have a structural relationship to the diphtheria and other bacterial toxins. They consist of two parts, an A sub-unit and a B sub-unit. The B sub-unit binds to sugars on the surface of the cell and, therefore, is a lectin. The A sub-unit traverses the membrane and affects a cellular function.

In the case of ricin, the A sub-unit binds to a cellular organelle, the ribosome, and blocks protein synthesis.

Markov's high fever and slow death are consistent with the action proposed for A sub-unit of ricin.

On the practical side, antidotes to *Pseudomonas* and *Shigella* (bacteria) toxins, the toxin of the death angel mushroom and the poison of the scorpion, may result from basic studies with the sugar-binding lectins.

BROWN OCTOBER ALE
NOT ALWAYS GOOD

WILLIAM DOEMEL

A cool beer was the beverage the English and Dutch settlers who first colonized this country enjoyed most.

To make beer, only barley, hops, and good water were needed, but good beer, like that served in the pubs and brewhouses of the homeland, required artistry and perhaps a little magic.

At first, the colonists relied upon ships to bring beer from the old world, but too often the beer arrived "stinking."

In the Netherlands (now New York City) colony, the Dutch found they could grow their own hops and barley. By 1629 they had a small brewery operating, and though they claimed their brew to be as good as that found in their homeland, there is much evidence that suggests otherwise.

By the time of the Revolutionary War, whisky and rum had replaced beer as the most popular beverages. Americans rediscovered beer only after German immigrants introduced them to good German beers. The English brew, known as ale, and the German lagers are the main topic of this article. The impact of new knowledge on the brewing industry in America also is discussed.

Beer is a fermented beverage made from malted barley and flavored with hops. The English version of beer is called ale. There are several kinds—draught (draft) bitter ales, draught mild ale, and bitter and sweet stout.

Bitter ale always has been the most popular of these drinks. Copper-colored and heavily hopped, this beverage has little carbonation and thus seems quite flat to those unaccustomed to its flavor. When fewer hops are added during brewing, the result is a mild ale.

Stout, as its name implies, has a thick consistency like cream. Also, it has a dark brown to black color. Neither the ales nor the stouts were too successful in America, and up to the mid-nineteenth century, Americans favored the much more alcoholic rye and bourbon whiskies.

When German immigrants introduced Americans to a milder aged beer in the mid-nineteenth century, they became once again beer drinkers. The German version of beer, once brewed, was stored or lagered in casks for several months.

Most American beers are similar to a beer that was first brewed in Pilsen, Czechoslovakia. This Pilsener style lager has a pale golden color and although well-hopped, it has a milder flavor than the English ales. It also is much more lively, being heavily carbonated.

Another popular lager is the Munchener style. Either dark or pale, it has a distinctive malty flavor and in its dark form is sweeter than other lagers.

One German lager has come to be known in parts of Germany as "the springtime beer cure." Known as bock beer, this lager is brewed usually in the spring. It traces its origins to Munich, where monks from the Order of St. Francis of Paula brewed a special beer that was almost black in color and had a sweet and malty taste. Having a higher alcohol content than other lagers, 6 percent compared to 4 percent, bock beer gave the drinker a lift from the winter doldrums.

The success of the German lagers in this country may be linked to major improvements in the technology of brewing and to an improved understanding of the microbiology and chemistry of the process. Until the mid-nineteenth century, most brewers did not understand the role of organisms, called yeasts, in the process.

Louis Pasteur, a French microbiologist, demonstrated the essential role of yeasts in the fermentation of malted barley to beer. He also showed that the beer could be preserved from spoilage if contaminating bacteria were killed by gentle heating, pasteurization.

During the same period, Emil Christian Hansen, a biochemist employed by the Carlsberg Breweries in Copenhagen, Denmark, isolated one type of yeast from the ale fermentation, Saccharomyces cerevisiae, and a second type from the lager fermentation, Saccharomyces carlsbergensis. How interesting that in two countries, by chance, two different yeasts had been enriched through many brewings. Both produce palatable fermented products from malted barley, yet the products taste very different.

American brewers quickly incorporated the new technology and utilized their increasing understanding of fermentation to make a less variable and more stable beer.

As with cars, beer also came to be produced on the assembly line. The introduction of Budweiser, the first American beer to be pasteurized and bottled, by the Anheuser-Busch Brewery in 1875, was the knell for the hundreds of small breweries that had been established throughout the country. In 1879 there were seventy-six breweries in Indiana; today, only two remain.

Recently a new, less caloric beer was introduced by the Miller Brewing Co. called Miller Lite. The beer was advertised as having the same taste as Miller High Life but with fewer calories. Now beer drinkers could enjoy twice the amount of beer, yet maintain their intake of calories.

It was an immediate success and has been imitated widely by other brewers. These light beers also have increased the profitability of the companies, for although costing about $2 to $3 a barrel less to brew, they sell for $2 to $3 a barrel more than regular beer.

Today, chemists, microbiologists, and engineers have joined the brewmaster to control the quality of the product. As a result, the brewing processes of today bear little resemblance to the lager process brought to this country in 1847.

AMERICAN PRAIRIE COVERED
ONE MILLION SQUARE MILES

DAVID KROHNE

Can you imagine a sea of grasses extending unbroken from Indiana all the way to the Rocky Mountains?

The North American prairie that once covered nearly 1 million square miles now is gone. But what a sight it must have been. There are accounts by explorers and pioneers of grass so tall and thick it could hide a man on a horse. When it burned, the fire easily could overtake a man on horseback.

The North American prairie can be divided into three sections based on rainfall:

- The short-grass prairie of Colorado and western Kansas.
- The mid-grass prairie of eastern Nebraska and Kansas.
- The tall-grass prairie of Iowa, Illinois, and Indiana.

In the West, in the rain shadow of the Rocky Mountains, rainfall is too low for many crops and much of the original prairie still exists as rangeland. In the tall-grass prairie region, an annual precipitation of forty inches and some of the most fertile soils in the world once led to the phenomenal grass growth described by the pioneers.

A few remnants of this prairie exist along old railroad rights-of-way and in prairie cemeteries where virgin prairie sod never was plowed.

Such remnants have provided scientists with much of the information they have about the composition of the prairie. Studies of these remnants have shown the original prairie was composed of perennial grasses with special adaptations for their environment.

Underground Meristem

The growing point or meristem of these grasses is underground, a feature that protects the plant from grazing and from fire.

Many nonprairie grasses have their meristems above ground. If they are eaten by a buffalo or if a fire sweeps through the area, the meristem is destroyed and the plant soon dies. The native prairie grasses, however, simply begin growing again from their well-protected meristems.

The prairie was a very dense community of plants in which reproduction by seed was very difficult. There was very little bare ground in which seeds could germinate and thrive in competition with mature plants.

Consequently, many prairie grasses reproduce vegetatively by sending out stolons or underground stems that produce a new plant. The new plant can draw on all the resources of the mature plant. The dense mat of these underground stems connecting young plants with their parents formed the prairie sod that was so difficult to plow.

Also Wildflowers

Studies of prairie remnants also have shown that the prairie was not simply a sea of grasses. Hundreds and hundreds of wildflowers, many of which now are all but extinct, grew in the prairies.

Shooting stars, sunflowers, prairie violets, gentians, orchids, lupines, blazing stars, and many others grew in profusion.

In the dense, luxurious growth of the prairie, competition for light and insect pollinators was intense. As a result, these wildflowers tended to time their flowering so that each species would bloom at a particular time during the summer. The effect then was a constantly changing panorama of color.

The lush grass and hundreds of wildflowers were, however, only the tip of the iceberg. As much as 80 percent of the prairie was underground in the form of large and deep root systems. Although rainfall is relatively high in the tall-grass prairie region, there still was tremendous competition for water, especially during the late summer when many of the species were most actively growing.

Because these plants were perennials, the above-ground portions would die each year, but the root systems could continue to grow and develop.

A mature specimen of big bluestem, one of the dominant grasses, might have a root system ten or twelve feet deep. Compass plant, a sunflower-like species, produces a tap root that extends sixteen feet into the soil. Many of these plants continued to grow for decades and some individuals lived more than 100 years.

Fire Was Important

Fire played an important role in the ecology of the prairie. The accounts of the pioneers show that fires were frequent, especially in the spring and fall when the grass was not actively growing and much litter had accumulated from the previous summer's growth.

Many of the fires were started by lightning, but the Indians apparently also set fires to clear the perimeter of their camps or to drive game in hunting.

Recent studies have shown fire is beneficial to true prairie plants and actually stimulates growth. Fire releases nutrients into the soil where they can stimulate growth. It also opens up bare areas for reproduction by seed.

Finally, fire benefited the prairie by killing back the seedlings of trees. If left unburned for many years, the forest would continue to encroach upon the prairie and eventually would replace the grassland with forest.

Have you ever wondered why the black midwestern soils are so fertile? The answer lies in the prairie.

After the last ice age, huge amounts of loess, rock pulverized to the consistency of flour by the glaciers, were deposited over the midwest. This material was rich in minerals, but contained no organic matter.

Nutrients Near Surface

When the prairie grasses invaded this recently glaciated region, they began to increase the organic content of the soil. The tremendous production of the grasses each year went back into the soil through decomposition and the effects of fire.

The deep root systems pulled nutrients up from deep in the soil and deposited them near the surface when the above-ground parts of the plant died each year.

In addition, many of the wildflowers are legumes. These plants greatly increase soil fertility. They have associated with their roots special bacteria that pull nitrogen from the atmosphere and convert it to a form useful to plants.

The combination of loess with its mineral richness and the constant addition of organic material and nitrogen to the soil resulted in the deep, black soils that are among the richest anywhere in the world.

BONSAI GROWING—
HOBBY WITH TWISTS

ROBERT PETTY

In an ill-kempt country cemetery beside a busy highway, a botanist strolled intently with a garden trowel and small bucket.

Suddenly he stopped, fell to his knees, and after several moments announced, "This is the one."

There, growing among recently mowed weeds in a rather dry, stony soil, was what appeared to be a small seedling of Eastern red cedar or oldfield juniper. On closer examination, it was evident that this "seedling" was several years old and that it had adjusted to intermittent mowing, an impoverished soil, and possible roadside sprayings.

If one changed the scale of his vision, there clearly, was a rather well-proportioned tree, in miniature.

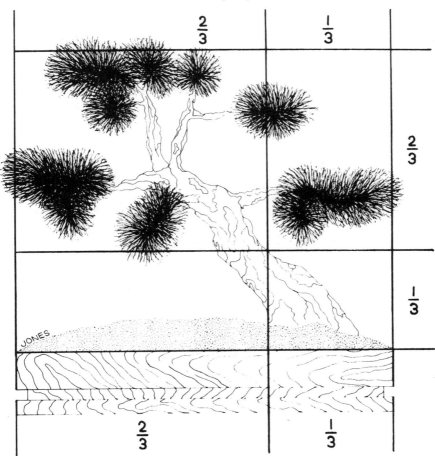

| $\frac{2}{3}$ | $\frac{1}{3}$ |

$\frac{2}{3}$

$\frac{1}{3}$

| $\frac{2}{3}$ | $\frac{1}{3}$ |

"Rule of Thirds" Illustrated

The botanist is one of a growing number of bonsai enthusiasts, and he had found some promising "raw material."

"Bon-sai" literally means "potted-tree." When miniature landscapes are created as a setting for the "sai," or tree, the art is termed "sai-kei," "kei" meaning "scenery." Or if the artist's emphasis is strictly a miniature landscape, "bonkei" is the proper term.

For centuries the Japanese have been practicing the unusual art forms of miniature tree and landscape culture. No one knows exactly how long ago it began, but it was known at least as early as the sixth century. Someone became intrigued by the tiny gnarled trees he found growing in rock crevices high up in the mountains of Japan. The small trees eventually were cultivated in the emperor's courtyard.

Trial and error produced an art of maintaining and training the miniature growth. Trees were grown singly or in groups and even as miniature forests.

As wealthy patrons, following the cue from the palace landscape, began paying large sums for the best available specimens, others began the practice. The sudden monetary value encouraged perfecting a science of treatment that could produce such miniature growth. In recent years in this country, bonsai has become a popular horticultural hobby.

The first trick is to simulate the conditions that caused such retarded growth as occurs in those original rigorous mountain habitats. Various techniques are used. One of the easiest is simply to pinch back the growing tips of stems and roots. This involves repeated root pruning and repotting. This pruning usually is combined with a restricted nutrient and water budget—one just sufficient to sustain outward appearing health, especially in the coloration of the foliage.

As the slow growth occurs, the shape of the little tree is determined by wiring the flexible branches into the growth form of a much older tree, spreading the "crown" and twisting the stems to accentuate a gnarled old-growth appearance.

One method that works extremely well for certain root-sprouting trees such as spruce is the initiation of several new sprouts from a single section of horizontal root. The young sprouts often are naturally dwarfed and produce especially well-proportioned bonsai. One section of an older root can give rise to many clumped sprouts and can be arranged to give the effect of a miniature forest.

As the art has developed, patterns of growth have been classified into five basic categories—the formal erect, the informal upright (where tops are bent), slanting (trunk and bottom branch go in opposite direction), semi-cascade (approaches horizontal growth), and cascade (tree bends over the side of the pot).

Many growers follow the "rule of thirds," whose fibonaccian fractions define a supposedly ideal form. To achieve the best mature form may take fifteen to twenty-five years of patient pruning and training. It is little wonder that superb specimens, many years old, may cost hundreds of dollars at a retailer's shop.

Many kinds of trees are suitable for bonsai culture. The small-needled evergreens, having flexible branches, are the most popular. Eastern red cedar, common in many grazed pastures and along mowed roadsides, makes an excellent bonsai. In addition to native junipers, the Japanese cryptomeria, black and white pines, and various spruce are widely used.

Among deciduous shrubs and trees, cotoneasters, flowering quince, various Oriental elms, and maples are known to be successful.

Fall is the best time to transplant or repot evergreens, while spring is safest for deciduous species. To qualify for bonsai status, the tree must be less than three feet tall at "maturity." Many bonsai are less than a foot tall.

While numerous books are available on the do's and don'ts of bonsai care, the practice is still very much an art. The finest artisans often are deliberately vague about exact procedures. However, the Department of Agriculture's Home and Garden Bulletin No. 206, "Growing Bonsai," by H. M. Cathey, is a great bargain for the beginner.

The tree chosen, the form achieved, the plain or decorative pot, tray, or setting all go toward an expression of individual personality and artistic preference. Bonsai can be a most satisfying pastime for those with proper patience. For the impatient enthusiast, there are two alternatives: buy a bonsai at a florist's shop or go scale a mountain.

APPENDIX E

Selected Bibliography: Research on Mass Media Science Communication

Sharon Dunwoody

Although not exhaustive, this annotated bibliography offers citations from the research literature in the United States in the area of mass media coverage of science and technology. A few "seminal" pieces from the 1950s and 1960s are included, but the bulk of the entries are from the 1970s to the present. The bibliography is current as of November 1984. To make scanning this document easier, the entries have been divided into the following nine categories:

The Audiences for Mass Media Science Messages

BURGOON, MICHAEL, BURGOON, JUDEE K., and WILKINSON, MIRIAM. "Dimensions and Readership of Newspaper Content." *Newspaper Research Journal 3* (October 1981): 74–93.

This study by a research group at Michigan State concludes that in general, government, politics, economics, and professional major sports are of greater interest to readers than is content related to life-style and business investments. But they note that exceptions to this rule seem to be consumer information, science, health, and psychological information, all of which seem to have high readership appeal. The same data are also discussed in "Dimensions of Content Readership in Ten Newspaper Markets," *Journalism Quarterly* 60 (Spring 1983):74–80.

CRONHOLM, MARGARETA, and SANDELL, ROLF. "Scientific Information: A Review of Research." *Journal of Communication* 31 (Spring 1981):85–96.

This article is a recent attempt to summarize existing science communication research; most of the citations are of American research endeavors. The goal, the authors state, is to examine factors that "contribute to the effects of science communication."

FREIMUTH, VICKI S., and VAN NEVEL, J. PAUL. "Reaching the Public: The Asbestos Awareness Campaign." *Journal of Communication* 31 (Spring 1981): 155–167.

The authors analyze an attempt by the Department of Health, Education, and Welfare in 1978 to inform the public of the risks of asbestos exposure. Many of the messages were designed for mass media dissemination, and the authors content-analyzed both print and broadcast outlets to determine the level of dissemination of the materials. They found great variability; some media organizations used lots of the materials while others did not. Although surveys showed that members of the public became more knowledgeable about the risks of asbestos during the campaign period, the authors warn that the effectiveness of such a campaign depends upon media gatekeepers, who decide whether or not to publish materials and when to do so.

GANZ, C. "The Role of Scientific Communication in the Process of Technological Innovation." *Aslib Proceedings* 28 (November/December 1976):385–391.

Ganz describes a survey funded by the National Science Foundation that examines the communication behaviors of a group of innovative persons. Most interesting was the finding that the only *common* elements among formal media used by these creative respondents were popular science publications such as *Scientific American.*

GRUNIG, JAMES E. "Communication Behaviors and Attitudes of Environmental Publics: Two Studies." *Journalism Monographs,* no. 81, March 1983.

Grunig suggests that the use individuals make of environmental information depends on situational variables such as the amount of control a person thinks she has over her own surroundings and the person's level of involvement in the issue at hand. In this monograph he presents his own "situational theory" as a means of incorporating these variables into general attitude-behavior theories.

GRUNIG, JAMES E. "Research on Science Communication: What Is Known and What Needs to Be Known." *The ACE Quarterly* 62 (October/December 1979):17–45.

In this paper Grunig summarizes some of the science communication research available and places it within his own theoretical framework. He spends a considerable amount of space on science audience studies, an area in which his own research has been concentrated. (This article is also available in a compilation of papers presented at a national agricultural science information conference; see citation under "Special Publications.")

KRIEGHBAUM, HILLIER. *Science and the Mass Media.* New York: New York University Press, 1967.

The author devotes considerable space to an examination of the publics for mass media science information. Results of a large-scale study of public attention to the Russian launching of *Sputnik* in the 1950s are detailed here. Krieghbaum was a participant in that landmark study.

LARSON, MARK A., ZIMMERMAN, DON, and SCHERER, CLIFF. "Communication Behavior by Environmental Activists Compared to Non-Active Persons." *The Journal of Environmental Education* 14 (Fall 1982):11–20.

A survey of media use habits of environmental activists compared with similar data from nonactivists found few differences. The environmental activists did not differ from nonactive respondents in habitual mass media use except in magazine use and in wanting to find out more about environmental issues.

MAZUR, ALLAN, and CONANT, BEVERLIE. "Controversy over a Local Nuclear Waste Repository." *Social Studies of Science* 8 (May 1978):235–243.

The authors asked if exposure to media coverage of a controversy over a proposed long-term nuclear waste storage site could affect attitudes toward the technology. They interviewed a sample of 124 persons at the height of such a controversy in New York and then reinterviewed 85 percent of the sample four months later. They found that people who had heard about the controversy were more likely to oppose the storage site than were people who had not heard about it. The second round of interviews showed a persistence of attitudes over time, with men being more consistent than women.

MAZUR, ALLAN. "Media Coverage and Public Opinion on Scientific Controversies." *Journal of Communication* 31 (Spring 1981):106–115.

The author finds one consistent relationship between media coverage of a scientific controversy and public attitudes: when media coverage increases, public opposition to the technology in question increases. He supports his argument with data from several of his studies of such controversies.

National Association of Science Writers. *Science, the News, and the Public.* New York: New York University Press, 1958.

This study was conducted in 1957 with the cooperation of NASW, the Survey Research Center at the University of Michigan, and New York University. It polled a national sample on interest in science news, sources of science news, and the public's image of science and scientists.

NUNN, CLYDE Z. "Readership and Coverage of Science and Technology in Newspapers." *Journalism Quarterly* 56 (Spring 1979):27–30.

This secondary analysis of surveys by the Newspaper Advertising Bureau suggests editors underestimate public interest in science news.

O'KEEFE, TIMOTHY. "The Mass Media as Sources of Medical Information for Doctors." *Journalism Quarterly* 47 (Spring 1970):95–100.

A survey of 283 doctors found that although 71 percent considered medical information obtained from the mass media to be either "very" or "fairly reliable," only 24 percent said the information was of any importance to them.

PATTERSON, JOYE. "A Q Study of Attitudes of Young Adults About Science News." *Journalism Quarterly* 59 (Autumn 1982):406–413.

This analysis of attitudes of young adults in a midwestern city found general support for science but also isolated three attitudinal types: "the true believer," "the anxious dissenter," and "the seasoned supporter."

PATTERSON, JOYE, BOOTH, LAUREL, and SMITH, RUSSELL. "Who Reads About Science?" *Journalism Quarterly* 46 (Autumn 1969):599–602.

This study examined what people read about science and, given a choice, what they might select to read. The experimental setting makes generalization difficult, but the researchers found differences in topic selections based upon such things as gender.

SHAW, DONALD L., and VAN NEVEL, PAUL. "The Informative Value of Medical Science News." *Journalism Quarterly* 44 (Autumn 1967):548.

In contrast to the O'Keefe study cited above, this one found that 60 percent of the 229 doctors queried said they sometimes picked up information about new research developments within their own specialties from the mass media. The authors suggest that doctors may rely on mass media to point out new developments to them.

SWINEHART, JAMES W., and MCLEOD, JACK M. "News About Science Channels, Audiences, and Effects." *Public Opinion Quarterly* 24 (Winter 1960): 583–589.

The authors compared the findings of the pre-*Sputnik* National Association of Science Writers survey (see citation above) with a post-*Sputnik* national survey. They found that the wide circulation of news about science—and particularly about the Russian satellite—seemed to have little effect on the public's reading habits or on attitudes toward scientific topics. They did find that coverage of *Sputnik* increased public awareness of the satellite, but it did not increase levels of knowledge about satellites in general.

UBELL, EARL. "Science in the Press: Newspapers versus Magazines." *Journalism Quarterly* 40 (Summer 1963):293–299.

The author, a full-time science writer, also was involved in the National Association of Science Writers national survey of public interest in and use of science news cited above. In this article he summarizes the results of that survey. He particularly notes the public's preference for print as a source of science news.

WADE, SERENA, and SCHRAMM, WILBUR. "The Mass Media as Sources of Public Affairs, Science, and Health Knowledge." *Public Opinion Quarterly* 33 (Summer 1969):197–209.

This analysis of data from four national surveys found that while television was the chief source of public affairs information, newspapers and magazines were preferred for science and health information. Print users, on the average, had more specific information about science and health than did persons who chiefly used the broadcast media. The authors argue that the interaction between education and mass media use explains much of what they found. The more education the person has, the more likely he or she is to use print as the major source of news and information.

Describing Mass Media Science Communication

ALTIMORE, MICHAEL. "The Social Construction of a Scientific Controversy: Comments on Press Coverage of the Recombinant DNA Debate." *Science, Technology, & Human Values* 7 (Fall 1982):24–31.

In a content analysis of coverage of the recombinant DNA controversy in *The New York Times* and the *Washington Post* from 1974 to 1980, the author looks for evidence that the issue is dealt with not only as a scientific or technical problem but also as a philosophical and political one. He finds that the coverage largely excluded the last two elements.

BOWMAN, J. S., and HANAFORD, K. "Mass Media and the Environment Since Earth Day." *Journalism Quarterly* 54 (Spring 1977):160–165.

The authors sought environmental stories published in eight U.S. mass circulation magazines during 1971 to 1975. They analyzed the frequency of stories and the topics dealt with, concluding that readers of "most of the leading mass circulation magazines" are unlikely to get an adequate exposure to environmental problems. The most popular environmental topics in these magazines were management of resources and water quality, while air quality and environmental additives were least popular.

BURGER, EDWARD J., JR. *Health Risks: The Challenge of Informing the Public.* Washington, D.C.: The Media Institute, 1984.

Through a series of case studies, the author argues that the media have done a less than adequate and sometimes destructive job of conveying risk information. Among the press's faults, he notes, are tendencies to sensationalize and to oversimplify.

COLE, BRUCE J. "Trends in Science and Conflict Coverage in Four Metropolitan Newspapers." *Journalism Quarterly* 52 (Autumn 1975):465–471.

A content analysis of four newspapers at three times—1951, 1961, and 1971—indicated that more controversy was reported in 1971 science articles than in the previous years, and the controversies were reported across a much broader range of subject matter in 1971. The study also indicated that science writers may be less likely to report controversy in science than are general staff reporters.

CULBERTSON, HUGH M., and STEMPEL III, GUIDO H. "Possible Barriers to Agenda Setting in Medical News." *Newspaper Research Journal* 5 (Spring 1984): 53–60.

The authors content-analyzed more than 2000 medical news articles, editorials, and columns from ten Ohio daily newspapers and surveyed more than 400 Ohio residents about their health care beliefs. They found no relationship between topics considered important by readers and those given prominent play in newspapers. For example, while medical costs and insurance matters were mentioned by 74 percent of the survey respondents, the topics accounted for only 12 percent of all newspapers mentioned. In contrast, while newspapers devoted 34 percent of their stories to diseases, only 3 percent of the public mentioned diseases as an important health problem in America.

FREIMUTH, VICKI S., GREENBERG, RACHEL H., DeWITT, JEAN, and ROMANO, ROSE MARY. "Covering Cancer: Newspapers and the Public Interest." *Journal of Communication* 34 (Winter 1984):62–73.

The authors compared coverage of cancer in 50 daily newspapers from 1977 and 1980. While they found that coverage of risk factors had increased dramatically between 1977 and 1980, they also found that the more recent stories continued to focus on "fast-breaking" events, giving the coverage a fragmented appearance.

GERBNER, GEORGE, GROSS, LARRY, MORGAN, MICHAEL, and SIGNORIELLI, NANCY. "Scientists on the TV Screen." *Society* 18 (May/June 1981):41–44. Idem. "Health and Medicine on Television." *The New England Journal of Medicine* 305 (October 8, 1981):901–904.

Since the late 1960s, Gerbner and his colleagues have been trying to determine "the conceptions of social reality that television tends to foster in different groups of viewers." Their massive content analyses of prime-time television content have included measures of images of scientists and of science, and in these articles the investigators offer some preliminary data supporting their contention that "science is bad news but good drama" on TV.

GLYNN, CARROLL J., and TIMS, ALBERT R. "Sensationalism in Science Issues: A Case Study." *Journalism Quarterly* 59 (Spring 1982):126–131.

In this content analysis, the authors examine the manner in which two newspapers handled the Tellico Dam controversy. They conclude that although the newspapers did not sensationalize the issues, they often concentrated on peripheral issues (such as the snail darter), sometimes to the detriment of larger issues such as the potential impact of the dam.

GREENBERG, RACHEL H., FREIMUTH, VICKI S., and BRATICK, ELAINE. "A Content-Analytic Study of Daily Newspaper Coverage of Cancer." In Dan Nimmo, ed., *Communication Yearbook 3*. New Brunswick, N.J.: Transaction Books, 1979, pp. 645–654.

More than 2000 newspaper stories from 49 daily newspapers were examined in this analysis of stories about cancer. The researchers found that the stories spent little space discussing prevention or detection, two high priority topics among cancer specialists and health communicators. Also lacking was information about such contextual factors as incidence rates and risk factors.

KRISTIANSEN, CONNIE M., and HARDING, CHRISTINA M. "Mobilization of Health Behavior by the Press in Britain." *Journalism Quarterly* 61 (Summer 1984):364 –370, 398.

The authors content-analyzed stories about health issues appearing in seven British national newspapers in 1981. They found that health articles were given a "meager" amount of newsplay, with disease getting more attention than any other topic. Most articles were event-oriented and contained little detailed information about the topics. The authors did find, however, that the press rarely described treatments as "miracle cures."

The Media Institute. *Television Evening News Covers Nuclear Energy*. Washington, D.C.: The Media Institute, 1979.

The institute, a nonprofit organization that receives funding from major corporations, conducted a content analysis of 469 television network newscasts about nuclear energy that were aired within the ten-year period of August 5, 1968, to April 20, 1979. This time period includes the Three Mile Island accident. Analysis indicated that network broadcasts did not provide sufficient information to enable a viewer to "make a rational assessment of the risks and benefits of nuclear power generation"; indeed, the institute concluded that the network programming contained a general antinuclear bias.

Newspaper Advertising Bureau. *Readership and Coverage of Science and Technology in Newspapers*. New York: Newspaper Advertising Bureau, 1977.

This report is an expanded version of Nunn's *Journalism Quarterly* article cited in the previous section. Content analysis of newspapers in 1971 and 1977 found that the percentage of newspaper items allotted to science and technology remained small, hovering in the 5 percent range. Copies of this report are available from the bureau at 485 Lexington Avenue, New York, N.Y. 10017.

OATES, WILLIAM R. "Social and Ethical Content in Science Coverage by Newsmagazines." *Journalism Quarterly* 50 (Winter 1973):680–684.

This content analysis of the coverage of human heart transplantation in 1967 found that all three major U.S. newsmagazines—*Time, Newsweek,* and *U.S. News & World Report*—provided social and ethical context along with the hard news itself. However, as the news aspects of the story waned, the social and ethical discussion of heart transplantation disappeared as well.

RICH, JONATHON T. "A Measure of Comprehensiveness in News Magazine Science Coverage." *Journalism Quarterly* 58 (Summer 1981):248–253.

By reading the research literature related to two major scientific issues (Legionnaires' disease and the birth of the first test-tube baby), the author was able to compile a list of "pertinent" facts about each. These lists were then compared with the facts offered by the coverage of both issues in three newsmagazines: *Time, Newsweek,* and *U.S. News & World Report.* The author concluded that of the three, *Time* offered the most complete coverage and *U.S. News* the least complete coverage.

RUBIN, DAVID M., and HENDY, VAL. "Swine Influenza and the News Media." *Annals of Internal Medicine* 87 (6 December 1977):769–774.

A content analysis of swine influenza stories during a one-week period in nineteen daily newspapers, the UPI wire service, and the evening news broadcasts of the three television networks found that coverage of the inoculation campaign was "generally superficial and marked by a 'body count' mentality, but it was rarely inaccurate or sensational." This article also offers suggestions drawn from the study to doctors interested in improving press coverage of medical subjects.

SCHOENFELD, A. CLAY. "The Press and NEPA: The Case of the Missing Agenda." *Journalism Quarterly* 56 (Autumn 1979):577–585.

Some mass communications researchers argue the media have an agenda-setting effect; by publicizing a topic they make it more salient to the public. In this article, Schoenfeld looks for an agenda-setting effect related to the passage of the National Environmental Policy Act in 1969. He finds none. Media coverage of the evolution of the legislation was sparse; the author argues that media thus played only a minor role in making the landmark piece of legislation salient to the public before it became law.

SCHOENFELD, A. CLAY, MEIER, ROBERT F., and GRIFFIN, ROBERT J. "Constructing a Social Problem: The Press and the Environment." *Social Problems* 27 (October 1979):38–61.

The authors examine the role of the press in the early construction and delineation of environmental problems as a new social reality. They found that newspapers in the 1960s did not contribute much to the dialogue surrounding emerging environmental issues. The authors then try to make sense of the lack of coverage through sociological explanations of news making.

Science in the Streets. Report of the Twentieth Century Fund Task Force on the Communication of Scientific Risk. New York: Priority Press, 1984.

Dominating this task force report is a background paper by sociologist Dorothy Nelkin, who discusses several case studies of media coverage of scientific risk.

SHERBURNE, E. G. "Science on Television: A Challenge to Creativity." *Journalism Quarterly* 40 (Summer 1963):300–305.

This content analysis of prime-time television programming in San Francisco in March 1963 revealed that only 6 percent of all programming was devoted to science, with 75 percent of that small proportion focusing on medicine and psychology.

STEPHENS, MITCHELL, and EDISON, NADYNE G. "News Media Coverage of Issues During the Accident at Three Mile Island." *Journalism Quarterly* 59 (Summer 1982):199–204, 259.

This article offers details of the content analysis that dominated the review of media coverage of TMI done in 1979 by a presidential task force. The analysis found relative balance in the media coverage and concluded that rather than offering an alarming or negative picture of the accident, media coverage "was predominantly reassuring or positive."

Accuracy

BORMAN, SUSAN CRAY. "Communication Accuracy in Magazine Science Reporting." *Journalism Quarterly* 55 (Summer 1978):345–346.

Scientists evaluated the accuracy of mass circulation magazine articles that dealt with three major scientific events. The author found the accuracy level of the articles as a whole to be good. The major area of criticism was omission of relevant information, and the most frequently cited omission was the failure to mention the names of the primary investigators.

BROBERG, KATIE. "Scientists' Stopping Behavior as Indicator of Writer's Skill." *Journalism Quarterly* 50 (Winter 1973):763–767.

This analysis of corrections made by scientists to press releases prepared about their research found that of all changes made, additions accounted for the highest number. As the material in a press release became more complex, the scientist tended to add more detail. The analysis also found that scientists changed more technical terms to lay terms than the reverse. The author concludes that none of the writers of the press releases being studied could "satisfy the scientists' penchant for explaining their research in greater detail."

DUNWOODY, SHARON. "A Question of Accuracy." *IEEE Transactions on Professional Communication* PC–25 (December 1982):196–199.

This brief article reviews the research literature on accuracy of mass media science coverage and suggests that when scientists claim something is inaccurate, they are in most cases saying a piece is incomplete and lacks details. That, in turn, suggests that scientists may be using inappropriate criteria to evaluate the accuracy of journalistic accounts.

PULFORD, D. L. "Follow-up Study of Science News Accuracy." *Journalism Quarterly* 53 (Spring 1976):119–121.

Pulford asked scientists to rate the accuracy of media stories about their work and found that 73 percent of the 143 respondents judged the articles to be generally accurate.

TANKARD, JAMES W., and RYAN, MICHAEL. "News Source Perceptions of Accuracy of Science Coverage." *Journalism Quarterly* 51 (Summer 1974):219–225, 334.

The researchers asked sources to rate the accuracy of stories about themselves and their work. Findings indicated that scientists were strongly critical of the accuracy of science news reporting in general and found a mean number of 6.22 errors in their own stories. Most of the errors were those of omission rather than misstatements of fact.

TICHENOR, PHILLIP J., OLIEN, CLARICE N., HARRISON, ANNETTE, and DONOHUE, GEORGE. "Mass Communication Systems and Communication Accuracy in Science News Reporting." *Journalism Quarterly* 47 (Winter 1970):673–683.

Using a very different measure of story accuracy, the researchers asked individuals to read science stories and then to recall the main content of the stories. The scientists quoted in the articles were then asked to judge the accuracy of the audience recall of the stories. Nearly two thirds of the audience recall of the average article was judged acceptably accurate by the scientist quoted. Another interesting finding: a scientist was very critical of science writing in general but expressed satisfaction with the accuracy of specific articles that quoted him or her!

Readability

BOSTIAN, LLOYD R. "How Active, Passive and Nominal Styles Affect Readability of Science Writing." *Journalism Quarterly* 60 (Winter 1983):635–640, 670.

In a quasi-experimental setting, the author found that readers considered science stories written in active voice to be more interesting and easier to read than the same stories written in passive voice and in nominal style (substituting nouns for verbs). However, comprehension of the information didn't vary across the three types of writing.

FUNKHOUSER, G. RAY. "Levels of Science Writing in Public Information Sources." *Journalism Quarterly* 46 (Winter 1969):721–726.

The author examined textual variables in science stories published in magazines aimed at different audiences and then compared audience demographics with the textual data. He found that as the proportion of college graduates reading any single magazine increased, so did the sentence length and the number of difficult words used in that magazine's science articles.

FUNKHOUSER, G. RAY, and MACCOBY, NATHAN. "Communicating Specialized Science Information to a Lay Audience." *Journal of Communication* 21 (March 1971):58–71. Idem. "Tailoring Science Writing to the General Audience." *Journalism Quarterly* 50 (Summer 1973):220–226.

Both these articles were based on a National Science Foundation–funded study of the relationship of textual variables in science articles to audience information gain, enjoyment, attitude change, and the tendency to seek further information about the topic in the story. Among the findings were that scientists in the study enjoyed the "simplified" version of the science articles being used as much as did the nonscientists.

GRUNIG, JAMES E. "Three Stopping Experiments on the Communication of Science." *Journalism Quarterly* 51 (Autumn 1974):387–399.

In a series of experiments, Grunig tested the ability of such readability devices as parables and analogies in economics stories to cause readers to stop and think about the material. He found that the style of the stories was less important than whether the content was relevant to the perceived situation of the reader. For readers who found the content relevant, parables and analogies stimulated thinking and possible understanding. Examples, on the other hand, seemed to stimulate even less thinking than did a straightforward, simple treatment of the story content.

HUNSAKER, A. "Enjoyment and Information Gain in Science Articles." *Journalism Quarterly* 56 (Autumn 1979):617–619.

In an experimental setting, the author compared reader enjoyment and information gain among subjects who read one of three versions of a psychology journal article. The three varied only in language simplicity. Findings indicated that while reader enjoyment increased as the writing became simpler, information gain remained the same. He concluded that science can be written in a form that lay people would enjoy without sacrificing the amount of information being ingested.

Science Newsmaking: Sources, Journalists, and Their Interactions

CARTER, ROY E. "Newspaper 'Gatekeepers' and the Sources of News." *Public Opinion Quarterly* 22 (1958):133–144.

This study found that reporters' rankings of news values were more similar to physicians' rankings than they were to physicians' estimates of reporters' values. The study also offers a number of factors that influence relationships between journalists and physicians as sources.

DENNIS, EVERETTE E., and MCCARTNEY, JAMES. "Science Journalists on Metropolitan Dailies." *The Journal of Environmental Education* 10 (Spring 1979): 9–15.

This survey of seventy-five reporters from fifty-two different media organizations examines journalists' perceptions of their working conditions, including notions of their audiences and the reporters' relationships with their sources. The researchers found "many" of their respondents to have special credentials and training in science.

DUNWOODY, SHARON. *Science Writers at Work.* Research Report No. 7. Bloomington, Ind.: School of Journalism Center for New Communications, 1978.

The study examines the news-selection behaviors of some of the top mass media science writers in the United States as they covered a large scientific meeting. Findings emphasize the high degree of cooperation among journalists as well as their dependence on the meeting planners to determine what was news about the meeting itself.

DUNWOODY, SHARON. "The Science Writing Inner Club: A Communication Link Between Science and the Lay Public." *Science, Technology, & Human Values* 5 (Winter 1980):14–22.

This article makes the argument that a relatively small group of prestigious science journalists plays a substantial role in determining what news the public sees about science in media. The "club" is examined as an informal group that, among other functions, serves as a pool of resources for its participants. (Reprinted in Chapter 12, this volume.)

DUNWOODY, SHARON, and SCOTT, BYRON. "Scientists as Mass Media Sources." *Journalism Quarterly* 59 (Spring 1982):52–59.

Scientists in this two-university survey were found to have much more contact with journalists than was expected. In fact, 75 percent of the respondents indicated they would welcome further contact. This study also found that a scientist's rank was positively related to both frequency of contact with journalists and evaluation of the quality of mass media coverage of science. But it found no relationship between a scientist's productivity and his or her level of exposure in the mass media.

DUNWOODY, SHARON, and RYAN, MICHAEL. "Public Information Persons as Mediators Between Scientists and Science Writers." *Journalism Quarterly* 60 (Winter 1983):647–656.

This study of scientists' perceptions of the roles played by public information personnel found that although scientists generally viewed such personnel favorably, they did not view them as integral to the dissemination of science.

DUNWOODY, SHARON, and RYAN, MICHAEL. "Scientific Barriers to the Popularization of Science via Mass Media." *Journal of Communication* 35 (Winter 1985):26–42.

Scientists who responded to this national survey agreed that science as a culture does not reward scientists for becoming involved in efforts to increase the public understanding of science.

FRIEDMAN, SHARON M. "Blueprint for Breakdown: Three Mile Island and the Media Before the Accident." *Journal of Communication* 31 (Spring 1981): 116–128.

In one of the more interesting analyses related to the accident at Three Mile Island, Friedman conducted interviews with utility personnel and journalists and analyzed documents from both groups in order to characterize the types of information dissemination that took place in the Harrisburg, Pa., area prior to the accident. She found serious gaps in both the utility's and the regional media's efforts to keep residents aware of the operating conditions of the TMI facility. (Updated version is printed in Chapter 14, this volume.)

GOODELL, RAE. *The Visible Scientists*. Boston: Little, Brown & Co., 1977.

The author has interviewed articulate science celebrities and discusses not only their pervasiveness in mass media science communication but also how and why they got there. The book examines science journalists to a limited degree.

JOHNSON, KENNETH. "Dimensions of Judgment of Science News Stories." *Journalism Quarterly* 40 (Summer 1963):315–322.

In this experimental setting, a group of editors evaluated the newsworthiness of science news stories primarily on the basis of color and excitement, while groups of science writers, scientists, and both readers and nonreaders of science news all emphasized accuracy and significance.

JONES, GRETA, and MEADOWS, JACK. "Sources and Selection of Scientific Material for Newspapers and Radio Programs." *Journal of Research Communication Studies* 1 (1978):69–82.

The authors examined nearly 200 items selected by two BBC radio departments for science programming over a period of several months. They also interviewed a number of science journalists about their sources of news. Among their findings are that formal sources of information for science reporters are limited in number and "not necessarily representative of scientific research as a whole."

LASSAHN, PAMELA HENRY. "Comparison of Judgments About Agricultural Science News." *Journalism Quarterly* 44 (Winter 1967):702–707.

The researcher asked groups of farmers, newspaper editors, county extension directors and extension editors, and agricultural scientists to sort a group of agricultural research stories according to personal interest in the topics. Farmers, the ultimate audience for the material, indicated a high level of interest in stories with economic implications. Lassahn found that the newspaper editors and the information service editors predicted farmer preferences for stories.

PFUND, NANCY, and HOFSTADTER, LAURA. "Biomedical Innovation and the Press." *Journal of Communication* 31 (Spring 1981):138–154.

The authors examined media coverage of industry involvement in recombinant DNA research in an attempt to describe the level of complexity with which the media approached the issues. Among other things, they found journalists relying on "mainstream" scientists as sources, with little attention paid to dissident scientists or other individuals who did not offer consensual views. They also found coverage of continuing issues to be disjointed, with many articles failing to provide scientific contexts for reported discoveries. Although the authors deal only with DNA coverage in this article, their original research also included analyses of media coverage of the use of diethylstilbestrol (DES), the swine flu vaccination program, and the development of an artificial heart.

RYAN, MICHAEL. "Attitudes of Scientists and Journalists Toward Media Coverage of Science News." *Journalism Quarterly* 56 (Spring 1979):18–26, 53.

On the basis of a survey of scientists and science reporters, Ryan concludes that the attitudes of scientists and journalists toward science news coverage are "remarkably similar." But each group perceived a larger attitudinal gap than actually existed.

SHEPHERD, R. GORDON. "Science News of Controversy: The Case of Marijuana." *Journalism Monographs*, no. 62, August 1979. Idem. "Selectivity of Sources: Reporting the Marijuana Controversy." *Journal of Communication* 31 (Spring 1981):129–137.

This study investigated how well the press functioned in popularizing scientific views and findings on a controversial issue. Shepherd's main interest was in the credentials of "experts" used by journalists for issues such as marijuana. Among other findings, he concluded that the actual marijuana expertise of authorities quoted by the press was quite low; the majority of "experts" had themselves done little or no research on marijuana.

TANNENBAUM, PERCY H. "Communication of Science Information." *Science* 140 (May 10, 1963):579–583.

Tannenbaum asked the general public, mental health experts, and persons who produced television programs dealing with mental health themes about their attitudes toward mental health. He found that "while the judgments of the public, the experts, and the communicators are all quite far removed from the image presented by the media, the communicators' perception of the audience's beliefs corresponds quite closely with that image." Furthermore, the public's actual beliefs and the communicators' view of the public's beliefs were quite different.

Media Coverage of the Social Sciences

Since few researchers have looked specifically at mass media treatment of the social sciences, this section contains a small number of empirical studies, but also it includes several articles and book chapters of commentary on the topic.

DUNWOODY, SHARON, and STOCKING, S. HOLLY. "Social Scientists and Journalists: Confronting the Stereotypes." In Eli Rubinstein and Jane Brown, eds., *The Media, Social Science, and Social Policy for Children*. Norwood, N.J.: Ablex Publishing Company, 1985, pp. 167–187.

The authors suggest that relationships between social scientists and journalists are sometimes based more on stereotypical images of one another than on reality. In this book chapter, they explore some of the more common stereotypical portrayals of journalists utilized by scientists.

HIGBIE, CHARLES E., and HAMMOND, PHILLIP E. "A Mildly Sociological View of the Press Coverage of a Sociological Convention." *The American Sociologist* 1 (May 1966):145–147. Hammond, Phillip E., and Higbie, Charles E. "This Time a More Personal View of the Press Coverage of a Sociological Convention." *The American Sociologist* 3 (February 1968):51–53.

The authors and some of their graduate students observed journalists and sociologists interacting at the 1965 American Sociological Association meeting in Chicago. The first article publishes their findings, along with recommendations for making the meeting more accessible to journalists who know little about sociology. The second article recounts the authors' own attempts to make the 1966 meeting more accessible; on the basis of their first article they had obtained a grant from the Russell Sage Foundation specifically to implement some of their recommendations.

HIXSON, VIVIAN SCOTT. "Caveat Lector: Reviewing Popular Social Science." *Journal of Communication* 31 (Spring 1981):168–177.

The author argues that book publishers are likely to publish bad social science—or bad "anything"—if the market prospects are good. Thus, she says, "post-publication reviewers inherit the major responsibility of providing substantive criticism." In this study she analyzes the book reviews in various media of selected social science books and finds that while reviewers in specialized periodicals do a competent job, those in daily newspapers, library journals, and literary and entertainment magazines fail to provide critical and informed opinions.

Knowledge into Action: Improving the Nation's Use of the Social Sciences. Report of the Special Commission on the Social Sciences of the National Science Board. Washington, D.C.: Government Printing Office, 1969.

Included in this report are a number of recommendations regarding the mass media's potential to increase public understanding of the social sciences.

McCALL, ROBERT B., and STOCKING, S. HOLLY. "Between Scientists and Public: Communicating Psychological Research Through the Mass Media." *American Psychologist* 37 (September 1982):985–995.

This article describes some of the differences between how social scientists operate and how journalists operate and then provides some practical hints on how scientists can work more productively with journalists.

STOCKING, S. HOLLY, and DUNWOODY, SHARON L. "Social Science in the Mass Media: Images and Evidence." In Joan E. Sieber, ed., *The Ethics of Social Research: Fieldwork, Regulation and Publication.* New York: Springer-Verlag, 1982, pp. 151–169.

This chapter examines the small amount of research related to coverage of social science by the mass media. Additionally, the authors pose questions that could be addressed by future researchers to begin to add to what we know about this area.

WALUM, LAUREL RICHARDSON. "Sociology and the Mass Media: Some Major Problems and Modest Proposals." *The American Sociologist* 10 (February 1975):28–32.

A research presentation by Walum at a meeting of the American Sociological Association generated a flurry of media attention. The author describes what happened to her and her research, ultimately arguing that social scientists must take a more active role in the dissemination process.

WEIGEL, RUSSELL H., and PAPPAS, JEFFREY J. "Social Science and the Press." *American Psychologist* 36 (May 1981):480–487.

The authors analyzed media coverage of some of the initial findings by sociologist James Coleman on the effects of school desegregation. They found that the media uncritically disseminated the research, even in the face of dissenting voices from within the sociological community.

YU, FREDERICK T. C., ed. *Behavioral Sciences and the Mass Media.* New York: Russell Sage Foundation, 1968.

This book contains the proceedings of a 1966 conference of social scientists and journalists who explored ways of increasing and improving the public understanding of the behavioral sciences.

Teaching Mass Media Science Reporting

Again, while some researchers have begun to examine the training of science communicators as well as the quality of science communication courses, many of the citations below fall into the realm of commentary.

FRIEDMAN, SHARON M., and TRIMBLE, WALTER. *Science Writing Workshop.* Bethlehem, Pa.: Lehigh University, 1981.

This report summarizes a three-and-a-half-day workshop for general assignment reporters on dealing with science-related topics. The workshop was funded by a National Science Foundation grant and administered by Friedman, who directs a science writing program at Lehigh. The report offers details on teaching strategies as well as analysis of a followup study of the potential effects of the workshop on reporters' working habits.

GRIFFIN, ROBERT J., and SCHOENFELD, CLAY. "Environmental Impact: University Programs in Journalism." *The Journal of Environmental Education* 14 (Fall 1982):4–10.

A survey of the environmental content of journalism courses throughout the country found that about 10 percent of the programs have separate courses in environmental reporting, while environmental content otherwise tends to surface in public affairs reporting courses. The best predictors of environmental writing content in programs, the researchers found, were the presence of an environmentally interested faculty member and of a graduate-level environmental program.

ROGERS, CAROL L., and DUNWOODY, SHARON. "Using Mass Media Science Materials in the Classroom." *Journal of College Science Teaching* 13 (March/April 1984):340–349.

The authors discuss strategies for utilizing media science stories in the science classroom both as science teaching aids and to bolster critical reading of mass media science on the part of students.

RYAN, MICHAEL, and DUNWOODY, SHARON. "Academic and Professional Training Patterns of Science Writers." *Journalism Quarterly* 52 (Summer 1975): 239–246, 290.

Although already dated, this study is the most recent one on a national scale to look at the educational backgrounds of science reporters. The study additionally asked respondents to recommend training for future science reporters.

SCIPHERS. A quarterly newsletter of the Science Writing Educators Group (SWEG).

Available since 1979, SCIPHERS devotes its pages to a variety of information tailored to teachers of science communication. For further information, contact Sharon Dunwoody, School of Journalism and Mass Communication, University of Wisconsin, Madison, Wisc. 53706.

STOCKING, S. HOLLY. "Don't Overlook the 'Social' in Science Writing Courses." *Journalism Educator* 36 (April 1981):55–57.

The author argues that the social sciences are an important source of scientific information and advises that teachers of science writing make a special effort to include them in courses. She suggests some specific tactics for integrating them into course structures.

"Teaching Science and Environmental Writing." *The Journal of Environmental Education* 10 (Spring 1979).

This special issue of the journal published papers presented in 1978 at a science writing symposium in Seattle. Entitled "Teaching Science and Environmental Writing: The Journalism of Uncertainty," the symposium drew papers on a number of aspects of teaching. Included are a survey of science journalists on metropolitan daily newspapers, a discussion of the structures and goals of science and environmental writing courses being taught at colleges and universities, and a number of articles on specific teaching techniques.

"Teaching Scientific Writing." *The English Journal* 67 (Spring 1978).

This special issue emphasizes teaching scientific writing in English classes. Nearly twenty authors have contributed short articles on techniques, goals, and perspectives on teaching.

Special Publications on Mass Media Science Communication

ALBERGER, PATRICIA L., and CARTER, VIRGINIA L., eds. *Communicating University Research.* Washington, D.C.: Council for the Advancement and Support of Education, 1981.

This 226-page handbook was compiled from the proceedings of a Fall 1980 conference conducted by CASE for university science writers. Included are summaries of panel discussions and talks as well as reference materials. Issues tackled include the importance of communicating university research, the public's perception of research, reaching specific audiences, handling controversial research, translating research language for the general public, and retaining journalistic credibility while serving institutional interests.

GASTEL, BARBARA. *Presenting Science to the Public.* Philadelphia: ISI Press, 1983.

The author, both a physician and a science-writing educator, offers in this volume some practical advice to the scientist who serves as a source of information to journalists or who may wish to do some public communicating directly. The book is specifically geared to the scientific audience.

GOODFIELD, JUNE. *Reflections on Science and the Media.* Washington, D.C.: American Association for the Advancement of Science, 1981.

Although more of a personal essay than a comprehensive look at the state of mass media science communication, this book raises a number of issues concerned with relationships between scientists and journalists. It also briefly describes a number of "case studies" in which relationships became problematic.

GREENBERG, MARK L., ed. *Writing and Teaching in a World of Business, Science, and Technology.* Proceedings of the Fall 1980 conference of the Delaware Valley Writing Council. Philadelphia: Drexel University, 1981.

In October 1980 writers, teachers, and students of writing in business, science, technology, secondary schools, and universities joined to discuss the theory and pedagogy of writing. The proceedings have been divided into seven sections: Writing for Business; Business and Science Writing in High Schools; The Composing Process; Communicating with the Public; Teaching Technical Writing, and Science Writing for Children; Special Applications of Technical Writing; and Writing for Professional Publication.

Popular Reporting of Agricultural Science: Strategies for Improvement. Proceedings of the National Agricultural Science Information Conference, Iowa State University, Ames, Iowa, 1979.

This conference offered papers on a wide range of science communication topics. Included are remarks on the process and problems of science communication by scientists, farmers, science writers, and news consumers. Papers from the conference have been printed in *The ACE Quarterly* 62, no. 4 (October/December 1979).

Report of the Public's Right to Information Task Force. Washington, D.C.: U.S. Government Printing Office, 1979.

The task force, appointed by the President's Commission on the Accident at Three Mile Island to evaluate media coverage of the now-famous accident, concludes in this report that coverage reflected the information available to reporters at the time. It also takes to task the Nuclear Regulatory Commission and TMI owner Metropolitan Edison for doing such a poor job of utilizing their public information personnel to disseminate timely information about ongoing events.

"Science: News, Controversy, Drama." Special section of the *Journal of Communication* 31 (Spring 1981):84–189.

This special section is devoted to recent research in science communication. Science communication is broadly defined to include images of science found not only in news programming but also in mass media entertainment content. Please see other parts of this bibliography for details about some of the individual articles.

SIPIscope, the newsletter of the Scientists' Institute for Public Information, 355 Lexington Avenue, New York, N.Y. 10017.

Editor Fred Jerome devotes part of each bimonthly issue to science communication topics. Among more recent topics explored by *SIPIscope* have been "Informing the Public: Why Bother?" (January/February 1982); "How the Media Cover Cancer" (September/October 1983); and "Why Is Science Writing So Uncritical of Science?" (January/February 1984).

"Special Issue on Interpreting Technology for the Nonspecialist." *IEEE Transactions on Professional Communication* PC–25 (December 1982).

This issue includes several articles on writing strategies useful in "translating" scientific languages into plain English.

"Technology: The New Media Superstar." *Professional Engineer,* September 1981.

In this special issue of the quarterly magazine of the National Society of Professional Engineers, five articles articulate the problems of communicating technology to the public. Some of the articles deal with the broader area of science communication in general.

Other Science Communication Bibliographies

BOWES, JOHN E., STAMM, KEITH R., JACKSON, KENNETH M., and MOORE, JEFF. *Communication of Technical Information to Lay Audiences.* Seattle: School of Communications, University of Washington, May 1978.

Making extensive use of computerized retrieval systems, the authors of this bibliography attempted to locate and review communication research relevant to the relationship between people and technology. The result is an excellent compilation of more than 160 studies.

GUILLIERIE, RENEE, and SCHOENFELD, A. CLAY. *An Annotated Bibliography of Environmental Communication Research and Commentary: 1969–1979.* Columbus, Ohio: ERIC/SMEAC Clearinghouse for Science, Mathematics, and Environmental Education, 1979.

This bibliography covers ten years of environmental communication research. With few exceptions, only articles published in refereed U.S. journals are abstracted. Each annotation includes a brief discussion of the problem, methodology, findings, and conclusions. Copies of the bibliography are available from ERIC/SMEAC Clearinghouse for Science, Mathematics, and Environmental Education, Ohio State University College of Education and School of Natural Resources, 1200 Chambers Road, Columbus, Ohio 43212.

APPENDIX F

Science in the Mass Media: A Selected Guide

Carol L. Rogers

Compiling a guide to science in the mass media is almost like writing yesterday's news. It is old and dated before it even gets printed. Since most of the public gets its science information from the mass media, however, there is still some value in looking at what the public gets to read, listen to, or watch about science.

The following guide is not exhaustive; rather, it provides some specific examples of science in the mass media in the United States and Canada in the fall of 1984. In addition, the television entries include several major public television series that might be rebroadcast and are available for rental and/or purchase. The entries are divided into five sections:

Science on Radio

Canadian Broadcasting Corporation. CBC National Radio News, Box 500, Station "A," Toronto, Canada M5W IE6.

CBC National Radio News produces "Quirks and Quarks" (see entry below). Science features also are incorporated into the regular radio news programs, specifically "The World at Six" and "Sunday Magazine."

"Dimensions in Science." American Chemical Society, 1155 16th Street, NW, Washington, D.C. 20036.

Formerly called "Man and Molecules," this program was first aired in December 1960 and is one of the longest running science series on radio. The weekly series consists of fifteen-minute segments that are sent without charge to seveal hundred radio stations in the United States. It also is carried overseas. ACS estimates its total audience at about 6 million. The Society produces two spinoffs from the series: "Science Log," a one-and-a-half-minute weekly, and "Science Chronicle," a three-minute show. ACS also produces occasional radio specials, such as "Are We Alone in the Universe?" (produced and aired in 1979) and "DNA: The Architect of Life" (produced and aired in 1982).

"Focus." American Association for the Advancement of Science, 1333 H Street, NW, Washington, D.C. 20005.

AAAS produces eight of these thirty-minute radio programs per year. They consist of interviews or panel discussions with scientists on such topics as heart disease, effects of low-level radiation, climate change, and science and secrecy. "Focus" is sent to some 230 public radio stations in the United States and to larger National Public Radio stations via the NPR satellite.

"Horizon." National Geographic Society, Washington, D.C. 20036.

Since 1980 the National Geographic Society has produced daily radio spots under the name "Horizon." These ninety-second spots are aired regularly on 200–250 of the more than 1000 Associated Press subscription stations. Based on interviews with scientists, adventurers, and photographers, "Horizon" programs reflect the broad interests of the National Geographic Society.

National Public Radio. 2025 M Street, NW, Washington, D.C. 20036.

The NPR Science Unit produces regular segments for NPR's two daily news programs, "All Things Considered" and "Morning Edition." NPR does both short and long features, as well as investigative pieces. The science unit, which operates out of the Washington office, has correspondents on the East and West coasts and stringers around the country.

"Quirks and Quarks." Box 500, Station "A," Toronto, Canada M5W IE6.

This hour-long current affairs science program runs nationally on Canadian Broadcasting Corporation (CBC) radio Saturdays at noon. The show can be received in the United States by border stations and through CBC Northern Service (shortwave). The show has a magazine format which combines documentary and straight interview in the coverage of six to eight items per week.

"Report on Science." American Association for the Advancement of Science, 1333 H Street, NW, Washington, D.C. 20005.

This daily, ninety-second science news program is produced by AAAS for the CBS Radio Stations News Service. It airs on the CBS–owned and operated stations in several large cities, including New York, Boston, and Los Angeles, plus other cities in the United States and in San Juan and Toronto. Estimated audience is several million people each week. Topics cover all of science and technology from anthropology to zoology.

"Science and Man." UPI Audio Network, 220 East 42nd Street, New York, N.Y. 10017.

This sixty-second radio feature by the UPI science editor is transmitted five times a week (weekdays) to radio stations subscribing to the UPI Audio Network (about 1000 affiliates). "Science and Man," which has been on the air for more than ten years, covers topics in science and medicine, from new information on diseases to hazards in the workplace.

"Science Editor." News Office, University Hall, University of California at Berkeley, Berkeley, Calif. 94720.

Produced by the University of California at Berkeley, this three-minute radio show reports science news from within the University of California system. "Science Editor" is distributed nationwide by CBS Radio Network and regularly broadcast over about 100 stations. It has been on the air since 1948.

"Science Report." American Institute of Physics, 335 East 45th Street, New York, N.Y. 10017.

This radio show, which deals with topics in physics and the physical sciences, is distributed to a total of about 500 public and commercial radio stations. Produced three times a year, each show consists of five pairs of two-minute segments.

Science on Television

"The Body in Question." KCET–TV, 4401 Sunset Boulevard, Los Angeles, Calif. 90027.

This thirteen-part PBS series on health and the human body is hosted by Jonathan Miller, noted British physician, writer, actor, lecturer, and theater director. Filmed on location throughout the world, the series uses special effects, art, architecture, historical recreation spots, and live experiments to focus on personal, historical, and cultural patterns. Topics include how the heart works, human development beginning with conception, "miracle cures," and native medicine. First aired in September 1980, this program is rerun occasionally.

"The Brain." WNET/Thirteen, 356 West 58th Street, New York, N.Y. 10019.

"The Brain," an eight-part series of one-hour documentaries, premiered on PBS in October 1984. It is designed to explore what we know and don't know about the brain and its role in behavior, perception, intelligence, memory, and emotion. "The Brain" was produced as part of the Annenberg/CPB Project.

"Connections." Time-Life Video, Rockefeller Center, New York, N.Y. 10020.

This is a ten-week series coproduced by the BBC and Time-Life Television and aired on PBS stations. Written and narrated by BBC science journalist James Burke, each one-hour documentary portrays the interdependence of scientific and technological innovations throughout history. Examples include programs showing how the modern production line can be linked with the invention of the clock; how changes over time have affected changes in energy sources; how materials have altered the course of history; how television has affected our lives. "Connections" is still being distributed.

"Cosmos." KCET–TV, 4401 Sunset Boulevard, Los Angeles, Calif. 90027.

This thirteen-week series, created and hosted by Carl Sagan, premiered on PBS in September 1980 and has been rerun since then. A joint production of Carl Sagan Productions, Inc., and KCET–TV, each one-hour episode is devoted to astronomy and space exploration in the broadest possible human context. The premiere of the series drew one of the largest audiences in the history of PBS. Program segments deal with spacecraft missions of discovery to the planets, black holes, the origin of matter, the human brain, alternate universes, time travel, communication among whales, death of the sun, and the search for life on other planets.

"Hard Choices." KCTS/9, University of Washington, Seattle, Wash. 98195.

These six one-hour documentaries first aired on public television stations in January/February 1981. Produced by KCTS in Seattle, these programs examine the ethical challenges brought about by the ongoing revolution in medicine and biology. They cover selecting the sex of our children, modifying human behavior, life-prolonging technology, genetic screening experiments with human subjects, and the problem of providing a fair distribution of health care. An average of 2 million households originally saw each segment; the series has been rerun.

"Health Week." Cable News Network (CNN), 1050 Techwood Drive, NW, Atlanta, Ga. 30318.

These twenty-minute shows air Saturdays and Sundays on the Cable News Network. They are directed toward a general cable television audience and reach an estimated 546,000 homes. Started in 1980, "Health Week" includes news reports as well as some extended features and a viewer quiz.

"How About . . . . " Mr. Wizard Studio, 132 Stagecoach Road, Canoga Park, Calif. 91307.

Some 130 commercial television stations carry these eighty-second science features produced and hosted by Don Herbert, who produced and starred in the early "Mr. Wizard" television programs. The features, which use film, tape, slides, photographs, and other visual material, are typically inserted into news and other informational programs. Topics are wide-ranging and include such items as the latest research on volcanic eruptions, wind power, aging, acid rain, and bioluminescence. "How About" was first aired in 1979.

"Innovation." WNET/Thirteen, Gateway One, Newark, N.J. 07102.

"Innovation," Channel 13's weekly science series, had its pilot season in Spring 1983. It had a twenty-six-week run in 1983–1984 and came back for its third season in late October 1984. The only one-subject science magazine television program, "Innovation" includes a mini-documentary, a technology update, and a conversation segment with an expert on the topic being covered each week. Programs cover such subjects as oceanography, childhood development, phobias, alternate fuels, lasers, and technology for the disabled.

"Life on Earth." WQLN–TV, P.O. Box 10, Erie, Pa. 16512.

This series of thirteen one-hour programs first aired on PBS in January 1982. Produced by the BBC and hosted by David Attenborough, the series traces the emergence and development of life on this planet. It focuses on the rise and fall of species, the endless struggle for survival, and the adaptation to new and hostile environments. The United States presenter of the series is WQLN–TV.

"National Geographic Specials." National Geographic Society, Washington, D.C. 20036.

This continuing, popular series of one-hour specials is produced by the National Geographic Society and WQED–TV in Pittsburgh and aired on PBS. Topics covered include the Galapagos Islands, the human brain, sharks, national parks, and animals of the night. The 1975 production "The Incredible Machine" held the record for the largest audience ever viewing a PBS telecast until 1982, when the National Geographic's "Sharks" set a new one. "National Geographic Specials," which have won numerous Emmys, have been broadcast continuously since 1965. Four programs are produced yearly, each of which is seen by approximately 13 million people.

"The Nature of Things." Canadian Broadcasting Corporation, Box 500, Station "A," Toronto, Canada M5W IE6.

The CBC has been producing these one-hour programs for twenty-five years, and the series is now the longest-running science show on television in North America and one of the most popular shows in Canada, boasting an average weekly audience of 1,300,000. "The Nature of Things" is broadcast as a series or in segments by close to 100 PBS stations. An episode may deal with three to four subjects using a magazine format or cover a single subject for the full sixty minutes. The series covers all of science, including natural history, medicine, physics, psychology, technology, and sociology.

"Newton's Apple." KTCA–TV, 1640 Como Avenue, St. Paul, Minn. 55108.

After only one year on the air the program's producer, James Steinbach, and writer/host Ira Flatow won the 1983 AAAS-Westinghouse Science Journalism Award for television. Broadcast locally in the Minneapolis–St. Paul area beginning in Fall 1982, "Newton's Apple" began airing nationally on PBS in October 1983. It was picked up by 276 PBS stations, with an estimated audience of 4 million viewers for the show. This thirty-minute program is a combination of field production and studio segments.

"Nova." WGBH–TV, 125 Western Avenue, Boston, Mass. 02134.

The first "Nova" program aired in March 1974. Since then, this series of one-hour documentaries has grown to be one of the leading attractions of the Public Broadcasting Service. It is produced by WGBH–Boston. Programs aired in 1984 have included such topics as time, population in China, animal communication, climate, aquaculture, space, and biological warfare. WGBH produces twenty new "Nova" programs per year, coproduces and acquires others, and repeats broadcasts as well.

"Odyssey." Public Broadcasting Associates, Inc., 566 Centre Street, Newton, Mass. 02158.

This twenty-seven-part anthropology series was produced by Michael Ambrosino, creator of "Nova," and first aired on PBS in Spring 1980. The series of one-hour documentaries explores many of the unique and rapidly disappearing life-styles of the world's people. Topics covered include the early Americans, women of the Masai tribe in Kenya, hunter-gatherers in the African bush, and the life and work of Franz Boas, "the father of American anthropology." All programs now aired on PBS are reruns.

"Science Notes." KQED–TV, 500 8th Street, San Francisco, Calif. 94103.

KQED–TV began producing these regular three- to five-minute science spots in 1981. About twenty of the mini-programs have been produced each year. Topics covered include volcanoes, dinosaurs, computerized pacemakers, rheumatism, AIDS, and genetic engineering. The presentations often have a regional slant to make them particularly relevant to viewers in the San Francisco Bay Area.

"Science TV Report." American Institute of Physics, 335 East 45th Street, New York, N.Y. 10017.

These two-minute features are produced in sets of five with themes such as sports or astronomy. For four years the AIP has been presenting these news spots to about sixty local television stations nationwide at no cost. AIP produces about three of these shows each year.

"Smithsonian World." 1752 N Street, NW, Washington, D.C. 20036.

This series of one-hour documentaries is coproduced by the Smithsonian Institution and WETA–TV in Washington. Seven programs were planned for the first season, the first of which premiered in January 1984. This ambitious program combines science with art and history, reflecting the interests of the Smithsonian. Examples are the programs on "Crossing the Distance," which describes how people got from point A to point B; "Time and Light," which explores time-measurement tools and methods; and "Speaking Without Words," which looks at how humans and other creatures communicate.

"3–2–1 Contact." Children's Television Workshop, One Lincoln Plaza, New York, N.Y. 10023.

"3–2–1 Contact" is the first major series on science and technology for the eight- to twelve-year-old audience. First aired in 1980, it is designed for both at-home and in-school viewing. The first season consisted of sixty-five half-hour shows, broadcast each weekday for thirteen weeks. The series uses a magazine format that includes documentary footage shot on location, animation, stock footage, and a five-minute mystery serial called "The Bloodhound Gang."

Science in Newspapers

National Geographic Society. 17th and M Street, NW, Washington, D.C. 20036.

The National Geographic Society sends weekly feature stories on a wide variety of topics to daily and weekly newspapers throughout the country. The articles are designed to appeal to a mass audience and can be reprinted as written.

"Science Times." The New York Times. 229 West 43rd Street, New York, N.Y. 10036.

This regular science section appears every Tuesday in The New York Times. Begun in 1978, the section carries features about all areas of science, profiles scientists at work, reports new developments in science, reviews books, and answers questions about scientific phenomena. The articles frequently cover topics in greater depth than is usual in newspapers and are syndicated to newspapers that subscribe to The New York Times wire service. The New York Times was one of the first newspapers to include a science section, and its coverage is one of the most comprehensive.

NOTE: An increasing number of newspapers throughout the United States are now featuring special science sections. These range in length from a half-page to several pages once a week. Topics typically include all the sciences, medicine, and technology.

"Science Today." United Press International, 220 East 42nd Street, New York, N.Y. 10017.

This column moves on UPI wires three times a week for afternoon newspapers. It deals with all areas of science and medicine and is written by UPI staff members. It is edited by Al Rossiter, Jr., UPI science editor, based in Washington, D.C.

Smithsonian Institution. 900 Jefferson Drive, Washington, D.C. 20560.

This service of the Smithsonian Institution's Public Affairs Office provides four illustrated articles per month to weekly newspapers throughout the United States. The articles, which highlight research being done at the Smithsonian, cover diverse topics ranging from animal communication to flowering plants.

Science Magazines

American Health. 80 Fifth Avenue, Suite 302, New York, N.Y. 10011.

This magazine, launched in 1981, is published ten times a year. Subtitled "Fitness of Body and Mind," it is designed for a general audience. Each issue combines short news and health-fitness items with longer feature articles written by scientists, physicians, and journalists.

American Scientist. Sigma Xi, The Scientific Research Society, 345 Whitney Avenue, New Haven, Conn. 06511.

This bimonthly research publication contains original research reports in all scientific disciplines, plus a large number of science book reviews, commentary, and articles. The journal is written by scientists for scientists, primarily for members of Sigma Xi.

Bioscience. American Institute of Biological Sciences, 1401 Wilson Boulevard, Arlington, Va. 22209.

This monthly journal (with a combined July/August issue) is published for the membership of the American Institute of Biological Sciences and over 4500 institutional subscribers. The journal contains state-of-the-art articles covering a broad range of biological areas, research report condensations, short primary research papers, long and short features and news items, and book reviews.

Chemical and Engineering News. American Chemical Society, 1155 16th Street, NW, Washington, D.C. 20036.

This weekly magazine is published for a professional audience and provides an overview of current developments in academia and industry. The publication includes short news items as well as longer, special round-up articles. Special sections on business, government, technology, science, and international developments keep readers up-to-date on topics of particular interest in these areas.

Discover. Time, Inc., Time-Life Building, Rockefeller Center, New York, N.Y. 10020.

This monthly magazine, which made its appearance with the October 1980 issue, is designed for the educated layperson. Its contents include news briefs, short features, profiles of scientists, science applications, and reviews of science in the media. It covers all the scientific disciplines.

High Technology. High Technology Publishing Company, 38 Commercial Wharf, Boston, Mass. 02110.

This monthly publication premiered with the September/October 1981 issue. It is designed to keep the reader abreast of important developments at the frontiers of technology and to explain, in detail, how the technologies work, how they'll be applied, and how they interact. Each issue contains several feature articles plus regular departments on such things as investment opportunities in high technology, new patents and processes, and opinion and commentary.

IEEE Spectrum. 345 East 47th Street, New York, N.Y. 10017.

This monthly magazine is designed for professionals. Each issue contains several general articles on a wide range of topics of interest to engineers, with relevant photographs and charts; short news items; book reviews; and commentary. It occasionally deals with particular topics in greater depth, such as the accident at Three Mile Island.

Issues in Science and Technology. National Academy of Sciences, National Academy of Engineering, Institute of Medicine, 2101 Constitution Avenue, NW, Washington, D.C. 20418.

The first issue of this quarterly publication appeared in Fall 1984. Designed as roughly the science equivalent of *Foreign Affairs*, the magazine covers a broad range of topics that deal with policy implications of developments involving science and technology. The first issue included articles on science and the public process, ballistic missile defense, Medicare's prospective payment system, the air bag regulatory process, and the reindustrialization of America.

Mosaic. National Science Foundation, Washington, D.C. 20550.

Mosaic is an interdisciplinary magazine of basic and applied research published six times a year by the National Science Foundation. It is written by science journalists and edited for nonspecialists. The magazine contains long feature articles on all areas of scientific research that NSF supports in the natural and behavioral sciences.

National Geographic. 17th and M Streets, NW, Washington, D.C. 20036.

This monthly publication goes to the more than ten million members of the National Geographic Society. It relies heavily on high-quality, four-color photographs and other visuals to cover a variety of topics about the world we live in. Entire issues have been devoted to energy, the space shuttle, sharks, Saturn, Mount St. Helens, and paleoarcheology.

Natural History. American Museum of Natural History, Central Park West and 79th Street, New York, N.Y. 10024.

This monthly magazine features all the natural sciences. It is designed to appeal to persons interested in the social and natural sciences, human environment, and wildlife. It includes feature articles, book reviews, reading lists, news about the museum, and a monthly sky observation chart and commentary.

Nature. Macmillan Journals, Ltd., 4 Little Essex Street, London WC2R 3LF England.

This weekly science magazine, published in England, largely consists of short research and news items covering all fields of research. A small number of articles in each issue provide more in-depth coverage of major research developments. Designed for a professional audience, the journal also publishes an extensive technical letters section (actually brief reports of original research of wide interest) and book reviews.

New Scientist. Commonwealth House, 1–19 New Oxford Street, London WC1A 1NG England.

This weekly science magazine, published in England, covers the international science scene. It contains many short news items, three- to five-page reports on current research, and several commentaries on science and technology. It carries a mix of articles written by magazine staff and items contributed by other scientists and journalists.

Omni. 909 Third Avenue, New York, N.Y. 10022.

This monthly science magazine was launched by Penthouse Publications in October 1978 to appeal to a broad general public. It was the first of the new wave of science magazines and one of the few to blend science fact and science fiction. The glossy, four-color magazine relies heavily on dramatic visual presentation.

Physics Today. American Institute of Physics, 335 East 45th Street, New York, N.Y. 10017.

This monthly magazine contains feature articles written by physicists for physicists, book reviews, stories on recent developments in physics and science policy, and other features.

Popular Science. 380 Madison Avenue, New York, N.Y. 10017.

This monthly magazine is designed to inform technically curious readers about the world and universe in which they live. Subjects range from space to geothermal energy, from computers to automobiles, from housing technology to photography. For do-it-yourselfers, a portion of the magazine advises on projects and maintenance for the home and car.

Psychology Today. 1200 17th Street, NW, Washington, D.C. 20036.

This monthly publication is read by lay people and many professionals who are interested in learning more about human behavior from new findings in psychology and the other social sciences. One of the first "popular" science publications to appear, it is now published by the American Psychological Association.

Science. 1333 H Street, NW, Washington, D.C. 20005.

This weekly journal is published by the American Association for the Advancement of Science largely for a professional audience. Each issue contains original research articles and technical research reports written by scientists; staff-written news and comment and research news sections; and book reviews covering all fields of science, medicine, technology, and science policy. The magazine occasionally publishes special issues devoted to such topics as recombinant DNA, high-technology materials, energy, health care technology, and electronics.

Science 85. 1333 H Street, NW, Washington, D.C. 20005.

This award-winning magazine was launched by the American Association for the Advancement of Science in October 1979. Published ten times a year, it is designed for an educated general audience. Each issue makes extensive use of four-color photographs and other visuals and contains in-depth articles and quick wrap-up reports on new developments in science, technology, and medicine; science cartoons; books and media reviews; sports features; and commentaries.

Science Digest. 888 7th Avenue, New York, N.Y. 10106.

Hearst Publications began testing full-size special editions of this forty-three-year-old, digest-size publication in the fall of 1979. It was converted to the full-size format with the November/December 1980 issue. Now monthly, *Science Digest* relies heavily on four-color visual presentations and includes short items plus long features written by both scientists and journalists.

Science News. 1719 N Street, NW, Washington, D.C. 20036.

This is the only weekly newsmagazine of science in the United States. Edited for readers who are primarily science professionals and other science-oriented adults, it provides concise, current news of science. Each sixteen-page issue contains many short items with usually one or two longer trend or frontier-of-science articles.

The Sciences. 2 East 63rd Street, New York, N.Y. 10021.

This publication of the New York Academy of Sciences appears ten times a year and contains articles, book reviews, commentary, program activities of the Academy, and news briefs. Originally intended for Academy members, the magazine now appeals to a much broader audience within the scientific community.

Scientific American. 415 Madison Avenue, New York, N.Y. 10017.

This illustrated monthly magazine is addressed to readers who already have a strong interest in science, technology, and medicine. The articles, which cover the physical, biological, and social sciences, are written by the people who have done the research they are describing. Each September issue is devoted to a single topic such as industrial microbiology, economic development, and the brain. Regular feature departments include "Books," "The Amateur Scientist," and "Science and the Citizen."

Technology Review. MIT, Room 10–140, Cambridge, Mass. 02139.

Originally an MIT alumni magazine, *Technology Review* is now a national magazine on technology and its implications. It is edited for a sophisticated general audience. Each monthly issue contains several long articles on topics such as lead exposure and human health, energy alternatives, urban transportation, technology and privacy, and scientists as whistleblowers. Columns, book reviews, and short news items also appear regularly.

Science in Nonscience Magazines

Columbia Journalism Review. Graduate School of Journalism, Columbia University, 700 Journalism Building, New York, N.Y. 10027.

This bimonthly publication contains articles about the media in general and about media coverage of various topics. It has featured articles on press coverage of Three Mile Island and recombinant DNA and on environmental reporting. In addition to the longer articles, each issue contains media news, book reviews, and letters.

Fortune. Time-Life Building, Rockefeller Center, New York, N.Y. 10020.

This fortnightly business magazine, published by Time, Inc., occasionally features science and technology articles designed to appeal to *Fortune's* primary audience: corporate managers and others interested in business.

Mother Jones. 625 Third Street, San Francisco, Calif. 94107.

This magazine, published ten times a year, is one of the few periodicals to include investigative science journalism. Designed to appeal to a liberal audience, the publication has taken a critical look at such things as the medical establishment, energy issues, and drugs.

Newsweek. 444 Madison Avenue, New York, N.Y. 10022.

This weekly newsmagazine contains special sections on science, medicine, and the environment; they are among the most closely read of all its regular departments. *Newsweek* cover stories on science- and medicine-related topics have consistently been among the top sellers on newsstands.

New Yorker. 25 West 43rd Street, New York, N.Y. 10036.

Over the years this weekly magazine has contained some of the most readable, detailed, and accurate science articles found in any nonscience publication. It also periodically profiles scientists. Among topics it has treated especially well are recombinant DNA (in a three-part 1978 series) and chlorofluorohydrocarbons (in a 1975 prizewinning piece).

Smithsonian. 900 Jefferson Drive, Washington, D.C. 20560.

This general monthly publication of the Smithsonian Institution covers everything from art and music to culture and scholarship. Many of the feature articles are science-oriented.

Time. Time-Life Building, Rockefeller Center, New York, N.Y. 10020.

This weekly newsmagazine contains regular science, medicine, environment, and behavior sections. In addition, it carries periodic cover stories on science and medicine topics, which are consistent best-sellers.

Index

THE RUBY DICE

Catherine Asaro

Baen Books by Catherine Asaro

Sunrise Alley
Alpha

The Ruby Dice

THE RUBY DICE

Catherine Asaro

THE RUBY DICE

Copyright © 2008 by Catherine Asaro

A Baen Books Original

Baen Publishing Enterprises
P.O. Box 1403
Riverdale, NY 10471
www.baen.com

ISBN 10: 1-4165-5514-5
ISBN 13: 978-1-4165-5514-8

Cover art by Alan Pollack

First printing, January 2008

Distributed by Simon & Schuster
1230 Avenue of the Americas
New York, NY 10020

Library of Congress Cataloging-in-Publication Data:

Asaro, Catherine.
   The ruby dice / Catherine Asaro.
      p. cm.
   "A Baen Books Original"—T.p. verso.
   ISBN-13: 978-1-4165-5514-8
   ISBN-10: 1-4165-5514-5
   I. Title.
   PS3551.S29R83 2008
   813'.54—dc22

                    2007037314

Printed in the United States of America

10 9 8 7 6 5 4 3 2 1

F
ASA
(sf)

To Jim Baen
1943-2006

*In memory of one of
the great publishers*

Acknowledgments

I would like to thank the following readers for their much appreciated input. Their comments have made this a better book. Any mistakes that remain are mine alone.

To Aly Parsons, Kate Dolan, Sarah White, and Maria Markham Thompson for their excellent reading and comments on the full manuscript; to Aly's Writing Group for insightful critiques of scenes: Aly Parsons, Simcha Kuritzky, Connie Warner, Al Carroll, J. G. Huckenpöhler, John Hemry, Bud Sparhawk, and Bob Chase. To my editor and publisher, Toni Weisskopf; to Hank Davis, Marla Anspan, Danielle Turner (Managing Editor), Mary Ann Johanson (copy editor), and all the other people at Baen who did such a fine job making this book possible; to my excellent agent, Eleanor Wood, of Spectrum Literary Agency; and to Binnie Braunstein for her enthusiasm and hard work on my behalf.

A heartfelt thanks to the shining lights in my life, my husband, John Cannizzo, and my daughter, Cathy, for their love and support.

Prologue

The Emperor of the Eubian Concord ruled the largest empire ever known to the human race, over two trillion people across more than a thousand worlds and habitats. It was a thriving, teeming civilization of beautiful complexity, and if it was also the greatest work of despotism ever created, its ruling caste had managed to raise their denial of that truth to heights greater than ever before known, as well.

Lost in such thoughts, the emperor stood in a high room of his palace and stared out a floor-to-ceiling window at the nighttime city below. The sparkle of its lights created a visual sonata that soothed his vision, if not his heart. At the age of twenty-six, Jaibriol the Third had weathered nine years of his own rule. Somehow, despite the assassination attempts, betrayals, and gilt-edged cruelty of his life, he survived.

Tonight the emperor grieved.

He mourned the loss of his innocence and his joy in life. His title was a prison as confining as the invisible bonds that held the billions of slaves he owned and wished he could free.

Most of all, he mourned his family. Ten years ago tonight, his parents had died in a spectacular explosion recorded and broadcast a million times across settled space. In the final battle of the Radiance War between his people and the Skolian Imperialate, the ship carrying his parents had detonated. He had seen that recording again and again, until it was seared into his mind.

1

Jaibriol's father had descended from a long line of emperors, every one of them dedicated to the destruction of the Imperialate. On that day, the Skolian Imperator had captured his father. Rather than see him imprisoned, his own people had destroyed the Imperator's ship. So had come the death of Jaibriol's father, the Emperor of Eube.

And so had come the death of Jaibriol's mother—the Imperator of Skolia.

How two interstellar potentates ended up in the midst of a battle, Jaibriol would never know. Perhaps they had been fleeing into exile, seeking a place where the hatred between their peoples couldn't destroy them. Whatever the truth, they had taken it to their graves. Now both were ten years dead, and Jaibriol sat on the Carnelian Throne. His mother had ruled the empire of his enemies. He carried the secret of his heritage like a bomb ready to detonate within him.

He kept his bedroom darkened as he gazed at the city below, Qox-ire, the capital of his empire. He could no longer see the lights that glistened on the lofty towers, nor could he see beyond the city to the thundering waves that crashed on a shoreline of dazzling black sand. The scene's luster blurred into luminous washes of color, for tonight the emperor wept.

A door hissed across the room. He tensed, knowing it could be only one person. His bodyguards would stop anyone else. Unless they were dead and this was an assassination attempt. He felt more sorrow at the thought of their possible deaths than the thought of his own. He continued to gaze out the window. If an assassin had come upon him tonight, perhaps he should let the killer free him from the agony of his so-called glorious reign.

Footsteps whispered on the deep-piled rug. Someone stopped behind him, and he heard breathing.

"If you have a knife," Jaibriol said, "I would suggest placing it between my third and fourth ribs."

A woman spoke in a dusky voice. "I never carry knives. They're too obvious."

Jaibriol turned around. The woman stood at nearly his height, her leanly muscled body taut with coiled energy. Glittering black hair brushed her shoulders, and her upward-tilted eyes were as red as gems. Her high cheekbones underscored her aquiline beauty, giving her the profile that graced several Eubian coins. Her black jumpsuit resembled a uniform, except that it fit snugly, accenting her sultry, pantherlike sensuality. She could have passed for thirty-five, but Jaibriol knew the truth. His wife was more than a century in age.

"You don't need a knife," he said. "You cut to the bone without it."

Her lips curved upward. "I thank you for the compliment."

"What would you consider an insult?" he asked dryly. "If I called you sweet and accommodating?"

She raised her sculpted eyebrow at him. "For what possible reason would you say such a thing?"

Perhaps because just once, he thought, *I would like a wife who showed even one of those traits.* She didn't catch his thought; she had no telepathic ability. Although she wasn't an empath, either, she was far more attuned to his moods than he would have thought possible for a member of the Highton Aristo caste. Of course, he was supposedly Highton as well. He had the shimmering black hair, red eyes, and alabaster skin. No one had any idea he possessed the forbidden abilities of a psion.

"I was curious to see your reaction," he said. It was even true.

"No games, Jai. Not tonight." She sounded tired. Or more accurately, she let her fatigue show. Although she presented a perfect, cool exterior to the world, he knew her too well to be fooled.

"Why not tonight?" he asked. It was refreshing to ask a straight question. In normal discourse, Hightons never did. Direct speech was an insult, for Aristos used it only with their slaves. Except, of course, between lovers. He had long ago decided not to dwell on the implications, that they used the same form of speech with lovers and slaves.

His wife, Tarquine, walked away, across the dimly lit room. "It's the mercantile Lines," she said, sounding distracted.

Well, hell. If Tarquine decided some group posed a threat, she could do a great deal of damage. As Finance Minister, she wielded far too much influence over the economics of the Eubian empire; her reach could affect even the other two civilizations that shared the stars with them, the Skolian Imperialate and the Allied Worlds of Earth.

"Merchants in general?" he asked. "Or one in particular?"

She turned to him. "The Line of Janq."

"They're the ones who own so many export corporations in Ivory Sector, aren't they?" As Diamond Aristos, they dealt with Jaibriol less than his Highton Aristo advisors.

"If this consortium they are putting together succeeds," Tarquine said, "they will own all of them."

Jaibriol frowned. That would give one Aristo Line a lock on nearly one quarter of the empire's most lucrative export institutions. "Can you get me a report on what you know?"

"A report." She watched him, her eyes dark in the dim light. "So you can prepare for a meeting with them that will allow us to negotiate this situation in a reasonable manner."

His jaw ached, and he realized he was clenching his teeth. He forced himself to relax. "That's right."

She came back over to him. "Of course, Jai. I will provide you with a report."

He hated it when she agreed that easily; it almost always meant trouble. She unsettled him as much today as when he had met her, perhaps even more now that he knew her better. Nine years ago, his joint commanders of Eubian Space Command, or ESComm, had conspired to kill him and nearly succeeded twice, including on his wedding day, though no proof existed. In the end, they had both died by assassination. Three civilizations believed they had arranged each other's deaths. How could it be otherwise? No one could touch those two warlords who led the massive, relentless military machine of the Eubian empire.

Except Tarquine.

She would never acknowledge it, but Jaibriol knew. She had arranged the death of the admiral through the explosion of his ship, making it look as if the other commander killed him. The retaliation of the admiral's kin had been fast; before Jaibriol knew even one of his commanders had died, both were gone.

"Tarquine," he warned. "Keep out of it."

"I am the Finance Minister," she said mildly. "I cannot 'keep out of it.'"

"You know what I mean."

"You worry too much," she murmured.

"When you say 'don't worry,' I get hives."

She laid her finger on his cheek. "It will be fine."

He folded his hand around her fingers and moved them away. He was no longer the naïve youth who had married her out of desperation, because he was safer with her as his empress than as his enemy. He was still young compared to his advisors, hardly more than a boy by Highton standards, but he had learned a great deal over the past ten years. And if it meant he had lost his innocence, it also meant he kept his life.

Jaibriol had never lost his dream—to make peace between his people and the Skolians. He would never have the chance to know his family, the Ruby Dynasty who ruled Skolia. Their Imperator, Kelric Valdoria, would never know he was the uncle of Eube's emperor. That secret would remain locked within Jaibriol. But perhaps they could meet at the peace table. It was the only way he knew to honor his mother and father, who had dreamed of ending the hostilities between their two peoples.

He didn't want his parents to have died in vain.

The night mourned with silence, as if it were a sonata with no music left to play. More than ever, tonight Kelric Skolia—Imperator of the Skolian Imperialate—felt his age. The years weighed on him.

He sat on the bed, in the dim light, and watched his wife sleep. White hair curled around her face. Her skin was smooth, with only a few wrinkles, but it had a translucent quality. Her torso barely rose and fell with her shallow breaths. The crook of her nose, broken decades ago, shadowed her cheek. She had never wanted it fixed, though he could have given her anything, anything at all, any riches or wealth or lands or gifts.

Anything except her life.

"Jeejon," he said. A tear formed in his eye, and he wiped it away with the heel of his hand.

She seemed small under the blankets, wasted away. He had searched out every remedy medical science could provide, but it was too late. By the time he had met Jeejon, nine years ago, her body had nearly finished its span of life. She had been born a Eubian slave. They designed her to last sixty years, and she had been fifty-seven when his path crossed hers. His age. But he had benefited his entire life from treatments to delay his aging, even nanomed species passed to him by his mother in the womb. Jeejon had received nothing; her owners considered her a machine with no more rights than a robot. Kelric had managed to extend her three years to nine, but now, at sixty-six, her body had given out.

A rustle came from the doorway. He looked around to see Najo, one of his bodyguards, a man in the stark black uniform of a Jagernaut, with a heavy Jumbler in a holster on his hip.

"I'm sorry to disturb you, sir," Najo said. "But you have a page on your console."

Kelric nodded. Nothing could stop the Imperialate in its vibrant life, nine hundred worlds and habitats, a trillion people spread across the stars. It slowed for nothing, not even him, its Imperator.

He rose to his feet, watching Jeejon, hoping for a sign she would awaken. Nothing happened except the whisper of her breath.

Kelric went with Najo. His other bodyguards were in the hall outside: Axer, a burly Jagernaut Tertiary whose shaved head was tattooed with linked circles; and Strava, tall and stoic, a Jagernaut Secondary, her hair cut short. They had accompanied him here to his stone mansion above a valley of green slopes and whispering trees. He lived in the Orbiter space station, which had perfect weather every day. The big, airy spaces of his home accommodated his large size, as did the lower gravity, two-thirds the human standard. He didn't need bodyguards in this house; the entire habitat protected him. Najo and the others had come with him today as a buffer, to shield his privacy in these last days with Jeejon. His moments with her seemed faded by antiqued sunlight, as if they were aged gold.

His officers had to be able to reach him, however. As Imperator, he commanded all four branches of Imperial Space Command, or ISC: the Pharaoh's Army, the Imperial Fleet, the Jagernaut Forces, and the Advance Services Corps. He didn't rule the Skolian Imperialate; that job went to a contentious, vociferous Assembly of elected representatives and to his aunt, the Ruby Pharaoh. But Kelric had the loyalty of ISC.

He crossed his living room, limping slightly from an old injury that even biomech technology had never fully healed. The large space of polished grey stone soothed him. This mansion had belonged to his half-brother, Kurj, a previous Imperator. Kurj had been a huge man, tall and massively built, and Kelric looked a great deal like him. The house was all open spaces and stone, with no adornment except gold desert silhouettes that glowed on the walls at waist height. Kelric had thought of adding color to the grey stone, but with Jeejon here, the place had always seemed warm.

When he reached the console by the far wall, he found glyphs floating above its horizontal screen. The message was from his aunt, Dehya Selei. The Ruby Pharaoh. She descended from the dynasty that had ruled the Ruby Empire thousands of years ago. As a scholarly mathematician, she was far different from those ancient warrior queens; Dehya wielded a vast and uncharted power in the shadowy mesh of communications that wove the Imperialate together.

Her message glowed in gold:

Kelric, we've a diplomatic glitch with the Allied Worlds of Earth. It isn't urgent, but as soon as you have a chance, I'd like to brief you.—Dehya.

He rested his palm on the screen, and the holos faded above his skin. She could have paged his gauntlet, but it would have been an intrusion. *Thank you,* he thought to her, for understanding he needed this time with Jeejon before his voracious duties devoured his attention.

As a member of the Ruby Dynasty, Kelric had inherited his title as Imperator after the death of his sister, the previous Imperator. He commanded one of the largest militaries in human history—yet all his power, all his titles and lineage and wealth meant nothing, for they couldn't stop his wife from dying.

Kelric's bedroom was huge and spare, all polished stone and high ceilings. Breezes wafted in through windows with no panes. The bed stood in the middle of the stone floor; walking to it, he felt as if he were crossing a desert. The room echoed, and Jeejon hadn't stirred.

With a sigh, Kelric lay beside his wife.

"Kelric?" Her voice was wispy.

He pushed up on his elbow to look at her. She watched him with pale blue eyes, worn and tired, wrinkles at their corners.

His voice caught. "My greetings of the morning."

"Is it . . . morning?"

"I think so." He hadn't been paying attention.

Her mouth curved in the ghost of a smile. "Come here . . ."

He hesitated, wanting to hold her but afraid. He was so large, with more strength than he knew what to do with, and she had become so fragile.

"I don't break that easily," she said.

Kelric drew down the covers. She was wearing that white sleep gown he loved. He pushed off his boots, then lay on his back and pulled her into his arms. She settled against his side, resting her head on his shoulder. They stayed that way, and he listened to her breathing. Each inhale was a gift, for it meant she lived that much longer.

"I remember the first time I saw you," she said.

"At that mining outpost."

"Yes." She sighed. "You were so incredibly beautiful."

He snorted. "I was so incredibly sick."

"That too."

The memories were scars in his mind. He had been one among millions of refugees caught in the aftermath of the Radiance War that had devastated both the Imperialate and Eubian empire. Alone and unprotected, he had feared to reveal his identity lest he risk assassination. Not that anyone would have believed him. He had been dying, stranded on a mining asteroid, his body in the last stages of collapse. Jeejon was processing people through the port. A former Trader slave, she had escaped to freedom during the war. If she hadn't taken him in, he would have died, alone and in misery.

He laid his head against hers. "You saved my life." If only he could do the same for her.

She was silent for a while. Then she said, "You were kind."

Although he laughed, his voice shook. "I made you a Ruby consort. That's more cruel than kind." One reason he lived here, instead of on the capital world of the Imperialate, was so she wouldn't have to deal with the elegantly cutthroat world of the Imperial court.

"It has been a treasure." Her voice was barely audible. "I was born a slave. I die a queen."

His pulse stuttered. "You won't die."

"It was a great act of gratitude, to marry me because I saved your life."

"That's not why I married you." He wasn't telling the full truth, but he had grown to love her.

She breathed out, her body slight against his. "When we met, you were wearing gold guards on your wrists."

Kelric tensed. "I took them off."

"They were marriage guards."

Had she known all these years? "Jeejon—"

"Shhhh," she whispered. "I never knew why you left her."

"Don't."

"You never went back to her. Even though you love her."

"You're my wife. I don't want to talk about someone else. Not now." Not when they had so little time left.

She pressed her lips against his chest. "No one knows what happened to you during the war, do they? It isn't just me . . . you never told anyone about those eighteen years you vanished."

"It doesn't matter." Moisture gathered in his eyes.

Her voice was low. "Such a tremendous gift you have given me, waiting while it took me nine years to die."

"Jeejon, stop."

"Someday . . . you must finish that chapter of your life you left behind for me."

He cradled her in his arms. "You can't die."

"I love you, Kelric."

"And I, you." His voice broke. "Always."

"Good-bye," she whispered.

"Don't—" Kelric froze. Her breathing had stopped. Somewhere an alarm went off, distant, discreet, horrifying.

"*No.*" He pulled her close, his arms shaking, and laid his cheek against her head. "*Jeejon, no.*"

She didn't answer.

Kelric held his wife, and his tears soaked into her hair.

I

Hall of Circles

The Highton language was rife with allusions to the Carnelian Throne that symbolized the reign of the Eubian Emperor, phrases such as "He commanded with magnificence from the throne" or "His glorious Highness sat on the esteemed Throne of Carnelians" or "Only a fool would put a half-grown boy on the damn throne." None of those phrases referred to the emperor actually sitting on a chair, of course. Unfortunately, however, the Carnelian Throne did exist. And it was about as comfortable as a rock.

Jaibriol sat in the throne, leaning to one side, his elbow resting on its stone arm. He was alone in the Hall of Circles except for his guards. The room was like ice. Its white walls sparkled, designed from a composite of diamond and snow-marble. Rows of high-backed benches ringed the chamber, all snow-diamond and set with red cushions like drops of blood on frost. A white dais supported his throne, and red gems glinted in the chair, as hard and cold as the Hightons who sat atop the empire's power hierarchy.

His bodyguards were posted around the walls, three of the mammoths where he could see them and four others behind him. They wore the midnight uniforms of Razers, the secret police who served the emperor, their dark clothes jarring against the brilliant white walls. These Razers had so much biomech augmentation, they were considered constructs rather than human beings. Their thoughts lurked at the edges of his mind, mechanical, not quite human.

The captain of his guards waited by the dais, alert and still, his feet apart, his arms by his sides. Although his face remained as impassive as always, Jaibriol never felt ill-at-ease with him. He had selected these men over time, choosing those with no Aristo heritage.

It disturbed Jaibriol that the Aristos identified their Razers only by serial numbers. His guards seemed more human to him than the supposedly exalted Aristos. He had named the captain Vitar, because the guard resembled Jaibriol's younger brother. But he had come to think that wasn't right, either; he should have asked the Razer what he wanted to call himself.

A chime came from his wrist comm. Jaibriol lifted his arm and spoke into the mesh. "Yes?"

The voice of his personal aide, Robert Muzeson, came out of the comm. "Your joint commanders are here, Your Highness."

"Send them in," Jaibriol said. His pulse ratcheted up, and he took a breath, schooling himself to calm. He had summoned them to this frozen place rather than to his office because the presence of the throne accented his authority.

The towering doors across the hall swung open like cracks widening in ice. Vitar's biomech arm flashed as he communicated with the other Razers, and they moved into position, flanking the entrance. A retinue of military types swept into the hall, a general and an admiral, with six other officers in a crisp formation. The Razers fell in around the retinue and accompanied them down the central aisle.

General Barthol Iquar strode at the front of the group. He was Tarquine's nephew, a powerfully built man in a dark uniform. Admiral Erix Muze, a leaner man in cobalt blue, walked with him. Both commanders were Hightons, members of the highest Aristo caste, which ran the military and government. They topped the hierarchy of ESComm; together, they commanded the Eubian military.

Jaibriol remained relaxed on his throne while they came to him. He allowed neither his posture nor expression to reveal his discomfort. Their minds were great weights pressing on his, smothering him; as they came nearer, his perception shifted and they seemed like chasms that could pull him into darkness and pain and swallow his sanity. He shored up his mental shields, both protecting himself and hiding his mind, for he could never let them suspect he was a psion. He carried out this farce that defined his life, every day of every year, until he felt as if he were walking down an infinite corridor of frost.

Seeing their hard faces, it was hard for Jaibriol to remember they existed because of an attempt to *protect* empaths. That well-meant research had produced a monstrous result. The geneticists tried to mute the painful emotions empaths sensed, but instead they created a race of antiempaths. Aristos. When an Aristo's brain detected the pain of a psion, it shunted the signals to its pleasure centers. The stronger the psion's agony, the greater the effect. Aristos considered the resulting explosion of ecstasy they experienced the greatest elevation a human being could experience. They named it "transcendence" and called the psions they tortured to make it possible "providers."

In their brutally warped logic, the Aristos believed their ability to transcend raised them into a superior form of life, and that the agony of their providers elevated them. If the Aristos ever suspected their emperor was a Ruby psion—the ultimate provider—his life would become a hell almost beyond his ability to imagine.

Almost.

Watching the approach of his commanders, Jaibriol fought to maintain his mask of indifference. Robert, his personal aide, came in after the retinue. His presence both calmed Jaibriol and stirred his guilt. Robert's unusual name came from Earth. Eubian merchants had "liberated" Robert's father from his ship. Of course they weren't merchants and they hadn't liberated anyone, but that sounded so much more palatable than saying pirates had kidnapped him and sold him into slavery. Jaibriol couldn't undo the sins of every Aristo, but he had managed to bring Robert's father to the palace and reunite him with his son after decades of unwanted separation.

The retinue stopped at the dais, and Barthol and Erix bowed to Jaibriol. None of the aides were full Aristos, so they all went down on one knee. Jaibriol had to stop himself from shifting his weight. He had never liked having people kneel to him. His parents had raised their children in secret on a world with no other people, so they never bothered with court protocols. He wasn't certain which disturbed him more, that Eubians believed all human beings except Aristos should kneel to their emperor or that he was becoming accustomed to that treatment.

He didn't immediately tell them to rise, not because he had any desire to see people kneel, but because to do otherwise would be viewed by Hightons as a weakening of his authority. Early on in his reign, he had learned the hard way: behave as expected or deepen the risk of assassination.

A memory jumped into his mind of the day ESComm had found his father and taken him away. Jaibriol had been fourteen. ESComm had wrested his father from his world of refuge without knowing the man they found had a family. After that shattering day, Jaibriol's mother had hidden her children on Earth with one of the few people she trusted, Admiral Seth Rockworth. Then she had started the Radiance War. Almost no one knew she had done it to reclaim her husband. Jaibriol had ascended to his throne with the foolish hope that he could end the hostilities between the empires of his parents, but after ten years among the Aristos, he despaired that he would ever make headway.

Finally he moved his hand, palm down, permitting the aides to stand. Although their gazes were downcast, they caught his gesture. After they rose to their feet, he stood up and descended the dais, taking his time, studying the general and admiral. Both were tall, especially Erix Muze, who stood nearly eye to eye with Jaibriol when the emperor stopped in front of them.

"I am pleased," Jaibriol said. He wasn't; he liked neither of his arrogant joint commanders. But even if they loathed him, especially Barthol, at least they were more loyal than the previous two, who had kept trying to murder him.

Jaibriol motioned toward the closest bench. He didn't invite them to sit; such a direct comment from one Aristo to another would be a profound insult.

As soon as Robert saw Jaibriol lift his hand, he spoke with deference. "General Iquar and Admiral Muze, it would please the emperor if you would join him."

The three of them took their seats on the bench, Jaibriol on one end and his commanders in its middle. It was an awkward arrangement for a conference, but he had no intention of making this easy. He was tired of their delaying tactics. If he had to spend time in their mind-torturing presence, he wanted them off balance. He had discovered that the more uncomfortable he made the Aristos around him, the less likely they were to notice his discomfort, or his "penchant" for treating non-Aristos as if they were human.

Captain Vitar stationed himself next to Jaibriol, a stark reminder of the power wielded by the emperor, that he could command ESComm's billion-credit Razers as his private bodyguards. Vitar wore the face of a mechanical killing machine with no emotions. He didn't fool Jaibriol. His guards loved, hated, laughed, and wept like other humans. He sometimes had the odd sense that Vitar enjoyed intimidating Aristos he knew Jaibriol didn't like. The Razer would of course never do anything to suggest he harbored such inappropriate sentiments, so Jaibriol could never be sure. He had difficulty picking up moods from his guards because the extensive biomech augmentation to their brains changed their brain waves.

Barthol Iquar spoke the requisite formal phrases. "You honor the Line of Iquar with your presence, Esteemed Highness."

Erix spoke. "You honor the Line of Muze, Esteemed Highness."

Jaibriol inclined his head. In the convoluted Highton language, it meant he accepted their words without rancor, but without any particular encouragement, either. To Barthol, he said, "I understand you have acquired a new corporation."

"Indeed," Barthol said, cautious. "A good business. Furniture."

Good business, indeed. The general was leaving him no openings. No matter. Jaibriol had expected this. "Perhaps I might look at your inventory. I understand you have an excellent selection of tables."

Although neither commander showed a reaction, they knew what he meant. The peace table. Their negotiations with the Imperialate. He felt the spark of their anger even with his mental barriers up. They would have to live with it. The negotiations had been stalled for years, and he was heartily sick of their maneuvers to avoid the talks.

"I will have an inventory sent to you," Barthol said smoothly.

Jaibriol just sat, letting the silence lengthen. The tactic sometimes prodded Aristos to speak, as if they couldn't bear a hole in the convoluted webs of discourse they wove. These two were too well versed in Highton to show discomfort, but their moods trickled over Jaibriol: unease and anger. Neither had any desire for peace with the Skolians. Barthol also thought him a callow youth with peculiarities that bordered on intolerable.

After several moments, Jaibriol said, "I'm sure you know best what inventory would suit my interests. Perhaps the most knowledgeable of your people can assist my review."

The general's eyes were hard and clear, like the gems in the Carnelian Throne. "Of course, Sire."

"I would particularly like to see any unusual pieces." Jaibriol didn't say *Skolian,* but they knew. He intended to reopen the talks, if he could convince the Skolians, and he expected at least one of his joint commanders in attendance. Barthol had a close relation to Tarquine, as her nephew, but he harbored a greater antagonism toward Jaibriol than Admiral Muze.

"We are always happy to seek the betterment of the empire," Erix Muze said.

"It pleases me to know." Jaibriol didn't doubt he meant it. He also had no doubt that "betterment of the empire" didn't include negotiations with Skolians.

He dismissed the commanders with body language, a slight shifting of his weight, a glance to the side. Suddenly Robert was there, escorting the officers away. He had developed his ability to read Jaibriol's Highton gestures to an art.

Captain Vitar directed the other bodyguards using commands Jaibriol couldn't see, except for the lights flickering on his biomech arm and those of the other Razers. The captain had biomech limbs, nodes in his spine, bioelectrodes throughout his brain, and threads and high-pressure hydraulics networking his body. Yet when Jaibriol looked into his face, he saw a man.

After his commanders were gone, Jaibriol stood up and beckoned to Vitar. The guard came over, looming above even Jaibriol, and bowed. The conduits on his dark uniform glinted. Although protocol demanded that everyone except other Aristos kneel to the emperor, Jaibriol shared one trait in common with his predecessors on the throne: he preferred his guards on their feet and ready to defend his person.

"Vitar, do you like your name?" Jaibriol asked.

"Most certainly, Sire. It is an honor." Disappointment flashed in his gaze, though he quickly hid the emotion. "But if you wish to withdraw it, I will be honored to obey your wishes."

"No, I didn't mean that." Jaibriol rubbed his chin. "I just thought you might like to choose your own."

The Razer paused only a moment, but for someone with a brain as much biomech as human, it was a long time. Then he said, "I would never presume to such. But it is a most esteemed offer."

"It's not a presumption," Jaibriol said. "If you could pick any name, what would you choose?"

Vitar thought for a moment. "Hidaka. Sam Hidaka."

"All right. If you would like, I will call you Hidaka."

For one of the few times in the years Jaibriol had known him, the captain grinned in an all-out smile. "Thank you, Sire! You are most generous."

Jaibriol didn't feel generous, he felt like a cretin. He should have asked Vitar years ago what name he preferred. No, not Vitar. Hidaka. He would have to remember.

He regarded the Razer curiously. "It's an unusual name. Did you make it up?"

The captain shook his head. "It is the name of the founder and chief executive of the most successful coffee business on Earth." Then he added, "Coffee is one of the Earth people's greatest achievements."

Startled, Jaibriol smiled. He wondered what other Aristos would say if they knew his Razers admired or even knew about any aspects of cultures outside the euphemistically named Eubian Concord, which as far as Jaibriol could see had achieved "concord" only in the Aristos' united desire to subjugate the rest of humanity.

"Well, Hidaka, you have an excellent name," Jaibriol said. "Your men may choose names as well, if they wish."

The captain bowed. "You honor us."

Jaibriol couldn't answer. It wasn't an honor, it was appalling it had taken this long for him to offer the choice.

They left the hall then, and as Jaibriol walked through the black marble halls of his palace, he brooded. He wished his joint commanders were as straightforward to deal with as his guards. He doubted he would ever convince Barthol Iquar or Erix Muze to endorse his wish for peace. And without support of the military, he didn't see how any talks with the Skolian Imperialate could even succeed.

"Jeremiah Coltman," Dehya said.

Kelric looked up from the console where he was scanning files on army deployments. He and Dehya were in a room paneled in gold and copper hues. It was one of many offices that honeycombed the hull of the Skolian Orbiter space station used as a command center by the Imperialate.

"Jeremiad what?" he asked.

Dehya regarded him from her console, a slender woman with long hair, sleek and black, streaked with white, as if frost tipped the tendrils curling around her face. Translucent sunset colors overlaid her green eyes, the only trace she had of her father's inner eyelid. Kelric didn't have the inner lid either, but he had his grandfather's metallic gold eyes, skin, and hair, modifications designed to adapt humans to a too-bright world.

"Jeremiah Coltman," she repeated. "Do you remember?"

"I've no idea," he said, rubbing his shoulder to ease his stiff muscles. He had many aches these days; he hardly recalled the years when he had been bursting with youth and energy.

"That boy from Earth," Dehya said. "About a year ago we had trouble with the Allied Worlds over him."

Kelric searched his memory, but nothing came. **Bolt,** he thought, accessing his spinal node. **You have anything on him?**

His node answered via bioelectrodes in his brain that fired his neurons in a manner he interpreted as thought. **Jeremiah Coltman was detained on a Skolian world. I'm afraid my records are spotty.**

Kelric remembered then. It had come up the day Jeejon died. He recalled little from that time, and he had recorded nothing well in the long days that followed. Even now, nearly a year later, he avoided the memories. They hurt too much.

"I thought the man they locked up was an adult," Kelric said. "A professor."

"An anthropology graduate student." Dehya was reading from her console. "He spent three years on one of our worlds while he wrote his dissertation. Huh. Listen to this. They didn't throw him in prison. They like him so much, they won't let him go home."

Kelric turned back to his work. "Can't somebody's embassy take care of it?" It surprised him that she would spend time on it. Dehya served as Assembly Key, the liaison between the Assembly and the vast information meshes that networked the Imperialate in space-time—and in Kyle space. Physics had no meaning in the Kyle; proximity was determined by similarity of thought rather than position. Two people having a conversation were "next" to each other no matter how many light-years separated them in real space. It allowed instant communication across interstellar distances and tied the Imperialate into a coherent civilization. But only those few people with a nearly extinct mutation in their neural structures could power the Kyle web. Like Dehya. As Assembly Key, she had far more pressing matters to attend than a minor incident from a year ago.

"Ah, but Kelric," she said. "It's such an interesting incident."

Damn! He had to guard his thoughts better. He fortified his mental shields. "Stop eavesdropping," he grumbled.

She smiled in that ethereally strange way of hers, as if she were only partly in the real universe. "He won a prize."

"Who won a prize?"

"Jeremiah Coltman. Something called the Goldstone." She glanced at her console. "It's quite prestigious among anthropologists. But his hosts won't let him go home to receive it. That caused a stir, enough to toggle my news monitors."

Kelric felt a pang of longing. Had he been free to pursue any career, he would have chosen the academic life and become a mathematician. He and Dehya were alike that way. Those extra neural structures that adapted their brains to Kyle space also gave them an enhanced ability for abstract thought.

"Why won't they let him go?" Kelric said. "Where is he?"

"Never heard of the place." She squinted at her screen. "Planet called Coba."

He felt as if a freighter slammed into him. Jeejon's words rushed back from that moment before she died: *You never told anyone where you were those eighteen years.*

"Kelric?" Dehya was watching him. "What's wrong?"

Mercifully, his mental shields were in place. He didn't think she could pick up anything from him, but he never knew for certain with Dehya; she had a finesse unlike anyone else. So he told the truth, as best he could. "It reminded me of Jeejon."

Sympathy softened her sculpted features. "Good memories, I hope."

He just nodded. His family believed he had been a prisoner during those eighteen years he vanished. He let them assume the Eubians had captured and enslaved him, and that he didn't want to speak of it. That was even true for the final months. But he didn't think Dehya ever fully believed it. If she suspected he was reacting to the name *Coba,* she would pursue the lead.

He had to escape before she sensed that his disquiet went beyond his memories of Jeejon. Dehya's ability to read his moods depended on how well the fields of her brain interacted with his. The Coulomb forces that determined those fields dropped off quickly with distance; even a few meters could affect whether or not she picked up his emotions.

He rose to his feet. "I think I'll take a break."

She spoke softly. "I'm sorry I reminded you."

His face gentled, as could happen around Dehya. She was one of the few people who seemed untroubled by his silences and reclusive nature. "It's all right."

He left the chamber then, his stride long and slow in the lower gravity, which was forgiving to his huge size. Alone, he headed back to his large, empty house.

II

A Debt to Life

Kelric sat in his living room with no lights except the gold designs on the walls. No sunlight slanted through the open windows, but the bright day diffused into his home. He had settled on the couch, almost the only furniture in the huge room.

He sat and he thought.

Coba. It had taken eighteen years of his life. What would it do to Jeremiah Coltman? Would the young man's unwilling presence stir that world as Kelric's had done, until its culture erupted into war? Compared to the Radiance War that had raged between the mammoth Eubian and Skolian empires, Coba's war had been tiny. But it ravaged its people. And he, Kelric, had caused it. Coltman was a scholar, not a warrior, but the youth's presence would still exert an influence.

Kelric spoke to the Evolving Intelligence, or EI, that ran his house. He had named it after an ancient physicist who had illuminated mysteries of relativistic quantum mechanics.

"Dirac?" he asked.

A man answered in a deep baritone. "Attending."

"Find me everything you can about Jeremiah Coltman."

Dirac paused. "He was born in Wyoming."

"What's a wyoming?"

"A place on Earth."

"Oh." That didn't help. "What about his graduate school?"

"He earned a doctorate from Harvard for his study of human set-
tlement on the planet Coba. He spent three years working on a
construction crew there while he wrote his dissertation. One year ago,
a Coban queen selected him for a *Calani*. I have no definition of
Calani."

"I know what it means." Kelric leaned back and closed his eyes.
Queen was the wrong word for the women who ruled the Coban city-
estates. They called themselves Managers. In Coba's Old Age they had
been warriors who battled constantly, but in these modern times they
considered themselves civilized. Never mind this atavistic penchant
of theirs for kidnapping male geniuses.

Dirac continued. "Coltman's family and members of the Allied diplomatic corps have tried to free him."

"Any success?" Kelric asked.

"So far, none. He agreed to abide by Coban law when they let him
live on their world."

"What about this award he won?"

"Apparently the Coban queen relented enough to send his doctoral
thesis to his advisor at Harvard. The advisor submitted it to the
awards committee. At twenty-four, Coltman is the youngest person
ever to win the Goldstone Prize."

Kelric was grateful the fellow had received the honor, not because
he knew anything about anthropology, but because it had caught
Dehya's attention, which meant Kelric had found out about Coltman.
It also gave him a reason to ask about the planet.

"What do you have on Coba?" Kelric asked. His outward calm
didn't match his inner turmoil. He had avoided directly speaking that
question for ten years, lest someone notice and want to know why he
asked. As long as he seemed to ignore Coba, no one had reason to suspect its people had imprisoned a Ruby heir for eighteen years.

"Coba is a Skolian world," Dirac said. "Restricted Status. No native
may leave the planet. They are denied contact with the Imperialate.
The world has one automated starport, a military refueling post that's
rarely used. Skolians who voluntarily enter the Restricted zone forfeit
their citizenship."

Kelric waited. "That's it?"

"Yes." The EI sounded apologetic.

Relief washed over him. It was even less than he expected. Restricted Status usually went to worlds inimical to human life or otherwise so dangerous they required quarantine. The Cobans had *asked* for the status, and ISC had granted it because Coba was so inconsequential that no one cared.

Kelric's Jag starfighter had crashed on Coba after he escaped a Eubian ambush. The Cobans should have taken him to the starport. He would have died before they reached it, but the Restriction required they do it. Instead they saved his life. His legs had been pulverized by the crash, and the Cobans had healed him the best they could. But their medicine had limitations; even with additional work done by his people two decades later, his legs would always bear the internal scars of those injuries.

On Coba, by the time he recovered, they had decided never to let him go. They feared he would bring ISC to investigate the Restriction. They had been right. That had been before he understood how the Imperialate could destroy their unique, maddening, and wondrous culture.

Kelric couldn't fathom why they let Coltman study them. He rose to his feet, and his steps echoed as he walked through the stone halls of his house, under high, unadorned ceilings.

His office had a warmer touch. Jeejon had put down rugs, dark gold with tassels. Panels softened the stark walls with scenes of his home world, plains of silvery-green reeds and spheres adrift in the air. In some images, the spindled peaks of the Backbone Mountains speared a darkening sky.

He sat at his desk, and it lit up with icons, awaiting his commands. He turned off every panel. Then he opened a drawer and removed his pouch, a bag old and worn, bulging with its contents. Often he wore it on his belt, but other times he left it here, in the seclusion of his private office. He undid its drawstring—

And rolled out his Quis dice.

The pieces came in many forms: squares, disks, balls, cubes, rods, polyhedrons, and more. Not only did he have the full set carried by most Cobans, his also included unusual shapes such as stars, eggs, even small boxes with lids.

Dice and Coba. They were inextricably blended. All Cobans played Quis, from the moment they were old enough to hold the dice until the day they died. It was one giant game, the life's blood of a world.

They gambled with Quis, educated with it, gossiped through the dice, built philosophies. The powers of Coba used it to gain political influence. For a Manager to prosper, she had to master Quis at its topmost levels.

Then there were Calani.

The few men honored as Calani were extraordinarily gifted at Quis. They spent their lives playing dice. They provided strategy for the Manager, a weapon she wielded in the flow of power among the Estates. Managers had ten to twenty Calani; together, they formed her Calanya. The stronger a Calanya, the more a Manager could influence Coban culture. Quis meant power, and a Manager's Calanya was her most valuable asset.

Only Calani owned jeweled dice. The white pieces were diamond; the blue, sapphire; the red, ruby. But Calani paid a steep price for the spectacular luxury of their lives. They remained secluded. They saw no one but the Manager and the few visitors she allowed. They swore never to read, write, or speak to anyone Outside the Calanya. Nothing was allowed to contaminate their Quis, for anyone who succeeded in manipulating their game could damage the Estate, even topple the Manager from power. Managers shielded their scholarly Calani from Outside influences with the single-minded resolve of their warrior queen ancestors.

To symbolize Jeremiah, Kelric chose a silver ball. He built structures around it and let them develop according to complex and fluid rules. His skill molded the structures, but the complexity of the game and its often unexpected evolution informed their design just as much. Calani and Quis: they created each other.

He had intended to model Coban politics and examine what they revealed about Jeremiah. Instead, the dice patterns mirrored the history of his own people. He wasn't certain what his subconscious was up to, but he let the structures evolve.

Six millennia ago, an unknown race had taken humans from Earth and moved them to the world Raylicon. Then they vanished, leaving nothing but dead starships. Over the centuries, using libraries on those ships, the humans had developed star travel. They built the Ruby Empire and established many colonies, including Coba. But the empire soon collapsed, stranding the colonies. Four millennia of Dark Ages followed.

When the Raylicans finally regained star travel, they split into two opposed empires: the Eubian Concord, and Kelric's people, the Skolian

Imperialate. Skolians referred to Eubians as "Traders" because they based a substantial portion of their economy on the sale and trade of human beings.

Since that time, Skolia had been rediscovering the ancient colonies like Coba. The people of Earth had a real shock when they reached the stars: their siblings were already there, two huge and bitterly opposed civilizations. The Allied Worlds of Earth became a third, but unlike their bellicose neighbors, they had no interest in conquering anyone. They just sold things. In his more philosophical moments, Kelric thought neither his people nor the Traders would inherit the stars. While they were throwing world-slagging armies at each other, the Allieds would quietly take over by convincing humanity they couldn't survive without Allied goods. Imperial Space Command had an incredible ability to expand to new frontiers, but it paled in comparison to Starbytes Coffee.

Earth's success in the interstellar marketplace, however, depended on maintaining civil relations with Skolia and Eube. They obviously had no intention of upsetting their relations with the Imperialate over one graduate student. The moment Jeremiah had set foot on Coba, he had forfeited his rights as an Allied citizen and become subject to the Restriction.

Kelric blew out a gust of air. He had to get Jeremiah out of there, and do it without alerting anyone. The Restriction protected Coba's extraordinary culture.

And it protected Kelric's children.

He sat back, staring at the Quis structures that covered his desk. "Dirac."

The EI's voice floated into the air. "Attending."

Kelric knew if he continued to ask about Coba, someone might notice. His interactions with Dirac were shielded by the best security ISC had to offer. But he knew Dehya. If she became curious, she could break even his security. He was taking a risk. But it had been so long, and he had so little time left.

"I need you to find a Closure document," he said. "It was written ten years ago, just after the Radiance War." He leaned his head back until he was gazing at the stone ceiling. Outside his window, wind rustled in the dapple-trees like children whispering together.

"Did you arrange it?" Dirac asked.

"That's right," Kelric said. "I was serving on a merchant ship. The *Corona*." He had escaped Coba in a dilapidated shuttle that had barely managed to reach another port. He hadn't had credits enough even to buy food, let alone repair the aging shuttle. The job on the *Corona* had offered a way out.

"I have records of a vessel fitting that description," Dirac said. "Jaffe Maccar is its captain."

"That's it. I filed a Closure document with the ship's legal EI."

A long silence followed. Finally Dirac said, "I find no record of this document."

Maybe he had hidden it better than he thought. Either that, or it was lost. "It's encrypted," he said, and gave Dirac a key.

After a moment, Dirac spoke crisply. "File six-eight-three. Marriage to Ixpar Karn Closed. If Closure isn't reversed in ten years, Kelric Garlin Valdoria Skolia will be declared dead, and his assets will revert to his heirs. Ixpar Karn and two children are named as beneficiaries." The EI paused. "Your listed assets are extensive."

"I suppose."

"In one hundred eleven days," Dirac said, "Ixpar Karn will become one of the wealthiest human beings alive."

Even though Kelric had known this was coming, it rattled him. "Ixpar doesn't know."

"Do you wish me to cancel the document?"

"I'm not sure."

"You aren't dead," Dirac pointed out.

"If you cancel it, I'll be married to Ixpar again." It was a dream he desired, but it meant too much danger to her and his family. The Closure didn't become permanent until the end of ten years. It was usually done when someone's spouse vanished, to declare that person legally dead. Generally, the abandoned spouse invoked the Closure, not the person who had disappeared.

"Is marriage to Ixpar Karn a problem?" Dirac asked.

He thought of Jeejon. His marriage to her had been valid because of the Closure. She had been dead a year, but grief didn't end on a schedule. It receded, yes, but it crept up on you like a mouse under the table, until one day you looked down and saw it crouched in your home, watching you with pale eyes, still there after all this time. It was true, he had married Jeejon in gratitude. Maybe he had never felt the soul-deep passion for her that he had with Ixpar, but he had loved Jeejon in a quieter way. She had given up everything she owned to save his life, even believing he was deluded to think he was the Imperator.

She had never expected anything in return, but he had sworn to stand by her.

Dirac spoke. "Sir, the three people named as your heirs live on Coba. I don't think it's legal for inhabitants of a Restricted world to inherit from a Skolian citizen."

"I'm the Imperator," Kelric growled. "If I say it's legal, it's legal."

"According to Imperialate law, that isn't true."

Kelric scowled at the ceiling. Unlike his officers, his EI had no qualms about contradicting him.

"Who is going to tell me no?" Kelric asked.

"That would be complicated," Dirac acknowledged. "May I ask a question?"

"Go ahead."

"Why set up the Closure?" The EI sounded genuinely puzzled, as opposed to an AI, which only simulated the emotion. "You aren't the deserted spouse."

"I was unprotected, in a volatile situation." Painful memories rose within him. "I left my children on Coba so they would be safe and taken care of in case anything happened to me. If I died, I wanted to make sure they and Ixpar inherited."

"Yet nothing happened to you."

He grimaced. "I was kidnapped and sold as a slave."

"Oh." Another pause. "Are you saying you became a Trader slave after you signed this document?"

"That's right."

"But the document is only ten years old. Less, in fact."

"Yes."

"It was my understanding the Traders captured you twenty-eight years ago. Not ten."

Kelric didn't answer.

"When you die," Dirac added, "this document becomes public."

"My heirs could hardly inherit otherwise." He had wrestled with that decision, knowing it would draw attention to Coba. As long as he could shield both Coba and his family, he would do so. But if he ever had to choose, his wife and children came first. While he lived, the Closure document would remain secret even if it defined him as officially dead. When he actually died and could no longer look after Coba, the will within the document would become public, ensuring his heirs had his name and the multitude of protections that came with it.

And yet . . . he could protect Coba now in ways he couldn't have imagined ten years ago when, as a desperate refugee, he had written that will.

Dirac suddenly said, "This Closure document gives a new twist to the Hinterland defenses."

Kelric stiffened. "I have no idea what you mean."

"The Hinterland Deployment. One of your first acts as Imperator ten years ago. The military presence you established in sector twenty-seven of the Imperialate hinterlands."

"It was vital," Kelric said. "We needed to stop Traders from using that region of space."

"No indications existed that they were using it," Dirac said.

Kelric's advisors had told him the same. He gave Dirac the same answer he had given them. "That was the problem. No one paid attention to that sector. Had ESComm set up covert operations there, we might never have known."

"This is true." Dirac waited a beat. "How interesting that the Coban star system is the most heavily guarded region of that deployment."

Damn. It was how he protected Ixpar and his children without revealing his attention to their world. "Delete that from your memory."

"Are you sure?"

"Yes."

"Deleted. You have sixty seconds to undo the deletion before it becomes permanent."

Kelric knew erasing parts of an EI's memory was ill-advised. It always lost associated data as well. Such deletions could have unexpected results. But erasing one small fact wouldn't cause trouble. Still . . . perhaps he should reconsider.

"If I don't cancel this Closure," Dirac added, "you are going to be destitute in one hundred and eleven days."

A voice called from another room. "Kellie?"

"For flaming sakes," Kelric muttered. "Dirac, end session." He got up and stalked out of his office.

A woman was standing in his living room. Roca. Gold hair cascaded down her body and curled around her face. She had the same metallic gold skin and eyes as Kelric, but it looked much better on her. In her youth, men had written odes to her beauty and songs lauding her grace. Hell, so had women.

He scowled at her. "My name is Kelric, Mother."

"My apologies, honey. I forget sometimes."

Honey was almost as bad. He wondered when she would notice that her "baby" had grown into a hulking monster who commanded one of the deadliest war machines ever created.

"Don't glare at me so," she added, smiling.

"I thought you were going to Selei City for the Assembly."

Her good mood faded. "That's what I came to see you about." She walked to his console and stood facing it, her palm resting on the surface, though he didn't think she was looking at anything.

He went over to her. "What's wrong?"

She looked up at him. "The Progressive Party wants to abolish the votes held by Assembly delegates with hereditary seats."

That didn't sound new. The Progressives considered it appalling that the Ruby Dynasty and noble Houses held seats even though no one had elected them. As Pharaoh and Imperator, Dehya and Kelric were among the Assembly's most influential members. Roca had won election like any other delegate and become Foreign Affairs Councilor. With her hereditary votes added to that, she was also a great force. Kelric's siblings all held seats, but their blocs were smaller. Each of the eleven noble Houses had two seats, but those were mostly titular, with few votes.

Kelric smiled wryly. "One of these days, the Progressives will call for eradication of the Assembly on the grounds that EIs instead of people should run the government. The Royalists will agree we should abolish the Assembly, but only so Dehya becomes our sole ruler. The Traditionalists will insist a woman command the military and stick me in seclusion. The Technologists will blow up the Assembly with hot-air bombs. Meanwhile, the Moderates will urge everyone to please get along."

Roca laughed, her stiff posture easing. "Probably." She leaned against the console with her arms folded. "The problem is, I think the Progressives can make headway this time."

He didn't see how. "Every time they introduce one of those brain-rattled amendments, the Royalists vote them down. Usually the Traditionalists do, too. Your Moderates don't care, and they're the biggest party. Given that Dehya and I are both Technologists, I doubt our own party would vote to weaken our influence."

She stared across the room. "It seems the deaths in our family offer them a political opportunity."

Kelric stiffened. He hated that he had gained his title through the deaths of his siblings. "It may offend them that I inherited Soz's votes when she died, and that she inherited them from Kurj, but they can't deny the law. The Imperator holds a primary Assembly seat." Although technically the military answered to the Assembly, the loyalty of ISC to their Imperator was legendary. He doubted the Assembly wanted to push the issue of whom the military would obey. The last time they had faced that question, ISC had thrown its might behind the Ruby Dynasty and put Dehya back on the throne. In the end, she had chosen to split her rule with the Assembly because she genuinely believed it was best for the Imperialate. But few people doubted that, if put to the test, ISC would follow the Imperator.

"They won't touch your votes," Roca said. "They aren't stupid." Her voice quieted. "It's your father's bloc. No one objected to my inheriting it after he died because they knew how it would look. But it's been ten years." She sounded tired. "Before he became Web Key, we had only two Keys, the positions you and Dehya now hold. Those two Keys powered the Kyle web. It was a fluke that your father's mind differed enough from theirs to add a third mind without killing them. Many people don't believe we can duplicate that achievement. They say those votes should cease to exist unless we find another Web Key."

Kelric swore under his breath. The Progressives had grounds for their objection. He had expected them to raise it years ago, and when they hadn't, he had grown complacent. They had bided their time until they could no longer be accused of traumatizing the widow or her grieving family. They had even waited a year after Jeejon's death, though Kelric had no direct connection with his mother's votes. Yes, they had been careful. He could see why Roca was worried. They might win.

He didn't want her to lose those votes. She was one of the Assembly's greatest moderating forces. Many citizens felt the Imperialate subjugated its people with militaristic occupations and harsh laws. Facing the relentless threat of the Traders, Kelric understood all too well the draconian measures instituted by previous Imperators. He had enough objectivity to admit that in defending the Imperialate, he was capable of acts many would consider oppressive. They *needed* temperate voices. Roca offered a counterbalance. The day he rejected that balance was the day he became a tyrant.

"You have a plan?" he asked.

"I'm going early to the session," she said. "See if I can sway votes. It would help if you attended in person. Spend time softening up delegates with me."

"I couldn't soften a pod fruit."

"You're damned effective when you want to be."

He glowered at her. "Doing what? I hate public speaking."

"I'm not asking you to speak in the Assembly." She smiled with that too-reasonable expression that always meant trouble. "I just plan to give some dinners. Small, elegant, elite. People consider it a coup to be invited. They will think it even more so if the Imperator attends. We wine them, dine them, and convince them to support us."

Kelric stared at her. "You want me to attend dinner parties with the Imperial court?"

"Yes, actually."

"I would rather die."

Exasperation leaked into her voice. "It's not a form of torture, you know."

"It's not?"

"Do you want to win the vote or not?"

I'm going to regret this, he thought to her. "Fine," he growled. "I'll do it."

"Good." Then she thought, *The dinners will be fun.*

Gods forbid.

Her sudden smile dazzled. *Which ones would forbid it?*

Kelric glared at her. He had grown up on the world Lyshriol, steeped in its mythology of deities for the moons, suns, and mountains. He was named after Kelricson, the god of youth, though he hardly felt young anymore. He had become more pragmatic after he left home, but deep inside, a part of him still remembered when he had believed those luminous stories.

All of them. He let his thought grumble. **Especially Youth.**

Roca laughed good-naturedly. *Maybe even even he will enjoy himself.*

After Roca left, Kelric returned to his office and gazed at the dice on his desk. He thought of his children on Coba, the only he had ever fathered. In standard years, his son would be twenty-six now and his daughter sixteen. Ixpar was forty-two. She wasn't the mother of either child; she had only been fourteen when Kelric met her, and twice that age when she married him. He had never been allowed to see his son, and he had known his daughter only a few months after her birth. The ache of that lack in his life had never stopped, even after all this time.

Kelric often wanted to go to them. Then he would remember the devastation he had wrought on Coba, how cities had roared in flames while windriders battled in the skies. He had brought death and ruin to their world.

He would die before he let that happen to his children.

III

The Guards

A natural arch of black marble domed the mausoleum. It was set in cliffs high above the city of Qoxire on the planet called Eube's Glory, named by Jaibriol's unsubtle ancestor, Eube Qox, the monumental egotist who had founded the Concord. The crypt had stood for centuries, sheltering the ashes of the Qox Dynasty.

No wall blocked Jaibriol's approach to the crypt; nothing separated the inner sanctum from the chill morning except a row of black columns. In some ways, the vaulted spaces reminded him of Saint John's Church in the Appalachian Mountains on Earth. Seth Rockworth had taken Jaibriol and his siblings there each Sunday during the two years they had lived with him. But Saint John's had filled Jaibriol with warmth, with its stained-glass windows, graceful arches, and wooden pews. For all the majestic elegance of this mausoleum, its black marble spaces felt cold.

Accompanied by his Razers, he walked between two giant columns. Mist curled around the pillars and shrouded their tops. He pulled his jacket tighter, grateful for its warmth. With the climate controls in his clothes, he could survive almost anything, even a blizzard. But no climate system could protect him from the snowfall of his emotions.

Inside the mausoleum, light orbs glowed above him and dimmed after he passed. Pearly mist softened the marble statues and wreathed the orbs, giving them an ethereal quality, as if he had entered a realm of translucent life. The obelisks he sought stood together, two thin pyramids of marble, all slanted lines, no square corners. They guarded the ashes of a man and a woman: Ur Qox and Viquara Iquar.

His grandparents.

The stark monuments mesmerized him. The reign of Ur Qox had been a long one. His son—Jaibriol's father—had spent only two years on the throne, imprisoned by Viquara and her new consort while they ruled from the shadows.

Jaibriol turned away, struggling with his confused pain. He wasn't certain why he had come here. Leaning against the steep side of the obelisk, he stared into the shadows of the mausoleum. Fog brushed his face with its damp kiss, and he wiped his palm along his cheek, smearing the clammy moisture.

Viquara Iquar had died in the Radiance War. Some said she had stepped in front of a laser shot meant for her son. Had she saved his life? Jaibriol didn't understand why it mattered so much to him, but he needed to believe she had loved her son.

Her Ruby son.

Jaibriol's great-grandfather had sired Ur Qox on a provider so he could breed a psion, an heir with a mind powerful enough to create a Kyle web. But the traits that created psions were recessive; a child had to get them from both parents. So Ur Qox had repeated the process, siring a son on one of his providers. She gave birth to a Ruby psion. Jaibriol's father.

Ur Qox had been no saint; Jaibriol had no doubt that if the emperor could have impregnated his empress with another woman's child and tricked her into believing it was her own, he would have done it to protect the secret. But no Aristo could carry a Ruby child. The baby needed a psion as its mother, and an Aristo could never be a psion; they considered the traits a weakness and deliberately kept the DNA out of their bloodlines. The fetus of a psion responded dramatically to its environment. Nurturing it in a lab or even within a surrogate proved difficult and clones were rarely viable. The stronger a psion, the greater the problems. Ruby psions were almost impossible to birth except through natural methods. Had Viquara Iquar tried to carry a Ruby child, it would have died. She had to have known her son was another woman's child. Yet she had never revealed him.

Jaibriol laid his hand against the obelisk. Its polished surface chilled his palm. He was aware of his guards in the shadows, tall and silent, like the marble edifices. Tendrils of fog drifted above him, obscuring the light spheres until they became luminous blurs, as if they were ghosts of the Qox dynasty that had lived and died before him.

"Could you love him?" Jaibriol whispered. "You called him son, and he called you mother." Only Viquara would ever know the truth.

And what of his grandfather? Jaibriol knew Ur Qox only through the eyes of his son, Jaibriol's father. Ur Qox had been a distant parent, chill in his affections. Although Ur had been half Ruby, none of the traits had manifested, for Aristo genes dominated. Ur Qox had been an Aristo. Yet he never harmed his son. He had isolated Jaibriol's father in seclusion to protect him, not only against other Aristos, but even from himself.

The solitude had left Jaibriol's father craving love. He had only been twenty-four at Jaibriol's birth, three years younger than Jaibriol was now. He had been the finest man Jaibriol had ever known, a loving parent who taught him more than he felt he could ever give his own child. He knew now why it mattered so much to him to believe his grandparents had loved their son. Jaibriol's father had lived with the specter of Aristo brutality embodied by his own parents, both of them epitomes of a Highton. For Jaibriol, it would be the reverse, for his child would receive the Ruby genes only from him. Not from Tarquine.

His heir would be an Aristo.

Kelric met Admiral Barzun in the Skolian War Room.

Consoles filled the amphitheater, and robot arms carried operators through the air. Far above, a command chair hung under a holodome lit with stars, so anyone who looked up saw it silhouetted against the nebulae of space. When Kelric worked here, coordinating the far-flung armies of the Skolian military, he sat in that technological throne. It linked him into the Kyle web, which stretched across human-occupied space. Any telop, or telepathic operator, could use the Kyle web, but only Kelric and Dehya could create that vast mesh and keep it working.

Chad Barzun was waiting on a dais in the amphitheater. Crisp in his blue Fleet uniform, he was a man of average height, with a square chin, a beak of a nose, and hair the color of grey rock. As one of

Kelric's joint commanders, he headed the Imperial Fleet. Kelric liked him because Barzun spoke his mind, with respect, but he said what needed saying even if he knew Kelric might not like it.

Barzun had commanded the fleet that returned Dehya to the throne. The shock of that coup had paled, though, compared to her next action, when she returned half her power to the Assembly. On his own, Kelric would never have split the power, but he understood her reasons. The time for a dynasty as sole rulers of Skolia had passed. They needed the Assembly. But unlike before, the Ruby Dynasty now had equal footing with that governing body.

Chad saluted Kelric, extending his arms at chest level and crossing his wrists, his fists clenched.

Kelric returned the salute. "At ease, Chad."

The admiral relaxed. "My greetings, sir. Are you leaving soon?"

"Later today." Kelric grimaced. "Unfortunately."

Chad smiled slightly. "I don't envy you this vacation."

Kelric didn't envy himself, either, having to attend dinner parties with the Imperial Court. "I'm taking a few days alone first."

"Very good, sir." Chad's voice quieted. "Let yourself rest. Gods know, you've earned it."

"I'll try," Kelric lied.

They spent the next hour going over the Imperator's duties, which Barzun would oversee in Kelric's absence. If necessary, Chad could reach him through the Kyle web. Given that he believed Kelric was taking a long-overdue vacation, though, Kelric knew he would make contact only in an emergency.

Later, Kelric rode the magrail to a secluded valley of the Orbiter. He limped across the gilt-vine meadows, past Dehya's house. Holopanels on her roof reflected the sky and Sun Lamp several kilometers above. The spherical Orbiter was designed for beauty rather than efficiency; half its interior was just a sky. He could see the tiny figures of people walking by the sun. If they looked up, they would see the ground with its mountains and valleys curving above them like a ceiling of the world.

He hiked up the slope to his house. Inside, his duffle was where he had left it, on the desk in his office. He took his dice pouch out of the desk and tied it to his belt. Then he went to a black lacquered stand in the corner. Resting his hand on its top, he slid his thumb over its design, the Imperialate insignia, a ruby triangle inscribed within an amber circle. The gold silhouette of an exploding sun burst past the confines of the triangle. The symbol of an empire. The Imperialate claimed it was civilized, but a heart of barbarism beat close beneath its cultured exterior.

Bolt, his spinal node, interjected a thought into his musing. **Kelric.** He roused himself. **Yes?**

According to your schedule, you depart from docking bay six in twelve minutes.

Kelric pushed his hand across his close-cropped hair. He couldn't put this off any longer. With a deep breath, he tapped out a code on the sunburst insignia. A hum vibrated within the stand as if it had come to life after a long sleep, and a drawer slid out. His Coban wrist guards lay inside.

The ancient guards were crafted from gold. Their engravings showed a giant hawk soaring over mountains, the symbol of Karn, largest and oldest city-estate on Coba. He picked up one of the guards and snapped it open. The hinge worked, though he had left it untouched for a decade.

Kelric couldn't put on the guards, however. He already wore gauntlets. He brushed his thumb over the massive cuff on his forearm, a marvel of mesh engineering. He had found the gauntlets in the Lock chamber. His ancestors had lost the knowledge to create Locks, and his people had yet to recover it, but they could use the machines they found derelict in space. These gauntlets were part of that ancient technology. They provided him with a mesh node, a comm, and a means to link to other systems. He felt certain they had intelligence, probably beyond his ability to understand. He had worn them for a decade, yet he still didn't know how they had survived for five thousand years or why they let him use them.

He clicked open a switch on his gauntlet—and it snapped closed. He pried at the switch, but this time it didn't move at all. Trying to open the entire wrist section didn't work, either. Odd. The gauntlet looked normal: small lights glowed on it, silver threads gleamed, and the comm glinted.

Come off, he thought. He didn't want to damage it; the gauntlets could never be replaced. Destroying them might even be murder. **If you won't open,** he added, **I can't put on my wrist guards.**

Both gauntlets snapped open.

Kelric blinked. Apparently they liked his Coban guards.

A socket showed in the skin of his left wrist. Normally the gauntlet jacked into that socket so it could link with his internal biomech web. He took his Coban guard and clicked it around his wrist, lining up a hole in the gold with his wrist socket. Before he could do anything else, his gauntlet snapped around his arm and fitted to the Coban guard as if they had always been joined. Filaments wisped out from the gauntlet, protecting the soft gold.

"Huh." Kelric squinted at his arm. He cautiously snapped his second Coban guard around his other wrist. That gauntlet immediately closed, repeating the same procedure as the first.

Bolt, Kelric thought.

Attending, Bolt answered.

Why did my gauntlets do that?

I don't know. Bolt projected a sense of puzzlement.

Do you know why they wouldn't come off before?

Based on past incidents, I would say they believe it would endanger you to remove them.

What, by my standing in my perilous office? I might stub my toe.

It does seem far-fetched.

He touched the wrist guard. Its gold seemed warm compared to the silver and black gauntlet. **Can you find out why they did that?**

If you mean can I talk to them, the answer is no. But we exchange information all the time. I sometimes read patterns in their data. If I direct our exchange, with your wrist guards as the subject, I may glean some insights.

See what you can find out.

I will let you know.

He gazed at the lacquered stand. His Calanya bands still lay in its drawer, gold rings that could be worn on the upper arms as a sign of honor, if a Calani wished. They indicated his Level, the number of Estates where he had lived in a Calanya. Most Calani were First Levels. Attaining a higher Level was a matter of great negotiation, for what better way for one Manager to gain advantage over another than to obtain one of her Calani? His Quis held immense knowledge of her Estate, strategies, plans, everything.

Toward the end of his time on Coba, Kelric had lived at Varz Estate. His Quis had vaulted the already powerful Estate into world dominance, but his submerged fury had also gone into the dice. His life had

been hell. Harsh and icy, the Varz queen had been a sadistic nightmare. By that time, Ixpar had ruled Coba, a young Minister full of fire. She had freed Kelric from Varz—and so provoked the first war Coba had seen in a thousand years.

I've an analysis of your gauntlets, Bolt thought.

Kelric put away his memories. **Go ahead.**

They consider whatever you plan to do dangerous enough that you need them for your protection. However, apparently they deem your wrist guards acceptable, even beneficial, to your needs or emotions.

His emotions? Even he wasn't sure how he felt. He stared into the drawer. One of his Calanya bands was missing. It had come off during his escape from Coba and probably lay buried somewhere in the ashes of Ixpar's Estate.

Kelric gathered the bands and packed them into his duffle. Then he left for the docking bay.

"Prepare for launch," Kelric said. The cabin of the ship gleamed, small and bright. An exoskeleton closed around his pilot's chair and jacked into the sockets in his spine.

As the engines hummed, Bolt thought, Your bodyguards aren't here.

Kelric didn't answer.

Mace, the ship's EI, spoke. "Bay doors opening."

A hiss came from around Kelric as buffers inflated to protect sensitive equipment in the cabin. His forward screens swirled with gold and black lines, then cleared to reveal the scene outside. Two gigantic doors were opening, their toothed edges dwarfing his vessel, and the rumble of their release growled through his ship. Beyond the doors lay the glory of interstellar space, its gem-colored stars radiant against the dust clouds and the deep black of space.

Bolt's thought came urgently. You must not leave without security.

I have it. Kelric laid his hand on the massive Jumbler at his hip. The gun had to be big; it was a particle accelerator. It carried abitons, antiparticle of bitons, the constituents of electrons. With a rest energy of 1.9eV, bitons and abitons produced nothing more than orange light when they annihilated. But that was enough. In the atmosphere, the beam sparkled as it destroyed air molecules; when it hit anything solid, the instability of the mutilated electrons blew apart the object.

One gun is not enough to guard the Imperator, Bolt thought. **The ship is armed. And I used to be a weapons officer.**

Even so. You should have—

Bolt, enough.

With a great clang, the docking clamps released Kelric's ship. He maneuvered out of the bay, leaving the Orbiter along its rotation axis. The great notched edges of the doors moved slowly past, as thick as his ship was long. Communication between Mace and the dock personnel murmured in his ear comm. To them, the launch was routine. No one knew he was alone. He had told Najo, Axer, and Strava he was taking his other guards, and he told the others he would be with Najo, Axer, and Strava.

As his ship moved away from the Orbiter and through its perimeter defenses, Kelric spoke into his comm. "Docking station four, I'm switching off your network and onto the Kyle-Star."

"Understood," the duty officer replied. "Gods' speed, sir."

"My thanks." Kelric cut his link to the Orbiter, but contrary to his claim, he made no attempt to reach Kyle-Star, the interstellar mesh of communications designed to guide starships.

Bolt, he thought. **Download my travel coordinates to the ship.**

I don't think you should do this alone.

I've made my decision.

I'm concerned for your safety.

I appreciate that. Now send the damn coordinates.

You are sure you want to do this?

Yes! I'm also sure I don't want to argue with a node in my head.

Bolt paused. Then he thought, Coordinates sent.

"Coordinates loaded," Mace said.

"Good." Kelric took a deep breath. "Take me to Coba."

IV

Viasa

Jaibriol ran. Struggling for breath, he raced through tunnels of dark rock that absorbed the light. A void was gaining on him, drawing closer, closer. A talon grasped his arm—

"No!" Jaibriol sat upright in bed, his heart beating hard.

It was several moments before his adrenaline eased enough for him to breathe normally. "Father in heaven," he whispered—and then realized he had spoken in Iotic. When seeking comfort, he instinctively lapsed into his first language, though only Skolian nobility used it. Or he spoke English. He had converted to Seth's Catholic faith on Earth, finding refuge from his nightmares in the sanctuary of his adopted religion. The one tongue he never associated with succor was Highton, supposedly his "true" language.

Night filled the imperial suite. He had woken up alone, but it wasn't unusual; his wife needed only a few hours of sleep compared to his nine or ten. Although he could now manage with sleeping every other day, he had never truly grown used to the sixteen-hour cycle of this planet.

Cloth rustled across the room; with a start, he realized someone was sitting in one of the wing chairs. He didn't think it was an Aristo;

41

he felt none of the pain their presences caused. He reached out mentally—and sensed Tarquine. He exhaled, his rigid posture easing. She was one of the few Aristos whose mind didn't injure him.

He spoke in Highton. "My greetings, wife."

"Did you have another nightmare?" she asked from the dark.

"It was nothing." He often dreamed he was trapped, and he probably would for as long as he remained emperor, which would be the rest of his life, however long that lasted.

The glint of her eyes was visible even in the shadows. "It's been a strange day."

"Strange how?" Jaibriol doubted he wanted to know, but he couldn't afford to be oblivious.

"It seems a major mercantile firm in Ivory Sector has experienced a sudden reversal of fortune. Odd, that."

Hell and damnation. What had she done? "What reversal?"

"The Janq Line that manages the firm has financial woes," Tarquine said. "Apparently their investments in several merchant fleets have collapsed." Her words flowed like molasses. "It seems these fleets were actually pirates. They preyed on Skolian space lines, kidnapping people to sell as providers. In Skolian space. Which of course we know is illegal."

What startled him wasn't that the Janq Line sent pirates into Imperialate space; half the Aristo Houses had fleets raiding the Skolians. But they were rarely caught. Of all the ways Tarquine might have brought down the Janq Line, he never would have expected this. For one, it would be difficult to achieve, given how well Aristos protected their fleets. More to the point, it was understood that no Aristo Line touched the "merchant" fleets of another. If Tarquine had aided in the Janq downfall, she had broken an unwritten law of her own people. Why?

"I'm surprised they were prosecuted," Jaibriol said.

"Well, the Skolians caught them in Skolian space with Skolian captives. They had plenty of evidence."

He wanted to demand *How?* but she would never admit any involvement, and he was certain no evidence existed that could link her to the situation. The idea that one of their own would leak such information to the Skolians was anathema to any Aristo—except him. He would have liked to throw all their "merchants" in chains.

He recalled his discussion with Tarquine about the Ivory Sector corporations trying to corner the export market. He spoke warily. "I find myself wondering if the Janq corporation that suffered this set-back was involved in the consortium that hopes to attain a monopoly on the Ivory mercantile system."

"Oddly enough," Tarquine said, "they seem to be the major players. Or they were, before this fiasco. With their affairs in such disarray, they've had to step back from the mercantile venture. It appears the consortium will collapse."

"Imagine that," Jaibriol said sourly. He had been preparing for talks with them, to limit their monopoly. "So negotiations with the Janq Line won't be needed after all."

"Apparently not."

"And of course you had nothing to do with it."

If she heard his sarcasm, she gave no hint. "Of course."

Jaibriol sometimes thought she was like a night-panther stalking the palace, sleek and dark, deadly in her beauty. She slipped among the corridors of power as if they were trees in a jungle, her form visible and then gone as if she had never been there. How or when she attacked, he rarely knew. Telling her to stop was like trying to catch a shadow, for no proof ever connected her to the results of her operations.

"Why are you sitting over there?" he asked. It gave him an eerie feeling, as if she would fade into the night, only to reappear later with no blood on her hands, but her lovely, feral eyes glinting with triumph.

Cloth rustled. Tarquine coalesced out of the shadows, walking toward him. She sat on the bed, sleek in her silken black nightshift. "Azile spoke with me today."

"Azile speaks with you many days." Azile Xir was the Minister of Intelligence, after all, and she the Minister of Finance. The fact that they didn't like each other didn't negate their need to work together.

"Some days," Tarquine said sourly, "his words are less sublime than others."

He rubbed his knuckles down her cheek. "*Sublime* is an overrated word."

"Particularly in the matter of reminders."

"Reminders?" He had no idea what she meant, and she had shielded her mind.

"About heirs," she said. "Ours, to be specific." Only a hint of anger touched her voice, but from Tarquine, that was a great deal. "Or our lack thereof."

Jaibriol gritted his teeth. Azile wasn't the first to bring up the matter, not by far. No matter how young Tarquine looked or how good her health, she was well past the age when most women could conceive. She had eggs in cryogenic storage, but she would need the help of specialists to carry a child.

"I've learned to ignore hints about our nonexistent progeny," he said. "Sublime or otherwise."

"You need an heir, Jai. Our firstborn will also inherit my title as head of the Iquar Line." A fierce pride infused her voice. "We must both ensure our successions."

Jaibriol did want to have this conversation. He had avoided it for years. He had spent his childhood surrounded by the warmth and love of his family, and that was what he had imagined for his children. Not the chilly world of Aristos. In his youth, he had looked forward to fatherhood, inspired by the example of his parents; now he never wanted heirs.

He said only, "It isn't safe here."

"We can protect our child. It is well known your father isolated you in your childhood." She waited a beat. "To protect you against assassins, of course."

"Of course." His palms felt clammy. Tarquine knew the truth about him. She kept his secret just as he kept hers, that she had altered her own brain so she could never transcend. It was a change Aristos considered unforgivable. If they knew, they would destroy her. It was also why Jaibriol had married her; she was the only Highton woman he could live with, for she would never transcend with him. It also gave him leverage over her to keep his secret. That over the years he may have fallen in love with his deadly wife was a thought he avoided, for he didn't know how to deal with the idea he could love an Aristo.

Tarquine knew his grandfather had secluded his father until adulthood because his father was a psion. The Qox Dynasty had wanted a Ruby psion among its ranks, someone who could wrest the Kyle web from the Ruby Dynasty. With Jaibriol's father, they finally succeeding in breeding the psion they wanted—and he rejected Eube. Instead, he sought out one of the few people like him: Soz Valdoria of the Ruby Dynasty. Jaibriol's mother.

He spoke in a low voice. "Our heir will be more you than me." It could never be a psion; Tarquine didn't have the genes. The child would grow up to transcend on the pain of his own father. It was a prospect too gruesome for him to contemplate.

"The longer we wait," she said, "the greater the chance one or both of us will die before the child reaches maturity, or even before its birth. Is that what you want?"

"No." He shifted his weight. "But I would rather have this conversation another time."

"We've avoided it for ten years."

"I know." He pulled her closer. "Tomorrow, Tarquine. We will talk about succession then."

She put her arms around his neck. "Very well. Tomorrow."

He drew her down to lie with him, deep into the silk sheets and the shadows of the night. But as he caressed her soft skin, he felt as if he were drowning. Tomorrow he would put her off again, as he had for years, but someday he would have to decide: sire an Aristo child or die without an heir and leave Eube in the hands of those who would seek to subjugate humanity.

Kelric played dice.

The cockpit of the Skolian scout ship curved around him in bronzed hues. He was traveling in inversion, which meant the speed of his ship was a complex number, with an imaginary as well as a real part. It eliminated the singularity at light-speed in the equations of special relativity. He could never go *at* light-speed, so he went around it much as a cyclist might leave a path to ride around an infinitely high tree. Once past the "tree," he could attain immense speeds, many times that of light. During such travel, his ship needed only minimal oversight, which meant he had little to do. So he swung a panel in front of himself and played Quis solitaire.

He built structures of the Trader emperor. Jaibriol the Third had only been seventeen when he came into power. Kelric could barely remember being that young, let alone imagine ruling an empire at that age. Jaibriol had compensated for his deadly lack of experience by marrying his most powerful cabinet minister, Tarquine Iquar. Kelric knew Tarquine. Oh yes, he knew her, far too well. While he had been serving aboard the merchant ship *Corona,* the Traders had captured it and sold him into slavery. Tarquine had bought him. If he hadn't escaped, he would still be her possession.

Uncomfortable with the memory, he shifted his focus to politics. His structures evolved strangely. They implied Jaibriol Qox genuinely wanted peace. Kelric found it hard to credit, yet here it was, in his Quis.

The peace talks had foundered years ago. He had represented ISC at those talks, a military counterbalance to Dehya. They made an effective team: she the diplomat and he the threat. But for it to work, they had to *get* to the peace table. He had hoped Roca might sway the Assembly away from its current intransigence and back to negotiations. If they and the Traders didn't hammer out a treaty, their empires were going to pound away at each other until nothing remained.

Patterns of the upcoming Assembly session filtered into his Quis. The structures predicted an unwanted result: his mother would lose the vote. He varied parameters, searching for models that predicted a win, and found a few. They relied on her ability to sway councilors outside of the session, with a greater chance of success if he helped her. Which meant he couldn't avoid attending her infernal dinner parties. That put him in a bad mood, and he quit playing dice.

Sitting back, he gazed at the forward holoscreen, which showed the stars inverted from their positions at sublight speeds. He could replace the map with a display of dice and play Quis with the ship's EI. It seemed pointless, though. He had taught it the rules, and it played just like him, but without creativity. For ten years, he had done almost nothing but Quis solitaire. He was starved for a session with a real dice player, a good one. He had wanted to teach Dehya, had even given her a set of dice, but then he changed his mind. She was too smart. When she mastered Quis, she could unravel his secrets from his play. He couldn't trust anyone with that knowledge.

On Coba, he had sat at Quis with many Calani, saturating their culture-spanning game with his military influence until the war erupted. Ixpar claimed that capacity for violence had always been within her people, that in the Old Age, queens had warred with one another until they nearly destroyed civilization. Finally, in desperation, they subsumed their aggression into the Quis. He believed her, but he also saw what they had achieved, a millennium of peace, one that ended when he came to their world.

Kelric would never forget the windriders battling in the sky or Karn roaring in flames. In that chaos, he had stolen a rider and escaped. By then, he had known all too well why the Cobans wanted the Restriction. If he, only one person, could have such a dramatic effect, what would happen if the Skolian Imperialate came to Coba in full force? He had sworn that day to protect his children, Ixpar, and Coba.

Which was why he had to go back.

The voice droned on the ship's comm. "Identify yourself immediately. This world is Restricted. Identify yourself . . ."

The automated message kept repeating, an eerie reminder of the day, ten years ago, when Kelric had flown to this starport so he could escape Coba. It was the only warning anyone received, either in space or on-planet. The port was fully automated and usually empty. ISC didn't care who landed as long as they stayed in the port. Any Skolian who entered the Restricted zone, which consisted of the entire planet outside of the port, essentially ceased to exist. Kelric doubted anyone in ISC bothered to keep track, though. It would matter only if the Cobans held someone against his will. Unfortunately, they had done exactly that with him, for eighteen years. It had nearly killed him.

Had ISC discovered the Cobans had imprisoned a Ruby prince, they would have considered it an act of aggression subject to military reprisals. They would have put the Cobans under martial law, prosecuted the Managers involved, absorbed Coba into the Imperialate, and never realized until too late, if ever, that they had destroyed a remarkable culture. He had the authority now to prevent the military actions, but he couldn't stop his family from turning their relentless focus here if anyone discovered his interest—which they might if the port recorded his landing. So he wouldn't go to the port.

"Mace," he said. "Get a map of the Coban Estates from the port. Hide your presence from the mesh system there."

"Accessing." Then Mace said, "The files are locked."

"Use my keys." His security should top any port safeguards.

"I have the map," Mace said.

"They're keeping Jeremiah Coltman in a city called Viasa," Kelric said. "It's in the Upper Teotec Mountains, the most northeast Estate." He was fortunate the Viasa Manager had bought Jeremiah's contract. Kelric had never been to Viasa, and his inviolable seclusion in the Calanya of other Estates meant that none of Viasa's citizens had ever seen him.

"I've identified a city that fits your description," Mace said. "But it's called Tehnsa."

"Oh. That's right." He had forgotten. "Viasa is below Tehnsa, near Greyrock Falls and the Viasa-Tehnsa Dam."

"I have the coordinates," Mace said.

A holomap formed to Kelric's left, a dramatic image of the towering Upper Teotec Mountains. The winds in those peaks were brutal. His ship was a Dalstern scout, designed for flight in planetary terrains as well as space, but it would need guidance. At least Coba had aircraft beacons. Although their culture had backslid during their millennia of isolation, they had redeveloped some technology even before ISC rediscovered them. Their windriders were small but respectable aircraft.

"The dam has a beacon that can guide us," Kelric said.

"I can't find it," Mace said. "And this map is wrong. We're passing over what appears to be Tehnsa, but the map places it southwest of here."

Kelric frowned. Although Mace continuously updated the holo-map, it could only calculate the changes as fast as the scout's sensors could provide data about the mountains.

"How are you handling the winds?" Kelric asked.

"So far, fine. They're increasing, though, as we go lower in the atmosphere." After a pause, Mace added, "This port map is appalling. It hardly matches the one I'm making at all."

"Can you find the beacon?"

"So far, no."

"Keep looking."

"I'm getting a signal!"

Relief washed over Kelric. "From the dam?"

"No. It's a mesh system."

What the blazes? "Cobans don't have mesh systems."

"It's from Viasa," Mace said. "Not a guidance beacon. It's a general comm channel."

He couldn't imagine where the Viasans had obtained equipment to produce such a signal. He toggled his long-range comm and spoke in Skolian Flag, which was used by his people as a common language to bridge their many tongues. He didn't want to reveal he knew Teote-can, the Coban language, unless it was necessary.

"Viasa, I'm reading your signal," he said.

No response.

"Mace, can you increase my range?" Kelric asked.

"Working," the EI said.

"Viasa, I'm receiving your signal," Kelric said. "Can you read me? I repeat, I'm reading your signal. Please respond."

Still nothing. The scout was lower in the mountains now, and peaks loomed around them.

The comm suddenly crackled with a man's voice, words that made no sense.

"What the blazes was that?" Kelric asked.

"He's speaking Flag," Mace said. "Very *bad* Flag. I believe he said, 'Know English you? Spanish? French?'" The EI paused. "Those are Earth languages."

Kelric wondered if he was speaking to Jeremiah. **Do I know any of those?** he asked Bolt.

I have a Spanish mod, Bolt replied. I can provide rudimentary responses.

Go, Kelric thought.

Bolt gave him words, and he spoke into the comm, grappling with the pronunciation. The Skolian translation glowed on one of his forward screens.

"This is Dalstern GH3, scout class TI," he said. "Viasa, I need holo-maps. These mountains are much trouble. The wind make problem also."

"Can you link your computers to our system here?" the man asked. "We will help guide you down."

"Computers?" Kelric said, more to himself than the man.

"I think he means me," Mace said. "I will make the link."

Kelric spoke into the comm. "We try." At least he thought he said *we*. The translation came up as *I*. He continued to navigate, relying on Mace to map the terrain and feed data to his spinal node. He could hear winds screaming past the ship.

"I'm having trouble linking to Viasa's mesh," Mace said. "It's manufactured by Earth's North-Am conglomerate and is only partially compatible with ours."

Kelric shook his head, wondering if anyone existed who had escaped buying products from the Allied Worlds of Earth. Coba, though? He hadn't expected that.

The man's voice came again. "Dalstern, can you send your data in an Allied protocol?"

"Which one?" Kelric asked.

Symbols transmitted from Viasa appeared on Kelric's screen, and he immediately saw a problem. The Viasa system wasn't set up to deal with starships, only windriders. It was trying to specify his trajectory in a system defined on the planet, in coordinates only they used.

"Viasa, we are maybe close to what we need," Kelric said. "Can you transform the coordinate system you use into the Skolian standard system?"

More silence. Kelric hoped his Spanish was intelligible. What he wanted to say didn't match what was coming out. Mace translated his last sentence as *Can you send the equations that transform the coordinate system in your primary nav module to the system we use?* He hoped it made sense to the people in Viasa.

A peak suddenly reared up on his screens. With accelerated reflexes, he jerked the scout into a vertical climb. G-forces slammed him into his seat as he veered east and dropped past another crag with a sickening lurch. The scout leveled out and shot through the mountains.

"Gods," he muttered. He spoke into the comm. "Viasa, where is beacon to guide aircraft in these mountains?"

A woman answered in terrible Spanish. "Say again?"

"The warning beacon. Where is it?"

"Broken." Her accent didn't mask her suspicious tone. He had just revealed he knew more about Viasa than almost any offworlder alive.

The man spoke. "Dalstern, we have holomaps for you, but we still have a mismatch in protocols. We are working on it. Please stand by."

"Understood." Kelric wiped the back of his hand across his forehead. "Mace, how is our speed?"

"Too fast. The deeper we go in these mountains, the more complex the terrain. I can't recalculate the map fast enough."

Kelric leaned over the comm. "Viasa, I need maps."

"I'm sending what I have," the man answered.

"Received!" Mace said. A new holomap formed, centered on a magnificent waterfall that cascaded down a cliff. In the east, a pass showed in the mountains. With a rush of relief, Kelric veered toward that small notch.

"Dalstern, did that come through?" the man asked.

"I have it," Kelric said. "I pull up."

"Viasa should be beyond the cliffs," Mace said. "I don't have the landing coordinates yet."

Kelric grimaced at the thought of setting down in a mountain hamlet without guidance, on a field that was probably too small. "Maybe we'll see it when we get through the pass."

The holomap suddenly fragmented. In the same instant, Mace said, "I've lost the Viasa data stream."

Damn! Kelric spoke into the comm. "Viasa, we have problem."

"We too," the man said.

Sweat dripped down Kelric's neck. Mace was doing his best to reconstruct the holomap, but they needed more—

With no warning, a wall of stone loomed on his screens. Kelric had no time to be startled; Bolt accelerated his reflexes, and he swerved east before his mind grasped what he was doing. Cliffs sheered up on his starboard side as they leapt into the pass. Closer, too close! He careened away, but that brought him too close to the other side.

Suddenly they shot free of the cliffs. Ahead and below, the lights of a city glittered like sparkflies scattered across the mountains. The rest of the majestic range lay shrouded in darkness beneath the chilly stars. Bittersweet memories flooded Kelric, and incredibly, a sense of *homecoming*, all of it heightened by the adrenaline rushing through him. He had never seen Viasa, but he knew the way of life, culture, language, all of it. Until this moment, he had never let himself acknowledge how much he missed those years he had spent submerged in Calanya Quis. He had given up everything for that privilege: his freedom, heritage, way of life, even his name. It had almost been worth the price.

"We need a place to land," Mace said. "Or I'm going to crash into that city."

"They must have an airfield."

"I don't see one."

Kelric spoke into the comm. "Viasa, I need set-down coordinates."

The man answered. "We're working on it!"

Kelric could guess the problem. They didn't know starship protocols. The Cobans learned fast, but no one could jump from elementary physics to astronavigation in ten minutes. Jeremiah was an anthropologist. Although most college students learned the rudiments of celestial mechanics, he had no reason to know how to guide down a starship.

"I'm mapping a landing site," Mace said. "I'll try not to hit too many buildings."

Kelric spoke into the comm. "Viasa, I have no more time. I guess coordinates."

"Dalstern, I have it!" the man shouted. Holomaps of Viasa flared above Kelric's screens.

"Received," Kelric said. Then he realized he was going to career right over the origin of the signal, which meant he might hit their command center. "Suggest you get out of there," he added with urgency.

A sparkle of lights rushed toward the ship, and towers pierced the starred sky. A dark area ahead had no buildings. With a jolt, Kelric realized they had sent him to the Calanya parks, probably the largest open area in Viasa, even bigger than the landing field.

The Dalstern was dropping fast, past domes and peaked roofs. A wall sheered out of the dark and grazed a wing of the ship, sending a shudder through it. Gritting his teeth, Kelric wrestled with the Dalstern, struggling to avoid the Estate buildings.

The scout slammed down into the park and plowed through the gardens with a scream of its hull on the underlying bedrock. Trees whipped past his screen as the Dalstern tore them out of the ground. A wall loomed ahead of them, and he recognized it immediately, though he had never seen this one before. A huge windbreak surrounded every Calanya in every Estate, and he was hurtling straight at Viasa's massive barrier.

With a shattering crash, the scout rammed through the wall. Kelric groaned as the impact threw him against his exoskeleton. The ship came to a stop balanced on a cliff that sheered down beyond the windbreak. Debris from the wall cascaded across the front of the ship. His lamps revealed a spectacular view; the Teotec Mountains rolled out in fold after magnificent fold of land, a primal landscape of dark mists and snow-fir trees.

The Dalstern began to tip over the edge.

Kelric tore off the exoskeleton and jumped to his feet. So much for his plans to land discreetly.

"We don't have much time," Mace said. "I can take off now, but if I tip too far, I'm going down that cliff."

"Coltman will come," Kelric said, more to assure himself than Mace. Jeremiah was smart. If a way existed to reach the ship, he would find it. At least, Kelric hoped so. He cycled through the air lock and jumped to the ground, into a wild night, with the notorious Teotecan winds blasting across his face. Two people were running across the parks toward him, a tall woman and a husky man.

He knew the man.

Kelric froze. His hope of managing this without anyone recognizing him had just vanished.

Pounding came from the other side of the ship. Kelric ran around the fuselage and found a youth banging on the hull.

"You have to get out!" the young man shouted in Spanish.

Kelric reached him in three ground-devouring strides. He grabbed the youth's arm and swung him around. The fellow looked up with a start, like a wild hazelle caught in a hunter's trap.

"I come for man called Jeremiah Coltman," Kelric said in his miserable Spanish.

The man inhaled sharply. "I'm Coltman."

Kelric took his chin and turned his face into the starlight. His features matched the images. He lifted one of the man's arms and read the glyphs on the armband: *Jeremiah Coltman Viasa.*

Relief washed over Kelric. "So. You are. We must hurry."

The Dalstern creaked as it tipped further. Alarmed, Kelric took off, pulling Jeremiah with him as he ran for the air lock.

A woman's voice called in Teotecan. "Jeremiah, wait!"

Kelric spun around. The woman and man had stopped a short distance away. The woman's attention was on Jeremiah, but the man stared at Kelric as if he were a specter from the graveyard.

Kelric's hand fell to his gun—and Jeremiah caught his arm. The youth had courage to touch a man with a Jumbler, the weapon of a Jagernaut, one of ISC's notorious biomech warriors. Had Kelric had less control of his augmented reflexes, Jeremiah's impulsive action could have just ended his young life.

"Please," Jeremiah said in Spanish. "Don't shoot them."

Kelric lowered his arm. Watching them, the woman came closer. She was tall and elegant, with a regal beauty. A thick braid dusted by grey fell to her waist. The man was about forty, and he wore three Calanya bands on each arm. Third Level. He had been a Second Level when Kelric knew him.

"Don't go, Jeremiah," the woman said.

The youth's voice caught. "I have to."

"Viasa has come to care—" She took a deep breath. "I have come to care. For you."

"I'm sorry," he said with pain. "I'm truly sorry. But I can't be what I'm not." He glanced at the Third Level, then back to the woman. "And I could never share you. It would kill me." He sounded as if he were breaking inside. "Oh God, Khal, don't let pride keep you apart from the man you really love. Whatever you and Kev said to each other all those years ago . . . let it mend."

"Jeremiah." The starlight turned the tears on her face into silver gleams.

The ship scraped and shifted position as if warning them, impatient in its precarious balance. Kelric spoke to Jeremiah in a low voice. "We have to go."

The youth nodded, his gaze on the woman.

"Good-bye, beautiful scholar," she said.

Jeremiah wiped a tear off his face. "Good-bye." Then he turned and climbed into the ship.

With one hand on the hatchway, Kelric stared at the Coban man. The Third Level looked stunned, but his gaze never wavered.

Kelric spoke to him in Teotecan. "Don't tell anyone. You know why."

The man inclined his head in agreement, silent as he kept his Calanya Oath.

Then Kelric boarded the scout.

V

Scholars' Dice

Jeremiah sat in the copilot's seat while Kelric piloted the Dalstern. The youth said nothing, but he didn't barrier his emotions well. His pain scraped Kelric's mind. Kelric pretended to be absorbed in his controls, giving the fellow as much privacy as they could manage in the cramped cabin.

An image of Jeremiah showed in a corner of Kelric's screen. The fellow hardly looked more than a boy. He wasn't tall, and his lean physique lacked the heavy musculature valued in Earth's culture. His rich brown hair was longer than most Allied men wore it. He had a wholesome, farm boy quality, and a shyness Kelric associated with scholars. Those traits might not have made him a male sex symbol on Earth, but Coba's women probably adored him. Quiet, brilliant, scholarly, fit but slender, neither too large nor too strong: he matched their most popular ideal of masculinity. Kelric had unfortunately fit another ideal, albeit one less common, the towering, aggressive male they wanted to tame.

It didn't surprise him that Jeremiah's armbands differed from those worn by most Calani. Kelric recognized them because his were the same. Jeremiah was Akasi, the Manager's husband. Making him a

Calani without his consent was coercion, which meant the union could be annulled if Jeremiah wanted. Whatever the youth decided, Kelric suspected it wouldn't be easy for him.

Jeremiah sat with his eyes downcast, and Kelric busied himself with checks that didn't need doing. They were high enough now that the winds and abysmal port map didn't endanger the ship.

Eventually, when Jeremiah began to look around, Kelric spoke in his clumsy Spanish. "Are you all right?"

The youth answered in the same voice Kelric had heard over the Viasa comm. "Yes. Thank you for your trouble."

"It is not so much trouble."

"You could have been killed."

Kelric suspected the biggest risk had been to the Calanya park. He would find a discreet means to recompense the Viasa Manager for repairs.

"I have seen worse," Kelric said. "I expect to have beacon, though. It help that you know the transform for the coordinates." Without Jeremiah's quick thinking, he would have had to land blind. The Dalstern would have survived, but not whatever part of Viasa it hit.

"I was guessing," Jeremiah said. Mortification came from his mind. "Playing dice with your life."

Kelric wondered if the young man realized just what he had accomplished. "Such a problem take more than guesses."

"I was lucky."

Kelric's voice gentled. "You are not what I expect."

Jeremiah watched him with large brown eyes that had probably turned the women of Coba into putty. "I'm not?"

"The genius who make history when he win this famous prize at twenty-four?" With apology, Kelric added, "I expect you to have a large opinion of yourself. But it seems not that way."

"I didn't deserve the Goldstone." Jeremiah hesitated. "Besides, that's hardly reason for your military to rescue me."

"They know nothing about this." Kelric wasn't certain how much to tell him. "I take you to a civilian port. From there, we find you passage to Earth."

Jeremiah's brow furrowed. "At Viasa you spoke in Teotecan. You even knew how to read my name from the Calanya bands. How?"

Kelric thought of Ixpar, his wife, at least for one hundred and nine more days. He answered, but not in Spanish this time. He spoke in Teotecan. It had been ten years, but it came back to him with ease.

"It doesn't seem to bother you to speak," Kelric said.

Jeremiah's eyes widened, and he just stared at Kelric. It was a moment before he answered, this time in the Coban language. "Well, no. Should it?"

Kelric spoke quietly. "It was years before I could carry on a normal conversation with an Outsider." He used an emphasis on *outsider* only another Coban would recognize, as if the word were capitalized. Calani were Inside. The rest of the universe was Outside.

Jeremiah froze, his eyes widening. He shifted his gaze to Kelric's wrist guards, and his jolt of recognition hit Kelric like mental electricity.

"You were a *Calani*?" Jeremiah asked.

Kelric took a gold armband out of his pocket and handed it to him. "I thought this might answer your questions."

Jeremiah turned the ring over in his hands, and his shock filled the cabin. "You're him." He raised his astonished gaze. "You're *Sevtar*. The one they went to war over."

Sevtar. Kelric hadn't heard the name in a decade. Sevtar was the dawn god of Coban mythology, a giant with gold skin created from sunlight. He strode across the sky, pushing back the night so the goddess Savina could sail out on her giant hawk pulling the sun.

"Actually, my name is Kelric," he said. "They called me Sevtar."

"But you're *dead*."

Kelric smiled. "I guess no one told me."

"They think you burned to death."

"I escaped during the battle."

"Why let them think you died? Did you hate Coba so much?"

Kelric felt as if a lump lodged in his throat. It was a moment before he could answer. "At times. But it became a home I valued. Eventually one I loved." He extended his hand, and Jeremiah gave him back the armband. Kelric ran his finger over the gold, then put the ring back into his pocket. Those memories were too personal to share.

"Some of my Oaths were like yours," Kelric said. "Forced. But I gave the Oath freely to Ixpar Karn. When I swore my loyalty, I meant it." He regarded Jeremiah steadily. "I will protect Ixpar, her people, and her world for as long as it is within my power to do so."

Sweat beaded on Jeremiah's forehead. "Why come for me?"

"It was obvious no one else was going to." Dryly Kelric added, "Your people and mine have been playing this dance of politics for years. You got chewed up in it." He touched his wrist guard. "I spent eighteen years as a Calani. Everything in me went into the Quis. I was a Jagernaut. A fighter pilot. It so affected the dice that the Cobans went to war. I had no intention of leaving you in the Calanya, another cultural time bomb ready to go off."

Jeremiah didn't seem surprised. After spending a year in the Viasa Calanya, he probably had a good idea how influential the Calani could be with their Quis.

"You knew Kev," Jeremiah said.

Kelric thought of the Third Level he had seen. "He lived at Varz Estate when I was there. Kevtar Jev Ahkah Varz. He called himself Jev back then, because people mixed up our names." As a Third Level, he had an even longer name, now. Kevtar Jev Ahkah Varz Viasa. He would be one of the most powerful men on the planet.

"Why did you tell him not to say anything?" Jeremiah asked.

Kelric wondered if he could ever fully answer that question, even for himself. "I don't want my family seeking vengeance against Coba for what happened to me. They think I was a POW all those years. I intend for it to stay that way."

Jeremiah's posture tensed. "Who is your family?"

Kelric suspected Jeremiah would recognize the Skolia name. It was, after all, also the name of an empire. For most of his life, Kelric had used his father's second name because fewer people could identify it.

"Valdoria," Kelric said.

Jeremiah stared at him. Although he seemed to recognize the Valdoria name as belonging to an important family, he gave no indication he realized the full import of what Kelric had just told him.

"Maybe someday I can return here," Kelric said. "But not now. I don't want Ixpar dragged into Skolian politics unless I'm secure enough in my own position to make sure neither she nor Coba comes to harm." Wryly he added, "And believe me, if Ixpar knew I was alive, she would become involved."

Jeremiah smiled shyly. "Coban women are—" Red tinged his face. "Well, they certainly aren't tentative."

It was an apt description of Coba's warrior queens. Kelric couldn't bring himself to ask more about Ixpar; he didn't want to hear if she had remarried. So he said only, "No, they aren't."

"I thought I would never see my home again," Jeremiah said.

"Your rescue has a price. If you renege, you'll face the anger of my family. And myself." Kelric thought of his children, those miracles he had hidden within Coba's protected sphere. He could sense their minds like a distant song. No matter who might claim it was impossible over such distances, he felt his link to them even now, perhaps through the Kyle. They were happy. Well. Safe. He wanted them to stay that way.

"I'll never reveal you were on Coba," Jeremiah said.

"Good."

"But how do I explain my escape?"

Kelric smiled. "It's remarkable. You managed to fly a rider to the port on your own." He motioned at the controls. "I've entered the necessary records and had the port send a message to Manager Viasa, supposedly from you."

"So she will tell the same story?"

"Yes."

Jeremiah spoke softly. "I'll miss her."

Kelric thought of Ixpar, of her brilliance, her robust laugh, and her long, long legs. "Coban women do have that effect." Then he remembered the rest of it, how they had owned and sold him among the most powerful Managers. "Gods only know why," he grumbled. "They are surely maddening."

Jeremiah laughed softly, with pain. "Yes, that too."

Kelric hesitated. "There is a favor I would ask of you."

"A favor?"

"I should like to play Calanya Quis again."

The youth sat up straighter, as if Kelric had offered him a gift instead of dice with someone who hadn't done it properly for ten years. "I would like that."

Kelric pulled a table-panel between their seats as Jeremiah untied his pouch from his belt. The youth rolled out a jeweled set similar to Kelric's, though with fewer dice. Soon they were deep in a session, their structures sparkling in towers, arches, pyramids, and curves. Kelric could see why Manager Viasa had wanted the youth's contract even though Jeremiah had no formal training for a Calanya. His Quis had clarity and purity. He made creative moves. Kelric had no problem anticipating them; Jeremiah had a long way to go before he mastered his gifts. Kelric could have turned his game around, upside down, and inside out. But he didn't. He didn't want to discourage the fellow.

With subtle pressure from Kelric's Quis, Jeremiah built patterns of his first years on Coba. During the day he had worked in Dahl, a city lower in the mountains, and at night he had worked on his doctoral thesis. He considered it an idyllic life. He never had a clue that Manager Viasa had noticed him during her visits to Dahl—until it was too late.

After a while, Kelric realized Jeremiah was trying to draw him out. So he let his life evolve into the dice. Twenty-eight years ago, his Jag fighter had crashed in the mountains, and the previous Dahl manager had rescued him. Ixpar had been visiting Dahl, a fiery-haired child of fourteen. Kelric later learned it was Ixpar who had argued most persuasively that they should save his life, though it would violate the Restriction.

When he had realized they never intended to let him go, he had tried to escape. But the crash had damaged his internal biomech web and injured his brain. While fighting to free himself, he had lost control of the hydraulics that controlled his combat reflexes and killed one of his guards. Desperate to save the other three, who had befriended him during his long convalescence, Kelric had crippled himself to stop his attack.

The Cobans had been terrified that if he escaped, ISC would exact retribution against their world that would make the guard's death look like nothing. They had been right. They should have executed him, but instead they sent him to the prison at Haka Estate. What swayed the Minister who ruled Coba to let him live? The arguments of her fourteen-year-old successor. Ixpar.

"Good Lord," Jeremiah murmured. "I never learned any of this in Dahl."

"I doubt they wanted it in your dissertation," Kelric said.

The youth regarded him with a look Kelric had seen before, that awed expression that had always disconcerted him. "The way you play Quis is extraordinary," Jeremiah said. "And you were holding back. A *lot*."

Kelric shifted in his seat. "It's nothing."

Jeremiah made an incredulous noise. "That's like saying a supernova is nothing compared to a candle."

His face gentled. "Your Quis is far more than a candle."

"Do you miss Calanya Quis?"

"Every day of my life."

"Perhaps you and I could meet sometimes—?"

Kelric wondered what Jeremiah would do when he realized he had just asked the Skolian Imperator to play dice with him. No matter. It was a good suggestion. But unrealistic.

"Perhaps," Kelric said, though he knew it wouldn't happen. He doubted he would see Jeremiah again after they parted.

"You know," the youth said. "It could work in reverse."

"What do you mean?" Kelric asked.

"Quis. We worry about Outside influence on Coba, but think how Coba might affect the rest of us." He gathered his dice back into his pouch. "They're so peaceful here. Imagine if they let their best dice players loose on all those barbaric Imperialate warmongers." He froze, his hand full of jewels, staring at Kelric as he realized he was talking to one of those "warmongers."

"I'm sorry," Jeremiah said, reddening. "I shouldn't—I didn't—that is, I didn't mean to offend."

"You didn't," Kelric said. He knew all too well how the Allied Worlds viewed the Skolian military. He also preferred peace to hostilities. In theory. In reality, he fully intended to build up ISC; they needed more defenses against the Traders, not less. But he wasn't blind. Jeremiah had reason for his views. Only a thin film covered the Imperialate's conquering soul. It gleamed, bright and modern, but it could rip all too easily and uncover the darkness under their civilized exteriors.

Aristos filled the conference room, their gleaming black hair reflected in the white walls. Jaibriol felt as if he would suffocate from the pressure of their minds. After ten years of guarding his mind, his defenses were mental scar tissue, gnarled and rough. He had to deal with the Aristos or they would destroy him, but he could manage it only by locking himself within layer after layer of soul-smothering mental defenses, until he felt as if he were dying from a lack of air.

He met often with his top Ministers: Trade, Intelligence, Finance, Industry, Technology, Diamond, Silicate, Foreign Affairs, Domestic Affairs, and Protocol. High Judge Calope Muze also attended the meetings at Jaibriol's request. Lord Corbal Xir came, too. Both Corbal and Calope had been first cousins to Jaibriol's grandfather, and until Jaibriol sired an heir, they were next in line to the Carnelian Throne, first Corbal, then Calope. It bemused Jaibriol that he, a man of only twenty-seven years, had two people over a century old as his heirs. At 141, Corbal was the oldest living Aristo.

Corbal's son Azile served as Intelligence Minister. In the convoluted mesh of Aristo Lines, Jaibriol was even related to Tarquine; she had been the maternal aunt of his grandmother, Empress Viquara.

Except the empress hadn't truly been his grandmother. He couldn't fathom how his grandfather had convinced her to participate in that mammoth fraud, one that would tear apart the Qox dynasty if it ever became known.

With Jaibriol on the throne, Corbal had expected to rule from the shadows, with Jaibriol as the figurehead and Corbal hidden. But he had found the new emperor less malleable than he expected. Jaibriol had been painfully naïve, yes, and so unprepared to deal with Aristo culture he had practically signed his death warrant the day he asserted his right to succeed his father. But he had never been malleable. He and Corbal had existed in a constant state of tension since then.

The worst of it was, Corbal was the closest he had to a friend. His few pleasant memories among the Aristos came from dinners with Corbal, Azile, and Corbal's provider, a woman named Sunrise. Corbal never admitted he loved Sunrise or that he never transcended with her. Although many people knew he favored her, he hid the full extent his feelings, perhaps even from himself. He would never reveal such affection for a provider, for it was considered aberrant to love a slave.

Today, Jaibriol sat at the gold octagon table and listened to his advisors argue about reopening treaty negotiations with the Skolians. They disguised their maddeningly convoluted discourse as small talk. Corbal sat across from him, watching everyone with a scrutiny Jaibriol knew well, given how often Corbal turned it on him. Calope Muze sat next to Corbal, cool and aloof, shimmering pale hair curling around her face, her elegant features suited to a classical statue.

Calope had let her hair go white. So had Corbal. Tarquine had a dusting of white at her temples. Jaibriol knew they allowed the color to change because it gave them an aura of authority. When everyone had beauty and youth, those who also had age found subtle ways to accent their experience. Only Jaibriol realized their hair had turned white as a side effect of changes they made to themselves. They were the only Aristos he knew who had eliminated their ability to transcend. That it had taken more than eighty years for each of them to develop compassion was sobering, but it also meant Aristos had the capacity to be other than the sadistic monsters he had thought defined their essence.

Tarquine sat at Jaibriol's left, apparently relaxed, but he wasn't fooled. Although she didn't really want a treaty either, she saw advantages to settling matters with the Skolians enough to open up trade. New markets increased the wealth of Eube, which of course included her own prodigious assets. She was already obscenely rich; she needed more money about as much as Jaibriol needed rocks in his head. But she thrived on the machinations that increased her assets. She might even be willing to establish peace with the Skolians if she thought she could exploit the treaty for financial gain.

At least, she implied such in response to veiled inquiries from other Aristos about whether or not she thought they should do business with the Skolians. Yet incredibly, deep in the night when Jaibriol held her in his arms, he glimpsed another reason his barracuda of a wife didn't oppose the negotiations. For him. In the light of day, when passion no longer clouded his mind, he suspected he only interpreted her motives in a way that made him less lonely. But whatever the truth, she didn't fight him on the treaty.

Trade Minister Sakaar loathed the negotiations. Jaibriol had hoped Sakaar would support opening trade relations because it would increase export markets for Eubian goods. But Sakaar's Ministry dealt primarily with the slave economy, and the Skolians refused to discuss any trade as long as the inventories included humans. Jaibriol agreed with the Skolians, but he could hardly tell that to his Ministers, at least not if he wanted to survive.

All the people of Eube except a few thousand Aristos were slaves. The bulk of them, nearly two trillion, were taskmakers. They led relatively normal lives, some even achieving a certain amount of authority and prosperity. But none were free and all wore collars indicating they were property. It sickened Jaibriol that he owned Robert, his bodyguards, and most everyone on this planet, as well as several hundred others, but if he ever let that sentiment slip, the Aristos would turn on him with a vengeance. It wasn't only that the economic structure of their empire depended on the trade; they also considered it their supposedly exalted right to own anyone who wasn't an Aristo.

Providers, or pleasure slaves, were at the bottom of the slave hierarchy. Only a few thousand existed. They lived in incredible luxury, but they had no power. Aristos acknowledged only one reason for a psion to exist—to provide transcendence. Their attitudes about the torture they inflicted horrified Jaibriol, especially because they would do the same to him if they ever learned the truth.

"Paris is a decadent city," Azile was saying. "I have no desire to tour France again."

Jaibriol tried to focus on the discussion. Azile's comment referred to the Paris Accord, the unfinished treaty they had hammered out with the Skolians eight years ago, before the talks stalled. They had "met" on a neutral planet, Earth, which sided with neither Skolia nor Eube. No one actually went to Paris, of course; no one would risk putting so many interstellar leaders together in one place. Rather, they convened as holographic simulations through the Kyle web.

Jaibriol wanted to rub his aching temples. Or better yet, leave. But he didn't dare show any sign they would interpret as weakness. He hid his raging headache behind an icy Highton veneer. "Paris is one of humanity's most remarkable cities."

"Of course we esteem Earth," the Trade Minister said sourly. His hand rested on the table with his thumb and forefinger together, a sign that his real opinion opposed his words.

"We should visit our birthplace of our race," Jaibriol said. It was the closest he would come to stating his intent to resume the talks.

Corbal smiled slightly. "That would be an unusual vacation party: the emperor of Eube, his empress, his ministers, the high judge, and a doddering old man."

Jaibriol almost snorted. Doddering indeed. Corbal was as hearty as they came. He considered his cousin. "We should ask my joint commanders to join us."

The Silicate Minister spoke, a stately man of about fifty. "I suspect the commanders of ESComm have more important matters to attend than jaunts to Earth."

Jaibriol regarded him with a decided lack of enthusiasm. He had never liked Highton discourse, and the Silicate Minister was less proficient at it than most Aristos, with the result that his comments grated even more than usual. He spoke coolly. "More important than attending their emperor?"

The Silicate paled, realizing the insult he had given. "One always esteems Your Glorious Highness."

Sakaar leaned forward. "The Allieds have a penchant for theft. It makes me leery of supporting their tourist economy."

Jaibriol would have laughed if they hadn't all been so serious. He could well imagine the Allied reaction if the Eubian emperor, his ministers, and his joint commanders all showed up for a vacation on Earth. Panic hardly began to describe it. But he understood Sakaar's meaning; the Allieds refused to return slaves who escaped into their territory.

"Perhaps they just need to know our position better on the matter," Jaibriol said.

Sakaar snorted. "Assuming we all agree on that position."

Tarquine spoke in her husky voice. "I'd wager that's an impossible assumption."

Iraz Gji, the Diamond Minister, gave a discreet laugh. Jaibriol wasn't certain why it surprised him that Aristos had a sense of humor; maybe because he never felt like smiling when they came near. But Gji always enjoyed a joke, especially at the expense of his foes, which seemed to include Minister Sakaar. Gji represented the Diamond Aristos, who managed the means of commerce for the empire, so he and Sakaar both dealt with trade. They often came down on different sides of an issue. Like Tarquine, Gji had no love for the Allieds or Skolians, but an avid interest in their spending power.

A buzz came from the comm button Jaibriol had set in his ear. As his ministers continued arguing, he tapped the button, appearing as if he were simply touching his ear.

Yes? He barely moved his throat. Sensors in his body picked up the muscular changes, translated them into speech, and sent it to his comm. He said only that one word: anyone who could contact him on his private comm didn't need the usual overblown honorifics and responses.

The voice of his aide Robert came over the comm. "Sire, we have a report on the Skolian Assembly I thought you would want to know immediately."

Foreboding stirred in Jaibriol. The Skolian Assembly was always doing things he didn't want to hear about, but this sounded worse than usual. *Go ahead,* he answered.

"They introduced a measure to eliminate the votes that Roca Skolia inherited from her late husband."

Jaibriol stiffened. Roca Skolia—his grandmother—was a leading moderate in the Assembly. If her influence weakened, so did his hopes for resuming any talks. He not only had to persuade his people; he had to convince the Skolians as well.

A vote like that can't pass, can it? he asked.

"Apparently it might." Robert sounded miserable. He was the only person Jaibriol knew who actually supported the idea of peace for altruistic reasons rather than economic gain.

It was the final blow in a miserable day. His ministers were going on about tourism and the supposed decay of Paris, and he wanted to shout in frustration. He braced his elbows on the table and pushed back his chair with an abrupt scrape of exorbitantly expensive wood against polished bronze tiles.

They all went silent. His jarring interruption wasn't technically unacceptable, since he hadn't spoken directly, but it balanced on the edge. He looked around at them. "This has been a most auspicious discussion." It hadn't, it had been an exercise in circuitous evasion, but the phrase would get him out of the meeting without irredeemably insulting anyone.

After the barest pause, while they absorbed his dismissal, they each nodded to him, some with a veiled hostility they had no idea he could detect. He rose to his feet, and with a rustle of black diamond clothes, everyone else stood around the table.

His advisors departed through the main entrance, an elegant horseshoe arch with bronze columns, leaving in groups of two or three as they continued to confer among themselves. Jaibriol headed for a hexagonal arch in the back of the room with Captain Hidaka and four of his Razer bodyguards.

Corbal was standing by the table, talking with the Protocol Minister. When he saw Jaibriol leaving, he excused himself from Protocol and started toward to the emperor. Tarquine immediately came over to Jaibriol, deftly inserting herself between him and Corbal. Hidaka didn't block her, but Jaibriol had the sense that if the captain had thought he didn't want to see his empress, the Razer would have intervened even with Tarquine. Hidaka was a remarkably courageous man.

Right now, Jaibriol didn't feel ready to deal with either Corbal or Tarquine. One he could handle, but not both. He nodded to his cousin in an accepted gesture of farewell. Corbal frowned, but he had no choice except to stay back. Tarquine walked at Jaibriol's side, her laserlike gaze smoldering at Corbal.

Within moments, Jaibriol and Tarquine were striding down a hall outside the conference room, flanked by Razers. As with everything built by Hightons, the corridor had no right angles; its walls curved into the floor and ceiling. The halls that intersected the corridor came at acute angles.

Eventually Jaibriol slowed down. "Damn tourists," he grumbled.

Tarquine gave a startled laugh. "Was that a joke?"

He slanted a look at her. "I'm allowed a sense of humor, my lovely wife."

Her lids half closed. "So you are."

He wasn't certain how to interpret her response. He had the feeling he fascinated her. Perhaps that was what kept her interested in him; she couldn't predict his behavior.

"What did you think of the meeting?" he asked.

"They will never agree to more talks."

"I could order them to do it." He didn't need all of them, just one of his joint commanders, Corbal, and the Intelligence and Foreign Affairs Ministers. And Tarquine, of course.

"Without their cooperation," she said, "the negotiations would be a disaster."

He knew it was true. "The Skolians probably won't agree anyway."

Tarquine drew him to a stop. "If you try to catch stardust, you will die from a lack of air."

"I won't give up."

"Then look to the Diamonds."

His brow furrowed. "The Aristo caste? Or the rocks?"

"Aristo." Her eyes glinted. "They failed in their attempt to dominate the Ivory export corporations, so they will be looking for new ventures. Perhaps even among the Skolians? Just think what a huge, untapped market our enemies offer."

He raised an eyebrow at her. "No doubt that market could benefit the Finance Ministry as well."

"Perhaps."

He knew she had probably figured out many paths to profit, like a fractal that became ever more intricate the more closely one looked at it. "I don't suppose you have an idea how to interest the Diamonds in supporting us."

She started walking with him again. "I'll think on it."

That didn't reassure him. Whenever she turned her prodigious talents to solving a problem, he never knew whether to be grateful or terrified.

VI

A Court of Rubies

The world Metropoli boasted the largest starport in all of the Skolian Imperialate, teeming with people and vehicles. Kelric's small scout ship went unnoticed in all the tumult, especially with his stratospheric clearances, which invoked veils of security most people had no idea existed.

He dulled the metallic sheen of his skin and hair so he appeared more his age. Then he donned clothes that made him look overweight. His passenger, Jeremiah Coltman, watched him with puzzlement, but he didn't push the matter. He would figure out the truth soon enough. Kelric avoided news broadcasts when he could, but his likeness was out there on the meshes. If Jeremiah worked at it, he could identify his rescuer.

They walked to the gate where Jeremiah would board a transport to Earth. The youth was wearing a blue pullover and "jeans" interwoven with mesh threads. He had purchased them at a store that sold Allied imports. Several women gave him appreciative glances, but no one otherwise paid attention to them. It amused Kelric that he could so easily hide in plain sight.

At the gate, Jeremiah offered his hand. "Thank you for everything."

When Kelric hesitated, Bolt prompted him. **Put your hand in his and move it up and down.**

Oh. That's right. He clasped Jeremiah's hand and shook until Jeremiah winced. Embarrassed, Kelric let go. He sometimes forgot to moderate his strength.

"You're sure you have enough funds?" he asked.

"You've been incredibly generous," Jeremiah said. "You must let me pay you back."

"It's nothing." Kelric didn't know the value of what he had given Jeremiah. He could multiply the amount by a million and it would still be insignificant to his estate. At least, that would be true for one hundred and eight more days. He had to decide what to do, or he would soon be penniless and officially dead.

A female voice spoke from the air. "Mister Coltman, please board the shuttle. We are ready to leave."

Jeremiah swung his new smart-pack over his shoulder and smiled at Kelric. "Good-bye. And good luck."

Kelric inclined his head. "You also."

After Jeremiah boarded, Kelric stood at a window-wall and watched the shuttle take off. *Good-bye,* he thought, to Jeremiah and to Quis.

But an idea was lurking in his mind. It had hidden in his subconscious, and now it crept into his thoughts like mist, blurring the outlines of his reality.

Had the time come to stop hiding Coba?

When Kelric visited the world Parthonia, to attend Assembly sessions in person, he stayed at the Sunrise Palace. It was built of golden stone, with arched colonnades. Trees shaded its wings, silver-bell willows and ghost elms with pale green streamer-leaves draped from their branches. Three million people lived in Selei City far below, but this region of the mountains was off-limits except to guests of the Ruby Dynasty. Tomorrow, the Assembly would convene in the city; tonight, the elite of that legislative body had invaded the palace.

Kelric wore his dress uniform. After many studies, the ISC protocol experts had designed it from a dark gold cloth that glimmered. The sheen seemed superfluous to Kelric, but it thrilled the analysts who charted how his appearance affected the public. The tunic had a gold stripe across his chest, and a gold stripe ran up the trousers, which Protocol claimed accented the length of his legs. It wasn't clear to him why anyone would give a buzz in a battleship about the length of his legs, but his bewildered comments had no effect on their efforts. They polished his boots to a shine and fastened a dark gold belt around his waist, all the time rhapsodizing about how the uniform complimented his physique. It was mortifying.

He put off going downstairs as long as he could, but finally he descended the staircase that swept into the foyer of the Grand Opera Hall. Chandeliers dripped with sunburst crystals, and gold shimmered on the walls. Guests filled the room, sparkling in their finery. Human servants rather than robots moved among them, carrying platters of drinks or pastries. So much for his mother's "small" dinner party.

As Kelric entered the Hall, he fortified his mental barriers until the emotions of the crowd receded. He was actually prodding his mind to produce certain chemicals. They blocked the neurotransmitters necessary to process the brain waves he received from other people. If he produced too many blockers, it damped his ability to think; at the extreme, to protect himself from Aristos, it could cause brain damage. But for a party, he needed only levels that were a natural and normal precaution.

A man carrying a tray of goblets bowed to him. With a self-conscious nod, Kelric took a glass of a gold drink that bubbled. He would have preferred Dieshan pepper whiskey.

A woman in a long green dress was talking to several people nearby. She glanced idly at Kelric, then froze with her drink raised, staring at him. It was odd. He lived here, after all. They were attending an affair hosted by the Ruby Dynasty; seeing a member of that dynasty shouldn't elicit surprise.

Everyone in her group was staring at him now. They bowed, all except the woman, who kept gaping, her face flushed. Then she jerked as if remembering herself and bowed as well. Bewildered, Kelric nodded to them and kept going.

After he passed the group, he glanced at himself. Nothing looked wrong, and he didn't think he had done anything strange, unless they noticed his slight limp. He eased down his defenses to search for clues, but the pressure against his mind increased, and his head throbbed. The moods of his guests swirled, too many to distinguish, a thick stew of emotions flavored by anticipation, curiosity, jealousy, avarice, boredom, and sensuality. Ill at ease, he reinforced his barriers until they muted the onslaught.

"I haven't seen you at one of these in ages," a man drawled.

Kelric tensed as he swung around. Admiral Ragnar Bloodmark stood there, idly holding a goblet of red wine. Tall and lean, with sharp features, he had an aura of menace, as if he were ready to strike. His dark coloring came from his Skolian mother and evoked a lord of the noble Houses, but his grandfather had actually hailed from a place called Scandinavia on Earth. Ragnar was a Skolian citizen, however. His impressive military record and seniority should have made him the top choice to head the Imperial Fleet. Kelric had never trusted him, which was why he had promoted Chad Barzun instead, and he doubted Ragnar would ever forgive him that decision.

Although Ragnar bowed, he somehow made the gesture mocking. Kelric had always wondered how he managed that, following Imperial protocols to the letter, yet projecting disdain rather than respect. If he meant it to bother Kelric, the ploy failed; Kelric had never felt any need to have people bow to him.

"My greetings, Admiral." Kelric kept his voice neutral.

"And mine." Ragnar watched him closely. "So you will attend the Assembly in person this time?"

"I imagine so." Kelric wondered if Ragnar was probing for clues about his vote. The admiral was a Technologist. Although Ragnar had supported Dehya's coup, Kelric had no illusions about his motives. He had helped her for two reasons, the first being because he thought she could win. He hid his second, but as an empath Kelric knew; Ragnar coveted the title of Ruby Consort and the power that came with it. That Dehya already had a consort didn't deter him. Kelric had no proof that Ragnar had plotted against her husband, nor would any tribunal accept empathic impressions as evidence; even if a way existed to verify them, they were too vague. But he had no intention of trusting the admiral.

"Your mother looks lovely," Ragnar was saying.

Distracted, Kelric followed his gaze. Roca stood across the hall in a sleeveless blue gown, talking with several councilors, her gold hair piled elegantly on her head. Diamonds sparkled at her throat and dangled from her ears. One man was paying especially close attention to her, and Kelric doubted his interest had anything to do with politics. He hated it when men noticed her that way. They were intruding on his father's memory.

"You're talkative tonight," Ragnar said. A laconic smile curved his lips. "As always."

Deal with it, Kelric told himself. He motioned at the crowd. "They all glitter tonight. But tomorrow in the Assembly, it will be a different story."

"The ballot on your father's votes comes up, doesn't it?"

Kelric shrugged. "Votes on the hereditary seats come up every year." He eased down his barriers so he could probe the admiral. "And always fail."

"Perhaps not this time." Ragnar had worked with Ruby psions for decades and knew how to shield his mind. He also wasn't an empath, which meant Kelric couldn't receive impressions from him as well as from a psion. Although Kelric felt his ambivalence, he couldn't tell if it was because Ragnar wasn't certain how to vote or because he doubted the vote would succeed.

"It would be unfortunate for our party if the vote passed," Kelric said.

Ragnar gave an incredulous snort. "It's ridiculous that a technology party supports hereditary rule within a democracy."

Kelric cocked an eyebrow. "Ridiculous?" Ragnar wasn't the only one to make that assertion, not by far, but most people didn't say it to Kelric's face. He saw their point perfectly well, but he had no intention of giving up his power.

"I apologize if I gave offense," Ragnar said.

Kelric doubted he felt the least bit apologetic. He sipped his drink. "It's only half a democracy."

"So it is." An image jumped into Ragnar's mind, his memory of Dehya in the command chair of an ISC flagship while a million vessels gathered in support of her coup. He had helped put her there despite his objections to her throne. His motives were purely self-interested; her ascendancy worked to his advantage if he backed her. However, he had no wish to support Roca's moderating voice in the Assembly. He wanted to conquer the Eubian Traders. Period.

Kelric couldn't keep up even his minimal link to Ragnar. His head was swimming from the flood of moods. He raised his shields, and the deluge eased.

A woman spoke at his side, her voice rich with the Iotic accent of the nobility. "So what are you two plotting?"

Kelric turned with a jerk, even more edgy. Naaj Majda had joined them. At six-foot-five, she commanded attention. Gold braid glinted on her dark green uniform, and her belt had the Majda insignia tooled into it, a hawk with wings spread. Iron-grey streaked her black hair; she was almost eighty, but she looked fifty. As General of the Pharaoh's Army, she served as one of his four joint commanders. She was also matriarch of the House of Majda and a ranking member of the Royalist Party. In the interim after the war, following the death of Kelric's sister but before Kelric assumed command of ISC, Naaj had acted as Imperator.

She was also his sister-in-law.

Ragnar bowed to Naaj in perfect style and managed to make it even more sardonic than with Kelric. "My greetings, General." He raised his glass to her. "Oh, my apologies. You prefer the dynastic address, yes? Your Highness."

Naaj cocked an eyebrow at him. "Apology accepted." She knew perfectly well he was baiting her.

Kelric nodded to Naaj, and she nodded back, both of them excruciatingly formal. The House of Majda was the most powerful noble line, and thousands of years ago they had been royalty in their own right. Now their empire was financial, with holdings vast and lucrative. They had served the Pharaoh's Army since before the Ruby Empire and provided many of ISC's top officers.

Over forty years ago, Kelric had wed Naaj's sister—and lost her soon after to assassination. After the Radiance War, when Kelric had shown up to claim his title as Imperator, he had feared Naaj would refuse to relinquish either the title or the substantial Majda assets he had inherited from her sister. As Matriarch, however, she was honor bound to protect the widower of the former matriarch. If not for that kin-bond, he wasn't so sure she wouldn't have tried to depose him.

She spoke with impeccable courtesy. "Your House does honor to your guests, Your Highness."

Well, that was safe. He gave a safe response. "We value the honor of your presence." He eased down his barriers, but Naaj was guarding her mind, and she blocked him.

"We were discussing my father's votes," Kelric said.

She inclined her head. "His memory lives with honor."

He returned the gesture. That seemed the extent of their ability to relate tonight: nods and platitudes about honor. At least she spoke with respect. Kelric's father had been a farmer from a relatively primitive culture, which had appalled the Royalist Party. Personally, Kelric would have far rather spent his time on a farm than in the royal court, but he could hardly tell Naaj that, not if he wanted her votes.

"We venerate his noble memory," Ragnar told Naaj, his eyes glinting.

"So we do." Her expression remained neutral despite his use of *noble* for a farmer. Kelric wondered why Ragnar bothered trying to bait her. No one could fluster Naaj.

As Naaj and Ragnar parried with barbs disguised as small talk, Kelric began to wonder if Ragnar provoked Naaj more than she let on, for her shields slipped, and Kelric sensed her mood in unexpected detail. She intended to back Kelric tomorrow even if he counseled peace. She preferred action against the Traders, but she would follow Kelric's recommendations even if her House wished otherwise—because she respected his judgment.

That floored him. She sure as hell hadn't felt that way when he had assumed command of ISC. As the head of a conservative House, she followed ancient customs from a time when men were property and kept in seclusion. Modern Skolia had an egalitarian culture, and Naaj was too savvy to let her personal views destroy her career; she knew she had to deal with him as Imperator. But she had obviously doubted his leadership ten years ago. He hadn't realized how much had changed since then.

And you? he asked himself. *Do you see Coba the same way Naaj used to see you?* He had never considered it in that light.

"Good gods," a sensual voice said. "Kelric, what have you gotten into, caught by these two?" A woman with dark eyes and night-black hair was strolling up to them. Her glistening red gown could have been painted onto her prodigiously well-toned body. Ruby balls dangled from her ears, and her ruby necklace was probably worth more than a fully armed Starslammer warship.

Naaj gave the woman a dour look. "You're out of uniform, Primary Majda."

"So I am, cousin." The woman, Vazar Majda, smiled lazily, with the ease of someone who was both off duty and out of Naaj's line of command. A former fighter pilot, Vazar now served in the upper command echelons of the Jagernaut forces, or J-Force.

Ragnar bowed to Vazar, and this time he even looked as if he meant it. He raised his goblet. "You're stunning tonight, Primary Majda."

"Thank you, Admiral," Vazar said. With a wicked gleam in her eyes, she grasped Kelric's arm. "I'm rescuing this golden apparition from you two." Then she dragged him away.

Laughing, Kelric tried to extricate his arm. "Vaz, you'll give people ideas about us."

"Oh, they'll get them anyway." She drew him through an alcove and onto a balcony above the palace gardens. Out in the balmy night air, she closed the doors and sagged against the wall. "Gods, I thought I was going to suffocate in there. How can you stand these parties?"

He leaned against the wall and smirked. "That's a good question. The place is teeming with my sisters-in-law."

"Given all the brothers you have, that's no surprise." Her smile faded. "Had."

Kelric's mood dimmed. He had lost a sister and a brother in the Radiance War. Soz and Althor. Althor had been married to Vazar.

"Ragnar is right," he said, offering her a less painful subject. "You could be a lethal weapon in that dress."

Mischief returned to her eyes. "What about you, eh? Roca's greatest weapon, her gorgeous, powerful, bachelor son."

Kelric grimaced at her. "ISC needs an entire protocol division to make me look this way." He grinned as a wicked thought came to him. "We should set them loose on the Trader emperor. He'll surrender just to make them go away."

Vazar's laugh rumbled. "I imagine so." Then she said, "Roca wants you to sway votes."

He couldn't let that opening go by. "What votes?"

"That's why we're all here, isn't it? If the Assembly eliminates your father's votes, your mother loses power."

Well, that was blunt. It was one reason he liked Vazar; she didn't play at intrigue. He lowered his barriers. It wasn't as painful out here, where distance and several walls muted the torrent from the Opera Hall. He probed at her mind.

"The drawbridge is up and the moat full of sea monsters," Vazar said. "You can't come in."

He squinted at her. "What?"

"You've a luminous, powerful mind, Kelric, but subtlety was never your strong point. Quit snooping."

He lifted his goblet to her. "I was knocking at the door."

She stood against the wall, facing him, curved and deadly in her glittering red dress. "If you want to know how I plan to vote, the answer is 'I don't know.'"

Damn. Her Assembly seat was hereditary. How could she not know her position on a ballot that jeopardized her own votes?

"I didn't realize a question existed," he said.

"I'm not Naaj. There's a reason I'm a Technologist instead of a Royalist." She shook her head. "If anyone should wield those votes, it's Roca. But should we concentrate so much power in unelected seats? Even without them, she's one of the most influential councilors in the Assembly."

Kelric's voice cooled. "That's right. She earned it through election."

"No one elected her to your father's votes."

"Better her than anyone else."

"Why should *anyone* have them?"

He spoke quietly. "My mother lost two sons and a daughter in the Radiance War. The Traders captured and tortured her husband, several of her children, and herself. She more than any of us should hate them. And believe me, she's capable of it." He knew Roca's darker side, the anger she wrestled with, but when she walked into the Assembly Hall, she put it behind her. "Yet *she* counsels peace, now that we have a Trader emperor who claims he will negotiate with us."

"She's an invaluable voice of moderation," Vazar said. "But if we reaffirm that power for Roca, what happens when the next person wants it? And the next?" Her gaze hardened, reflecting the pilot who had become infamous in battle. "And maybe moderation is the wrong counsel."

He couldn't argue. Sometimes, when his anger or grief became too great, he wanted to launch his war fleets and destroy the Traders, even knowing his forces and theirs were too evenly matched to ensure any outcome but misery.

"If we don't negotiate peace," he said, as much to himself as to Vazar, "this hostility will never end. Do you want a thousand years of war?"

Vazar pushed back her hair. "No." She stared down at the gardens. "Have you talked to Brant?"

He followed her gaze. In the garden below, Brant Tapperhaven was walking with a woman. As head of the J-Force, Brant was another of Kelric's joint commanders, and like most Jagernauts, he had a fierce streak of independence. He also abhorred the idea of inherited votes. Kelric was glad Brant didn't hold an Assembly seat; he might have gone against Kelric tomorrow.

"We've discussed it," Kelric said, and left it at that.

"Who is that girl with him?" Vaz asked.

"I don't know." He watched the couple stroll under colored lamps strung from silver-bell willows. The woman was lovely with her dark hair and sensual grace. She reminded Kelric of Rashiva, the Manager of Haka Estate on Coba. Haka ran the prison where he had spent one of the worst years of his life, after he killed his guard trying to escape. Then Rashiva had taken him out of prison and made him her Calani and husband, under coercion. It had outraged the Minister who ruled Coba, for Haka was an antagonist of the Ministry, whereas Kelric's former Estate, Dahl, had been the Ministry's strongest ally. Within a year, the Minister had pardoned him and he had no choice but to return to Dahl.

They had never allowed him to see Rashiva again, but seven months later, she had given birth to a son. She claimed the boy was premature, the son of another man, but rumors spread about his violet eyes, a color never before seen on Coba.

The same color eyes as Kelric's father.

Something was building within Kelric, something ten years in coming. He kept hearing Jeremiah's words: *They're so peaceful here. Imagine if they let their top dice players loose on all those barbaric Imperialate warmongers.*

Watching the woman in the garden, he spoke quietly. "She looks like my ex-wife." It was the first time he had mentioned anything about his life on Coba to any Skolian. It felt as if alarms should blare or bells toll.

"You think so?" Vaz peered at the woman. "Corey wasn't that pretty." She flushed and quickly added, "I mean no offense to her memory."

"I know. None taken."

She gave him an odd look. "Why would you call my cousin Corey your ex-wife? You two were married when she died."

Softly he said, "I wasn't talking about Corey."

"Who else could you mean?"

Ten years of caution, ten years of silence: he couldn't break it so easily.

"We should go back inside," he said.

Vaz was watching him intently. "All right." For now she let it go.

But he knew her silence wouldn't last.

VII

The Gold Die

Jaibriol ran hard, his feet pounding the dirt path. Above him, the sky vibrated in the blue-violet splendor of the high mountains, streaked with wispy clouds. Six tiny moons glittered in different phases, but none of the big ones were visible. Even this high above the coast, in the crystalline silence of the mountains, he could hear the thundering tides ripped from the ocean by those moons and hurtled against the shore far below.

Although the thin air up here bothered most people, Jaibriol enjoyed the challenge. Hidaka ran with him. Given all his augmentation, the Razer wasn't the least bit out of breath, which could get annoying, but Jaibriol would far rather exercise with him than with another Aristo. He reveled in the sheer joy of running in the clear, cold morning. His doctor claimed his body was a tuned instrument in its prime, bursting with health. He didn't know about that, but he felt as if he could live forever.

A hum came from the comm plug in his ear. Loping along, he said, "Yes?"

"Sire, it's Robert. Are you all right?"

"I'm fine. Why wouldn't I be?" Surely Robert didn't think jogging a few kilometers would harm him.

"The Amethyst Wing of the palace blew up," Robert said.

"*What?*" Jaibriol came to an abrupt stop. Hidaka halted next to him, and his other three guards stopped behind and before them.

"A pipe detonated under the Columns Hall," Robert said. "The section with the gold tiles and black pillars. The columns shattered on the floor and the walls collapsed."

Good Lord. Had someone attacked the palace? Remarkably, it had actually been several years since anyone tried to assassinate him or any of his advisors. "Was anyone hurt?"

"No one," Robert said. "The hall was empty."

Jaibriol didn't see why anyone would bomb an empty hall. He glanced at Hidaka, who was undoubtedly wondering why the emperor was talking to thin air. Jaibriol tapped his ear and mouthed *Robert,* and Hidaka nodded.

"Is security checking it out?" Jaibriol asked.

"I called them immediately," Robert said. "They're making sure it's safe for the repair teams. And for you, of course."

"Good," Jaibriol said. "I'll be down as soon as I change."

Jaibriol stood in the ebony and gold hall, half hidden by a column that hadn't fallen, and watched the repair crews. Gilded dust swirled and mounds of glinting rubble were piled everywhere. The techs were calculating the cost of the robots they would need to replace those destroyed in the blast. More durable and less emotional than human beings, the robots needed neither sleep nor food. When Jaibriol realized the techs would have rather lost taskmakers than robots, bile rose in his throat. They ranked a machine above a human.

With Robert at his side, he resumed his walk through the hall, past crushed marble and melted gold, as much to escape the techs as to survey the damage. The dust would have bothered his nose, so he was glad his updated nanomeds neutralized its effect. Hidaka stayed with them, tall and silent, towering over even Jaibriol. The other three guards went ahead or behind them.

"Any report yet on why this happened?" Jaibriol asked.

Robert had his hand cupped around his ear where he was wearing a comm. "A pipe exploded." He paused, listening. "A pressure differential in the gas it carried may be the culprit."

Jaibriol stepped over chunks of a fallen column, a mess of gleaming marble shot through with jagged cracks. "That wouldn't cause a blast this big."

Robert nodded his agreement. "But security has found no trace of a bomb."

"Was anyone scheduled to be here?"

"Not a soul."

Jaibriol didn't like it. In his experience, nothing ever happened in the palace without reason, because someone was plotting this or that, anything from humbling a rival to seeking their demise. "Let me know as soon as you find out more."

"I will, Sire."

As they continued through the wreckage, Jaibriol's unease grew. He would have to ramp up his defenses even more; in the relative calm of the past few years, he had almost become fatally complacent.

People overflowed the Amphitheater of Memories where the Skolian Assembly met. Tiers of seats rose for hundreds of levels; above them, balconies held yet more people. Delegates filled the amphitheater, and images glowed at VR benches where offworld representatives attended through the Kyle web. Controlled pandemonium reigned as thousands conferred, bargained, and argued, all the gathered powers of a civilization struggling find an accommodation between dynastic rule and democracy.

Kelric sat at the Imperator's bench with Najo, Axer, and Strava standing on duty. They hadn't stopped scowling at him since they had discovered he took his "vacation" with no guards.

A dais was rising in the center of the amphitheater. The Councilor of Protocol sat at a console there, preparing to call the vote. Tikal, the First Councilor of the Assembly, and so the elected leader of the Imperialate, waited at a podium. Dehya was standing next to Protocol's console, gazing out at the amphitheater. On principle, Kelric would have preferred Dehya attend through the web; that way, his people could protect her even better than the stratospheric level of security he already had in place. But he knew why she came in person. Although she was one of the savviest people here, her waiflike face and small size made her appear fragile. It inspired protective instincts in people and helped counterbalance his presence, which many people found alarmingly militaristic.

The session had started only an hour ago, and already the debate regarding his mother's voting bloc had finished. Few speakers had commented. Those who did, including Naaj Majda, orated eloquently in Roca's favor. The lack of counterarguments didn't fool Kelric. No one wanted to speak openly against the Ruby Dynasty. Unfortunately, their reluctance only went so far; it wouldn't stop most of them from voting against her even in an open ballot. He could see Roca on his screens. She sat across the amphitheater, appearing relaxed at her console with a composure that he doubted came easy today.

The number of votes a delegate held depended on the size and status of the populations that elected them, or in the case of hereditary seats, on the power of the family. As populations fluctuated, so did the voting blocs, continuously updated. No one ever knew exactly how many votes everyone had, though they could estimate it with good accuracy. The Ruby Pharaoh and First Councilor held the largest blocs. The next largest went to Kelric, then to the councilors of the Inner Circle: Stars, Intelligence, Foreign Affairs, Finance, Industry, Judiciary, Life, Planetary Development, Domestic Affairs, Nature, and Protocol. For the First Councilor, Ruby Dynasty, Inner Circle, and Majdas, the size of their blocs depended on a complicated and oft-debated algorithm that took into account their political influence as well as the populations or hereditary position they represented.

Protocol spoke into her comm. "Calling the vote."

The words flashed on Kelric's screen. They also came over the audio system, almost lost in all the noise. She waited while people quieted. Then she said, "The measure is this: The voting bloc of the Web Key should cease to exist until another Web Key ascends to the Triad. A vote of Yea supports abolishing the bloc: a vote of Nay opposes the measure."

She called the roll, starting with the delegates of lowest rank, who had the fewest votes. Their names appeared on Kelric's screen, their *Yea* or *Nay,* the number of votes they carried, and the overall tally. The results also showed on a large holoscreen above the dais.

Bolt, Kelric thought. **Project the outcome based on the current results and your expectations for delegates who haven't yet voted.**

Your mother will lose, Bolt answered.

Damn. At the moment, the tally favored Roca. Most of the noble Houses had already cast their ballots, though, and they supported her. Ragnar's name came up—and he voted against her. Kelric gritted his teeth as her edge shrank. The vote continued inexorably, and when it turned against Roca, murmurs rolled through the hall. Kelric heard a snap, and pain stabbed his palm. Startled, he looked down. He had gripped the console so hard, a switch had broken and jabbed his hand.

"Cardin Taymor," Protocol called.

Kelric glanced up, at a loss to recognize the name.

She's new, Bolt informed him. **From Metropoli. Given her record in their Assembly, she will undoubtedly vote Yea.** He accessed Kelric's optic nerve and produced an image of Taymor. Kelric blinked; she was the woman in the green dress who had done a double take last night when he walked into the party.

His screen flashed with Taymor's vote: *Nay.*

Hah! Kelric grinned. **You calculated wrong.**

Perhaps I had too little data. Bolt paused. **Or maybe your protocol analysts know what they are doing better than you think. She did seem taken with you.**

Dryly Kelric thought, **Thanks for your confidence in my intellect.**

Voices rumbled in the amphitheater; apparently Bolt wasn't the only one who had misjudged Taymor's intent. Coming from the most heavily populated world in the Imperialate, she wielded an impressive bloc. The tally swung back in favor of Roca.

Update, Bolt thought. **I now project you will win.**

Kelric exhaled. The broken switch fell out of his hand and clattered onto the console.

As the vote continued, the tally fluctuated, but remained in Roca's favor. Two of Kelric's brothers had attended: Eldrin, his oldest sibling and the Ruby Consort; and Denric, who had earned a doctorate in literature and now taught children on the world Sandstorm. Both voted with Roca, and she cast proxies for Kelric's other siblings, also in her favor.

Then Protocol said, "Vazar Majda."

Across the amphitheater, the Majda queens were sitting at their consoles, tall and aristocratic. Only their women held Assembly seats; even in this modern age, they followed ancient customs that forbade their men to inherit power.

When Earth's people had finally discovered the Imperialate, they had scandalized the noble matriarchs of Skolia. Apparently on Earth, men historically held more power than women. The matriarchs claimed this was why it had taken Earth's people so long to reach the stars. They asserted that if women had been in charge, Earth would have achieved that pinnacle of technology thousands of years earlier.

Their arguments conveniently ignored the fact that their ancestors had developed star travel because they had starships to study.

Earth's annoyed males responded by pointing out that Earth had achieved a far greater degree of peace than the Imperialate, which surely had to do with the fact that bellicose, aggressive women had been in charge of the Imperialate rather than peaceful men. Naaj Majda hadn't understood why Kelric found this so funny. She even acknowledged the Earth men had a point. Kelric told her to go read Earth's military history.

By the time Earth and Skolia discovered each other, both had evolved toward equality, though men still tended to hold more power on Earth and women more among the Skolians. The Traders had always been egalitarian; they enslaved everyone equally, male and female alike.

The way the Majda queens secluded their princes reminded Kelric of the Calanya on Coba. He had lived in over half of Coba's cities, yet he knew almost nothing about them, for he had spent almost his entire time in seclusion. He had never done anything as simple as buy a sausage at market. They had imprisoned him in luxury as if he were a ruby die locked in a treasure box, withholding something far more precious than all the wealth they had lavished on him—his freedom.

Protocol's words came over the audio system. "Vazar Majda, does your console have a problem?"

With a start, Kelric realized Vazar hadn't voted.

Her answer came over the audio. "No problem."

"Please place your vote," Protocol said.

Why isn't she responding? Kelric asked Bolt. He could see her arguing with Naaj.

I don't know, Bolt thought. **However, my projection of your win assumes the Majdas support you.**

He didn't believe Vazar would go against them. But she had worried him last night.

"Vazar Majda, you must respond," Protocol said.

The buzz of conversation in the amphitheater died away. Such a wait was unprecedented. Then Kelric's console flashed—like a punch to the gut.

Yea.

Voices swelled as the tally swung solidly against Roca. Naaj's face was thunderous. Protocol called her next, and she struck her console with her adamant *Nay,* negating Vazar's vote. Then the Inner Circle voted—and doubled the tally against Roca. Roca went next and took a huge bite out of their gains.

"Kelric Valdoria," Protocol said.

He stabbed in his answer, and it flared on his screen. *Nay.* The tally careened toward a balance, almost evening the sides.

Two voters remained: the Ruby Pharaoh and First Councilor. Their blocs were almost identical, but Dehya always had a few more votes— because she had staged the coup that deposed Tikal. Her decision to rule jointly with him had been contingent on those extra votes, and with them the ability to break a deadlock.

"First Councilor Tikal," Protocol said.

His answer was no surprise: *Yea.* The tally shifted firmly to his side, and the amphitheater went silent as if the Assembly were holding its collective breath.

"Dyhianna Selei," Protocol said.

Dehya's vote flashed: *Nay.*

The tally careened toward Roca's side. When it finished, the result glowed in large red letters above the amphitheater.

By a mere six votes, Roca had lost.

Kelric brooded in the Corner Room, an alcove well removed from the amphitheater. Someone had shoved a divan in a corner, so he sat on it with his back against the wall and his legs stretched out along its length. A line of blue and white glyphs bordered the wall at shoulder height, more artwork than words.

Leaning his head back, he closed his eyes. He was clenching his Quis pouch, and dice poked his hand through the cloth. He told himself today's vote didn't matter. If anything, it strengthened his position as Imperator. But he feared it boded a more intransigent Assembly and a future of greater hostilities with the Traders, the Allieds, even his own people.

A creak broke the silence. As Kelric opened his eyes, the antique door across the room swung inward on old-style hinges designed for aesthetics rather than practicality. A slender man with curly blond hair stood in archway. Beyond him, Kelric's bodyguards were talking to another guard in Jagernaut leathers. Kelric's visitor came in and closed the door.

"My greetings, Deni," Kelric said.

Denric, his brother, crossed the room. "It's good to see you."

Kelric felt the same way. He saw Denric only a few times a year. When had that streak of grey appeared in his brother's hair? Denric had always seemed young, though he was a decade older than Kelric. Perhaps it was his boyish face or small size compared to his towering brothers. Or maybe it was his idealism, his belief he could bring about a more peaceful universe by schooling young people. Kelric suspected the universe would resist tranquility regardless of how well its inhabitants educated themselves, but that had never decreased his admiration for his brother. Denric had taken a teaching post that paid almost nothing in an impoverished community and dedicated his life and personal resources to its youth.

Denric settled into an upholstered chair and swung his feet up on the footstool. "Well, that was certainly a rout."

"We only lost by six votes," Kelric said. "That hardly qualifies as a rout." Not that it made him feel any better.

Denric considered him for long enough to unsettle Kelric. Then his brother said, "I suppose for you, it has advantages."

"You think I *wanted* that to happen?"

"It supports you." Denric's voice was atypically cool. "It will help you continue to build up the military beyond our needs and to increase ISC control over our people."

Kelric couldn't believe he was hearing this from his own brother. "You ought to know me better than that."

"I thought I did." Denric shook his head. "But sometimes it seems like I hardly know you at all. You've become so focused on ISC, people are comparing you to Kurj."

Kelric stared at him. People had called Kurj a *dictator*. Yes, Kelric physically resembled him. Even their names were similar. But he had little else in common with his half-brother.

"If I don't build up ISC," Kelric said harshly, "the Traders will conquer us. Then we'll all be slaves."

Denric gave him an incredulous look. "So you need military threats against our own people?"

"Of course not."

"Which is why all our worlds have such a strong ISC presence."

"It's to protect them." Kelric eased down his shields. **We have to be ready. If the Traders attacked today, we would lose.**

Denric's cultured thoughts came into his mind. ⏐ had heard nothing of our situation being that bad.

It is hardly something I want to broadcast.

Then why don't they attack us?

They probably don't know they can win. After a moment, Kelric added, **Or maybe this emperor of theirs genuinely desires peace.**

Maybe. Denric didn't hide his doubt.

Kelric's head throbbed from the contact. Releasing the link, he shielded his mind and exhaled as the ache in his temples receded. He doubted psions could survive without the ability to raise shields. The onslaught of emotions could drive a person insane.

Kelric thought of his only face-to-face meeting with the Trader emperor. He had felt certain Jaibriol the Third was an empath, though Aristos supposedly lacked the "contaminating" genes that created a psion. The youth protected his mind well; only a Ruby psion would have guessed. Maybe this emperor had reasons no one expected for wanting connections with Skolia.

The door opened again, and this time Dehya stood framed within its arch. Yet more black-clad bodyguards had gathered outside, dwarfing her delicate form. They were human components in the myriad of defenses that protected the dynasty, especially the Dyad.

"Well." Denric pulled himself out of his chair. "I'll leave you two to talk."

A smile touched Dehya's face. "My greetings, Deni."

He swept her a gallant bow. Court etiquette didn't require he do so with his own family, but he always treated Dehya that way. Straightening up, he winked at her. "Don't intimidate my little brother."

Her laugh was musical. "I'll try not to terrorize him."

After Denric left, closing the door behind him, Kelric smiled at his aunt. "I'm quaking in my boots."

Dehya dropped into the chair, taking up much less of it than Denric had done. "Roca isn't happy."

That had to be an understatement of magnificent proportions. "She's still one of the most influential voices in the Assembly."

Dehya regarded him wearily. "It isn't only the vote. She believes Vazar betrayed us. She used words that—well, let's just say it was language my sister the diplomat rarely employs."

"I don't blame her." Yet for all his anger, Kelric knew Vazar too well to call her decision a betrayal. "Vaz follows her conscience, not anyone's political agenda."

The door slammed open and Roca stalked into the room. "She dishonored him." She closed the door with a thud. "She *inherited* Althor's votes. Now she disrespects his memory."

"I doubt she sees it that way," Dehya said.

"Why aren't you angry?" Roca demanded.

Dehya grimaced. "I'm worn out with being angry. It seems to be a constant state where the Assembly is concerned."

Roca scowled at Kelric.

"What?" he asked.

"First Denric, then Dehya, now me. What is this, we must come to petition the mighty Imperator?"

"Why are you angry at me?" he asked.

"You spoke to Vaz last night."

"I speak to Vaz all the time."

"Did you encourage her to change the vote?"

"You think I *plotted* this with her?"

Roca met his gaze. "Did you?"

"No." He barely controlled his surge of anger. "I can't believe you would even ask."

"Her vote benefits you."

"For flaming sakes," Kelric said. "If I had wanted to vote for the damn ballot, I would have."

"Having Vaz do it makes her the traitor." Roca's gentle mental tap came at his mind, at odds with her tense words. *Kelric?*

He crossed his arms and strengthened his mental shields.

Kelric, come on. Her thought barely leaked through.

She wanted to talk? Fine. He lowered his barriers and let his anger blast out. **You have no business accusing me.**

Roca took a step back and her face paled. *I know.*

So why the bloody hell say it?

It was Dehya who answered. *We think someone has compromised security.*

What? Is this supposed to be a test?

Roca winced at the force of his thought. *Yes. If we argue and rumors of strife within the Ruby Dynasty spread, it implies a leak in our security.*

He was the one who oversaw security. If they trusted him, they would have told him. **Why didn't you warn me?** This time, though, he moderated his thought so its power didn't blast them.

We had to make it convincing, Roca thought.

She had a point; he was a terrible actor. But they were testing him, too, regardless of what she claimed. He gave her a dour look. **Did you ask Denric to challenge me?**

Surprise came from her mind. *No. I didn't.*

Although that troubled Kelric, he knew Denric had never been easy with the military. **The problem isn't Vazar. The Assembly doesn't like our hereditary seats. If they could remove them all, they would.**

Roca crossed her arms. *After all this, I can't believe they still expect us to do the Promenade.*

Kelric couldn't either, but he had always felt that way. Every seven years, the Assembly asked the Houses to walk in a ceremonial promenade. The public loved it, which was why the Assembly promoted the whole business, because it inspired the public to love them, too.

We can refuse, he thought.

I'd like to. Roca uncrossed her arms. *But it would make us look ill-tempered.* She resumed pacing. *I need to talk to Councilor Tikal.*

Dehya glanced at Kelric with a slight smile. *I think we should let her loose on the Assembly to work her magic.*

Maybe she'll convince them to take another vote. Aloud, in case someone actually was eavesdropping, he added, "If you believe I plotted with Vaz, you should, uh, leave." He winced at his dreadful acting, and a swirl of amusement came from Dehya.

"Very well," Roca said. "I will." With that, she swept out of the room. In the wake of her departure, the chamber seemed smaller.

Dehya sat back in her chair. "She won't stay angry."

Kelric just shrugged. He was still simmering.

"I spoke to Vaz before I came here," Dehya added.

He hadn't caught *that* from her mind. He always kept his shields partially up when he mind-spoke with her, though; she had more mental finesse than he would ever manage, and he didn't want her to learn too much from him.

"About the vote?" he asked.

"She didn't want to discuss it," Dehya said. "I think she's as upset with herself as we are."

Kelric scowled. "That didn't stop her from doing it."

She told me something peculiar, Dehya thought.

Wary, he let her see only the surface of his mind. **Peculiar how?**

Her answer had an odd stillness. *That you had an ex-wife.*

Kelric was suddenly aware of the dice pouch in his hand. **I do.**

I thought providers were forbidden to marry. Her thought was muffled.

They are.

Then how could you have had a wife?

He couldn't respond.

Kelric? Dehya asked.

His answer came like a shadow stretching out as the sun hovered above the horizon. **I wasn't with the Traders all those years.**

Neither her posture nor her face betrayed surprise, but it crackled in her mind, not from what he told her, but because he finally admitted what she had always suspected.

Kelric couldn't explain. He had been married against his will too many times. Jeejon was the only woman *he* had ever asked. He had been bought, enslaved, kidnapped, forced, and otherwise had his life arranged, often with no regard to his own preferences. He had never perceived himself as pleasing, but apparently women found him so, enough even to do something as mad as launch a thousand windriders in war over him. He didn't understand why.

But gradually he had come to understand his responses. If a woman treated him well, he became fond of her even if he resisted the emotion, as he had with Rashiva wo had forced him into an unwanted marriage. As an empath, he thrived on affection. The better his lover felt, the better he felt. All psions experienced that effect to some extent, but for him it seemed unusually intense. The more he gave his lover, the more she gave back. When she desired and cherished him, he felt those emotions. So he sought to make his lover happy. He liked to see her smile, hold her, laugh with her, pleasure her. Her contentment became his.

It wasn't love, though. When he truly loved a woman, it blazed inside him, until she became imprinted on his heart, even his soul. In his seventy years of life, only two women had seared him with that mark. Ixpar would always be his greatest love, but it had taken him years to realize—for she had come second, when he had believed he could never feel such passion again. She had waited, giving him the time he needed, knowing his ability to love had been crippled, leaving emotional scar tissue in his heart.

The words wouldn't come for him to tell Dehya. So instead he lowered his barriers and formed an image in his mind.

Savina.

She had brought sun into his life. She laughed often, and her yellow hair framed an angelic face. She had stood only as tall as his chest, but that never stopped her from doing outrageous things to him: climbing the tower where he lived and hanging on a rope while she proclaimed her love; carrying him off, up to a ruined fortress; getting him drunk so she could compromise his honor in all sorts of intriguing ways. Somewhere in all that, their play had turned to love, and it had changed him forever.

Kelric couldn't bear the memory. He hid it deep in his mind.

"Saints almighty," Dehya murmured. "What *happened* to you?"

He just shook his head.

After a silence, she said, "Do you want to be alone?"

He nodded, staring at his dice pouch. He listened to the sound of her retreating footsteps and looked up just as she set her hand on the crystal doorknob.

"Do you remember," Kelric said, "when I asked you to make copies of my dice?"

She turned to him. "I still have them."

"Tonight, at home, will you join me for a game of Quis?"

"Quis?"

He shook his pouch, rattling the dice. "This."

Surprise jumped into her expression. "I would like that."

He said no more. That had been enough. Maybe too much.

After Dehya left, Kelric poured his dice onto the divan. He picked up the gold ball. He almost never used it. For him, it symbolized one person. Savina. She had been an empath, a mild talent, but she carried all the genes. Living with primitive medical care, in a place with infant mortality rates higher than on almost any other settled world, Savina had brought an empath into the world. Incredibly, the baby girl had survived the agonizing birth.

Not so for Savina. She had died in Kelric's arms.

On a distant world, protected by the inimitable Hinterland Deployment, a child with gold eyes was growing to adulthood. She had been born of Kelric's greatest sorrow, but she was an even greater treasure, hidden by the Restriction and by one of the greatest military forces known to the human race.

VIII

Sunsky Bridge

"Peace talks be damned!" Corbal faced Jaibriol across the glossy black expanse of the desk in Jaibriol's office. "With this vote, the Skolians have made their intentions clear. They intend to ramp up hostilities, not flaming chat with us in Paris."

They were on their feet with the desk between them. It was as if they stood within the void of space; today, the walls of emperor's office gleamed with nebulae, and blue points of light glowed in the cobalt floor. A sapphire lamp hung from the domed ceiling. The entire room felt as cold and distant to Jaibriol as any hope for the negotiations.

"The vote was a protest against hereditary rule," he said. "Not peace."

Corbal's red gaze didn't waver. "It was a vote to give Imperator Skolia more power."

Jaibriol stiffened. He could never live up to Tarquine's memory of Kelric, the man who had been her provider and lover, who had escaped from her habitat, shredded her security, and infiltrated one of the largest military complexes in Eube, the Sphinx Sector Rim Base. The Lock that ESComm had stolen from the Skolians was in that complex. Kelric had used it to join the Dyad—to become a Key, which only a Ruby psion could do. Now he was the Imperator. The Military Key. The Fist of Skolia.

Compared to Kelric, Jaibriol had no doubt he seemed young, callow, and inexperienced. Tarquine claimed she no longer wanted Kelric, but Jaibriol didn't believe her. He could never compete with a legend.

Only Corbal and Tarquine suspected Jaibriol could also use the Lock. Except no one would ever use it again, for Kelric had killed it, or whatever one did to deactivate a singularity where Kyle space pierced their universe. Jaibriol had found Kelric in the Lock that day—and he had let the Imperator go free, an act many would consider treason. *Meet me at the peace table,* Jaibriol had told him. But the Paris Accord had fallen apart and now Kelric had even more power. Enough to conquer Eube? All Jaibriol saw was the long, slow dying of his dream.

He sank into his high-backed chair, put his elbows on his desk, and leaned his head in his hands. He was so very tired, a bone-deep exhaustion that sleep never cured. The longer he lived among the Aristos, the more hopeless it seemed that they would ever deal with the Skolians, a people they didn't consider human. They weren't capable of understanding why Skolians abhorred the Concord. After all, Eubian taskmakers had a high standard of living. It took no genius to see why Aristos maintained it; only a few thousand of them controlled two *trillion* taskmakers. The Aristos didn't care about the soul-parching effects of that control, how they crushed the spirit of those who resisted them. The slagged remains of several worlds served as testament to how far Hightons would take their reckoning against definace.

But no sane Aristo wanted genocide. They knew perfectly well that too much repression inspired rebellion. Taskmakers formed the backbone of civilization; even a fool could see that keeping them satisfied worked better than oppression. Aristos might be arrogant, amoral, and without compassion, but they were never stupid. They ensured their taskmakers lived good lives—as long as they obeyed.

Providers were another story. Aristos believed they had one and only one purpose: to please Aristos. In their twisted world view, torturing providers "elevated" those slaves to a higher form of existence. But the Aristos knew the truth, no matter how much they masked it with the convolutions of their speech. It was why Corbal hid his tenderness toward Sunrise; his love for her threatened the fabric of an empire. Lurking in every Aristo's mind was the specter that one day their slaves would rise against them, not a city, a world, or a star system, but all of them. Trillions. Then nothing could stop the fall of Eube.

Jaibriol lifted his head to regard his cousin. "We will deal with the Skolians as we must."

Corbal was studying him. "Never show signs of weakness. Your enemies will devour you."

Jaibriol just stared at him, and wondered if he could ever resurrect his dream.

Dehya sat at the round table with Kelric, and they each rolled out their dice. While the rest of the Assembly slept, celebrated, or brooded, the Dyad played Quis.

Words had never been Kelric's forte, so instead of explaining the rules, he showed them to her. He placed a regular tetrahedron, a ruby pyramid, in the center of the table. Then he waited.

Dehya looked from the die to Kelric. When he continued to wait, she smiled slightly, then took a gold pentahedron and set it next to his piece.

That surprised him. Did she know she had started a queen's spectrum? She had probably studied records of his solitaire games, trying to figure them out. Building a spectrum against an advanced player was difficult. An augmented queen's spectrum was almost impossible; to his knowledge, he was the only person who had done it in Calanya Quis.

He rubbed his fingers, which ached with arthritis even his nanomeds couldn't eliminate. Then he set a yellow cube against her die. She followed with a green heptahedron. Well, hell. She *was* making a spectrum.

Kelric played a sapphire octahedron. "My game."

She looked up at him. "You can win Quis?"

He grinned. "Of course. You're lucky we aren't betting; you would owe me ten times whatever you had risked."

Dehya cocked an eyebrow. "Why should I believe you won?"

Despite her outward skepticism, he could tell she was enjoying herself. It was the advantage of being an empath; it helped him learn gestures, body language, and expressions until interpreting them became second nature. He could read Dehya even when she shielded her mind.

He tapped the line of dice. "These increase in rank according to number of sides and colors of the spectrum. Five make a queen's spectrum. Three of the dice are mine and two are yours. That means I have advantage. So I win."

"I was helping you, eh? If you start the spectrum, you win no matter what."

"You can block my moves." He took his dice and slid hers across the table. Then he set an amethyst bar in the playing area. "Your move."

"Are we gambling?"

"If you would like."

She laughed softly. "Ah, well, you made up the rules, I don't know them, and you've been playing for decades. I *don't* think I want to bet." She set her amethyst bar on top of his.

Kelric stared at the bars, frozen. He felt her amusement fade to puzzlement. Finally, still not looking at her, he said, "I didn't make up the rules."

"Who did?" Her voice had a waiting quality.

He set a diamond sphere near the structure. "Your move."

She waited a while. When he said nothing else, she said, "Spectrums go by color, yes?"

He glanced up. "That's why they're called spectrums."

"And white is all colors, as in light."

"Yes!" She was going to be formidable at Quis. He wondered if she realized he had used the diamond ball, the highest ranked piece, to symbolize her. Dehya wasn't hard like a diamond, but its strength fit her, as did the way it refracted light into many vivid colors.

She set a gold dodecahedron apart from the other dice. *Interesting.* The dodecahedron came next in rank after the sphere. What did she mean? Possibly nothing. He could never tell with Dehya, though; her complex, evolving mind often startled him.

He set down an onyx ring, one of his symbols for himself. She thought for a moment, then balanced a topaz arch so it connected the diamond ball and gold dodecahedron.

"That's a sunsky bridge," Kelric said. "It suggests a cooperative venture."

She tapped the gold dodecahedron. "Roca." Then she touched the diamond ball. "You."

He regarded her curiously. "Why assign names to the dice?"

"I've watched you play. Your structures evolve. It's almost as if they have personalities."

It gratified him that she understood. "They tell stories. Or make the story. The dice shape events as much as portray them."

"I don't see how gambling can spur events." With a wry smile, she added, "Except to lower my credit account."

Kelric waved his hand. "Gambling is for Outsiders. It isn't true Quis."

"Then what do you do with it?"

He leaned forward. "Suppose everyone played. Everywhere. Throughout the Imperialate."

She was watching him closely. "And?"

"I put my stories into my Quis when I sit in sessions with other people. Then they play with others. The better designed my strategies, the more it affects their Quis, and the more they pass on my intentions."

"So your effect spreads."

"Yes."

"And if, say, Vaz Majda played Quis, you might affect her opinions with your influence."

Good! She understood. "But other people also input stories. Ragnar might build patterns of war. Councilor Tikal would focus on politics. Naaj would bring in heredity. Their input goes to the public, who all play Quis. Everyone affects the game, but most people don't play well enough to do much beyond accepting, refusing, or transmitting ideas."

Her voice took on a careful quality. "And when everyone is playing Quis this way, what do you call your world?"

He knew what she was asking: where had he spent all those years? He gathered his dice and put them in his pouch. "Thank you for the game."

She started to speak, but whatever she was going to say, she let it go. Instead she asked, "Who won?"

"Both of us."

"So you and I, we don't gamble."

Calani and Managers never do. But he kept that thought shielded from her. "With you, I would rather work together."

She met his gaze. "So would I."

He stood and bowed. "We will play again."

Dehya rose to her feet. "I hope so." Her thoughts swirled with unasked questions, and he knew if he let down his barriers, they would flood his mind. But she didn't speak. Perhaps she knew he couldn't bring himself to answer.

Not yet.

IX

Plaza of Memories

Jaibriol unexpectedly found Sunrise.

He went to the opulent wing of the palace where Corbal lived. His cousin stayed there when he wasn't seeing to his business affairs or meddling in Jaibriol's life. Hidaka came with Jaibriol, along with three Razers who were like extensions of the captain's biomech-enhanced mind.

His unannounced visit shook up the taskmaker who looked after Corbal's suite. She and her husband had served the Xir Lord for decades. She was trembling as she knelt to Jaibriol, and tendrils of her auburn hair wisped around her face.

"Please rise," Jaibriol said, far more gently than Hightons were supposed to speak to taskmakers.

She rose to her feet, her gaze downcast. "You honor us with Your Most Glorious Presence, Your Highness."

Jaibriol winced. He had managed to stop his staff from talking that way, but everyone else did it regardless of what he said. He just nodded and walked into the living room of Corbal's suite. Plush cushions were scattered across a carpeted floor that sparkled with holographic tips on the pile. Blue-lacquer tables shone and the walls gleamed blue. The room glistened.

With a start, Jaibriol realized someone was sleeping on a large pillow in one corner. It was Sunrise, Corbal's provider. She lay curled on her side with her eyes closed in her angel's face. Her hair fell across her body in glossy waves, as bright as a yellow sun. She wore nothing more than a scant halter of gold chains, with sapphires that barely covered her enlarged nipples. A gold chain around her hips held the gold triangle of her G-string. She was lushly, voluptuously desirable, full and round where Hightons were lean.

Jaibriol stopped, his face heating. Even while she slept, her contentment soothed. He blocked her, not because he didn't appreciate the healing balm of her mind, but because if she awoke, she might suspect him. Sunrise was a powerful empath, able to detect far more than most Aristos realized.

Jaibriol never knew how to act around her. He had spent the first fourteen years of his life with only his family. On Earth, he had been shy around girls, unsure how to behave. As emperor, he had slept with a provider once, a sweet, silver girl who had taken his virginity and left him with a treasured memory. Then he had married Tarquine, and he hadn't touched any other woman since.

He spoke self-consciously to Hidaka. "I'll come back later. Lord Xir doesn't seem to be here." Corbal obviously had been, though, given Sunrise's state of dress, or lack thereof. He felt like an intruder.

A deep voice came from behind him. "Your Highness?"

Jaibriol turned with a start. Corbal's son Azile was walking through the archway and unfastening a long coat, which he wore over a silk shirt and elegant slacks. His cheeks were red from the wind, which probably meant his flyer had just landed on the roof of the palace.

Jaibriol inclined his head to his Intelligence Minister, his closest kin after Corbal and Calope Muze. He used the minimalist Highton greeting appropriate for family. "Azile."

The older man bowed. "You honor my father's home."

"I came to talk to him." Jaibriol indicated where Sunrise slept. "But I didn't want to wake her."

Azile glanced idly toward the corner, then did a double take. His startled, instinctual response was so intense, Jaibriol felt it despite the muting effects of his shields. Azile sensed Sunrise's unprotected mind, but in a far different manner than Jaibriol. In that instant, the desire to transcend hit Azile so hard, an image jumped into his thoughts of Sunrise crying in pain.

Bile rose in Jaibriol's throat. How the blazes could Azile desire to hurt her that way? He wanted to throw his Intelligence Minister across the room.

The blood drained from Azile's face. Shock surged from his mind, and a deep loathing for himself. He spun around and strode from the room through a smaller archway. Jaibriol watched in amazement, not because it offended him to have his cousin walk out, not even because it was a crime to leave the emperor's presence in such a manner, but because he had never felt such remorse from an Aristo capable of transcending. Azile was only in his fifties, much younger than Corbal or Tarquine had been when they changed.

When Hidaka motioned for two of the Razers to go after Azile, Jaibriol held up his hand, stopping them. Then he followed his cousin into a small alcove stocked with liqueurs. Azile was leaning on a counter, his face ashen. As Jaibriol entered, the Intelligence Minister jerked up his head and comprehension of his trespass against the emperor flooded across his face.

"Your Highness!" Azile straightened up abruptly. "Please accept my most humble apology."

"Accepted," Jaibriol said, sparing Azile an arrest. He had never seen his cousin disturbed this way. Sweat sheened Azile's forehead. Could he be more like his father than Jaibriol had realized? He knew Azile transcended; even now, with his shields full strength, he sensed the crushing pressure of Azile's mind.

"One might be distracted by many things," Jaibriol said, probing. "It is always my hope that my kin are well and serene."

Azile inclined his head to the right, indicating gratitude at Jaibriol's response. "Most serene, Your Highness."

"I'm pleased to hear it." Jaibriol studied him. "Tell your father I visited."

"Certainly. It will be my pleasure to serve the throne."

Jaibriol doubted it; he knew Azile disliked him. But maybe this was a start toward better relations between the two of them.

Jaibriol found Tarquine at a crystal table in the Atrium, surrounded by lush trees, with sunlight filtering over her from the polarized glass of the ceiling and walls.

"My greetings, husband." She was spearing sea delicacies in a porcelain dish using a sharpened ivory prong.

"Tarquine." He sat down, preoccupied with his thoughts.

She studied him for a moment. "Distraction becomes you."

Jaibriol had no idea how to take that, which he told her in suitably convoluted Hightonese. "I would never say incomprehensibility becomes you, my lovely wife, since you are always comprehensible, but should that ever change, I'm sure it would reflect just as well."

Tarquine smiled, a slow curve of her lips. "I do believe I've just been insulted."

Jaibriol grinned at her. "Never."

She blinked, staring at him.

"Astonishment also becomes you," he added amiably.

"'They say his smile is like the sun that rarely rises,'" she murmured. "Carzalan Kri wrote that in one of his poems."

"You think my sun doesn't rise enough?" Jaibriol supposed it was true. He rarely felt like grinning at anyone.

"It's another sign of your distraction," Tarquine decided.

He took a tobin-plum out of a bowl and bit into the pale blue fruit. "This is good."

"Indeed."

He gave her a dour look. "If Highton words were a form of nourishment, that one would have no nutritional value at all."

She sat back, relaxed, regarding him as if he was a rare and valuable acquisition. "You look well today."

"Don't do that."

"What? Compliment you?"

"Look at me like I'm your dessert."

Her smile turned sultry. "My dessert was never so sweet."

Jaibriol wanted to groan. Sweet, indeed. He was an emperor, not a slice of cake.

"I've been wondering something," he said.

She regarded him curiously. "And what could that be?"

"Is it unusual for a man to feel affection toward his father's provider? I don't mean desire. More like kinship."

"Not particularly." She swirled a melon-shrimp around in the sauce on her plate and took a bite.

He sat back, thinking. "Perhaps Azile was affected by something else."

"An intelligence matter, I would imagine."

He knew she was fishing to find out if his comment connected to Azile's work as Intelligence Minister. Her mind never rested when it came to politics.

"It's Sunrise," Jaibriol said.

"Providers always affect Aristos." Tarquine finished her melon-shrimp. "I'm told she has a high Kyle rating."

"I wouldn't know," he lied.

She spoke quietly. "Corbal values the dawn. He would never let its radiance dim."

Jaibriol knew she was right. Despite Corbal's attempts to disguise his affection, Tarquine had long ago realized how he felt about Sunrise. She was the radiance in his life.

"It's always intriguing when people act out of character," Tarquine said. "Don't you think?"

Jaibriol stiffened. "No."

She was probing about Azile, which meant she was thinking of looking into the matter. He didn't want her investigating his Intelligence Minister, at least no more than usual. He had no doubt she and Azile kept dossiers on each other. But he had managed to keep their mutual ill will at bay.

He sincerely hoped it stayed that way.

Sunlight flooded Selei City on the planet Parthonia. Skyscrapers pierced the lavender sky, which had never taken on the bluer hue intended by the world's terraformers. The mirrored buildings reflected clouds as if they were part of the sky. Kelric strolled across a plaza tiled with blue stone. Government officials walked in pairs and trios through the area, their executive jumpsuits glossy in the sunshine. They gave Kelric and his heavily armed guards a wide berth.

Kelric was always aware of the stronger gravity here and its effect on his heavy build. He felt slowed down, and he fatigued more easily. The beautiful weather contrasted with his mood. He had no desire to attend the Assembly after yesterday's loss. But the sessions continued regardless of his mood. At least he could escape during this break.

"Nice day," Strava commented as they strolled along.

"It is." Kelric needed to say no more. It was one reason he liked these guards. They were as taciturn as he.

He stopped at the plaza's fountain, a jumble of geometric shapes with water cascading over them. It looked like a big pile of wet Quis dice. What would happen if he introduced Quis into Skolian culture? It could just become a fad, but he knew it too well to believe that. Quis would fascinate his people. Scholars would write papers on it. Gaming dens would proliferate. Schools would teach it. The game was too powerful to fade away.

Maybe it would even spread to Eube. The Coban queens had sublimated their aggression into Quis. He doubted it could affect the Traders as much, but even a small change might get the stalled treaty negotiations back on track.

A silver spark flashed in Kelric's side vision.

Combat mode toggled, Bolt thought.

What the hell? Kelric spun around as his body toggled into combat mode and accelerated his motions.

Najo shoved him to the ground, and Strava and Najo threw themselves across Kelric as he hit the pavement. Axer stood over them with his feet planted wide, firing, his massive Jumbler clenched in both hands. He swept the beam across the plaza with enhanced speed, his reflexes powered by the microfusion reactor within him. Strava and Najo were shooting as well, even as they protected Kelric with their bodies. Sparks glittered in the air, and when the beams touched ground, it exploded in bursts of orange light. Debris flew and dust swirled around the fountain.

Kelric lay with his palms braced on the ground, tensed like a wire drawn taut. He wanted to throw off his guards and vault to his feet; it took a great effort to stay put and let them do their job. His enhanced vision picked out projectiles headed toward him and also their demise in flashes of light.

After an eon, his bodyguards stopped firing. The air had the astringent smell of annihilated bitons, and sirens blared throughout the plaza. Engines rumbled overhead as military flyers soared through the sky.

"Imperator Skolia?" Najo asked, getting to his feet. "Are you all right?"

Kelric pushed up on his elbow. "I'm fine. Are we clear?"

"Looks like it," Strava said. She was kneeling over him, her calves on either side of his legs while she surveyed the ruined plaza. Najo scanned the area with his gauntlet monitors, and Axer was speaking into his wrist comm.

Kelric stabbed a panel on his own gauntlet. "Major Qahot, what the hell is going on?"

The voice of his security chief came out of the mesh. "The shooters are dead, sir," he said. "It doesn't look like they expected to survive."

"Suicide assassins," Kelric said.

"Apparently. Are you all right?"

"I'm fine," he growled. "I want to know how the blazes they got in here." The Assembly drew delegates from all over Skolia. Some attended through the web, but many gathered in Selei City. ISC had ramped up security so high, they should have known if anyone within a hundred kilometer radius even breathed oddly.

Strava climbed to her feet, freeing Kelric. He stood up and spoke quietly to his bodyguards. "Thank you."

Najo inclined his head, and Strava lifted her hand in acknowledgment. Axer was getting updates on his gauntlet and probably his ear comm, too. ISC police were already combing the plaza, and no doubt every nearby building. The flyers overhead gleamed gold and black, reflected in the mirrored skyscrapers.

Kelric finally let himself absorb that he had almost died.

"They never had a chance," Major Qahot said, pacing across the security office beneath the Assembly Hall. A stocky man with bristly hair, he moved as if he were caged, unable to break free until he solved the mystery of Kelric's attackers.

People filled the room, officers, aides, guards. And Roca. Kelric had arranged to have Dehya and his brothers transferred to safe houses, as well as the First Councilor and Inner Circle. Roca, however, refused to leave. His people would take her if he ordered it, but he knew it would antagonize her. For now, in the depths of this secured command center, he let her stay. She stood by a wall, listening while his officers investigated the attempt on his life. Kelric sat at a console that monitored the Assembly Hall, Selei City, the countryside, even orbital traffic. From here, he could access any system on the planet.

"The assassins could never have reached you," Qahot said as he paced. "Their clothes were shrouded against sensors, but the moment they drew their weapons, it triggered alarms all over Selei City. Their shots would never have hit home."

Roca spoke, her voice like tempered steel. "They should never have gotten close enough to shoot."

Perspiration beaded on Qahot's forehead. "It won't happen again, Your Highness."

"Imperator Skolia." Strava spoke from her seat at another console. "We've identified the security hole that let the assassins slip their guns by our systems."

"A hole?" Kelric said. "How did that happen?"

"It migrated from another system." She was reading from one of her screens. "The Hinterland Deployment."

Kelric froze. The Hinterland Deployment guarded Coba. "How could it affect us? That's a different region of space."

She rubbed her chin as she studied the data. "It's odd. A few bytes are missing from a security mod in the Hinterland codes. Almost nothing. But the hole propagated to other systems." She looked up at Kelric. "The mesh-techs couldn't locate the cause, but they're patching the hole."

It was all Kelric could do to remain impassive. One little hole in Hinterland security. Just one, but it had spread. Because it hadn't been properly coded. Because it should never have existed. Because he had made it in secret.

Kelric had told Dirac to "forget" Coba was the focus of the Hinterland Deployment. He should have known better. The deletion had ended up drawing far more attention than if he had done nothing. Hell, it had nearly killed him.

"Keep me apprised of their progress," he told Strava.

"Will do, sir."

He swiveled his chair to Axer, who was standing by a console with his hand cupped to his ear as he listened to his comm. "Do you have anything on the three assassins?" Kelric asked.

A frown creased the broad planes of the guard's face. "They were delegates in the Assembly. The police found records in their quarters."

His careful expression didn't fool Kelric. His guards shielded their minds and didn't talk much, but he knew them well. Axer was worried.

"What do you have on them so far?" Kelric asked.

"They feared what would happen if Councilor Roca lost the vote." He glanced at Kelric's mother. "I'm sorry, ma'am."

"Why would they fear the vote?" she asked. "Their seats aren't hereditary."

"Apparently they thought it gave Imperator Skolia too much power and you too little."

Kelric stared at them. "They would assassinate me to support my mother?"

Roca's voice hardened. "Then they deserved to die."

Don't, Kelric thought to her.

No one tries to murder my child and gets away with it.

Kelric recognized her cold fury. Normally she was a gentle woman, but threats to her family brought out a ferocity that startled even him. He thought of his ordeals on Coba. Had she known, she would have retaliated against the Cobans. And if today's assassination had succeeded? Roca was next in line to become Imperator. It was among the more bizarre ramifications of their extended lifespans, that a parent could be her child's heir. She didn't want the title; she was trained to succeed Dehya as Assembly Key. But she was better qualified as Imperator than Kelric's siblings, and only a Ruby psion could join the Dyad.

Had Kelric died, the Closure document would have released to the authorities as soon as the news became public. ISC would have gone to find Ixpar and his children. He had always known that could happen, but when he had written his will, he had seen no other choice.

Kelric? Roca's forehead furrowed. *You think I will retaliate against the families of the assassins?*

Startled, he strengthened his shields. At least his defenses had been strong enough that she misread his thoughts. **Let the courts deal with it.**

She regarded him impassively.

I mean it, Mother. Let Legal handle this. He was aware of his guards watching. They had probably figured out he and Roca were mentally conversing. As Jagernauts, they were psions, but if even Roca picked up so little through his shields, it was unlikely they would get anything. They had nowhere near her mental strength. Kelric had become a master at hiding from his family, but he was worn out by cutting himself off that way.

Security suspected something was up, Roca thought. *But not this.*

So you really were trying to start a rumor yesterday.

Yes. To trace its source.

Apparently its source found us first.

Roca exhaled. *It seems so.*

Kelric glanced at Qahot, who was leaning over a console to read its screen. "Major, do we have leads on who the assassins were working with?"

Qahot straightened up. "So far, it looks like only those three were involved. Records of their correspondence indicate they've grown disaffected over the years." Then he added, "Yesterday, one of them told another delegate you should be 'voted out' of your seat permanently."

It was a sobering response. Kelric had known the Imperator wasn't well-liked, but he hadn't thought anyone wanted him dead. Had he lost sight of his humanity in the performance of his duties?

Axer was watching his face. "Sir, they were fanatics. No matter what you did, they would have objected. It was the office of Imperator they opposed. Not the person."

Kelric knew Axer meant well, and it was one of the longer speeches his guard had ever made to him. But he suspected the assassins protested the man who held the title as much as the title itself. He had to do his job, even if people hated him for it. He nodded to his guard, then spoke to Qahot. "Do checks on all the Assembly delegates and their aides. Make sure no one else was involved."

"Right away, sir," Qahot said.

A door across the room opened to admit a Jagernaut in black leathers. Vazar. She strode to Kelric's console. "Primary Majda reporting, sir."

Kelric stood up, regarding her coolly. "Are my joint commanders safe?"

"Yes, sir." Her posture was ramrod straight. "General Majda and Primary Tapperhaven have left Parthonia. Admiral Barzun is on the Orbiter. General Stone is on Diesha. All are under increased security."

"Good," he said. Her tension practically snapped in the air. Yesterday she had voted against the Ruby Dynasty; today she was tasked with protecting their interests. Neither of them missed the irony. He went around the console to her and spoke in a low voice only she could hear. "You're on duty here until I get back. Don't disappoint me."

She met his gaze. "I won't, sir."

He felt her mood: regardless of her vote, she would protect his family with her life. As angry as he felt toward her, he had to respect the integrity that spurred her to choose what she believed was right even when she knew it would alienate him and imperil her own Assembly seat.

Kelric beckoned to Roca, and she left the command center with him and his guards. Her anger at Vaz simmered, but she said nothing. She rarely spoke aloud to him when he was dealing with ISC, and he had realized she didn't want to appear as if she were interfering with his authority. He doubted she would, but he appreciated the consideration. The Assembly needed more of that sensitivity she brought to the table, not less.

Her bodyguards were outside, three instead of the usual two. They fell into formation around Kelric and Roca, along with Najo, Strava, and Axer. They all walked down the metallic tunnel deep below Selei City.

"With supporters like those assassins," Roca said in a low voice, "I don't need enemies."

"It's not your fault," he said.

She glanced at him. "You're a damn fine commander, Kelric. Don't let what happened today make you believe otherwise."

He rubbed his neck, working at stiffness his nanomeds couldn't seem to ease. "Doubt is good for the soul."

"I'm just so immensely grateful you're all right."

"I, too," he said wryly.

Her normally dulcet voice turned icy. "Everyone involved with this attempt against your life will pay."

She reminded him of the clawcats that prowled the Teotec Mountains on Coba. "Let the courts deal with it."

"Of course."

Kelric didn't trust *that* answer. She never gave in that easily. He knew she wouldn't rest until they had caught everyone connected with the attempt on his life.

The assassins had forced him to face certain facts. If he died and Roca became Imperator, then at the same time she was taking command, the Closure document would come to light. And he would no longer be alive to protect Coba.

X

King's Spectrum

Jaibriol sat sprawled on a sofa in the sitting area of his bedroom, his eyes closed. His mind brimmed with the bittersweet memories that crept up on him when he didn't fill his days with enough work to make him forget. Tonight he remembered how his mother had brought him and his siblings to Earth, deep in the night, to a starport in Virginia. She had asked Admiral Seth Rockworth to meet them, and he had been waiting.

Seth had looked after Jaibriol, his sister, and his two younger brothers for two years—while their mother waged war against their father's empire. They had lived in a gorgeous area of the Appalachian Mountains. Everyone had known Jaibriol as Jay Rockworth. He could have gone by Gabe; some historians believed his name derived from *Gabriel*. But it felt wrong to call himself after an angel when he descended from Highton Aristos. No one who knew him had dreamed he had a claim to both the Carnelian and Ruby thrones.

The loneliness of those days had weighed on him, for he could never acknowledge his parents. But it had also been a gentle time when he made friends, went to school, played sports, attended church, and had the closest he would ever come to a normal life. He and his siblings had cared deeply for Seth. Their mother had taken them to the retired admiral because he had been the Ruby Pharaoh's first consort, an arranged union that established a treaty between Skolia and the Allied Worlds. That he and the pharaoh later ended the marriage hadn't dissolved the treaty. Although technically Seth was no longer a member of the Ruby Dynasty, Jaibriol's mother had trusted him, enough to leave her children and their secret in his care.

Jaibriol didn't know what had happened to his sister and brothers; he had been offworld when he claimed his throne, and they had been on Earth. He had searched the meshes for them and found nothing. He feared to investigate too far, lest he endanger them with his attention, but he mourned the loss of their companionship as much as he grieved for his parents.

Tarquine had erased the few images of him on the meshes from that time on Earth. He hadn't looked Aristo then, with gold streaks in his hair and brown contacts that covered his red eyes. She wanted no questions. Not long after their marriage, she had cracked his secured medical files and discovered he had the same nanomeds in his body as Kelric. Roca Skolia had passed the meds to her children in her womb, and Jaibriol inherited them from his mother. From that, Tarquine had deduced the truth. Only she could have found that damning shred of evidence because she had owned, ever so briefly, a member of the Ruby Dynasty.

Tarquine had destroyed the files.

Why she protected him, Jaibriol didn't know, though surely it was because he held a similarly damning secret about her, that she no longer transcended. It seemed impossible it could be because she loved him.

Slumping back on the sofa, he put his feet on the table in front of him. Gold and midnight blue brocade glimmered on the sofa and the wing chair at right angles to it. Far across the suite, his canopied bed stood on a dais. The bedroom gleamed, gilt and ivory, with blue accents and tiered chandeliers.

His guards were outside. This bedroom suite was one of the few places with enough safeguards to allow him privacy even from his formidable Razers. They were infamous for their supposedly inhuman nature, but Jaibriol wondered, especially about Hidaka. He felt certain the guard knew when he wanted to be alone and when he wanted visitors, and did his best to ensure Jaibriol's wishes were met.

Why Hidaka would care, he had no idea, but he appreciated the results.

His wrist comm buzzed. Lifting his arm, he said, "Qox."

One of his guards answered. "Robert Muzeson is here, Your Highness. Shall we let him in?"

"Yes, certainly," Jaibriol said.

As Jaibriol sat up, the arched door to the entrance foyer opened. Its corners were curved, avoiding the right angles Aristos abhorred. Squared-off corners, like direct speech, were for slaves. Aristos considered abstraction elevated; Jaibriol considered it maddening.

Hidaka escorted Robert inside and bowed deeply to Jaibriol.

"Thank you," Jaibriol told the guard. Then he added, quietly, "For everything, Captain."

For an instant something showed on Hidaka's face. Shock? Jaibriol wasn't certain. He tried to pick up a mood from the captain, but he couldn't read the Razer's mental processes, which had been substantially altered by the extensive biomech in his brain.

After Hidaka withdrew, Jaibriol motioned Robert to the wing chair. "Relax, please."

"Thank you, Your Highness." Robert settled in the chair and leaned back, though he wasn't truly relaxed. Jaibriol slouched on the sofa, his long legs on the table. He knew it wasn't regal, but he really didn't care.

Robert looked as professional as always, a fit middle-aged man with brown hair. He dressed in elegant clothes of muted colors with peculiar names like *ecru*. To Jaibriol, it just looked like pale brown. Robert didn't have the stunning appearance of his father, Caleb, but from what Jaibriol had gathered about Caleb's life before he came to the palace, those good looks had brought him only grief. He had been a provider for Robert's mother. Now Caleb spent his days painting, as he had done before he was sold as a slave.

Jaibriol exhibited Caleb's work in one of the palace galleries. He never considered his patronage a favor; Caleb had great talent and was developing a well-deserved renown. The gratitude Robert and his father expressed made him want to crawl in a hole. How could they thank him? He *owned* them. They wore slave cuffs on their wrists and collars threaded with picotech that included ID chips and security monitors. They ought to hate him. Maybe they felt that way about other Aristos; he had certainly sensed it in Caleb. But never about him.

Right now, he sensed calm from Robert. Although Jaibriol could pick up moods, he couldn't always tell *why* a person felt that way. The emotions might be vague or mixed together. He received the clearest impressions from other psions. As a telepath, he might glean hints of a person's thoughts, but only if they were strong, well-articulated, and on the surface of the mind. Even to do that, he had to lower his barriers. He could mind-speak only with his family. One of the many reasons he appreciated Robert was because very little ruffled the aide. He wasn't a psion, so Jaibriol didn't have to shield his mind, and Robert's even temper often eased Jaibriol's agitated moods.

"Do I have any appointments?" Jaibriol asked. He had slept last night, so tonight he would work.

Robert unrolled his mesh film onto a board in his lap and read from the screen. "Nothing for the next three hours. A report came in on that explosion in the Amethyst Wing."

Jaibriol leaned his head against the headrest on the sofa and closed his eyes. "What caused it?"

"That's the rub of it, Your Highness. They found nothing wrong with the pipes and no indication of explosives."

Jaibriol opened his eyes. "That makes no sense."

"It doesn't appear to, no." Robert squinted at his screen. "It says here that about three centimeters above the pipe, space imploded. The surrounding region of space-time collapsed into the hole left behind in the, uh, weave of space and time." He looked up to meet Jaibriol's incredulous stare. "I'm sorry, Sire. That is what it says."

"They expect me to believe it?" Maybe they thought he was an idiot. "How would repair techs know that?"

"They forwarded a report to Professor Quenzer in the physics department at Qoxire University," Robert said. "Her research team came to examine the blast area and data. They are the ones who proposed the theory."

"Oh." Although Jaibriol knew very little about physics, even he had heard of the renowned Quenzer group. If they said space was falling apart, he would have to take them seriously. "It's an odd theory." To put it mildly.

"That's not all," Robert said. "Three other explosions took place, one on this planet, one in space, and one on a starliner in Sapphire Sector."

Jaibriol swung his legs off the table and sat up straight. "All like the one here?"

"It appears so."

"Was anyone hurt?"

"Several people on the liner had to be treated for minor injuries they sustained during a hull breach. But the situation was contained without any serious problems."

"What about the second blast here?"

"It happened in the Jaizire range." Robert looked regretful. "I'm afraid it destroyed a portion of one of your mountains."

Jaibriol loved the peaks and their wild, primordial forests, but he would far rather lose a mountain than people. "Why would space implode in four different places? It sounds crazy."

"No one seems to know," Robert said.

"Do they think it will happen again?" The prospect of space falling apart that way was just too eerie.

"They don't know that, either."

"Well, have them investigate it. The physicists, I mean." Jaibriol rubbed his eyes. "I want to know why it's happening."

Robert bent over his mesh screen. "I will see to it."

Jaibriol hesitated. "I have a question for you, Robert."

His aide looked up. "Yes, Sire?"

"Did I say something strange to Hidaka just now?"

"I don't think so. Why do you ask?"

Jaibriol felt odd, asking if he had offended his biomech guard. "He seemed taken aback when I thanked him."

Robert's puzzlement vanished. "You didn't trouble him, I'm sure. Surprised him, perhaps."

"Why?"

"You thanked him."

Jaibriol waited. When his aide said nothing more, he spoke wryly, "Aristos do say thank you, you know."

Robert met his gaze. "Not to machines."

"He's not a machine. None of them are."

Robert didn't answer. They both knew that not only would other Aristos disagree, they would find Jaibriol's statement offensive, a threat even. If they started acknowledging their slaves as human, their carefully crafted worldview would crumble. They had far too much power and wealth at stake to let that happen.

A beep came from Robert's mesh. Peering at the screen, he flicked his finger through several holoicons. "I'm getting a message for you." His eyes widened. "Good gods."

Jaibriol leaned forward. "What is it?"

Robert looked up, his face pale. "Someone tried to kill Imperator Skolia."

Hell and damnation. "Who did it?" Jaibriol could guess. "Someone who didn't think the Imperialate military should have as much power as the Assembly handed him with that vote, yes?"

Robert scanned the screen. "It looks that way. His people aren't releasing much information. The attempt took place in public, though, and monitors in the area recorded it."

"So they can't hush it up," Jaibriol said, shaken. He had almost lost another family member. "He's all right, isn't he?"

Robert looked up with a start, then caught himself and said, "According to these broadcasts, he's fine."

Jaibriol didn't need to ask Robert why he gaped. A normal Eubian emperor, upon learning that his greatest enemy had suffered a murder attempt, wouldn't seek assurance his foe was all right.

"They would claim everything is fine no matter what," Robert said. "It does look true, though." He indicated his screen, and Jaibriol leaned over to peer at it. The news holo showed Kelric climbing to his feet in the middle of a plaza, surrounded by three huge Jagernauts with gigantic black guns.

"So," Jaibriol said. As much as he wished the specter of Kelric Skolia would disappear from his life, or at least his wife's memory, it relieved him to see his uncle well. Of course, that assumed the broadcasts told the truth.

"Imperator Skolia doesn't have an heir," he said. "If he dies, it will destabilize the Imperialate."

"His mother is his heir," Robert said.

Jaibriol didn't want to think about succession in the Ruby Dynasty, because it meant considering the death of people his mother had loved. He had never met her family, but through her, he felt as if he could love them as well, given the chance. It would never happen; they would probably rather see him dead first. And no matter how uncomfortable it made him, he had to consider the ramifications should any of them die.

"If Roca Skolia became Imperator," Jaibriol said, "she might be more amenable to the talks."

"If Roca Skolia became Imperator," Robert said flatly, "she would destroy the galaxy to avenge the murder of her child."

Jaibriol couldn't argue with that. She might be moderate politically, but rumor claimed she was fiercely protective of her family. The ferocity didn't surprise him in the least. Her daughter—Jaibriol's mother—had been the same way.

The emperor shook his head. He didn't want to imagine the consequences if Kelric took the mandate offered to him by that vote. Jaibriol knew that going to war against his own family would destroy him.

It had been ten years since Kelric walked in the desert of Coba. Hot wind tugged his leather jacket and the pullover he wore underneath. Gusts pulled at the Talha scarf hanging around his neck. Woven from coarse white and black yarn, the Talha resembled a muffler, with tassels along its edges.

Carrying his duffle, he walked down the sand-scoured street of the starport. Najo, Axer, and Strava stalked at his side, sleek and lethal, each with the bulk of a Jumbler on his or her hip. They scanned the area continually and monitored it with their gauntlets. They weren't happy about this trip, even less so because he had told them almost nothing of his intentions.

They encountered no one. The place consisted of a few wide streets bordered by unused buildings. Robots kept the tiny port in shape, and travelers rarely visited. Nothing more than a low wall surrounded the base; beyond it, desert stretched in every direction, punctuated by sand dunes mottled with spiky green plants, and by bluffs streaked with red and yellow layers of rock. It reminded Kelric of ballads his father had sung about a starkly beautiful desert that separated the world of mortals from the land of the two sun gods.

They soon reached a wide gap in the wall. A pitted windrider stood beyond it, partially buried in drifts of sand. That was it. No gate. Nothing. On this side, they were Skolians: on the other, their citizenship ceased to matter. Even knowing that, his guards didn't hesitate to walk with him into the Coban desert. Restricted territory.

Kelric spoke into his gauntlet. "Bolt, connect me to the port EI." He could have thought the command to his node, but he wanted his guards to witness what he had to say.

Bolt's voice came out of the mesh. "Connecting."

The EI that ran the port spoke. "ISC-Coba attending."

"ISC-Coba," Kelric said, "I'm sending you some codes. Use them to access the Kyle web and contact the EI called 'Dirac' on the Orbiter space station."

"Understood," ISC-Coba said.

Najo watched him with that uncanny ability of his to seem utterly still. Strava rested her hand on her Jumbler while she scanned the desert. Axer was checking the area with his gauntlet.

"Contact made," ISC-Coba said.

Dirac's rich baritone rumbled. "My greetings, Imperator Skolia."

Kelric gazed north to mountains that reared against the pale sky. It had been so long. "Dirac, how many days until my Closure becomes permanent?"

"Ninety-seven," Dirac said.

Najo stiffened, his eyes widening. Axer raised his head, and Strava snapped her attention back to Kelric. Learning he would be legally dead in ninety-seven days had to be unnerving for the people tasked with ensuring he stayed alive.

Kelric turned toward the nearby windrider. It was painted like a giant althawk, with red wings and a rusted head that had once gleamed. The landing gear resembled black talons, or it would have if he could have seen under the sand dunes drifted around the aircraft.

"Dirac," he said. "Cancel the Closure."

A pause. "Cancelled," Dirac said.

Najo started to speak. Kelric didn't know how he looked, but whatever Najo was about to say, he changed his mind. Axer and Strava exchanged glances.

"Closing connection," Kelric told Dirac.

"Orbiter connection closed," ISC-Coba stated.

"ISC-Coba," Kelric said. "Verify my identity."

"You are the Imperator of Skolia."

Kelric stopped then, unable to take the final step. He tried to go on, but no words came.

"Do you have a command?" ISC-Coba asked.

"Yes." He took a deep breath. "Change the status of this world from Restricted to Protected."

"That requires a review by Imperial Space Command."

"I'm the Imperator. That's review enough."

Silence.

In truth, Kelric knew of no cases where ISC had altered a world's status without a review. The process could take years. However, nothing prohibited him from doing it. In theory.

Then ISC-Coba said, "Status changed."

Kelric exhaled. A human probably would have protested. "End communication."

"Connection closed," Bolt said.

Najo spoke. "Sir, to protect you, we need to know what's going on."

Kelric indicated the mountains. "We're going to a city up there. The air is even thinner than here, so use caution in any exertions. The food varies from irritating to toxic, at least to us, but our nanomeds can deal with it. Boiling the water helps. For a short stay, we should be all right." Eighteen years here, with his meds failing, had nearly killed him. By the time he had left, he had been dying. His capture and subsequent escape from Trader slavery had worsened the injuries to his body and biomech, until he had gone deaf and blind, and lost the use of his legs. Jeejon had given up everything she owned to get him help; without her, he wouldn't have survived.

A wave of grief hit Kelric. He remembered what Jeejon had told him just before she died: *Someday you must finish that chapter of your life you left behind for me.* It was true, but he had needed this year to say good-bye to her.

Kelric looked out over the desert. **Be well, love.** He sent his thought into the wind, across the sands, as if it could float into the pale sky, to the stars and beyond, until it reached her spirit.

"Sir, I don't understand," Strava said. "Why are we here?"

Kelric continued to gaze at the desert. "So I can see the city. Walk down a street." He turned to them. "Buy a sausage at market."

They regarded him with bewilderment.

Finally Axer said, "What are the threats?"

"To me?" Kelric asked. The greatest threat here was him, to Coba.

"Yes, sir."

Kelric answered wryly. "People in the city might gawk at my metallic skin. They will probably stare more at you three, with those Jumblers. Their city guards just carry stunners."

"You seem to know this place," Najo said.

More than I ever admitted, he thought. The sight of the land, the smell of the air, the feel of the wind: it was achingly familiar. "I spent eighteen years here," he said.

"Gods above," Strava said. "Sir! Is this where—"

Kelric held up his hand. "None of you can talk about this without my leave." He had known them for years and trusted them, at least as much as he trusted anyone. But he had left a trail this time, and if and when questions arose, he wanted to be the one who responded.

"We won't say anything," Najo told him. Axer and Strava nodded their agreement.

"I'm not sure what will happen at the city." Kelric rolled a tassel of his Talha between his fingers. "For personal reasons, I may find it hard to speak. You won't know the language. It has roots in common with ours, but it has evolved in isolation for thousands of years. Your nodes can analyze it and eventually provide translations, but at first it may sound like gibberish."

"What hostiles should we be aware of?" Axer asked.

Kelric would have laughed if this hadn't hurt so much. "These people are peaceful. Treat them gently."

"We need a flyer to reach the mountains," Strava said.

Kelric indicated the windrider. "I flew that here ten years ago. If it still works, we can take it to Karn."

"Karn?" Najo asked.

Softly Kelric said, "My home."

The voice on the radio sent a chill up Kelric's spine. The woman spoke in normal tones—in Teotecan. "Sky Racer, I've received your ID. Are you new here? I don't recognize your codes." She paused. "Or your accent."

"It's an old windrider," Kelric said, self-conscious about his rusty Teotecan. "And I haven't been to Karn in years."

"Welcome back." She sounded wary.

"My thanks." Talking to an Outsider was strange. Keeping an Oath of silence for so many years had reinforced his taciturn nature. As Imperator, he had to overcome his reticence to speak, but being here brought it back. In all his time on Coba, he had never had a conversation like this. Piloting a rider wasn't that different from the antique aircraft he flew as a hobby, and he had overheard pilots during his trips as a Calani, so he had an idea of protocols. But this felt surreal.

"Request permission to land," Kelric said.

"Go ahead," the woman said. "Lane Five."

Quis patterns appeared on his screen, providing directions. In the copilot's seat, Najo peered at the symbols, his brow furrowed. Axer and Strava had the two seats in back, and Kelric felt them concentrating on his Teotecan. He could have translated, but he wanted the privacy of his adopted language for a little while longer.

He spread the wing slats of the great metallic hawk and circled the airfield, fitting into the pattern of two other riders. At most Estates, he would have been the only one; Karn, however, had the largest airport on Coba. The woman in the tower tried to draw him into conversation, but he remained noncommittal. She was more curious about a man piloting a rider than about his accent.

Kelric landed reasonably well, though the craft bounced a couple of times. While his guards unstrapped from their seats, he went to the locker in the back. He hung his jacket on a seat. As he pulled off his shirt, a surge of pleasure leaked around Strava's mental shields, which she immediately clamped down. Facing away from her, Kelric smiled. Her appreciation of her shirtless commander embarrassed her far more than him.

He removed his duffle from the locker and donned the white shirt with loose sleeves he had packed. It matched the ones he had worn here, even the embroidery on the cuffs. Next he took out his armbands. For a moment he stood, staring at the engraved circles of gold. Finally he slid them on his arms. They felt strange. He almost took them off again, then decided that for this one day he would wear these signs of his former life.

He shrugged back into his jacket, in part against the chill winds of the Teotecs, but also to hide his bands and gauntlets. His dice bag hung from his belt and his Talha around his neck. Seeing the scarf, people would assume he came from Haka Estate, which was far from Karn in both distance and culture. It would, he hoped, account for his accent and bodyguards. He didn't have the dark coloring of the Haka-born, so he obviously wasn't native to that shimmering desert land. People would probably assume that was why he neither covered his face with the Talha nor wore a robe. In this age, only Haka men went robed. And Calani. But of course no sane person would believe that even a guarded Calani would be out on his own.

Finally they disembarked from the rider. He stood on the tarmac with his guards, wind tugging his clothes, surrounded by spectacular scenery. To the west, the Teotec Mountains rolled out in forested slopes; to the south and east they dropped down in endless ripples of green. The city jumbled north of the port, and the Upper Teotecs towered starkly above it. Clustered beneath those peaks, Karn basked, yellow and white in the morning sunshine from a cloud-flecked sky.

✧   ✧   ✧

The lane of blue and white cobblestones was as familiar to Kelric as a picture seen a thousand times but never touched. He walked with Najo, Strava, and Axer, marveling at the city he had lived in, yet never experienced. Shops crowded both sides of the street, and wooden signs hung from bars above the doors, creaking in the wind. He passed glassblowers, potters, butchers, and dice makers.

The pure mountain air, exhilarating in its clarity, stirred memories edged with beauty and pain. After Savina had passed away, he had ended up at Varz Estate, even higher in the Teotecs. The Varz queen had been a nightmare. She had forced him into a marriage the day after Savina died, respecting neither his grief nor his need to see his child. He hadn't known which was worse, the physical brutality of her obsession with finding ways to hurt and control him, or the cruelty she could inflict with words. His repressed fury had saturated the Quis and roused the sleeping dragon of violence the Cobans had so long submerged.

It had been more than a year before Ixpar brought him to Karn. In the exquisite serenity of her Calanya, he had begun to heal, but it had been too late by then. His influence had saturated the Quis for nearly eighteen years. Nothing could have stopped the war.

A pack of boys burst out of a side lane, laughing and calling to one another. They gaped at Kelric but kept going, jumping over invisible obstacles with shouts of delight.

"Happy kids," Najo commented.

Kelric couldn't answer. His memories brought such longing. He *missed* Coba. Despite everything he had gone through on this world, he had also spent the best times of his life here.

He knew the location of the market only from maps he had studied as a Calani, and he wasn't sure he could find it. He heard it first, a rumble of voices in the street. The lane crooked around a corner and opened into a bustling plaza like a tributary feeding a great lake. Merchants, stalls, and customers thronged the area. Buildings two or three stories high bordered it, many with balconies. Chains adorned with metal Quis dice hung from their eaves, clinking in the ever-present wind. A tumult of voices poured over him like Teotecan music. So much color and vibrancy and *life*.

"Too many people," Axer said, his hand on his holstered gun.

Kelric barely heard. He walked forward and Cobans flowed around him. Merchants called out wares; children ran and hopped; street artists sang, fiddled, or acted out skits. He looked around for a sausage stand. In the first Quis game he had ever played, the Dahl Manager had bet him one tekal, "enough to buy a sausage in the market." He had owed her Estate that tekal for twenty-eight years. He didn't know the cost of a sausage now, though, besides which, he had no Coban money.

Although people noticed him, they paid less attention than he had expected. Just as he started to relax, a lanky woman in the red and gold of the City Guard stared hard at him. Then she spun around and strode across the plaza.

"Not good," Strava said, watching the woman.

"She knows we're out of place," Najo said. "She's going to tell someone."

"Probably at the Estate." Kelric indicated a fortress of amber-hued stone high on a hill across the city. "The Manager lives there." He might soon see Ixpar, perhaps his children. Just as he had needed time alone after Jeejon had died, so now he needed to prepare; in matters of emotion, it always took him time to adjust. Before he faced Ixpar, he wanted to know how it felt to be part of Coba in a way he had never known when he lived here.

Strava was studying him with that penetrating gaze of hers. "What is a Manager?"

"The queen of a city-estate," Kelric said. "The Manager of Karn, this city, is also the Minister. She rules Coba."

Najo tensed. "Does she pose a danger to your person?"

Danger indeed. He wondered how such a funny question could hurt so much. "No," he said. The only danger was to his heart.

Nearby, a man was sitting against the yellow-stone wall of a shop. He wore fine clothes: a well-tailored white shirt, suede trousers with gold buttons up the seams, and suede boots. His air of confidence evoked a king in his milieu. Quis dice were piled on his low table.

"Someone you know?" Strava asked.

"I've never seen him before," Kelric said.

A woman had sat down at the table, and a crowd was gathering. Kelric stayed back and acted like a Haka man, never smiling. With so many people around, he absorbed a sense of their moods even through his shields. They found him exotic, but he didn't think anyone realized he was more than a visitor from a distant city. Although his guards disconcerted people, no one seemed to realize the Jumblers weren't just big stunners.

The man at the Quis table cleared off his extra dice, and the woman rolled out her set, all their pieces carved from wood. The two players were talking, setting a bet that involved many coins and goods. When they finished, the woman opened the game by playing a blue cylinder.

Conversations drifted around Kelric from the crowd.

"I heard she came all the way from Ahkah to challenge him," a man was saying.

"His reputation is spreading," a woman replied.

"I can't figure why he isn't in a Calanya," another woman said. "Everyone says he's good enough."

"Maybe he has some problem," someone else said.

A man snorted. "Right. A problem with living in a cage."

"Why go in a Calanya?" another man said. "He's making pots of coins here, and he doesn't have to abide by an Oath straight out of the Old Age."

"Did you hear about the offworld Calani in Viasa?" a woman asked. "Viasa Manager kidnapped him, just like in the Old Age."

"Heard he was good-looking," a second woman said.

A third one chuckled. "You want to carry one off, too?"

The other woman bristled. "I don't need to kidnap a man to get a husband."

"You haven't heard?" a man said. "The fellow escaped."

"He did not," a woman said.

"Play Quis with someone from Viasa," he countered. "It's in their dice. Stole himself a windrider and whisked off."

Kelric listened as people embellished Jeremiah's tale. Manager Viasa had built her cover story well; he heard no hints of his own involvement. So he returned his focus to the game. The players competed rather than studying problems or plotting the ascendance of their Estate. They were opposed rather than aligned. It reminded him of the Quis played among Managers, but on a less intense scale, for fun rather than politics.

Both players surely rated the title of Quis Master. They built towers, arches, stacks, bridges, rings, claws, and more. Whenever one gained advantage, the other wrested it back. The man was probably the better player, but the woman seemed more experienced. They vied solely for advantage, without the complexity of Calanya Quis. Kelric had no doubt the man would thrive in a Calanya: he had the gift. He would find such Quis far more satisfying than anything Out here. That he chose freedom despite the price it exacted—never to play true Quis—hinted at far-reaching changes in Coba's social structure.

Suddenly the man grinned. "My game."

"What?" The woman looked up with a start.

Murmurs rolled among the crowd. "He hasn't won . . ."

"His tower has more dice then hers . . ."

"She collapsed his tower . . ."

"But look! He hid an arch."

Axer spoke to Kelric in a low voice. "Do you have any idea what these people are saying?"

"They're arguing over the game," Kelric said, intent on the dice. The man had bridged several structures with an elegant arch, increasing their worth enough for him to claim victory. He had managed it despite his opponent's vigilance because he used dice of a similar color to the surrounding pieces, so it looked as if he were creating lesser structures. A camouflage.

The woman ceded the match, and applause scattered as people slapped their palms against their thighs. After arranging to pay her debt, the woman stood and bowed with respect to the Quis Master. Then she went on her way.

Kelric walked forward.

The gleam in the man's eyes when he saw Kelric was the same as in any culture on any planet, the calculation of a master sizing up a rube. Kelric temporarily eased down his barriers. With so many people at market, it was hard to distinguish moods, but he gathered the man didn't see him as a challenge. Good male Quis players were in a Calanya. He also associated Kelric's large size with low intelligence. The crowd that had watched the last game was dispersing.

"Have a seat," the Quis Master said. "I'm Talv."

As Kelric sat down, he wondered if he had somehow let on that he didn't know market-style Quis. He had never learned to gamble, and he had played nothing but Quis solitaire for ten years. He wasn't certain he could beat Talv. But if he could win a few tekals, he could buy a sausage and indulge his admittedly whimsical desire to repay his old debt.

Talv glanced at the pouch on Kelric's belt. "You've brought your set, I see." He started to remove his extra dice.

Kelric knew if he rolled out jeweled Calanya dice, the game would end before it started. As much as a Quis Master might want to challenge a Calani, he would never risk the ire of a Manager. So he indicated Talv's extra dice. "I prefer those." Speaking with an Outsider was even harder when he was about to play Quis. "Your extra set."

"Are you sure?" Talv yawned. "Most people find it easier to use their own dice. They will be more familiar to you."

It was, of course, something any child knew. "Yours will be fine," Kelric said.

"All right." Talv smirked at him. "What shall we bet?"

"How much for a sausage?"

"A *sausage*?" Talv wasn't even trying to hide his disdain. "One tekal."

So. Same price. "Let us play for two tekals."

Talv shrugged. "Oh, all right. You can start."

"Shouldn't we draw dice?" Going first was an advantage.

"If you insist." Talv pulled a disk out of his pouch and handed over the bag. Kelric took out a lower-ranked piece, a flat square.

"Your move," Kelric said.

"So it is." Talv set a red pyramid in the playing area. He seemed bored, but Kelric could tell he believed the game would be over fast enough to make the tedium bearable.

A sense of *opening* came to Kelric. After so many years of solitaire, sitting here made him feel . . . expanded. It hadn't happened with Jeremiah or Dehya, but he had held back in those games. Now he envisioned a myriad of elegant patterns stemming from that single die that Talv had placed. He set down a grey pyramid with curved sides.

Talv looked up at him. "If your die doesn't touch mine, you aren't building a structure."

"I know," Kelric said.

"Are you sure you want to play that piece?" Talv said. "Nonstandard dice are difficult to use."

Kelric was growing irritated. Calani never disrupted a session, especially not with unasked-for Quis lessons. "It's your move."

"Suit yourself." Talv set down an orange pentahedron.

Kelric saw his intent: a queen's spectrum. Few players could manage them; they were too easy to block. Kelric had slipped one past Dehya because she hadn't known the rules, but he wouldn't be that lucky with her again. To succeed against someone who knew Quis,

Talv either had to camouflage the spectrum or else hope his opponent was too stupid to see it. He hadn't bothered with a camouflage.

Kelric had met only one other player who could consistently build a queen's spectrum in high-level Quis: Mentar, the Fourth Level at Karn Estate, the elderly widower of the previous Minister. Mentar's Quis had fascinated Kelric. Ixpar had claimed that when he and Kelric played dice, the world shook.

This callow player was no Mentar. Kelric slid an aqua piece against the orange die, disrupting the spectrum. Talv grunted and placed a yellow cube. So. He was trying to recover by turning his spectrum at an angle. Kelric blocked him with an ocher cube.

"Huh." Talv rubbed his chin. He set down a green die, again turning his spectrum.

Enough, Kelric thought. He bridged Talv's pyramid and his own cube with an arch. The cube had a higher rank, so the advantage went to Kelric. He had no idea what points went with it, but he doubted he had enough to win. And indeed, Talv continued playing. Good. Kelric didn't want to stop; he was envisioning an exquisite design with the dice. His Quis thoughts pleased him, and he set about making them reality.

Talv became quieter as they played. His sneer vanished, and he spent more and more time considering his moves. Then he began to sweat.

Kelric built for the sheer beauty of it. Dice spread in patterns of platonic solids, and geometric elegance covered the table. After a while, Talv stopped sweating, and his game took on a new quality, as if he were appreciating a work of art. When he quit fighting Kelric, he became a better Quis partner. The structures flourished.

With regret, Kelric pulled himself back to here and now. As much as he would have enjoyed playing for hours, he had business to attend. He set down a white sphere. When Talv started to place a ring, Kelric spoke quietly. "It's my game."

Talv lifted his head like a swimmer surfacing from a dive. "Your game?"

A woman behind them said, "I don't believe it!"

Startled, Kelric looked around—and froze.

People.

They had crowded around, more even than for the last game. The woman who played before, the other Quis Master, was gaping at the table. Others looked from her to the board with bewildered expressions.

"What is it?" Talv said.

Kelric turned back to him. He tapped a line of dice that wound across the table, around and through other structures: grey, orange, gold, yellow, yellow-green, green, aqua, blue, indigo, purple, and finally the white sphere.

Murmurs swelled in the crowd. Talv stared at the structure for a long time. Finally he lifted his gaze to Kelric. "I don't think I've ever heard tell of anyone, even the highest of the Calani, building a grand augmented queen's spectrum."

XI

Hawk's Queen

Murmurs spread through the crowd like the hum of dart-bees swarming together. Kelric hadn't intended to draw attention; he had become too caught up in the game. He had to admit, though, it was a good spectrum.

He inclined his head to Talv. "You play well."

"I had thought so," Talv said. "Now I know better."

"You have talent. It's wasted on market Quis."

Talv's voice heated. "You won't lock me in a Calanya!"

"Find other ways to use your talent," Kelric said. "Join the Minister's staff. Work your way up in the Estate Quis."

Talv snorted. "In case you haven't noticed, I'm the wrong sex."

"No laws forbid it."

"Sure they do," Talv said. "They're just unwritten."

"So break them."

"Who *are* you?"

Kelric smiled slightly. "I believe you owe me two tekals."

Talv squinted at him. "Just two?"

"That was the bet."

Talv shook his head, but he handed over two coins. Kelric turned the copper heptagons over in his hand. One side showed a Quis structure, a nested tower that symbolized protection. The other had the portrait of a regal queen.

"That's Ixpar Karn," Kelric said.

"Haven't you ever seen a tekal before?"

He looked up to see Talv watching him oddly. Kelric rose to his feet. "Thank you for the game."

"The honor was mine." Talv stood as well. "That was Quis like nothing I've ever played or even heard of in a Calanya."

It was the highest compliment among Quis Masters. Kelric nodded to indicate honor to his opponent. His guards gathered around him, and he could tell they wanted him away from this attention. He left the table, and people stepped respectfully aside as he walked through the crowd. He felt their awe and curiosity.

Kelric went deeper into the market until he lost himself among the crowds. A familiar aroma teased his nose, wafting from a stall with yellow slats. A sausage merchant stood behind the counter, a plump man with a white apron pulled across his large belly. He beamed as Kelric paused. "What can I get for you, Goodsir?" He motioned at sausages hanging from the rafters. "I've the best spiced-reds from here to Haka."

Kelric indicated a fat specimen. "Kadilish."

"Ah! A man after my own tastes." The merchant wrapped the sausage in waxy paper, accepted Kelric's tekal, and handed over the purchase as if it were the most natural thing to do. For him, it was. To Kelric, it was another watershed.

"Sir," Najo said, his voice uneasy.

Kelric looked up at his worried guard, then turned in the direction Najo indicated. Across the plaza, a street opened into the market. Far beyond it, on its distant hill, the Estate glowed amber in the sunlight. Someone was entering the plaza from the street. Many someones. They came in formation, all wearing the uniform of the City Guard, and they were headed straight for him.

Strava stepped closer, and Kelric was aware of Axer behind him and Najo, tall and solid. He had no idea if the City Guard members approaching him suspected his identity, but if they did, and if Ixpar had sent these guards, then she might well hate him for bringing his people to her world. He had no reason to think she wanted to see him.

Najo, Axer, and Strava drew their guns, the black mammoths glittered harshly in the streaming sunlight, a forbidding contrast to the small, light stunners worn by the Coban guards. Then Najo sighted on the group coming across the market.

Kelric grabbed his arm. "Don't harm them!"

All three of his bodyguards waited, poised and ready. It was in that instant that Kelric realized who walked in the center of the approaching retinue. She had to see the monstrous guns his guards had drawn, but she kept coming without hesitation. She was tall even among Cobans, and her hair blazed like fire, pulled loosely into a braid. Her suede trousers did nothing to hide the muscular lines of her long, long legs. She had a powerful beauty, wild and fierce under a veneer of elegance—a face that could inspire armies and conquer a world.

For Kelric, time slowed down. In this crystalline moment, he thought the two of them would be here forever. She came closer, closer still, and then she was in front of him, her gray eyes filled with incredulity. He had thought of a million words for this moment, planned for days. Seasons. Years. Now the words left him.

"Kelric?" she whispered.

She was one of the few Cobans who had known him as Kelric rather than Sevtar. Seeing her filled him with an emotion he couldn't define, jagged and painful and miraculous. They stood together as if they were inside a bubble, and he wanted to touch her, feel her cheek, her hair, her lips, but he feared to move, lest it burst this tenuous sphere.

He spoke in a voice rough with the feelings he couldn't express. "My greetings, Ixpar."

XII

The Last Band

"It cannot be!" Ixpar reached into her pocket and drew out a half-melted ring of gold. She held it up so he could see the remains of his twelfth armband. "This is all that remains of Kelric Valdoria."

He pulled up his jacket cuff and uncovered the wrist guards embedded in his gauntlets. It astonished him that his hand didn't shake. "These, too."

Ixpar stared at the heavy gold for a long moment. The engraving of a hawk soaring over mountains gleamed in their ancient engravings. Then she looked up at him and spoke in her husky voice, so familiar to him and yet also so new.

"If the god of the dawn has come seeking vengeance," Ixpar said, "I entreat him to reconsider."

"Vengeance?" He blinked. "For what? My shattering Coba?"

Moisture gathered in her eyes. "Ten years is a long time."

Too long. He wanted to say so much, but he could neither move nor speak. It was several moments before he found his voice again, at least enough to ask the question that was always with him. "My children?"

Her face gentled. "They are well."

Softly he asked, "And who came after me?"

"After?" She seemed as lost for words as him.

He forced out the question. "As your Akasi."

"None now."

"You have no husband?"

"I thought not." Her voice caught. "It seems I was wrong."

A sense of homecoming came over him then, more than he had felt since he set foot on her world. He took her into his arms and embraced the wife he had never expected to see again. She stiffened, and his bodyguards loomed around them. Gods only knew what they thought.

Then Ixpar exhaled and put her arms around him, leaning her head against his. He held a stranger, yet he recognized her curves and strength, the sensual power of her body. If he had erred in coming here, it was too late to turn back.

In this incredible instant, he didn't care.

XIII

Space-time Enigma

The fifth implosion happened in Sphinx Sector, in deep space. Jaibriol heard about it while he was dining with Iraz Gji, the Diamond Minister, and Gji's wife, Ilina. Gji and Ilina were impeccable Aristos, their black hair glittering in the cool light, their eyes a clear, crystalline red. Just like Jaibriol. He had even become used to seeing himself that way. In his youth, gold had streaked his hair. Never again. Now he looked the perfect Highton.

Jaibriol had expected Tarquine to join them, but she had vanished, he had no idea where. He had no intention of admitting he couldn't keep track of his empress, so he asked his cousin Corbal to join him instead, to make her absence less noticeable.

They relaxed in the Silver Room, a parlor with holoscreens for walls and plush divans where they could recline, sipping wine and watching the broadcast about the implosion. A taskmaker read the news, which meant she could speak as directly as she pleased; indirect speech was only required from Aristos with other Aristos.

"Space-time ripples have spread outward from the disturbance in every direction," she said. "It is by far the most extreme of the five events."

Jaibriol grimaced as he listened, stretched out on his divan. If this last blast had happened here, it sounded like it could have destroyed the palace and the surrounding coast.

"As to why the disturbances are occurring," the broadcaster continued, "scientists postulate that the fabric of space-time has weakened in the region of space where an implosion takes place."

"Weakened?" Gji asked, incredulous. "That's like saying the sky or the air weakened. It makes no sense."

Jaibriol sat up, swinging his feet to the floor while he touched a finger-panel on his wrist comm.

Robert's voice came out of the mesh. "Muzeson, here."

"Robert, get me the head of the team at the university studying this implosion business," Jaibriol said.

"Right away, Your Highness."

"Odd little events, aren't they?" Ilina said languidly. She was lying on her divan, sleek in a black diamond bodysuit that fit her like a second skin. She sipped her Taimarsian wine. "Perhaps a Highton sneezed and his exhalations shook up space."

Her husband laughed, relaxed in a lounger. Although he had drunk several glasses of wine, he hardly seemed affected. Either he held his liquor remarkably well or else meds in his body kept him from becoming intoxicated. "Such exhalations would surely do more than shake space, eh?" Gji said. "Perhaps they could cause a black hole such as the one at the center of the galaxy."

Jaibriol didn't know whether to be astounded or exasperated. Eube and Skolia might be on the verge of war, assassination attempts threatened to destabilize the Imperialate, space-time was falling apart, and all they could talk about was the purported superiority of Hightons, even to the extent, it seemed, of causing galactic formation. He had learned to deal with Aristos, but sometimes it truly taxed his diplomatic skills.

The feeling was probably mutual. He knew Gji and Ilina were irritated that he hadn't offered them providers as part of tonight's entertainment. He had no intention of letting them transcend with the slaves he had inherited from his grandfather. By not doing it, he weakened his standing with them, but good Lord, he couldn't let them torture the people in his care. He hadn't lost that much of his soul.

Most Aristos considered him eccentric, particularly in his avoidance of providers. True, fidelity to one's spouse was expected; in castes where heredity and genetics meant everything, adultery brought high penalties. But that didn't preclude Aristos doing whatever they wanted with providers. Such slaves weren't considered human. It baffled Aristos that Jaibriol eschewed the pleasure girls offered to him and instead preferred his wife.

What stunned Jaibriol most, though, was that Tarquine did the same for him. She refused to discuss the matter, yet during nine years of marriage, she had never to his knowledge taken a provider. He told himself she made that choice for him and not because no one could measure up to Kelric. Sometimes he almost believed that.

Corbal was reclining on his divan as he watched the broadcast, which had shifted into a scientific discussion about bubbles frothed in space-time. "Who would have thought," he mused, "that carbonation could be such a problem?"

Jaibriol smiled, just slightly, as supposedly befitted the emperor. He was aware of Gji watching him with a speculative gaze. When he glanced at the Diamond Minister, Gji bowed his head to indicate respect. Jaibriol tried to probe his mind, but as soon as he relaxed his defenses, the pressure from Gji and Ilina swamped his empathic reception. He wanted to flee the agony of their presence, and he had to force himself to keep his barriers down. Gji's ire at what he considered Jaibriol's lack of hospitality came through strongly, and also a hint of something else. Suspicion? Something to do with Corbal.

The pain was unbearable. Jaibriol gave up probing and raised his barriers. He knew some Aristos suspected Corbal of showing too much affection for Sunrise, his provider. He didn't think Gji's concern involved Corbal's private life, though. Whatever disturbed Gji went a lot farther than Sunrise.

Jaibriol's comm crackled, and Robert's voice came through. "Sire, I have Professor Cathleen Quenzer on comm."

"Put her through," Jaibriol said.

A woman spoke. "My honor at your esteemed presence, Your Highness."

Relieved to speak with a taskmaker, Jaibriol slipped into direct speech. "Doctor Quenzer, what is going on with these implosions?"

"We just received word of the fifth," she said. "We are optimistic it will provide us with more information."

Apparently she was used to dealing with Aristos; that sounded like Hightonese for *We don't have a clue.*

"Why do they keep happening?" he asked.

She spoke carefully. "Think of space-time as cloth. It's fraying in some places. When it gets too thin, it rips, and we register that as an implosion."

"But why is it happening?"

"We're working nonstop to understanding the causes."

Jaibriol knew she wasn't going to admit to the emperor that she didn't know. He doubted the scientists would believe he had no intention of taking punitive steps if they didn't give him immediate answers. His predecessors had unfortunately ensured that such an atmosphere reigned in Qoxire. So he just said, "Keep me informed."

"Absolutely, Your Highness." She sounded relieved.

After Jaibriol signed off, Corbal said, "It would hamper repairs in the Amethyst Wing if the damage spread."

Jaibriol wasn't exactly sure what Corbal meant, but he thought his cousin was asking if they expected more implosions in the palace. So he said, "One can never be certain."

Gji had his full concentration on Corbal, with a hardness in his attitude he hadn't shown before. "It would certainly hamper repairs to spread damage, whether in a palace or an entire sector of space."

Corbal met his gaze with a guarded expression. "Indeed."

Jaibriol wondered what Minister Gji thought Corbal had done. He didn't think Corbal knew, either. It apparently had some link to a repair. Probing, Jaibriol said, "In the end, though, repairs usually have the desired effect. Improvement."

Gji took a sip of his wine. "Assuming the need for them didn't cause a grounding elsewhere."

Grounding? What the blazes—

Then it hit Jaibriol. Gji meant the scandal with the Janq pirate fleet. The grounding of the Janq ships had dealt a fatal blow to the Ivory Sector mercantile coalition. For some obscure reason, Gji believed Corbal had something to do with that fiasco.

Jaibriol took a swallow of the wine he had barely touched. Then he said, "One could always go to sea somewhere else." It seemed glaringly obvious to him; if they quit trying to sell Skolians *as* Eubian goods, they could sell Eubian goods *to* Skolians.

"Sailing to new shores can be a risk," Gji said cautiously. He seemed uncertain how to interpret Jaibriol's remark.

Ilina waved her hand. "Oh, sailing is a pleasure. I do love cruises. Perhaps, Your Highness, you know of some good ones."

"I wonder if we might try new routes," Jaibriol said.

"One can always look," Gji said. He glanced from Corbal to Jaibriol. "However, no reason exists to give up the old." An edge had entered his voice, and in Highton, that had layers of meaning, none of them good.

Corbal was as cool and as unreadable as always, so Jaibriol fell back on his advantage that no other Aristo shared; he probed Corbal's mind. He couldn't lower his barriers much, but it was enough to sense that his cousin understood his idea about trade with the Skolians far better than he let on—and that Corbal didn't like it at all.

With Gji and Corbal both on edge, Jaibriol suspected that if he pushed the idea now, they would reject it. So he said only, "Indeed," relying on that annoying but useful all-purpose word.

Then Jaibriol changed the subject by appearing not to change the subject. "These implosions add many layers to the idea of giving up the old," he said. It meant absolutely nothing, but what the hell. It would distract their attention while they tried to puzzle it out.

Corbal slanted a look at him. "I should not like to see space imploding everywhere, like bubbles popping in froth. Or words."

Jaibriol almost laughed. He knew Corbal meant his words were froth, which was quite true at the moment. "That would be strange," he said. "Five events already, from here to—"

Then he stopped, as the realization hit him.

He knew where the implosions were headed.

Kelric stood with Ixpar by a high window that overlooked Karn. Houses clustered along the streets and down the hills, and plumberry vines grew in a profusion of purple and blue flowers, climbing walls and spiraling up street lamps. So many times he had stood savoring the view from this window.

"I'd forgotten how beautiful it is here," he said.

Ixpar was leaning against the wall across the window from him. "I never did."

He turned to find her looking at him, not the city. She had that quality he remembered well, a serenity that came when she wasn't preoccupied with politics or war. Soon she would be pacing and planning again, her agile mind occupied with affairs of state. But she let him see this reflective side she showed so few people, indeed that few knew existed. She had always been compelling, but the years had added a maturity that made it difficult to stop gazing at her face.

"You look good," Kelric said.

Her expression gentled. "To see you again is a miracle." Then her smiled faded. "But I fear your reasons for coming. What happens now? Will Skolia retaliate against Coba?"

"I won't allow it."

"You can't stop the Imperator."

Softly he said, "Yes, I can."

Her posture stiffened. "You said otherwise ten years ago."

It was hard to tell her. Once she knew what he had become, this bubble that held them would disintegrate. So he said only, "The Imperator has changed the status of Coba."

"We no longer have the Restriction?"

"As of this morning, no. Coba is Protected."

She clenched the window frame, and her face paled. "What does it mean?"

His words were coming out all wrong; he had meant to reassure her, not cause alarm. He tried again. "In some ways it's like Restriction. A Protected world is even harder to visit. But you decide who comes here. You control what happens. And your people now have Skolian citizenship."

She stared at him. "Why would your brother do this thing?"

"He didn't."

"Then who did?"

The world was too quiet. Muffled. His voice seemed far away. "Me."

For a long time she just looked at him. Finally she spoke in a low voice. "Do I say Your Majesty? Or Imperator Skolia?"

Heat spread in his face. "Call me Kelric. Hell, Sevtar."

She started to answer, then stopped as if she had glimpsed something truly strange. "Am I your wife by Skolian law?"

He thought of the Closure he had cancelled. "Yes."

"Doesn't that make me the Imperator's consort?"

The answer welled up within him, one word he had waited so long to say. "Yes."

"Winds above," she murmured. "I am honored. But Kelric, that changes nothing. Your empire can still destroy us."

He knew she would never have allowed Jeremiah Coltman to study them if she had felt all offworld influence would bring harm. "Change *will* come. You can't hide forever. Must it be for the worse?"

Her gaze never wavered. "We would be just as wrong to deny the danger now as we were when we took you into the Calanya."

Kelric knew her fear. He shared it. Then he thought of the Assembly vote that had strengthened his position. "I control ISC now. My influence becomes more established every year. I can set it up so no Skolian ever sets foot here." He struggled for the words. "A parent has to let a child become an adult. Coba can't live protected all its life."

She regarded him dourly. "We are not children."

He suspected he would make it worse if he continued these inarticulate attempts to express himself. So he said, "Play Quis with me."

Ixpar placed the first die.

They sat at a table by the window and played dice at its highest level. Ixpar had always been brilliant, and the years had added even greater depth to her Quis. She wove patterns of other Managers into her structures, other Calani, other Estates. She synthesized a world into her Quis with a virtuosity that took his breath. Her patterns spoke of how the war had drenched Coba in violence and ruin. The recovery had taken years, but they were healing. He would destroy their hard-won stability.

Kelric molded the structures to portray positive offworld effects. New technologies. Better educations. Health care. The mothers of his children had received nanomeds from him and passed them to his son and daughter; they would all live longer, healthier lives as a result. All Cobans could have those advantages. He wove patterns of Jeremiah; in allowing an offworlder here, Ixpar had dared take a chance. He had expected Jeremiah to create turmoil, but the youth's Quis had told another story, how he benefited Coba.

Ixpar turned his patterns into comparisons of Skolia and Earth, symbolized by Kelric and Jeremiah. One aggressive and large; the other gentle and scholarly. One overwhelming; the other seeking friendship. Jeremiah would never hurt anyone; Kelric was the military commander of an empire.

He saw himself through her Quis and wasn't sure he knew that man, one with great strength of character, but also one who wielded a power so immense, he could crush them without realizing it. He created patterns showing her how he would work with the Managers of Coba. He would sit at Quis with them. Ixpar's eyes blazed as she played fire opals, garnets, rubies. Angry dice. Never would she agree to have her Calani play Quis with other Managers! Her vehemence startled him. That he sat in the Assembly as Imperator—*that* she could deal with. But for him to reveal his Quis to other Managers went against every principle she held true.

So he showed her harsher reality: someday the Imperialate *would* find Coba. Without his intervention, it could do them great harm. Or perhaps, despite his best attempts to prevent it, the Traders would conquer her world and enslave her people. Coba should join the interstellar community on their terms. They should open or close their world according to *their* choice. They needed a gatekeeper. Him.

Ixpar countered with jagged patterns of destruction, of his life on Coba and the upheavals that followed. Her dice never accused, never damned. She blamed Coba. But he knew the truth. He had left terrible wounds here.

Kelric paused, subdued. This intense session, with someone he hadn't seen for ten years, drained him. She believed that to protect Coba, they should strengthen its isolation until they could survive even if he died. He took a breath and continued the session. With the utmost care, he molded new patterns. All the finesse he lacked in the blunt power of his mind and body, he put into his dice. He had been a prisoner before, on Coba, with neither the understanding nor opportunity to control his effect on the Quis. Now he and Ixpar had that knowledge. Together they could make a better world.

Her Quis called him idealistic. Her patterns revealed the deep differences between his people and hers, his way of life and that of Coba. Skolia would saturate the Quis until it swamped Coba's unique, irreplaceable culture.

It doesn't have to be that way, he answered. He sifted a new idea into his dice: Quis was like the mesh his people had created in Kyle space. To open a gate to the Kyle, they needed only a telop, or telepathic operator. The most gifted telops managed the star-spanning net that wove the Imperialate into a coherent whole. The Dyad created and powered that mesh.

Quis was a web. It, too, linked a civilization. Cobans communicated and took information from the world-spanning game; the more adept players acted as operators; the rare geniuses who dedicated their lives to Quis defined its highest levels. The best players read moods, even thoughts, from the dice. With both Quis and the Kyle, it became hard to tell where the web left off and the mind began. Intellect and emotion; technology and art; communication and intuition: it all blended. If Coba and Skolia combined their remarkable cultures, with care, they could achieve great marvels. At their best, they could produce a civilization greater than the sum of the two alone.

And at their worst? Ixpar asked.

He made no false promises; she could pick up nuances in his Quis he never meant to reveal. She knew his doubts, which had never left him. But she would also recognize his belief that he could protect Coba. She would have to choose which to trust.

Their session lasted hours. He had to return to Parthonia, yet long after he should have left for the starport, they continued to play. Their guards kept anyone from disturbing them. The people of Karn surely knew by now their Minister was playing Quis with a Calani returned from the dead. Windriders would carry the news to other cities.

Within days, all Coba would know: the Minister had sat at Quis with the Imperator.

Afternoon had melted into evening by the time Kelric and Ixpar pushed back from the table. He stood up, his joints creaking. "A good session," he said. More than good. It was worth ten years of solitaire.

"So it was," Ixpar murmured. She rose to her feet, and they stood together at the window above Karn. Long shadows from the mountains stretched across the city.

Leaning against the wall, Kelric gazed across the window at his wife. She looked as fit today as ten years ago. And as erotic. Quis with her had always had a sensual undercurrent.

"It's been a long time," he said.

She regarded him with smoky eyes. "Too long."

Kelric heard the invitation in her voice. He grasped her arm and drew her forward, into his embrace. But she resisted, her palms against his shoulders.

"I have a thing to say," she told him. "You should know."

That didn't sound good. "Know what?"

"I remarried."

Kelric stiffened. Had he misinterpreted her mood? His voice cooled. "You said you had no Akasi."

"I don't." Sadness touched her voice. "He passed away."

"Oh." *Idiot,* he told himself. "I'm sorry."

"It's been several years." Her face was pensive. "After the war, the Council felt I should remarry. As expected."

As expected. By law, the Minister had to marry a Calani, preferably the man with the highest level among the suitable candidates. "You mean Mentar?" As the previous Minister's consort, the Fourth Level had been more than twice Ixpar's age.

She nodded. "Together, he and I knew more of the Quis than anyone else alive. We had much in common."

He heard what she didn't say. "Did you love him?"

"I always had great affection for him."

"More as a father figure, I thought."

"I loved him." She paused. "In a quiet sort of way."

Kelric told her about Jeejon then. When he finished, Ixpar spoke with pain. "We have each done as we should. But sometimes, I wish . . . we hadn't lost so much."

"I, too," he said.

Ixpar took his hand. Then she led him to a private door of the Rosewood Suite.

That evening, in the last rays of gilded sunlight slanting through the windows, they lay in the rosewood bed where they had loved each other so many years ago. Outside, in the city below and the world beyond, life continued, people working, bargaining, playing Quis. Beyond Coba, stars shone, worlds turned in their celestial dance, and ships streaked among the settlements of thriving humanity. They were all oblivious to two people, neither of them young, who had lost so much in their lives, but for a brief time in each other's arms, found a bittersweet happiness.

XIV

Cathedral

Jaibriol was working at his private console when Tarquine strolled into their bedroom. Her windblown hair was tousled around her shoulders, and she had on a violet jumpsuit and boots suitable for weather far colder than here in the seaside capital.

"Where have you been?" Jaibriol asked.

She came over and leaned down to kiss him. "My pleasure at your company as well, my esteemed husband."

"Tarquine, don't."

She straightened up, her face composed as if she had just been out for a moment rather than slinking into the room three hours late. "You look tired. Perhaps you brood too much."

Jaibriol sat back and crossed his arms. "And I imagine you must be hungry, my dear wife, since you missed dinner."

She went to the antique wardrobe against the wall and took out a silken black nightshift. "I'm sure I'll satisfy my hunger," she murmured.

Jaibriol flushed, and tried not to stare as she changed into the shift. She had a beautifully toned body, long and lean, with flawless skin and legs that could wrap around him in ways that right now he didn't want to think about.

145

"I'm not as distractible as you think," he said, though she never deliberately played such games. Just being herself, she affected him even after ten years, perhaps more now that he knew what waited for him under the velvet bedcovers. But he couldn't let her sidetrack him. "Where were you tonight?"

She smoothed her shift into place around her thighs. "You could have asked Corbal to that dinner with Minister Gji." Her gaze darkened. "I'm sure he would have been pleased to join you. He's always happy to insinuate himself."

"He's my kin. And as a matter of fact, I did ask him."

"You trust him too much."

"Do I now?" He narrowed his gaze. "For some inexplicable reason, the Diamond Minister seems to think our good Lord Corbal is responsible for exposing the Janq merchant fleets as pirates."

Her response was barely detectable, just a quirk of her eyebrow. But Jaibriol noticed, and he dropped his barriers in time to catch a flicker of her hidden emotions. She hadn't expected him to figure out the business about Corbal.

Tarquine came over with that slow walk of hers that made his throat go dry and sweat break out on his brow. At times like this, he thought she ought to be required to register it as a deadly weapon.

She leaned against the console, her gaze languorous. "You seem flushed."

Jaibriol spoke coolly. "Corbal Xir is one of the savviest people I know. He's too smart to let someone divert blame to him for something he didn't do. No one could manage it." He paused. "Almost no one."

"I wouldn't know."

"No, of course not. You never do." He stood up, facing her eye to eye. "Don't undermine my advisors."

"You worry too much."

"I mean it, Tarquine." Married to her, he would be a fool not to worry. "And where the hell were you tonight?" Perhaps direct speech would startle her into an admission.

It didn't work. Her lips curved, and her lids lowered over her tilted eyes. "Such passionate language."

Jaibriol couldn't get anything from her mind except arousal. Over the years, she had learned to shield her thoughts, but at the moment, she wasn't trying. Knowing he excited her that much was more stimulating than any seduction. Hightons were supposed to marry for political or economic reasons, not passion, but with Tarquine, he was never sure about anything. She kept him forever off balance.

He turned and walked away from her. Unfortunately, that meant he was approaching the bed, which led to the obvious train of thought. Even as he tried not to imagine her body stretched across the sheets, he caught a hazy, sexualized image from her mind: himself, his eyes full of desire, his muscles straining against her as they made love. He almost groaned aloud. He had to get a grip.

Jaibriol swung around. "You set him up."

"Him?" Her gaze went up his body, and he remembered he had on only his trousers and a shirt open at the neck, not even his shoes. And of course, the more direct the speech between lovers, the more erotic the invitation.

"Corbal," he said, flustered. "You set up Corbal."

"How could I do that? I had no idea you would invite him in my stead."

"Like hell."

She frowned at him, and her exasperation felt real, though he wasn't certain if his claim about Corbal caused it or his insistence they keep talking instead of going to bed.

"Jai, I went to a meeting with the chief executive officers of the Onyx Sector textile guilds," she said. "It lasted longer than I expected."

He felt as if he had run into a wall. Such meetings were her job, after all. After a moment, he said, "Was it productive?"

"As much as ever, I suppose." She tilted her head. "What about your dinner with Gji?"

"I set the groundwork for suggesting trade relations with the Skolians." He shrugged. "We'll see." She would figure out soon enough the dinner had gone nowhere.

She glanced down at his console. "You're studying physics?"

"Just those implosions." He came back and touched a panel. A holomap formed in the air showing the locations of the five events. Although they were scattered in space, they lay roughly in a line, the most recent on the edge of Sphinx Sector. It was a long way from the Sphinx Sector Rim Base, but if they veered in their path, they would go through that military complex. He was convinced they were headed in that direction, though where the next implosion would occur, if it did at all, he had no idea.

The Lock was at the SSRB. Jaibriol had met Kelric there ten years ago, just after the Imperator killed the singularity. Now he wondered if Kelric had simply put it to sleep.

Maybe it was trying to wake up.

Tarquine trailed her finger over his lips. "If you relaxed more, you would worry less."

Jaibriol gave up trying to resist then and pulled her against him. As he closed his arms around her, she kissed him, her lips full and hungry. With a groan, he drew her to the bed, and they tumbled onto the velvet covers. He dragged off the shift she had so recently donned, ripping it apart. He was barely aware of her undressing him. She was fire and ice, tempting him into the depths of her passion, until he lost all sense of himself and melded with her, body and mind.

And when they lay sated and tangled in the rumpled sheets, he wondered if he had also lost part of his soul to her.

On the world Parthonia, Kelric waited in the Cathedral of Memories. Its sweeping wings graced Selei City, where elegant towers rose into the lavender sky. He gazed out a one-way window with a gold tint from its polarization. Like him, perhaps? Metal man, people said. A war machine.

Years ago on Coba, a friend had taught Kelric an ancient phrase that the fellow said was more about people than metal: "Iron chills whatever life it can hold, but never frozen is the touch of gold." In the times when Kelric wondered if he had lost his humanity as Imperator, he reminded himself of that saying. At least one person had seen him as warm rather than the case-hardened warlord.

The Royal Concourse, a wide path of white stone, led from the cathedral steps outside to an open-air coliseum about half a kilometer away. Metallic dust sparkled in the walkway, tiny nanosystems that monitored pedestrians, just as ISC security monitored every micron of the city. People lined the concourse and thronged the coliseum. Sunlight streamed everywhere, vendors sold food, and military police paced among the crowds. Breezes stirred flags with the Imperialate insignia on tall poles in front of the coliseum.

The Promenade was among the most popular Skolian festivals. A person needed stratospheric connections to obtain a ticket. But the spectacle would be broadcast throughout the Imperialate, and people everywhere would celebrate. Kelric hoped they enjoyed themselves.

As exciting as it might be for the rest of the universe, it was excruciating for him and his security teams.

A door swooshed behind him, and he turned to see Najo, the captain of his bodyguards. The Jagernaut crossed the chamber and saluted, arms out, wrists crossed, fists clenched.

Kelric returned the salute. "Any news from the port?"

"Nothing, sir." Sympathy showed in his eyes. "I'm sorry."

Kelric felt heavy. He wanted to withdraw from the too-bright day and sit in private. He couldn't, so he just said, "Thank you."

"They still might come."

"Perhaps." But Kelric knew it was too late for Ixpar to change her mind. He had failed to convince her.

Ten days had passed since his trip to Coba. Ixpar had declined to return with him, and he hadn't even had a chance to meet his children yet. He wanted them all by his side so much it hurt. But the day he had sworn his Calanya Oath to Ixpar, he had vowed to protect her Estate. He would keep his Oath. Just as he had spent all those years secluded in a Calanya, so now he would do the same for Coba, secluding a world.

Music filtered from outside into the chamber where Kelric stood. It was the Skolian anthem, "The Lost Desert." Its rapturous melody could lift the spirit, but its bittersweet quality often brought people to tears.

The House of Jizarian began the Promenade. A man announced them, his voice resonating from spinning orbs that floated above the concourse and coliseum. As the music shifted into the brighter theme of their House, the Jizarians poured out of the cathedral. Children ran down the steps and onto the Concourse. The adults followed in traditional costume, the women in red silken tunics and trousers, the men in shirts and trousers sewn with glinting threads. Their hair gleamed, mostly dark, but a few with lighter coloring. Kelric even saw a redhead.

The matriarch came last, normally with dignity and age, but this one was barely twenty-four, full of exuberance and vim, having inherited her title when her mother passed away several years ago. Her hair bounced about her shoulders as she waved to the crowd. The spectators cheered and threw flowers as the Jizarians nobles walked the concourse.

"An attractive House," Najo said. "Vibrant."

"So they are," Kelric said, intent on his console. Everything looked secure. He had an odd feeling, though, like a pressure on his mind. He checked the room where his family waited: Dehya, Roca, his siblings and their families, including children. It hurt to see them. In all his time on Coba, he had never been allowed to share in the lives of his children, nor did it seem now that it would ever happen.

Najo was watching his face. He spoke quietly. "They are happy and well, sir. Safe."

Kelric couldn't answer. He knew Najo didn't mean his brothers and sisters. His guard was too perceptive, and Kelric didn't think he could talk about it, not now, maybe never.

Outside, the Jizarians were entering the coliseum. The House of Nariz left the cathedral, a small family of moderate lineage in conservative dress, dark pants and blue shirts. The Akarads came next, a line of merchants with thriving fleets. The men wore red-brown robes over their clothes, but in a casual manner, letting them billow behind them in the breezes. The Shazarindas followed, less strict in their demeanor, wearing a great deal of yellow.

Kelric shifted his weight, restless and unsettled. He cycled through views of the city and countryside. Then he paged his intelligence chief in the orbital defense system.

The chief's voice came over the comm. "Major Qahot." She was the sister of the Qahot who worked for Kelric down here; together, they formed an inimitable security team.

"Any problems?" Kelric asked.

"None, sir. Is anything wrong?"

"No. Nothing." Kelric wished he knew what bothered him.

Outside, the women in the House of Kaaj were descending the cathedral steps. Just the women: they kept their men secluded. In their traditional garb, they resembled ancient Ruby warriors, with leather and metal armor, curved swords at their hips, and glinting spears. In real life they ran robotics corporations, but right now they reminded Kelric of paintings he had seen of Old Age queens on Coba.

He spoke into the comm. "Qahot, let me know if you notice anything strange."

"Aye, sir." She paused as voices spoke in the background. Then she said, "We had an unauthorized ship request to land about an hour ago."

Kelric tensed, afraid to hope. "Who? And why?" He had left authorization for Ixpar, but the Coban port and its ships were decades out of date. Maybe security here hadn't recognized the codes. Maybe

Ixpar hadn't realized that. Or maybe he was raising futile hopes within himself.

"They're tourists," Qahot said. "They didn't realize the festival is off-limits. We have them in custody, five men and six women, name of Turning. We're running checks."

"Did any of the women give her name as Ixpar Karn or ask for me?"

"No, sir," Qahot said. "Are you expecting someone?"

"No, not really." Kelric pushed down his disappointment. "Keep checking them out. Let me know if anything comes up."

"Yes, sir."

Outside, the Vibarrs were striding toward the coliseum. Their late matriarch, an aggressive powerhouse, had broken with tradition and named her son as her heir. Now he led the House, all bankers and lawyers and wildcatters, secure in their power and wealth. The Rajindias came next, the House that provided ISC with biomech adepts, the neurological specialists who treated psions. They were fierce, but less so than the hawklike Kaajs.

Hawk.

Insight came to Kelric like a rush, as a fire might flare at a campsite. Turning. *Tern*. A bird, yes, but they had the wrong one, probably because of language differences. Not *tern*. *Hawk*.

He spoke into his comm. "Qahot?"

"Here, sir," the major said.

"The leader of those tourists—is it a woman?"

"Yes, sir."

"With red hair?"

"No, sir."

Disappointment flooded over Kelric, even though he had kept trying not to hope.

Then Qahot added, "Her hair is orange. Like copper."

Kelric exhaled, long and slow, absorbing her words. Then he said, "I want to talk to her."

When the Majdas walked the Concourse, they left no doubt who dominated the noble Houses. With their black hair, high cheekbones, and great height, they embodied the quintessential Skolian aristocrat. Most of the women wore uniforms, primarily the dark green of the Pharaoh's Army, but also the blue of the Imperial Fleet. Vazar strode along in her Jagernaut leathers, skintight black with glinting silver studs.

The Majdas also secluded their princes. But the same indomitable will that infused their women manifested in the men. More than a few of their brothers and sons had defied tradition. They walked with the House, professors, architects, scientists, artists, and military officers, tall and imposing.

Naaj came last. Queen of Majda. She neither waved nor smiled. She simply walked. It was enough.

Najo stood with Kelric at the window. "Impressive."

Kelric smiled dryly. "They've raised it to an art."

Then the announcer said, "The Ruby Dynasty."

A deluge of children flooded out of the cathedral, Kelric's nephews and nieces, grandnephews, grandnieces, and on down the generations. They waved enthusiastically at the crowd, who cheered their approval of the dynasty's beautiful progeny. Kelric had intended that effect; the more his young kin charmed the public, the better. It was good public relations.

His siblings came next, first his sister Aniece, small and curved, with dark curls and gold eyes. Her husband Lord Rillia walked at her side. Kelric's brother Shannon followed, a willowy Blue Dale Archer with a bow and quiver on his back. Then Denric the schoolteacher. Soz should have been next; since her death, they had left a gap in the Promenade, in her honor.

After a moment, Havryl walked down the steps, his bronzed hair tossing in the wind, his toddler nestled in the crook of his arm. His wife came with him, holding their baby. Kelric's brother Del and his sister Chaniece, who were twins, would have followed, but they had stayed home, tending to the family duties. Another lull came in the Promenade, in honor of Althor, who had died in the Radiance War.

A hum sounded behind Kelric. He turned to see that Najo had moved to the door.

"Sir?" Najo looked at him with a question in his gaze.

Kelric nodded as if he were ready, though he wasn't and might never be. But he had set these events in motion and he would never turn back.

Najo tapped his gauntlet and the door shimmered open. A woman stood in the archway. She had piled her hair on her head and threaded it with blue beads. Her leather and bronzed clothes evoked the warriors of her ancestors, and a keen intelligence filled her gaze.

As Kelric crossed the chamber, the tread of his boots on the tiles seemed to echo. He stopped in front of her, trying to absorb that she stood *here,* out of context with every memory he had of her, in a place he had never expected to see her.

"Ixpar." For him, that one word, at this moment, held more meaning than he could sort out. He knew only that his life had improved immeasurably.

She inclined her head. "My greetings."

He indicated the window. "Will you join me?"

"It would be my honor."

He felt painfully formal. He knew her so well, yet he barely knew her at all. As they reached the window, exclamations from the crowd swelled over the monitors. With Ixpar at his side, Kelric turned to look out the window.

A woman was descending the steps, a vision in rose-hued silk that rippled around her figure. The announcer said, "Roca Skolia, Foreign Affairs Councilor."

"That is your mother?" Ixpar asked. When Kelric nodded, she said, "No wonder."

He glanced at her. "No wonder what?"

Her voice had that smoky quality. "No wonder you were the man whose face launched a thousand windriders into battle."

He crooked a smile at her. "What, it scared them that much?"

"Hardly," she murmured.

It didn't surprise him that she knew the tale of Helen of Troy from Earth's history; she would never have allowed Jeremiah to study Coba if she hadn't first studied him and his people. Kelric took her hands. "It's not too late to change your mind." He needed her to be sure she wanted this.

She spoke quietly. "I thought a long time before I boarded that ship in the port. Is this a mistake? No clear answer shows itself when I project futures with my Quis. Some patterns evolve into ruin. Others are incredible. Even beautiful." She stopped. He waited, and finally she said, "The time comes when we must take a risk. To decide our own future."

An odd silence fell over the room, coming from outside. Kelric hadn't realized how noisy the crowds were until they quieted. He glanced at the window—and froze.

A robed and cowled figure with four guards stood at the top of the cathedral steps. A Talha scarf wrapped around his head within the cowl, hiding his face, except for his eyes.

Kelric shot a look at Ixpar.

She answered his unspoken question by saying, simply, "Yes."

His emotions swelled, too jumbled to untangle. He stared at the robed figure. "I can't see him."

"He's never gone in public without robes," Ixpar said. "He's never even left the Calanya."

Dismay surged within him. "I would never force—"

She set her hand on his arm. "He *wanted* to come." Dryly she added, "Manager Varz was the one who balked. It took a lot to convince her."

It didn't surprise Kelric. It stunned him that she had allowed her Calani to travel at all, let alone off the planet. Apparently the current Varz Manager was more human than the monster he had known.

The announcer hadn't spoken; he was probably reading whatever notes Kelric's officers had delivered to him when the geneticists finished their tests. Kelric had ordered the tests the moment Ixpar told him who had come with her. He could almost hear the question whispered among the spectators. *Who is that?* It had been Kelric's question as well, for twenty-eight years. Finally he would have an answer.

With firm motions, the man pushed back his hood and pulled down his Talha. Kelric doubted anyone watching right now except he and Ixpar understood the significance of that action. A Hakaborn prince never showed his face to the public.

The man had large eyes. Violet eyes. His curly hair was as dark as the Hakaborn, but it glinted with metallic highlights. He stood tall and strong, his head lifted. He had a strange look, though, as if he were about to step off a cliff. Kelric knew the courage it took for him to do this, he who had surely never expected even to leave seclusion, let along walk before trillions on an interstellar broadcast. It was a quieter bravery than the dramatic acts of the Jagernauts Kelric had known at that age, but that made it no less real.

Then the announcer said, "Jimorla Haka Varz Valdoria."

Startled voices erupted among the crowd, and Kelric released a silent exhale. To use the Valdoria name at this point in the Promenade identified Jimorla as his child, as binding a declaration as any legal document. He had hoped and believed it for so long, but he had never been sure. Jimorla wasn't a Ruby psion, so he couldn't use the Skolia name, but he was Kelric's firstborn in every other aspect and would take his place in the line of succession to the Ruby Throne.

Jimorla visibly braced his shoulders. He descended the stairs with his guards and strode along the Concourse, his robe billowing out behind him. For the first time, a Calani walked openly on another world. Coba—and Skolia—were changed forever. Quis would come to the Imperialate.

A strained voice interrupted his thoughts. "Sir," Najo said.

Kelric turned to see Najo standing by the console, which blazed with lights. Najo had that same expression he had worn when Kelric revealed he had spent eighteen years on Coba, the look of a man who knew he stood witness to the making of history.

"People are trying to contact you," Najo said.

"Who?" Kelric could guess: the leaders of an empire. They had just learned they had a new crown prince.

"The First Councilor of the Assembly," Najo said. "General Majda, Admiral Bloodmark, Primary Tapperhaven, your mother, your brothers, your sister, the gene team you summoned, and several councilors of the Inner Circle."

Kelric noticed the list didn't include Dehya. She had just discovered the existence of a prince who preceded her own son in age, yet she waited. She understood Kelric in a way few others could.

"I imagine they're surprised," Kelric allowed.

Najo looked as if he considered that a monumental understatement. But he said only, "Yes, sir."

Kelric wasn't ready to talk. He wanted these moments for himself. "Tell them I'll contact them after the Promenade."

Voices surged outside. Startled, Kelric turned back. A young woman had appeared at the top of the cathedral stairs—a girl whose skin, hair, and eyes shimmered gold.

The announcer said, "Roca Miesa Varz Valdoria—" He took a breath that everyone on thousands of worlds and habitats in three empires would hear, a sound that would become another page of history. Then he added, "Skolia."

Until that moment, Kelric hadn't been one hundred percent certain. By using the Skolia name, the announcer verified what he had always believed: his daughter was a Ruby psion.

Someday she would take her place in the Dyad.

She descended the steps alone, but the defenses of an empire protected her. Her true name was Rohka, the Coban version of Roca. Kelric felt as if he were sundering in two. Rohka, the miracle he and Savina had given life sixteen years ago, had come into the world as her mother died. The hours Kelric had spent cradling his infant child in his oversized arms had been the only light in his grief-shattered life.

He would be forever grateful to Ixpar for freeing him from Varz, but he had mourned, too, for the Varz Manager had retaliated by denying him his child.

Jimorla had reached the coliseum, and officers ushered him to the area reserved for the Imperator's children. He was the first person to sit there in a century. On the Concourse, Rohka's stride never faltered, though Kelric recognized the overwhelmed look she tried to hide. He had seen the same expression on her mother's face when Savina felt daunted but refused to let fear diminish her spirit.

Welcome, Kelric thought to his children. They couldn't reply; even if they had known how to interpret mental input, they were too far away. He didn't even know if his son was an empath or had the rarer telepathic traits Kelric shared with his family.

And yet . . . he felt certain a man answered, distant but clear, the thought in Teotecan: *It is my honor.*

A girl's thought suddenly resonated in his mind, young and raw, untrained but full of power. *And mine, Father.*

The speaker said, simply, "Kelric Skolia, Imperator of Skolia, and Ixpar Karn, Minister of Coba."

Kelric and Ixpar descended the cathedral steps together. The crowds had cheered the Houses and Ruby Dynasty. They were silent now, whether in shock or respect, he didn't know. He had never been comfortable in public displays; he preferred to stay in the background. But he had waited ten years for this—no, twenty-eight. That was when he had first seen Ixpar, as he awoke in a sickroom on Coba with the fourteen-year-old Ministry successor leaning over him. It had taken nearly three decades to bring that moment full circle, decades that had changed him more than he would ever have imagined. Today, his life was complete.

XV

The Bitterfruit Tree

The Opal Hall in the Qox Palace gleamed like an iridescent pearl. Its luminous moonstone walls shifted with traces of aqua and marine. Jaibriol sat on a white couch across from Parizian Sakaar, the Highton Aristo who served as his Trade Minister. Jaibriol's aide, Robert, had taken one of the wing chairs at the opal table. So had Tarquine, who had at least showed up this time.

Jaibriol felt ill. They were going over reports from the guilds that bred and trained providers. Before he had claimed his throne, he had served in the Dawn Corps of the Allied Worlds, which had helped newly freed worlds recover after the war. He had seen the pavilions where Silicate Aristos "designed" providers, the labs and examination tables, the discipline, memorization, testing, erotica, and isolation rooms. He had met providers huddled in their cubicles, slaves his own age or younger, staggeringly beautiful. The collars and cuffs they wore extended picotech into their bodies until the threads became so interwoven with their neural systems, it was impossible to remove them without surgery.

None of those providers had a name. None knew their age. None could read or write. An inventory had listed them by serial number.

That night, Jaibriol had walked out among the whispering trees and been violently sick in the beautiful forest the Silicates had grown to adorn their pavilion. He had leaned over with his arms around his stomach and retched again and again until he felt as if he were tearing out his insides.

The Trade Minister sitting here had no idea of Jaibriol's reaction. Sakaar didn't consider his job abhorrent. He went over the files on the trillion-dollar industry as if he were reporting on inanimate objects. Jaibriol could tell the meeting disturbed Robert, whose father had been "trained" in a Silicate facility. But his aide accepted it as part of Eubian life. He had never known anything different. The other aides didn't think about it at all; they were simply doing their jobs, recording files and organizing statistics.

As Finance Minister, Tarquine tracked Silicate corporations and ensured they followed accepted business practices, at least as defined by Aristos. She hid her response behind the icy façade she had perfected, but Jaibriol caught the truth from her mind. The meeting revolted her. It was why she had altered herself so she could no longer transcend; late in her life, she had developed a trait shared by no other Aristos he knew except Corbal and Calope Muze. Remorse. His empress might be one of the most prodigiously crooked human beings alive, but she wasn't brutal. She could no more bring herself to inflict pain on providers than could he.

Yet sometimes in the sultry hours of the night, when Tarquine held him in her arms, he felt the hunger within her, her memory of transcendence. Deep within, a part of her wanted to hurt him, and that darkness chilled Jaibriol.

At the moment, she was frowning as she studied a holofile Sakaar had handed to her, a copy of the one he gave Jaibriol with reports on various Silicate facilities.

"This entry on the Garnet sale during the third octet last year," Tarquine was saying. "It appears less eminent than the predictions of my Evolving Intelligence codes."

Jaibriol blinked. "Less eminent" sounded like her way of saying the profits were lower than expected. Outwardly, the Trade Minister seemed unaffected by her observation. When Jaibriol concentrated on his mind, though, he realized Sakaar was hiding an unease greater than such a minor comment deserved.

"It is difficult to estimate eminence with elevation," Sakaar said.

Jaibriol almost laughed at the bizarre phrasing. Sakaar had a point, though; such predictions often weren't accurate.

Tarquine scanned another holopage. "And here, under the Mica Class Three-Eight product line, the fifth octet subprofits margin is only one-third as eminent as one might foresee."

Jaibriol wasn't even certain what she had said. Whatever it was, though, Sakaar didn't like it. With his mental barriers at full force, he could tell only that Sakaar was uncomfortable. Too uncomfortable. Her comments didn't sound threatening to Jaibriol, but the Trade Minister thought otherwise.

Jaibriol had long ago learned the value of letting his people probe and strike while he listened. Among Hightons, whose discourse branched like verbal fractals, an emperor who spoke so little frightened people. It could be useful; they often attributed more intrigue to his silence than it warranted. In his first years as emperor, when he had been a desperate teenager totally out of his depth, the silences had protected him, hiding just how thoroughly he had no idea what he was doing. Now they had become a tool.

"Claims of inconsistency would be premature," Sakaar said.

That caught Jaibriol's attention. It sounded as if Sakaar had warned Tarquine to stop accusing him without proof. Among Aristos, where appearance and reputation were everything, an unsubstantiated accusation ranked as a crime worse than marrying outside one's caste. Which of course turned such accusations into valued currency, but only if the accuser could make them stick. If not, the accuser suffered censure, loss of reputation, even legal penalties if the accused went to the courts. Sakaar's reaction was way out of proportion to Tarquine's comments, which made Jaibriol suspect his Trade Minister far more than if Sakaar had said nothing.

"Perhaps they would be premature," Tarquine answered, her voice smooth. "But premature development is no longer a danger with so many advances in modern science."

"Unless the development is itself flawed," Sakaar said.

Watching Tarquine, Jaibriol suspected she had evidence of some Machiavellian scheme Sakaar had concocted, and she wanted him to sweat. Either that, or she was bluffing the hell out of the Trade Minister.

Robert's wrist comm beeped. An instant later, Jaibriol's buzzed, Sakaar's pinged, and Tarquine's hummed.

"What the blazes?" Sakaar said.

Jaibriol lifted his comm. "Qox here," he said. As soon as he moved, the others responded to their pages.

Corbal's urgent voice came out of the mesh. "Jai, turn on the Third Hour broadcast. You'll want to see this."

Puzzled, Jaibriol nodded to Robert, who had somehow managed the feat of simultaneously being attentive to the emperor and answering his comm. Robert flicked his finger through a holicon above the mesh film in his lap, and a holoscreen activated on the wall across from Jaibriol. As the others turned around to look, images formed in front of the screen. It was a Skolian transmission. The Eubian translation scrolled beneath it in three-dimensional glyphs, but he didn't need them; he was fluent in Skolian Flag.

The broadcast showed the Cathedral of Memories, a building of sparkling white stone, windows of blue glass, and flying buttresses that were works of art. A tall man was striding with four guards along a concourse to a huge arena. His dark skin had a disquietingly familiar gold sheen.

". . . must be his son," a newscaster was saying, her voice taut with excitement. "It's the only way he could walk in the Promenade *after* the Ruby Dynasty, but before Imperator Skolia.

A chill started at the bottom of Jaibriol's spine and crept upward. Did she mean Kelric Skolia's son? *What* son?

"Who the flipping hell is that?" Sakaar demanded.

Jaibriol had no doubt that normally some Aristo would have responded with a veiled barb at the Trade Minister's lapse of language. But the only other Aristos present were Tarquine and himself, and he was far too riveted by the broadcast to give a flaming jump about what Sakaar said.

If he understood the broadcaster, the next person to walk the concourse would be Kelric. It meant the promenade was almost done; only the Ruby Pharaoh and her family followed the Imperator. But when the cathedral doors opened, a girl with gold skin walked out onto the top of the steps, the wind blowing back her distinctive gold hair.

"This is incredible!" the newscaster said. "A *second* child has appeared."

A man spoke, apparently another commentator. "I don't think much doubt exists as to her parentage, with that coloring."

"Why aren't they announcing her name?" the woman said.

Jaibriol was wondering the same thing. Didn't Kelric know his own children? The girl stood waiting, her head held high. He could tell what she felt, though, even if sensing her mood was impossible across interstellar distances. After a lifetime of associating emotions with people's behavior, and ten years among Hightons, whose language was as much gesture and posture as words, he read body language like a book. She was scared.

A new voice spoke, what sounded like the official announcer at the Promenade itself. "Roca Miesa Varz Valdoria—" The man inhaled deeply. Then he said, "Skolia."

"It can't be!" Sakaar shouted.

"Gods forbid," Tarquine muttered. "*Another* one of them?"

Jaibriol stared at her, his hands clammy. "Did you know?"

"I had no idea," she said. "But they must be legitimate heirs. He was wearing marriage guards when I bought him. He told me his ex-wife gave them to him."

This was news to Jaibriol; none of ESComm's files on Kelric included anything on an *ex*-wife. "Why was he still wearing them?"

"He said he loved her."

Jaibriol tried to fathom her reaction. If what she had just said bothered her, it showed on neither her face nor the surface of her mind. With Sakaar in the room, though, he couldn't let down his barriers enough to be certain.

The broadcasters continued talking, excitement spilling into their words. Jaibriol tuned them out, his focus solely on the scene. The doors of the cathedral opened again—and the Imperator walked out. He towered, broad of shoulder, long in the legs, massive in physique, huge and gold. His square chin, chiseled features, and close-cropped hair enhanced the effect, as did the grey at his temples. When Jaibriol had met him ten years ago, Kelric had been dying. Even then his presence had overpowered. Now he stood like an indomitable war god surveying his realms.

Nor was he alone. A woman stood at his side, nearly as tall as Lord Skolia. Fiery hair was upswept on her head, and her eyes blazed, fierce and flooded with intelligence. She was one of the few people Jaibriol had ever seen who could match the sheer force of personality that Kelric projected.

And this time Jaibriol *felt* Tarquine's reaction. It jumped within her, so intense it burst past his barriers. *Anger.* In her mind, she owned Kelric, though he had attained his freedom ten years ago. To see him with another woman violated her sense of balance at a level so deep, it burned within her. In that moment, Jaibriol didn't want peace with Kelric's empire, he wanted to obliterate the Imperialate.

The Promenade announcer said, "Kelric Skolia, Imperator of Skolia, and Ixpar Karn, Minister of Coba."

"Minister?" Tarquine raised an eyebrow. "It seems you and the Imperator have something in common."

Jaibriol felt as if she had socked him in the stomach. The Aristo edge to her sarcasm came from her anger at discovering Kelric had a wife again—this one astonishingly formidable—and Jaibriol couldn't bear to see how much it affected her. He had one thing in common with Kelric: Tarquine. He couldn't reply, he could only stare at the broadcast as Kelric and his long-legged wife strode down the concourse.

Then the Ruby Pharaoh and her consort walked out onto the cathedral steps. The first time Jaibriol had seen a Promenade, seven years ago, they had appeared alone. Today their son accompanied them, a boy of eight. They had named him Althor, in honor of his uncle, who had died in the Radiance War.

Normally their heir would go first, as Kelric's had done. But not this child. Jaibriol knew about him from the ESComm files. The pharaoh and her consort were too closely related; they carried the same deleterious mutations in their DNA. The boy had been born without substantial parts of his body, including his legs. Hightons would never have allowed such a birth, but Althor's parents had cherished him. Over the years, surgeons had worked on the boy, giving him biomech limbs and organs, and an internal web more extensive than even for a Jagernaut. He appeared normal now, tall for his age, though thin. He walked slowly with the stiff gait of someone unused to his limbs, and his parents stayed with him. But he walked.

An exhale came from the crowd at the sight of the pharaoh's heir. The Promenade had served its purpose, assuring the Skolian people that their leaders were strong and well, and that their ruling house would thrive for generations to come.

Jaibriol wished he could stop the broadcast. He felt as if he had eaten from the bitterfruit tree of Aristo mythology. He lived a nightmare day after day, with no reprieve and no hope of escaping the pain or fear. He had to sit here and watch his family, knowing they shared the Ruby bonds forever denied to him, that they would always have the joy of that love. He would never know those gifts they took for granted. He couldn't even risk siring an heir with his own wife.

Jaibriol stood up abruptly, knocking the holofile on his lap to the floor. He had to leave before his crumbling defenses fell apart. Everyone scrambled to their feet. He nodded curtly to Robert and his guards, indicating they should accompany him.

Without a word, Jaibriol strode from the room.

Kelric stood with Ixpar at a starburst window in a tower of the Sunrise Palace on the planet of Parthonia. Outside, the mountains stretched in every direction, rolling in swell after swell of green, with blue-violet sky above and lowering dark clouds misting their peaks. Late afternoon sunrays slanted across Ixpar's face, silvering her grey eyes.

"Shall we?" Ixpar murmured.

Kelric took a breath. "Yes." It had taken years for this moment to come, and he had thought it never would happen. He would wait no longer.

She touched his arm with a gesture he remembered, as if she were simultaneously offering support and assuring herself he was real. Then she flicked her finger across the panel of the wrist comm he had given her this afternoon. It was odd to see her with Skolian technology, which had been forbidden to Cobans for so long. Even after only a few hours, she used it with ease. It had always been that way with her; sometimes she seemed to pick up ideas faster than he could articulate them.

A deep voice came out of her comm mesh. "Najo here, sir."

Ixpar quirked her eyebrow at Kelric and mouthed, *Sir?*

"He thinks you're me, because it's my comm." Kelric motioned at the device. "Go ahead."

Ixpar lifted her arm and spoke in accented but fluent Skolian Flag. "Secondary Najo, this is Ixpar Karn. Have Imperator Skolia's children arrived yet?"

Silence followed her words. Although Kelric was separated from his bodyguards by a wall and enough distance to mute his reception of their moods, he knew them well enough to interpret Najo's response; hearing Ixpar jolted him. His guards had been laudably discreet, given the curiosity he felt consuming them. They had no idea what to make of Ixpar.

Then Najo said, "Their flyer is en route, Your Majesty."

Ixpar blinked as if the comm had sprouted two heads. She touched the mute panel so Najo couldn't hear her. "My what?"

Kelric smiled. "Majesty. It's your title, as my consort."

"Are you one of these, too?"

"Well, yes. I go by Lord Skolia, though."

She regarded him dubiously. "*Majesty* seems rather grandiose. More like a mountain than a person."

"You can use your Coban title if you prefer. Just tell him."

She touched the send panel. "Thank you, Secondary Najo. Also, you may call me Minister Karn."

"Understood, ma'am." He paused. "Are you with Imperator Skolia? I have a message for him."

Kelric had no doubt "a message" was a prodigious understatement. Gods only knew how many people wanted to reach him. He and Ixpar had escaped the coliseum by the roof, where they boarded a flyer. They had spoken with no one. His children had sat below his box in the coliseum, and he had had them escorted to the palace as soon as the Promenade ended. If he had asked them to wait while he came through the tunnel to their box, people would have had time to catch up with them. He had waited twenty-six years for this moment. Maybe his children would accept him, maybe not, but he wanted whatever happened to be private.

He activated his comm. "Najo, tell anyone who wishes to speak with me that I will talk to them this evening."

"Yes, sir. They are rather urgent, though."

Kelric could imagine. "They'll have to wait." Ixpar was watching him, her stately figure silhouetted against the arched window. "Let me know as soon as my children arrive."

Najo answered quietly. "They're here, sir."

Kelric froze. What if they rejected the father they had never met?

After a moment, Najo said, "Imperator Skolia?"

Kelric took a deep breath. "Please escort them in."

An eternity passed for Kelric in the moments before anyone entered. The world seemed caught in another bubble, but this time he wasn't certain if he was within it or on the outside. The door opened, leaving Najo in its archway, a towering Jagernaut in black with a huge gun on his hip. He had a strange look, as if he had gone through a tunnel packed with the unexpected and come out the other end, no less stunned than before but able to accept whatever he found. He stepped aside, into the room—

A girl appeared in the doorway.

In that moment, Kelric *knew*. He needed no DNA, Promenade announcers, or Coban historians to tell him. Like knew like. Her mind glowed like the sun, as it had even before her birth, when she was barely more than a dream. She stared at him with his own eyes. She wore suede trousers and a gold shirt, so much like her mother, Savina; but unlike Savina, his daughter was tall, nearly the height of her namesake, Roca Skolia.

It was several moments before he could speak. Finally the Teotecan words came to him. "My greetings, Rohka."

His daughter inhaled abruptly, as if his voice reminded her that she needed to breathe. She walked forward, and if she knew anyone else but Kelric was present, she gave no sign. She stopped a few paces away from him. "Father?"

Somehow he smiled. "It seems I have that good fortune."

"Cuaz and Khozaar me!" she said, invoking Coba's capricious wind gods.

Her flustered expression so reminded him of Savina, he didn't know whether to laugh or cry. "Your mother used to say that."

Rohka hesitated. "Will you tell me about her?"

His voice softened. "Gladly."

He hadn't spoken about Savina since her death. Perhaps talking to Rohka would help him close the chapter on that terrible loss, so he truly felt free to love Ixpar. His bond to Ixpar had begun to form that first day he saw her leaning over him like a fire-haired angel, but so much had intervened in the fourteen years between when he met her and married her. Including Savina. It took him a long time to grasp his emotions; he was like a glacier flowing down a mountain. Patience wasn't a common trait of Coban women when it came to love. Savina had burst into his life like a solar flare, melted his reticence, and loved him passionately for five years. Losing her had nearly killed him. Only Ixpar had understood, and given him the time he needed to come alive again.

It finally dawned on Rohka that Kelric was standing next to the leader of her civilization. She flushed, her cheeks rosy, and bowed to Ixpar. "My greetings, ma'am."

Ixpar inclined her head. "And mine to you, Rohka."

A rustle stirred in the doorway. Looking up, Kelric saw Strava enter the room. She gave him a questioning look.

Taking a breath, Kelric nodded. Strava didn't turn around, but lights flashed on her gauntlets, as happened when his guards used their bio-mech to communicate. Then she stepped to the side of the entrance.

A man walked through the doorway.

Kelric saw him, but his tension was so high, he couldn't focus on the man's face. It was a blur. Then everything snapped into place and his heart wrenched. Jimorla. His firstborn. His heir.

Jimorla's face was achingly familiar, though Kelric had never seen him before today. He had the same violet eyes as Kelric's father. His brown hair curled in disarray, tousled from the wind. A gold shimmer overlaid his skin, but he had inherited his darker coloring from his mother, Rashiva. He also had her exotic beauty and upward tilted eyes, but in him it had the dramatic masculine strength of his desert ancestors.

His son showed no hint of a smile. By custom, a man from a desert estate never smiled in the presence of a woman unless only his kin were present. His Oath forbade him to speak to anyone Outside the Varz Calanya. Even knowing that, Kelric hadn't been able to stop himself from hoping Jimorla would speak, for his son had already defied tradition by traveling to Parthonia and walking in the Promenade. But those were breaks with custom, not the Oath. As much as Kelric knew that intellectually, he couldn't help but wonder if Jimorla's impassive silence came from more than his Oath.

Kelric spoke in Teotecan. "I am pleased you are here." It sounded as stilted as it felt.

And his son said, "I am honored."

An ache swelled within Kelric, one hard to define, for he had never understood his own emotions as well as he read those from other people. This came from deep within him, full of warmth, as if it held his heart.

"How is your mother?" Kelric asked.

"She is well." Defiance flashed in Jimorla's eyes. "As is my father, Raaj."

It felt like a punch. *What did you expect?* Kelric thought. Raaj had raised Jimorla. It hadn't been until age thirteen that Jimorla learned the identity of his biological father. Kelric knew he would have to work to become a father to his children. They were part of him, yet they were strangers. Their lives had been so different than his, they had no intersection with him.

Except for Quis.

He couldn't suggest playing Quis to Jimorla; it would be a great offense, especially given that his son had come without the Manager of his Estate. It astonished him that Stahna Varz had let her Calani travel to another world. It went against every tradition, custom, and expectation of her people. It violated Jimorla's Calanya Oath. No Manager would allow such, yet the most rigid of all Coban queens had done exactly that.

"I'm grateful Manager Varz accepted this visit," Kelric said. That sounded so paltry for what he felt.

"It wasn't Stahna who made the decision," Ixpar said.

Kelric stiffened and stared at her. *What had she done?* Started another war?

Whatever Ixpar saw in his expression, it made her smile. "Don't worry," she said. "I haven't kidnapped anyone."

Jimorla looked from her to Kelric, his gaze intent. Then he shrugged off the robe he wore over his shirt and trousers and folded it over his arm. At first Kelric wasn't certain why, except for the room being warm. Then he saw the gold bands in his son's sleeves, partially covered by the loose cloth. Three Calanya rings gleamed on each of his upper arms. The top band showed the rising sun insignia of Haka Estate, where he had been born, and the middle one had the Varz clawcat.

The third ring bore the Karn althawk.

Gods almighty. His son was a Karn Calani. Ixpar had made him a Third Level, probably one of the few on the planet, and he had achieved it at an incredibly young age. Jimorla had lived in the Calanya at two of the most powerful Estates, Haka and Varz, both adversaries of Karn. That combined with his heritage would make his Calanya contract exorbitantly expensive. It must have put even Ixpar's Estate into debt.

Another realization hit him. His son could have refused the Third Level. That he had accepted it, though it meant leaving his home to live at an Estate he probably viewed as hostile, meant more to Kelric than he knew how to say.

Jimorla was watching him, and Kelric saw the uncertainty in his eyes. He had no more idea how his father would accept him than Kelric did about his son.

Kelric's voice caught. Looking at both his children, he said, "Welcome to my home."

And to my heart.

XVI

Pillar of Light

Jaibriol stood in the Silver Room of the Qox Palace and studied the life-size holo image before him. It showed two military men, but they weren't ESComm officers. No, these were the warlords of his enemies. They were standing on a stage, listening to a speech. The one with steel-grey hair was Chad Barzun, who headed up the Skolian Imperial Fleet. The other was Admiral Ragnar Bloodmark.

A door hummed behind Jaibriol. He didn't need to turn; he saw his visitor's face reflected in the screen behind the holos. Tarquine came to stand at his side, studying the image of the Skolian commanders. Her faint scent drifted to him, astringent and bracing.

"An interesting couple," she said. "Did you know Bloodmark is one-quarter Scandinavian?"

"I didn't realize you were that familiar with ISC." He knew about Bloodmark because he had read the ESComm dossiers on all the top Skolian officers, but he hadn't thought she was interested in military details.

"I make it my policy to know the major players." She indicated Bloodmark. "He may look like a nobleman, but his mother was space-slag poor. Bad economics in that bloodline."

"That may be," Jaibriol said. "But he operates now at the top level of Skolian hierarchies."

Tarquine waved her hand in dismissal. "That can't be too difficult. They are only Skolians, after all."

He raised an eyebrow. "As opposed to, say, Iquars?"

She gave him a half-lidded stare, like a feral cat. "Iquars are in a class by ourselves."

When she looked at him that way, it could make him forget why he didn't like being the emperor of Eube. "So I've noticed."

She tilted her head at the images. "Why are you interested in these two?"

He refocused his attention on less flammable matters than his wife. "Of all the Skolian commanders, Barzun seems the one most likely to support a peace treaty."

"That's hardly saying much," Tarquine said, "given the allergic reactions they all have to the concept."

"I suppose. Bloodmark was more intractable at the talks, though. He carries a great deal of weight with ISC." Jaibriol rubbed his chin. "In fact, he has more seniority than Barzun. But the Imperator promoted Barzun over him. I wonder why."

"I take it you have a hypothesis?"

"I'm not sure." As much as he disliked discussing Kelric with her, she knew the Imperator better than did any other Aristo. "I had the impression during our negotiations that the pharaoh was the only one willing to talk peace. But maybe Imperator Skolia isn't as intransigent as we thought."

"Don't let them fool you," Tarquine said. "The Allieds have a very old saying. 'Good cop, bad cop.'"

"What is a 'cop?'"

"Police officer. When you want something from adversaries, you set two people to work with them. One person is easy on the target. Softens them up. The other is tough. Of course it's never true; they play off each other." She flicked her finger through several holicons on her wrist comp, and the image in front of them changed to one of the Ruby Pharaoh.

Jaibriol almost jerked; the pharaoh looked like a delicate version of his mother. The pharaoh was ethereal rather than robust, and where his mother had been fierce, the pharaoh seemed gentle. But both women had the same large green eyes and heart-shaped face. It hurt to see. He longed just once to talk to his Ruby kin, not about politics or war, but about the family he would never know.

"See how fragile she looks," Tarquine mused. "But she isn't in the least. She is steel."

"I wouldn't know." He kept his gaze on the holo, unable to meet Tarquine's gaze.

His wife spoke in a low voice. "They say the Ruby Pharaoh and her niece—the previous Imperator—were more alike than anyone realized."

Jaibriol felt as if she had caught him with a rope and spun him around. What did Tarquine expect, to hear him admit Soz Valdoria, the late Imperator, was his mother?

"People say many things," he told her.

"So they do. For example, that gold is softer than steel."

Gold? He gave her an incredulous look. "You think the *Imperator* is more likely than the pharaoh to consider peace?"

Tarquine thought for a moment. "I'm not sure. He's every bit the military commander. But I suspect he is less adamant against it than he seems."

As uncomfortable as this discussion made Jaibriol, her interpretations intrigued him. "Pharaoh Dyhianna is the ruler, though. Imperator Skolia answers to her and the First Councilor."

Tarquine gave him a dour look. "What sort of brain-addled decision was that? She deposes that Assembly, a very sensible thing to do. And then what. She gives them back half of the power. Maybe she would give me half if I asked."

Tarquine on the Ruby Throne. What a terrifying concept. He said only, "The blended government works."

She waved her hand. "That's a non sequitur."

"What, that their government is sound?" As much as he found her canny mind fascinating, she could exasperate the blazes out of him. "How the hell is that a random comment?"

"Well, they are Skolians," she allowed. "I guess one should make allowances for their bizarre notions."

Given that he was half Skolian, Jaibriol decided his blood pressure would remain lower if he changed the subject. He touched his wrist comp and replaced the holo with an image of Barcala Tikal, the First Councilor, who shared the rule of Skolia with the Ruby Pharaoh. A lean man with regular features, he had brown hair streaked with grey.

"What do you think of him?" Jaibriol asked.

She considered Tikal. "Sounder finances in his Line. But he could do a lot better if he paid more attention to his finances and wasted less time on the Assembly."

Jaibriol threw up his hands. "Tarquine, he's the Assembly leader! That's his job, for flaming sake."

She regarded him through sleepy eyes. "We certainly are direct today."

Jaibriol crossed his arms, refusing to let her distract him. "We would also like to be enlightened today, sometime before the sun sets."

Her lips curved upward. "Indeed. About what?"

"Tell me more about Tikal."

She studied the holo of Tikal as if he were a puzzle. "The pharaoh took a possibly fatal risk when she let him live. I doubt he has ever stopped thinking how much safer he would be if the Ruby Dynasty no longer held power." She tilted her head. "Of course, he is Skolian. You never know how they will act."

"That's because they aren't as predictable as Aristos." He didn't say "as unimaginative," but she knew what he meant.

"*Predictable* isn't the word for us," Tarquine murmured. "We're efficient. When methods work, why change them?"

"That assumes everyone shares the same view of what works."

"Oh, they never do," she said. "Consider your Diamond Minister, Izar Gji. He wants to increase commerce. He's far more interested in wealth than in war. The export coalition he and the other Diamonds were putting together had the potential to be highly lucrative. But they needed the Janq Line to make it work. After the Skolians stole the Janq merchant ships and caused such a ruckus, the coalition fell apart."

"The Skolians didn't 'steal' anything," Jaibriol said, annoyed. "They confiscated pirate ships that committed criminal activities in Skolian space."

She waved her hand in dismissal. "It doesn't change the outcome. Now that the coalition has fallen apart, Minister Gji will be looking for other ventures to achieve his goals." She paced in front of the holo, thinking. "Gji wants to expand trade routes. Approached in the right way—" She stopped in front of Jaibriol, blocking the holo of the First Councilor. "The *predictable* way—he may even consider exotic options."

He knew "exotic" meant Skolian. "He didn't seem interested to me," Jaibriol said, remembering his lackluster dinner with the Minister. "Nor is it only Gji I have to convince. I need the support of my Trade Minister." Flatly he added, "And Sakaar sure as hell won't give it to me."

Tarquine's gaze darkened. "Trade Minister Sakaar has many concerns he needs to consider."

Jaibriol thought back to what she had said to Sakaar during their meeting about the Silicate pavilions, her implication that she had discovered a problem in his reports. He had been so rattled by the broadcast about Kelric's unexpected children that he hadn't yet followed up on the Sakaar matter.

"Concerns such as—?" Jaibriol let the question hang.

"Sakaar hides well," she said. "So well, in fact, that he could vanish from almost anyone's sight. Unfortunately for him, he has to deal with me rather than 'almost anyone.'"

Jaibriol didn't envy the Trade Minister. But Sakaar was clever. "He deals well, Tarquine."

"Very well," she murmured. "Astonishingly, extensively, extravagantly well." She waited a heartbeat. "After all, fraud is a form of dealing."

Good Lord. Sakaar's crime would have to be massive indeed if even Eube's unrepentantly corrupt empress considered it astonishing, extensive, and extravagant. "Such dealing," he said sourly, "has been known to give emperors mammoth headaches."

"Heads should only ache if one gets caught," Tarquine said. "You don't need medicine at all." In her dusky voice, she added, "But I do believe Minister Sakaar has a raging pain in his head."

"And precisely what caused this dire health of his?"

"Let us just say he misplaced the revenue of a few trades. For a little while."

He squinted at her. "What little while?"

"Well, perhaps the last five years."

Five *years*? "What the hell?"

Her lips quirked up. "That was articulate."

"Yes, well, I would very much like you to articulate more on the subject of Sakaar."

She switched into that terrifyingly incisive mode of hers. "Our illustrious Sakaar routed ten percent of the profits from every transaction he oversaw as Trade Minister into a series of hidden Allied financial institutions. He disguised his actions through an exceedingly labyrinthine process. It was brilliant."

"*Every* transaction?" He stared at her. "Tarquine, there are *millions* of those a year, some for millions of credits."

"Indeed. He is a very wealthy man." She paused a beat. "Or he was, before someone froze his assets."

Hell and damnation. "He must be brilliant, to have hidden this from you for five years."

"Actually," she hedged, "the pertinent time span in that case would have a different numerical value."

"Tarquine."

"So to speak."

"What numerical value?"

"Perhaps three."

"He hid it from you for three years?"

She scratched her ear. "Perhaps one might use the word months."

"*Months?*" She had known within three months and said nothing until now? "Then why the holy blazes did it continue for five years?" If she had made some deal with Sakaar, he would have her hide. And a very, very bad headache. "Just when did he find out you knew he was stealing my empire blind?"

"You needn't look so alarmed." She was almost purring. "I let him know at that last meeting we had with him. I imagine he was quite relieved when that broadcast about the Ruby Dynasty distracted you." Satisfaction saturated her voice. "Think of this, husband. A crime committed constantly for more than five years is far more serious than one done for three months. And the more serious the crime, the greater leverage it gives to the discoverer of that peccadillo."

"Peccadillo?" He could only stare at her. She was talking about fraud on a massive scale. He had never heard of anything like this before.

"Don't worry," she added. "I will deal with it."

"When you deal with things, I get hives," he muttered. "I want a report, Tarquine, and it damn well better include the evidence you've gathered. I want everything. *Everything.*"

"Of course," she said smoothly.

Jaibriol wanted to groan. Whenever she agreed that easily, he knew it was time to worry.

✧　✧　✧

The sixth implosion destroyed a gas giant in an uninhabited star system of Sphinx Sector.

Jaibriol strode across the launch hexagon with Robert and his bodyguards. Glory's sun was just rising. Seven of the fourteen moons were in the sky, four of them tiny chips barely visible to the eye. The largest, a huge red disk, glittered on the horizon opposite to the sun. Eube Qox, the first emperor, had surfaced it with ruby and named it in honor of his empress, Mirella. Overhead, the third largest satellite sparkled as a half-moon. Jaibriol's grandfather had named it Viquara after his empress and surfaced it in diamond.

The fifth largest moon was called Tarquine. Jaibriol had altered it both within and without. He surfaced it with a steel-diamond composite, brilliant and hard, but inside it had a beautiful crystalline structure in violet, blue, and white. A geode. It was the most fitting tribute he could think of for his wife.

The fourth moon should have been named after his mother. His father supposedly never had the chance, so Jaibriol inherited the decision. He couldn't call it Sauscony, after a Skolian Imperator, which was undoubtedly why his father had never named it, either. Jaibriol finally christened it Prism, in honor of the world where his family had lived in exile. He let people think it was his father's nickname for his mother. He didn't know how to resurface Prism, though the name cried out for a substance that would split light into its colors. The choice should have been his father's, and it felt wrong for him even to choose the name, let alone decide how to change the moon.

All this business with moons and wives seemed hollow this morning. After seeing Kelric with his family—and knowing his own empress desired the Imperator—Jaibriol felt broken inside. Tarquine would never admit any desire for Kelric; she refused even to acknowledge the huge price she had paid for him. But he had felt her anger at seeing Kelric's imposing wife. Kelric had everything Jaibriol could ever want, and if Eube and Skolia ever found their way back to the talks, Jaibriol would have to meet him at the peace table without letting his envy interfere. Somehow, someway he had to find accommodation with the knowledge that he could never again have what he craved, the love of a family of psions. It was good he had matters to take him away this morning, for he didn't think he could have borne another day of the icy Aristo world that imprisoned him.

As Glory's small sun edged above the horizon, Jaibriol boarded his yacht. Robert sat next to him, and his bodyguards took other seats, with Hidaka as the pilot. They blasted off into a dawn of splintering clarity. Their destination: Sphinx Sector Rim Base. Jaibriol's purported intention: to discuss with the commanders there the possibility that the implosions could be a weapon of Skolian design. It could be coincidence that the path of the events pointed roughly toward the SSRB, but neither Jaibriol nor ESComm intended to take chances.

Jaibriol kept to himself the real reason for his visit. He didn't believe the Skolians had anything to do with the implosions. He feared a more ancient intelligence was at work, one he neither understood nor had reason to believe intended good will.

The Lock.

The War Room on the Skolian Orbiter served as one among several centers of operations for the Imperialate military. It was a Skolian counterpart to the Eubian SSRB complex. In the War Room, Skolian commanders planned strategies against the Eubian military.

Today the amphitheater in the command center thrummed with energy: officers worked at consoles, telops focused on the meshes, pages ran errands, and cranes with console cups swung through the air. High above the amphitheater, a massive arm held a command chair under the dome of holostars. Conduits from all over the War Room fed into the blocky chair and sent data directly into the brain of whoever sat in that technological throne.

Kelric entered the War Room in the holodome, far above the busy amphitheater, striding along a catwalk that stretched to his chair. Yesterday he had walked the Promenade with his wife and children on the planet Parthonia; today he brought them to the Orbiter to see where he lived. He tried to forget they had to return to Coba. As much as he wanted them here, they had lives elsewhere; Ixpar ruled on Coba, his daughter was her successor, and his son a high-ranked Calani. But they were here now, and perhaps, just perhaps, they would consider staying.

The rest of his family wanted to know where the blazes he had acquired a wife and children. He had so far said little, except that he spent eighteen years on Coba. He intended to tell them more, but neither words nor expressing emotions had ever come easy to him. He needed time to answer their questions.

Dehya left him alone, patient with his silences, though he had no doubt she was investigating Coba. Roca also understood he needed time. She would have gone to Coba if he hadn't forbidden it and had a military force to back up his wishes. But in other ways her response was gentle. He remembered her pleased surprise: *You named your daughter after me?* Well, of course he had. Roca had been the greatest female influence in his youth. Surely at least part of the reason he loved so deeply was because his parents had loved their children that way.

The rest of his kin took their lead from Roca and waited, trying to be patient, but their frustration felt like a cloud of smoke. It was another reason he had come to the Orbiter; he needed time alone with his family. He and his children needed time to adjust to one another before he could open up to everyone else.

As Imperator, he also had to work. So today he had come to oversee the roaring, star-flung military known as Imperial Space Command, squeezing in a few hours while Roca spent time with the daughter-in-law and grandchildren who were so new to her.

Holographic starlight from the dome silvered his blocky throne. As he settled into the chair, it folded a mesh around him and clicked prongs into his ankles, wrists, spine, and neck, linking to his biomech web. The hood lowered, and a spider-web of threads extended into his scalp. Data poured into Bolt, and the node organized the input, leaving Kelric free to think.

He laid his arms on the rests and sat back. This chair was almost identical to the one in the SSRB Lock command center. He would never forget. He had met an emperor there. He was almost certain Jaibriol the Third was a telepath, yet that was impossible; Hightons had deliberately eliminated the DNA from their gene pool. Gods help humanity if that had changed, and the Eubians created their own Kyle web.

Three Locks had survived the fall of the Ruby Empire. The Orbiter was one; this space station had drifted in space for five millennia before Kelric's people found it. Although modern science couldn't replicate the Locks, they still operated. They had opened Kyle space to humanity. A person didn't physically enter the Kyle; they accessed it with their mind. The laws of physics didn't exist there, including limitations imposed by the speed of light. The content of someone's thoughts determined their "location." As a result, the Kyle mesh, or psiberweb as some called it, gave telops instant communication across interstellar distances. ESComm's military inventories and personnel dwarfed ISC, but ISC could outmaneuver, outcalculate, and outcommunicate ESComm. The Traders lumbered and Skolia sailed. It was the only reason Kelric's people survived against Eube.

A sense of stirring came from Kelric's gauntlets. A warning.

Bolt? Kelric asked. **Did you get that?**

You'll have to be more specific than "that," Bolt answered. I'm receiving a large amount of data.

My gauntlets. Kelric didn't know how to describe it. **They're warning me.**

About what?

I don't know. You didn't sense anything?

I can't get impressions the way a human does.

At times Kelric thought the node was more human than some humans. **Did the gauntlets send you any data?**

Nothing. They seem quiescent. Bolt paused. Not quiescent, exactly. More as if they are waiting.

That sounded like an impression to Kelric, regardless of what Bolt might think of his ability to form them. **Waiting for what?**

I'm not sure. You, maybe.

Kelric concentrated on the gauntlets. **What are you telling me?**

HOME. It came from his gauntlets as a feeling rather than a word.

Where is your home? Kelric asked.

No response.

Bolt suddenly thought, Kelric, have you been reading the broadcasts from the Selei Science Meshworks?

No. Should I be?

I don't know. One just came up in my memory. I believe your gauntlets inserted it.

Kelric stiffened. **They can affect your memory?**

It's never happened before. However, I detect a sense of urgency.

What's in the broadcast?

It regards some space-time anomalies. Bolt gave him a summary of the implosions. Apparently no cause has yet been found.

Kelric rubbed his chin, bewildered. **They started on Glory?**

Yes. But they've moved into space. And grown more disruptive.

Where are they going?

Bolt accessed his optic nerve and presented a map that appeared to hang in front of the chair. It showed a region of space with the implosions highlighted in red. The line is roughly toward the SSRB, where the Traders have the Lock. Which is where you found the gauntlets and could be the place they consider "home."

Kelric concentrated on the gauntlets. **Is this linked to the Lock?**

No response.

Bolt, did they put anything else in your memory?
Nothing.

Kelric studied the massive gauntlets on his wrists. **What are you trying to tell me?**

A sense of an alien intellect washed over him. **HOME.**

Home. If they wanted the SSRB Lock, he didn't see how he could help. He stared down at the War Room, and Bolt let the map fade. The dais on the far side of the amphitheater was empty, and the corridor to the First Lock lay beyond it. Transparent columns bordered the corridor, and ancient mechanisms gleamed within them, moving gears and levers that flashed lights. The path extended away from the dais until it dwindled to a point of perspective, as if it went on forever.

Have you detected anything unusual from this Lock? he asked Bolt.

Nothing. But I don't normally communicate with a space-time singularity.

Kelric smiled at its phrasing. A Lock didn't communicate, it simply existed. Even that wasn't certain. If someone who wasn't a psion tried to enter the Lock, they found nothing in the chamber at the end of the corridor. He suspected they could find the singularity only if they entered the room when a Ruby psion was already there. He had never tried to bring in someone else; it seemed wrong. The Lock wanted only its Keys to visit that surreal place where two universes intersected.

A psion who wasn't a Ruby *could* sense the singularity. They knew it was there, unlike someone with no Kyle ability. But the farther they went down the corridor, the greater the pressure on their mind, until they had to turn back or black out. Only a Ruby psion could endure its power and reach the chamber.

The Lock had never bothered Kelric. It felt *right.* He was always aware of it at the edges of his mind, and Dehya described a similar effect. That was the closest they came to communication with it. Kelric rarely walked that corridor. He had no reason to; he was already a

Key. Whether formation of the Dyad was its purpose or simply a side effect, he had no idea. He and Dehya took care never to disturb it, except in emergencies. He had no idea of such a situation now, but the warning from the gauntlets disturbed him. They either couldn't or wouldn't tell him more, and he couldn't go to the Lock where he had found them.

But he could go to the one here.

The Sphinx Sector Rim Base formed one of several command centers for the Eubian military. The base consisted of many space stations executing intricate orbits around one another. From far away, they sparkled like jewels in deep space; closer in, they resolved into giant habitats bristling with weapons, antennae, and space debris. The Lock that ESComm had stolen from the Skolians orbited in the center of the system. Most of the habitats supported lush biospheres and populations in the millions, but the Lock was small and purely functional, only machinery and metal.

Colonel Vatrix Muze had been in charge of the Lock station the first time Jaibriol had visited, ten years ago, and he still held the prestigious post. In the convoluted kinship relations among Aristos, Muze had ties to both Jaibriol and Robert. The colonel was the grandson of High Judge Calope Muze, Jaibriol's cousin, and Calope's uncle had sired Robert's mother, which meant Jaibriol and Robert were also distantly related.

Colonel Muze and a retinue of officers met Jaibriol in the docking bay. Muze bowed to him. "We are deeply honored by your visit, Your Glorious Highness."

Jaibriol knew he was lying. The colonel's mind grated even through his protections. Muze was no happier to see him today than the first time they had met, ten years ago. It wasn't only the relentless pressure of Muze's mind that bothered Jaibriol; he also felt the man's covert hostility, the most dangerous kind, antagonism hidden behind a veneer of deference.

Muze escorted him along a corridor that curved upward in the distance, following the curve of the rotating station. They were essentially walking on the inside of a huge donut in space. Jaibriol's guards surrounded them, Robert stayed at his side, and Muze's aides followed. Jaibriol felt as if his mind were splitting open. It wasn't only Muze; the colonel's three aides all had enough Aristo lineage to manifest that searching hunger for transcendence. It pressed down on

Jaibriol, wore at him, exhausted him, until it was all he could do to keep from lurching forward. Robert glanced at him with concern, but Jaibriol didn't dare acknowledge it or otherwise reveal any sign of weakness.

"We have optimism," Colonel Muze was saying. "A team of distortion physicists is attending our discourse on the fabric of space-time. It is auspicious that they bring their ideas into our sphere."

Jaibriol wished the colonel would just come out and flaming say that the scientists sent to study the implosions had arrived. Nor had he ever heard of distortion physics. For all he knew, Muze had made it up. It would be a typical Highton ploy to ridicule someone.

"One would hope they don't distort their own name," Jaibriol said.

Muze glanced at him with a bland expression. "Your wit dazzles, Your Highness."

Wit, indeed. Muze's veiled antagonism jabbed at Jaibriol's shields. He lowered his barriers so he could probe the colonel's mind, but the pressure immediately increased, and he stumbled as his vision darkened.

"Your Highness?" Muze spoke smoothly, watching Jaibriol like a hawk that had spotted prey.

Jaibriol caught his balance and gave no sign he acknowledged Muze's implied question about his health. He struggled to rebuild his barriers. Mercifully, the onslaught receded, and the haze faded from his vision. It didn't bode well that Muze had caught his lapse; Hightons were experts at reading body language. Muze would interpret his dizziness as weakness, and when Aristos saw weakness, they attacked, often subtly, but they found ways to exploit any failing they perceived in a foe. And Jaibriol had no doubt Muze saw him in those terms. He had made enemies in ESComm when he opened negotiations with the Skolians.

Jaibriol had read the files on all his top ESComm officers. Many of them abhorred the Skolians. He had once thought their hatred derived from their conviction Skolians were a lower form of life. And that was part of it. They considered it repellent that a dynasty of "providers" had established an empire to rival their own. But as much as they refused to admit it, the Aristos also felt beaten down by the constant hostilities. They wanted to conquer Skolia because they were tired of war. It didn't create a desire in them to negotiate; the only solution they considered acceptable was eradication of the Imperialate and the enslavement of all Skolian peoples.

❖   ❖   ❖

The Lock corridor in the Skolian Orbiter lay in front of Kelric. Its lights seemed faster today. As a Key to the web, he was more attuned to the Lock than anyone else alive except Dehya. It was agitated, if one could apply a human emotion to a physical place. The corridor stretched out in front of him to that seemingly infinite point. Even knowing it lay inside a space habitat only a few kilometers in diameter, it unsettled Kelric. Perhaps it *did* go on that incredible distance, twisting into another place that wasn't aligned with this space-time.

Behind him, the War Room registered as a subdued hum. The Orbiter's thirty-hour cycle was deep into night. Even this late, telops were at work, monitoring the far-flung forces of an empire. Kelric knew they were aware of him, probably wondering what he intended to do. It was a good question: he wasn't sure himself.

He began to walk the corridor.

His boots clanged on the diamond-steel floor. He continued on, inundated with brightness from the brilliant surfaces, the pillars, the glow suffusing the area. On he walked, toward a point that never came closer.

And walked.

And walked.

Time seemed bent, as if it had curved away, around a corner. Surely it hadn't taken this long to reach the SSRB Lock. He felt as if he were walking forever down an endless path. He experienced none of the pressure other psions described in the corridor. Maybe he *couldn't* feel it; he lacked mental finesse, having an immense but blunt power.

The point of perspective finally began to change, growing into an archway that glowed as if it were white light. He stopped in front of it and set his hand against the side, convincing himself of its solidity. Then he stepped into the Lock chamber. Radiance enveloped him; with so much light, he could barely see the room. It was only ten paces wide, but its walls rose high over his head, lost in a luminous fog.

The Lock pierced the center of the chamber in a radiant column of light. It rose out of the floor and disappeared into the haze overhead. This was the singularity, the point where another universe punctured space-time. Kelric steeled himself, unsure what he would find but certain he needed to find out.

Then he stepped into the pillar of light.

XVII

Pillar of Darkness

"Your meeting with Colonel Muze and his staff is tomorrow at First Hour," Robert said. He rolled his mesh film out on the desk next to the armchair where Jaibriol had slumped. Glancing over, he spoke carefully. "They are all Aristos."

Jaibriol barely heard. He sat sprawled in his chair, too worn out to move. Tonight's dinner with the colonel and his top officers had been interminable. It battered his mental defenses. Nor did it help that the twenty-hour day here threw off his sleep cycle, which had adjusted to the sixteen-hour day on Glory. Muze had given him the best quarters on the station, but they were cramped and utilitarian. Jaibriol didn't care; he just wanted a reprieve from the pain in his head. He suspected his dinner companions had been transcending at a low level, unaware their good moods came from their emperor's splintering headache. In one of the grimmer ironies of his life, the very trait that made them so dangerous to him also improved their temper in his presence and ameliorated his tendency to antagonize them.

"Luminos down," Jaibriol said. He should answer Robert, but he barely felt able to talk. He needed time for the health nanomeds in his body to help him recover.

The lights dimmed, and the walls softened into soothing views of space with spumes of interstellar gas. With an exhale, Jaibriol slumped lower in his chair.

Robert was watching him with that concerned look he had worn ever since they had arrived. "Can I get you anything?"

"Thank you. But I'm fine." Jaibriol wasn't and never would be, but nothing Robert could do would change that miserable fact.

It felt strange to be so close to a Lock and sense nothing. No life. When ESComm had stolen this Lock from the Skolians, they had also captured Eldrin Valdoria, Kelric's older brother. As a Ruby psion, Eldrin could have become a Key, and with both a Lock and Key, the Aristos could have created their own Kyle web. The day they had enslaved Eldrin, the dream of Jaibriol's parents had ended, for Eube had gained the final ingredient it needed to conquer Skolia.

At the time, Jaibriol had been traveling as a member of a humanitarian organization, the Dawn Corps of the Allied Worlds. Desperate to protect both his parents' dream and his uncle, he had offered Corbal a trade: himself for Eldrin. It was the only exchange Corbal would consider for his captive Ruby psion: a Qox emperor he believed had the energy to conquer Skolia and raise Eube to greater heights, in exchange for the Skolian prince who might make it possible to conquer Skolia despite having no Qox heir to assume the throne. The death of Jaibriol's father had left Eube tottering on collapse; a vibrant young emperor could mean the difference between survival and breakdown.

Corbal's decision to accept Jaibriol's offer had outraged many Aristos. They also questioned why Corbal gave up his claim to the throne. Jaibriol had no doubts on that—Corbal had expected to rule from the shadows, manipulating the boy emperor. It had taken him longer to realize that Corbal had recognized his secret; Jaibriol lacked the same neural structures Corbal had eliminated in himself so he would no longer transcend. Only someone who had done the unthinkable among the Aristos would have uncovered the truth:

Jaibriol's great-grandfather had been Aristo.

His grandfather had been half Aristo, half Ruby.

His father had been a Ruby psion.

Jaibriol was a Ruby psion.

The Qox Dynasty had created its own Key.

Corbal hadn't just wanted to rule from behind the throne; he wanted Jaibriol to join the powerlink, make the Dyad a Triad, build a

Kyle web, and conquer the stars. Corbal had sought to rule the sum total of humanity, all of it, Skolia and the Allieds included, through a puppet emperor. Except Jaibriol had proved far less malleable than he expected. Jaibriol couldn't deny the lure of the power, but he could no more inflict Aristo rule on all humanity than he could transcend. He had also realized his cousin didn't transcend, for Corbal didn't have that immense cavity in his mind. So the two of them had reached an impasse; they each kept the other's secrets.

Jaibriol could never trust his cousin. And yet . . . over the years, something had happened. Corbal's attitude toward him had changed. If Jaibriol hadn't known better, he might have called it familial love. He did know better, of course; he wasn't that naïve.

A chime sounded. Disoriented, Jaibriol opened his eyes and blinked at Robert. "What is that?"

Robert frowned at his mesh film. "Colonel Muze wishes an audience with you."

Jaibriol swore under his breath. "Tell him I'm asleep."

"If that is what you wish," Robert said formally, "I will take care of it."

Jaibriol wanted to groan. He hated it when Robert talked that way. "In other words, you think I should see him."

"You need his good will," Robert said. "Or at least the best relation you can establish with him. It isn't unreasonable for the station commander to pay his courtesies during a visit such as this. Refusing his request would be an insult."

Jaibriol didn't feel up to dealing with Muze, but what he avoided today could escalate tomorrow. "Very well," he said tiredly. "Bring him in."

As Robert set up the audience, Jaibriol sat up and rested one elbow on the arm of his chair, a posture he had learned by studying portraits of his ancestors, who were often shown seated this way in some imperially elegant place. He had noticed the posture had a subtle effect on people; they viewed him as more regal. It disquieted him that it felt so natural.

His bodyguards ushered Colonel Muze into the room. Hidaka walked at Muze's side, looming over him, his boots clanking. All of Jaibriol's guards were present, six counting Hidaka, one at each wall of the hexagonal chamber. They had that preternatural stillness of Razers, like waiting machines.

Muze bowed to Jaibriol. "My honor at your revered company, Glorious Highness."

Jaibriol nodded stiffly, an acceptance of the greeting with no indication the honor was either returned or refused. He didn't want to alienate Muze any more than he did just by being himself, but neither did he want to encourage the colonel. He lifted his hand, indicating a brocaded armchair identical to his. Both had extensive mech-tech that read body language and adjusted for comfort. On this utilitarian habitat, though, the brocade was more of a rarity than the smart tech.

After Muze was seated, Jaibriol waited. The colonel had requested the audience and he was lower in status than the emperor, so protocol required he broach the discussion first.

"Your visit brings fortune to our station," Muze opened.

"It would appear the vagaries of space-time also bring theirs," Jaibriol said, referring to the implosions. His nanomeds had eased his headache, but it was growing worse again.

"It is great bravery to set oneself in a path of the inexplicable." Muze tilted his head slightly to the left, a hint of contradiction.

Jaibriol knew what he implied; only a fool traveled into the path of an unexplained violent phenomenon. He gritted his teeth, but he could live with the barb. As long as Muze viewed him as callow and ill-advised, he wouldn't suspect Jaibriol's real reason for coming here. Muze didn't seem surprised by his interest; the Lock was, after all, their most valuable acquisition from the Skolians. No one knew if it could revive, and securing a Ruby psion had proved inordinately difficult, but as long as they had the Lock, the chance of creating their own Kyle web remained.

Jaibriol said nothing and let Muze stew. Eventually the colonel would get around to his reason for inflicting this audience. Jaibriol just hoped his head hadn't split open by then.

"It is rare that we have the pleasure of such a magnificent visit," Muze said.

"Indeed," Jaibriol said, and hoped his agreement stuck in Muze's craw. It probably wouldn't; Aristos expected their emperor to think of himself in grandiose terms.

"Would that we could offer your Glorious Highness a better environment," Muze added, his expression cagey.

Jaibriol didn't mind about the small quarters; he would be just as miserable in a bigger room. He said only, "It would be auspicious." He was running out of inflated adjectives.

Muze's eyes glinted. "Perhaps we could provide Your Magnificence a small token of our esteem."

With his headache, it took Jaibriol a moment to absorb what Muze meant. Then he felt sick. The colonel had just offered him a provider so Jaibriol could torture some psion even more unfortunate than himself. He wished he could toss the colonel out, but he didn't dare stir suspicion, especially during this visit. Jaibriol usually avoided "gifts" of providers using his fidelity to his wife as the reason, which was considered bizarre but not abhorrent. But at times, he couldn't avoid it without crossing what Aristos considered an unacceptable line, which meant he had to be present when they transcended. Sometimes it made him so deeply ill, he thought he would lose his mind, and right now he felt close to the edge.

Somehow he managed to say, "Your magnanimous character is noted." He almost gagged on the words.

Muze should have been pleased with the response. But he only seemed warier. Wary . . . and something else. What?

Then it hit Jaibriol. The colonel was *transcending*. With growing horror, Jaibriol realized Muze suspected his good mood was linked to the emperor. Jaibriol shored up his barriers, but it didn't help; his defenses were too strained.

"I shall arrange matters to your taste," Muze was saying.

Alarm flared in Jaibriol. He had to stop Muze from bringing a provider. He would experience the psion's agony as if it was his own, and if that happened in his current weakened state, he would crack open. But he couldn't form the words to extricate himself for the situation. His thoughts fled the intricacies of the Highton language like a cornered animal in pain.

"Your Highness?" Muze asked, his gaze hard.

A chime sounded.

Jaibriol blinked. As he turned toward the sound, Robert looked up from the desk where he had been occupying himself. Until now, he had apparently been too inconsequential for Muze to bother noticing.

"Your Glorious H-highness." Robert sounded terrified. "Please excuse my deplorable interruption. I beg you to forgive me. It is an urgent message from his eminence, Lord Corbal Xir. He requests you attend it soon. Sire!" He slipped out of the chair and knelt with his head down. "I beg you, forgive me."

Jaibriol would have gaped in utter astonishment at his aide's peculiar behavior, except the agony in his head overcame every other reaction, even his falling over in shock. Whatever had afflicted Robert?

It took him a moment to realize Robert was giving him an out. Corbal ranked well above Vatrix Muze in Highton levels of power and influence, enough so the colonel would have to accept a dismissal. At the same time, Robert implied the emperor would see that his aide paid for such an unwelcome interruption from an evening of pleasure. With his mind so raw, Jaibriol knew Robert *was* terrified, not of him, but *for* him. Robert feared that if this audience continued, the emperor would reveal himself in ways better left unknown.

Jaibriol lifted his hand to Muze, palm upward, the gesture meant to indicate apology and displeasure with the source of the infraction, Robert in this case. "It appears my cousin is more eminent than usual," he said wryly.

Muze gave a startled laugh. Apparently Jaibriol's attempt at a Highton joke hadn't fallen flat. He didn't know whether to be relieved he could pull it off or dismayed he was becoming that much of an Aristo.

He initiated the process of dismissing Muze without insult. The entire time, Robert stayed on his knees, shaking. When Hidaka escorted the colonel from the room, Jaibriol had an odd sense, as if Hidaka stayed too close to Muze. It wasn't enough to be an overt threat, but he wondered if the Razer was subconsciously trying to intimidate the colonel. It couldn't be conscious; Razers were designed to consider Aristos supreme beings. It was imprinted in their biomech webs and neural nets. Unless Muze endangered or attacked the emperor, Hidaka could no more threaten him than he could turn inside out. Given that Muze had done nothing more than offer Jaibriol a pleasure girl, the Razer could hardly consider him a danger.

After Muze was gone, Jaibriol said, "Thank you, Hidaka. You all may go as well."

"If it pleases Your Highness that we leave," Hidaka said in his deep voice, "we will esteem and honor your wishes." Then he added, "But I beg you to ask us to commit suicide instead, for we would rather take our own lives than leave yours undefended."

Hell and damnation. The last thing he needed was his Razers arguing with him under the guise of spurious threats to commit suicide. "Hidaka," he said softly. "Go. My head hurts."

The captain stared at him. Hightons never admitted weakness. The shock of it had the desired effect; Hidaka offered no more objections, just motioned for the other guards to leave with him.

As soon as he and Robert were alone, Jaibriol slid down to the floor next to his aide and slumped against the desk. Robert had scanned the room earlier for monitoring devices, but Jaibriol didn't want to take chances. Audio bugs were harder to find than optical, so instead of speaking, he tapped a message on his wrist comm and held it so Robert could see it even with his head bowed.

=Why are you on the floor?= Jaibriol asked.

Robert raised his head. Then he tapped out a message on his comm. =You must not let them harm you.=

=I am the emperor. They cannot.= That wasn't true, but he had endured too much truth for the night. He just wanted to go to bed and give his meds a chance to treat his aching head.

=They can,= Robert wrote. =And they will.=

Robert never openly contradicted him. It scared Jaibriol. =I'll be all right.

=We must leave this place,= Robert answered. =It is worse for you here.=

A chill went through Jaibriol. Just how much did Robert suspect? =I can't go yet.=

=Cancel the meeting tomorrow. A crisis has arisen. Lord Xir bids you to attend it.=

Jaibriol thought he must be even more dazed than he had realized, to have forgotten what elicited Robert's reaction in the first place. Reorienting, he wrote, =If Corbal sent a message by starship and it's already arrived, he must have sent it just after I left Glory.=

Robert met his gaze squarely. =Forgive me. I lied.=

Jaibriol gaped at him. Robert was supposed to be incapable of misleading a Highton. That he admitted it without a flinch also put the lie to his performance of terror in front of Muze. When Jaibriol didn't immediately respond, Robert paled. But he never averted his gaze.

Jaibriol took a deep breath. =Very well. I will leave for this "emergency."= As relief suffused his aide's face, he added, =But first I must visit the Lock.=

Robert's brow furrowed. =You are already in the Lock.=

=Not the station. The singularity.=

=But it is dead, Sire.= Robert grimaced. =Unless evil spirits haunt its grave. This station is a grim place.=

=It has no spirits. Just technology.=

Robert didn't answer, and Jaibriol doubted his aide believed him. Jaibriol rubbed his head with his fingertips. Regardless of his condition, he couldn't leave before he did what he had come here to do. He feared that what had begun as a small anomaly could become an interstellar catastrophe by the time it reached the SSRB. The implosions had started where he lived. Maybe it was coincidence, but he didn't believe that. The Lock was seeking him. Maybe it wanted any Ruby psion, and he happened to be closest.

He had to find out what it needed before it was too late.

XVIII

The Ward of Lives

Radiance filled Kelric Skolia.

Light flowed, liquid and brilliant.

A thought formed in his mind, with the sense of an alien intelligence. **KEY.**

Yes, Kelric thought. **I am your Key.** His body no longer existed. He had become thought. Light. Radiance.

NOT KEY, the Lock answered.

I am your Key. He could never stop being one. His brain was so thoroughly intertwined with the Dyad, it would cause fatal brain damage if he tried to withdraw.

DEATH. The luminosity dimmed around Kelric.

Whose death? Kelric asked.

ALL.

Foreboding rose in Kelric. If the Lock ceased with him in it, he would stop existing as well. His gauntlets had thought of "home," which suggested the SSRB where he had found them. Could that Lock be dying because he had deactivated it?

How can I help? Kelric asked. **What do you need?**

STRENGTH.

That I can do. He gathered his power into a great wave and flooded the Kyle. The fading of the light slowed, but it didn't stop.

ENDING, the Lock thought.

Then I must go, Kelric answered. If he didn't return to his own universe, he could vanish here. The first time he had entered a Lock, he had no trouble leaving. He had thought of doing it and found himself stepping out of the singularity. But now, when he tried, it didn't work—and without a body, he had no other way to go back.

The universe darkened. **END.**

NO!

The Kyle vanished.

Jaibriol Qox, Emperor of Eube, stood at the threshold of the corridor that led to the SSRB Lock and stared down the dead, dark pathway. Columns rose on either side, shadowed and filled with motionless gears. Nothing glowed here except a small Eubian safety light on the dais behind him.

He had come alone into this graveyard. He had evaded his guards by leaving his quarters through a disguised exit Robert had discovered when he swept the room for monitors. Convincing Robert to let him go by himself had been more difficult. His aide feared the Lock and had no desire to enter it, but he had even less desire for the emperor to do so. When Jaibriol told him to remain behind, he had thought for one astonishing moment that Robert would refuse an Imperial order. Then his aide had knelt to him, his face flushed, and Jaibriol had felt smaller than an insect.

No sense of life awaited him. No intellect tugged at his mind. Before Kelric had killed this Lock, Jaibriol had felt its presence. It had filled the station. Apparently no one else sensed it, certainly no Aristo or taskmaker, possibly not even a provider. But Jaibriol had known. Now that presence was gone.

Are you dead? he thought. Maybe he was deluded, to imagine this place as anything more than a big room with defunct machines and a path that led . . .

Where?

He started down the Lock corridor.

Darkness surrounded him. The wan light from the dais dimmed to nothing. It should have trickled down the pathway, yet nothing penetrated the gloom. He walked in blackness.

Jaibriol stopped, uneasy. He looked back the way he had come, but he could see no more in that direction. Turning forward again, he took another step. The darkness drew closer. He knew, logically, that a lack of light wasn't "close." Yet he felt as if it wrapped around him, heavy and dense.

He continued on.

Jaibriol had no idea how long he walked. Unable to see even his hand in front of his face, he felt dissociated from reality. This place between space-time and some other universe had gone wrong. He considered returning to the dais room, but he feared if he walked the other way, he would never reach the end of the path in that direction either. He existed in a limbo of nothing.

His hand hit a surface. With a relieved grunt, he felt along the barrier and found an opening. When he stretched out his arm, his hand hit another side. And archway, perhaps. He leaned against the lintel, his heart beating hard. Although he had no idea where he had ended up or if he could escape this place, at least it *was* a place.

When his pulse settled, he took an exploratory step through the archway. He almost fell; the floor on the other side was a hand span lower than on his side. He felt his way along a cool, smooth wall and figured out that he had entered a small room with eight sides. An octagon chamber. It had an octagonal depression in its center about two paces wide.

Jaibriol rubbed his hand over his eyes. Worn out, he slid down one wall and sat on the floor. He was no closer to discovering if the Lock had a connection to the implosions.

"What should I do?" he asked the air.

Silence.

After he rested, he climbed to his feet and made his way along the wall again, headed toward the doorway. Maybe he should go back to his quarters and sleep, before his body gave out.

His knee hit a hard surface.

Jaibriol paused, startled. Then he explored the barrier. It felt like a console. Yes, here was the seat. He sat down and slid his palms over the panels until his fingers scraped a line of engraved hieroglyphics. He felt it carefully. He didn't recognize the language, but it had elements in common with both Iotic and Highton, which derived from the same roots. He pieced out the inscription:

To you, Karj, comes the ward of lives.

Karj? Could it mean Kurj, the man who had been Imperator before Jaibriol's mother? But he had died only twelve years ago, and this inscription was probably thousands of years old. The name Kurj dated from before the time when Skolia and Eube had split apart, back when they had all been one people.

He tried to activate the console, but nothing worked. Finally he gave up and went back to the center of the chamber. Kneeling in the depression, he felt around the floor, searching for clues to understand this place. The sleek surface offered no answers.

Frustrated, he sat with one leg bent and his elbow resting on his knee. His thoughts felt muted, but at least it eased the damage from his exposure to Aristos, especially Colonel Muze, whose mind had grated like sandpaper on a raw wound. The darkness settled over him like a blanket and muffled his brain.

In the darkness of a space that didn't exist, Kelric Skolia strained to keep his identity intact.

Begin.

He shored up Kyle space like the Atlas of Earth's mythology holding up the world.

Begin.

His power beat like a deep pulse.

Begin.

The darkness stabilized, an absence of light but no longer of existence. And Kelric began to understand.

When he had deactivated one of the Locks, he had eliminated one of three nodes that sustained Kyle space. The Locks balanced the Kyle web; with only two operating, it strained and snapped. Humanity had created million of gates that connected the Kyle to space-time, and each one added to the strain. Just as earthquakes relieved pressure in a planet's crust, so the implosions relieved stresses between the two universes. The instabilities had built for ten years, until something had to give. When the disruptions reached the SSRB, they were going to rip apart space-time between the three Locks like fault lines cracking. It would be an interstellar disaster of unprecedented proportions.

Kelric saw no choice. He had to reactivate the Lock. A universe where the Traders had access to Kyle technology wasn't one he wanted to contemplate, but destroying a substantial portion of space could be even worse. Gods only knew how many people would die and star systems perish.

He had no idea if he could restart the Lock from so far away, but as a Key, he had more resources than anyone else, probably more than he had plumbed. The SSRB Lock existed at the fringes of his awareness, quiescent, distant and vague, but alive.

Resume, he thought.

No response.

I am your Key. Come to me.

Like a leviathan awaking, the Lock stirred.

Jaibriol sat in the darkened SSRB Lock and tried to understand its emptiness.

Come to me, he thought, he wasn't certain why, except that the words felt right.

The Lock stirred.

Jaibriol froze. **Who?** he asked.

NOT KEY. It was as if a distant monolith turned toward him.

I'm not a Key, that's true, he admitted.

DEATH.

He swallowed, wondering if it thought he had killed it. **Do you mean this Lock?** Uneasily, he added, **Or me?**

ALL.

Both of us?

NO.

I don't understand.

END.

His frustration built. **What ends?** He felt foolish questioning a thought that was probably a figment of his imagination.

THE CORRIDOR OF AGES.

I don't understand. He didn't know if the thoughts came from the Lock, the machinery, or something else.

Nothing.

You have to help me. That felt wrong. He delved deeper into his mind—and words came as if Kyle space itself revealed them.

Come to me, Jaibriol thought. **I am your Key.**

Kelric's thought thundered throughout the Kyle.

RESUME.

With a gigantic, shattering surge of power, the Lock awoke.

Light flooded the chamber where Jaibriol sat, brilliant and painful. He cried out and covered his eyes. In that instant, the Kyle singularity shot up through the floor and pierced the chamber—

Right through Jaibriol.

XIX

A Chilling Blue

Crush the petals of a night-fragrant vine,
In bitter dreaming sweetness.
Hold its vulnerable, frail beauty,
Cherished beyond all reason.

The night offers surcease, heart-aching hope,
Or painful, streaming cruelty.
Pray withhold your chilling blue transcendence
In the deep, purpling dawn.

The singing of the ancient provider broke Jaibriol's heart, for the music was impossibly beautiful and impossibly sad. He grieved for the love of the family he had lost, for the family he would never know, and for the crushing, bitter weight of Aristo cruelty that would be his for the rest of his life.

Deep within the Kyle, the emperor wept.

XX

Triad Quis

Jaibriol dragged himself out of the singularity on his hands and knees. He sprawled on the floor while his head reeled with power. It was unbearable. He would drown in the streaming blue of the Kyle.

His fingers spasmed as he clawed the floor. For ten years he had hidden, repressed, constrained, and constricted his mind, and now the Lock had ripped it wide open. Power flooded him as his thoughts encompassed a universe. He wanted to scream, but he could barely breathe.

His muscles clenched as if he were convulsing. It could have been seconds, minutes, hours. Then they released, and he choked out a sob. He crawled another few feet, pulling his body along the floor. Light filled the chamber, mercilessly bright. With tears streaming down his face, he pushed up on his hands—

And stared into the maw of a laser carbine.

Too much in shock even to register fear, Jaibriol raised his head. In the brilliance of the Lock, he could barely see the man who held the gun. But he recognized the eyes. They were the only color in the chamber, red and hard. And when the man spoke, Jaibriol knew his voice.

"The fates of Eube are truly capricious," Colonel Muze said from behind the gun, "that they would give us a Ruby Key in the person of our own emperor."

The Lock had shredded Jaibriol's defenses, and the Aristo mind of the colonel surrounded him in a great icy void that froze his thoughts, his heart, his being. He felt Muze transcending, and he silently screamed with the torment. In one horrifying moment, he had given Eube everything it needed to conquer the Skolians and condemned himself to a life of agony so much worse than what he already lived that he knew he would go insane.

"**No.**" Jaibriol thought he whispered, but the word thundered in the chamber as if he were one of those fates Muze had evoked.

The colonel backed away from him. "Get up."

Jaibriol couldn't move.

"*Get up!*" Muze shouted, and his fear saturated the air.

Jaibriol dragged himself to the console, which glowed like alabaster. Clutching the chair, he pulled up to his knees. With his arms shaking, he struggled to his feet. Then he just stood, staring at Muze. The violation couldn't have been worse than for an Aristo to enter the Lock.

"For ten years, you've corrupted the throne." Loathing filled the colonel's voice. "I always knew you were flawed, but I had no idea just how great the filth you brought among us. We will cleanse Eube of your stain." His voice was harsh with revulsion. "And you will serve us, provider. Have no doubt; you will pay for this crime beyond all crimes."

The light suddenly flared even brighter, blinding him. A backlash of violence hit Jaibriol, not physically, but crashing through his mind. He stumbled away from the console and tried to scream, but no sound came. He teetered at the edge of the pillar of light, the singularity that had thrown him into Kyle space, and he knew without doubt that if he fell into it again, the power would kill him.

The singularity died.

Darkness dropped around Jaibriol. The pillar was gone. He no longer felt the presence of the Lock. The astringent smell of a laser shot and the stench of melted composites filled the air—that, and another smell he couldn't identify but that raised bile in his throat. He couldn't handle the sensory onslaught; his mind was shutting down.

He staggered backward and hit a wall. The blackness wasn't complete; dim light filtered into the chamber from the corridor, enough to show him that whatever had killed that Lock had also slagged the console. Vatrix Muze no longer stood anywhere Jaibriol could see. He didn't understand why the colonel had fired. Did he sicken Muze so much that the Aristo would seek to destroy a Ruby Key who had joined the Triad? If that were true, Aristo thought processes were even more alien than he had ever comprehended.

He stumbled toward the entrance, a vague octagon of lighter shadows. A towering figure appeared there, silhouetted against the dim light. Jaibriol lurched to a stop, unable to push himself any farther.

A deep voice spoke. "Can you walk, Your Highness?"

Jaibriol wanted to weep. "**Hidaka?**" He barely whispered it, and yet his voice echoed.

"I have stopped the assassination attempt." Hidaka's usually impassive voice sounded shaken. "You must leave this place, Sire."

Jaibriol stared at his bodyguard. Hidaka had to know what he was seeing. He had to have heard what Muze had said. Why would a Razer call a false emperor *Sire*?

Something grotesque lay in a twisted, smoldering pile across the chamber. Then Jaibriol recognized the stench that filled the room. Cauterized human flesh.

Hidaka was holding a laser carbine. His bodyguard had murdered a high-ranking Aristo who had just made possibly the most valuable discovery in the history of the Eubian empire.

"**Ah, no.**" Jaibriol swayed, and his vision dimmed.

"Sire!" Hidaka lunged into the chamber.

Jaibriol's legs buckled, and Hidaka caught him as he fell. The giant Razer lifted Jaibriol into his arms as easily as if the emperor were a broken doll, and blackness closed around him.

Kelric slowly lifted his head. He was sitting sideways at a console in the Lock chamber on the Skolian Orbiter. The singularity glowed next to him, but it seemed oddly dim. Although his head throbbed, he sensed no damage to himself. None of his internal warning systems had activated.

Bolt? he asked. **Are you there?**

Yes. I'm fine.

How did I get here? The last Kelric remembered, he had been deep within a fracturing Kyle space. He had reactivated the SSRB Lock many light-years distant at a Eubian military complex.

I don't know. Bolt, who was supposed to have no personality, sounded bemused. My memory has a gap. I have no other data until you became conscious of sitting here.

Kelric gazed at the pillar of light. He no longer had to squint against its brilliance. **Something damaged the Lock.**

I detect no damage here.

It's weakened.

Perhaps the problem isn't with this one.

Kelric rubbed his temple. **I feel strange.**

Are you injured?

I don't think so. After a moment, he added, **I've a shadow.**

All people have shadows, assuming proper light conditions.

Not that kind, Bolt. In my mind.

Is your link as a Key weakened?

No. It has a— He struggled to define his impression. **Not a shadow, exactly. When you have a solar eclipse, the moon shadows the sun. The moon is present, but you don't see it, only the shadow. It's as if a moon cast its shadow across Kyle space.**

"Kelric?"

He jumped to his feet and whirled around, his body toggling into combat mode as he raised his arm to strike.

Dehya had entered the chamber and stood bathed in radiance from the singularity. Small and frail, she was little more than a third his weight. She looked up at his giant fist raised above her head.

Kelric stared at her, dismayed. What if he hadn't stopped his reflexes in time? He could have killed her with one blow.

He lowered his arm. **"You surprised me,"** he said—and froze. He had spoken in low tones, but his words resonated with power.

"What did you do?" Her voice sounded as if it came from far away, blowing across the blue spaces of the Kyle.

I called the Lock at the SSRB, he thought. Usually mind-speech drained him, but in this interstice separating space-time and the Kyle, it felt right. **Something went wrong.**

It died, she answered. *Or ended somehow.*

I can't tell what happened. My mind is too blunt.

I can't tell, either. My mind hasn't the strength.

We must combine efforts.

Kyle space is damaged. If we go in together, we could strain it too far.

Kelric feared she was right. With the combined power of their minds focused in the Kyle, they might destabilize its weakened structure and accelerate the implosions. But if they didn't find out what was wrong, they could be inviting a catastrophe of interstellar proportions. Something had happened when he touched the SSRB Lock, something so intense it had pushed him out of the singularity and seared his memory.

Dehya was watching his face. *It called to me for help, too, I think.*

My gauntlets sent me a warning about the SSRB Lock. A memory leapt in Kelric's mind: he had met Jaibriol Qox there, ten years ago.

Dehya's thought drifted over him like mist. *Let me see.*

Here in the chamber, his mind flexed as it never could in normal space. And he and Dehya were Keys. Their minds linked in ways no other humans could manage. He lowered his barriers so she could see pieces of the memory he had stored in Bolt ten years ago . . .

The emperor stood at his full height, over six feet tall. He was a boy, no more than seventeen. He crossed the dais to Kelric. When he stopped, only a rail separated them.

"Go now," Jaibriol said. "While you can."

"You would let me go?" Kelric asked, incredulous.

Jaibriol regarded him steadily. "Yes."

Kelric didn't believe it. "Why?"

The emperor answered in cool, cultured tones. "Meet me at the peace table."

"You want me to believe you wish peace," Kelric said, "when you have a Lock and two Keys."

"What Lock?" The youth spread his hands. "It no longer works."

Kelric knew Jaibriol had seen him suspend the singularity. Yet the emperor hadn't asked if he could bring it back alive.

"We had one Key," Jaibriol added. "We gave him back."

"Gave who back?"

"Your brother. Eldrin Valdoria."

"Don't lie to me, Highton." Kelric knew the Eubians would never free his brother. Now that they had a Lock and a Key, nothing would convince them to surrender either.

"Why would I lie?" Jaibriol asked.

"It's what you Hightons do," Kelric said. "Lie, manipulate, cheat."

It happened then. Jaibriol's aloof mask slipped. In that instant, his face revealed a terrified, lonely young man trapped in a role beyond his experience. And his gaze was wrenchingly familiar. Kelric *knew* him, but he didn't remember how.

Then Jaibriol recovered, and once again the icy emperor faced Kelric. "I've little interest in your list of imagined Highton ills," he said. His disdain was almost convincing.

Kelric tried to fathom him. "Eube would never give away its Key. Not when you had a Lock. Nothing is worth it."

"Not even me?"

That stopped Kelric cold. "You, for Eldrin?"

"Yes."

It was the one trade Kelric could imagine them making. A vibrant young emperor on the throne would revitalize Eube. But at the price of their Key? It must have ignited furious debate.

"You are right," Jaibriol said. "It wasn't a universally popular decision. But it is done. I am emperor and your brother is free."

Kelric wondered if his face betrayed that much of his thoughts. He didn't fool himself that they had let Eldrin go. This new emperor was toying with him while guards waited outside.

"I am alone," Jaibriol said.

Kelric froze. "Why did you say that?" If he hadn't known better, he would have thought Jaibriol was an empath. But no Aristo could be a psion.

"You didn't wonder if I had guards?" Jaibriol asked. "I find that hard to believe."

"And you just happened to come in alone when I was here."

"Perhaps you could say I felt it."

"Perhaps," Kelric said. "I don't believe it."

"I suppose not." Jaibriol rubbed his chin. "I detected your entrance in the station web."

Kelric knew the boy was lying. But why? And why did Jaibriol look so hauntingly familiar?

"Imperator Skolia." Jaibriol took a breath. "Meet me when we can discuss peace."

"Why should I believe you want this?"

Jaibriol motioned upward, a gesture that seemed to include all Eube. "It's a great thundering machine I hold by the barest thread. If I am to find a way road to peace, I need your help."

It hit Kelric then, what he had known at a subliminal level through-out this surreal conversation. He felt the youth's mind. Jaibriol had mental barriers. They had been dissolving as he and Kelric talked, probably without the young man realizing it. His luminous Kyle strength glowed.

Jaibriol the Third was a psion.

Kelric spoke in a stunned voice. "You're a telepath."

"No." Pain layered Jaibriol's denial. He became pure Highton. Pol-ished. Cold. Unreal. "I am what you see. Qox."

"At what price?" Kelric asked. "What must you suffer to hide the truth?" He couldn't imagine the hells this young man lived, sur-rounded by Aristos, never knowing surcease.

Jaibriol met his gaze. "Was anyone here when I came into the Lock? I never saw him."

Kelric spoke softly. "Gods help you, son."

Strain creased Jaibriol's face. "Go. Now. While you can."

Kelric stepped into the Lock corridor. Then he turned and started the long walk down the corridor. His back itched as he waited for the shot, a neural blocker to disable him or rifle fire that would shred his body.

"Lord Skolia," Jaibriol said.

He froze. Would the game end now? He turned to face the emperor. "Yes?"

"If you make it to Earth—" Jaibriol lifted his hand, as if to reach toward him. "Go see Admiral William Seth Rockworth."

"I will go." He wanted to ask more, but he didn't dare stay longer. He set off again. As he strode down the corridor, he had a strange sense, as if Jaibriol whispered in his mind:

God's speed, my uncle . . .

The memory faded, and Kelric became aware of Dehya. He didn't recall moving, but they were both sitting on the floor. The light of the singularity rippled the air in the chamber.

He is a psion. She didn't make it a question.

It took Kelric a moment to reorient. **Yes, I think so.**

We need to know more about him.

Have you had contact with Seth Rockworth? Qox lived with him for two years. He regretted needing to ask the question; he knew she avoided the topic of her former husband. Nei-ther the Imperialate nor his government had formally acknowledged their divorce for fear it would invalidate the treaty established by their marriage. For Eldrin's sake, she kept the subject out of their lives.

I haven't spoken to Seth in years, she thought. *I doubt the Allieds would let me near him. They've watched him continually since they learned he had Jaibriol Qox as his ward.*

I'm not surprised.

I too have wondered about Qox, though.

Kelric tensed. **In what way?**

It's hard to explain.

He waited, but she said no more. It was her way; she often thought in patterns or equations that evolved in subshells of her mind before she spoke of them. It disconcerted most people, but it never bothered him. When she felt ready, she would explain.

In any case, he had another way to communicate with her. He took off his pouch and spilled his Quis dice onto the floor. The gems sparkled against the silvery-white composite, but the light that saturated the chamber washed out their glitter. He lowered his defenses carefully, so he wouldn't injure her mind with the force of his own. He wanted her to understand Quis at a level deeper than even she could glean from a few sessions.

Kelric offered his knowledge of Quis, and he felt her mind blending with his as she absorbed the concepts. He placed the first die, an onyx octahedron he used for the Qox dynasty. Dehya studied it and then set down a gold dodecahedron. They built patterns of the Traders, the Imperialate, and the Ruby and Qox dynasties. At first, she did little more than mimic his moves. Then she began to mold the structures on her own. He felt the change on a visceral level, as her Quis took on the luminous character of her extraordinary intellect.

Kelric wasn't certain when he realized what Dehya was trying to show him. She knew too little about the game to clarify her patterns, but she learned fast. Incredibly fast. Her theory became clear; the implosions began on the planet Glory because the Lock was seeking the nearest Ruby psion.

Jaibriol the Third.

No! He built structures to overpower hers, yet no matter how hard he tried, they evolved back to the same pattern: the Lock sought a Key. It hadn't reached out to the Orbiter or Parthonia or anywhere else the Ruby Dynasty called home. Instead, it had touched the Qox Palace.

As to why Dehya believed Jaibriol was a Key, either she didn't know Quis well enough to develop the pattern or else she was holding back.

Kelric pushed harder, building structures centered on the Aristo compulsion with the so-called purity of their lines. They were fanatical about their genetics. They would consider it an abomination for a psion to sit on the throne.

Dehya's patterns echoed his, but a stronger one swamped them out. Aristos had an even greater obsession: subjugating the Ruby Dynasty. They found the power wielded by the House of Skolia more intolerable than diluting their DNA, enough even for the Qox Dynasty to breed a Ruby psion in their Line.

Kelric exhaled. He had to acknowledge the possibility. He already believed the emperor was an empath. If Qox had the sensitivity of a Ruby psion, the young man's life had to be a never-ending hell.

A grim thought hit him. **If I restarted the Lock, Qox can use it.**

Dehya looked up. *We must discover what happened and decide what to do.*

Affecting the SSRB Lock from so far away is difficult. I'm not sure what I'm doing.

I may be able to tell.

The Kyle might not support both of us at the same time.

We must try.

Kelric nodded, his motions slowed in the space of this interstice chamber. He put away his dice, and they stood up, regarding each other. Whether or not they would survive, neither of them knew, but the consequences of trying nothing were too serious to ignore.

Together, they stepped into the column of radiance.

XXI

The Broken Pillar

Jaibriol awoke into dimness. He lay on his side with blankets pulled over his shoulders. Opening his eyes, he stared across the room, which was lit by no more than a small night-panel next to an unfamiliar door. He felt queasy and dull . . .

His memories trickled back then: the Lock, Colonel Muze, Hidaka, the nauseating stench of scorched flesh. Jaibriol groaned, and his stomach lurched.

A rustle came from across the room. "Your Highness?"

Hidaka? Jaibriol thought he spoke the name, but nothing came out. His giant bodyguard was walking out of the shadows, a projectile pistol large on his belt, his boots thudding on the floor, his tread slowed in the lower gravity of the space station. The gunmetal collar around his neck glinted.

Jaibriol laboriously pulled himself up to sit in bed. The covers fell around his waist. He still wore the black trousers and shirt from before, but someone had taken off his shoes.

Hidaka stopped by the bed, looking down, his face shadowed. "Are you repaired?" he asked.

Jaibriol squinted at him, disoriented. When his Razers talked that way, they did sound like machines. "I don't know." His voice was thick. "How long have I been unconscious?"

"Six hours, thirty-two minutes, and twelve seconds."

That long? His fear grew. "You shot Colonel Muze."

"Yes, Your Highness. He threatened you. I am tasked with guarding your life. So I removed the threat."

"What did you see?"

"You went into the corridor. It was too dark, and I couldn't find you."

"You followed me into the Lock?" Jaibriol hadn't had any idea. He had thought he gave his bodyguards the slip.

"Yes, Sire. So did Colonel Muze. When the Lock activated, it lit up the dais room. I saw him at the start of the corridor. He did not see me. He went down the corridor, and I followed."

Good Lord. Hidaka must have heard everything. But maybe he didn't realize what it meant.

"Do you know who I am?" Jaibriol asked. He wished Hidaka didn't loom so ominously over him.

"You are the Emperor of Eube." Hidaka seemed puzzled by the question.

A cautious relief spread over Jaibriol. "Yes, that's right. I was checking the Lock to see if it had sustained damage related to the implosions."

"Yes, Sire."

"That is what you saw."

"Yes." Then Hidaka added, "I didn't see the emperor join the Triad."

Jaibriol felt the blood drain from his face. He stared at Hidaka, and the captain met his gaze steadily. In a voice more human than many Aristos, Hidaka said, "I would never see anything, Your Highness, that would bring harm to your reign." His gaze darkened. "Nor would I let anyone else."

Everything about Jaibriol's life as he had understood it these past ten years was tilting askew. "What have you told the station authorities?"

"That Colonel Muze tried to murder you."

Sweat broke out on Jaibriol's brow. "Has anyone tried to take you into custody?"

"No, Sire."

"An Aristo is dead, Hidaka." He strove to keep his voice even. "No one can kill a Highton with impunity."

"I was protecting you." The captain paused. "Security here does wish to question me. They also wish to ascertain you are alive."

"Why haven't they ascertained it yet?"

"We will let no one near you, Sire, until we are assured of your safety."

We? If more people than Hidaka were involved in this business, he could be in even more trouble than he thought. "Who is 'we'?"

"Myself and your other bodyguards."

"You have protected me well. I'm immensely grateful." He meant every word. At the moment, he was also terrified of the Razer, who had broken God only knew how many supposedly inviolable restraints on his actions. "I must speak now with the station authorities."

"I cannot risk your safety."

He wasn't certain if Hidaka was holding him prisoner or guarding him. The captain had been conditioned to protect Aristos. *Only* Aristos. Then he had seen the emperor revealed as a Ruby psion. He should have *helped* Muze make the capture. Jaibriol wouldn't wish anyone's death, but he was grateful Hidaka had intervened. Now, though, he had no idea what the captain intended for him.

"Is Robert here?" Jaibriol asked.

"He has been staying in his quarters."

"Is this his suite?"

Hidaka shook his head. "Mine, sir."

"Ah." Jaibriol spoke firmly. "I must speak with Robert."

Hidaka's gaze never wavered. "I cannot bring him, Sire."

Jaibriol thought he must be hearing wrong. Hidaka couldn't refuse, not if he acknowledged Jaibriol as emperor. Jaibriol lowered his barriers and probed Hidaka's mind, but he received only a metallic sense of thought.

"You must bring him," Jaibriol said.

"I cannot put you in danger."

Jaibriol rubbed his face, groggy and disoriented. "What are you going to do with me?"

"No harm will come to you." Incredibly, strain sounded in the captain's metallic voice. "I have sent a starship to the Qox Palace, summoning backup. When the rest of your Razers arrive, we will escort you to Glory."

"Because you trust the other Razers."

"Yes, Sire."

Jaibriol's hand clenched on the blanket. "Are you going to tell anyone what you saw in the Lock?"

Hidaka met his gaze. "I saw nothing except an attempt by Colonel Muze to murder you."

He didn't know whether to be relieved or afraid. Hidaka had the ultimate case for blackmail. "What do you expect in return?"

For a moment the Razer looked confused. Then comprehension washed over on his face. Jaibriol almost missed it; in the dimness, he could barely see the cybernaut's shadowed features.

Hidaka went down on one knee and bent his head. "I ask nothing in return, Your Highness, but that your reign be long and glorious. I serve you today, tomorrow, next year, and for as long as I live."

Jaibriol stared at him, astonished. When he had ascended to the throne, his Razers had disturbed him, for they had been more than half Aristo. He had gradually replaced them with these guards who couldn't transcend, but he never forgot that his secret police were conditioned to hold Aristos and their principles above all else, including the emperor's life, should it turn out he violated those principles by his very existence. Never in a thousand years would he have thought Hidaka would, or even could, choose loyalty over that conditioning.

When Jaibriol found his voice, he said, "Captain, I—Rise. Please, rise."

Hidaka rose to his feet, towering. Jaibriol looked up at him, aware of how vulnerable he would be if Hidaka ever decided to act against him. "I am grateful for your protection and your loyalty. I will never forget, Captain. But I must see Robert."

"He is called Robert Muzeson." Hidaka's voice was steel.

Then Jaibriol understood. Robert was related to the colonel. Distantly, but still, he had a kinship tie with Vatrix Muze.

Jaibriol spoke quietly. "I'll be safe with him. And you'll be here."

It was plain Hidaka wanted to object. Jaibriol would see now how far his bodyguard could go in holding him captive.

For a moment, Hidaka did nothing. He finally took a deep breath and bowed to Jaibriol, then crossed the room to the door. When he opened it, Jaibriol glimpsed his other guards outside. Hidaka spoke to them, four giants conferring, then closed and secured the door.

The Razor turned back to Jaibriol. "I have sent for Muzeson."

Jaibriol's grip on the blanket eased. If he was a prisoner, at least they didn't intend to completely isolate him.

Robert arrived within moments, and strode across the room. He looked as if he hadn't slept in ages. Dark rings showed under his eyes like smudges and his hair was a mess. Jaibriol could imagine him raking his hand through it as he argued with Hidaka.

When Robert reached the bed, he knelt and bowed his head. "My honor at your presence, Esteemed Highness." His voice shook.

"Robert, you don't need to do that." When his aide looked up, Jaibriol motioned to the chair by the nightstand. He congratulated himself that his arm only trembled a bit, for he felt as wobbly as a newborn pup. "Sit. Be comfortable. Tell me what's going on."

Robert sat in the chair, stiffly, on its edge, obviously anything but comfortable. "Are you all right, Sire? I've been so worried. They refused to let me near you."

"I'm all right. Hidaka didn't want to do anything until I woke up." That wasn't exactly true, but it would do. "How much has he told you?"

Robert's posture tensed more, though Jaibriol wouldn't have thought that possible. "He said Muze tried to kill you and destroyed the Lock instead. Hidaka managed to shoot him before he shot you."

Jaibriol could pick up more from Robert than with Hidaka, enough to know his aide believed the tale. "I'm grateful for Hidaka's quick action." More than grateful. Indebted for life.

Robert glowered at him. "It is my fervent wish, Most Glorious and Esteemed Highness, that you will remain glorious and esteemed by resisting the impulse the next time you feel inspired to dodge your bodyguards."

Jaibriol almost smiled. He didn't, knowing that if he softened, Robert would continue the lecture. He thought of Muze, and his humor faded. "The colonel's staff must be upset."

Robert answered dryly. "You've a gift for understatement."

"Have they demanded we turn Hidaka over to them?"

Robert gave him an odd look. "You are the emperor. They can't make demands against the captain of your guards, especially after Muze tried to kill you. They are treading with care. And Hidaka sent for backup before anyone knew what he was doing."

Jaibriol was beginning to reassess his fear of the guard. Maybe Hidaka had been the only one thinking straight. "Is the situation here that bad, that we need backup?"

"I'm not sure," Robert said. That he made such an admission relieved Jaibriol; the aides who served most Hightons would never risk such a statement, lest they bring down punishment on themselves. Jaibriol thought it was a stupid way to manage staff. In his experience, people did better work when they weren't afraid they would be skewered for problems beyond their control.

"The colonel's aides are terrified," Robert continued. "I suspect they are waiting to see who you want executed." After a moment, he added, "If you do."

Jaibriol stared at him. "Executions for *what*? Were they in a conspiracy with Muze?" He doubted it, given that Muze hadn't actually tried to assassinate him. But he would have asked the question if Hidaka's cover story were true. Besides, one never knew with Aristos. Their plots and counterplots bubbled everywhere like overactive carbonation.

"I haven't seen evidence of one," Robert said. "That doesn't mean it doesn't exist, of course."

"So they expect me to kill a few of them just to make sure."

"Yes, Sire."

It sounded to Jaibriol like a good way to decimate the station. He didn't intend to execute anyone. However, he needed to appear as if he were acting from a position of power rather than waiting to see if the station authorities would demand an investigation.

"I want Muze's people questioned." He glanced at Hidaka, who was standing back, a dark figure in the dim light. "Captain, you're in charge of the interviews. I want to know how far this conspiracy went." They both knew it went nowhere, but he had no doubt Hidaka could make it look as if he believed otherwise.

Jaibriol started to say more, but his vision blurred and the room swirled around him. Although Robert was saying something, Jaibriol couldn't concentrate. As he sagged to one side, Robert jumped up and reached to catch him. Suddenly Hidaka was there, his large hand covering Robert's shoulder, holding him back with that huge grip.

Robert froze, staring up—and up—at Hidaka. Moving with great care, the aide straightened, keeping his arms at his sides and his hands in plain view.

Jaibriol rubbed his eyes, trying to regain his equilibrium. "What did you say?" he asked Robert.

Robert spoke carefully. "You need a doctor."

Jaibriol shook his head, then stopped as his nausea roiled. He didn't dare see a doctor. He had no idea what a physician could tell about his condition. Did becoming a Key alter him in a measurable way? He didn't feel any three-way Triad link, but he was too shaken to think straight. Power roared within him like an ocean, but it was all muddled and confused. He dreaded what it could mean. His uncle had killed his great-grandfather by joining the powerlink. Their minds had been too alike; it couldn't support them both. Jaibriol prayed he hadn't harmed his kin, the Ruby Pharaoh or the Imperator.

With a sigh, he collapsed onto the bed. He was aware of Hidaka pulling the covers over him. Then he passed out.

DARKNESS.
INJURY.
DEATH.

Kelric?

The name reverberated in the darkness.

Dehya? he thought.

I am here.

They existed in blackness. The Lock Chamber on the Orbiter had vanished the moment they stepped into the singularity. But where light normally inundated Kyle space, now only the dark surrounded them.

Kelric poured out his power. Dehya added her nuance—

Kyle space burst into existence, a radiant blue ocean under a sky roiling with dark clouds. Kelric swelled in a giant wave, a tsunami that could drown a person by breaking on the shores of their mind. Dehya existed everywhere as texture, detail, color, the *essence* of this space. Had Kelric had a body here, his breath would have caught. He had never seen the Kyle in such vivid beauty. When he was by himself, he experienced it only as a sense of light.

It's incredible, he thought.

I've never seen it so strongly, Dehya thought.

Or vast. In the far distance he saw blackness.

That's not a landmass, Dehya thought. *It's just gone.*

He swept through the ocean toward the empty place. As he neared the dark shoals, he arose in a tidal wave. His power roared into the darkness—

Into nothing—

Nothing—
Destruction—
Death—
Come back! Dehya's shout reverberated.

With a wrench, he pulled out of the void. The sea and skyscape reformed, but now they wavered and rippled.

Home, he thought.

Kelric became aware of his body. He was sitting at the console in the chamber again. Dehya stood on the other side of the octagonal room, partially hidden by the singularity. The light washed out his vision; he could barely make her out.

For a while he sat, unfocused. Eventually he realized Dehya was walking toward him. Each of her steps lasted a long time. Her mouth moved, but it took endless time for her to form one word. It vibrated in his mind, distant, long, drawn out.

Goooooooo . . .

Her slowed-time walk mesmerized him. How many hours would she need to cross the chamber? How long to say one sentence?

Dooooown . . . she thought.

Go down . . . ? He was comfortable on his stool. He could sit here forever.

Avennnnuuuuuue . . .

She had taken three steps, and the singularity no longer hid her from view. Her body was ephemeral, translucent, caught in transition from the Kyle.

Of Aaaages . . .

Go down the Avenue of Ages. She wanted him to leave the chamber. Urgency touched her voice despite her languid approach.

He slowly stood, rising to his full height, the floor receding below him. Dehya was partway into her fourth step. He turned toward the entrance. The corridor should stretch from that opening back to the Orbiter, but he could see nothing beyond the arch. He stepped toward it, and the thud of his boot reverberated as if he were some massive giant out of Lyshrioli mythology. He stepped again, but the entrance came no closer. Again. The opening was only four paces away, yet it seemed unreachable.

Huuurrrryyy . . .

Step.

Step again.

The archway was out of reach.

Reach . . .

Reach out . . .

Reach out his arm . . .

His hand closed on the edge of the arch.

Pull . . .

Pull body . . .

Pull body forward . . .

Lift foot . . .

Lift foot to Lock corridor . . .

Kelric lurched into the corridor and stumbled along its glittering floor. His time sense snapped back to normal, and he heaved in a breath, his chest expanding as he gulped air. Then he swung around. Dehya was inside the chamber, barely visible in the radiance. She had one foot lifted and one arm outstretched, but viewed from out here, her motion was so slow, he couldn't even see a change in her position.

Dehya!

Kelric had a strange sense, as if she strained to answer his mental shout, but her thoughts existed in a slowed time and couldn't mesh with his own. He grabbed the archway and stretched his arm back into the chamber. He felt as if he were pushing through invisible molasses. With maddening slowness, his hand closed around her forearm. He braced himself against the archway, one foot against the wall and the other planted on the floor behind him—and he *heaved*.

Dehya came out of the chamber like a child birthed by ancient forceps. Her body solidified and suddenly she was moving at normal speed—straight into Kelric. The force of his pull had already unbalanced him, and as she crashed into his body, he stumbled back, losing his hold on her. She lurched away and slammed into a pillar, her cheek bouncing against its transparent surface. The lights inside the column flashed as if panicked.

Kelric regained his balance like a tree almost felled, but still standing. When he started toward Dehya, she shook her head, warning him away. Her face was pale and her eyes large. She spoke, or at least her mouth moved, but he heard none of her words. He stretched out his arm, pointing to the corridor that should—he hoped—take them to the Orbiter War Room.

Dehya slowly pushed a straggle of hair out of her eyes and started down the corridor. Far in the distance, a point of light glittered.

They walked together.

And walked.

And walked.

For hours.

The point of perspective never came closer. They were in a broken corridor, forever trapped between two universes.

XXII

The Path Home

Jaibriol awoke, slept, and awoke again. Robert hovered over him, his face strained, always with Hidaka nearby, like a bulwark.

The next time Jaibriol awoke, he was lying in a new bed. Someone had changed his clothes into silk pajamas with the imperial seal of a Eubian jaguar on the shirt. The small light on a nearby wall illuminated very little, but he could tell this room was smaller than his quarters on the station. Although the hum around him was familiar, he couldn't place it. He lay on his back and stared at a white ceiling curving above his head, so close he could touch it if he lifted his arm.

Eventually it came to him. The hum was an engine. He was on a star yacht. He didn't recognize this cabin, but his own yacht had a bulkhead that arched above the bed this way. As he turned on his side under the silver covers, a beep came from nearby. Undoubtedly a panel somewhere had just notified some person he was awake. He didn't know how the monitors could tell the difference between his turning over while he slept and while he was awake, but they seemed to know.

Sure enough, someone soon appeared: Corbal Xir, his elderly cousin. "Elderly" was relative; Corbal had the health of a man in his prime. Only his eyes showed his age. Jaibriol wasn't sure how to define what he saw in them. Wisdom, perhaps, but other Aristos possessed that trait. A human being could be wise and still be harsh. It wasn't the presence of something he saw, but its lack. No cruelty. His cousin might be avaricious and power hungry, but he wasn't brutal. Jaibriol had no doubt Corbal would manipulate him for gain if he could, but he felt closer to the Xir lord than to any other Aristo except Tarquine.

Corbal walked quietly through the cabin, his pace slow in the low gravity created by the yacht's rotation. When Jaibriol realized his cousin thought he was sleeping, he sat up and swung his legs over the edge of the bed. Corbal paused, his face unreadable in the dim light.

"Luminos, half power," Jaibriol said. The lights brightened, though not enough to bother his eyes.

"My greetings, cousin," Corbal said. He came over and sat in a chair near the bed.

Jaibriol rubbed his eyes. "Is this your yacht?"

"It is indeed." Corbal frowned at him. "I thought you had outgrown this penchant of yours for traipsing all over Eube without proper guard or backup."

"My guard is fine," Jaibriol said coolly. "Hidaka sent for more Razers."

"He did. I came, too. I thought you might prefer a yacht to a military transport."

He was right, but he was also evading the point. "How did you know Hidaka had sent for more guards?"

"Why wouldn't I know? Your safety is my concern. Your bodyguards know this."

Jaibriol wasn't fooled. His bodyguards didn't trust Corbal any more than he did. "They wouldn't tell you if they thought I was in danger. For all they know, you plotted with Colonel Muze, another of my dear relatives." He scowled at Corbal. "Your spies are nosing into my affairs again. I want you to cut it out."

His esteemed cousin looked as if he didn't know whether to feign offense or astonishment. "I cannot 'cut out' what I haven't done."

"You know what I mean. How did you get past Tarquine?"

Corbal crossed his muscular arms. "I fail to understand why I would need to pass the empress."

"Oh, I don't know. Maybe because her spies are watching your spies watch me to make sure they report nothing back to you that she doesn't want you to know about me."

Corbal snorted, and this time his annoyance sounded genuine. "Your wife has a high opinion of her intelligence. Someone should remind her that the point where self-confidence becomes folly is closer than most people realize."

Jaibriol had long ago learned never to underestimate the force of nature he had married. "I'm glad to hear you say that. It eases my mind to know you won't let it happen to you."

Corbal raised an eyebrow. "You might warn the empress of the same. Otherwise someone might turn her merchant fleets over to the Skolians."

Well, hell. So he also suspected Tarquine of helping the Skolians catch Janq pirates. Corbal would never accuse her without proof; otherwise, the accusation would do him more harm than Tarquine. And they both knew that if Tarquine had leaked covert information to the Skolians, she would never leave a shred of evidence.

Jaibriol thought of his dinner with Diamond Minister Gji, the one where Tarquine had never shown up and Corbal had come instead. "I can well imagine what might happen if an Aristo Line lost its fleets and believed the wrong person had caused it."

Corbal's voice hardened. "I would like to believe that the throne supports its allies."

"Well, you should believe it," he said, irritated Corbal had misunderstood his warning. He wasn't the one Corbal needed to fear. "I can't promise, however, that those who sit next to that rock-hard chair of mine don't have their own agenda."

Corbal raised his eyebrows. "Your Glorious Highness would never accuse, without proof, those who sit next to him."

"Well, guess what. I wouldn't accuse her *with* proof. Maybe I'm just worn out with the two of you bickering all the time."

Corbal shook his head at the direct speech and didn't respond, but Jaibriol could tell he appreciated the warning even if the craggy Xir lord would never make that admission.

"It pleases me to see you well," Corbal said instead. "The Line of Muze has much to answer for, but at least murder isn't among their crimes. Not that a lack of success makes the attempt any less of a betrayal."

If you only knew, Jaibriol thought. He said only, "Indeed." He had to admit, that word could come in useful.

"Muze's sentence fit his crime," Corbal said. "But now we will never know what he could have told us. Others may have plotted with him."

Dryly Jaibriol said, "Along with how many other Aristos who don't consider me fit to rule?"

"Of course you are fit to rule. The Emperor of Eube is exalted beyond and above all humanity."

"Corbal, don't." He wasn't up to listening to the standard Aristo line. It didn't help that most of his trillion subjects believed it, and even many Aristos, those who weren't convinced he was going to bring about the fall of Eube through his youth and "eccentric" notions of peace.

"Don't what?" Corbal said. "You must never express doubt. It only invites more such incidents."

He knew what his cousin meant: *Don't slip up.* But today Jaibriol could barely maintain his façade; his mind was too thick to form coherent thoughts. If Corbal ever learned what had happened, he would do everything within his prodigious power to use Jaibriol as a member of the Triad. Jaibriol felt ill when he contemplated the potential interstellar ramifications. He didn't even know why the Lock had awoken. The words he had thought while sitting in it hadn't felt like his own. Nor did he know what it meant to join the Triad. Should he sense the other two people in the link? He prayed the destruction of the Lock hadn't also killed them.

"How long have I been out?" Jaibriol asked.

Corbal had an odd expression, as if Jaibriol were a riddle for him to solve. "About six days, planet time. Ninety hours."

Jaibriol leaned against a bulkhead. "What do the doctors say is wrong with me?"

"Well, that is a problem."

That wasn't what Jaibriol wanted to hear. "It is?"

"The captain of your Razers says you gave him an Imperial order. No doctors. He says he will kill anyone who violates your order."

"Oh." Jaibriol couldn't recall giving the order, but it was a good one. "I didn't trust anyone on the station."

"You are no longer on the station."

"Razers are very literal."

Corbal was studying him. "They are designed like machines. Yours, however, seem to have more personality."

Jaibriol had no intention of letting Corbal interrogate him about his bodyguards. Hidaka had saved his life in more ways than he could count, but it also put Jaibriol at risk. It wasn't like with Corbal and Tarquine; he knew secrets about them as damaging as what they knew about him. They kept their silence to protect themselves as well as him. He had nothing, however, to ensure Hidaka never revealed him, and the Razer held an even greater secret. Corbal and Tarquine knew he could join the Triad; Hidaka knew he had *done* it. That the Razer hadn't yet tried to blackmail him offered no guarantee it wouldn't happen.

An image tugged at Jaibriol's mind: the light in his room reflecting off the Razer's gunmetal collar. He realized then his mistake. He kept forgetting his bodyguards were taskmakers. He saw them as free men, deserving of the same respect as every human. But they always knew: he could turn them off, reprogram them, kill them with impunity. Even if he forgot that ugly truth, they never would. No Razer would blackmail the emperor. In Highton culture, it would be an immediate death warrant. If he had been thinking clearly, he would have realized that sooner.

Nor could a guard betray him to another Aristo in the hopes of furthering himself. The Aristo might go along with it until he learned the emperor's secrets, but then he would destroy the Razer. Hidaka should have let Colonel Muze take Jaibriol prisoner. He should have served as a witness. Instead, he defied a lifetime of conditioning to protect the emperor, choosing fidelity over the brainwashing that had defined him since birth. Why, Jaibriol didn't know, but it was finally soaking into his overwhelmed brain that Hidaka genuinely wanted to protect him.

Jaibriol exhaled as if he were a balloon losing air. It was good his guards looked out for him, because he felt too dazed to do it himself. He closed his eyes and slumped against the wall.

Corbal spoke quietly. "You should see a doctor."

"I'm only tired." Jaibriol lifted his eyelashes halfway, just enough to see Corbal. "I will speak with you later."

His cousin obviously wanted to object. But even he couldn't defy an Imperial dismissal. "As you wish, Your Highness." He rose and bowed, then took his leave. At the doorway, though, he paused to look back. Jaibriol met his gaze with no encouragement in his expression or body language, and after a moment, Corbal nodded with reserve and left the room.

Jaibriol slid back down into bed. He wondered if he would ever feel normal again. Did all Triad members live with this vertigo and sense of mental displacement? He hated it. And what good did it do him? He had no idea how to build a Kyle web or anything else. If he could have left the Triad, he would have done so in a second. But Hidaka had sacrificed the Lock to save him, and no one knew how to repair the ancient, arcane technology. If Jaibriol needed it to stop the implosions, he was out of luck, because that Lock would never again operate.

The dreamlike universe of the Lock corridor was neither spacetime nor the Kyle, but somewhere in between. Kelric and Dehya walked in limbo. When Dehya mouthed words, he couldn't decipher them. Their thoughts interfered like waves and cancelled each other out. The too-bright corridor sparkled until it hurt Kelric's eyes.

Bolt, he thought. He had an odd sense, as if his node responded, but the firing of its bioelectrodes was out of phase with his brain. Its thoughts were waves whispering against the shores of his mind.

He and Dehya walked and walked and went nowhere.

Kelric became aware of a tug on his thoughts. **Dehya?** he thought. **Is that you?**

Nnnnnnnn.

He wasn't certain if that came from her, but he took it as *No.* An image flickered in his mind . . .

A Quis die?

That didn't come from Dehya. Kelric focused inward, and the image of a topaz octahedron intensified. It was the piece he used to symbolize Haka Estate, where his son had grown up. A second image formed: a gold octahedron. His daughter. He wasn't forming the images; they came from outside of him.

Rohka? he thought.

Come hooooome . . .

The thought originated from beyond this corridor. It coiled like a rope, and he grabbed it with his mind. He grasped Dehya's shoulder to ensure they didn't get separated in this endless place, his huge hand covering her from neck to upper arm. Dehya glanced up at him, but she didn't object.

Kelric followed the mental rope of Quis dice. Nothing changed in the corridor: it remained an infinite pathway that ended in a point. But the image of the dice stayed in his mind, drawing him home . . .

Like a shutter opening, the point ahead of them suddenly expanded into an archway a few meters away, its transparent columns filled by gold, silver, and bronze gears, with lights racing across them like sparkflies. Kelric lengthened his stride, afraid the arch would disappear before he and Dehya reached that portal back into their own universe.

As they staggered under the arch, his mind *rippled* as if it were a lake and the thoughts of people in his universe were stones dropping into the water, creating circles that expanded outward in ever widening waves. In that moment, he saw the Lock corridor as if he were watching it through hundreds of eyes, all the people in the War Room. He and Dehya were stepping out of a white mist, she staggering in slow motion, he with his limp exaggerated, his large hand gripped on her shoulder.

Kelric's thoughts snapped back into his mind as abruptly as they had jumped outward. He and Dehya stumbled onto the dais in the War Room, and people surged around them. With a groan, he sank to his knees, reeling with vertigo. Doctors knelt around him, monitoring him with scanners and asking questions he couldn't hear. Dehya collapsed a few paces away, and one of her huge Jagernaut bodyguards knelt protectively over her while people crowded around.

Kelric didn't realize his bodyguards were also on the dais until Najo brushed his shoulder. Looking around, Kelric saw Strava on his other side, her stoic face impassive, and Axer behind him, huge and bulky, a giant with a bald, tattooed head.

Chad Barzun, the commander of the Imperial Fleet, knelt next to Kelric. Even as short as he kept his iron-grey hair, it looked disheveled, as if he had raked his hand across it. Wrinkles creased his blue uniform, though it was designed from smart cloth that could smooth out normal crumples. Dark circles showed under his eyes.

Kelric's mind swam, thick and woozy, with a sense of mental dislocation. Chad was talking, but Kelric couldn't understand him. It wasn't that Chad spoke out of phase, but rather that Kelric had spent so long in a distorted space-time, his mind couldn't readjust to his natural universe.

He looked past all the people and commotion. At the edge of the dais, his mother Roca and his brother Eldrin stood waiting—with a tall woman whose regal face would have caught his eye in any crowd. Ixpar. His wife. He had never seen her so pale. He didn't know how long he had been gone, but during that time, she would have been stranded in a place she had little context to understand and where she knew almost no one. She had taken the irreversible step of breaking Coba's isolation, risking the well-being of her people, even their identity, all based on his vow that he could protect them. And what had he done to honor her tremendous act of faith? Vanished the day after she came to him. Gods only knew what she thought now of his promises.

An ISC doctor was wrapping a med-string around Kelric's arm to monitor his blood pressure. Another medic was studying holos of Kelric's body that rotated above a screen he had unrolled on the floor. Kelric couldn't follow the discussion of the doctors at all, and Chad had given up trying to talk to him. The admiral was just sitting on the floor, an elbow on his bent knee, watching the doctors and Kelric.

Bolt? Kelric thought.

I'm here, his node answered.

Relief washed over Kelric. **Can you communicate for me? I can't understand anyone.**

I will access your gauntlets.

Good. Also, how long was I in the Lock?

I don't know. The singularity disrupted the atomic clock in your biomech web.

See what you can find out.

A deep voice came out of the comm on his right gauntlet. "Admiral Barzun, can you understand me?"

Chad jerked, then peered at Kelric and at the gauntlet with that alert, wary style of his that Kelric knew well. When the admiral answered, his words were garbled and indistinct.

Do you understand him? Kelric asked.

Yes, Bolt answered. It's muddled, but I believe he said, "To whom am I speaking?"

Explain it to him.

"I am the primary node in Imperator Skolia's biomech web," Bolt said to Chad. "He is having trouble hearing you. I will interpret. Also, he wishes to know how long he has been gone."

As Chad answered, Bolt thought, He says you went into the corridor four days ago and Pharaoh Dyhianna about three.

No wonder I'm so hungry. He should have been starving; he needed huge amounts of food to fuel his large body. **Is Dehya all right?**

Bolt relayed the question. He says the pharaoh is having less problem communicating. However, she won't tell anyone what happened.

Kelric glanced at Dehya over the heads of the people around them. She was sitting up and talking to another doctor. Her guards hulked over her, dwarfing her body.

Dehya, Kelric thought. **Can you hear me?**

She glanced at him. *Are you still out of resonance?*

Resonance with what? And why doesn't it affect you?

I think whatever damaged Kyle space threw the Lock here out of phase with our universe. My mind adjusts faster than yours, that's all. It's probably the price you pay for all that power. She paused as someone spoke to her. Then she thought, *Kelric, we need to talk. We have to get rid of all these worried people.*

Worried indeed. The people around them were pretending they didn't notice the pharaoh and imperator having a silent conversation. Although he and Dehya were trying to be subtle, it was hard not to use gestures or facial expressions when they communicated; he did it reflexively. It was awkward, like whispering in front of others, but at the moment he had no other option.

We can't talk just yet, he thought, tilting his head toward Roca, Eldrin, and Ixpar. **We must see to our families.**

Yes. Her face gentled as she gazed at Eldrin. He looked calmer now than when she had come out of the corridor, but Kelric could imagine how frantic he must have been after she vanished. Guilt washed over him for the worry he had caused.

Dehya's thought rippled. *You didn't do it. Something happened, I don't know what, but it's not good.*

It's still affecting us.

Can you speak at all with the people here?

Kelric turned his attention to the admiral, who had sat back on the floor. "Chad, do you understand me?"

Everyone around him froze, and the people tending Dehya turned with startled jerks. Ixpar had been lifting her hand to her face, probably to brush away a fiery tendril of hair, but now she stopped with her arm in midair.

For flaming sake. **Bolt, why is everyone staring at me?**

Your voice sounds odd, Bolt thought. It is unusually loud and it echoes. I believe it is the type of sound humans associate with an elevated being.

Elevated, my ass.

It wasn't until Dehya laughed that he realized he hadn't shielded his mind from her. When he glowered, she thought, *I doubt your gluteus maximus has anything to do with it.*

Funny, he growled. Her doctors were asking if she was all right, probably because she had laughed for no obvious reason.

He climbed stiffly to his feet, his joints crackling and his knees aching. He towered over everyone. Chad and his doctors stood up as well, and the doctors backed away. Although Chad stayed put, sweat sheened his forehead.

"I'll need to meet with you and the other joint chiefs," Kelric said to him. From the way the admiral blanched, Kelric thought his voice must still sound strange.

"I'll take care of it, sir." Chad's answer had an oddly distant quality, as if he were far away. But he spoke with the same efficient confidence Kelric had always appreciated. Chad Barzun might not have Admiral Ragnar Bloodmark's brilliance, but Kelric would far rather have Chad backing him than Ragnar.

Kelric rolled his shoulders to ease his sore muscles. "Chad, did anyone try going into the Lock to find us?"

"We've been trying," Chad said. "No one with a trace of psi ability has been able to enter the corridor. Normally they can walk a short way before they have to turn back, but this time they couldn't even go under the archway. The path, well—disappeared. We sent in people with a zero Kyle rating, and they found the path, but they couldn't reach the end. They just kept walking. They couldn't communicate with us, either, until they came back. We finally found someone with a negative rating. She reached the end, but the chamber was empty. No singularity. She waited a day, until she ran out of water, but she never found a trace of you or Pharaoh Dyhianna."

"Gods," Kelric muttered.

"It was bizarre," Chad said. "No sensor registered either you or the pharaoh as anywhere on the Orbiter."

"Doesn't that always happen when we go in the Lock?"

"I don't know," Chad admitted. "We have so few records of anyone using this one."

It was true, Kelric realized. He and Dehya called on the Lock as sparingly as possible, for they had no idea what, if anything, might stir a backlash. Exactly what that backlash might be, he neither knew nor desired to find out.

"Sir, what happened in there?" Chad asked.

A good question. "I'm not sure. I'll brief you at the meeting." Kelric wanted to speak to Dehya before he discussed it with anyone else. He could also see Ixpar watching him, which made it difficult to concentrate on Chad.

The admiral followed his gaze and smiled. "Shall I see you at the meeting then?"

"Yes, that would be good." Kelric started toward his wife, but as soon as he took a step, one of his doctors blocked his way.

The man's face paled as he looked up at Kelric, but he didn't move. "I'm sorry, Lord Skolia. But we don't know if your phase shift can affect your family."

That gave him pause. He wasn't sure what was wrong with him, but he certainly didn't want to shift anyone out of normal space or cause some other bizarre effect. After a moment, he said, "Please tell my wife what you just told me. It's her decision as to whether or not she will come over."

Ixpar was watching him with that intense quality of hers, as if she were barely contained energy. Her red hair had escaped its braid and was curling about her face. It reminded him of her personality, civilized on the surface, but with the atavistic queen simmering just below. She had always fascinated him, a study in contrasts, an enlightened leader dedicated to the advancement of her people with the soul of an ancient warrior burning within her.

Although the doctor was obviously uneasy, he went over to where Ixpar stood with Kelric's mother, Roca. Eldrin wasn't there anymore. Glancing around, Kelric saw Eldrin embracing Dehya, his head bent over hers, tears on his face. Kelric was feeling worse by the moment for causing all this upset.

He turned back to see Ixpar walking toward him in her graceful, long-legged gait. She didn't look the least perturbed by the prospect that her husband might suddenly phase out of space-time. A smile curved her lips. She might be the newcomer here, submersed in a culture strange and sometimes inexplicable, but if she felt any apprehension, neither her posture nor her mood revealed it. But then, Ixpar had never been easily daunted.

Roca stayed back. Kelric doubted she was worried about Kyle space anomalies; more likely, she knew he wanted to see Ixpar alone. It was an aspect of her personality he had always appreciated, for all that she frustrated him at times. However much she might want to talk to him, she stayed back, respecting his privacy. Although she had raised her mental shields, he could sense her response to Ixpar. She approved of his new wife. As well she might; they were both formidable women.

He detected more than that, though. She had always feared he would overwhelm his loves with the sheer force of his personality and mind. With Ixpar, she had no worries.

Ixpar stopped in front of Kelric, almost eye to eye with him. He wanted to embrace her, but he felt restrained with so many people on the dais: doctors, bodyguards, telops, and mech-techs studying the entrance to the Lock Corridor. He had never had Eldrin's ease with expressing his emotions even one on one, let alone with other people present.

Ixpar brushed a curling tendril out of her face and spoke in formal tones. "It's good to see you."

His voice softened, as it so rarely did nowadays. "I'm glad you're here."

"Kelric—" Her self-assured exterior slipped, and in that instant her worry for him showed. Then she took a breath and once again became the composed queen.

The hell with restraint. Kelric pulled her into his arms, feeling the smooth sweep of her hair under his cheek. With a sigh of release, she put her arms around him, supple in his embrace. She felt like a tiger, slim and sleekly muscled.

"I thought I had found you only to lose you again," she murmured.

"Ai, Ixpar, I'm sorry. I had no idea that would happen."

"Where did you go?"

"I'm not sure." He drew back, his arms around her waist. The faint sprinkle of freckles across her nose was almost impossible to see, except this close up. "You sent that message. The Quis dice."

She touched the dice pouch hanging from her belt, though he didn't think she realized she had taken that reflexive action. "No one could send you messages," she said. "Your officers tried to contact you, but it didn't work."

"You didn't send me mental images of Quis dice?"

"I wouldn't know how."

He realized it was true. Although she empathized strongly with others, he didn't think she was a full psion, certainly not a telepath who could send mental pictures. If she hadn't done it, though, then who? Neither his mother nor his siblings knew anything about Quis.

"Were either Rohka or Jimorla here?" he asked. He had been silent about his children for so long, it felt odd to say their names, as if it made both him and them vulnerable.

"We've been taking turns." She shifted her arms, and her muscles flexed against his back, stirring pleasant memories of their evening together on Coba.

"Hmmm." Kelric drew her closer and nuzzled her cheek.

She laughed softly. "We have an audience, you know."

Well, hell. He lifted his head with reluctance and let her go. "Were either of them here just before Dehya and I came out?"

"Rohka was here until a short time ago," Ixpar said. "She was tired, though. In fact she almost passed out. Your mother sent her to the house so she could rest."

Perhaps his daughter had almost passed out because she had reached between universes to contact him. She had the Ruby power, but no training; such an effort would probably exhaust her. He didn't know who else besides Jimorla would send images of dice, and he didn't think Jimorla had the Kyle strength.

"Has she ever talked about mind pictures?" he asked.

Ixpar shook her head, her brow furrowed. "Nothing. If she has a talent like that, she lets no one know."

It didn't surprise Kelric. Cobans didn't believe psions existed. If Rohka talked about what she could do, they would think her daft. He doubted she had told anyone here, either. Being sixteen years old was difficult enough even without the culture shock she was facing. She had no context to understand her gift. The moment the speaker at the Promenade had given her name as Skolia, almost everyone across three interstellar civilizations had understood its import—except Rohka herself.

"I need to talk to her and Jimorla," he said.

Ixpar's face gentled. "It would be good. They need to see you're all right."

Kelric didn't know if he could assure them of that. He feared none of them were all right, that what he and Dehya had discovered in the Kyle threatened the stability of space itself.

XXIII

The Lost Covenant

Corbal's yacht landed at a private spaceport in the Jaizire Mountains on Eube's Glory, capital planet of the Eubian Concord. Jaibriol had no doubt Corbal told his crew to make sure no one notified the empress. Corbal's spies would triple-check their security to ensure she didn't know her husband had come home.

Tarquine was at the port, of course.

She had come with a flyer, ready to whisk Jaibriol away to his private retreat in the untamed forest of the high peaks.

Corbal scowled as he stood in Jaibriol's cabin, watching the emperor prepare to meet his wife. "You should return to the palace," Corbal growled. "Not gallivant around the mountains."

Jaibriol shrugged into a conservative black-diamond shirt and sealed it up the front. Corbal was trying to unsettle him with the direct speech, but his cousin should know by now it wouldn't work.

"I need a rest, remember?" Jaibriol said. In truth, he was heartily sick of resting. His vertigo had receded, and he felt almost human again.

Corbal crossed his arms and leaned against a table. The furniture was genuine wood, a rarity on any space-faring vessel. Jaibriol liked it,

233

though not for the reason most Hightons approved of such extravagance, because it showed their wealth. During his first fourteen years of life, he had lived on a world where his family had only what they made themselves. He didn't know if the planet had been terraformed or developed flora on its own, but the mountains had been lush with trees. His family had built everything they needed from that wood. He would never tell his cousin the true reason he liked the tables on Corbal's yacht: they reminded him of home.

"Hiding in the hills will hardly present a courageous face to your subjects," Corbal said. "They want to see their emperor hale and hearty." Dryly he added, "And alive."

Jaibriol fastened his elegant sleeves with carnelian links at the cuffs. "Surely you don't suggest they know I might not have been alive." If someone had already leaked news of the murder attempt, he would have their hide. Not literally; he wasn't that much like his ancestors.

"No." Corbal straightened his posture, which in Highton meant he intended to convey a supposed truth. "But they will suspect problems exist if you don't attend your duties."

"Robert is going back with you." He cocked an eyebrow at Corbal. "If any dire duties come up that need attending, I'm sure he'll let me know."

His cousin frowned. "Sarcasm doesn't become an emperor."

"Oh, admit it, Corbal. You don't want me with Tarquine." Jaibriol finished fastening his cuffs. He could have had a valet dress him, but he had never liked other people doing what he was perfectly capable of doing himself. For public appearances, he let his protocol people work on him, mainly because they wouldn't leave him alone until he agreed, though somehow they always made it seem as if it were his idea.

"Your wife is most esteemed," Corbal said, holding his thumb and forefinger together. "So exalted, in fact, that she is up in the ozone. Such lofty heights can asphyxiate a person."

"Yes, well, she doesn't trust you, either."

His cousin made an exasperated noise. "Jai, your language will be your downfall just as surely as your empress."

Jaibriol scowled at him. "Stars forbid I should actually say what I mean."

"You want direct speech? Fine. Your manipulative wife is power mad."

Jaibriol went over to him. "If power is what she wants, why would she cause my downfall? If I go, so does she."

"A desire for a man's power isn't synonymous with a desire for a man's best interests."

The corners of Jaibriol's mouth quirked up. "I believe her desire is for the man."

"Then you have my sympathy," Corbal said sourly.

"Whereas you of course have no desire for my power."

Corbal met his gaze. "You were safer with Colonel Muze and his laser carbine than you are with Tarquine Iquar."

Jaibriol walked to the doorway, where he paused and looked back at his cousin. "I will see you when I get back."

Then he went to meet his wife.

Tarquine was waiting on the landing hexagon with her own Razers. Jaibriol could usually read her expressions even when she was a cipher to everyone else, but today her face was inscrutable, and he didn't dare lower his mental shields with his mind so sensitized by the Triad.

Her clothes bothered him, though he couldn't say why. She wore a violet jumpsuit, fur-lined jacket, and boots, all suitable for the cold mountain weather. Her hair hung in glittering perfection around her face and shoulders, and her sculpted features showed no hint of strain. But something was wrong. He was as certain of it as if someone had shouted the news.

Captain Hidaka stepped down from Corbal's yacht, his carbine gripped in both hands. Jaibriol followed, and then the rest of his guards. The conduits on Hidaka's arm were flashing, as were those of the captain for Tarquine's guards, as they communicated via implants in their bodies. The entire time, Tarquine stared at Jaibriol with no hint of emotion. He didn't know what to think. She didn't seem angry, nor did he know of any new crises beyond the usual state of Aristo life.

Hidaka turned to Jaibriol. "You and Her Highness are cleared to approach each other."

Jaibriol nodded, wondering if it sounded as bizarre to Hidaka as it did to him, that they had to clear the empress and emperor to meet each other like ships cleared to land.

Tarquine approached Jaibriol, her walk stirring him in ways he tried to ignore. She wasn't trying to be seductive; she never showed or sought affection in public. But he knew the way her muscles were moving under that jacket and jumpsuit. He had been alone for days, and he wanted his wife. More than that, he wished she had come to meet him because she wanted him, not because she had to assert to Corbal that she wielded greater influence over the throne.

"My greetings," Jaibriol said.

She stopped in front of him. "Are you all right?"

Her directness jolted him. In Highton, it could be an invitation to intimacy. It would shock other Aristos, not because of the sexual overtones; given the bondage orgies some of them had with their providers, a subtle hint of sensuality would hardly outrage anyone. But in this case, it came from an Aristo to her spouse in public. Rather than inviting his warmth, she would normally follow the strictures of their caste, including a reserve so extreme, it felt like a straightjacket to Jaibriol. Today she seemed distracted.

"I'm fine," he lied. He wondered if she sensed a difference in him. Space-time had literally shifted under his feet, yet everyone treated him exactly as always, even Hidaka, the only person alive who knew the truth.

"I find myself pleased," Tarquine said, her voice duskier than usual.

Jaibriol realized what he sensed in her. Strain. He could believe she would worry about an attempt on his life. It threatened her position as empress, especially given that he had no heir. If he died, the line of succession would go to Corbal. And he believed—or perhaps deluded himself—that she cared for him in her own Highton way. But he wasn't certain why her concern would translate into strain *with* him.

"It pleases me to see you looking so well," he said, which was more tasteful than *I want to throw you onto a bed.*

"It should," she murmured. "Much better than Corbal."

"It was generous of him to pick me up," Jaibriol said. Wryly he added, "Magnanimity is always a virtue."

"How very Highton," she said. "Using a five-syllable word where one or two would suffice."

He gave a startled laugh. "Now you sound like me."

"Far better to sound like you—" Her gaze shifted to a point beyond his shoulder. "—than certain others."

He turned to the yacht. Corbal was standing in the hatchway, leaning against one side, his arms crossed as he watched them. Although his shirt and trousers didn't look as if they had climate controls like the clothes Jaibriol was wearing, the Xir lord seemed unaffected by the cold.

Jaibriol walked back to the ship. He took care, when he was with both Tarquine and Corbal, never to appear as if he favored one over the other, at least not too much, lest their subtle war escalate to uglier proportions.

When Jaibriol stopped below the air lock, Corbal waited a moment before jumping down, just the barest pause—but it could get him arrested, for no one, even the highest of the Hightons, could deliberately stand above the emperor. Corbal was pushing to see how much favor Jaibriol would show in front of Tarquine. It irritated Jaibriol, because it forced him either to do nothing about Corbal's lapse in respect, and so appear weak by Highton standards, or else to think of some stupid punishment he had no wish to apply.

Jaibriol frowned at him. "I should invite you to dine with Tarquine and myself."

His cousin cocked an eyebrow at him. "What offense have I given, that you would threaten me with such?"

"Corbal, if you ever do that again, you won't be happy with the result."

The Xir lord answered in a deceptively mild tone. "Be assured, whatever point I might have intended is already made—and obvious to the only people who need a reminder of it."

Jaibriol knew he meant Tarquine. "Asserting favor with the throne by depending on the good will of kin has risks. Don't leave me no choice but to take actions I would far rather avoid."

"Favor works in two directions."

Jaibriol understood his point: enmity also went two ways. He didn't want Corbal as an enemy any more than Corbal wanted his disfavor.

"My greetings, Lord Xir," Tarquine said as she came up next to Jaibriol.

Corbal bowed to her. "My greetings, Your Highness."

"I do hope the cold doesn't bother you," she murmured. "I've never put any credence in the maxim that blood thins with age, but I wouldn't want you to inconvenience yourself for us."

Jaibriol almost groaned. It was a double barb, both against Corbal's age and her suggestion that his relationship with Jaibriol would weaken over time.

"How kind of you to express concern," Corbal said. "I've heard it said that advanced years bring with them a greater understanding of others."

"Oh, I'm sure," she replied. "Or even, say, advanced decades. All fourteen of them."

"Or eleven," Corbal said. "An unusual number that. Eleven. It's prime, you know."

"Of course," she said. "Always prime. At the top."

Enough, Jaibriol thought. They were giving him a headache. He had no desire to hear them taunt each other about the supposed decrepitude of their advanced age when they were so obviously hale and hearty. It only heightened how raw he felt around them.

"Prime," Jaibriol said. "As is the hour." Which meant absolutely nothing, but might distract them.

Corbal was focused on Tarquine. "A prime number has no divisor, you know. Except one and itself." Softly he added, "One. Not two."

Jaibriol blinked. What the blazes? Tarquine, however, apparently knew exactly what he meant. She said, "As in father and son, hmmm?"

"One's heir is his immortality." Corbal seemed puzzled by the reference to his son, but his voice had that too smooth quality Jaibriol dreaded, because it never boded well. "Assuming one has an heir."

For flaming sake. So that was the point of Corbal's barbs about prime numbers. The empress had yet to give birth to the Highton Heir.

Jaibriol was about to tell them to cut it out when Tarquine said, "Immortality comes in many guises. Intelligent—or otherwise. Of course, what one would like immortalized varies. Some things are better left to their mortality."

Ah, hell. That sounded like she had discovered some misdeed of Corbal's son Azile, the Intelligence Minister, and was threatening to expose him if Corbal didn't quit insulting her.

"I find myself wishing to dine," Jaibriol said shortly. He held out his hand to Tarquine. "Attend me, wife." He had no doubt she would find his order inexcusably abrupt, but he didn't have the energy to deal with the two of them. If he didn't put a stop to this, he might end up with his Intelligence Minister discredited and Corbal as his enemy, which could be a disaster. He needed both Corbal and Tarquine, and just *once* he wished they would try to get along, if only for his sake.

Tarquine regarded him with her unreadable crystalline gaze, and for one nerve-wracking moment he thought she would refuse him in front of Corbal, forcing him to lose face or reject her. Then she laid her hand in his. Instead of releasing her, as protocol demanded, Jaibriol lowered his arm and stood holding hands with his wife.

"I thank you for bringing me home," he told Corbal. "May the gods of Eube smile upon you."

Corbal bowed, and Jaibriol caught the flicker of relief in his eyes. He hadn't wanted his son discredited, but neither had he been willing to back down in front of Tarquine.

Jaibriol took leave of his cousin and returned to the flyer with Tarquine. They boarded with all eight of their oversized bodyguards. Inside, she waited until the molecular air lock solidified, hiding them from Corbal's yacht and undoubtedly from his spy sensors as well. Then she jerked her hand out of Jaibriol's hold as if he had developed a plague.

She spoke icily. "Never speak to me that way again."

"Damn it, Tarquine, I need my Intelligence Minister." He was painfully aware of their guards listening. Most Aristos assumed that Razers thought only of military matters, but he knew better. "And I need Corbal's good will."

He expected her to tell him why he needed neither. Instead she just shook her head. "Let's go home, Jai. I'm tired."

Concern replaced his anger. "Are you all right?" She never admitted anything she considered a weakness.

"Of course." She waved her hand. "We have better matters to concern us than your inconsequential cousin."

He wasn't fooled. If she considered Corbal inconsequential, she wouldn't devote so much effort to monitoring his activities or spying on his spies.

"I would have rather awoken on your yacht," he said. His smile quirked. "In your cabin." And bed.

She gave him a quelling look, but it wasn't convincing, given the spark of desire in her mood. "Then where would I have slept?"

He pulled her toward him. "I can think of someplace."

She tensed in his hold, and at first he thought she would pull away. Then she exhaled and relaxed into his kiss.

After a moment, Jaibriol drew back, though he kept his arms around her waist. "I was surprised to see Corbal," he admitted. He would have expected Tarquine to reach the SSRB ahead of even his shrewd cousin.

She started to speak, then shook her head.

"What is it?" he asked

"I was—preoccupied."

His unease stirred. "By what?"

"It isn't important." She took his arms and pulled them away from her waist. "We should go."

It isn't important was as bad as *Don't worry.* And her rebuff stung. He turned away and went to a passenger seat at the front of the craft. Hidaka took a seat against the hull that faced inward. Two of Tarquine's guards took the pilot and copilot's seats, and the others settled into passenger chairs.

Tarquine sat next to Jaibriol. "Don't sulk," she murmured as if he were a boy. At least she said it too softly for anyone else to overhear. Then again, all their bodyguards had biomech-augmented ears.

"You tell me not to give you orders," he said. "You don't like it. Fine, Tarquine. Don't treat me like a child."

He expected her to respond with a convoluted Highton remark that meant, *Then don't act like one.* Instead she said, "You know, for all that Corbal offends the bloody hell out of me, he's right. Both he and I are old. Maybe too old." She glanced at him. "I can't help it if you seem young to me. But I don't mean to offend."

It was a fair comment, and more than he had expected. "You seem pensive today."

"No. I just—" She shook her head as if to discard the mood. An aloof smile came to her face, and she was Tarquine again, Empress of Eube, and Finance Minister of the wealthiest empire in human history.

"It is interesting the news one hears," she said.

He regarded her warily. "I'm afraid to ask."

"The Diamond Minister has suggested, rather obliquely, that we consider Skolians as a possible market for Eubian products."

Jaibriol stared at her. "You talked to Gji?"

"I talk to him often. We are both Ministers, after all."

He remembered now why her clothes tugged at him. She had been wearing that same outfit the night she hadn't shown up for his failed dinner with the Diamond Minister. "That time Gji and his wife dined at the palace and you didn't show up—was it because you were up here?"

She gave him an odd look. "Why would I have been here? I had a meeting in the city." She stretched her arms. "Minister Gji actually has the notion that opening trade negotiations with the Skolians is a good idea."

He couldn't help but smile. "How did you convince him it was his idea?"

"You know, Jaibriol, you waste many of the resources at your disposal." She wouldn't look at him, which was odd, because she could stare him in the eye even when she was committing financial fraud on an interstellar scale.

"What resources?" he asked, which was about as direct as a person could get, and it wasn't an invitation to intimacy, but she had him worried enough to slip out of Highton.

Her eyes flashed at his unintended insult. "Oh, I don't know. Maybe all those providers you ignore."

Jaibriol suddenly felt ill. She couldn't mean what that sounded like. "We had an agreement."

"What agreement? I don't recall signing anything."

No. She *couldn't* had done what he thought. Neither of them touched their providers, and they never offered them to any other Aristo. They had kept that agreement for ten years. "You know what I meant."

"Sometimes," she said, "bargains must be rethought."

"You hosted Minister Gji and his wife at a dinner." He was having trouble breathing.

"A dinner, yes. I invited many of the Diamonds."

"Many?" Jaibriol knew what they would expect. "Tarquine, who served the meal?"

"You know, your providers lounge around all day, using your wealth and giving nothing in return."

He stared at her. According to the books, he had sixteen providers on Glory. They lived in a wing of the palace distant from where he spent most of his time, and he told Robert to give them whatever they wanted. He avoided them assiduously, not because he disliked them, but because they might recognize what no Aristo could sense, that he was a psion. Like them.

Somehow he spoke calmly, though he was raging inside. "You had them serve at the dinner."

She met his accusing gaze. "As they should. I entertained the Blue-Point Diamonds in the most esteemed style of the palace. You made many allies that night, Jaibriol." Then she added, "Despite yourself."

She might as well have punched him in the stomach and kicked him while he was down. He had protected the providers entrusted to his care for ten years, and in one night she had destroyed all that. The Blue-Point Diamonds numbered more than fifty. God only knew what horrors that many of them could inflict on sixteen helpless slaves. He felt sick. He had to hide his reaction, lest the guards grow suspicious; that for some merciful reason Hidaka had chosen to protect his secrets was no guarantee others would do the same. But the anger that surged within him was almost more than he could contain.

He sensed no satisfaction from Tarquine, only fatigue. She didn't like what she had done, either. Why do it, then? Knowing her mood didn't reveal the reason for it, and she was guarding her thoughts even more than usual. Maybe she truly did want to increase Eubian wealth, even if it meant doing business with their enemies. She had always valued finance over war. But it didn't fit. Plenty of other methods existed that didn't require dealing with Skolians or hurting his providers. The only reason she had suggested opening trade negotiations was because she thought it could restart the peace process.

Jaibriol couldn't bear to reach for his dream at the price of committing the very crimes that caused hatreds between his people and the Skolians. Tarquine knew he would never do what she believed necessary to win support for his ideals. So she had waited until he was gone, and then she had done it herself.

He had known her nature when he married her, and yes—he had known it worked to his advantage. That he chose at times to forget that knowledge didn't make it any less true or him any less responsible.

God forgive me for the day I married you, he thought. *For I don't think I can.*

XXIV

A Father's Debt

"It is like an enormous, glaring machine," Rohka said. "It flashes and rings, with too many parts to count, and it has so much light, it blinds you." Her voice had that same quality Kelric remembered in her mother, a sweetness and energy he had never forgotten.

They were sitting on the sofa in the sunken living room of his house on the Skolian Orbiter. The place had seemed empty in the year since Jeejon's death. Having Ixpar and the children here changed that, but it was hard to absorb. It always took him time to adjust to new circumstances. Yet for all that he struggled to adapt, it brought him great pleasure to know he would find them in the big stone rooms of his house when he returned at night.

"I've never heard Skolia described quite that way," he said, smiling, more for the joy of her presence than for her less than complimentary depiction of his civilization.

Rohka winced, with no attempt to hide her emotions. She was open and unjaded, like a fresh wind blowing through his life. "I don't mean to insult your home. It's all so much to understand." Her large eyes were like his mother's. "When you vanished down that corridor, we feared never to see you again. I thought your people knew so much, but no one could say what happened."

"I didn't mean to frighten you."

"I'm just so glad you came back."

He agreed heartily with the sentiment. "How did you know to send me the Quis images?"

"Jimorla suggested it. He said a Sixth Level Calani would have to respond to dice." She shifted her weight on the couch. "Ixpar told your military people, but I don't think they believed it. She tried sending the images, but she can't do it. Jimorla said he wasn't strong enough. Your family tried, but they don't know Quis. So I did it."

He spoke with gratitude. "I don't know if either I or the pharaoh would have made it back, otherwise."

"I don't understand." Her young face brimmed with emotions: uncertainty, curiosity, fear, relief. She didn't hesitate to let him know how she felt, and to Kelric, that was a gift. "I study physics with my tutors. But none of it sounds like anything your family tells me about space and time and these places where neither exist."

"You can learn." He was balanced over an emotional chasm. If he asked and she said no, it would be worse than if he never asked. But the words came out before he could stop them. "We have a school on the Orbiter. It's among the best in the Imperialate. If you would like— you could study here." Then he stopped, for fear of her refusal.

"Stay here?" Rohka seemed relaxed on the other end of the sofa, turned sideways to face him, one hand on a large cushion. But he saw the way her posture tensed. Nor did she know how to shield her thoughts. Her mind was a blaze of warmth, golden and untouched by the harsh universe beyond Coba. She was a miracle, and she had no idea.

"If you would like to stay," he said, self-conscious. "It's your choice."

"I don't know." Her smile flashed like sun breaking through the clouds. "It's so incredible! All my life, I've known my father was Skolian. But I never understood what it meant."

Kelric grinned at her. "Just think of what you could see."

Her mood doused as fast as it had flared. Her emotions changed so quickly, it was hard to keep up. It was like sunlight glancing off a sparkling lake, then suddenly banished by clouds.

"I have duties to my people," she said.

He spoke quietly. "You will someday rule Coba. You'll live through the era when your world becomes part of the Imperialate. What better way to prepare yourself for that responsibility than by getting an Imperialate education."

She regarded him with approval. "That's a good argument. I will try it on Ixpar."

That was so much like something Savina would have said, it made Kelric want to laugh and cry at the same time. "Does that mean you would like to stay?"

"Maybe. But I have to talk to Ixpar."

His heart swelled. Her response might not be a ringing agreement, but it was a start.

"Kelric?" A man spoke in a rich voice.

"Eldrin!" Kelric jumped to his feet and turned to look over the couch. "My greetings."

Eldrin stood in the wide entrance across the room. He was about six feet tall with broad shoulders but a leaner physique than Kelric. He wore an elegant grey and white shirt and blue trousers. He had violet eyes, and his lashes glinted with a hint of metal. Burgundy hair, glossy and straight, brushed his collar, longer than most Skolian men wore it, or at least those in the military, which defined Kelric's world. It was no coincidence Eldrin looked like an artist; he was known throughout settled space for his singing. His spectacular voice had a five-octave range that normal humans couldn't achieve, a gift he had inherited from his father, the Dalvador Bard.

Eldrin inclined his head. "It's good to see you."

Rohka stood up, watching Eldrin with wide eyes.

Kelric smiled at her. "This is my oldest brother. Eldrin. Your uncle."

Rohka bowed to Eldrin, charmingly awkward. She spoke Skolian Flag with a heavy accent. "I am honored, Your Majesty."

Although it pleased Kelric that she knew Eldrin's correct title, he didn't want her to think she had to address his family with such formality. He regarded Eldrin with an intent focus and tilted his head. His brother nodded almost imperceptibly and walked over to them.

Eldrin smiled at Rohka. "It is a pleasure to meet you. But please, call me Eldrin." He hesitated. "Or if you like, Uncle Eldrin."

Rohka's cheeks turned rosy. "I would like that."

Eldrin glanced at Kelric, but he sent no mental images or thoughts. Rohka might "overhear." He could tell Eldrin wanted to talk to him alone, but Kelric didn't want Rohka to think he was pushing her away when they had just begun to know each other.

Rohka glanced from Eldrin to Kelric. Then she spoke with courtesy to Kelric. "Is it all right if I go talk to Ixpar now? I would like to tell her what we discussed."

"Yes, certainly," Kelric said, touched by her sensitivity. In that way, too, she was like her mother, rather than blunt like him. "Ixpar went to the pharaoh's home to get Jimorla."

"They're still there," Eldrin said. He gave Kelric a bemused look. "Mother and Dehya are asking your wife about that dice game. It seems Minister Karn plays it rather well."

Minister Karn. The title startled Kelric, for he would always think of her as Ixpar. But to the rest of humanity she was the enigmatic minister who had appeared out of nowhere. The broadcasters knew nothing about her, and Kelric didn't intend to tell them. He had promised Ixpar no one would bother her world, and he meant to keep his oath. With the defenses around Coba fortified even more than before, no one could even go near the solar system without having their ship confiscated.

"Ixpar knows Quis better than most anyone else alive," Kelric said.

"She trounces me all the time," Rohka grumbled.

Kelric couldn't help but smile at her irate expression. "Give it time. You'll see."

Rohka blushed and smiled. Then she took her leave, as charming in her departure as her presence.

After Rohka left, Kelric walked outside with Eldrin. They went higher on the hill, above the house. The weather was, as usual, perfect. They strolled under trees with shushing leaves.

"She's quite striking," Eldrin said.

"Do you mean Rohka?" Kelric asked, pleased. His daughter, it seemed, was brilliant, beautiful, and charming.

His brother glanced at him and grinned. "You should see the look on your face. Yes, she is impressive. Mother is delighted with her, as you've probably noticed." He stopped under a tree and leaned against its papery trunk. "I meant your wife, though."

Kelric rested his weight against another tree. "Ixpar is more than striking."

"Imposing might be a better word."

Kelric thought of the time he had seen Ixpar striding across the Calanya common room, her waist-length red hair in wild disarray, belts of ammunition criss-crossed on her chest, and a machine gun gripped in her hands. "Yes. Much better."

"Your son is—" Eldrin paused. "I want to say reserved, but that isn't right. He seems almost in shock."

It was what Kelric had feared. "He's lived in seclusion his entire life. I'm astonished he was willing to come here at all."

Eldrin was watching him closely. "Those bands he wears on his arms—they're like the ones you have in your office."

"Hmmm," Kelric said.

"Just hmmm?" When it became clear Kelric didn't intend to add anything more, Eldrin spoke curiously. "Does wearing those bands mean living in seclusion?"

"Possibly," Kelric said.

His brother waited. Then he thought, *Kelric?*

Kelric kept up his shields. He didn't feel ready to speak about this. It wasn't that he intended to cut out his family; he would tell them about Coba. But it didn't come easy. Although he had always admired Eldrin, they had never been close in his youth. Eldrin was fifteen years his senior and had left home a year after Kelric's birth. Their lives hadn't intersected much; Kelric had joined the J-Force as a Jagernaut, and Eldrin had already been a singer. Only in these last ten years, with both of them living on the Orbiter, he had begun to know his brother.

"I don't mean to intrude," Eldrin said.

"You're not." Kelric exhaled. "I just need more time."

Eldrin smile wryly. "Your son is a lot like you. He won't talk to me at all. To no one, in fact, except Minister Karn. He never smiles, either."

"He doesn't mean it as a rebuff." At least, Kelric hoped not. "A Calani never speaks to anyone Outside his Calanya. And men from the desert never smile in the presence of women, except their wives or kin."

Eldrin was watching him with fascination. "Good gods, did you live like that?"

"For a while." The topic was making him uncomfortable. "I wanted to ask you about the Lock. You were there when Dehya and I came out this afternoon, weren't you?"

Eldrin obviously wanted to stick with the subject of his "little" brother living in seclusion. But he relented and said, "It was eerie. The two of you appeared in the corridor, slowed down. You looked translucent. You solidified as you came through the arch and started to move normally. It was about twenty minutes, though, before your voice sounded normal."

"Did you feel anything? Mentally, I mean."

Eldrin thought for a moment. "When I reached out to Dehya's mind, it felt strange. Disorienting."

"Is it still that way?"

"Not anymore. But something is bothering her." He regarded Kelric uneasily. "She says you and she must talk. That was why I came to get you."

Kelric rubbed his hand over his eyes. "Yes."

Eldrin waited. Finally he made a frustrated noise. "You're a regular fount of information today."

"I'm not trying to be obscure. I just don't know what to tell you."

"According to Chad Barzun, before you went into the Lock, you looked up those implosions. He thinks it could be important."

"Possibly." Kelric had thought it destabilized Kyle space to have two Locks carrying the load of three, but in trying to reactivate the SSRB Lock, he feared he had damaged it. Whether or not his efforts had eased the strain on the ancient centers, he had no idea, but if they hadn't, he dreaded the results.

"I've never seen Dehya like this," Eldrin said.

"Like what?"

"Scared, but she won't tell me about it."

Kelric understood the feeling. "I'll talk to her."

"Right now you have company." Eldrin indicated the hill below them. Four people were climbing it: Ixpar, Roca and her namesake Rohka, and a robed, cowled figure that could only be Kelric's son, Jimorla.

"First I need to talk to someone else," Kelric said. It was his son who had realized how to pull them out of the corridor.

Jimorla wandered with Kelric through the house, inscrutable in his robes. His cowl covered his head and the Talha hid his face except for his eyes. He had inherited the height of the Valdoria men, but with a slimmer build. Apparently in his youth, he had trouble eating some foods and had to boil his water, following the same diet Kelric had used on Coba. But whatever illness Jimorla had endured as a child, in the end Coba had agreed with him; as an adult, the young man was strong and fit.

When Kelric had caught up with Jimorla on the hill, Roca had taken one look at his face and ushered everyone else off, leaving him alone with his son. Kelric wasn't sure how she managed it so smoothly, but he was grateful. She seemed to realize that without privacy, he and his son couldn't converse.

Jimorla stopped in a doorway. "Is this your office?"

"That it is." Kelric lifted his hand to invite him inside.

Jimorla walked to the desk, which was stacked with jeweled Quis dice. He glanced up, only his eyes showing within his cowl.

Kelric understood his unspoken question. "Those are mine."

His son pushed back his cowl then and pulled down the Talha so the scarf hung around his neck. With a start, Kelric realized his son considered this office the closest equivalent of a Calanya, and therefore a place he might relax.

The light pouring through the window struck metallic glints in Jimorla's hair. His violet eyes were a color never seen in Coban natives. Prior to his son's birth, Kelric had assumed he didn't carry the gene for violet, because it was dominant on his home world and his eyes were gold. But the genetics of eye color had always been convoluted, and his people had altered their own DNA over the millennia, further complicating the patterns of their inherited traits.

"I feel as if I should ask for a Speaker," Jimorla said.

Kelric understood. In a crisis, if a Calani needed to talk to an Outsider, he could do it through the Calanya Speaker.

"You and I are in the same Calanya," Kelric said. "Now that you're at Karn. So we can talk."

"It's true, isn't it?" Jimorla seemed bemused. "I never expected to leave Varz."

"But you said yes." It meant the world to Kelric.

His gaze darkened. "How could I refuse? It would be tantamount to defying the Imperator."

Dismayed, Kelric said, "Is that how you saw this, as an order from me to come here?"

"Isn't it?"

"No. It's your choice. Always."

Jimorla gave no outward hint of his thoughts, but he didn't shield his mood any better than his sister. His mind evoked the aqua waters of a sun-drenched ocean. Thoughts swam below the surface like silvery fish, a flash of color, then shadows. Kelric couldn't follow most of the emotional currents, but he felt Jimorla's resentment. It wasn't only that his son hadn't wanted to come here; the anger went much deeper.

Jimorla? Kelric thought.

The youth tilted his head. "Did you say something?"

Kelric suspected his son rarely mind-spoke on Coba, if ever. Rohka was the only one strong enough there, and his children would rarely have the chance to interact.

"I thought it," Kelric said.

The color drained from Jimorla's face. "Don't."

"My apology." With regret, Kelric raised his barriers. He seem less able to connect with his son than his daughter.

"Why do you want us here?" Jimorla asked.

Kelric searched for the right words. "I hoped we could get to know one another." It sounded so bland for such a great longing within him. He hoped he hadn't acted precipitously by contacting them, that his wish to know them hadn't outweighed his common sense in protecting them.

Anger flashed on Jimorla's face. "Why would you want to meet me now, after ignoring me for twenty-seven years?"

"I had no choice on Coba. I wasn't allowed to see you."

"You didn't have to leave my mother."

That felt like a blow to the chin. "She said I left her?"

"No. She didn't say anything."

"She turned away from me."

His son looked incredulous. "Why would she do that?"

"She didn't want me."

"Yes, she did." Now Jimorla seemed bewildered. "Why else would she refuse to fight in the war?"

That was unexpected. In military terms, Jimorla's mother had been the strongest ally of Ixpar's greatest foe. "I didn't know she refused."

"She was in love with you." Defiance sparked in his voice. "But she loves my father more."

My father. The words cut like blades. With difficulty, Kelric said, "Raaj is a good man."

Jimorla hesitated. Then he spoke in a quieter voice. "Why did she turn away from you?"

Kelric wondered if the young man had any idea of the knives he was turning. But he owed his son the answers. "She didn't like my past."

"That you had been in prison for murder?"

"No. She could live with that."

"What else could it have been?"

"Tell me something. Have you ever kissed a woman?"

Deep red flushed Jimorla's face. "Of course not."

"Have you ever smiled at one? Besides your kin."

"No. You know I'm not married." His voice tightened. "Why do you ask these insulting questions?"

Kelric couldn't imagine living the constrained, controlled life of a Haka nobleman since birth. It had been hard enough for just one year. "I don't consider them insults."

"And that offended my mother?"

"In a sense. I had lovers before I married her."

Jimorla stared at him for a long moment. When he found his voice, he said, "Oh."

Kelric had no regrets for the women he had loved. But in the rigid culture of the desert Estates, it was illegal for a man even to smile at a woman. Even now it angered and bewildered him that Jimorla's mother had been able to look past the fact that he had killed someone, but not that he had taken lovers outside of marriage.

Jimorla could have reacted many ways, most of them negative. Rather than offended, though, he looked puzzled, perhaps because he had lived away from the desert long enough to adapt to less restrictive customs. But he seemed unable to fathom his own father having such freedoms.

After a moment, Jimorla said, "When I was thirteen, my mother said you wanted to meet me."

Kelric nodded. "I always did. But it wasn't until then that the Managers agreed to let you visit me."

"What changed?"

It was almost more than Kelric could bear to talk about those days. But he forced out the words. "I was dying. By the time the doctors figured it out, I had only a few months to live."

The tense set of Jimorla's face softened. "I didn't know."

"The war started before you and I had the chance to meet."

"Everyone thought you died in the fires."

"It was better that way."

"Why?!" Jimorla's anger surged. "Why was it better for us to grieve for your death?"

Kelric spoke grimly. "I caused the first war your people had seen in a thousand years. It tore Coba apart, and as long as I was part of your culture, that would continue. I wouldn't—I *couldn't* be responsible for more death and misery." Quietly he added, "Especially not of my own children."

Jimorla breathed out, his face strained, but he didn't dispute Kelric's words. As a Calani, he had to know the truth; it saturated the Quis of Coba.

"You waited ten years to come back," Jimorla said. It was an accusation more than a statement.

"It took that long to make certain I could protect you." Kelric wished he were better with words. "I haven't always been Imperator, Jimorla. And having a title is no guarantee of power. Had I revealed Coba when I had no power base, it could have done great harm to your world. I can stop that from happening now. I couldn't when I first escaped."

"You could have found a way."

"I did," Kelric said quietly. "That is why you're here." He lifted his hands, then dropped them. "I'm no good with explanations. I'm sorry."

He feared his son would find that answer a poor excuse. Instead, Jimorla said, "I've never been good with words, either." He glanced at Kelric's dice. "But with Quis . . ."

Kelric exhaled. Technically, they were in the same Calanya. So they could sit at dice. In reality, Kelric was as far Outside as a man could go, and Jimorla's Oath to Ixpar forbid him to play Quis with Outsiders. Yet here he stood, waiting, and Kelric could no more turn down his son than he could cut off his arm.

Forgive me, Ixpar, he thought. He gathered up his dice and indicated a table. He and Jimorla sat across from each other.

Then they rolled out their dice.

XXV

The Fountain

The Qox retreat for the Emperor of Eube had no name. No map listed its location. No mesh address existed for it. The retreat nestled within a valley hidden among the highest peaks of the Jaizire Mountains, and no one could visit that range without permission from the emperor. Forests surrounded the boar-wood lodge. The trees grew unusually tall, their trunks huge and gnarled, clustered close together as if they had joined ranks to repel invaders. Vines dripped from their spiked branches like tatted lace in dark shades of green. Tangle-wolves and blue-spindled pumas stalked the peaks.

Jaibriol loved the retreat. It didn't remind him of home; the land here was too stark and brooding. The wild beauty, untamed and untainted by Aristos, called to something within him. Usually he enjoyed the time he spent here with Tarquine, a respite from the grueling days of his reign. But today they walked into the lodge in cold silence.

The walls had no tech to distract him, only smooth wood with whorled knots. A boar-wood exterior surfaced the console against one wall. The floor had the best available controls to remove insects and dirt, and keep the temperature comfortable, but it looked like simple wood softened with rustic throw rugs.

Jaibriol went to a bar by one wall and poured a drink of the strongest liqueur he could find. The label on the fluted crystal bottle said, simply, "Anise I." The Anise burned a path down his throat and flared heat throughout his body. Ten years ago he would have gagged at its strength; now he hardly blinked.

Tarquine poured a tumbler of Taimarsian brandy. Unable to look away, Jaibriol watched her raise it to her red lips. The muscles of her alabaster throat barely moved as she swallowed. She was physical perfection by Aristo standards, and it suddenly made him ill.

"Did you join them?" he asked.

She glanced at him, the tumbler at her lips. She took another sip, then slowly lowered the glass. "Join who?"

"At your 'dinner' for the Blue-Point Diamonds." His voice was low and dark, like the anger within him. "Did you join their orgy and use my providers?"

"Your language seems to have lost its elevation." Her oh-so-perfect voice had a chill that symbolized everything he hated about Aristos, but today it also had an edge, as if she were struggling to keep her icy veneer.

"Don't play Highton games with me." Something was building in him, something hard and full of misery. "Answer me."

"Why should I?" Her voice was heating up. Tarquine—the ultimate ice queen—was losing her cool. "You violate all standards of Highton decency and then accuse *us* of immorality."

"You did, didn't you?" He felt as if acid were burning inside of him. "Oh, I'm sure it was sublimely tasteful by Highton standards, right, Tarquine? You were all discreet when you tortured and raped the providers I expected no one ever to goddamned *touch*." His fists clenched at his sides. "Did you enjoy it? I know it's still in you. I feel it at night, when you 'make love' to me. Or whatever you call it."

Her voice struck like a weapon. "At least other providers didn't talk while I enjoyed them."

He stared at her. *Other* providers. Had she forgotten their guards were here, that they could hear her imply the emperor was a slave? It was insane to argue; he and Tarquine were losing the hard-fought composure they needed to survive. But too much had happened, and his life was out of control. The thought of her spending time with some pleasure boy while he agonized in the crucible of the Lock was more than he could bear.

"Did you enjoy committing adultery?" he said, his voice honed like a knife. It was an insult even more grave than the accusation that she betrayed their vows, for an Aristo could only commit that crime with another Aristo. To suggest that for her, lying with a provider was adultery, put her on the same level as the slaves lowest in the hierarchy of the Eubian empire. "I don't even know how many male providers I have. Or maybe you didn't care—male, female, they're all good."

Jaibriol didn't know she was going to strike until her palm hit his face, and his head snapped to the side. Her voice was deadly. "Never speak to me that way. *Never.*" She set her drink on the counter. Then she turned and walked away from him, her back stiff under her jumpsuit.

He stared at her, his fist clenched on the bar. Her betrayal affected him at a deeper, more primal level than he ever wanted to admit. It killed him, and he hated knowing he had come to need her so much. That her actions might motivate the Diamond Aristos to support his foolish dream of peace made it even worse. The contradictions of his life had become more than he knew how to endure, but he had no choice, he had to live with them no matter how they ravaged his soul.

Jaibriol downed his drink in one swallow. Then he swung around and hurled the glass with biomech-enhanced strength. It flew across the lodge and shattered inside the antique hearth. Hidaka had been bending over the console, but now he straightened up with a jerk, glancing from Jaibriol to the pulverized glass strewn across the stone. The guards posted around the walls came even more alert, if such was possible. They were all being discreet. None gave any hint they had just heard the emperor and empress have an argument that could tear apart Jaibriol's claim to the title. They probably assumed he and Tarquine had been so angry, they hurled unforgivable insults. Even that violated the icy code of Aristo behavior. Since his experience in the Lock, he was losing the restraint so vital to his life.

Jaibriol walked over to Hidaka, his adrenaline racing even as he tried to appear calm. Although the captain regarded him with a neutral look, Hidaka was expending so much effort to hold the expression, Jaibriol could practically see his strain.

"Do you need the console, Your Highness?" Hidaka asked.

Jaibriol nodded, not trusting himself to words. As Hidaka moved aside, Jaibriol settled into the cushioned seat and entered his mesh-globe, the "world" tailored to his needs, where he kept records, personal data, and correspondence, what people had called their "account" in the antique world of early mesh systems. He knew he should leave this business with Tarquine alone, but he couldn't stop himself. He accessed the list of his providers, the "inventory" he hated, for he lived in fear that someday he would become an entry in that seductive, brutal catalog.

He had inherited fourteen of them, not from his father, who according to the records had never even visited them, but from his grandfather. Despite their gorgeous and sensual appearance of youth, most were in their thirties or older. One was even fifty-two, though in her holo she looked fifteen.

The last two providers, both women, were gifts given to Jaibriol by other Aristos. Although six of his grandfather's were male, it said nothing about his grandfather's preferences; an Aristo could transcend with a psion of either sex. Pain was pain regardless of who experienced it. He didn't see how Aristos lived with themselves, let alone considered it their exalted right to hurt other human beings, especially those who were so helpless. He hated knowing the providers had suffered during his absence, and he loathed even more knowing that heritage was within his own DNA, that he was one-eighth Aristo.

Unexpectedly, the records for Corbal's providers came up as well, apparently because Tarquine had nosed into his private affairs. Sunrise was the only one Corbal lived with. She had a physical age of sixteen, but Jaibriol was startled to discover Corbal had first bought her decades ago, during his marriage. His Highton wife had sent her away, which suggested his interest in Sunrise had been considered more than acceptable even then. After his wife passed away, Corbal brought Sunrise back to his home. The sweet "girl" Jaibriol knew was actually a woman over twice his age.

He locked Corbal's files. It wouldn't keep Tarquine out if she put her mind to breaking in, but he didn't see why she cared. Even if she hadn't already copied the record, it wasn't anything that offered her economic or political advantage.

The holos of his providers remained. They stood on a screen in front of him, each about one hand span high, the beautiful pleasure slaves he owned. He couldn't stop wondering who Tarquine had slept with. Probably the men; his wife was definitely heterosexual. The thought made him want to smash the console. Gritting his teeth, he took a long look at the women. In the reflection of the console, he saw Hidaka behind him, gazing at one of the images with a strange look

Jaibriol couldn't interpret. The girl's large bronze eyes glimmered in the holo, and her hair shone like polished bronze, falling to her waist in huge curls. She wore nothing but a glittery G-string and a chain halter with a few topazes hiding the parts of her he most wanted to see.

Jaibriol stared at the image. "Hidaka, contact Robert and let him know I am returning to the palace." He indicated the bronze girl. "Tell him to have her ready for me."

Robert was waiting when Jaibriol stepped out of the flyer on the roof of the palace. He hadn't told Tarquine he was leaving. He hated himself for expecting her to act as anything but an Aristo, and he couldn't bear to look at her. His loneliness crashed in, the pain that he kept at bay only by the intricate delusion he had built for his life, that no matter what miseries he endured as emperor of this sadistic empire, he had the respite of an empress who, beneath her chilly exterior, actually loved him.

He was a fool a thousand times over, for believing in his dream, for believing in her, for believing anyone could ever change this hell known as the Eubian empire. They had the strongest, wealthiest, largest civilization humanity had ever known and someday they would probably take over the entire human race. Nothing he did, nothing he endured, no desperate hope he carried within him would ever change that.

Robert stood in the circle of the flyer's lamps. They didn't need the light; it was never truly dark on Glory with so many moons. Tonight, Jaibriol counted nine, some crescents, some fuller, some tiny, others dominating the sky. The tormented ocean crashed so loudly against the glittering black shore beyond the city, he could hear the waves even here, atop his palace.

"Welcome back, Your Highness," Robert said.

"Thank you, Robert." Jaibriol strode past him, toward the bulb tower with the lift that would take them into the palace.

Robert caught up with him. "Should I tell the staff to prepare for the empress's arrival?"

"No." Jaibriol kept going. "Did you have the girl brought to my rooms?"

"Yes, Your Highness." He sounded upset.

"Good." Jaibriol stopped at the onion dome. A molecular air lock shimmered in its side and vanished, leaving a horseshoe arch. He stalked through it, headed for the collapse of his personal life.

The bedroom suite was dark; only a red crystal lamp burned on the nightstand, and its dim light barely reached the voluminous bed. Even from so far away, Jaibriol saw the mound under the covers. He crossed the room silently, past the sitting area and breakfast niche. At the bed, he stared down at the girl sleeping under the velvet spread. Her hair veiled her face, leaving it only partly visible. Bronze lashes sparkled against her cheeks.

He pulled down the bedspread, uncovering her. She was wearing even less than in the holo, just the G-string. Her body was full and curved, and her face so pretty that his breath caught. She had a tiny waist and breasts surely too large to be natural, with huge nipples that looked permanently erect. From her file, he knew she had enhanced pheromones as well, designed to attract and intensify a man's sexual response.

Jaibriol didn't even take off his shoes. He slid onto the bed and sat against the headrest, still wearing his leather jacket, and under it, his black-diamond clothes with carnelian at his cuffs and belt. When he pulled the girl between his legs and slid his hand over her breast, she murmured in her sleep.

"Wake up." He rolled her nipple between his fingers, trying to recall her name from the file. "Wake up, Claret."

She sighed and opened her eyes, her lashes taking forever to lift. "My honor at your glorious presence, Most Esteemed Highness," she murmured drowsily.

Jaibriol bent his head and kissed her hard, too full of anger and hunger to be gentle. He gripped her between his knees, with her torso against his chest. The conduits on his coat scraped her skin, but if it bothered her, she gave no sign. She molded against him, pliant in his hold, far more lush than an Aristo, compliant in a way he would never find in his wife. Her scent surrounded him, intoxicating, and he should have savored every moment with her. He owned the most desirable sex slaves alive—and he couldn't enjoy them even after his wife had goddamned cheated on him.

Jaibriol stopped kissing her and sat with his head bent over the girl, his arms around her. He wanted to smash something inanimate, because he didn't want her, he wanted Tarquine. Even immersed in the aphrodisiac of this lovely girl's pheromones, he couldn't make love to her because he couldn't be unfaithful to his wife.

Claret pulled herself up so she could look into his face. "Why are you sad, Your Highness?"

"I'm not sad," he lied.

She slid her hand across his chest. "What would you like?" she murmured. "Whatever you want. Anything."

He folded his hand around hers. "I couldn't imagine a sweeter night. But it seems sweet isn't what I want."

Fear sparked in her gaze. A brutal image jumped into her mind, what she had endured at the hands of the Blue-Point Diamond Aristos, and Jaibriol felt as if he would die.

"Claret, I'm not going to hurt you." He brushed the tousled hair from her face. "How could I harm such a gift?" Her Kyle strength was a balm on his traumatized mind. He kissed her again, more gently. "You can sleep here tonight. Whatever you need, just let the house staff know."

Her puzzlement washed over even his guarded mind. She had no mental barriers. Of course Aristos never taught their providers how to shield their thoughts. The more open a psion, the more the Aristo received their pain. Jaibriol couldn't imagine how they could have tortured this tender girl and taken enjoyment from it, and for a moment he hated them so much, he felt capable of murder. The only person he hated more was himself, for not protecting the people in his care.

"I'm sorry," he whispered. It was an insane thing for the emperor to tell a provider, but he couldn't stop the words.

Claret touched his temple. "You hurt so much."

"No." He could never let her know. "I don't."

"It's in you." Her eyes were luminous. "Such terrible pain. It is yours rather than mine. And you have no void."

"No. It isn't true." Tears he could never shed burned in his eyes. He had known he couldn't hide from a psion, but he had thought for just one night he could keep his nature a secret.

She leaned her head against his shoulder. "That you are a gift of the gods," she whispered, "we have always known."

His voice rasped. "What does that mean?"

"You are kind."

He had no answer to that. He wasn't kind, he was a monster who had let them be misused on a terrible scale.

"If only I could give you kindness," Jaibriol said.

"You have given me all I need," she answered, but she was lying, for an image jumped into her mind of what she wanted and could never have.

Hidaka.

In her memory, that taciturn monolith he knew as one of his deadly cybernetic guards was instead a man full of affection and loving words, though the two of them had never dared act on their feelings, lest they be caught and punished, even executed. Jaibriol wanted to die then, as he realized what Hidaka's "odd" look had meant at the lodge. It was a man in pain and trying to hide it. Hidaka had saved Jaibriol's life in a thousand ways when he shot Muze, and in return Jaibriol had taken the woman he loved.

The foyer outside of Jaibriol's bedroom was dim. Hidaka was standing with his feet apart and his arms crossed, his face a study in impassive neutrality. He lowered his arms and bowed as Jaibriol walked into the foyer.

"Are my other Razers outside?" Jaibriol asked.

"Yes, Sire." Hidaka guarded his voice well. If Jaibriol hadn't realized what had happened, he wouldn't have noticed the captain's strain. But he couldn't miss it now. He remembered Hidaka leaning over the console in the lodge. He had assumed the guard was checking security, but now he wondered if Hidaka had been trying to discover whether or not Claret was all right. Jaibriol had noticed her because of the intensity of Hidaka's response to her holo, and he felt like a swine for not realizing *why* his guard had reacted that way.

"I'm not going to stay," Jaibriol told him.

The captain nodded, and if Jaibriol hadn't been looking for it, he might have missed the relief in Hidaka's gaze.

"But I want you to remain here," Jaibriol added. "Tonight."

"Sire?"

Jaibriol spoke gently. "She is yours, for as long as the two of you want to stay together. She can move into your rooms in the palace if you would like."

Emotions burst across the face of his guard—his stoic, mechanical Razer. Alarm, fear—and hope. "I would never presume—"

Jaibriol lifted his hand, stopping him. "Just promise me this. You will treat her well."

Hidaka took a deep breath. Then he said, simply, "I will."

"Go on." Jaibriol tilted his head toward the bedroom. "The suite is yours tonight."

For one instant a full smile lit the Razer's face, a flash of white teeth. It only lasted a second, but that single moment spoke volumes against his supposed mechanical nature.

Jaibriol felt even smaller than before. They acted as if he had given them a great gift simply by allowing them to love each other. He could never say the words they deserved, never free Claret or Hidaka or Robert or anyone else, and most of all, he could never reveal his aversion to the foundations of Aristo life, for if he did, he could end up in the same inventory where he had found Claret.

Glory's six-hour night was half over by the time Jaibriol returned to his mountain lodge with his three guards. He couldn't find Tarquine. The central room was empty except for one of her Razers monitoring the console. That the guard had stayed here had to mean she was in the lodge. He could have one of his Razers find her. But he couldn't bring himself to show even that hint of how much he needed the woman he had insulted beyond forgiveness.

She wasn't in any room, including the bedroom. They should have been asleep together, but apparently neither of them could rest. Guilt and insomnia seemed to be partners tonight.

Standing by the perfectly made bed, he noticed a line of light across the room, under the antique door to the bathing chamber. Puzzled, he went over and pushed it open. No one was visible in the room beyond, with its round pool and earthen colors. A lamp with a blueglass shade glowed on a table in one corner, and a fountain burbled in the center of the blue-tiled pool.

Jaibriol turned to the Razer with him. "Wait here."

His bodyguard bowed. "As you wish, Sire."

Jaibriol went into the chamber and closed the door. The fountain was a scalloped bowl shaped like a flower with arches of water that curved up into the air and sheeted down the bowl.

He found Tarquine on the other side.

The empress was sitting by a sculpted bowl at the edge of the pool, hidden from the door by the water spuming through the air. She had leaned over the bowl, her head bent, her hair hanging around her face.

"Tarquine?" He stopped, bewildered by the strange tableau. He had seen her look many ways, but never vulnerable like this.

She lifted her head. Dark circles rimmed her eyes, and her pallor frightened him. Jaibriol knelt beside her, dismayed that while he had been stealing away to the palace, his wife had been sick. Except she couldn't be ill. Like him, she had health nanomeds, molecular laboratories that patrolled her body.

"What happened?" Jaibriol asked.

"Nothing." Her voice was low. "Where have you been?"

"At the palace."

Her voice turned acid. "Did you enjoy yourself?"

"No." He whispered the word.

"Neither did I." She pulled a lock of hair out of her eyes. "I never touched your providers."

He stared at her, incredulous. "You sure as blazes made it sound like you did."

She rested her elbow on the edge of the bowl and rubbed her eyes. "Perhaps I wanted to hurt you."

"Why?" She had succeeded, more than she knew.

"Because you make me care too much." She lowered her arm and met his gaze. "You force me to care if you are happy, if you are well, if you are satisfied with your life. And you never are, Jaibriol. Your sorrow saturates everything."

"I thought you had betrayed our vows."

She didn't tell him an Aristo could never betray a spouse with a provider. Incredibly, she said, "So you had to as well?"

"I couldn't." He spoke bitterly. "I don't know what hells our marriage exists in, Tarquine, but it seems I love you too much to act in a manner any other Aristo would consider normal."

Her voice softened. "You express your love in strange ways."

So do you, he thought, but he couldn't say it, for he was never certain of anything with her, especially whether or not she loved him, and it hurt too much to ask her, for she would never acknowledge anything she believed made her weak. So instead he touched the bowl where she was leaning. Its purifying systems had cleansed its water to a pristine perfection, but he had no doubt she had thrown up in it.

"How can you be sick?" he asked.

"I'm not." She said it with a straight face, though she looked too exhausted even to stand.

"You just happen to be hanging over this bowl?"

Her gaze never wavered. "I lied to you, Jaibriol."

He didn't know which amazed him more, that she admitted it or that she stated it so simply. "About what?" He could think of so many possibilities, he hardly knew where to start.

"About why I missed your dinner with Minister Gji."

"You were in a meeting that night."

"No. I was here, in the mountains."

Although he had suspected as much since he saw her clothes, her confession made no sense. "Why lie about that? The lodge is here for us to use."

"I didn't come to the lodge."

"Where did you go?"

"A clinic."

"What clinic?" He had no idea what she was about, and he couldn't bruise his mind further by lowering his barriers.

"The Jaizire Clinic. The late Empress Viquara, my niece, established it, accessible only to the Qox Line." Bitterly, she added, "Modern medicine can accomplish almost anything our glorious empire requires it to do."

Jaibriol was beginning to understand, but he shunned the knowledge, as if doing so would protect him from this new agony she was about to inflict. "Tarquine, don't."

"It is already done," she said. "That night, after I came back, when we made love."

"*No.*" His hand spasmed on the edge of the bowl.

"You need an heir," she said tiredly. "You will have one."

"You cannot!" He refused to believe it. "You're too old."

She gave him a dour look. "How complimentary."

"I don't mean an insult. But it can't happen."

"Yes, well, that which can't happen is making me very sick."

"You have to see a doctor!" Alarm flared through him. "I'll summon—"

"No!" She caught his hand before he touched his wrist comm.

"*Why?*" His mind reeled. This woman who sat slumped here, her face pale from illness, might carry the Highton Heir. "Haven't you gone to one?"

"Not once." She had that unrelenting quality he knew all too well. "Nor will I."

He took her hand. "You must take proper care of the baby. And yourself."

"That is why no doctor must see me." She squeezed his fingers, then released his hand so she could motion at the room around them. "And why I came here to rest."

"You aren't resting. You're sick."

"I'm fine. *Only* in here can you know otherwise."

"Why?" His heart was beating too hard.

"I've secured this room to the best of my ability."

Jaibriol knew that euphemism. *To the best of my ability* meant she had turned her prodigious and shady resources to the task. If any place existed where they could talk in private, she could create that refuge.

"Why would you hide the event the entire empire is waiting for?" he asked. The unending speculation as to if and when she could provide him an heir had been a bane on their lives.

"Because any child of yours," she said, "won't be what the doctors expect."

He wanted to rage then, for she was right, and he would have seen it right away if he hadn't been so shell-shocked. She carried the full Aristo genes, but he was only one eighth. It was why he avoided medical experts, and why he had doctored his own DNA to appear more Highton, both within and without. Could a physician discover the Highton Heir wasn't Highton? As his great-grandfather had protected his grandfather, and his grandfather protected his father, so Jaibriol would protect his heir. But how had they managed without endangering the mother or the baby? They had left no records that could help Tarquine.

He stared across the bowl at her. "You can do checks on yourself, can't you? To see if the child is well?"

"Yes, to both." With exquisite misery, she said, "It is a boy. The next emperor."

Jaibriol wanted to feel joy, but his emotions were ripping him apart. "My grandfather was only half Aristo."

"*Never* say it. Never *think* it. Even with my safeguards, you never know."

She didn't understand. "Whatever his genes, he was Highton." Like a train hurtling over a cliff, Jaibriol couldn't stop. "He thought like a Highton. Behaved like a Highton. Valued being Highton." He spoke in a low voice. "Aristo genes are dominant, Tarquine. The Kyle genes didn't manifest in the Qox Line until my father, who inherited them from both his father and his provider mother."

Her fist clenched the rim of the bowl. "Your grandmother was the empress Viquara. My niece. Your mother was the Highton empress Liza. *Never forget.*"

"Our child will transcend." She had to acknowledge the truth. "He will grow up to crave his father's agony. And he'll know what I am. I can hide from my Ministers, my advisors, my judges and military officers and aides. But I can't hide from my own child."

"No child of mine will betray his father."

He felt as if his heart were cracking open. "You don't know that. My grandfather was a monster."

"Your grandfather was the esteemed emperor of Eube."

"That doesn't change his brutality."

"He didn't have you as a father."

That caught him off guard. "What?"

She spoke quietly. "Bring your son up as your father brought you up, and the Highton Heir will be a far better man than any of those around him."

He didn't know where to put her admission, one no other Aristo would even think let alone speak, that raising their child without Highton influence would make him a better human being. "I can't live in exile with him. Secluding him won't change the fundamental nature of what he and I are. My grandfather stayed away from my father to protect him. But who will protect me from my son?"

She started to speak, stopped.

"What is it?" he asked.

"It can be done."

Something in her expression set off his alarms. "You know of another case?"

"It doesn't matter."

"Yes, it does!"

"Ah, Jai, no, I don't know. We will handle what comes."

"You had no right to do this without telling me."

"That may be," she said. "But I will not undo it."

"I wouldn't ask you to."

"Your grandfather survived."

"I would rather die," he said flatly, "than have my son follow the brutal footsteps of my grandfather."

Tarquine watched him as if her cast-iron heart were breaking. "Love our son. It's all you can do."

His life was disintegrating, and he didn't know how to stop it. "Even if he never betrays me, what if someone uncovers the truth? What will happen to our son then? If I am unmasked, so is he."

She pushed back the hair tangled around her face. That she had let it become so disarrayed told him far more about her distress than any claim she might make to feel otherwise.

"Go to the Skolians," she said.

"They would never accept the son of Jaibriol II, grandson of Ur Qox, great-grandson of Jaibriol I. To them, I embody everything evil in the universe."

"You are their kin. They will accept you."

"And leave Eube in the hands of whom? You? Corbal? Calope Muze? My joint commanders? What sins against humanity would our empire commit because I was too great a coward to face my own reign?"

"Then endure, husband." Her gaze never wavered. "Endure and never grieve for what you cannot have."

"If I am ever discovered," he said, "you must take our son and yourself to safety, even if you have to go to the Ruby Dynasty. They won't like your Aristo heritage or his, but they won't turn away family." He could never know for certain if what she believed about his kin was true, but what he knew of them through his mother supported her conviction. And they had the means to shield his family.

"I will protect our child no matter what it takes." A fierce light glinted in her eyes. "But I will never throw myself on the mercy of the Ruby Dynasty."

He thought of the power roiling within him, tearing apart his carefully built defenses. "I can't promise we will survive."

"We are Qox and Iquar. We do more than survive." She was darkness and whiskey, mesmerizing. "We thrive. And we conquer."

Jaibriol had no wish to conquer humanity. But the moment he joined the Triad, that possibility had come within his grasp. Even knowing his child would be everything he feared, pride stirred within him, and another emotion as well, one so intense and painful, it might be love. He had within him the power to give his child an empire greater than any ever known.

The events whirling around him had gone beyond his control. He would do anything to protect his son, even if it meant he had to become the greatest tyrant in human history.

XXVI

Tides of Sorrow

Kelric had known the best Quis players on Coba. He had sat in the Calanya of the most powerful Estates. He recognized the hallmarks of brilliance even after years away from Coba.

His son had no parallel.

Jimorla's talent blazed. No wonder Ixpar had been willing to put her Estate into debt for him. Had Kelric not been the Imperator, he doubted the Varz Manager would ever have agreed to trade such a spectacularly gifted player to her greatest foe.

He didn't have the words to tell Jimorla how proud he was of his son. So he put it into his dice. Jimorla responded with a vibrancy totally unlike his enigmatic demeanor. They built structures of Coba. Kelric told his son about his life. He wasn't certain Jimorla truly understood; the culture that had molded his son was so different, Jimorla might never comprehend the life Kelric had known. But the young man's hostility faded.

Kelric's concerns for the Imperialate percolated into his dice. He hadn't intended it to happen, but his worries were too big, and Jimorla was too talented to miss them. His son grasped his concerns exactly as would a Calani playing Quis with his Manager during a session dedicated to studying problems faced by the Estate. It was a gift of trust Kelric hadn't expected, and it meant as much to him as if Jimorla had spoken words of welcome.

Kelric described the Lock, the Keys, and the history of his people. He modeled what he knew of Jaibriol Qox, their meeting ten years ago, and his suspicion about Qox's mind. As the picture unfolded, Jimorla evolved it with his prodigious Quis. Untouched by anything Skolian, he offered Kelric a view unlike any other Kelric had considered. His son compared the Locks to three great dice, vital pieces in an interstellar game of Quis. He played them in structures that defined which empire gained advantage.

Yet despite Jimorla's luminous talent, his models of the Eubian emperor faltered. He described Qox as Kelric's son. It made no sense. It was impossible for Kelric to have fathered Qox; he had been on Coba fathering Jimorla. Yet his son remained convinced. Kelric soon realized Jimorla knew too little about the Ruby Dynasty to understand what he implied. He had no context. As Kelric told him more about his family, his son's structures changed. Yet still he persisted in making impossible patterns. He developed a convincing model to explain all of Qox's actions given one simple—and terrifying—assumption.

The Trader emperor was a member of the Ruby Dynasty.

Kelric hiked with Dehya up behind his house, and they sat at the top of a long hill that dropped into a gorge. Far below, a river frothed and rushed through the valley.

The walk had tired him. He had never fully recovered from his years on Coba and his escape from the Traders, and he felt his age even more lately in the many aches of his body.

"A void as large as the one you found in Kyle space," Dehya said, "could mean a substantial part of *that* universe imploded."

"Maybe the strain there is as great as here." As far as he knew, no implosions had occurred in their space-time since he found the void. "I couldn't sense the Lock, just emptiness."

She regarded him uneasily. "If the implosions start again, we may have little recourse without that third Lock."

Frustration welled within him. "I was sure I did nothing more than wake it up. If I hadn't already been a member of the Dyad, I doubt I could have done even that much. But from so far away, it's impossible to tell what happened."

Dehya grimaced. "Gods only know what Jaibriol the Third might do with access to a working Lock."

In that splintering moment, watching her, Kelric knew she suspected what Jimorla had tried to tell him with Quis, that Qox was a member of the Ruby Dynasty. A chill ran through him.

"No," he said. *No.*

"Soz and the previous Trader emperor spent fifteen years stranded together on some planet," Dehya said.

"They weren't stranded together." Damn it, Dehya knew that. "ISC had imprisoned him. He escaped and Soz went after him in another ship." Everyone knew the rest, that Soz had spent fifteen years searching for Qox.

"Convenient how it looked as if they had died," Dehya said. "Yet here they were on some unknown world."

"A planet is a large place to hide."

"So it is." Dehya looked at him, and he at her. Neither of them wanted to think it, what Soz and Qox might have done *together* in fifteen years. Soz couldn't have been anywhere near Qox when ESComm pulled him off the planet, for they would have blasted the entire region to make certain no one survived. By all accounts, she and Qox had never found each other. Kelric thought surely a person could go insane if they spent fifteen years alone, struggling to survive. As emperor, Qox had been reclusive; no one knew anything about him. From all accounts Soz had been single-minded in her pursuit of victory against the Traders in the Radiance War, driven, obsessed even. But insane? It didn't fit with what Kelric knew of his sister's indomitable strength of will.

He and Dehya could never reveal their suspicions to anyone else, for the more people who knew, the greater the chance it would leak and endanger Jaibriol, ending the reign of the only emperor who might actually negotiate with them.

"Jaibriol the Third can't be a psion," Kelric said, a protest as much to himself as to Dehya.

Dehya regarded him uneasily. "His parents *both* would have had to have had the genes. So his grandfather would have had them as well."

"I find it hard to believe even an adult psion could survive among the Aristos. In my time with Tarquine, I could hardly bear to be around her colleagues." Kelric shook his head. "I can't imagine how a child would bear it. He would go crazy."

"Unless he was kept separate from the Aristos."

And there it was. Jaibriol the Third had been secluded throughout his childhood. No one knew he had existed until he was an adult, for all appearances the perfect, ultimate Aristo.

Kelric thought of Tarquine, the only Aristo he had met whose mind didn't exert that suffocating pressure. The empress. Was that why Jaibriol had married her? Kelric knew he and Dehya might be mistaken about their fears; they had no way to tell, not without meeting Jaibriol Qox. But they couldn't take any chances.

And so, in one of the greatest ironies of their lives, they would protect the Emperor of Eube.

"You cannot!" The words exploded out of Barcala Tikal, the First Councilor of the Skolian Assembly. He and Kelric were both on their feet, facing each other across the table on the dais of the Orbiter War Room. Dehya, Eldrin, Roca, Chad Barzun, and Ragnar Bloodmark were all seated, though Kelric thought they were ready to jump up, too, and argue with him. No matter. He didn't intend to change his mind.

"I can," Kelric said. "And if he agrees, I will."

Tikal hit the table with his fist. "No. It's insane."

Kelric planted his fists on the table and leaned forward. "But it's perfectly sane for our armies to hammer each other and slag planets instead?"

"We have no choice," Tikal said.

"We make our choices!" Kelric shot back at him.

"Gentlemen, stop," Roca said quietly. "Sit down. Please."

Kelric and Tikal continued their hostile stares. Then Tikal took a breath and settled in his chair. Kelric stood for a moment, his adrenaline racing, annoyed at Roca for being so blasted *moderate*. Then he grunted and sat down as well.

His brother Eldrin was watching him with a puzzled frown. "Interstellar leaders never meet in person even when they are allies," he pointed out to Kelric. "For you and Jaibriol Qox to meet, even through the Kyle mesh, would be unusual. What makes you think he would ever agree to a face-to-face meeting?"

"He might very well refuse," Kelric admitted. "But we'll never know unless we ask."

"Oh, I don't know," Ragnar said lazily, tapping a light-stylus against his other hand. "Our Imperator seems to have no trouble meeting with the wives of interstellar leaders."

Kelric gritted his teeth. Years had passed since his meeting with Tarquine, and still Ragnar wouldn't let it go. She had contacted him during the initial peace talks and requested the private conference, using the Kyle connection that Skolia had set up for Eube. When Kelric met with her, she claimed she wanted to know his intentions, whether or not his people honored the Eubian emperor's "desire for peace." It was absurd, and Kelric hadn't believed her, but he had spoken with her anyway. Why? They had each been taking the measure of the other. The Allieds had a phrase for it: Know thy enemy.

Although neither he nor Tarquine had committed a crime, it took no genius to see that a meeting between the Skolian Imperator and Eubian Empress—who had once been lovers—could be considered improper, to put it mildly. He had secured their communication, but it hadn't surprised him that Dehya found out. Unexpectedly, Ragnar had also broken his security and recorded the meeting. The admiral hadn't trusted him since.

Dehya spoke tiredly. "Ragnar, let it go."

"Why should he let it go?" Tikal demanded. "It has a direct bearing on this discussion."

"The problem," Roca said, "isn't some long ago meeting where nothing happened." She regarded Kelric. "What you want to do goes against every diplomatic protocol. Those protocols exist for a reason. They make it possible for our governments to deal together without destabilizing our already volatile relations. What you suggest endangers that balance. As Foreign Affairs Counselor, I strongly advise against this meeting."

"I also, as commander of the Imperial Fleet," Chad said. "Even if Qox did agree, where would you meet him? Certainly not in Eubian territory. It would be impossible for us to guarantee your safety. If the Eubians tried to capture or kill you, it would start the very war you say this meeting is meant to avoid. The only way ISC could assure your safety would be for Qox to meet you in our territory. And of course he won't, for the same reasons you can't go to him."

"Then we'll meet on Earth," Kelric said.

"That's even worse!" Tikal told him. "The last time you went to Earth, they wouldn't let you go."

"That was during a war," Kelric said. "They held onto the members of the Ruby Dynasty who sought refuge there because they didn't believe ISC had the resources to pull us out. They were wrong then, and they know they would be wrong now, even more so, given our current military strength. They aren't stupid, Tikal, and they want a war even less than the rest of us."

Chad leaned forward. "No one 'wants' the destruction and death of war, but it can be far preferable to the alternative—Aristo dominance over the human race. Jaibriol the Third is a Qox. A Highton. The descendant of a line of despots. Talking to him in person won't change that."

"You also have to consider your safety in another sense," Ragnar said. "It's only been a few months since someone tried to kill you, Imperator Skolia. We don't know yet whether or not a more extensive conspiracy exists."

Unfortunately, he had a good point. Kelric looked up at Najo, who was standing near his chair. "Has any evidence surfaced to indicate a larger conspiracy?"

"As of yet, no," Najo said. "However, security hasn't finished their investigation."

Kelric knew they would keep on looking unless he told them to stop. To Ragnar, he said, "I admit, it's a risk. But some risks are worth the danger."

"Not this one," Roca said. "Kelric, I fear it will *increase* hostilities. The Traders know what that vote in our Assembly meant, that it handed you more support for ISC. We need to convince them we're interested in treaties rather than battles. If you ask the emperor to meet with you under the conditions you describe, it is going to look more like a threat."

"I have to agree," Chad said. "If anything happened at that meeting to you or their emperor, it would inflame both sides. That's why we never have two rulers meet this way."

Tikal spoke tightly. "Lord Skolia does *not* rule the Imperialate."

"No, he doesn't." Dehya spoke for the first time. "Nor does he have any wish to undermine either of us, Barcala."

Tikal scowled at her. "I haven't heard you objecting to this madness."

"Perhaps because I don't consider it madness," she said.

Everyone went silent. Kelric had little doubt he was the only one who wasn't surprised by her response.

"You support this idea?" Roca asked with astonishment.

"I trust Kelric's judgment," Dehya said.

"I don't hear you volunteering to meet Qox," Tikal countered.

"Only one of us should go," Kelric said.

"Why?" Chad asked. "Because it is safer than having both of you in the same place, yes?"

"That's right," Kelric said.

"It's even safer with neither of you there," Chad told him.

"One of us should go," Dehya said.

"Why?" Roca seemed bewildered. "And why Kelric?"

He couldn't reveal the truth, that he could only reach Qox's mind in person. As to why it had to be him, that was harder to explain. His son, who knew almost nothing of Skolia's tortuous politics with Eube, had interpreted Kelric's relationship with Qox as father and son. Kelric didn't understand why; as far as he knew, he had given Jimorla no reason to suspect he could be even the uncle of the Trader emperor, let alone his father. But that Quis session had convinced Kelric that if anyone went, it should be him. He was also the only one of them who had met the emperor in person. He couldn't put into words why he thought he had a bond with Qox, but nevertheless, the thought remained.

He could say none of that. So he spoke another truth. "Any mesh communication, no matter how well secured, can be monitored. Only if we meet in person can we be assured of confidentiality."

"And why do you need this confidentiality?" Tikal demanded. "What are you planning to discuss with the emperor that you want no one else to overhear?"

"An end to the wars," Kelric said. "We can never speak freely in front of our top people. Neither of us can show any sign the other side would interpret as weakness. But with just the two of us, we might find an accommodation."

"Or you might try to kill each other," Chad said. "You do realize that will be ESComm's first thought."

"I don't see why you think he would have any interest in finding an accommodation anyway," Tikal said.

"Jaibriol Qox was the one who suggested the peace talks ten years ago," Roca pointed out.

"Yes, well, look how successful those were," Ragnar said sourly. "His own military wouldn't support him."

Kelric scowled at him. "Neither would mine. It takes two sides to negotiate. Maybe if he and I meet, just the two of us, we can find common ground on our own."

The First Councilor shook his head. "When the Assembly voted to eliminate hereditary control over the Triad voting bloc, I knew it would increase your power base, even lead to military action against the Traders. It was my one hesitation in supporting the ballot. I did anyway, because I know someday we *will* face the Traders. We can't avoid it. Until one of our empires falls, we will remain set against each other. Our fundamental values and needs are too opposed. No common ground exists."

"We have to try," Kelric said, frustrated. "I need to do this, Barcala."

Tikal slapped the table. "The rest of humanity may view you as an Imperialate sovereign, but you don't rule here. You answer to me. And I say no."

"He answers to us both." Dehya said sharply. "I say yes."

"I won't give on this one," Tikal told her.

"My loyalty is always and firmly to ISC," Chad told Kelric. "But in this, I must agree with the First Councilor."

"I concur with Admiral Barzun," Ragnar said.

Damn. Kelric knew he could never sway them without the support of ISC. Technically, only Dehya and Tikal could make the decision. But with Tikal so adamant against the idea and no support anywhere else, he had little recourse.

Dehya met Tikal's gaze. "I won't give on this one, either."

"Then we're deadlocked," Tikal said. "We'll have to turn it over to the Assembly for a vote."

Kelric made an incredulous noise. "What the hell kind of secrecy is that? The whole point is that Qox and I would meet in private, unaffected by outside influences."

Tikal sat back and crossed his arms. "It's the only way to resolve a deadlock between Pharaoh Dyhianna and myself."

Even if Kelric had been willing to send it to the Assembly, he knew it would never pass. If Roca, the voice of the Moderate Party, refused to support him, he would never convince the more bellicose factions of that voting body.

Kelric spoke with difficulty. "Very well. I withdraw the proposal."

Tikal didn't look triumphant, only weary. No one else spoke. Kelric felt defeated on a much larger scale than with this one question.

Then he looked at Dehya.

Her face showed only disappointment. Nor did her mood hint at any other response. But she was the most nuanced empath alive; if anyone could hide from even the psions at this table, it was Dehya. Kelric understood her as no one else, because he had worked with her in a Dyad for ten years—and the moment he looked at her, he knew. She wanted to do this without Tikal's consent.

She wanted him to commit treason.

The Emperor of Eube sought refuge in the night, out on the sparkling dark beach. The waves roared and crashed, rising to the size of houses and hurling their fury against twisted black outcroppings along the shore. Their spray leapt into the sky, coruscating against a night washed with moonlight in gold, white, and red. Driven by the satellites of Glory, the violent tides battered the coast.

Jaibriol knelt in the sand with no company except Hidaka and three other Razers. They were like a wall separating him from the rest of the universe, one monolith with four parts. Hidaka had discussed names with them and they all had them now, but they hadn't responded to his oblique inquiries about what to call them. They lived in their own universe, intersecting humanity yet never truly like humans. But they never wavered in their protection.

Jaibriol was fragmenting.

He couldn't control the Triad power coursing through his mind. He didn't understand it. He had no context, no preparation, no training, no advisors. *Nothing.* He had only the incontrovertible knowledge that he had to hide what had happened, push it into a recess so deep, no one could ever detect it, neither the Aristos who would prey on his pain nor the providers who would recognize him. He didn't know how to suppress the forces raging within him like the tides driven against this tortured shore. Nor could he escape. Colonel Muze had destroyed the Lock, and no one knew how to rebuild it. To survive, he had to stop being a member of the Triad. And he couldn't.

Jaibriol pressed the heels of his hands against his temples and squeezed his eyes shut. He couldn't do this. He couldn't keep the secret. His life and mind were unraveling. If he continued as emperor, he would fall apart in front of everyone, the Hightons, his advisors, his aides, and his enemies.

"Sire." The deep voice rumbled.

Jaibriol lifted his head and stared through the veil of his pain at Hidaka. "I cannot," he whispered. He wasn't even certain what he was telling his Razer.

The captain spoke with atypical softness. "Shouldn't we return to the palace? Your absence will soon be remarked."

Jaibriol struggled to his feet. "You can protect my person," he said dully. "But what about my thoughts?"

Hidaka regarded him uncertainly. "You will recover."

Not this time. Wearily Jaibriol pulled himself upright. "Let us return."

He headed to the path that wound up the cliffs to the palace. The Razers fell in around him, and lights flashed on their biomech arms. Hidaka acted as a conduit, interpreting Jaibriol's actions for them. Jaibriol had no idea how deep a network among them could go, for to his knowledge no other Aristos had let their bodyguards develop such extensive links. When given the freedom to act as their own beings, they became neither machine nor human, but something else. Yet still they served him with deadly versatility. The best defenses on the planet guarded his person and his palace.

But nothing could protect him against his own mind.

XXVII

The Hall of Providence

"I trusted you." Ixpar's low voice pulled Kelric awake. Startled, he sat bolt upright, his pulse surging as his mind caught up with his reflexes.

Ixpar was kneeling next to him, wearing the silky shift he loved to take off her. But no invitation showed in her posture tonight. Starlight flooded the Orbiter, reflected through panels that had opened after the Sun Lamp set, and it poured through the windows of his bedroom, silvering her body. She knelt by him with one clenched fist resting on her thigh.

"You should trust me," Kelric said, trying to wake up the rest of the way.

"You knew you would contaminate his Quis if you sat at dice with him," Ixpar said. "It was bad enough you agreed. But to pour so much Skolian and Eubian politics into your first game? It is unconscionable."

"I'm not sure how it happened," he admitted. Caught by the luminous genius of Jimorla's Quis, he had instinctively sought his son's input.

"It's obvious how," Ixpar said. "He asked you to play Quis. You said yes. You should have said no."

"He is my son." He met her gaze. "I will not refuse him."

"So you make all Coba pay the price?"

"It was one session."

"One devastating session." The calm of her voice belied the anger in her gaze, which reflected the starlight. "Everything he took from you, he will bring to Coba. And his influence has no small effect on our Quis. He is a Calani like no other. You must know that after your session. His patterns of Skolia and Eube will flood Coba."

He knew it was true. "I'm sorry."

"And you would take my successor as well."

"Rohka talked to you?"

"She wishes to study at the school here."

"Will you say no?" he asked. Her anger was a fog around him.

"I cannot. By Coban law, she is an adult." She sounded worn out. "I hate the idea. It will contaminate her Quis past repair. But you spoke truly. She should know your people. To rule Coba well, in this era when we become part of your empire, she must understand Skolia."

"So must Jimorla," Kelric said. "Otherwise, he'll create distorted pictures, as he did with myself and Emperor Qox."

"It isn't the same." The heat faded from her voice. "I'm sorry, Kelric. But Jimorla wants to return home."

He made himself nod, though it hurt. He couldn't fight this. He even agreed. Rohka would serve as the conduit from the Imperialate to the Calanya, filtering the input they gave the Calani. It would protect the Quis of Coba. But knowing that made it no easier to hear how his son felt.

"And you?" Kelric asked. "Will you also go back?"

"I cannot stay."

What could he say? She couldn't stop ruling Coba because he missed her. He thought of Jaibriol Qox, who symbolized everything he could never have. Qox ruled Eube. Period. No Assembly, no First Councilor, no one to interfere. Tarquine stood by his side, brilliant and unmatched, she who had never seen Kelric as anything more than a slave. She would give Jaibriol heirs, and his children would honor their father as everyone esteemed the emperor. Kelric's son barely even acknowledged him.

You are a fool to envy Qox, he thought. The man probably lived in hell, if what Kelric suspected were true.

"I'm sorry," Ixpar said, watching his face. "Would that I could tell you otherwise." She spoke softly. "I wish you could return with me,

Kelric, live in my Calanya, be my husband." With pain, she added, "We both long for the impossible."

"We can visit each other." It was poor compensation, but it was better than nothing. He took her hand and ran his thumb over her knuckles. "Jimorla is truly a genius."

Her face gentled into a smile. "He is his father's son."

"Perhaps someday he will accept that."

"Ah, Kelric." She lifted his hand and pressed her lips against his knuckles. "I can only tell you what I tell myself; never grieve for what could have been. We do what we can."

Never grieve. He wondered if she realized she asked the impossible.

"If I defy a veto from the First Councilor," Kelric said, "I'm breaking the law." He and Dehya were walking on the hill behind his house, high above the gorge with the river.

"We could tell the Inner Council we think Jaibriol Qox is a psion," Dehya said. She even sounded serious.

Kelric slanted a look at her. "Either they would think we were crazy, or even worse, they would believe us. The more people we tell, the more likely it will hurt Qox."

"He's already in danger." She stopped and stared down at the foaming river that rushed against the rocks. "We need to talk to him."

"It's not that easy." Kelric had no way to contact Jaibriol outside of formal channels, which required extensive procedures through both governments. He didn't see what he would achieve by trying, except to get arrested. He might secure his part of the communication, but not the Eubian side. It wouldn't be private.

"I'll support any decision you make," Dehya said.

Kelric crossed his arms. "I don't want your support."

"Why the hell not?"

"Because the penalty for treason is execution."

She pulled him to a stop. "What, they're going to execute both the Ruby Pharaoh and Imperator?"

"When you overthrew the Assembly, you made enemies," Kelric said. "Blending the government may have been genius or madness, but either way, it's divisive." He rubbed the aching muscles in his neck. "You saw the ballot on Roca's votes. It was almost even. Take a vote on whether or not the Ruby Dynasty should share the rule of Skolia with the Assembly, and it would be even less in our favor. They can't take that vote; we have the power to enforce your decree that neither side can disband the combined government. But that power comes from ISC. If I were to lose my title—say by committing treason—our power base among the military would crumble." He thought of the day she had announced the blended government. "If you had disbanded the Assembly and returned to the days of pure hereditary rule, you would have had to execute Tikal. I doubt he's ever forgotten how close he came to death. At your hands."

"I didn't execute him," Dehya said.

"That just makes him more dangerous."

"He's an inspired leader," she said. "If my taking the Ruby Throne meant his death, it was wrong. We need the Assembly. The time for an empire ruled solely by a dynasty is gone."

"Yes, well, too many people agree with you, Dehya. In fact, a lot of them think the time for *any* dynastic rule is gone."

"The Traders don't," she said dryly.

"Unfortunately." He gazed at the river as it frothed and churned over the rocks. "We don't have a Prime line to Qox the way we do to the Allied President on Earth. We've had nothing but hostilities and war with the Traders for half a millennium. I can't imagine that changing."

"Yet here is Jaibriol Qox," she murmured, "acting oddly."

"Which is the greater treason," he asked. "To defy First Councilor Tikal and meet a tyrant in secret, or to obey and go to war when Qox may wish otherwise?"

Dehya met his gaze. "I wish I knew."

Jaibriol strode with Tarquine down a wide hall of the palace, under soaring horseshoe arches that shone with gold and emeralds. They were headed to the Amphitheater of Providence. The boots of his Razers rang on the jade-tiled floor, four mammoth human-biomech hybrids. But today they couldn't help him. It would be agony when he entered the amphitheater, for over two thousand Aristos had arrived to attend the economic summit. Tarquine would preside as Finance Minister, but Jaibriol couldn't avoid the sessions or attend via the mesh, not if he wanted to maintain the political edge that kept him sharp, even kept him alive. To give the appearance of neglecting such a confluence of powers could be ruinous.

As they neared the enormous doors of the amphitheater, a retinue of Hightons approached them from a hall that came in at an oblique angle to theirs. Jaibriol knew it had to be one of his top people, because no one else could get this close to him. With a sinking sensation, he recognized the tall man in the center of the retinue; General Barthol Iquar, Tarquine's nephew and one of ESComm's ruthless joint commanders.

He had no wish to see Barthol; the general's abhorrence of the peace process was matched only by his personal dislike of Jaibriol. But Tarquine was slowing down. As their two groups reached each other, everyone stopped. All of the aides and even Barthol's Razers went down on one knee to Jaibriol.

The general bowed to him with military precision. "You honor the Line of Iquar with your presence, Esteemed Highness." His harsh voice grated, and his Highton presence ground against Jaibriol's mind until he wanted to groan.

Jaibriol barely managed a nod. It was a marginal courtesy, one that suggested displeasure, but at this point it was all he could do without revealing his agony. He was about to resume his walk when he heard his wife speak through the haze of his pain.

"It pleases me to see you, Barthol," Tarquine said.

Barthol bowed to her. "It is my great honor to be in your presence." This time, he even sounded as if he meant the words.

"Indeed it is," Tarquine murmured.

Jaibriol thought of going on by himself, but he couldn't insult Tarquine by leaving her behind, and he had no intention of inviting his own incineration by ordering her to come with him.

"You look well today," Barthol told her.

"As do you," Tarquine said.

Barthol tilted his head slightly, a gesture that hinted at appreciation. "It esteems the Line of Iquar that its leaders are in good health."

"It does indeed," Tarquine said with a cool smile. "They plan to continue that way."

Jaibriol couldn't figure out what Tarquine was about. The contrast between his curt greeting and her welcome to Barthol hadn't been intentional on his part, but if it bothered her, she gave no sign. More to the point, he picked up nothing in her mood. He had a good idea what she meant by "continue," though. She headed the Iquar Line. No one knew yet she carried the heir to the Iquar title, and she hadn't chosen a successor to follow her if she died without an heir. Barthol was a logical choice, given his seniority within their Line and his power in ESComm.

"The throne wishes honor for your Line," Tarquine added to her brother.

Jaibriol blinked at her. *Your* Line? She and Barthol shared the same bloodline. Of course she wished them honors, but it was an odd way to say it, especially bringing in the throne. He had no desire to offer Barthol anything. The general had blocked him at every damn junction in the talks, adamant that Skolia pass a law requiring the return of any slaves who escaped into Skolian territory. Jaibriol had thought the Ruby Pharaoh had been willing to search for a compromise, but after Barthol took a hard line, her military became intransigent as well. It was a major reason the negotiations had stalled. As far as Jaibriol was concerned, Barthol could rot in perdition. He said nothing to the general, just met his gaze, an omission that glared all the more harshly given Tarquine's friendlier greeting.

"Your generosity benefits the Line of Iquar," Barthol told Tarquine, which meant zero given that she *was* the Line of Iquar.

"Indeed it does." Her words flowed over them, smooth and potent. "As it does for those who stand behind the head of any Line."

Jaibriol stiffened. If she was referring to heirs as those "who stand behind," she better not be planning to reveal she was pregnant. He couldn't let her do it with no warning or preparation, and without his agreement. Of course if he cut her off, she would turn him into metaphorical ashes, but he would have to live with it. He was already so beleaguered from his Triad entry, he doubted even Tarquine could make it worse.

Jaibriol couldn't read her intent; her face was inscrutable, and she had raised mental barriers, which no other Aristo would use, because they had no reason to learn. Barthol had his focus completely on her. His posture indicated caution, but he had turned his hand by his side so his palm faced away from his body, a subtle gesture that indicated curiosity. He wanted to know what she meant, too.

Barthol spoke smoothly. "It is the honor of those who stand behind them."

Well, hell. Was she leaving open the possibility she would name *Barthol* as her heir? That was bizarre. Whatever she hoped to achieve with such a temptation, it could only last a few months, until it became public knowledge she carried a child who was both the Highton and the Iquar Heir. If Barthol knew she had done it when she fully realized it meant nothing, he would only be angry.

Jaibriol didn't think he could take any more intrigues. He spoke curtly to Barthol. "It has been our pleasure to see you, General." He nodded to Tarquine, trying to make it appear as an invitation rather than an order.

To his relief, she inclined her head to her nephew. "May you fare well."

"And you always." Barthol bowed to Jaibriol. "I thank you for the honor of your presence."

Right, Jaibriol thought. He left with Tarquine, his retinue sweeping away. He expected Tarquine to frown at him for disrupting her machinations. Instead she put her hand on his forearm, as one would expect for the empress. Given that she never did the expected unless it served her purposes, it didn't set his mind at rest.

"An auspicious day," she said.

He spoke in a low voice. "Your esteem gives me hives, dear wife."

Her smile curved. "As often as you imply such to me, I have never seen a single hive on your beautiful body."

He flushed, and decided to keep his mouth shut on that one.

The doors to the Amphitheater of Providence rose to the height of ten men. They swung open as Jaibriol approached, apparently on their own volition, though he knew aides monitored his every step. As his retinue entered the hall, a thousand voices poured over him. He was coming in far above the floor, at a balcony that overlooked the gigantic hall with its many benches and the dais in the center.

Aristos filled the amphitheater.

Jaibriol's mind reeled from the thousands of them: Hightons, Diamonds, Silicates. He was dimly aware of Tarquine's hand on his elbow. To everyone else, it looked as if the emperor strode firmly into the amphitheater, attended by his empress and Razers. But he knew the truth; without the pressure of her hand, he would have stopped, frozen in place.

He and Tarquine took their seats in a balcony above the entrance, with his Razers around them like a human shield. This area was well removed from the rest of the amphitheater. He had selected it that way to protect his mind, but to the rest of Eube it was yet another example of his remote character. He had discovered it didn't matter. No one expected him to act normal. Broadcasters extolled his imperial demeanor. His behavior fit all too well with the Eubian belief that their emperor was a deity. Their attitude disturbed Jaibriol at a deep level; it felt like a trespass against the Christian religion he had converted to on Earth, which acknowledged only one God. But it also meant his people accepted his behavior, which at times was all that allowed him to keep from drowning in the cruelty of his life.

His distance from the other Aristos muted the effects of their minds, usually enough for him to tolerate these summits. Today even that wasn't enough. His head throbbed as the hum of voices swelled. Everyone knew the emperor had entered. They were an ocean of alabaster faces, glittering black hair, and hard carnelian eyes.

Tarquine turned to Jaibriol. "I must open the session."

He nodded stiffly, able to do little else. "Of course."

She didn't leave yet, though. Instead she spoke in a voice so low, even Robert wouldn't hear, though he sat only a seat away on Jaibriol's other side, reading holofiles. This was the best secured location in the amphitheater, with audio buffers for privacy, even visual buffers that hazed the air around them so no one could read their lips.

"Do you know why Corbal fears for his son, Azile?" she asked, intent on him.

Jaibriol narrowed his gaze. "Corbal fears no one. Not even you, Tarquine."

"He loves Azile, you know."

"I'm sure he does." Jaibriol even believed it.

"It is Admiral Erix Muze," she murmured.

"Why would Erix threaten Azile? They like each other."

"Suppose they were related."

"What do you say, 'suppose?'" Jaibriol couldn't see her point. "Azile is the grandson of one of Eube Qox's sisters and Erix is the great-grandson of the other. They're related to each other and to me." He pressed his fingertips into his temples, a sign of vulnerability no emperor should show in public, but he couldn't help himself.

"Erix married Azile's daughter."

"I'm aware of that." He was being too blunt, even for his wife, but he had no resources left for anything more. The impatience of the Aristos in the amphitheater grated against his mind like grit. "You have to start the session."

She leaned toward him. "Remember this, Jaibriol. Not all implications refer to your exalted self."

For flaming sake. She knew he didn't assume that. Unlike his predecessors. "Nor do all implications make sense."

"Erix loves his wife," she said.

Dryly Jaibriol said, "Truly astonishing."

"Just as Corbal loves the dawn. Except Erix doesn't know."

The dawn? That sounded like she meant Sunrise. He didn't see what this had to do with Erix's wife, who was Corbal's granddaughter and Azile's daughter—

A thought came to him, too impossible to consider, but he considered it anyway. Could *Sunrise* be Azile's mother? Azile looked and acted the perfect Highton, and he transcended. He had an Aristo wife and daughter. Of course his daughter was a Highton. Erix Muze would never have married her otherwise. If Erix felt an unusual affection for his wife, it might be seen as eccentric, but nothing more. He had no reason to think he might like her better because she had inherited traits not normally associated with an Aristo, such as kindness. Of course he would never suspect she was other than the ideal Aristo woman. Such an idea was preposterous. Outrageous.

Jaibriol stared at his wife and a chill swept over him. If Azile wasn't a Highton, Corbal had hidden a lie almost as huge as what he knew about Jaibriol. No one would discover it, not even Erix Muze. Corbal was too savvy. No one could outwit him.

Except Tarquine.

"What have you done?" Jaibriol said in a low voice.

"Prepared for the summit, of course." She rose gracefully, and he was aware of everyone below turning to look. The empress bowed to the emperor with perfect form and spoke in a voice that carried. "If Your Highness does so wish, we will began."

Jaibriol's pulse was racing, and his temples ached. He inclined his head, determined to keep his cool in front of the massed powers of his empire.

Tarquine walked with two Razers to the edge of the balcony. A robot arm had docked there, and she stepped into the Luminex cup at its end. As it ferried her across the hall, the dais in the center rose to meet them. A comm officer was seated at a console on that great disk, monitoring communications in the hall.

Within moments, Tarquine and her guards were stepping from the cup onto the dais. The robot arm withdrew, leaving her in full view. The shimmer of a security field surrounded her. It all had a surreal quality to Jaibriol, as he were watching a play through the veil of a mental haze.

Tarquine stood at the podium while the dais rotated, giving her a view of the entire hall. When she spoke, opaline spheres rotating in the air throughout the ampitheater sent her throaty voice everywhere.

"Welcome," she said. "The two-hundredth and twenty-second Economic Summit of Eube is now in session."

A rumble of voices greeted her announcement. Thousands of Aristos activated their consoles and settled in for the triennial meeting where the powers of the empire gathered to plot, argue, and conspire about increasing their already obscene wealth.

Jaibriol struggled to concentrate as the session proceeded. He neither spoke nor participated in either of the two votes, a ballot to increase Gold Sector tariffs and one to decrease the tax on merchant fleets. Technically, the vote didn't matter; the final decision rested with him. But he ignored the summit at his own risk. If he went against a vote, he weakened his power base with whatever group he opposed. It was an unending game of intrigue, and right now he couldn't handle it. Mercifully, he didn't have to. His aides were recording the session, and he would look at it in detail later.

When Iraz Gji, the Diamond Minister, stood up behind his console, Jaibriol thought he meant to speak in support of the tariffs. Gji had actively lobbied for their passage. Given Gji's stature as a Minister, the comm officer jumped him ahead in the queue, and the *active* light glowed on his console. The rumble of voices quieted; it was unusual for a Minister to address the proceedings, and delegates stopped their maneuvering to listen.

Gji's voice rumbled as spheres carried it throughout the hall. "I wish to enter a new form in these proceedings."

Jaibriol scowled. "Enter a new form" meant Gji wanted to call for a vote on a ballot that had neither been on the agenda nor discussed on the floor. No one had informed Jaibriol, and he never liked surprises, especially from his Ministers.

Tarquine inclined her head to Gji. "Proceed."

"The exaltation of Eube rises each summit," Gji began.

Jaibriol silently groaned. He might be dying in pain, but he swore, half of it came from the interminable ability of Aristos to speak for hours without saying anything. Given that this was an economic summit, Gji's "exaltation" undoubtedly referred to the wealth of the empire.

"It is our desire to see the rise continue," Gji said.

Jaibriol watched Tarquine, noting her perfect composure, and he suddenly knew she expected this. A tickle started in his throat. She claimed Gji had softened to the idea of trade with the Skolians, but that was only a first step. Surely Gji wouldn't put the matter to a vote now; without extensive preparation, probably over a period of years, such a vote would never pass.

"At its highest," Gji continued, "our exaltation will spread throughout settled space."

A ripple of chimes came from the amphitheater as Aristos tapped their finger cymbals in approval of his implicit suggestion that Eube should conquer the rest of humanity, as if owning two trillion people wasn't enough.

"Many avenues of commerce exist," Gji said. "Some venture into exotic realms. Fertile realms rich with resources."

More cymbals chimed, and Aristos discreetly opened their hands on their consoles with palms facing upward, expressing their curiosity. Jaibriol just wanted him to get to the flaming point. So far it sounded as if he were suggesting the usual, that they conquer those exotic realms, which was no more obtainable today than at the last two hundred summits.

"New avenues can mean new means of travel," Gji added.

No cymbals chimed. *New* was not a favored word among Aristos. They sought to operate, think, and act as one mind. Variation was anathema.

On the dais, Tarquine gave the appearance of listening with a posture that suggested wary attention. She no doubt fooled everyone else, but Jaibriol knew better. Gji had said exactly what she wanted to hear.

"New is always a risk," Gji said, acknowledging the unease in the amphitheater. "Unless, of course, it adds to the exaltation of Eube. It might then inspire a call for concord."

Ah, hell. Jaibriol clenched the edge of his console. A "call for concord" meant Gji wanted to vote *now*. Surely he didn't mean the trade expansion. They had no preparation. It would fail miserably.

Jaibriol stood behind his console, and the rumbles died in the amphitheater. Tarquine looked up at him with a calm face, but he sensed her alarm. He wasn't certain himself what he intended, he only knew he couldn't sit here while events spiraled out of his control.

Jaibriol spoke, and his comm sent his voice out to the spinning orbs. "You orate well, Minister Gji." In truth, Highton discourse annoyed Jaibriol no end, but what the hell. It was true Gji had mastered the style. "We are, after all, the Eubian Concord."

Gji bowed to him. Every screen in the amphitheater showed him as an inset, with Jaibriol as the main figure. Jaibriol hardly recognized himself. He stood tall and somber, broad-shouldered, dressed in black with his black hair glittering, his eyes like rubies, his face with the bone structure that supposedly made him one of the most handsome men alive. He hated what he saw, the Highton emperor.

"You honor our proceedings with your voice," Gji said.

Tarquine said nothing, but she lowered her mental barriers and let a warning fill her thoughts. She had no reason to hide her efforts; no one but Jaibriol could sense what she was doing.

"It pleases us," Jaibriol said, "that you wish for more concord in our exaltation."

"I am honored, Your Highness," Gji said.

That was certainly different from Gji's chill disinterest when Jaibriol had met with him over dinner. Jaibriol didn't want to remember what had changed the Minister's attitude.

"It would please us even more," Jaibriol said, "to hear how we might achieve this greater exaltation."

Gji raised his head. "The exotic realms of humanity control much wealth. To bring that wealth into concord with our own goals might be achieved by means other than Annihilators."

A shocked, discordant clamor of cymbals broke out. Often the cymbals expressed approval, but the syncopated beat the Aristos were using now told a different story. They were angry. It had taken Gji forever to get to the point, but when he finally reached it, no one missed his meaning. He had just called for a vote on opening trade relations with the Skolians.

Tarquine's voice rang out over the clamor. "Minister Gji, the Clerk in Session will attend your call."

Jaibriol stared at her. Her response was required; as the Minister who presided, she had to attend such details as whose clerk did what. But he knew her too well; she had set up this vote. Why? It was certain to fail. Perhaps that was the intent. She might have never wanted him to succeed.

Jaibriol had to make a decision. Only he could stop the call. No one would object if he made that choice, but it would do great damage to his hopes that it might pass another time. If he let the call go forward, it would also fail. Either way he lost. He watched Tarquine, wondering why she had done this.

He made his decision. As a clerk approached Gji, Jaibriol resumed his seat. That he hadn't objected didn't mean he agreed with the call, but it allowed the vote to proceed. For a ballot this outrageous, even if delegates suspected it had his support, that wouldn't stop them from voting against it. If anything, it would increase their determination to make their positions clear. Trade with the Skolians? Anathema. With carefully laid plans over time, he might have brought around enough Diamonds to garner the support he needed. This doomed the vote to failure, but at least he wouldn't go on record as opposed to the idea.

The clerk who took Minister Gji's call was a taskmaker and as such could present the ballot in direct language. It read simply: *Proposal: the Eubian Concord offer to open trade with the Skolian Imperialate for foods and curios.* Maybe Gji thought limiting the potential products for sale would make the idea more palatable. He might have been right if they had approached this in a rational manner. Nothing would help now.

As soon as the Clerk in Session read the ballot, Parizian Sakaar jumped to his feet. The Trade Minister's voice rang out above the turmoil. "Consorting with humanity's amoral dregs is no exaltation!"

Jaibriol had no doubt Sakaar meant the insult implicit in his blunt response. A widespread clash of cymbals indicated support for his outburst from the gathered Aristos. It sickened Jaibriol. He well remembered his meeting with the Trade Minister, when Sakaar had spoken about providers as if they were inanimate products. He called Skolians the "amoral dregs" of humanity because their psions were free rather than controlled by the brutal pavilions where his Silicate Aristos tormented providers.

Minister Gji stood again, another dramatic break with protocol, and regarded his Trade counterpart. "Indeed, Minister Sakaar, we would wish no loss of eminence due to consorting with dregs." He paused a beat. "Or due to other octet errors that create less exaltation."

Octet errors? What the hell? It sounded as if Gji was referring to the evidence of fraud Tarquine had found against Sakaar. None of the gathered Aristos showed any sign they caught the reference; as far as Jaibriol knew, Tarquine had told no one else. Members of the summit were talking agitatedly among themselves or notifying the comm officer they wanted to speak. The Trade and Diamond Ministers could get away with breaking protocol because of their high position, but Jaibriol suspected Sakaar wished now he had waited. Although his face maintained the Highton cool, Jaibriol recognized his strain.

Jaibriol rubbed his temples. His vision was blurring, and he had to wait until it cleared before he could search the hall. Both of his joint commanders had attended. Barthol Iquar was in the section reserved for the highest members of the Iquar Line. He wasn't speaking to anyone, just staring at Tarquine. It gave Jaibriol pause; he would have expected Barthol to assert the lack of military support for the vote.

Admiral Erix Muze was talking with his aides, and Jaibriol could see one of them preparing a statement. His protest would come soon. Tarquine was speaking into the comm on her podium, probably responding to a demand or question. The comm officer worked frantically, queuing requests to speak. Given the stature of the delegates who probably wanted to make their views known, Jaibriol didn't envy the officer her job, having to rank them.

The officer finally decided, and the *active* light glowed on the console of the Janq matriarch of the Diamond Aristos. Although the Janq Line had lost stature because of their economic troubles, few Aristos cared that the Janq had pirate ships. If anything, they admired Janq for the size of their fleet and their daring in pushing so far into Skolian space. The outrage, in their minds, was that the Skolians had "stolen" them.

Janq waited until the amphitheater quieted. Then she said, "The dregs of humanity have made clear their lack of eminence. It lowers us to consider them as a source of exaltation."

General Barthol Iquar rose to his feet.

Alarm flashed across the face of the besieged comm officer; she could hardly tell a joint commander to sit the hell down. Only Jaibriol could do that. She glanced up at him, almost imploring, but he didn't move. Barthol should have signaled the officer, but now that he was standing, Jaibriol had no intention of ordering him to sit. If he denied his joint commander the chance to speak against a ballot, especially one of direct concern to ESComm, it could backfire spectacularly.

The comm officer worked fast, and an *active* light glowed on Barthol's console. Even though he had violated protocol by interrupting the Janq matriarch, she offered no objection. He was a powerful ally. His protest added to hers would strengthen her position.

"Exaltation comes in many forms," Barthol said. "Dregs may be elevated through their association with superior life-forms."

Jaibriol gaped at him. *What the blazes?* Either he had lost his ability to understand Highton, or his bellicose General of the Army had just supported the Diamond Minister's call for trade with the Skolians.

For one moment, silence reigned. Then a roar of voices and cymbals erupted throughout the amphitheater. Tarquine would normally have called for order, but it looked as if she was swamped with messages blazing across her podium screen, the hologlyphs flaring like electronic fire.

Admiral Erix Muze, ESComm's other joint commander, stood up abruptly, the fourth time in moments that one of Eube's most powerful Hightons had broken the rules, this in an empire that prided itself on its lack of variation. The comm officer shot a panicked look at Tarquine, but she was too busy organizing the flood of messages she was receiving to respond.

The officer jabbed her console, and the *active* light blazed red on Erix Muze's console. The admiral's voice rang out. "It has been suggested here today that Eube may gain advantage by bringing rabble into concord with our goals. This, using means other than Annihilators and their kin." He fixed his gaze on Barthol. "However, it should be stated that fleets outfitted with such kin sail exotic seas far more profitably."

Jaibriol's shoulders relaxed. Although Admiral Muze had just declared his opposition to the ballot, he phrased it without offering challenge to his counterpart in ESComm. He seemed puzzled more than anything else, no doubt wondering what could possibly motivate Barthol to support the measure. Jaibriol had exactly the same question.

Barthol met Erix's gaze. With icily perfect intonations, he said, "And such profitable ships shall ride in the new dawn."

Jaibriol felt as if he were reeling. To anyone else, it must have sounded as if one joint commander had told the other that whatever their differences in this ballot, he expected to continue working profitably with him. But Jaibriol knew now what Tarquine had warned him about. Barthol had just hit Erix with a threat so huge, it could tear apart the Xir and Muze Lines. He could reveal Azile's daughter—Erix's wife—as the granddaughter of a provider.

Erix probably had no idea what it meant, but Jaibriol had absolutely no doubt Corbal knew. When Corbal rose to his feet, Jaibriol wondered if he should just kill himself now, because he didn't see how he would escape this madness unscathed. It was going to blow up in their faces rather than pass any vote. He glanced at Tarquine, but she was leaning over the comm officer's console, for all appearances doing her best to help sort the deluge of messages. The desperate officer turned on the *active* light of Corbal's console, her face flushed. Jaibriol sympathized. He had never seen even two speakers active at once, let alone five. It wasn't done. Period. Aristos were a great machine that operated in synch. They never deviated. If someone tossed a bolt into the proceedings, they scrambled in chaos.

Corbal's voice rang out. "Let us remember that those who ride in profit do so for the glory of the emperor."

Jaibriol felt like putting his head in his hands. Corbal had just invoked his royal heritage, that he was the son of Eube Qox's sister. On the surface, his statement was a suitably phrased Highton pledge of the loyalty they all gave to the Carnelian Throne, a reminder they were of concord and should behave accordingly. It sounded impeccably appropriate, but Jaibriol knew exactly what he meant. Corbal had just told Barthol Iquar to back the bloody hell off or Corbal would use his imperial connections to destroy him.

The head of the Janq Aristo Line was still standing. Her voice carried. "Such wisdom is of inestimable value, Lord Xir." Her words suggested she honored Corbal, but her stiff posture implied hostility. "As does all such wisdom—especially those truths about our sailing ships."

Jaibriol pressed his palms against the console as if that could stop him from falling when all these threats avalanched onto his throne. Janq believed Corbal had helped the Skolians capture her merchant fleets. She had to have evidence she believed good enough to withstand any claim of false accusation. She was telling Corbal that if he didn't either support her side or shut the hell up, she would reveal his treason to the summit.

"This is out of control," Jaibriol muttered.

"It is—unusual," Robert said. He sounded stunned.

Jaibriol had to stop this before it took him down with everyone else. Before he stood, he focused on Tarquine. She seemed unconnected to the monumental confrontation; her attention was on her work with the comm officer. She was simply doing her job, keeping order amid the blaze of emotions. No one suspected *she* told the Skolians about the Janq ships, she set up Corbal, she discovered Corbal's secret, and she had the evidence that would implicate either Corbal or else the Janq Line for a false accusation. No one—except Jaibriol.

Her bizarre exchange with Barthol before the summit made all too much sense now. Somewhere, someplace, she had promised to declare him as her heir instead of her own child. His branch of the Iquar Line would become ascendant after this generation and hers would lose the title. All he had to do was support this ballot. For Barthol, it would be a great coup. What did it matter to Tarquine? Her child would inherit the Carnelian Throne. Except Jaibriol knew she would never give up that power, especially not the rule of such a powerful Aristo Line.

Jaibriol rose to his feet, and the hall quieted as everyone turned to him. The comm officer seemed frozen, unable to deal with yet another break in protocol, this time from the emperor himself. It was Tarquine who leaned over and turned off the lights on the consoles of Janq, Barthol, Erix, and Corbal. They all sat down; to presume they had the floor after Jaibriol had taken it was a crime against the throne, as decreed by one of Jaibriol's particularly narcissistic predecessors.

His words rolled over the amphitheater. The first time he had heard his voice amplified, he had thought the techs did something to give it that deep resonance. But he had checked. They did nothing. He actually sounded this way.

He directed his first comment to Janq. "Your Line has always done great honor to our empire." Jaibriol let neither his posture nor the position of his hands refute his statement. She nodded with a hint of relief, accepting the support.

"It is our hope," Jaibriol said, "that such continues. And certainly it is within our power to see that it does."

Her eyes widened the slightest bit, enough to tell Jaibriol she had taken his true meaning, despite his apparent support. If she pursued an accusation against Corbal, the emperor himself would discredit her evidence. He hoped to high heaven that Tarquine could nullify whatever proof Janq thought she had, because he had no idea how to refute her evidence.

Corbal lifted his chin with triumph. So Jaibriol spoke to him next. "We are pleased with the words of Xir, that those who ride in profit do so for the glory of the emperor."

Corbal inclined his head in acceptance.

Jaibriol waited a heartbeat. The frightened boy who had no idea how to speak among Hightons had vanished years ago and in his place stood a stranger Jaibriol barely recognized as himself. To Corbal, he said, "May the dawn always shine on those who sail for you, from here to realms exotic and new."

His cousin froze. No sound came from the amphitheater. Everyone knew what Jaibriol meant by realms exotic and new; incredibly, the emperor looked with favor on the ballot. That was shock enough. Only Corbal would hear the hidden warning; if he went against the ballot, he endangered Sunrise, his son, and his granddaughter. Jaibriol didn't want any of them hurt, but he couldn't protect them if someone without Corbal's best interest in mind—such as Barthol Iquar—chose to expose him.

Seeing Corbal go pale, Jaibriol felt like scum. But he had to continue. He turned next to Erix. The admiral sat behind his console, his attention focused on Jaibriol as he undoubtedly tried to unwind the conflicting tangles of alliance and confrontation.

Jaibriol said, "Admiral Muze."

Erix inclined his head, his posture wary.

Amplifiers carried Jaibriol's words to every inch of the amphitheater. "It is interesting that to become an admiral one must first be—" He paused. "A colonel."

The blood drained from Erix's face. Although the palace had released no formal announcement about the "attempt" against Jaibriol's life, word had leaked. The Aristos knew: Colonel Vatrix Muze had tried to assassinate the emperor. Vatrix and Erix were first cousins. Jaibriol had no reason to act against Erix; according to the investigation, the admiral hadn't seen Vatrix in years, and they had been estranged for longer. But in the elegantly vicious universe of Hightons, none of that mattered.

In ancient Highton tradition, Jaibriol could execute Erix or any other Muze for the sins of his kin. It would create a crisis for ESComm; the precipitous loss of a joint commander was no small matter. But Jaibriol wouldn't be the first emperor to retaliate against a highly placed member of a Line that had trespassed against him.

For a long moment no one moved. Then a rustle came from the dais. The comm officer was looking up at Jaibriol with a questioning gaze. When he inclined his head, she spoke in a subdued voice, and her voice went out over the spheres.

"Your Highness," she said, "do you wish to respond to this call for concord?"

Jaibriol met her gaze. "I call for concord as well."

It felt as if a mental quake shuddered through the hall. Jaibriol no longer cared. He just wanted this to end. "It would please us," he told the officer, "for you to continue the call."

She nodded, her face pale, and called the roll, starting with the highest delegate present. "Minister of Intelligence, Azile Xir."

Azile rose to his feet. He stared at Jaibriol, his gaze hooded, and Jaibriol knew he had made an enemy. Azile spoke slowly. "I call for concord."

Voices rolled through the hall like a collective groan.

As Azile took his seat, the comm officer said, "Minister of Finance, Tarquine Iquar."

Tarquine straightened up from her attempts to organize the messages. She looked startled, as if she had been so busy, she had forgotten she was involved in the vote. Jaibriol didn't believe it for a moment, but she did a hell of a convincing job.

"I abstain," she said.

No surprise there. The Finance Minister often abstained, given her position as moderator of the summit. With her husband making his preferences known atypically early in the vote, she also chose the tactful response, neither going against him nor appearing to use her position to influence the call. With a sense of shell-shocked awe, he realized she would escape this entire business with no one ever suspecting her involvement.

"Minister of Diamonds, Iraz Gji," the officer said.

Gji stood up behind his console. "I renew my call for concord." He sat down again, his expression satisfied.

"Minister of Trade, Parizian Sakaar," the officer asked.

The Trade Minister rose heavily to his feet. For a long moment he stared at the Diamond Minister. Then he spoke as if he were gritting his teeth. "I call for concord."

"Saints almighty," Robert muttered.

My sentiments exactly, Jaibriol thought. Tarquine had stored up her evidence of his mammoth crimes for exactly such a time as this.

"General of the Army, Barthol Iquar," the officer said.

Barthol rose to his great height. "I call for concord."

The comm officer stared at him with her mouth open, and the rumbles in the hall swelled. Even having already heard Barthol sound as if he supported the measure, apparently few Aristos believed he would actually vote in its favor. They had probably thought his earlier comments were so elegantly abstruse that they hadn't yet figured out his true meaning.

The officer finally recovered enough to say, "Admiral of the Navy, Erix Muze."

Erix stood up as if he were going to his own funeral. He knew what he had to say if he wanted to avoid exactly that event. He answered in a tight voice. "I call for concord."

The officer inhaled sharply. "High Judge Calope Muze."

Jaibriol felt like crawling under his seat. He hadn't even realized Calope had attended the summit. She was the only other Highton he liked. She had always treated him with respect, as if she actually believed he made a good emperor. Now she had witnessed him threatening to kill her grandson without a shred of evidence. Every screen in the amphitheater showed her standing up at a bench far across the hall, her face strained. She stared in his direction for a long moment. Then she looked at Erix, her grandson. In a heavy voice, she said, "I call for concord."

I'm sorry, Jaibriol thought, though he knew she could never hear his thought. None of them ever would.

The comm officer looked as if she were having heart failure. Nor was she the only one. But she spoke evenly. "Lord Xir?"

Corbal rose to his feet, his face clenched. "I call for concord."

Jaibriol doubted Corbal would ever forgive him. Or Calope. Or any of them. He lived on an island of his own slow dying.

The roll call continued, but the rest made no difference. The major players had spoken—and with the exception of one abstain, they had agreed to support what would rank as one of the most stunning upsets in Eubian history.

Tarquine glanced up at him and inclined her head as was appropriate for a Minister to her emperor. No hint of triumph showed on her face.

But it blazed in her mind.

XXVIII

Mists of Discourse

Jaibriol left his bodyguards outside his office despite Hidaka's protests. The room was unlit when he entered, except for the light coming in the window across from the door. The sun of Glory had set, leaving the sky a vivid red. A tall figure stood at the window, gazing out at the burning sky.

"I don't know why anyone bothers to say I sit on the throne," Jaibriol said.

Tarquine turned to him. "You are the emperor, my husband. You handled yourself brilliantly in the summit today."

"You set them up." He didn't know whether to be horrified or grateful. "All of them."

"Ah, Jai." She walked over, more relaxed than he had seen her in days. "You have your chance to talk to the Skolians. This strong expression of support from your top people offers the opening you need to contact the Ruby Dynasty." She stopped in front of him. "What you do with that opening—sell curios or negotiate peace—is your choice."

This felt surreal. "It isn't that simple."

"No, it isn't. It never is. But you have the opportunity."

Knowing she was right didn't cool his anger. "Why bother to send me? I couldn't come close to your expertise."

"In what?" She set her palm against his chest. "Yes, if you put me on the Carnelian Throne, I could be the ultimate Highton sovereign. No other Aristo would match my reign."

"Or your modesty," he said dryly.

"Eube doesn't need the ultimate Highton sovereign."

"No? What does Eube need?"

Her voice had a sense of quiet. "Someone with the decency and strength of character to make the best *leader*. It isn't the same as the best Highton sovereign." She lowered her hand. "Go to the Skolians. Do what no one else among us can. Make the universe a better place for everyone, not just Aristos."

He stared at her. "If any Aristo overheard what you just said, they would consider it grounds for assassination."

"Do you?"

"Never." He couldn't believe she would give up the Iquar title for his hopeless dream. "You offer me the impossible, but the dreamer who sought that shiny hope has become tarnished past recovery."

"I will always be Highton." Her voice had a still quality. "I could no more change than I could alter the laws of physics. I am what I am." The dim light shadowed her face. "And you will always be decent."

Decent. He felt anything but. She had given him a second chance, but the boy who had approached the Skolians ten years ago was gone, and he feared the man who had taken his place had become too much of an Aristo to claim that dream.

The communication from the Eubians came into the Office of the Ruby Pharaoh on the planet Parthonia, capital of the Skolian Imperialate. They forwarded it to the equivalent office on the Orbiter space station. It went through twelve layers of security before it reached the Advisory Aide to the Pharaoh. At the time, Dehya was deep within the Kyle, working on the vast network of meshes. So the Advisory Office of the Pharaoh forwarded the message to the Advisory Office of the Imperator.

Seated in the command chair above the War Room, Kelric barely noticed when the light on the armrest turned blue. It was a moment before he touched the *receive* panel.

"Skolia, here," he said.

His aide's voice floated out of the mesh. "Sir, we have a communication from the Emperor's Office on Glory."

What the blazes? "Play it."

"Forwarding."

A new voice spoke, this one in elegant Iotic with a Highton accent. "My honor at your Esteemed Presence, Pharaoh Dyhianna. I am Robert Muzeson, Personal Aide to Emperor Qox." The light on the comm indicated the message was prerecorded; without access to the Kyle web, Eubians couldn't send in real time. They weren't without recourse to Kyle technology; they could always petition Skolia for the loan of a node. Of course they liked that idea about as much as they liked moldy food. Maybe less. Moldy food didn't taunt them by challenging their ascendancy.

The message continued. "His Glorious Highness, Jaibriol the Third, desires a mutual audience of himself and Pharaoh Dyhianna."

"Good gods," Kelric muttered. He had never heard of anything like this. It gave him one hell of an opening, though. He could have the techs bring Dehya out of her Kyle session, but that would take time— and involve her in ways he wanted to avoid.

Kelric tapped a panel. "Major Wills?"

A man answered. "Here, sir."

"Prepare the omega protocol." Kelric had designed omega himself, in case he ever wanted to hide his communications from ISC and the government. "Use it to send the following to Emperor Qox's people."

"Recording, sir." Wills sounded stunned. He couldn't miss the implication, that Skolia's Imperator wanted to conceal his contact with Eube's emperor.

"And Wills," Kelric said. "You are bound by the protocol confidentiality." It was the weak link in the process, that Wills knew he had sent the message.

"Understood, Lord Skolia."

"Message begin," Kelric said. "The Imperator desires a mutual audience of himself and Emperor Qox, real-time, virtual."

"Sending." Wills spoke with efficiency, but Kelric didn't miss the shock in his voice.

And you don't know the half of it, Kelric thought.

The Luminex console curved around Kelric. Normally a crew tended his VR sessions: today he came alone. He fastened himself into the chair. The mesh folded around his body and plugged into sockets in his wrists, ankles, and spine, linking to his internal biomech. He had told no one what he was doing, and he used security he had designed himself. If this worked as expected, no one else would ever know about this session. He didn't fool himself that it would be impossible to trace, but if someone did unravel what he had done, he hoped it would be too late.

He touched a panel in the arm of his chair. "Bolt?"

"Here," his node said. It had accessed the console through Kelric's biomech link to the chair.

"Do you have a Kyle node prepared for Emperor Qox?"

"Everything is ready," Bolt said.

A chill went through Kelric. No communication between Eube and Skolia at this high of a level had taken place for years, since the breakdown of the negotiations. In the beginning, their staffs had continued to speak, trying to restart matters, but when one attempt after another failed, those communications had fizzled as well.

"Let's go." Kelric lowered the visor over his head, and the world turned black.

"Wait," Bolt said, a disembodied voice in the dark.

"Is something wrong?" Kelric asked.

"Are you sure you want to do this?"

"He requested the communication."

"You know what I mean."

Kelric closed his eyes, not because it mattered in the dark, but out of reflex, as if that would let him evade the concern in the voice of his supposedly emotionless node. "Yes, I'm sure."

"Activating VR," Bolt said.

The surroundings lightened into a mist and took form: a glossy white room with no furniture or exits. As real as it seemed, he had to remind himself he was in a chair on the Orbiter. He had changed nothing in his appearance except his clothes; instead of the casual slacks and shirt he actually wore, here he had a dark gold uniform with the insignia of an exploding star on his shoulder.

Kelric walked toward one seamless wall, and a door appeared. He exited into a hall of blue marble columns and airy spaces. Normally the computer would create an honor guard and whatever other retinue his protocol people felt necessary for a meeting with the emperor. Kelric had activated none of those simulations. The less resources he used, the less likely he was to draw attention to his proscribed use of the Kyle web.

✧   ✧   ✧

Jaibriol stood by the Luminex console that curved around his chair. Robert waited a few paces back, checking a holofile. Hidaka was monitoring the area with his cybernetic arm, and Jaibriol's other guards stood posted around the chamber. Several Hightons waited with him: the Protocol Minister, the Diamond Minister, and Tarquine. Corbal hadn't approached him since the vote, and Jaibriol didn't blame him, given what had happened.

His head ached continually. No nanomeds could cure it. He wondered dully if he would have to endure this pain for the rest of his life.

A tech approached and knelt to him, her gaze downcast.

"Please rise," Jaibriol said.

She stood, favoring her knee. "We're ready, Your Highness."

He nodded formally and took his seat in the console. As she fastened him into the chair, its mesh folded around him, clicking prongs into his wrist, ankle, and spine sockets.

"Are you comfortable?" the tech asked.

"Yes, good," Jaibriol said. The taskmaker minds of the techs working around him offered a mental wall that eased the pressure of the Aristo minds in the room.

She tapped the console. "This will link to the Kyle web."

"You're sure they have a node we can use?" he asked. The Skolians had promised to create one, but unlike with the peace talks, this time no crew had contacted his people. They had dealt only with an EI that called itself Bolt. Jaibriol had no idea what it meant, and he didn't like it. But he wasn't meeting Kelric in person, only as a simulation. What happened at the other end couldn't physically affect him.

"The node is set," the tech said. "Ready, Your Highness?"

Jaibriol's pulse jumped. "Yes. Go ahead."

She lowered his visor, enclosing him in darkness. A voice said, "Initiate," and another said, "Activating VR."

The world brightened, and Jaibriol found himself standing in a white room. A *square* room. The right angles disoriented him. He expected a door to appear and an avatar to enter, to serve as his host. When nothing happened, he went to the wall, uncertain what to do.

A message in English lit up the surface: Privacy requested.

Jaibriol tensed. Kelric wanted to talk to him alone, with no one else in the connection? To call it a strange request was akin to saying it was odd that the vote on opening trade relations with the Skolians had passed.

Jaibriol had asked to meet the Ruby Pharaoh. The Imperator had answered. Technically, it was an insult; in theory, Kelric didn't rule Skolia. In practice, no one doubted his power, especially since the recent Assembly vote. But communications between potentates weren't done in private, not without inviting suspicion of collaboration with the enemy. In this situation, though, that verged on ludicrous. Jaibriol suspected that if he refused the private conference, he would never learn what Kelric had come to say. He also knew that if he cut his advisors out of the link, they would have collective heart failure.

He laid his palm against the wall. "I accept."

The surface shimmered and vanished, revealing a fog beyond.

"Emperor Qox!" The alarmed voice of his Protocol Minister cut the air. "You just activated a security field!"

Hidaka's deep voice rumbled. "Sire, please go no further."

"I've accepted the field," Jaibriol said.

"Jai, don't." That was Tarquine. "You don't know what it means."

"It's just a simulation," Jaibriol said.

Hidaka spoke. "Your Highness, simulations can be used to cause injury, even at a distance. You could risk brain damage."

Jaibriol hesitated. Then he said, "I'll be fine."

"Jai, no!" Tarquine's voice rang out.

I have to find out what your former lover wants. Then he walked into the mist.

Kelric didn't have to wait; Jaibriol soon materialized out of the fog. The emperor looked as if he were cloaked in the night. He wore black-diamond trousers and shirt, and a black belt studded with carnelians. Red gems glinted in his cuff links. His black hair splintered light, and his red eyes had a jeweled quality. Kelric was no judge of appearance, but even he could tell Qox was uncommonly good-looking even among Hightons, who raised the pursuit of narcissistic "self-improvement" to an art. The emperor exuded vitality, a man at his peak, broad-shouldered and tall, long-legged and narrow-hipped, the embodiment of every standard of perfection in Eube and across the stars.

Kelric hoped Qox had enhanced his avatar in the simulation, because if the emperor really looked like this, it had to violate some law of the cosmos. No one deserved so many advantages: the greatest wealth of any human alive, the highest title in what many considered the most powerful empire in human history, the worship of trillions who considered him a deity, and an empress whose sultry, devastating beauty was outdone only by her deadly efficiency as a political weapon. Kelric was acutely conscious of his advanced years, the grey in his hair, and the limitations on his power, his life, and his family. He had been nothing more than a high-priced slave to the woman this man called wife.

They stood taking each other's measure, neither willing to speak first, for it was an implicit admission that the other occupied the dominant position. They had held their titles for roughly the same time, but Jaibriol was hardly more than a third Kelric's age. He had also initiated contact, which meant he should go first. But Kelric's status wasn't formally equivalent to Jaibriol's title as emperor.

Then Jaibriol spoke in Highton. "Imperator Skolia."

Kelric responded in the Aristo language. "Emperor Qox."

"It intrigues us that you requested a secured conference," Jaibriol said.

Kelric's first reaction was that Qox had learned Highton discourse too well. Instead of simply asking why, he approached the question obliquely. Fast on the heels of that reaction came the shock; the emperor had spoken to him—a former slave—as he would to a Highton. As an equal.

Kelric could read nothing from Jaibriol except what Qox wanted him to see, the perfect, aloof, alabaster Aristo. If Jaibriol had ever been a naïve high school boy on Earth, those days were gone.

"Emperor Qox." Kelric spoke formally. "You honor me with your language. I haven't the proficiency in Highton to return the honor. If you will forgive my direct language."

Jaibriol inclined his head. "There is nothing to forgive."

"I come to you with a request."

Jaibriol watched him with his carnelian gaze. No, not carnelian. His eyes looked like rubies.

"Go on," the emperor said.

"Meet me on Earth. In person. Just the two of us."

Jaibriol's face showed no hint of his reaction to that outlandish suggestion. He spoke coolly. "Why would I do such a thing?"

"Because I can help you. I may be one of the only people who can. But only in person." If he and Dehya were right, if Qox were a psion, the emperor would know what he meant.

"I have many people who can help me," Jaibriol. "Billions, in fact. Why would I need the aid of a provider?"

Kelric gritted his teeth and was glad the simulation edited it out. "You once asked me to meet you at the peace table. We met. It failed. Are you willing to try again? We will get nowhere surrounded by aides, officers, and advisors who limit our discourse. Meet with me. Just me. If you truly meant what you said that day in the Lock."

Even in the simulation, Jaibriol's gaze darkened. "I spoke the truth."

"Then come to Earth."

For a long moment Jaibriol just regarded him, with no hint he would consider the suggestion, and Kelric's hope died.

Then Qox said, "Very well. Let us meet."

XXIX

Refuge and Fire

Jaibriol left Eube's Glory without telling Robert. He rose in the predawn stillness and went with Hidaka and three other Razers to the starport. Hidaka never balked. If he thought it bizarre that the emperor would steal away from his palace without telling even his most trusted aide, he said nothing.

Jaibriol couldn't fathom what Kelric wanted. At least he knew now that he hadn't killed his uncle by joining the Triad. He couldn't tell whether or not the pharaoh survived; if it was possible to detect the Triad across space, he didn't know how. But if she had died, surely he would have picked up some hint from Kelric of such a massive grief. And if anyone could help him deal with becoming a Key, it was Kelric. What would possess the Imperator to do such a thing, he had no idea. More likely Kelric would try to kill him.

By agreeing to see the Imperator in secret, Jaibriol knew he risked much. Despite the torment of his life, he had no desire to die, for he would soon be a father. He would love his child no matter what, even if his son might become everything he abhorred. But he could end up as a slave if he couldn't learn to control his mind better than he had done since he joined the Triad. And no Aristo could teach him that control.

So he went to meet his enemy.

Kelric's ship landed in a private berth at a starport in West Virginia. He came with Najo, Strava, Axer, and no one else. He had no wish to involve his bodyguards in actions that could end in an accusation of treason, and he had tried to leave them on the Orbiter. But ever since he had snuck off to Coba without them, they had been even more alert. They understood the stakes; if he was caught doing this, they all risked execution. They still refused to stay on the Orbiter.

As far as the port authorities knew, he was a rich Skolian who wanted no fanfare during his vacation on Earth. If his security worked as well as he intended, neither they nor anyone else would ever know otherwise.

Jaibriol would come in a similar manner. He hoped. That the emperor had agreed to the meeting supported Kelric's suspicion he was dealing with a psion, but he couldn't be certain until they met. Even then, he didn't know what he would find. If Jaibriol had lived among Aristos for ten years, gods only knew how badly it had damaged the Kyle centers of his mind.

Or maybe he was wrong about everything, and Jaibriol agreed to come because it offered a chance to kill the crazy Imperator.

Jaibriol's only stipulation had been that they meet in the Appalachian Mountains. It made sense; if the Aristos discovered what he had done, he would have an excuse, weak as it might be. He had gone on retreat in a place he had once called home. Kelric had no such cover for visiting Earth. The only time he had spent on this world had been against his will, as a political prisoner.

He went to an isolated mountain region, to a cabin owned by an elite establishment that catered to the wealthy. He spoke with no one and needed no check-in. Among the Allieds, one could buy anything if he paid enough, including anonymity. In some ways, it had been easier to arrange security here than for a military operation. Bolt had simply told his contact that his "patron" didn't wish to be disturbed and then arranged a large transfer of funds. Very large.

Kelric's guards were also securing the area. With all these precautions, he doubted a bug could get past them. On a solo mission like this, though, he still had significantly less protection than if ISC had been involved.

While Najo and Strava checked the rustically opulent cabin, Kelric sat at a desk built from knotted wood and unrolled his mesh screen.

Axer stood behind him, solid and silent, but Kelric felt his agitation. His guards hated this trip.

He scanned Earth's public meshes in their military, government, academic, and entertainment spheres. It was interesting from a cultural standpoint, but he couldn't concentrate on the entertainment sites and the rest offered nothing his security people hadn't told him in greater detail.

Kelric put away the screen and took the dice pouch off his belt. He played Quis solitaire for a while, but he couldn't focus on that, either. His structures kept evolving in patterns of tension, which was hardly eye-opening, or else predictions of his execution. Too much could go wrong, and his dice kept portraying every possible way. He finally stuffed them back in the pouch and sat back in his chair, rubbing his eyes.

Strava walked into the room. "Sir?"

Kelric looked up with a start. "Yes?"

"You have visitors." Her face was pale.

Kelric stood slowly, aware of Earth's uncomfortably heavy gravity. "Where?"

She tilted her head toward the front of the cabin. "They're on the forest road that leads up here."

"Do you have an ID?"

"Nothing," she said grimly. "We can't crack their system."

He met her gaze. They both knew what that meant. His guards had the best sensors available to a Skolian Imperator. None could match them—except those for a Eubian emperor.

"Keep me posted," Kelric said.

"I will, sir." Strava went to a window and edged aside the curtains so she could look out into the night. It wasn't necessary; she could have monitored the approach from within the security room she and Najo had set up within the cabin. But Kelric appreciated her presence and Axer's. He was more nervous than he wanted to admit. What if instead of Qox, a murder squad showed up? He had defenses, but so would they. Qox knew Kelric had come here alone, in secret, without ISC backup.

Kelric joined Strava and pulled back the curtains. Outside, pine trees rustled. The night otherwise had that deep silence of a land that knew no cities. Knowing his silhouette would be visible from outside, he let the curtain fall back, in case killers arrived instead of Qox.

Strava stood at his side with the poised look of a fighter ready to shoot someone, preferably a Trader, he had no doubt.

Kelric paced restlessly across the room. He was a fool to trust Qox. He had to be wrong. No psion could survive among the Aristos, not and retain his sanity.

One thought haunted him. When Jaibriol Qox had lived on Earth, the school authorities there had incorrectly recorded his birthday, listing him as a few months *younger* than his true age. The Qox Palace had fixed the mistake. The date on Earth had to be wrong; otherwise, Qox would have been conceived *after* his father "died." The previous emperor hadn't died, he had been lost on an unknown world, but he could hardly have impregnated his empress from there. Many people assumed she had used sperm stored by her husband to become pregnant after he disappeared. It went against Highton mores, however, which would explain why the palace found the "error," so Jaibriol didn't suffer the supposed shame of such a birth. Kelric had come to fear it hid a far greater bombshell, that Jaibriol's father had sired him while stranded on that planet.

Stranded with Kelric's sister, Soz.

He didn't want to believe it. Qox couldn't have forced her; she had been a Jagernaut Primary, one of the most versatile killing machines alive. But she would never have willingly birthed the Highton Heir. Unless . . . Qox had been a Ruby psion.

He pressed his fingers into his temples. The idea so disturbed him, his head throbbed. Usually the nanomeds in his body could fix a headache, but tonight even they didn't help. He felt disoriented, off balance.

"Sir?"

Kelric jerked. Turning, he saw Najo standing nearby. He focused his blurred vision on the guard. "Are they here?"

"About half a mile away." He watched Kelric with concern. "Are you all right?"

"My head hurts."

Najo tensed. "Sir! It's a trick!" His hand dropped to the Jumbler on his hip.

Kelric smiled slightly, aware of Strava and Axer watching. "The Traders often give me a headache, but I don't think we can accuse them of a nefarious plot because of it."

They regarded him dubiously.

Kelric's smile faded, for he knew if anything went wrong, he may have condemned these three to stand trial, even to die. For ten years, they had guarded him. They were more than officers; they had become an integral part of his life. They were willing to put their lives on the line for his hopeless dream of peace, and that meant more than he knew how to say. But he had to try.

"I want you all to know," he told them. "Whatever happens, I—" He stumbled with the words. "I thank you. For everything." It sounded so inadequate.

Najo said, "We wouldn't have it any other way, sir." Strava and Axer both nodded. They seemed to understand, feeling it from his mind if not his awkward speech.

Suddenly lights flashed on their gauntlets, which linked their bio-mech to the cabin security. Najo went to the door, standing to one side with his Jumbler up and ready. Strava returned to the window and nudged aside the cloth with her mammoth gun. Axer took up position by Kelric with his weapon drawn. Their tension filled the cabin, and Kelric feared they would jumble the first person that walked through that door.

"Put down your weapons," he said.

Strava turned to him, incredulity on her face. "Sir!"

"All of you," Kelric said. "Lower the guns."

"We can't do our job if you restrict us," Najo told him.

"If it were me coming here," Kelric said, "and we walked into a room full of Razers who had their laser carbines aimed at us and Jaibriol Qox standing behind them, what would you do?"

Najo regarded him steadily. "Defend you. Shoot, if necessary."

"That's my point," Kelric said. "Lower the guns."

Strava blew out a gust of air. She was clenching her Jumbler so tightly, her knuckles had turned white. Najo exhaled as well. Then he said, "Weapons down."

As the Jagernauts lowered their guns, an engine rumbled outside. Kelric's head felt as if it were splitting apart, but he knew now that nothing within his body caused the pain. It came from someone on the other side of that door.

Heavy footsteps sounded on the porch. The metallic sense of a mind came to him, one so augmented, it didn't feel human. The hair on Kelric's neck prickled. He hoped he hadn't made a mistake having his guards lower their weapons. A great deal could happen in the fraction of a second it took to raise a Jumbler.

Someone pushed the door. Perhaps they had expected it to be locked; Kelric didn't know. It opened slowly, swinging past Najo, who gripped his Jumbler, but with his arm straight down by his side, the tendons standing out along his tensed limb.

A giant stood framed in the doorway. A Razer.

Kelric had seen them on broadcasts. They served as the emperor's secret police and bodyguards. This one towered, his harsh features clenched. He did indeed hold a laser carbine—

Down by his side.

Kelric let out a breath, more relieved than he would ever admit. The Razer entered the room, his boots clanking on the wooden floor. Strava flanked his steps, matching him in height if not mass, her gauntlets flashing with so many warning lights, it cast an eerie red glow over her and the Razer.

Another man appeared in the doorway.

The moment Kelric saw him, he knew just how much the VR simulation had edited Qox's appearance. This man wasn't the perfect, untouched emperor. Jaibriol the Third stared at him with haunted eyes, his face haggard. But what Kelric felt most of all, undeniable and inescapable, was the raging Kyle pain in Jaibriol's mind. It was so huge, he wondered the cabin didn't catch fire and burn with its heat. No psion could miss it; he saw his own horror mirrored in the faces of his Jagernauts.

Incredibly, the Razer still didn't raise his weapon. He looked from Kelric to Jaibriol, his gaze far too perceptive.

Kelric found his voice. "Come in. Please."

Jaibriol entered the cabin, his gaze fixed Kelric. He spoke in that deep, spectacular voice that people all across the stars heard every time he appeared in broadcasts. It hadn't been doctored; he truly possessed that resonant voice—just as had Kelric's father, the Bard of Dalvador.

"You look the same as in the simulation," Jaibriol said.

Kelric blinked, startled. Of all the openings he had expected—an abstruse Highton greeting, stilted diplomacy, or questions—none included that statement. Jaibriol hadn't changed his appearance, either; physically he was the same. But no EI was here to edit out the agony in his gaze.

"I don't usually alter my appearance," Kelric said.

Jaibriol nodded stiffly, as if he didn't know what else to say and had been as caught off guard by his comment as Kelric.

Three more Razers entered, until the room was bursting with guards. Kelric felt how much it strained his own to keep their weapons down; the slightest hint of a threat, and they would fire. He didn't like the odds, either, four Razers and three Jagernauts. Despite the augmentation of the Razers, however, he suspected the Jagernauts were more formidable. But he doubted they cared a whit about their specs compared to Qox's bodyguards. They just wanted to shoot.

Jaibriol's splintered pain tore at Kelric. The emperor was struggling to hold the monstrous barriers he must have lived with every day of his life for the past ten years. But nothing could cut him off from Kelric, not when they were face to face. The mental defenses Jaibriol had built crumbled without Kelric doing anything. How could they help but come down to him?

The Triad knew its own.

Kelric knew then that matters were far worse even than he and Dehya had feared. Their nightmare had been given reality. Jaibriol Qox had become the third Key.

Qox stared at him with eyes that had seen more than anyone his age should have endured. "Father in heaven," he whispered.

In Iotic.

"Sire!" The Razer captain stepped toward the emperor as if to protect Jaibriol from himself. Strava jerked as if she had been struck. Najo gaped at Jaibriol, and Axer's confusion jolted over Kelric. Jaibriol had spoken the language of Skolian nobility, what Kelric would have taught his children had he raised them. Yes, certainly, the emperor knew Iotic, just as Kelric knew Highton. But what Eubian emperor would revert to perfect, unaccented Iotic under stress?

Jaibriol looked around as if he were trapped. Watching him, Kelric felt certain that if he bolted back to Eube without aid for his traumatized mind, he wouldn't survive. He needed help far more desperately than Kelric had ever guessed.

Strava cleared her throat. "Shall I close the door?"

Kelric started, as did everyone else. Then he glanced Jaibriol. The emperor took a deep breath and nodded.

"Yes, go ahead," Kelric told her.

They all waited while she swung the door shut on rustic but well-oiled hinges. Qox shifted like a thoroughbred racehorse ready to spook at the wrong word, the wrong gesture—or the wrong thought. Kelric could have mind-spoken to him; the emperor's Kyle strength filled the room. But it had a fractured quality, and Kelric feared to do more damage. How any psion could survive with such injuries, he had no idea. Jaibriol had to have a phenomenal strength of will. Kelric had known only one other person with that tenacious, enduring strength. Soz.

After another strained moment, Qox spoke in Highton, aloof and cool. "Well, we are here. Perhaps now you will tell me the reason for this."

"I needed to meet you in person," Kelric said.

A muscle twitched in Jaibriol's cheek. "Why?"

Kelric looked at the captain looming next to Jaibriol, his arms flickering with lights, except the Razer had no flesh and blood arm under all that tech.

Jaibriol glanced up at the Razer, then at Kelric. "What you have to say to me, you say to Hidaka. My guards remain."

Najo regarded Kelric, his gaze dark and tense.

"Stay," Kelric told the captain.

Relief flashed across Najo's face. He would have refused an order to leave, and Kelric had no intention of putting either himself or his guards in that position. But having so many people present hobbled him. He couldn't reveal Jaibriol in front of their guards.

Jaibriol ran his finger around the collar of his black tunic. "It always was hot and humid here in the summer."

Kelric almost smiled. Talking about the weather he could handle. "Is this where you lived while you were on Earth?"

"Not anywhere near here, actually. But the mountains around Seth's home are in the same range as these."

Kelric nodded. By "Seth," he had to mean Admiral Rockworth, the man who cared for Jaibriol and three other children during the two years of the Radiance War. Kelric wanted to ask him so much, especially if he was related to the other children, but he feared to push, or even nudge the emperor, lest it drive him away.

"Would you rather walk outside?" Kelric asked. From the alarmed expressions of their guards, he might have suggested he and Jaibriol throw themselves in front of a speeding magtrain.

Qox made a visible effort to relax his shoulders. "That would be good."

Strava scowled at Kelric, but when he gestured at the door, she stalked over and opened it. As he stepped forward, every guard in the room lifted their gun. Sweat gathered on his palms but he didn't wipe them on his slacks. When he came up next to Jaibriol, the emperor tensed, and the Razer he had called Hidaka clenched his half-raised carbine.

With care, Kelric lifted his hand, inviting Jaibriol to the door. The emperor inclined his head, and a line of sweat showed at his hairline. Together, they left cabin, accompanied by seven guards, all wound as tight as coils. Najo also had his Jumbler up and ready, but neither he nor Hidaka had aimed at anyone.

Although the humidity was worse outside, a cooling breeze ruffled the pines. Strava left the lamps on in the cabin so they had enough light to see. They stepped into a clearing ringed with trees, and Jaibriol exhaled, then breathed in the pine-scented air. The shattered sense of his mind eased.

"It's never this dark on Glory," he said. "The sky is full of moons."

"The Orbiter always has starlight," Kelric said.

Jaibriol hesitated, started to speak, then stopped. Finally he said, "Have you talked with Seth Rockworth?"

Kelric knew why he asked; ten years ago, when they met in the Lock, Jaibriol had suggested he go to the admiral. Rockworth had told the Allied authorities he had never known Jaibriol's identity, but Kelric had always wondered.

"I'm afraid not," Kelric said. "Earth's military won't let us near him."

"I'm not surprised." Jaibriol gave a tired laugh. "I doubt they were happy when one of his wards turned out to be a little more than a harmless schoolboy."

Jaibriol, Kelric thought.

The emperor froze, stock-still. Kelric waited.

Jaibriol's voice rasped. "The nights here are so strange. So long. Yet so short."

Kelric held back his impulse to try the link again. If Jaibriol had barricaded his mind at an extreme level for ten years, he might find any telepathic contact painful.

Kelric said only, "Long and short both?"

"Nights on Glory are only a few hours." Jaibriol began to walk. "But if you live on a world that is part of a binary system, with the planet orbiting one star, which orbits another star, the nights and days can last for hundreds of hours."

Kelric's breath caught. No one except the ESComm ship that had found Jaibriol's father knew the location of the world where he had been stranded. Rumor claimed the records had been lost and that the crew of the ship had died in the war.

"Did you grow up in a place like that?" Kelric asked.

"I lived with my mother," Jaibriol said. "Empress Liza."

Kelric could only nod. Everyone believed that story. But unless the last Highton empress had been a Ruby psion, it was complete fiction.

"Sir!"

The shout came from Strava in the same instant Najo shoved Kelric at the ground. Before Kelric had a chance to respond, his enhanced vision toggled on and the world slowed down.

The Razers leveled their guns at Kelric's bodyguards, but Strava and Axer weren't facing the Eubians, they were aiming at the trees. As Kelric's augmented speed kicked in, everyone seemed to move in slowed time. He hit the ground, catching himself on his palms, and his breath went out in a grunt. Najo shoved him down, protecting Kelric's body with his own. Strava stood above them, her feet planted wide while she fired into the forest. The beam from her Jumbler created sparks in the air and exploded the trees in a harsh orange flashes.

He was aware of Jaibriol falling next to him and the Razers firing their carbines. For one gruesome second Kelric thought they were shooting his guards; then he realized they were blasting the trees. Kelric twisted around to see Axer sweeping the area with his Jumbler. The trees disintegrated in orange explosions, lighting up Axer's body as if he were on fire. With his bald, tattooed head and muscled physique, he looked like an avenging demon.

And in that instant, as Kelric stared at the guard who had protected him for years, a projectile burst out from the trees—

And hit Axer.

The Jagernaut's body flew apart in gruesome slow motion.

"*No!*" The shout burst out of Kelric. He tried to jump up, but Najo shoved him down even as he fired. The trees around them truly were in flames now, from the Razer's carbine shots.

"It's you they're after," Jaibriol shouted at him. "They're trying to kill *you*. Are they insane? They could rid the universe of a Qox and they go for the good man instead?"

Kelric wondered what sort of nightmare Jaibriol lived, that he expected murder attempts to target him as the greatest evil. An explosion flared in the night, and a ball of fire ballooned above the trees barely fifty meters away. Another blast shattered the cabin, billowing debris, smoke, and flame.

Najo dragged Kelric to his feet. "Run," he yelled.

Hidaka heaved Jaibriol up so fast and so hard, he lifted the emperor off the ground. A third explosion rent the air, this one barely ten meters away.

"Go!" Hidaka shouted at Jaibriol, shoving him away from the blasts. "*GO!*"

Kelric grabbed Jaibriol's arm and took off with enhanced speed, literally dragging the Eubian emperor—

The ground exploded under them.

XXX

A Brace of Kinsmen

Jaibriol floated in a sea of flames. He had no sense of time or place, just dislocation.

Then he hit the ground and gasped as rocks stabbed his body. Debris rained around him. He tumbled down a slope, rolling, rolling, hitting rocks and underbrush, out of control. He smashed into a cluster of boulders and pain shot through him. With a groan, he scrambled to his feet, driven by adrenaline. Far up the slope, flames roared in the cabin. He couldn't see anyone; if Kelric or any guards still lived, they were no longer standing.

Jaibriol started up the slope—and tripped over a body. Lurching and dazed, he fell to his knees. A huge man lay sprawled in front of him, his lower leg twisted at a bizarre angle.

"Kelric?" His voice cracked. "God, no." Terrified to find the Imperator dead, he grabbed Kelric's wrist—and gasped with relief when he found a pulse. But Kelric wasn't breathing. Jaibriol pumped on his chest, using emergency techniques his parents had taught him on the planet Prism, where they had no medical care but what they could do for themselves.

Kelric suddenly jerked and choked in a breath. He coughed harshly, gulping for air.

"It's all right," Jaibriol said. "You'll be all right." He hoped it was true.

"Najo—" Kelric's voice rasped.

"Your guards are up there." Jaibriol stretched out his arm, pointing to where the fire blazed. "So are mine."

Orange light limned Kelric's face. "We must help them."

"Can you walk?"

Kelric paused, then said, "Bolt says my leg is broken."

Jaibriol scooted down to check Kelric's right leg. It had twisted back on itself in a way impossible even for a biomech joint. "This looks bad." He lifted his head. "Who is Bolt?"

Kelric pushed up on his elbows. "My spinal node."

"Can your meds administer pain medicine?"

"The hell with that. I don't want my focus dulled."

"We have to get out of here," Jaibriol said. "I don't think you can walk on this."

Kelric grimaced as he sat up. "I'll manage."

Jaibriol looked up the hill. With foreboding, he said, "No one has come down."

"They can't be dead." Kelric spoke as if his words could ensure their lives. "They *can't.*"

"Hidaka—he—" Jaibriol couldn't go on. He couldn't lose the captain. Angry at himself, he grabbed the outer seam on Kelric's slacks and ripped it hard, two-thirds of the way up Kelric's leg.

"What the hell are you doing?" Kelric shoved him away. "Finishing the job your people started?"

"They didn't start anything," Jaibriol said. "No one knows I'm here."

"You knew someone was trying to kill me."

Even realizing Kelric had sensed the truth about him, Jaibriol couldn't admit he had picked it up from the minds of their attackers. He had hidden too long. He couldn't reveal himself even to someone who already knew.

Jaibriol cast about on the ground. "They shot at you first."

"They could have been going after both of us. Maybe they just missed you. How could you know otherwise?"

Jaibriol found a long, straight branch and broke off its smaller twigs. "They didn't even know who I was." He gave a ragged laugh. "They could have killed the tyrant of Glory, and instead they went after you. What idiots."

Kelric's voice quieted. "You got it from their minds."

"Don't be absurd." He picked up several more branches and leaned over Kelric's leg. "I'm going to set this. So we can get out of here."

"Where did you learn how to splint a broken leg?"

Intent on examining the injury, Jaibriol spoke absently. "My mother taught me." He looked up at Kelric. "It's going to hurt. I'm sorry."

The Imperator had a strange look. The firelight from above glinted on his metallic skin. "It's all right."

Jaibriol carefully pulled away the shreds of cloth from Kelric's leg. He remembered when his mother had splinted his arm, after ESComm had pulled out his father and "cleansed" Prism. It was one reason everyone believed Soz Valdoria had been nowhere near the emperor. No one could have survived the mountain-slagging sterilization ESComm had inflicted on Prism.

Except.

As a Jagernaut Primary, his mother had had access to technology available to almost no one else. She had brought a quasis generator into exile. Just seconds before ESComm attacked, she enclosed her children in a bubble of the generator's field. Quasis froze the quantum state of anything within its field. Particles couldn't change state, which meant the bubble couldn't collapse, not even when a battle cruiser in orbit destroyed the mountain range. Jaibriol's arm had broken as the sterilization slammed around their bubble of safety, and his mother had splinted it while their family hunkered in the dark, bruised and terrified.

"Gods almighty," Kelric whispered. "What happened to you?"

Jaibriol jerked up his head. "I don't know what you're talking about." He struggled to fortify his mental barriers and hide his memory.

Kelric spoke in an unexpectedly gentle voice. "My mind is powerful, but blunt. I didn't pick up anything from the minds of our attackers up there. But other of my siblings have more mental finesse. They might catch what I missed." Quietly he added, "As might their children."

Sweat trickled down Jaibriol's neck. He could never answer Kelric's unspoken question about his parentage. He had hidden the truth for too long; he couldn't let go and speak of it. The secrecy was too ingrained within him.

"I'm going to set this now," Jaibriol said. "Are you ready?"

Kelric nodded, his face strained. "Go ahead."

Jaibriol went to work, gritting his teeth. He hated how it agonized Kelric; pain blazed in his uncle's mind. But the Imperator never cried out once. Jaibriol pulled off his black-diamond tunic, leaving only his undershirt, and ripped the tunic into cords so he could tie Kelric's leg to the splint. When he finished, he sat back, sweat streaming down his face. Kelric had one fist clenched on his thigh and he had dug the fingers of his other hand into the ground. He looked as if he had aged ten years.

"Yes, I'm an old man," Kelric said, his voice uneven.

"Don't say that." Jaibriol climbed to his feet and offered his hand. "You're going to live decades more. Centuries."

With help, Kelric struggled to his feet and stood with one hand on Jaibriol's shoulder, staring up the slope. The flames had died down rather than starting the forest fire Jaibriol had feared. He saw no one, neither his nor Kelric's guards.

"Do you sense anyone?" Kelric asked.

Jaibriol wanted to deny he could sense anything. But he wanted even more to survive. "No," he said dully. "No one. Not assassins and not bodyguards."

"I don't, either," Kelric said. "But it's hard to focus." Although he spoke calmly, he couldn't disguise the pain flaring in his mind.

"Can you walk?" Jaibriol asked.

"I doubt I can make it up that slope."

"I'll go look—no, I can't leave you here." Jaibriol stopped, torn with indecision.

"Go look," Kelric said.

Jaibriol took off, running up the hill. He slipped and slid on the steep slope, but compared to the peaks where he jogged in the Jaizires, this was nothing. He slowed as he neared the top and bent down to crawl the last few meters.

A blast crater spread out before him, and beyond it lay the scorched remains of what had been a beautiful tangled forest. The devastation bore no resemblance to the woods where he and Kelric had so recently walked. It looked like a battlefield.

Jaibriol sensed no one's mind except Kelric. Whoever had attacked them was either gone or dead. He searched the crater first, and then the smoldering remains of the forest beyond. He forced himself to account for everyone, identifying them by what little remained of their blasted, charred bodies: his Razers, Kelric's Jagernauts, and six commandos, which matched the number of minds he had felt in the attack. None had survived.

When Jaibriol found Hidaka's remains, he fell to his knees in the ashes next to the body. Working doggedly, he scraped a scorched, dead chip out of the dirt, all that remained of Hidaka's node. He had some grief-stricken idea he would bring it back to Claret.

Clammy from shock, Jaibriol went back to the hill and half slid, half ran down the slope. Kelric was sitting on one of the boulders that had stopped Jaibriol's roll earlier. The starlight of the bizarrely moonless night glinted on his gold eyes. He seemed more metal than human, but Jaibriol could tell a man of compassion inhabited that metallic body.

"All of them are gone?" Kelric asked, his voice low.

"Yes. Our guards. The attackers." His voice cracked. "All dead." He sat on the ground, braced his elbow on his bent leg, and put his forehead in his hand, too drained to move anymore.

"We can't stay here," Kelric said unevenly. He stood up and tried to take a step, but he immediately lurched and came down hard on his good knee.

"Ah!" The Imperator's sharp inhale ended in a groan.

Jaibriol raised his head. "Are you all right?"

"Fine," Kelric muttered. He grasped his splinted leg and maneuvered it around so it stretched in front of him. Then he just sat, silent. He obviously wasn't fine.

"I don't think you can go anywhere on that leg," Jaibriol said. "Not until you rest and your meds can start healing it."

Kelric started to speak, and Jaibriol thought he was going to object. Then his uncle just shook his head and fell silent.

Jaibriol felt something on his face. He touched his skin and his fingers came away wet with tears. Why did Hidaka have to die, one of the best men he had ever known? He was grateful beyond words that he hadn't told Robert or Tarquine he was coming. They would have insisted on coming with him. And they would be dead now; the first priority for his guards had been to save him, not his aides or even his spouse.

After a while, Kelric said, "Are their bodies destroyed?"

"That's a horrible question." Jaibriol's voice broke on the last word, and he decided to say no more.

"No, listen," Kelric said. "If their internal systems are even partially intact, it may be possible to revive them in new bodies."

Jaibriol stared at him dully until the words sank in. Then he said, "Not enough survived. It was bad."

"Oh." Kelric sounded subdued.

Jaibriol wondered if somewhere, some demon was laughing at them. He had so little, and now even that was gone.

"Hidaka saw." Jaibriol knew he should stop, but the words wrenched out of him. "He saw the whole thing. Yet still he supported me. He never wavered, never once."

"What did he see?" Kelric asked. The fires had died down, and his face was lost in shadows.

"Colonel Vatrix Muze caught me crawling out of the Lock," Jaibriol said. "So Hidaka shot him."

Kelric's voice went very quiet. "Why were you in the Lock?"

"The implosions." He took a ragged breath. "They were headed for the SSRB. I thought it might connect to the Lock. So I went to check."

"Did you find anything?"

"Nothing. It didn't work." He couldn't believe how calm he sounded. Inside he felt as if he were screaming.

"It was dead for ten years," Kelric said. "When I turned it back on, it was active for *one minute.* How could you know to be there for that one minute?"

"I don't know." Jaibriol wasn't even certain what Kelric meant. "I just sat there and the singularity appeared."

Kelric stared at him. "When the Lock reactivated, you were *sitting in it?*"

"Yes." He didn't know what else to say. "I will regret that moment for the rest of my godforsaken life."

"And you survived."

"If you call this survival."

"You had no preparation? No training? Nothing?"

"How would I?"

"Saints above," Kelric said softly. "What happened to you would have killed almost anyone else."

Jaibriol just shook his head. Although he was shielding his mind, Kelric's power was too great. It soaked into him, a great golden glow of warmth. These few minutes with his uncle had done more to ease the agony in his mind than anything else since he had become a Key.

"You need a medical facility with neurological experts," Kelric told him.

Jaibriol knew he would never get such treatment. Dully he said, "We both need help."

"Tell me that you betrayed our agreement," Kelric said. "Tell me that you let someone know you were coming here."

Jaibriol would have laughed if their situation hadn't been so bad. "No. I kept my word. Perhaps you told someone?"

"Not a soul. I secured the entire area."

"Enough to hide four explosions and a fire?"

Kelric exhaled. "I'm afraid so."

"The commandos were thorough. The cabin is gone. So are our vehicles."

"I picked this place because it was so remote."

"This is absurd," Jaibriol said, incredulous. "We're two of the most powerful people alive. We can't be without recourse."

Kelric didn't answer. His pain swamped out everything. After a while, though, Jaibriol felt it ease, and he suspected Kelric had let his meds dispense painkillers after all.

Eventually Kelric said, "We both have biomech enhancements."

Jaibriol nodded. "Even with your broken leg, we could probably walk out of here in a day or two."

"And then what?"

Jaibriol considered the question. "The moment we find help, we lose our secrecy. It will look strange for us to be together."

Kelric's laugh had a frayed edge. "You've a gift for understatement. Can the Emperor of Eube be executed for treason?"

Jaibriol jerked, startled. "I haven't committed treason."

Kelric spoke tiredly. "I have."

Good Lord. No wonder he seemed so subdued. "They can't execute the Imperator. ISC will stand behind you." The loyalty of his military to their commander was legendary.

"How do they know you and I aren't plotting here in secret? Why would they support me for committing the worst violation of ISC security in the history of the Imperialate?"

Jaibriol sat for a time absorbing the ramifications. He had come with such hopes, for a dream that never died no matter how much he lost. He took a breath and plunged ahead. "Then bring them a peace treaty."

"We don't have a treaty." Even in the dark, the lines on Kelric's face showed his strain. "Our generals and admirals and ministers and assemblies couldn't agree on one."

"Then let us agree, you and I." He tapped his temple. "I have the one we worked out years ago stored in my node. If you're willing to take a download into yours, we'll both have a copy. We can sign it with our neural and DNA imprints."

"Have you forgotten?" Kelric asked. "We never finished it. We couldn't come to terms on the most basic aspect of all."

It seemed to Jaibriol as if his whole life had narrowed to this moment. He knew the magnitude of what he suggested. But if they never tried, they would surely fail. He had nothing to lose by asking for the impossible.

He took a breath. "My joint commanders refused to sign because yours wanted to grant every escaped slave freedom. Yours refused to sign because mine demanded the slaves be returned."

"That hasn't changed," Kelric said. "My people will never agree to slavery. Not today. Not in a thousand years. My last wife was a task-maker. I was a provider. I'll never subject another human being to what we lived through." Softly he added, "To what you must suffer every day of your life."

"No." Jaibriol doggedly evaded the words. "Give me three months. Any Eubian slave found within your territory must be sent back if they have been free less than that. After three months, they are free." He willed Kelric to consider the compromise. "The Ruby Pharaoh almost agreed to that during our talks, before ESComm balked."

Kelric made an incredulous noise. "ESComm will never agree to that. Nor will your Trade Minister."

"They've already agreed to trade negotiations. That was why my office contacted the pharaoh's office. To start this dance we always do when we want to communicate with each other."

"Trade?" Kelric's voice sharpened. "Of what? *People?*"

"No! Gourmet delicacies. Curios. That sort of thing."

Kelric squinted at him. "Your people want to export food and souvenirs to mine?"

"Well, it's a start."

"Selling us those tentacled monstrosities you call gourmet food hardly seems a step to better relations."

Jaibriol smiled. "Ah, well." He agreed about the Taimarsian squid. "It isn't the goods, but the motivation."

"Whose motivation?"

"General Barthol Iquar for one. He wants the Iquar title."

"Tarquine already has it," Kelric said flatly.

Just hearing him speak her personal name cut Jaibriol. He steeled himself and went on as if he didn't care, though it felt like broken glass were inside of him. "She'll give it to him."

"Give up control of the strongest Aristo Line after Qox?" Kelric didn't look convinced. "She would never do it."

"She's the empress," Jaibriol said. "Her child will sit on the throne. She can afford to give up her Iquar title."

"It doesn't matter how much power Tarquine has. She always wants more."

"Nevertheless, it seems she is going to do it."

"For you." Kelric sounded tired, as if Jaibriol's words made him feel old.

"I don't know for what."

"You think the title would assure Barthol's agreement?"

"It's possible."

"That's only one of the signatures you need."

Jaibriol made himself speak, though he hated to go on. "Admiral Erix Muze will sign because he wants to live."

Kelric snorted. "You can't execute your joint commander for refusing to sign. ESComm would revolt against you."

Jaibriol spoke quietly. "No one except Colonel Vatrix Muze and Hidaka saw me crawl out of the Lock. Hidaka shot Vatrix."

"I'm not sure how this connects to Erix Muze."

"Hidaka told everyone Vatrix tried to kill me," Jaibriol said. "A Razer cannot lie about such a thing."

"Did he know what he was seeing in the Lock? About you."

"Yes. He knew."

"And he didn't reveal you?"

"No."

Kelric's voice gentled. "No wonder you mourn him so."

It hurt even to think on. "As far as anyone knows, Vatrix Muze tried to murder me. By Aristo custom, it is my right to have his kin executed in retaliation."

Kelric was watching him closely. "Did Erix Muze have anything to do with what happened?"

"Nothing."

"So you're telling me that with no trial or evidence, you can have one of your joint commanders executed for a murder attempt he knew nothing about. And no one would condemn you for it."

Jaibriol forced out the answer. "Yes."

"A murder attempt that didn't actually exist because your Razer killed the colonel and lied about it."

"Razers can't lie."

"Like hell."

"Assassination is a serious matter."

"Gods," Kelric muttered.

"No, the world of the Aristos isn't pretty," Jaibriol said. "But it is mine. I deal with it as I can."

"Would you actually put Erix Muze to death?" Kelric asked.

Jaibriol didn't know the answer to that himself. "What matters is that he believes I will do it."

"What about the Trade Minister, Parizian Sakaar? You need his support as well."

"He won't object."

"Why not?" Kelric demanded. "The trade of people is the life's blood of your economy. He'll set himself against any treaty that dilutes his control of that godforsaken industry."

"Let's just say he has other interests to protect."

"In other words, you have something on him."

"It would seem so." It was Tarquine who had something, but Jaibriol had no intention of discussing her further with Kelric.

"Is it enough to make him sign?"

"I think so."

"Corbal Xir is next in line for your throne," Kelric said. "He won't support a treaty that weakens his power."

"Corbal won't fight it." Jaibriol also doubted Corbal would ever forgive him.

"Why not?"

"Because I know many truths about him." Corbal also had truths about Jaibriol, but if he revealed those secrets, Jaibriol could drag down not only him, but also his son Azile, his granddaughter, and the entire Xir Line. And Sunrise. It killed him to threaten Corbal after his cousin had protected him, but his personal life meant nothing compared to what their peoples could gain. No matter how much the Aristos reviled him for seeking peace, he needed only four signatures on that treaty: himself, Corbal, Barthol, and Erix.

"If you and I sign this document," Jaibriol said, "I'll get the other signatures." He couldn't guarantee it, but he had a chance.

Kelric considered him. "For my people, the Ruby Pharaoh, First Councilor, and I must sign. And the Assembly has to ratify it."

"Will they?"

"The pharaoh, I think so. The First Councilor, I don't know." With a grimace, he added, "If I'm convicted of treason, my signature won't matter. In that case, our joint commanders must sign." Wryly he said, "You only have to deal with two of them. I have four." He thought for a moment. "Chad Barzun would probably sign. Maybe Dayamar Stone of the Advance Services Corps. Brant Tapperhaven of the J-Force? He's a wild card. But Naaj Majda, the General of the Pharaoh's Army, will never sign. She wants Eube broken. Period."

"They won't convict you." Jaibriol didn't know if he said it to convince himself or Kelric.

"Don't be so sure." Kelric sounded as if he felt heavy. "Many people abhor the split of hereditary and democratic rule in our government. If I'm accused of conspiring with you, it will weaken ISC support for the sovereignty of the Ruby Dynasty. The Assembly might well jump at the chance to remove me from my seat." He rubbed his eyes, his fatigue obvious. "As you may have noticed tonight, I am not universally liked."

"Nor I," Jaibriol said. To put it mildly. "But if we can complete this document tonight, would you sign it?"

For a long moment Kelric looked at him. Then he said, simply, "Yes."

Jaibriol couldn't believe he had heard the word. Fast on the heels of exultation came the sobering knowledge that even if he and Kelric signed, they had no guarantee their governments would support their agreement.

But they could try.

That night, beneath the stars of the planet that had birthed their race, two leaders sat together, a young man who was forever scarred and an aging man who had lost more in his life than he could measure. They had no lofty hall, no pomp, no protocols. They didn't go to work in a great amphitheater. No broadcasts covered their efforts. They sat on a rocky hill in the dark and went over the document step by step, sentence by sentence, word by word, until they agreed.

Then they signed together the first peace treaty ever established between their empires.

XXXI

The Meld

Kelric awoke as the sky began to lighten but before the sun lifted its orb above the mountains. The air smelled of smoke, ashes, and pines. Birds called in the distance. For a while he lay on his back, staring at the sky. Blue. On his home world, the sky had a violet tinge. As strange as Earth's looked to him, the color felt right in a way he couldn't define.

The events of last night soaked into his waking thoughts. Najo, Strava, and Axer were gone. He felt hollow without them.

Even with his nanomeds distributing painkillers, his leg ached. At least the hydraulics in his limb had kept it from snapping off. It would heal, he supposed, though his limp was going to be even worse. Of course, that wouldn't matter if he were dead. As much as he wanted to believe ISC wouldn't execute him, the realist in him knew otherwise. Too many people had too much to gain from his dishonor and death. Given who else had nearly died in this attack, he doubted the commandos had a link to ESComm. It wasn't that he didn't believe they might be involved in a murder attempt against their emperor; he wasn't that naïve. But Jaibriol claimed they hadn't known about him. With his mind so sensitized, he would have picked up an intent to kill him, and Kelric would have known if he lied about it.

The team investigating the last attack against Kelric had thought the would-be assassins operated alone. Either they were wrong or else other groups also wanted Skolia's Imperator dead. It was a grim thought. That the killers had known he was here suggested someone high in the government or ISC was involved.

Kelric slowly sat up. His muscles protested with stabs of pain, and he grunted, wishing he wasn't so stiff.

"My greetings," a voice said.

He looked around. Jaibriol was sitting on the rocks behind him, his booted feet braced on the ground, his elbows on his thighs, his hands clasped between his knees.

Kelric maneuvered around, dragging his leg until he was facing the emperor. "How long have you been awake?"

"About an hour." Jaibriol rubbed the back of his neck. "I looked for food, but I didn't find anything that seemed edible."

Although Kelric knew he was hungry, his biomech web muted the pangs by releasing chemicals that fooled his body into thinking he had eaten. It wouldn't stop him from starving, but it eased his discomfort.

"We should search the cabin," Kelric said.

"I did." Jaibriol lifted his hands, then dropped them. "Nothing is left but debris. Not even water. The blast and fire destroyed everything, even the plumbing."

"Water must be here somewhere." Kelric motioned at the forest. "Otherwise this wouldn't grow."

Jaibriol grinned, an unexpected flash of teeth that made him look years younger. "We can make history with our treaty, but we can't find a drink of water. Strange, that."

Kelric smiled. "I guess so." He picked up a staff of wood that was lying next to him. "This wasn't here last night."

"I made it while you were sleeping." Jaibriol rose to his feet with a supple ease that Kelric envied. "If you can walk this morning, I think we should leave as soon as possible."

Using the staff, Kelric struggled to his feet. By putting his weight on his good leg and leaning on the staff, he was able to stand. Jaibriol was right. They shouldn't wait for rescue. That no one else had been with their attackers didn't mean no one would show up. They could just as easily be picked off elsewhere, but at least they would be getting closer to help.

Kelric looked up the hill. "I'd like to go up." He wanted to pay his respects.

Jaibriol seemed to understand. He offered his arm.

"I'll be fine," Kelric said. He took a step—and his leg buckled. Jaibriol caught him before he fell, but Kelric's weight nearly knocked them both over.

Kelric swore under his breath. Then he pulled away and tried another step. He managed by using the staff as a crutch and keeping the weight off his broken leg. On flat ground it worked reasonably well, if slowly, but when he tried to climb the slope, his leg gave out. He couldn't manage even with Jaibriol's help.

The emperor spoke quietly. "I'm sorry."

Kelric couldn't answer; it hurt too much. *Good-bye,* he thought to his guards. *You will be missed.*

Jaibriol motioned to a notch across the small valley. "I think we can get out that way, and the land stays flat."

Kelric nodded, already tired. Then he began the painful process of walking. Jaibriol stayed at his side, moderating his stride to match Kelric's speed. It was humbling. It was hard to believe he had ever been young and full of energy. That was the man Tarquine had desired, the prince she had seen in broadcasts. Why she had paid that amorally ludicrous price for a dying man, he would never know.

They made their way through a narrow gap between two hills. Needles and twigs crackled under their feet, and branches rustled overhead, inundating them with the deep scent of pines. It was surreal, walking here with Jaibriol the Third as if the two of them were on a vacation.

Jaibriol's hair shimmered in the early morning light and his red eyes were visible from a good distance away. Anyone who knew anything about Eube would recognize him as an Aristo. Nor could Kelric hide his own offworld heritage. People on Earth didn't have metallic coloring.

After a while, Jaibriol said, "I think those implosions are connected to the Locks."

It took a moment for Kelric to reorient his thoughts. The space-time implosions. He felt too tired to talk. Given what he had done, though, activating the Lock while the emperor was in it, he owed Jaibriol more than silence.

"When my people built the Kyle web," Kelric said, "we knew almost nothing about the Locks. Everything was guesswork. But I'm starting to understand. I think the web strains the interface between Kyle space and our universe. Every time we add another gate, it adds to the strain. The Locks are a balance. When I turned one off, it destabilized the system. If we don't reactivate it, the implosions will get worse." Uneasily he said, "I think it could destroy large regions of space, entire solar systems. Maybe more."

He expected Jaibriol to be incredulous, ask a question, something. When the emperor had been quiet for too long, Kelric glanced at him. Jaibriol's face had gone pale. His fear hit Kelric like a bright light.

"What is it?" Kelric asked.

"The SSRB has no Lock." Jaibriol drew him to a stop. "When Hidaka fired at the colonel, we were inside that octagonal room that houses the singularity."

Kelric felt as if his pulse stuttered. "Are you telling me your guard fired a laser carbine inside the Lock chamber?"

Jaibriol nodded. "It missed me. But not much else."

"Ah, gods." Kelric suddenly felt bone weary.

"We've had no implosions I know of since then."

"Maybe it eased the pressure when I activated the Lock," Kelric said. "But I had the impression it only operated for about a minute."

"Yes." Jaibriol rubbed his neck again, a mannerism Kelric suspected came from the constant tension he lived with. "Three Locks. For a Triad."

Kelric resumed his painful limp. "As far as I know, the Triad doesn't require three Locks to exist."

"Then maybe neither does the Kyle. It had two Locks and two Keys. Now it has two Locks but thr—" He stopped abruptly, then spoke carefully. "If the Kyle once again had three Keys, maybe the two Locks would be enough."

"Maybe." It was plausible with what Kelric knew. He hoped it were true. In every way, the survival of his people depended on this young man. The emperor had gone to great lengths to attain the treaty, and Kelric had no doubt he wanted it. But if he changed his mind, he had within his grasp the ability to create a Kyle web for ESComm, negating the advantage Skolia had over Eube, the technology that kept them a step ahead of the Traders. Jaibriol didn't need a Lock to build such a web. The Triad Chair wasn't in the chamber, it was on a dais at the start of the corridor, well removed from the singularity. Jaibriol had been sitting in it the first time Kelric had seen him, ten years ago.

Back then, Kelric hadn't thought Jaibriol knew anything about the chair. Maybe that was still true. He strengthened his mental shields, blurring them, too, so Jaibriol wouldn't realize he had cut off his thoughts. Then he said, "You need the Lock to build a Kyle web."

"I don't have a Lock," Jaibriol said.

Kelric probed his mind as discreetly as he could manage. Jaibriol had no idea what to do with a Triad Chair. He just thought it was an uncomfortable throne. Nor did he comprehend what it meant to be part of the Triad. He only wanted free of its presence. He didn't know he could never leave the powerlink. Neurological changes had begun in his brain the moment he became a Key. To withdraw now would cause fatal brain damage.

Kelric didn't know how Jaibriol would survive among Aristos. His mind was a furnace, burning with power. Unless he learned to hide it better than this, the Aristos would soon realize the truth. Then what? They would have a Key. Jaibriol might have no interest in learning how to create a web, but if the Hightons turned their combined intellects to the problem, they would learn. And they would force him to build it for them.

"Kelric?" Jaibriol was watching him.

It startled Kelric to hear his personal name spoken by the Emperor of Eube. "Yes?" he asked.

"Your sister—" He stumbled over his words. "She was Imperator before you, wasn't she?"

Softly Kelric said, "Yes."

"Was she happy?"

"The last I saw her was almost thirty years ago." Kelric spoke with care. "Jaibriol, how could your mother teach you to splint a broken leg with tree branches?"

"She was good at—" He suddenly stopped, and panic flared in his eyes.

"That's an unusual skill for a sheltered Eubian empress," Kelric said.

Jaibriol turned his head away, and Kelric knew then that the young man could never speak the truth. It was locked within him by emotional scar tissue.

Kelric continued with the utmost gentleness. "When Soz was young, she loved to swim in a lake near our house. She would go up there when she wasn't supposed to be out and get into trouble when she came home."

Jaibriol gave an uneven laugh. "I can imagine."

Kelric remembered how Soz had laughed and teased, how she could grin one moment and glare the next. Seven brothers and one Soz, and they had never been a match for her. He smiled with his memories, though they hurt. "When I was eight and she was seventeen, we went hiking in the Backbone Mountains. We got caught in a storm. It frightened me, the lightning, the rain, the hail. It so rarely happened in the lowlands where we lived."

Jaibriol spoke softly. "You could have taken shelter in a cave."

A pain jumped within Kelric, a stab of loss and mourning and something else that felt like bittersweet joy. That hadn't been a guess about the cave. Jaibriol knew.

"Yes," he said. "A cave. We huddled in it while lightning cut the sky and thunder shouted. We were afraid. It comforted us to merge our minds. A full Rhon merge." Only Ruby psions could join minds that way, but they rarely did, for it was too powerful a link for most people to endure and too intense to sustain. But in those few moments, he and Soz had blended their thoughts down to a deep level. From that day on, he had shared a bond with her stronger than with his other siblings.

"Anyone fortunate to share such a bond," Jaibriol said unevenly, "would value it forever. She might—might even share the treasured memory with her children."

Kelric put his hand on Jaibriol's shoulder. "I can't help you leave the Triad." When alarm flared in the emperor's gaze, Kelric said, "Just listen. You don't have to admit anything." Softly he added, "You cannot return to Eube in your condition. I've been protecting your mind, but when we part, it will all come back, the agony, the loss of control, the pain. You'll be wide open to the Hightons."

"Don't," Jaibriol said.

"You must learn to control it."

"I can't," he whispered.

An idea was coming to Kelric, forming with the clarity of jeweled Quis dice in the sunlight. He looked around for support. A nearby deciduous tree had a thick branch, almost a second trunk, that grew horizontally a few feet above the ground. He limped over and leaned against it, half sitting, half standing. Then he untied the pouch from his belt. For a moment he stayed that way, looking at the worn bag bulging with dice. He had carried it for almost thirty years. The dice were as much a part of him as his limbs, his thoughts, his heart. They shaped his life. To part with them would leave a hole he could never fill even if he had a new set fashioned with identical pieces.

Kelric extended his arm with the pouch. "Use these."

Jaibriol's forehead creased. He came over and took the bag. Turning it over in his hand, he said, "What is it?"

"Dice."

The emperor opened the sack and shook a few gems into his palm. They flashed in the sunlight slanting through the trees and sparkled as if they were bits of colored radiance caught in Jaibriol's hand.

"They're beautiful." He looked up at Kelric. "What do you do with them?"

"Play Quis," Kelric said. "When pressure from the Hightons becomes too much, when you can't take anymore, when you fight for control and can't find it, play Quis. It will calm your mind, help your control, perhaps even ease the pain."

Jaibriol looked bewildered. "I don't know how."

In the short time he had with Jaibriol, Kelric knew it would be impossible to teach him Quis at a high enough level to help. But he did have a way.

Kelric took a breath. "If you meld with my mind, I can give you the knowledge. Store it in your spinal node to study at your leisure." He felt as if a part of him were dying. If he joined his mind with Jaibriol, the emperor would probably pick up more than Quis from him no matter how hard Kelric tried to limit their meld—including how to use the Triad Chair to create a Kyle web.

"You would offer me this trust?" Jaibriol asked.

Kelric nodded.

"What if it injures my mind even worse?"

"You have to trust me. Just as I must trust you."

Jaibriol clenched the pouch until his knuckles turned white. "I cannot."

"You have to trust someone."

"I don't trust my own wife. Why would I trust you?"

"You came here to see me," Kelric said. "I can think of no greater show of faith."

Jaibriol's voice cracked. "I can. Asking me to let you into my mind."

Kelric waited. The decision had to be Jaibriol's; if the young man felt pressured, they couldn't create the blend. They stood in the early morning with sunshine filtering through the trees, a fresh green light that softened the day. Butterflies flashed orange and black among the foliage.

Finally Jaibriol said, "Yes."

Kelric released his breath. "Good."

"What do I do?"

Kelric spoke gently. "Nothing." Then he closed his eyes.

Bit by bit, Kelric lowered the barriers he had developed over his lifetime. He didn't have the crushing mental defenses Jaibriol used; his were more layered shields that had become so integral to his personality, he wasn't certain he could lower them enough. He concentrated on his memories of Quis. He also accessed files in Bolt where he had stored Quis concepts, rules, ideas, strategies. When he had been a Trader prisoner, he had even tagged his interpretations of their customs with Quis structures. He readied it all for Jaibriol.

Then he reached out a luminous tendril of thought.

Their minds touched, and Kelric scraped Jaibriol's mental scar tissue. He had never wished for Dehya's finesse more than now, for he feared his raw power would injure the emperor even more. But the scars gradually melted, like gnarled ice under the warmth of a sun. Slowly, he and Jaibriol blended, first the outer layers of their minds and then those that went deeper. Kelric offered his knowledge to the young emperor, the files from Bolt, then his own memories, both the vibrant images and those time had dimmed and bleached.

And he absorbed memories from the emperor.

Kelric saw Jaibriol's father, the previous emperor, and knew that those who had called the man a monster had erred on a mammoth scale. The father in Jaibriol's memories was kind, gentle, vulnerable. That same decency defined Jaibriol beneath the hard exterior he had developed to survive. The son had inherited his father's purity of soul. Kelric also saw what Jaibriol didn't realize, that his father hadn't been strong enough to survive the Aristos. The tenderness that had made him such a beloved father would have destroyed him as emperor.

And it was true: Soz was his mother.

Jaibriol had her incredible strength. Kelric saw his sister through her son, and it broke his heart. Soz laughed more with her husband and children. She could be tender with her babies and fierce when protecting them. Jaibriol's sole model for an adult woman during the first fourteen years of his life had been one of the most complicated, strong-willed warriors of modern times, but what he remembered most about her was the depth of her love.

When Kelric opened his eyes, Jaibriol was kneeling on the ground, his head bowed, his shoulders shaking as tears flowed down his face. Kelric lowered himself next to the emperor, then put his hand on Jaibriol's shoulder and bent his head. He didn't know what Jaibriol had taken from his mind, but if the memories were as intense, as treasured, and as painful as those he had gained from the emperor, it was no wonder Jaibriol cried.

They knelt together in the forgiving beauty of a summer day and wept for the people they had lost.

XXXII

Stained Glass

On a summer day in the Appalachian Mountains, Kelric and Jaibriol reached the outskirts of a small town. Jaibriol sought help in a church, and they entered during Sunday services. Kelric could no longer walk on his own, even with the staff; Jaibriol supported him with Kelric's arm draped over his shoulders. Both of them were half-starved and dehydrated, and neither had slept much for two days. Jaibriol staggered inside the door, just enough to see they had found people. Then he sagged to his knees, no longer able to support Kelric's massive weight.

Kelric collapsed to the ground and rolled onto his back, his eyes closing. Jaibriol stayed with him, kneeling, while people rose from the pews, staring in bewildered shock. They approached with care, the reverend from the pulpit and parishioners from the pews. As they gathered around Jaibriol and Kelric, they spoke in English. Jaibriol peered at them, exhausted, unable to interpret the language he hadn't heard for ten years, and that he had never spoken as well as the Eubian or Skolian tongues he learned from his parents.

Jaibriol chose a church because he hoped they were less likely to turn away two people in need. After he had converted to Seth's religion, he

339

had been baptized and received First Communion. He didn't think this was a Catholic church, but it had the same serenity he remembered from St. John's. He stared over the heads of the people to a high, stained glass window aglow with sunrise colors and light.

Like Quis dice.

Patterns filled his mind, swirls of color and shapes.

The reverend knelt in front of Jaibriol and spoke in Eubian. "Can you understand me?"

Jaibriol tried to concentrate. "My friend is ill," he said. "He needs a doctor."

"We've sent for one." The man hesitated. "Can you tell me who you are?"

"You don't know?"

"No. I'm sorry."

It relieved Jaibriol that no one seemed to realize who had stumbled into their morning services. The idea that the Emperor of Eube and Imperator of Skolia would come into their church was probably too absurd for them to recognize either him or Kelric even if anyone had seen them on a news broadcast.

The other adults clustered around them. They were calm, but Jaibriol felt their confusion. Someone had taken the children away, or at least kept them back.

"Can you translate for him?" one of the women asked the reverend. She wore a blue dress with no shape.

"I speak English," Jaibriol said slowly.

Relief washed over their faces. "Can you tell us what happened?" the reverend asked.

"Someone tried to kill us." Jaibriol didn't know how much to say. "We need to contact your authorities."

"We've sent for the sheriff," the reverend said.

"What is sheriff?" Jaibriol asked.

"A law officer," the woman told him.

Kelric stirred and opened his eyes. He stared at the ceiling of the church and spoke in Iotic. "What is this place?"

"A church," Jaibriol said, his voice ragged. "They've sent for help." His head swam with dice patterns. He didn't know what they meant, but they soothed him.

Kelric laboriously sat up, huge muscles bulging under his sleeves. With difficulty, he grasped a pew and climbed to his feet. At nearly seven feet tall, with a massive physique, he had a build heavier than occurred in the gravity of Earth. He loomed over everyone like a titan. The parishioners backed away.

Jaibriol stood up next to Kelric. "Maybe you should sit," he said in a low voice. His Iotic sounded odd in this place.

Kelric nodded, his face clenched from pain, and eased into a pew. He crossed his arms on the pew in front of him, laid his forehead on his arms, and closed his eyes.

The reverend was one of the only people who had stayed with Jaibriol. He was watching Kelric with concern. "The doctor should be here soon. Will he be all right until then?"

"I don't know." Jaibriol had no doubt Kelric could recover from a broken leg. What would happen when he returned home was another story.

A boy of about ten years old had inched over to them. He looked up at Jaibriol. "Are you a Trader?"

"Sean!" A woman pulled him back. "Leave the man alone."

"He looks like those pictures on the holovid," the boy protested as she hurried him away.

Glancing around, Jaibriol realized no other children remained in the church. The adults stayed back, watching him. They seemed bewildered. He didn't know what to tell them. The past two days had drained him: the attack, signing the treaty, the miraculous and terrifying mental blend, and two days of stumbling through the forest. He had hoped the destruction of the cabin would activate some monitor, but if it had, no one had responded. He and Kelric had hidden their visit too well.

The door of the church creaked open and sunlight slanted across the worn pine floor. A burly doctor with a balding head strode inside carrying a med box. He headed toward Jaibriol, did a double take, and then stopped and gaped.

"Good God," he said. "You're an Aristo."

"Yes," Jaibriol said. "I am."

The doctor looked around at everyone. "You want me to treat a damn slave lord?"

"Grant, don't," the reverend said. "They need our help."

"Well, hell's hinges," the doctor muttered. Either he didn't know his words would result in his arrest on a Eubian world or else he didn't care. He came over to the pew and peered at Kelric, who had lifted his head.

"You the patient?" Grant asked in English.

Kelric glanced at Jaibriol, a question in his gaze.

"He asked if you're hurt," Jaibriol said. He turned to the doctor. "He has a broken leg."

Kelric slid along the pew, making room for the doctor, though he watched Grant warily. The doctor sat with no fanfare and bent over Kelric's leg. He poked and prodded, and checked it with a med tape. Glimmering holos rotated in the air above the tape like jeweled Quis dice.

Watching the doctor, Jaibriol realized it could help Kelric that everyone knew he had come in with an Aristo. It increased his chances of avoiding recognition, because no one in their right mind would expect the Imperator to be running around Earth with a Eubian nobleman. Kelric was wearing marriage guards, but if someone didn't know much about Eube, they could mistake them for the ID restraints of a taskmaker.

Whether or not Kelric could return home without anyone realizing he had been here was a different matter. If any news service picked up the story that an Aristo had walked into a church, that was it. One picture of him or Kelric on the meshes and their secrecy would evaporate. Even if they avoided that exposure, they had to get off-world without raising questions. They had also left thirteen dead people in the mountains along with a blasted cabin and burned out swath of land. Someone wanted to kill Kelric, and Jaibriol didn't believe for a moment that whoever masterminded the attempt had died with those commandos.

One powerful thought stayed with him; his wife and future heir were safe. He hadn't wanted an Aristo child, but it no longer mattered, for he already loved his unborn son.

"How'd you get this break?" Grant asked Kelric as he removed the splint. "You look as if you've been sorting wildcats." He squinted at the Imperator. "Guess that would be tough for them, eh?" He chuckled and went back to work.

Kelric blinked at him, then looked up at Jaibriol. "Do you know what he is saying?"

Jaibriol smiled. "He thinks you look tougher than a wild animal."

The doctor glanced from Kelric to Jaibriol, then went back to work. He spoke tightly to Jaibriol. "He your slave?"

"No," Jaibriol said. For people to make that assumption was one thing, but it could backfire spectacularly on him and their attempts to establish a treaty if Kelric's people learned he had made such an offensive claim.

"What language were you talking?" Grant asked.

"It's Iotic," Jaibriol said. In the same moment Kelric shot him a warning glance, someone inhaled sharply. Glancing around, Jaibriol saw the reverend staring at him in disbelief.

Jaibriol pushed his hand through his dusty hair. He had to be more careful. Only Skolian nobles and royalty spoke Iotic as a first language. That didn't mean Kelric was either, but it was a good explanation of why an Aristo would speak to him in that tongue. The chances of someone here knowing that were small but apparently not zero.

"Iotic, idiotic." the doctor muttered. "Never heard of it." He considered Kelric. "Who set your leg? He did a good job."

"I did it," Jaibriol said. He swayed, then caught himself. It occurred to him that he wouldn't stay on his feet much longer.

The doctor paused to study him. "When did you last have water or a meal?"

"We've found a lot of streams," Jaibriol said. "A few berries." He had to think about the food. "About two and a half days since an actual meal."

Grant scowled at the reverend, and then at the woman in the blue dress, who had come to stand with him. Seeing the reverend and the woman together, Jaibriol thought perhaps they were father and daughter.

"If we're going to help them," Grant told them gruffly, "I reckon we should get them some food. And a place to rest."

"Don't chew them out while I'm gone," the woman said. Then she bustled off.

"We can take them to the hospital," the reverend said.

"It couldn't hurt." The doctor stood up next to Jaibriol. "Does your friend speak English?"

"I don't think so." Jaibriol glanced at Kelric. "Can you understand any of what they're saying?"

Kelric shook his head. "My node can interpret Spanish, but not this language."

Jaibriol nodded and spoke to the doctor. "He doesn't, but I can translate for him."

"I need a release form to treat him," Grant said. "He has to sign it. We'll need your passports as well."

"Our what?" Jaibriol asked.

"Your documents. Your permission to be in our country, on our world, in our *free* space." Anger snapped in his voice. "No matter who you are, you need some authorization."

"No passport." Jaibriol decided he had better keep his answers short.

"How did you land?" Grant demanded. "They just let you traipse in here?"

"I don't know this word, *traipse*," Jaibriol said. "But if you mean, did I have permission to land, the answer is yes."

"Without a passport."

"Yes." He had no intention of describing the discreet and disguised manner he had used to enter Allied space.

The doctor jerked his thumb at Kelric. "He got documents?"

Jaibriol spoke to Kelric. "He wants to know if you have any papers allowing you entry into Allied space." Dice patterns swirled in his mind. He felt light-headed, as if he could float.

Kelric leaned back in the pew. "They were in the cabin." He lifted his gauntleted arm. "This comm has my military ID."

Jaibriol suspected Kelric wanted to give his identification as the Imperator about as much as he wanted another broken leg. He turned back to the doctor. "He doesn't have anything he can show you, either."

Grant shook his head. "This has to be the strangest case I've ever had."

The woman who had left earlier returned, walking into the sunshine that streamed past the open door of the church. She came to Jaibriol and spoke shyly. "We have rooms where you and your friend can stay. We've also a lunch for the two of you."

Jaibriol inclined his head. "I thank you." He barely stopped himself from using the royal "we." He felt her mood. She thought he was attractive, so much so, it intimidated her as much as his being a Highton. It was an odd reaction, but it took him a moment to figure out why. Hightons coveted beauty. They never had a simple appreciation for it; their possessive cruelty swamped out any softness. If a taskmaker noticed him that way, her reaction was lost in awe or fear. Providers were supposed to love him; they were bred, conditioned, and drugged for it. This woman's simple response so rattled him that it made him question whether, after ten years among the Hightons, he could ever again react like a normal human being.

✧   ✧   ✧

Jaibriol stood in the dimly lit parlor with the curtains drawn against the afternoon sun. Kelric had fallen asleep on the couch in the "bed and breakfast" where the people from the church had brought them. Kelric had refused to go to a hospital, so the doctor reset his leg in the church, covering it with a med-sheath from thigh to foot. In sleep, his legendary face was at repose for the first time since Jaibriol had met him.

The married couple that lived here had fed them, fussing as if they were any tourists who had stopped in town. Jaibriol had discretely looked into finding his siblings, but no trace of them came up in his searches and he feared to draw attention to their existence if he pushed any harder.

He had also spoken his request to his hosts, the other reason he had wanted to come to these mountains. It didn't have to be the Appalachians; he could have satisfied this request almost anywhere on this continent or several others. But he had once called this part of the world home, and it was here he turned for refuge.

His request had stunned his hosts. But they had been willing to help.

A soft knock came at the door. Jaibriol jerked up his head. He almost said, "Come," but stopped himself, not wishing to wake Kelric. Instead, he went to the door and opened it by the antique glass knob.

A priest stood outside. He wore a black collar with white underneath, and black slacks. Grey streaked his brown hair, and his calm face had a gentle quality. He started to speak, then noticed Kelric and stopped.

"Perhaps we should go somewhere else," Jaibriol said. "He needs to sleep."

The man nodded. His face was difficult to read, but he hadn't guarded his mind. Although he recognized neither Jaibriol nor Kelric, he had some idea what he was dealing with. What he thought about it, Jaibriol couldn't tell; except for his apprehension, the man's reactions were deep in his mind.

They went to a parlor with the curtains pulled. Jaibriol didn't turn on the lights; he preferred the dimness. Perhaps it made it easier to hide from himself.

"My name is Father Restia," the man said.

"Thank you for coming." Jaibriol knew he should introduce himself, but what could he say? His personal name was one of the most common among Aristos, but it was common because three emperors had borne it, including himself and his father.

"Missus Clayton didn't give me details," the priest said. "Normally I would ask that you come to the church. But when she described you, I understood why you preferred to remain in private." Quietly he added, "I've never spoken to a nobleman of any kind, let alone a Eubian. If I act in a manner that offers offense, please accept my apology."

It relieved Jaibriol that his hosts had found someone who didn't hate Aristos. "No need to apologize. I lived on Earth for two years, in another part of these mountains, in fact. I understand the customs."

Restia stared at him, and his face paled. So he knew. Only one Aristo had lived in the Appalachians for two years. Three empires knew that name. Jaibriol Qox.

The priest exhaled. "Is that when you became a Catholic?"

"My first year here. It gave me an anchor." Jaibriol had desperately needed something to give him hope while his parents waged war against—and for—each other.

"Then you know," Restia said. "Anything said between us remains in confidence."

Jaibriol inclined his head in acknowledgement. It made no difference. He had too much he couldn't say, and nothing this priest could tell him would change that. But perhaps Restia could offer a respite for Jaibriol's soul. He had little doubt that if hell existed, he would end up there, if he hadn't already, but he wasn't ready to give up yet.

He knelt at a small table and the priest sat on the sofa next to him. That in itself would have horrified Jaibriol's people, that their emperor knelt to any man, let alone one they considered a taskmaker. He put his elbows on the table and folded his hands so he could rest his forehead on them. It wasn't really a position of prayer; in truth, he couldn't look at the priest. After ten years, he had forgotten the proper phrases, so he went by what little he remembered.

"Bless me Father," he said. "For I have sinned. It has been ten years since my last confession. These are my sins." Then he stopped. What could he say? It would take a thousand years to confess.

After a moment, the priest said, "Go ahead, son."

Jaibriol sat back on the floor, leaning against a chair at right angles to Restia. Staring across the room, he said, "A man is responsible for

THE RUBY DICE   347

the sins committed in his name as well as his own. The roster is too long, Father. No one can absolve me for the crimes against humanity inflicted in 'honor' of my name."

"You are not the keeper of an entire race."

"No?" Jaibriol finally looked at him. "The Hightons think I am. They glorify my name while they torture, enslave, and kill, with impunity. I own billions of people. Hundreds of worlds. I descend from a line of monsters who considered genocide an appropriate response to defiance. The populations I control live with that specter, and if I've never slaughtered, neither have I acknowledged I consider it abhorrent. I could free my people. I could turn against the Hightons. I haven't." He felt the darkness within himself, and he feared Restia could do nothing for him.

The priest spoke in a quiet manner that fit like a cover over another emotion. If Jaibriol hadn't known better, he would have thought it was grief. But this man had no reason to mourn the tyrant of Glory.

"And if you did these things," Restia asked. "If you turned against the ways of the Hightons, what would happen to you?"

Jaibriol gave a harsh laugh. "What do you think? They would kill me." Bitterly he said, "Not that they don't try anyway."

"Then answer me this," Restia said. "If you can do more good by living with the evil, is that a greater sin than turning your back on what you can accomplish?"

"It's killing me," Jaibriol said.

"I wish I could offer you better counsel." Restia spoke softly. "Perhaps God has given you a greater trial because you have a greater purpose."

"Do you truly believe in this God?" Jaibriol asked. "So many cultures have a pantheon. Ask the man sleeping in the other room. His people believe in many gods and goddesses. Yet here on Earth, it is only one. A merciful god, you say. Yet what deity of mercy would create the Aristos?" He felt too heavy to continue, but the words he had pent up for so long poured out. "What mercy will be left when the Hightons hold sway over the entire human race, across all the stars, when no one is free but a race of monsters who would murder me in an instant if they saw me sitting here, speaking with you?"

"If I told you," Restia said, "that the greater humanity believes it has become, the greater the trials we must face, I would sound sanctimonious even to myself. I can't imagine what you face. Or what you endure. I know nothing of you but what we see on broadcasts."

Quietly he said, "If you have come to me for the absolution of confession, that I can offer. But the forgiveness you need isn't from me. It is your own."

"Then I will never have it," Jaibriol said. "I can reach for peace, Father, but I can't change the character of man, even within myself. In the coldest hours of my nights, when the specter of power lures with its siren call, will I turn away?" It haunted him, for he knew now what he had within his grasp. The knowledge had all been within Kelric's mind—the Triad Chair, the Kyle web. Kelric hadn't wanted to open that portion of himself, but Jaibriol had seen. In giving Jaibriol an inestimable gift that could allow Eube's emperor to survive, Kelric had also given him the knowledge to conquer humanity.

"Knowing I have within my grasp the power to rule it all," Jaibriol asked, "will I seek peace?"

Restia's face paled. "I pray you do seek it."

"So do I," Jaibriol whispered.

The rumble of an engine tugged Kelric out of his doze, back into a waking reality. He was sprawled on the couch in a pleasant room of the house. The people here seemed puzzled by his refusal to go to the hospital, but no one insisted. They couldn't know he wanted these last few moments of freedom before his world collapsed. Better a house than a hospital with doctors monitoring him on machines.

Kelric wondered what these people would do if they knew their two guests contained within their internal nodes a peace treaty of incredible proportions. Whether or not it would be ratified was a question he feared to look at too closely, for in giving Jaibriol the knowledge to protect himself, Kelric had also given him knowledge that would negate the need for any treaty, if the Highton emperor chose conquest instead of peace.

Jaibriol was standing across the room, gazing at holocube pictures on the mantel. Antique paper with flowers and leaves covered the walls, and the moldings that bordered the ceiling were painted a pale shade of rose. Kelric listened to the engines overhead and wondered if this soothing room would be his last sight of freedom.

He had watched with bemused fascination while Doctor Grant heckled Jaibriol all morning. He didn't have to understand English to figure out the doctor had thrown barb after barb at his Aristo guest. Jaibriol took it with equanimity, but still, it had to be strange for a man whose people considered him a god.

He sensed the haze of Quis patterns in Jaibriol's thoughts. It softened the scarred edges of the young man's mind. Given time and treatment Jaibriol might someday heal. He would never get that help, not as long as he ruled Eube, but perhaps Quis could give him relief. It had done so for Kelric, making his life bearable in times when he thought he could no longer go on. Seeing his dice pouch hanging from Jaibriol's belt wrenched him, all the more so because he knew what else he had given Jaibriol. If he was wrong about the emperor, he truly had committed treason at its highest level, and he deserved the execution looming before him. Jaibriol could return to Eube, erase the document he and Kelric had signed, and seek to enslave all humanity.

That Jaibriol was a decent man, Kelric had no doubt. But no one could live with the lure of that power and deny its hold. In the moment Kelric had offered him Quis, he had faced the most difficult decision in his life. He had based it not on concrete principles or logic, but on the unquantifiable patterns evolving in his mind. Whether he had done a great good or committed unforgivable harm against humanity, he didn't know.

The grumble of the engines intensified, until it sounded as if they were in the street outside. Jaibriol turned around and met Kelric's gaze. He looked as if he had aged years in the past few days, but he seemed much calmer now than earlier.

Someone had left Kelric's staff by the sofa. He grasped it with both hands and pushed himself to his feet. The doctor had done his job well; only a twinge of pain shot up his sheathed limb. He hoped Grant didn't have heart failure when he realized whom he had given so much grief today. Then again, someone willing to talk that way to an Aristo would probably survive knowing he had spoken to an emperor. It might be bravery, but more likely the doctor simply had no idea his words could have him put to death among Eubians. The people of the Allied Worlds lived a sheltered existence in the shadow of their violent neighbors.

The roar of the engine outside muted. A moment later, someone pounded on some part of the house. Kelric tensed, his hand tightening around the staff.

"They do that here," Jaibriol said. He came up next to Kelric. "It's called knocking on the door. It's how they announce their presence."

Kelric relaxed his grip on the staff. "We probably won't have another chance to talk."

Jaibriol bit his lip, and for one moment, he wasn't an emperor, he was a young man of twenty-seven caught in events too great to bear. It was hard to believe he was the same age as Kelric's son or Jeremiah Coltman, the youth Kelric had rescued from Coba. Jaibriol seemed years older, decades, centuries. No one should have to see in a lifetime what he endured every day.

"Be well," Kelric said. "No matter what happens, know that you can survive."

Jaibriol looked up at him. **God's speed, Kelric.**

The thought was an unexpected gift. Before Kelric could respond, steps sounded outside. They stopped—and the door creaked open. A man in the uniform of an Allied Air Force colonel stood framed in the rectangular doorway, and more uniformed men and women waited behind him in the hall, as well as the couple who owned the house. Dust motes swirled in a shaft of sunlight that slanted past them.

The colonel's face paled when he saw Jaibriol and Kelric. He walked into the room, his pace measured, and bowed deeply from the waist, a gesture part Skolian and part Eubian but one rarely seen on Earth in this modern age. With foreboding, Kelric inclined his head, aware of Jaibriol doing the same.

The colonel spoke in English. Bolt had been analyzing the language, developing a translation program. He interpreted the words as *My honor at your presence, Your Majesties.*

Kelric glanced at Jaibriol, wondering if he were offended. Eubians used Highness rather than Majesty. But the emperor didn't even seem to notice.

So they began the complex process of sorting out what Earth would do with the two potentates who had appeared out of nowhere in a church in West Virginia, beneath the wide blue sky of Appalachia.

XXXIII

Mists of Jaizire

ISC imprisoned Kelric on Parthonia.

His "cell" was a suite of rooms in a mansion that the army owned in the Blue Mountains far from any city. The officers who had picked him up on Earth had said very little. They had worn that same stunned look as the Allied Air Force officers. When Chad Barzun met them at the starport on Parthonia, his questions had broken over Kelric in shards. Kelric couldn't answer. He didn't know what would implicate him. Nothing like this had ever before taken place.

He had no idea what had happened to Jaibriol after the Eubian ambassador from the embassy in Washington, D.C., had showed up in Virginia with an octet of Razers. Someone in the church had contacted Washington as soon as they realized an Aristo had walked into their service. It had taken longer for the authorities to realize they should be doing the same with Kelric, but his own people had soon arrived.

And arrested him.

An ISC legal team questioned him. He said nothing. He allowed no one to access his gauntlets or Bolt. No one seemed to know what to do. Should they demand the Imperator submit to a biomech search?

Normally they could order a Jagernaut accused in an investigation to release his internal systems. But it didn't take a telepath to see they were afraid of him. Sooner or later, they had to decide what to do. He didn't deceive himself. He had done what they claimed. The only question was his sentence: prison or death?

Kelric was standing by a table, pouring a much-needed brandy when the door chimed. Apparently his momentary reprieve from questioning was over. As he turned around with the tumbler of gold liquid in his hand, the molecular air lock across the room shimmered away, leaving behind a horseshoe arch. The Ruby Pharaoh stood in the archway.

"Dehya." It relieved Kelric to see her far more than he wanted to show, given how many monitors were undoubtedly keeping track of his every motion, word, and breath. With Jagernauts on the job, they might even be trying to monitor his thoughts.

Jagernauts. As in Najo, Strava, and Axer. The memory broke over him with pain.

Dehya walked into the room, and Kelric could see guards outside, both his and hers. Except in his case they were no longer bodyguards. They were holding him prisoner.

Dressed in a blue jumpsuit, with her slight build and small height, her long hair drifting around her body, Dehya looked vulnerable. Fragile. Kelric knew better, but it reminded him how close she could have come to facing the same charges ISC had leveled against him. Fortunately, she hadn't known about the message from Qox.

As the door solidified, Dehya wandered around the room, looking at the glass statues on the glass shelves and peering at the luminous sculptures in the corners of the room. The diffuse light reflected off her glossy hair.

"Nice room." Her voice was quiet. Calm. Conversational. Kelric knew exactly what it meant. She was furious.

"I'm surprised they let you in," he said. "The prosecutors aren't allowing any other family members to see me."

Dehya turned to him, her slender form reflected in the mirrored wall behind the art objects. "I'm the Ruby Pharaoh. They can't refuse me." Her eyes blazed at him. "Unless of course they've neglected to tell me something. Like, oh I don't know, maybe that the Emperor of Eube contacted me while I was in the Kyle web. Just a little thing like that."

She certainly didn't waste time. "I didn't want you involved," he said.

Kelric, she thought.

He shook his head. Jagernauts were psions. He had trained many of them himself. Here, in the heart of an ISC facility, the chance was too great that someone might eavesdrop even on their minds if they dropped their shields and let their thoughts too close to the surface. *Someone* had figured out he went to Earth even though his security had been so effective that he and Jaibriol had staggered through the Virginia wilderness for over two days without anyone knowing. It had to be someone in ISC; no one else had access to that much of his security.

Kelric limped to the sofa in the center of the room, across the white carpet. His leg was healing, but not as fast as it would have when he was younger. Dehya watched him, her brow furrowed. When he eased down on the couch, she came over and sat on the one facing him across a crystal table.

"Are you all right?" she asked.

"I'll be fine." It was a lie, and they both knew it, but he didn't see the point in saying anything else. Instead he asked her what had haunted him the past three days. "Have the remains of my bodyguards been recovered?"

Dehya nodded, the anger fading from her eyes. She spoke with that infinite gentleness she could show. "I'm sorry, Kelric. Nothing is left."

He somehow managed to nod. He looked away, at the vases, the shelves, anywhere that would let him blink back the moisture in his eyes.

Dehya spoke softly. "Roca asked me to tell you that she will support you no matter what."

Kelric looked back at her. "Is she angry?"

"Furious," Dehya said. "Scared for her son. Worried. Relieved and grateful you're still alive."

For now, Kelric thought. "They won't let me see even her."

"Especially her."

He frowned at Dehya. "Why especially her?"

She spoke quietly. "Roca is your heir. If you die, she becomes Imperator."

It hadn't occurred to Kelric that anyone would think he and Roca would plot together. But if he really had intended to betray his people to the Eubians, of course ISC would keep him away from his successor.

He didn't want to talk to Roca, either, if it would bring down suspicion on her.

"The Allied authorities recovered the remains of both your and Qox's guards," Dehya said. "They found traces of the apparatus that set the explosions, and debris from weapons that don't correspond to those of our people or the Razers."

"But no commandos."

Her gaze darkened. "Someone else got there first."

He felt as if the ground were dropping underneath him. He couldn't reveal what he suspected. The three people who had tried to kill him in the plaza had seemed to act alone, but he had little doubt that someone else had arranged it. The commandos on Earth may not have known Jaibriol would be there, but whoever had masterminded the attempt would take advantage of the results. Kelric couldn't hide his meeting with Qox; news services all over had picked up the story. Whoever tried to assassinate him might have succeeded even though they failed. The attack hadn't killed him, but a conviction of treason probably would.

Dehya was watching him. "Jaibriol Qox."

"I don't think he planned it."

"It would be rather stupid to plan his own murder."

Kelric just looked at her. She looked back at him. They both knew what she wanted to ask: was Qox a psion?

Kelric said, simply, "Yes."

Her forehead furrowed. "He did plan the attack?"

"No."

Her eyes widened, just slightly, and he knew she understood. She pushed her hand through her hair, pulling the locks back from her face. She spoke in a murmur, reciting a line from a famous Eubian poem. "'So the gods turned in the void of stars, their frozen grave unbound.'"

Kelric clenched his hand around the brandy tumbler. "I need to address the Assembly."

"You can't address the Assembly if you're under arrest."

"You're the pharaoh. Order it."

"I can get you before the Assembly," Dehya said. "But they aren't going to let someone they consider a possible traitor speak as if nothing had happened. You would first have to let them vote on whether or not they judge your actions treason."

"All right." If he didn't face the Assembly soon, he might end up dead before he could bring them the treaty. He didn't know how much longer he could stop ISC from forcing him to download the records in his gauntlets and Bolt, but he doubted it would be long. Given the murder attempts, he had no idea what would happen to that download; right now he trusted his own people less than he had trusted Jaibriol Qox.

She clenched her fist and hit the arm of the sofa. "Kelric, listen! If the Assembly votes to convict you, that's it. You don't get a trial. You saw the ballot against Roca. It was almost even, including your votes, and you don't get a say in this. You have the most powerful hereditary seat. Gods, you wield a larger bloc than *anyone* except the First Councilor and me. And this isn't as simple as whether or not one of us can cast ballots for a dead spouse. A vote against you is a vote against hereditary rule. The only reason we keep that rule is because ISC backs us. ISC—which has arrested you for treason." Her voice cracked. "If you do this, and the vote fails . . ."

Kelric knew she was right. But it changed nothing. He had one shot. Nor was betrayal within ISC his only fear. The longer he went without bringing the treaty to the Assembly, the more time Jaibriol Qox had to change his mind.

"The Assembly is in session," he said. "Get me a hearing. Today."

Her face paled. "Are you absolutely sure?"

He forced out the answer. "Yes."

Dehya looked as if she were breaking inside. But she said, "Very well. You will have your vote."

Jaibriol found Robert waiting as he stepped down from his flyer onto the roof of the palace. How Robert had managed to keep everyone else away, Jaibriol had no idea, but he was immensely grateful.

"It's all over the mesh," Robert told him as they strode to an onion bulb on the roof with a lift down into the palace. "The Skolian and Eubian services picked it up almost as soon as the Allieds started broadcasting the story."

"Any speculation?" Jaibriol asked.

"They've arrested Imperator Skolia." Robert practically had to run to keep up with Jaibriol's long-legged stride. "That's fact. Speculation? Everyone believes you arranged to meet with him under false pretenses and almost succeeded in having him killed. The Hightons think you're brilliant."

"For flaming sake. That's ridiculous." Jaibriol stopped at the tower and smacked his hand on the entrance panel. "And assassinate myself in the process?" He wanted to hit something a lot harder than a panel.

Only one holo of him and Kelric had reached the meshes, a clip caught by a security camera across the street from the church. But the image had flooded settled space: him half carrying, half dragging Kelric into that church, the two of them covered in dirt and dust, exhausted, staggering. Broadcasters were calling it one of the most powerful images ever taken. Of course everyone had the same question: What did it mean? Jaibriol wished he knew.

The door shimmered open and he stepped into the lift with Robert and his quartet of Razers. These guards had no names. None showed any sign of humanity. They were part of an elite unit he had selected, but none of them had challenged decades of programming to save his life and his sanity in the Lock. He clenched his fist and bit the inside of his mouth until the pain stopped his tears.

"Where is my wife?" he asked Robert as the lift descended. "I'm surprised she isn't here demanding what the hell was I doing."

Sweat sheened Robert's forehead. "She isn't in the palace, Sire."

"Where is she?"

"I don't know. I'm sorry."

Hell and damnation. Didn't he have enough problems without Tarquine going off to do who only knew what? "What about my joint commanders, Barthol Iquar and Erix Muze?"

"General Iquar is downstairs. Admiral Muze has sent inquiries to the palace."

The last person Jaibriol wanted to see was Barthol. Ever since he had left Kelric, his mind had felt raw and unprotected. Barthol would be like sandpaper scraping over a bleeding wound. It didn't surprise him Muze kept away, given that Jaibriol had threatened to execute him.

"And Corbal?" Jaibriol asked.

"He is in your office." With impressive calm, Robert added, "He appears somewhat upset."

Jaibriol shot him a wry look. "And people tell me I'm the master of understatement. They haven't met you."

"Ah, well." Robert exhaled. "It is quite some business."

"Think they're going to arrest me for treason?"

Robert looked bewildered. "You are the emperor. No one can put you on trial. Who would you commit treason against? Yourself?"

"It was a joke, Robert."

"Ah." He gave Jaibriol a rueful look. "It has been lively here, Your Highness. But not with humor."

The door shimmered open and they stepped into a gold and black foyer that reflected their images in the polished marble. Jaibriol knew he had to talk to Tarquine. Her brother's agreement to sign the treaty would be contingent on what Tarquine did with the Iquar title.

If Jaibriol asked him to sign.

"It's insanity." Corbal slammed his hand on Jaibriol's desk. "Are you mad, meeting him on Earth so you can attempt to kill him and instead almost get yourself killed?"

"Why does everyone believe that happened?" Jaibriol asked. They were alone in his secured office, with his Razers outside.

"Didn't it?" Corbal paced back and forth. "Now his own people are going to kill him. Was that your intent, a false murder attempt followed by execution?" He turned to Jaibriol. "It's brilliant, worthy of the greatest Highton strategists." He came back over to the desk. "And it isn't your style."

"I never claimed to have plotted against the Imperator."

"No. You just met with him in secret." Corbal knocked a vase off the desk and it shattered on the floor. "Is that what you're trying to do to yourself?"

The archway across the room rippled open, revealing the captain of Jaibriol's bodyguards. Since Jaibriol had a security blanket in place, his Razers wouldn't know Corbal had knocked over the vase, only that something had crashed. He motioned with his hand, dismissing the captain, and the Razer bowed, then withdrew. The archway shimmered back into solidity.

Corbal was watching him, his jaw rigid. "Do you have any idea what could have happened if ESComm or your Ministers believed you orchestrated that meeting *with* Imperator Skolia instead of to kill him?"

Jaibriol came around the desk, his boots crushing the shards of glass. "You set this story in motion. To protect me."

"Why would I protect you?" Corbal asked bitterly. "After you threatened me, my son, my granddaughter, and my entire Line."

Corbal's words had gone so far beyond the accepted modes of Highton discourse even with one's kin that Jaibriol had no doubt he intended the insult. Jaibriol walked away, then swung around to face him. "I met with Kelric to talk about the treaty."

Corbal came over to him. "He will never sign. Not Kelric Skolia, not the Ruby Pharaoh, and not their aggravating First Councilor."

"You don't know that."

"It is the oddest thing," Corbal said coldly. "Who would have thought both your joint commanders *and* Trade Minister would all support opening trade relations with the Skolians. It is truly unprecedented."

"You voted for it."

"Funny, that." His voice grated. "And if you bring me a peace treaty, do you think I will sign that, too?"

Jaibriol met his accusing gaze. "Would you?"

Neither of them moved, both standing in the debris of a shattered vase, a work of art considered beyond price. Then Corbal said, "Some principles are more important than peace. And some are more important even than blood."

"Principles of Highton ascendance."

"That's right."

And if it means an end of your life as you know it? Jaibriol wanted to ask. If it became known Corbal had willfully passed off his son by a provider as a Highton, helped Azile rise to a position of great power, and let his granddaughter marry one of ESComm's joint commanders, Corbal would lose everything. Jaibriol had only to invoke that specter to force his agreement. But he couldn't do it. Corbal had protected him for years. He couldn't threaten him with exposure.

Jaibriol walked away from his cousin. When he reached the opposite wall, he turned around. "You have to do what you believe right," he said, knowing he was giving up his only leverage against Corbal. "And so do I. Know this, my cousin. For me, the rise of the sun is as precious today as it has always been, and as I hope it always will be."

Corbal's shoulders slowly relaxed as he breathed out. He came over to Jaibriol, but this time he stopped farther away, keeping the appropriate Highton distance. "That sounds like the man I have come to admire."

It was the first time Corbal had ever expressed the sentiment to him. "But not the brilliant Highton strategist."

"Look to your wife for that," Corbal said quietly.

"Robert says she isn't here."

"She went to your retreat."

Jaibriol stiffened. "What for?"

"I don't know. She wouldn't take her bodyguards."

"*What?*" Jaibriol strode toward the exit archway. It started to shimmer, but he burst through the air lock before it finished changing permeability. The membrane dragged along his skin.

"Robert!" he shouted.

His aide looked up from his desk. "I haven't found—"

"She's at the lodge," Jaibriol said. "Get my flyer. Now!"

Jaibriol jumped down from the flyer to the landing hexagon, his black jacket flying open. As he ran to the lodge with his guards, the harsh mountain wind whipped his hair back from his head. He burst through the front door into the main room.

The empty room.

"Tarquine!" he called. She could hear or see him on any screen; if she were here, she was either ignoring him—or she couldn't answer.

Jaibriol strode across the room. The lodge was too quiet, too still. He yanked aside the bead curtain in the morning alcove, but she wasn't there. He was running by the time he reached their bedroom. He turned in a circle in the middle of the room, looking around, his leather jacket crackling with the force of his motion, his hair disheveled on his forehead.

Then he saw it, across the room. Rumpled blankets lay bunched up on the mattress as if someone had lain in the bed. He strode over and jerked the covers off the mattress.

Blood covered the sheets.

"No!" He threw the blankets on the floor. The blood had spread in a terrifying stain. He looked frantically around for any sign of her, but there was nothing, *nothing*.

Jaibriol suddenly realized someone had closed the door to the bathing chamber. He ran to the wooden portal and threw it open. Mist filled the chamber beyond, rising from the pool, white and opaque. Heated water arched from the fountain into the air and sprayed across the pool, blue and clear. He went over and stared into the water, his heart dying as he looked for her body, a dark shape lying against the tiles.

The pool was empty.

Jaibriol gulped in a breath. He turned back and forth, looking, looking, but he saw no one. Steam and water dampened his hair and sheened his jacket. He was a dark shadow in a room of cloud. He strode around the pool and came into view of the back wall—

A woman was slumped there, a white shift dampened against her body, her black hair tangled over her face.

"*NO!*" Jaibriol ran to her, his boots hammering the tile floor, his Razers only steps behind him. Dropping to his knees, he heaved in air. "Tarquine." His voice broke as he cupped his hands around her deathly pale face.

She opened her eyes.

"Oh, God, my God." Jaibriol choked out the words. He pulled her into his arms, her slender weight limp against him. As he held her, his heart pounded in his chest and his arms shook.

"Your Highness," a voice said. "A doctor is on the way."

Jaibriol jerked up his head to see a Razer looming over them. "No," he said, knowing Tarquine would never want anyone to see her this way. "Leave us." He jerked his hand toward the door. "Go! No one is to disturb us."

"Yes, Your Highness." The startled guard bowed and quickly withdrew with the other Razers, closing the door behind them.

Jaibriol turned back to Tarquine and pulled the hair out of her eyes. "Are you all right?" He looked down, touching her, trying to find the injury. "Where are you hurt?"

She spoke in a dusky voice, as if her words were twilight. "Where is Hidaka?"

"Hidaka? What?" She was too pale; he was certain she had lost too much blood. "Who attacked you?"

She grasped his hand so hard, it hurt. "I have no injury. I am not the one they tried to murder on Earth."

"Ah, God. Hidaka is gone." He couldn't separate his shock over that loss with his fear for her. "You didn't know?"

"How could I not know?" Drops of water glistened on her hair. "Everyone across a thousand worlds knows. Your bodyguards died so that you could live."

"Tarquine, there's blood all over the bed."

"The blood of gods," she said. "Or is it slaves?"

"What are you talking about? Who hurt you?" He set his hand on his abdomen. "Is the baby all right?"

"No one hurt me," she said dully. "Your son, however, is dead."

He couldn't breathe. "It can't be."

Mist curled around them and blurred her face. "I can control the wealth of an empire and wield power our ancestors only dreamed of." Her voice cracked. "But it seems I cannot stop my body from losing a child."

He smoothed the tangles out of her eyes. "We'll call a doctor. The best. We'll—"

"Jai, stop." She laid her palm against his chest. "No doctor could have helped."

"I should have been here."

"It would have changed nothing."

"But why?" He couldn't see how his wife, a woman he had never seen ill, had lost her baby. "How?"

"Do you really believe I would birth a child who would grow up to crave his father's pain?" The murmur of the fountain muted her voice. "A child who might someday dethrone and enslave the man who most loved him?"

"What did you do?" he whispered.

"He was your son. Yours—and some long dead provider." She took a breath. "Your great-grandfather, Jaibriol the First, wanted a Ruby son. It took me years to unravel what he had done. The stored eggs still existed. Your great-grandmother wasn't the only candidate who carried Ruby DNA." In a low voice, she said, "I would have given you a Ruby son."

"Tarquine, no." He was breaking inside. "You can't. Only a psion can carry a Ruby child."

"I believed I could do anything," she said numbly. "If I were just strong enough."

It hit him then, why she had been willing to relinquish her title to Barthol: it would keep it within the Iquar bloodline—for the child she had carried had no Iquar blood. For him, she had made a sacrifice considered the ultimate crime for an Aristo.

Jaibriol pulled her into his arms and laid his head against hers, his face wet with the mist. It had to be the mist. He couldn't cry. Hightons never wept.

"Did you get what you sought on Earth?" she asked.

"Kelric and I signed the treaty."

"So we can sell his people Taimarsian squid?" Her voice shook with an incredulous laugh that held more pain than humor. "He risked execution for that?"

"No." Jaibriol drew back to look at her. "For peace."

She went very still. "You signed the peace treaty?"

"Yes." His pulse lurched while he waited for her response.

"It isn't valid unless Barthol, Erix, and Corbal sign," she said.

"Barthol will."

"You are astonishingly optimistic."

"Not if he expects the Iquar title."

In a deadened voice, she said, "And why would I do that?"

"For the son we will never have." His voice caught on what would have been a sob if he had let it free. "For the child who died because you loved your husband enough to offer him an heir who wasn't your own."

Incredibly, a tear formed in her eye and slid down her face. He had never before seen her cry, never once. "Erix and Corbal will never sign."

"They have motivation. As during the summit."

"Motivation is not enough," she said. "You must be willing to carry through the threats, my husband. Because if you can't, you are only bluffing, and they are far better at it than you."

Jaibriol no longer knew what he was capable of. To attain his goals, he would have to stoop to methods he despised, either with his people or the Skolians. He didn't know how much more of himself he would lose as he struggled to reach his dreams. He could think only that he would never know his son. He had thought Kelric sired a Ruby psion with his wife, the woman with the red hair, who wasn't a psion at all. He was wrong. He had seen Kelric's memories. The mother of Kelric's Ruby daughter had died in childbirth, in Kelric's arms while he wept. She couldn't survive the birth trauma of a child whose mind was so powerful, it tore hers apart.

"I can't lose you," Jaibriol said.

"If I cannot give you an heir to love you as you loved your father," she said in her throaty voice, "then someday I will give you an heir of unparalleled strength and brilliance. An Iquar heir." Darkness saturated her words. "But if you cannot raise a son, my husband, then raise an empire as none has ever been known, until all humanity everywhere, from here to the ends of space, kneels to you."

XXXIV

A Choice of the Ages

The Amphitheater of Memories overflowed with the session of the Skolian Assembly. No one knew Kelric was to appear. He entered the hall with Dehya and his guards through one of thousands of arches. A robot arm waited for them, with a console cup at the end large enough for six people.

All over the hall, the screens that usually showed speakers were instead replaying a broadcast that billions, even trillions of people had seen. Kelric stared at the images as they played throughout the amphitheater, larger than life. Less than two minutes of coverage had hit the meshes before the governments of three civilizations stopped it, but that was enough. Again he saw himself and Jaibriol stagger into the church. A few steps into the building, Jaibriol collapsed, half lowering, half dropping Kelric to the floor. Sunlight streamed over them, and Jaibriol's hair glittered. Exhaustion showed on his face, even desperation, but his haunted red eyes seemed to burn.

"Subtle," Dehya muttered. She sounded angry.

"His people think he set it up to kill me," Kelric said.

She looked up at him, and he knew her thought; if Jaibriol had set him up, Kelric was playing into his hands. By bypassing his right to a trial and throwing the decision for his fate to the Assembly, he left himself excruciatingly vulnerable. He saw no other choice; if whoever sought his death found the treaty, wiped it out of Bolt's memory, and denied knowledge of the document, no one would believe it existed. Without evidence, he could never justify his meeting with Jaibriol. Although the emperor had a copy, Kelric had no idea what he intended. He didn't believe Jaibriol had planned the attack, but Qox was perfectly capable of using it to his advantage. Jaibriol had a choice to make, and the fate of three empires hung on his decision.

Thousands of voices clamored in the hall. The tiers of seats started far below the level where he had entered and rose far above. Kelric felt as if he were entering a giant arena with himself as the gladiator set to fight for his life.

The dais was halfway up the height of the hall. Protocol sat at a console there, and First Councilor Tikal stood next to her, peering at one of her screens. Tikal suddenly jerked his head up and stared straight at Kelric. The robot arm was only one of many ferrying people through the hall, but Kelric had no doubt Tikal knew he was there. Protocol, who controlled the dais, apparently realized it as well, for the platform was rising to meet them.

Within moments the media wizards who controlled the screens had picked up his arrival. The images of Jaibriol blinked out, replaced by real-time views of Kelric and Dehya standing in the console cup. A surge of emotions flooded him like storm waves; no psion, no matter how strong, could shut out that many minds in one place, all concentrated on him. Their shock poured over him, their disbelief, curiosity, hostility, and confusion.

Kelric knew he frightened people with his power, his size, his taciturn nature, and his unpopular decisions to use ISC forces on Skolian worlds. In the past, the good he had done ameliorated the effect, and yes, so did the protocol officers who endeavored to portray him as the handsome, golden prince rather than the hardened, metallic dictator. But now screens all over the hall showed him dressed in black, towering over Dehya, his huge bulk dwarfing her delicate form, and he knew they should never have entered together. Next to her, he looked like a monster.

Across the hall, Roca was staring at him, her face pale as she leaned forward. Her aides were working furiously at the console, undoubtedly trying to figure out what the blazes was going on. At the pharaoh's bench, Eldrin was on his feet behind his console, his gaze fixed on Kelric and Dehya. Kelric was grateful Ixpar and his children were on the Orbiter. He wished he could have spoken to them before all this happened, but perhaps it was better this way. If ISC convicted him of treason, he didn't want it to backfire on his wife and children.

As the robot arm docked with the dais, Tikal came forward, his expression thunderous. He spoke flatly to Kelric. "You cannot address the Assembly."

"He has the right," Dehya said.

Tikal swung around to her. "He betrayed his people, his title, his oaths, and *your* family. By any law, this man has no right to stand before this governing body."

She met his gaze. "It is the Assembly's right to decide if he may address them. Not yours."

Tikal made an incredulous noise. "Imperator Skolia, you do realize, don't you, that you are asking the Assembly to decide your guilt or innocence? With no preparation?"

"That's right," Kelric said.

Tikal looked from him to Dehya. "Have you both gone mad?"

"He has the right to ask," Dehya repeated, her voice hollow. She looked up at Kelric. "If this is what you truly want."

He nodded, wishing he could tell her more. But he didn't dare. Too much was at stake.

Tikal shook his head. Then he motioned to the dais as if he were inviting Kelric to a guillotine.

As Kelric stepped out of the cup, the guards took positions on the dais that blocked him from Protocol's console. So he stood by the glass podium on the edge. When the robot arm swung away from the platform, only a force net that surrounded the great disk separated him from the chasm of air below.

Dehya was arguing with Tikal in low, heated tones. Kelric knew she was trying to convince him to let Kelric speak before they took the vote. Tikal would never agree. Before her coup, she and Tikal had been allies, even friends. As much as Kelric understood why she hadn't wanted to execute the First Councilor, her decision had left her open to any retaliation he sought against her or the rest of the Ruby Dynasty. Whoever had planned the attempts against Kelric's life didn't have to be in the military. Tikal had the necessary resources.

Bolt, Kelric thought. **Are you ready?**

I have prepared, Bolt answered. I don't think you can reach the console, however. If you go for it, the guards will shoot before you can do anything.

I know. But I'm right next to the podium.

It doesn't have what you need.

It can launch the emergency protocol.

Do you mean for evacuation?

That's right.

You don't want to evacuate the amphitheater.

No. I don't. But the protocol can link this dais to everyone's console.

The amphitheater techs have probably shut you out of the system.

It's been less than a day since the story broke, Kelric thought. **And no one had any idea I would come here. It's also a minor system, not one most people would think of first when closing me out.**

Perhaps.

Kelric watched Dehya and Tikal. **It doesn't look as if she's making headway.**

No. It doesn't.

Let's do it.

He leaned his arm on the podium as if he were resting, except he laid his wrist over a prong in the glass. The prong clicked into his socket through a hole in his gauntlet.

Downloading, Bolt thought.

Throughout the hall, red lights flashed on consoles, indicating the emergency protocol had activated. Kelric could have done without that glaring announcement that he had accessed the system, but at least it meant no one had closed him out.

"Councilor Tikal!" Protocol called. "He's sending out a file!"

"Block it!" Tikal shouted, whirling to face Kelric, his face contorted with anger.

Protocol's hands flew over the console. "Blocked, sir. I caught it in time."

I'm sorry, Bolt thought. I went as fast as I could.

Kelric felt as if his last supporting strut had broken. **You did your best.**

Tikal stared at Kelric with his fist clenched. "*Why?* Are you plotting the overthrow of your own Assembly? Gods, Kelric, what did they promise you?"

"I wasn't conspiring with Qox," Kelric said. "Let the file out."

"And give you access to every person in this hall?" Tikal asked. "Do you think I'm insane?"

"Kelric, what is it?" Dehya asked.

"It doesn't matter," Tikal said. "You asked for a vote from the Assembly on your guilt, Skolia. You're about to get it."

Kelric spoke angrily. "Was it you who tried to kill me, Barcala?"

"What?" Anger flooded the councilor's face. "You violate a ruling from your own government forbidding you to meet with Qox, you go in secret, you nearly get killed by his secret police, and then you have the gall to accuse *me?*"

"Councilor Tikal," Protocol said. "I have a copy of what he tried to send."

Tikal stared at Kelric, his face hard. "Erase it."

"Sir." Protocol spoke in a strained voice. "I think you better look first."

Tikal was still watching Kelric, but Dehya went to the console and stood by Protocol, reading the screen. Kelric saw the widening of her eyes.

"Gods almighty." Dehya lifted her head. "Barcala, *look* at this."

Tikal didn't move; he continued to stare at Kelric. Then the First Councilor took a deep breath and turned around. He stalked over to Dehya and clenched one fist by his side while he read Protocol's screen.

Comprehension dawned on Tikal's face—and something more, shock or anger, or both. Kelric wasn't certain and he couldn't risk lowering his defenses with so many minds pressing on him. The shock he understood. But he had an ugly sense Tikal would be angry only if he *wanted* Kelric to die, for he was staring at the only evidence that could clear Kelric's name.

Dehya looked up at Tikal. "Let him speak."

"This *has* to be false," Tikal said.

"Check the signatures," Kelric told him. "They're verified by DNA and neural fingerprints. We have records of Qox's from the negotiations ten years ago."

"You could have forged them," Tikal said.

"How?" Kelric demanded. "They're guarded by the best security available to ESComm."

"That's right," Tikal said. "Almost no one alive would have the knowledge, intelligence, and access to break that security. Except the head of ISC." He turned to Dehya. "Or the genius people call the Shadow Pharaoh." He shook his head when anger flashed across her face. "I've known you for decades, Dehya. We may have no proof you collaborated with him, but I don't believe for one second you didn't know about his plans."

"She had nothing to do with it," Kelric said. He had gone to great lengths to make sure nothing linked her to his actions. Tikal might have indisputable cause to remove him from power, but not Dehya.

No hint of the "frail" scholar showed in her face. "You have no proof, Barcala, because none exists. But know this—Imperator Skolia has my full support. Will you deny our people the only chance we've been offered for peace in *five hundred* years just to further your own power?"

Tikal looked more astonished than angry. "I'm not the one who overthrew the government. You damn near put me to death."

"But I didn't."

As they argued, thousands watched. No one could hear them, and during Assembly sessions images of the dais were blurred enough so no one could read the lips of the people there unless they were giving a speech. But anyone could see Dehya and Tikal were in a heated debate.

Tikal took a shuddering breath. Then he swung around with his fists clenched and spoke to Protocol. "Release the file."

Kelric sagged against the podium, and Dehya closed her eyes. As he straightened up, she looked at him, and he saw her shock over the treaty. It was probably one of the few times he had caught her by surprise. That he had brought them a peace agreement didn't mean they would absolve him of guilt. No guarantee existed Tikal would sign the document or that the Assembly would ratify it. But at least they had a chance.

Jaibriol Qox could still change his mind; instead of announcing a treaty, he could claim that one of his providers completed the Triad. If that happened, Kelric had no doubt ISC would kill him. The treaty would look like a lie. Even if he convinced them that Qox had betrayed him, he had still committed treason. And even if Jaibriol never revealed that Kelric had shown him how to use the Triad, ISC would suspect. The worst of it was they would be right—he would have betrayed everyone, his family, ISC, and the Imperialate. Eube would have its Kyle web and Skolia would fall. Only something as monumental as a genuine treaty would ameliorate his defiance of the First Councilor and his secret meeting with the emperor.

The ocean of voices in the amphitheater swelled as delegates received the treaty. Dehya stood with Tikal, both of them reading on Protocol's console while she paged through the file. Glyphs flowed across the screen, gold and black. Kelric waited, his pulse hammering. At first the delegates were quiet, with only a murmur rolling through the hall. As people finished the document, their voices rose, questioning, stunned, astonished.

Kelric steeled himself, for he had always dreaded speaking in front of crowds. Then he touched *send* on the podium. No one stopped him this time. His words went to every console and amplifiers in the hall.

"The treaty you are reading," Kelric said, "was signed by myself and Emperor Qox. For it to go into effect, five more people must sign: the Ruby Pharaoh, First Councilor Tikal, General Barthol Iquar of the Eubian Army, Admiral Erix Muze of the Eubian Fleet, and Corbal Xir, heir to the Carnelian Throne. It must also be ratified by this body." He took a breath. "I have done what I can. What happens now is in your hands."

The noise surged until it felt as if he stood in a maelstrom. Lights flashed all over Protocol's console as delegates demanded a chance to speak. In the midst of the furor, Dehya came to stand with him. Absurdly, the podium was too high. When she touched a panel on its edge, a column rose from the ground. She stepped up on it and spoke into the private comm, so only those on the dais heard. "Transfer the file on Protocol's console to here."

A record of the treaty appeared on the podium.

"End of holofile," Dehya said.

The display changed to the last paragraph, and below it, the signatures of Kelric and Jaibriol. The emergency protocol was still in effect, which meant the display on the podium showed on every console in the amphitheater. Dehya picked up the light-stylus that lay in a groove of the glass.

And she signed the treaty.

The session seemed suddenly distant to Kelric, as if he and Dehya were on a mountain with a jagged range below them. They stood on a precipice. They might plummet down that long drop, but in this one exhilarating moment they had scaled heights no one had believed they could ever surmount.

Dehya smiled at him, her eyes luminous. "So we have." She turned and extended the stylus to Tikal. "First Councilor?"

He stood looking at her. Kelric waited for him to denounce the treaty, to say what it would mean if Jaibriol refused to acknowledge it. Instead, he took the stylus from Dehya. Then he stepped over to the podium and wrote his name under hers.

Kelric's pulse surged. Would it happen? Would Skolia and Eube finally, after more than half a millennium, find peace?

Tikal touched the speaker's panel, and his words rumbled throughout the amphitheater. "We are offered a treaty. It has been signed; the wording is not up for dispute. We must choose a time to vote on ratification."

"We have to do it now," Kelric said in a low voice, just to Tikal and Dehya. "If we're going to ratify it, we need to before Qox's people have a chance to weaken his position."

Tikal considered him. Then he turned to Dehya. "Would you accept a vote now, rather than waiting for the Assembly to discuss the treaty?"

She regarded him steadily. "Yes."

The harsh light of the amphitheater threw Tikal's features into sharp relief. He took a breath, his face creased by strain. Then he touched the panel. As he spoke, his voice rang out through the amphitheater. "The vote will commence immediately. A *yea* accepts the treaty; a *nay* refuses the treaty."

Clamor erupted again, and Protocol's console blazed. Kelric could well imagine the objections; they needed time to digest this extraordinary news. Unfortunately, they had no time, and he hoped anyone who knew the dynamics of Skolia and Eube would understand rather than voting against the treaty.

Protocol spoke into her comm. "Calling the vote." Her words glowed on the podium and came over the audio. She started with the lowest-ranked delegates and went through the roster. Ballot by ballot, the tally appeared on every screen. Vazar Majda stabbed her console when she gave her *aye*. Naaj showed more reserve, but she abstained rather than going against the treaty.

When Protocol called Ragnar Bloodmark, Kelric watched the admiral—and saw the flash of hatred. Ragnar covered it immediately, even as his *abstain* registered on the tally. But a chill spread through

Kelric. He knew he would never find proof linking the admiral to the assassination attempts. But he no longer had a doubt who had masterminded them.

When the call came to Roca, she lifted her chin, staring straight at Kelric. Then she smiled, a radiant expression. Her huge bloc registered *aye* on every screen.

No one followed Roca; as signers, Kelric, Dehya, and Tikal couldn't vote. The tally glowed over the hall in bold red letters: 78 percent yea and 22 percent abstain.

"It is done," Tikal said, his voice resonant. "The Skolian Assembly accepts the treaty."

Kelric exhaled, flooded with relief. It was done. But they had only gone half way.

The rest depended on Jaibriol Qox.

XXXV

The Gift of Quis

Jaibriol kept his bedroom darkened as he stared out a window wall at the city below, Qoxire, capital of his empire. Its lights glistened, high above the thundering waves on the beach.

A door hummed across the room. Footsteps sounded on the deep-piled rug and someone stopped behind him. Jaibriol knew from his guards who had come, and he tensed as he turned around. Corbal stood about ten paces back, watching him, cold and hard. Behind him, on a table, the Quis dice Kelric had given Jaibriol lay in piles, sparkling in the gilded moonlight.

"Have you come to condemn me?" Jaibriol said. "Or bemoan your lost admiration for your emperor?"

"Ten years ago, you walked into my life," Corbal said. "Raw, unsophisticated, idealistic. Lethally innocent." He came over to Jaibriol. "That boy is dead. The man I saw in the meeting tonight—the man who blackmailed his joint commanders and his heir into signing that repellent treaty—is a Highton."

"Perhaps you wish to congratulate me, then." Jaibriol felt no triumph. They had signed—and he had become more an Aristo tonight than ever before.

373

"I find myself astonished at Barthol's cooperative nature," Corbal said. "He esteems you greatly, to offer such a success."

Jaibriol met his gaze. "You think much about succession."

"Of my Line, yes." His expression hardened. "Of my emperor's promises—or lack thereof, yes."

He doubted Corbal would ever forgive him for threatening to reveal his secret after Jaibriol had led him to believe he wouldn't do it. Yes, Jaibriol had been subtle with his threat. But Corbal had known.

"Many Lines have succession," Jaibriol said. "Say, Iquar."

"The Iquar Line may be one of great tribulation," Corbal said dryly, "but no one would deny its strength."

"Indeed. Barthol is a fortunate man."

"Barthol?" Corbal's forehead creased.

"Yes. Barthol." Tarquine had signed the documents making Barthol her heir directly after tonight's meeting.

Comprehension flooded Corbal's face, followed by disbelief. "*No one* is that fortunate. Not with the empress."

Jaibriol turned back to the window. "She is complicated."

Corbal joined him and stood staring out at Qoxire. "You know my thoughts on that."

"So I do." He also knew what Corbal really wanted to ask. Now that he had the signed treaty, what would he do? Even a few days ago, Jaibriol could have answered without doubt; he would seek peace. But everything had changed. In meeting Kelric, in coming to know his Ruby kin through his uncle's mind, Jaibriol had seen just how great was the paucity of his life, even more than he had already realized. It had forced him to confront what he had given up the day he claimed his throne. He would never share what Kelric and his family took for granted, the kinship, the love, the Ruby ties. Jaibriol was the wealthiest man alive, and he was dying from starvation.

But if he conquered Skolia, he could have his family. He could protect the Ruby Dynasty. No Aristo would touch his kin. He had learned an invaluable lesson tonight; he had within him the capacity to do whatever necessary to bend powerful Aristos to his will. In tonight's meeting, he had been more a Highton than ever before in his life.

A sovereign didn't have to be a tyrant. He, Jaibriol the Third, could give the human race peace by following a different path. He could do such great good for his empire if he wasn't locked in a constant struggle with the Imperialate. Perhaps someday he could even free all his people.

He would never have a Ruby son; all that survived of his child was his memory of Tarquine's ravaged voice as she told him their son had died. He bit the inside of his mouth, using the pain to stop the tears that welled in his eyes. Unless he conquered Skolia, he would never again know a Ruby bond.

Images of Aristos cut through his thoughts. If he brought them this treaty, they would revile him, condemn him, even seek to end his life. That avenue to peace would be an unending route to misery. But if he brought all humanity together under his rule, he could offer protection instead of tyranny.

Jaibriol stared past the city at the violent waves battering the shoreline and leaping into the sky. "It is amazing," he said, "how difficult answers can be to the simplest questions."

"So I've heard," Corbal said. "It is amazing, too, how one can think he knows a man and yet be wrong on so many facets."

Each time Corbal brought up his betrayal, Jaibriol died a little more inside. "Gems have facets," he said. "People are more complex."

"Except for rubies, wouldn't you say? One should never underestimate their effect."

Jaibriol wasn't certain what he meant. Better to imply Corbal misjudged the situation than to admit anything. "I've heard it said misjudgment can be as dangerous as underestimation."

"Misjudgment and underestimation are two facets." Corbal paused. "A dyad, so to speak. You need a third facet. A triad."

His pulse jumped. Corbal couldn't know he had joined the Triad. *He couldn't.* He kept his voice cool. "To get a third facet, you must cut it. That can't be done if the tools are ruined." He doubted the Lock would ever again work.

"This is true," Corbal said. "One has to guess at so much in life. We can never be sure if speculation is no more than air bubbles that vanish when we look too closely. But let us suppose, purely for conjecture, that the destruction comes *after* the gem is faceted. A gem such as, say, a ruby."

"I prefer carnelians." It was a lie, but Jaibriol could say nothing else.

"Think of announcements." Corbal's words flowed like rich, forbidden oil. "One can proclaim many things. A signed document, perhaps. Or other things. Perhaps a trio of things."

"You seem fascinated with the number three tonight."

Corbal's voice hardened. "And think about this. What some call peace, others might call robbery of what belongs to them."

Jaibriol couldn't answer. He knew what lay within his grasp. He had thought of nothing else for the past two days. He could conquer the entire human race.

A man can be a benevolent ruler. He could make the existence of humanity better by changing the Aristos.

You haven't changed them in ten years, he thought. *You've learned only how to survive.* Was he becoming like them, the Aristos who believed they were so much higher than the rest of the human race while they inflicted such atrocities?

"*Think* of it," Corbal said. "Humanity has reached across the heavens, multiplied to incredible proportions, created wonders beyond any imagining. Our numbers are greater than any ever before known, more than our ancestors could even dream. We have achieved empires greater than anything we've found among the stars. We stand at the pinnacle of human achievement." His voice was like the call of a siren. "One person could rule it all."

Jaibriol's heart was beating too hard. "The Skolians have a saying," he answered. "'Across the stars the dynasty may trod, but yet the gods of Skolia are flawed.'"

"I wasn't talking about Skolians."

"Neither was I."

"Unlimited power," Corbal murmured. "Unlimited wealth. Unlimited realms."

"An empire fit for a man's heir," Jaibriol answered coldly. Until he and Tarquine had a child, Corbal was his successor.

Corbal's gaze darkened. "Or his wife?"

He thought of how Tarquine had walked at his side into his meeting with Barthol, Corbal, and Erix only hours after she had miscarried. In the lodge, he had seen her vulnerable in a way she would never show another human being, yet when she went to face the powers of an empire, she showed no sign of weakness. Corbal had no place criticizing her.

Jaibriol answered with ice in his voice. "A man's wife is his concern. Not his kin's."

"Nor should she be the concern of any facet in a triad."

Jaibriol felt as if Corbal had slammed him against the wall. He knew what "facet" Corbal meant. Kelric. Jaibriol would never be free of his uncle's specter. He had seen Kelric's mind. The Imperator thought of himself as aging and tired. He didn't see the commander who stood like a war god, the survivor who had defied two empires to claim his throne, the legend over which an entire world had gone to war.

The man Tarquine had wanted.

Jaibriol knew he could never match Kelric, neither in ten years nor ten millennia. The Imperator's shadow would forever leave him in its chill.

The moonlight cast Corbal's face into planes of light and shadow, making him look even more like their ancestors, especially Eube Qox, who had founded the empire. "I've heard the Skolians ratified a treaty," Corbal said. "I've also heard an Imperator's life depends on who else signs." His words were dark gems, hard and brilliant. "Announce a triad instead and he will die."

Jaibriol didn't want to hear Corbal—and he couldn't stop listening. On Earth, Kelric had offered him a means to survive. Quis. What it would come to, Jaibriol didn't know, but Kelric believed it could help. It had been an act of compassion. He didn't want to envy his uncle. He didn't want to fear Kelric's effect on Tarquine. He wanted to put aside these insidious thoughts. But he couldn't forget.

Jaibriol also remembered the boy who had needed to believe the lives of his parents had mattered, the boy who thought he could make the difference they had dared envision. Yes, he remembered. He knew what had happened to that young fool.

The boy had died, replaced by a Highton emperor.

Kelric found Ixpar on the balcony of his bedroom in the ISC mansion. Starlight silvered her face. He stopped at the entrance, needing a moment to absorb that she was here and not on the Orbiter.

"When did you come?" he asked.

She turned with a start. "Kelric." Then she said, "I've been trying ever since you returned. They wouldn't let me until tonight."

He joined her at the retaining wall of the balcony, which came up to their waists. Below them, the tangled foliage of a dense forest carpeted the mountain slopes. "I'm surprised they let you at all. I'm still under arrest."

"Why would they convict you?" she asked. "You brought them the treaty."

"Emperor Qox hasn't acknowledged it."

She had a strange expression, as if an avalanche were poised above them, ready to fall. "And if he doesn't?"

He indicated at the forest. "Look at that."

She glanced at the trees, then back to him. "It's beautiful. But I'm not sure how it connects to the treaty."

Kelric answered softly. "When you know it may be the last time you see a view, it becomes that much lovelier." He was gazing at her rather than the forest. She had let her hair down, and tendrils curled around her face, glossy in the starlight. "So very lovely."

Her face gentled. "They won't kill you."

"Perhaps I deserve it."

"How can you say that?" She had that look he remembered, the one he could never avoid, as if she could see past his silences and into the heart of his fears. "You offered your people a miracle."

"At what price?" He turned to the forest and leaned his elbows on the wall, staring at the rich green life. "I took a chance. I may have been wrong."

She stood with him. "You don't have your dice pouch."

"I lost it on Earth."

Her voice quieted. "On Coba, in our Old Age, the men in the Calanya had a custom. It was rare even then, and it fell out of practice many centuries ago."

"Coba has gone through many changes," Kelric said. Most of the recent ones, unfortunately, were because of him. He had sworn to protect them, and he had genuinely believed he could. He regretted it more now than he could say, for all he had offered them was upheaval and possibly his death.

"In the Old Age, men couldn't inherit property," Ixpar said. "But Calani found a way around that."

He looked over at her. "How?"

"A father would give his son his Calanya dice. They called it the Gift of Quis. It symbolized the father teaching the son how he played. And the Quis of a Calani is his essence. Almost his soul." Softly she said, "It was a great act of trust."

Kelric had thought his son meant it literally when he portrayed him as Jaibriol's father, but now he wondered. "Does my son know about this custom?"

"I don't think so." She rested her palms on the wall as she looked over the mountains. "But sometimes, with the most gifted Calani, the line between their Quis and precognition blurs." She glanced at him. "I used to see that in yours."

"Jaibriol Qox sees me as a rival. Not a father figure."

"Perhaps. Or it may be that neither of you sees himself as well as he sees the other."

"I don't know." Tiredly, he said, "I just wish my own son would see me as a father."

"Kelric, he does, maybe too much. He fears to lose you. For ten years we believed you were dead. Then you appear like a miracle, offering dreams." Her smile seemed to hold more sorrow than anything else. "We had you for so brief a time. Then you vanished into this place you call a Lock. Then you disappeared again, and it turns out you are on Earth with your enemy. They say you are going to die. Execution. Then you offer humankind its first peace in how many centuries? Five? Six? Now you say you may yet die." She gave an uneven laugh. "And how many days have we been with you? Ten? You live an eventful life."

"I'm sorry." That sounded so woefully inadequate.

"Don't apologize." Her eyes were luminous. "I am grateful to know you lived. I understand better now, both why you wanted to hide us and why you wanted to ensure we were prepared if you could no longer do it."

"I should have left you alone." The words came hard. "Yes, I protected you, and my children. No one can take your heritage now." Then he said, "And if Qox chooses war instead of peace? He knows about my family, including a Ruby psion heir."

"He won't betray your trust."

"He faces temptation greater than you know, Ixpar."

"You think it is true he set all this up to destroy you?"

"No. But he can use it for those purposes. He may not even fully acknowledge the lure of that power. He might convince himself, if he tries hard enough, that he can do more good if we all unite under one sovereign. Him." He forced out what had to be said. "More than anything, I wish for you to stay with me. I know you cannot. Nor can Jimorla or Rohka." He thought of the hatred on Ragnar's face. "I have no evidence one of my own people tried to kill me. But I know. It may yet happen. Anyone close to me is close to that danger." With pain, he said, "Take them home, Ixpar. I can't promise you will be safe there, but it is far better than here."

"I will," she murmured. "I'm sorry."

"Don't be." His voice caught. "They are miracles."

She touched his hand. "Your son told me that playing Quis with you was a miracle, like riding on clouds or looking at the face of the sun and rising from its fire in rebirth."

Kelric swallowed. "Thank you."

"It is true."

"He will someday be better than me."

"He's like you. But he has played Quis almost from birth. It is a part of him in a way it never became with you." Her voice caught. "What he brings back with him, after his time here, will find its way into the Quis of Coba. Filtered through him. What Coba will do with that, I don't know, but I give you my oath, Kelric, we will seek answers for you. When you visit us—if ever you can come home—we will be waiting for you."

He drew her into his arms, bending his head over hers. His tears ran down his face, from the joy of knowing his family and the sorrow of losing them.

XXXVI

Duet

Dehya came to see Kelric after he sent away his protocol officers, when he could no longer take their fiddling with his clothes and hair. He was in a chamber near the Amphitheater of Memories where the Assembly met. Dehya stood by the door, and he could see her in the mirror. He pulled at his sleeves, trying to straighten them. He had dressed simply, despite the protests of his protocol team, choosing his unadorned black uniform.

"We've had a communication from the Qox Palace," Dehya said.

Kelric turned to her, and the room suddenly seemed too quiet. "What did they say?"

"The emperor will make an announcement today. They will time it to coincide with ours."

"Did they say what he was announcing?" It was a desperate question and they both knew it, but he asked anyway, in the groundless hope that he could know before he went before three civilizations and put his name, life, and empire on the line.

"They told us as much as we told them," Dehya said. She looked as if she had bitten into a sour fruit.

"Nothing, in other words."

She came over to him, small and slight in her sky-blue jumpsuit. "Whatever happens, know that I stand at your side."

"I don't want you at my side," he growled. "I want you to *live*."

Her voice gentled. "You hold so much within your heart, I think sometimes it may burst."

"Dehya, listen." He drew her to a table and sat across from her. "I can't go out there without warning you."

"I know you've secured this room." She sounded more as if she were warning him. "So did I. But nothing is certain."

"Even so." He had to do this. "Jaibriol Qox went to the SSRB to investigate the implosions." Kelric took a breath. "When I activated the singularity, he was sitting in the Lock."

Dehya stared at him for a full five seconds as her face paled. Then she said, "No."

"Do you remember what I told you about Soz and me?" Kelric asked. "What happened when we were children, during that storm?"

"I remember." Her voice had a deathly still quality.

"So does Jaibriol Qox, now. I showed him how to play Quis."

"Kelric—" Her hand clenched on the table.

"He needed something to give him control," Kelric said. He wanted to say more, to tell her that he believed Jaibriol's presence in the Triad had stabilized Kyle space and stopped the implosions. He didn't dare, even with mind-speech, given all the Jagernauts outside this chamber. He might have already revealed too much. But he didn't need to go on. He saw it in her eyes. She knew what Qox might do today.

"I'm sorry," he said.

"Don't be. I trust your instincts."

"I don't."

A chime came from the door. As Kelric and Dehya stood up, Dehya said, "I will see you in the amphitheater." Gently she said, "Be well, Kelric."

"You also."

Dehya left by a discreet exit that would put her in a hall with private access to the amphitheater. When he was alone, Kelric went to the main door. But he couldn't open it. Not yet. He stood with his palm against the portal, his head bowed as he centered himself. He felt as if a drum beat within him, steady, timeless. Perhaps it was his heart. Maybe it was a future his people had always faced and might now live. Or die for.

He touched a panel and the door shimmered. Eight Jagernauts waited outside. He saw it in their faces, what everyone wondered. Would Jaibriol give them a treaty today or destroy the military leader of his enemies?

Kelric set off down the hall, flanked by guards. His leg throbbed and his limp slowed him, but he kept going, headed for the Amphitheater of Memories.

Corbal came in when Jaibriol was alone, after the emperor had sent away his protocol officers. They were waiting in a chamber near the Amphitheater of Providence, where the Aristos had assembled. Corbal stood by the door, and Jaibriol could see him in the mirror. Jaibriol pulled restlessly at his sleeves, trying to straighten them. He shimmered from his hair to his black diamond clothes to his polished shoes. Carnelians glittered in his cuffs and belt.

"We've had a communication from the Skolians," Corbal said.

Jaibriol turned, and the room suddenly seemed too quiet. "What did they say?"

"They have set up a Kyle node for us, since we can't create one ourselves." His eyes glinted. "Yet."

Jaibriol nodded formally. "Of course."

"With the connection, we will see it live when Imperator Skolia makes his announcement. And send yours live to them."

"Very well." Jaibriol went over to him. But he couldn't open the door. He wasn't ready. Not yet. He felt as if a drum beat within him, steady, timeless. Perhaps it was the beat of his heart. Or maybe his empire.

He touched a panel and the door shimmered. Barthol Iquar and Erix Muze waited outside, both in black dress uniforms with red piping on their sleeves. Four Razers waited with them.

And Tarquine.

Her red gaze was so intense, it looked as if it could burn through him. He thought he caught triumph from her, but she masked her emotions too well for him to be sure.

The minds of his joint commanders pressed on him, but he could endure it better today. When he had rolled out the Quis dice this morning, he had only intended to distract himself. But as soon as he drew on the memories Kelric had given him, his fascination with the game had swamped everything else.

The Imperator had been right.

Quis settled Jaibriol. With Kelric's memories to learn from, he could center the raging turmoil of his mind. It didn't take away the pain or give him control yet of that surging power, but it was a start. He had years to learn Quis. He didn't know yet what he would do with it, but it offered a lifeline in the ocean of his misery. It would help him rule Eube—

And beyond.

Jaibriol strode out of the room. Tarquine fell in at his right and Corbal to his left, with Barthol and Erix on either side of them. So they headed down the long corridor, the warlords of a conquering empire.

Kelric stood in the console cup at the end of a robot arm. Guards had accompanied him to the amphitheater and more waited on the dais, but he rode alone, and they hadn't insisted otherwise. He had seen it in their eyes, just as with Dehya. It wasn't condemnation; it was, incredibly, respect. He had tried to offer humanity the impossible. Peace. They knew he hadn't betrayed them. If this moment crashed, ISC would have to go through with the execution; to let him live would be to allow treason of unprecedented proportions with nothing to answer for it. How could they trust him in the Triad? But he would die knowing they understood why he had gone to Earth.

The Amphitheater of Memories hummed with the people of a thousand cultures. Giant screens showed him riding to the dais. He hadn't looked at the numbers, but he could tell from the crowds, even in aisles and between consoles, that more people had come today than to any other session he had ever attended. He felt the life, the vibrancy, the sheer *energy* of that gathering.

Don't let it end, he thought to Jaibriol, though he knew his nephew couldn't pick up that thought across the stars.

The robot arm docked at the dais, and Kelric stepped out, aware of the guards watching him. No one moved. Protocol was at her console, and Barcala Tikal stood by her chair. Dehya was standing by the console. She nodded to Kelric, and he nodded in return, though he felt as stiff as ice. He went to the podium, and screens throughout the hall showed him taller than life.

Kelric touched the speaker's panel. His voice went out to the amphitheater, and from there to Skolia, to his family, to Ixpar and his children, to the Allied Worlds, to Earth, to Jeremiah Coltman and

Seth Rockworth and the people of a small Appalachian town. And to the Eubians. Three empires listened.

"Four days ago," Kelric began, "I met on Earth with Jaibriol Qox, the Emperor of the Eubian Concord."

The Razers swung open the great double doors, and Jaibriol walked with his retinue onto a balcony that overlooked the Amphitheater of Providence. Spread out before him, the hall hummed with Aristos, aides, officers, and guards, thousands in tier after tier. Giant screens showed images of Jaibriol, his hands braced on the waist-high balcony wall, Tarquine at his side, Corbal, Erix, and Barthol flanking them, Razers towering behind. He hadn't looked at the numbers, but it was obvious more people had come today than any other session he had ever attended.

He touched the speaker's panel on the wall and his words went out to three empires.

"My people of Eube." His voice resonated. "I come before you today to speak of triumph!"

"The treaty has also been signed," Kelric said, "by the Ruby Pharaoh and First Councilor, and ratified by the Assembly. All that remains is for the last three signers—the Highton Heir and joint commanders of ESComm—to add their names."

All across the amphitheater, people waited. Kelric looked at the private screen on the podium where a message would come only for him. It remained blank, and his heart thundered.

Jaibriol paused in the many honorifics expected from an emperor lauding his empire. He had said enough. He was tired of the overblown phrases. He glanced at Tarquine, and the intensity in her eyes terrified and exhilarated him.

"Four days ago," Jaibriol began, "I met on Earth with Kelricson Skolia, the Imperator of Skolia." He took a deep breath and lifted his chin.

Then he said, "Together, we signed a treaty for peace between Eube and Skolia."

A message flashed on Kelric's private screen. He read the words, and a roaring started in his ears. He didn't think he could speak, that his voice would shake.

Taking a breath, he raised his head. And somehow he addressed the Assembly. "I have just received word from the Eubians." Despite his intention to remain calm, his voice crackled with hope. "They have signed!"

His words rang out. "We have a peace treaty!"

Jaibriol stood above the hall while it roared with voices and cymbals. Their shock and fury pounded his mind until he thought he would disintegrate. He stared at Tarquine, and she met his gaze. He could feel her mind now, as the onslaught wore down his defenses. It hadn't been triumph he had caught from her before, but an emotion even more powerful, grief and joy mixed together, her sorrow for the crushing path he had laid out for himself, but also, incredibly, her fierce exultation that he had dared the impossible and won.

His declaration of the treaty had gone to thousands of disbelieving Aristos, millions of news services, billions of settlements, trillions of people. The Aristos would revile him, hate him as they had hated no other emperor. But it was done. He had gone beyond and reached for something greater. For the first time in the history of Skolia and Eube, they had peace.

Jaibriol grasped Tarquine's hand so hard, he felt the bones in her fingers. She never flinched. They stood together, looking over the amphitheater, and he knew he could survive. With her at his side, he had done what he set out to achieve, and though the price might be greater than he could imagine bearing, he wouldn't let it defeat him.

His parents had not died in vain.

Characters and Family History

Boldface names refer to Ruby psions, also known as the "Rhon." All Rhon psions who are members of the Ruby Dynasty use **Skolia** as their last name (the Skolian Imperialate was named after their family). The **Selei** name indicates the direct line of the Ruby Pharaoh. Children of **Roca** and **Eldrinson** take **Valdoria** as a third name. The *del* prefix means "in honor of," and is capitalized if the person honored was a Triad member. Most names are based on world-building systems drawn from Mayan, North African, and Indian cultures.

= marriage

Lahaylia Selei (Ruby Pharaoh: deceased) = **Jarac** (Imperator: deceased)

Lahaylia and **Jarac** founded the modern-day Ruby Dynasty. **Lahaylia** was created in the Rhon genetic project. Her lineage traced back to the ancient Ruby Dynasty that founded the Ruby Empire. **Lahaylia** and **Jarac** had two daughters, **Dyhianna Selei** and **Roca**.

Dyhianna (Dehya) Selei = (1) William Seth Rockworth III (separated)
= (2) **Eldrin Jarac Valdoria**

387

Dehya is the Ruby Pharaoh. She married William Seth Rockworth III as part of the Iceland Treaty between the Skolian Imperialate and Allied Worlds of Earth. They had no children and later separated. The dissolution of their marriage would negate the treaty, so neither the Allieds nor Imperialate recognize the divorce. *Spherical Harmonic* tells the story of what happened to **Dehya** after the Radiance War.

Dehya and **Eldrin** have two children, **Taquinil Selei** and **Althor Vyan Selei.**

Althor Vyan Selei = 'Akushtina (Tina) Santis Pulivok

The story of **Althor** and **Tina** appears in *Catch the Lightning*. **Althor Vyan Selei** was named after his uncle, **Althor Izam-Na Valdoria.** The short story "Avo de Paso" in the anthologies *Redshift*, edited by Al Sarrantino, and *Fantasy: The Year's Best, 2001*, edited by Robert Silverberg and Karen Haber, tells the story of how Tina and her cousin Manuel deal with Mayan spirits in the New Mexico desert.

Roca = (1) Tokaba Ryestar (deceased)
        (2) Darr Hammerjackson (divorced)
        (3) **Eldrinson Althor Valdoria**

Roca and Tokaba had one child, **Kurj** (Imperator and Jagernaut), who married Ami when he was a century old. **Kurj** and Ami had a son named Kurjson.

Although no records exist of **Eldrinson's** lineage, it is believed he descends from the ancient Ruby Dynasty. *Skyfall* tells the story of how **Eldrinson** and **Roca** meet. They have ten children:

Eldrin (Dryni) Jarac (bard, consort to Ruby Pharaoh, warrior)
Althor Izam-Na (engineer, Jagernaut, Imperial Heir)
Del-Kurj (Del) (singer, warrior, twin to **Chaniece**)
Chaniece Roca (runs Valdoria family household, twin to **Del-Kurj**)
Havyrl (Vyrl) Torcellei (farmer, doctorate in agriculture)
Sauscony (Soz) Lahaylia (military scientist, Jagernaut, Imperator)
Denric Windward (teacher, doctorate in literature)
Shannon Eirlei (Blue Dale archer)
Aniece Dyhianna (accountant, Rillian queen)

Kelricson (Kelric) Garlin (mathematician, Jagernaut, Imperator)

Eldrin appears in *The Final Key, Triad, Spherical Harmonic,* and *The Radiant Seas.* See also **Dehya**.

Althor Izam-Na = (1) Coop and Vaz
= (2) Cirrus (former provider to Ur Qox)

Althor has a daughter, Eristia Leirol Valdoria, with Syreen Leirol, an actress turned linguist. Coop and Vaz have a son, Ryder Jalam Majda Valdoria, with **Althor** as cofather. **Althor** and Coop appear in *The Radiant Seas.* Vaz and Coop appear in *Spherical Harmonic.* **Althor** and Cirrus also have a son.

Havyrl (Vyrl) Torcellei = (1) Liliara (Lily) (deceased)
= (2) Kamoj Quanta Argali

The story of Havyrl and Lily appears in "Stained Glass Heart," in the anthology *Irresistible Forces,* edited by Catherine Asaro, 2004. The story of **Havyrl** and Kamoj appears in *The Quantum Rose,* which won the 2001 Nebula Award. An early version of the first half was serialized in *Analog,* May–July/August 1999.

Sauscony (Soz) Lahaylia = (1) Jato Stormson (divorced)
= (2) Hypron Luminar (deceased)
= (3) **Jaibriol Qox** (aka **Jaibriol II**)

The story of **Soz** at seventeen, when she enters the Dieshan Military Academy, appears in *Schism,* which is Part I of the two-book work *Triad.* The second part, *The Final Key,* tells of the first war between the Skolians and the Traders. The story of how **Soz** and Jato met appears in the novella, "Aurora in Four Voices" (Analog, December 1998). **Soz** and **Jaibriol**'s stories appear in *Primary Inversion* and *The Radiant Seas.* They have four children: **Jaibriol III, Rocalisa, Vitar,** and **del-Kelric.** The story of how **Jaibriol III** became the Emperor of Eube appears in *The Moon's Shadow.* **Jaibriol III** married Tarquine Iquar, the Finance Minister of Eube. The story of how Jaibriol and Kelric deal with each other appears in *The Ruby Dice.*

Denric takes a position as a teacher on the world Sandstorm. His harrowing introduction to his new home appears in the short story, "The Edges of Never-Haven" (*Flights of Fantasy,* edited by Al Sarrantino).

Aniece = Lord Rillia

Lord Rillia rules Rillia on the world Lyshriol (aka Skyfall). His realms consist of the Rillian Vales, Dalvador Plains, Backbone Mountains, and Stained Glass Forest.

Kelricson (Kelric) Garlin = (1) Corey Majda (deceased)
= (2) Deha Dahl (deceased)
= (3) Rashiva Haka (Calani trade)
= (4) Savina Miesa (deceased)
= (5) Avtac Varz (Calani trade)
= (6) Ixpar Karn (closure)
= (7) Jeejon

Kelric's stories are told in *The Ruby Dice,* "The Ruby Dice" (novella, *Baen's Universe 2006*), *The Last Hawk, Ascendant Sun, The Moon's Shadow,* the novella "A Roll of the Dice" (*Analog,* July/August 2000), and the novelette "Light and Shadow" (*Analog,* April 1994). **Kelric** and Rashiva have one son, **Jimorla Haka,** who becomes a renowned Calani. **Kelric** and Savina have one daughter, **Rohka Miesa Varz,** who becomes the Ministry Successor in line to rule the Estates of Coba.

The novella "Walk in Silence" (*Analog,* April 2003) tells the story of Jess Fernandez, an Allied Starship Captain from Earth, who deals with the genetically engineered humans on the Skolian colony of Icelos.

The novella "The City of Cries" (*Down These Dark Spaceways,* edited by Mike Resnick) tells the story of Major Bhaaj, a private investigator hired by the House of Majda to find Prince Dayj Majda after he disappears.

The novella "The Shadowed Heart" (*Year's Best Paranormal,* edited by Paula Guran, and *The Journey Home,* edited by Mary Kirk) is the story of Jason Harrick, a Jagernaut who just barely survives the Radiance War.

Time Line

Circa 4000 BC   Group of humans moved from Earth to Raylicon
Circa 3600 BC   Ruby Dynasty begins
Circa 3100 BC   Raylicans launch first interstellar flights; rise of Ruby Empire
Circa 2900 BC   Ruby Empire begins decline
Circa 2800 BC   Last interstellar flights; Ruby Empire collapses

Circa AD 1300   Raylicans begin to regain lost knowledge
1843   Raylicans regain interstellar flight
1866   Rhon genetic project begins
1871   Aristos found Eubian Concord (aka Trader Empire)
1881   Lahaylia Selei born
1904   Lahaylia Selei founds Skolian Imperialate
2005   Jarac born
2111   Lahaylia Selei marries Jarac
2119   Dyhianna Selei born
2122   Earth achieves interstellar flight
2132   Allied Worlds of Earth formed
2144   Roca born
2169   Kurj born
2203   Roca marries Eldrinson Althor Valdoria (*Skyfall*)
2204   Eldrin Jarac Valdoria born; Jarac dies; Kurj becomes Imperator; Lahaylia dies

2205	Major Bhaaj hired by Majdas to find Prince Dayj ("The City of Cries")
2206	Althor Izam-Na Valdoria born
2209	Havyrl (Vyrl) Torcellei Valdoria born
2210	Sauscony (Soz) Lahaylia Valdoria born
2219	Kelricson (Kelric) Garlin Valdoria born
2227	Soz enters Dieshan Military Academy (*Schism*)
2228	First war between Skolia and Traders (*The Final Key*)
2237	Jaibriol II born
2240	Soz meets Jato Stormson ("Aurora in Four Voices")
2241	Kelric marries Admiral Corey Majda
2243	Corey assassinated ("Light and Shadow")
2258	Kelric crashes on Coba (*The Last Hawk*)
early 2259	Soz meets Jaibriol (*Primary Inversion*)
late 2259	Soz and Jaibriol go into exile (*The Radiant Seas*)
2260	Jaibriol III born (aka Jaibriol Qox Skolia)
2263	Rocalisa Qox Skolia born; Althor Izam-Na Valdoria meets Coop ("Soul of Light")
2268	Vitar Qox Skolia born
2273	del-Kelric Qox Skolia born
2274	Radiance War begins (also called Domino War)
2276	Traders capture Eldrin. Radiance War ends; Jason Harrick crashes on the planet Thrice Named ("The Shadowed Heart")
2277–8	Kelric returns home (*Ascendant Sun*); Dehya coalesces (*Spherical Harmonic*); Kamoj and Vyrl meet (*The Quantum Rose*); Jaibriol III becomes emperor of Eube (*The Moon's Shadow*)
2279	Althor Vyan Selei born
2287	Jeremiah Coltman trapped on Coba ("A Roll of the Dice"); Jeejon dies (*The Ruby Dice*)
2288	Kelric and Jaibriol Qox deal with one another (*The Ruby Dice* novel)
2298	Jess Fernandez goes to Icelos ("Walk in Silence")
2326	Tina and Manuel in New Mexico ("Ave de Paso")
2328	Althor Vyan Selei meets Tina Santis Pulivok (*Catch the Lightning*)